26

THE MINISTRY: CLERICAL AND LAY

THE MINISTRY: CLERICAL AND LAY

PAPERS READ AT
THE 1988 SUMMER MEETING AND
THE 1989 WINTER MEETING OF
THE ECCLESIASTICAL HISTORY SOCIETY

EDITED BY

W. J. SHEILS AND DIANA WOOD

PUBLISHED FOR
THE ECCLESIASTICAL HISTORY SOCIETY

BY

BASIL BLACKWELL

1989

© Ecclesiastical History Society 1989

First published 1989
First published in USA 1990

Basil Blackwell Ltd
108 Cowley Road, Oxford OX4 1 JF, UK

Basil Blackwell Inc.
3 Cambridge Center,
Cambridge, Massachusetts 02142, USA

British Library Cataloguing in Publication Data
A CIP catalogue record for this book is available from the British Library

Library of Congress Cataloging in Publication Data
Ecclesiastical History Society. Summer Meeting (1988: Magdalene
    College)
        The ministry: clerical and lay: papers read at the 1988 Summer
Meeting and the 1989 Winter Meeting of the Ecclesiastical History
Society / edited by W. J. Sheils & Diana Wood
            p.   cm.—(Studies in church history: 26)
    ISBN 0-631-17193-2
    1. Clergy—Office—History—Congresses. 2. Lay ministry—History—
—Congresses. I. Sheils, W. J. II. Wood, Diana 1940-. III. Ecclesiastical History Society.
Winter Meeting (1989: King's College, London) IV. Title.
    V. Series.
    BR141.S84 vol. 26
    [BV660.2]
    262'.1'09—dc20   89-38123

Typeset in 11 on 12 pt Bembo
by Joshua Associates Limited, Oxford
Printed in Great Britain by Billing and Sons Ltd, Worcester

CONTENTS

CONTENTS

CONTENTS

PREFACE

The theme of the conference held in the Summer of 1988 under the Presidency of the Reverend Professor Sir Owen Chadwick was 'Ministry: Clerical and Lay'. The topic proved a popular one with the membership, many of whom are themselves involved in varying forms of Ministry within their respective denominational callings, and a crowded programme occupied the Society for three days at the Divinity Schools in Cambridge and at Magdalene College. The society is grateful to the Master and Fellows of the College for their hospitality, as also to the Master and Fellows of Gonville and Caius College who made available their splendid dining hall on the occasion of the conference dinner. For the winter meeting the Society returned, as is customary, to King's College, London, where once again the college provided its usual hospitality. The papers here printed represent a selection of those offered at the meetings where, it is fair to say, the 'clerical' attracted considerably more attention than the 'lay'.

W. J. Sheils
Diana Wood

LIST OF CONTRIBUTORS

SIR OWEN CHADWICK O. M. (*President*)
Regius Professor Emeritus of Modern History, University of Cambridge

DAVID BAGCHI
Part-time Lecturer, Centre for Medieval and Renaissance Studies, Oxford

JULIA BARROW
Research Fellow, School of History, Birmingham University

CLYDE BINFIELD
Reader in History, University of Sheffield

CHRISTOPHER N. L. BROOKE
Dixie Professor of Ecclesiastical History, University of Cambridge

PATRICK COLLINSON
Regius Professor of Modern History, University of Cambridge

VIRGINIA DAVIS
Lecturer in History, Westfield College, University of London

PETER DOYLE
Principal Lecturer in History, Bedford College of Higher Education

SARAH FOOT
Research Student, Newnham College, Cambridge

DAVID B. FOSS
Lecturer in Doctrine and Theology, College of the Resurrection, Mirfield

GRAHAM GOULD
Junior Research Fellow, Trinity College, Oxford

IAN GREEN
Senior Lecturer in History, Queen's University, Belfast

DIANA GREENWAY
Senior Research Editor, Institute of Historical Research, University of London

JOHN R. GUY
  Archivist, Yeovil District Hospital

DAVID J. HALL
  Under-Librarian, Cambridge University Library

WAYNE J. JOHNSON
  Research Student, University of Keele

FRANCES KNIGHT
  Research Student, Christ's College, Cambridge

PETER LAKE
  Lecturer in History, Royal Holloway and Bedford New College,
  University of London

D. J. LAMBURN
  Research Student, University of York

ARTHUR STEPHEN McGRADE
  Professor of Philosophy, University of Connecticut

A. K. McHARDY
  Lecturer in History, University of Nottingham

STUART PIGGIN
  Senior Lecturer in History, University of Wollongong

D. M. NICOL
  Director, The Gennadius Library, American School of Classical
  Studies, Athens

W. JOHN ROXBOROGH
  Lecturer in Church History, Seminari Theologi, Malaysia

MATHIEU G. SPIERTZ
  Professor of the History of Dutch Catholicism, Catholic University,
  Nijmegen

BRIAN TAYLOR
  Rector of Guildford St Nicolas

W. R. WARD
  Emeritus Professor of Modern History, University of Durham

GEORGE YULE
  Professor Emeritus of Church History, University of Aberdeen

THE SEMINARY
(*PRESIDENTIAL ADDRESS*)

by OWEN CHADWICK

T HE language of the liturgy will always be a little different from the language of common speech, however carefully the drafters of ritual aim to make it understood by the people. It has in it a strand of poetry, and the nature of reverence carries inside itself a healthy dislike of bathos. Therefore: if ministers of a liturgy are expected to preach to the people, they will need instruction in how best to teach or to speak, not to mention education so that they have something to say and are not windbags. But even if a minister of a liturgy is not expected to preach, but is only there as voice to go through the set text, it will be done better if he does it with understanding; and therefore the minister will need the education to understand what is read, which in the western centuries where all this started would be in Latin. The minister also needs instruction on how not to drop the baby at baptism, and how to behave with a coffin, and what to do to a dying person. It is therefore expected that this will be an educated person, even if for much of the Middle Ages the sort of education for many ministers would be that which we should think specially appropriate to a sacristan rather than to a professional preacher. And since some such qualification was essential to do the job, bishops hardly liked to ordain persons who could not pass some sort of an educational test.

Early bishops, St Augustine of Hippo among them, organized a sort of diocesan school for future clergy. In 531 the second Council of Toledo decreed that those whom their parents wished to be put forward for ordination should receive the tonsure and be educated in a building belonging to the church and under the supervision of the bishop; and later those who decided for marriage should be let go. The development of the monastic houses had an effect because monks had leisure or even moral obligation to study, and before long there were learned monks, and everything that was accepted in the training of a good monk began to be accepted as right in the training of a good parish pastor. But it was not only the influence of the monks which helped the cathedral school. In England the synod of Cloveshoo in 747 ordered that children should be sent to school and that there they should be taught the understanding of the Bible.

The Carolingian reforms attempted to organize the cathedral schools.

I

Charlemagne ordered that they be created, so that it was now a legal obligation and no longer due to the initiative of the individual bishop. The emperor wanted able youths to be educated in languages so that they could enter better into the meaning of the Bible. A series of Carolingian regulations tried to make this into a system. They tried to make the *magister scholarum* an integral part of the cathedral establishment. Modern scholars investigated the library catalogues of the Carolingian cathedral schools and thereby proved the excellence of the standards which formed the ideal.

But these cathedral schools were good for training not so much the clergy as the higher clergy. In Germany an ordinand under the Ottonian empire and after, who went to the schools at Mainz or Cologne or several others, could have received a good education if he was capable of receiving it. But that was not enough in the multitude of priests. For the rest, everything was haphazard. People got the required qualification in any way they could. The universities came and overshadowed the cathedral schools and took over the effective training in theology. So they helped the general standards of clergy. It was hardly likely that most future priests would go to a university.

The third Lateran Council of 1179 ordered in chapter 18 that the cathedrals should provide a teacher who should teach not only poor scholars free of charge but also the clerics. Only a few decades later the fourth Lateran Council of 1215 ordered that every metropolitan church 'at least' should have a theologian who should teach the Bible to priests and others, and should specially tell them about the things that concern the cure of souls. The canon showed an advance in the expectation of what you needed from one of the ministers of the Church. Originally he is expected, as a minimum, only to be able to perform the rites accurately and sensibly; and if there were those who were expected to live up to such high ideals as those portrayed in Gregory the Great's book on Pastoral Care, no one expected everyone to be like that. Children got instruction from their elders as and when they could. But this canon of 1215 expects that the cleric shall know something of the Bible; and therefore that he shall be able to understand Latin in a way that is not only the Latin of the liturgy; and therefore that he shall be able to teach; and it expects that his job is the cure of souls. The canon was at first effective in very few places. In the longer run it was important to have laid down that rule.

The big men usually had a monastic training early in life or an education at some ecclesiastical school to which their parents put them. Thomas Aquinas was sent by his parents at the age of five to be educated by the

Benedictines at Monte Cassino and later was sent to various universities. John Fisher was sent by his parents to the school run by the canons at Beverley and then went on to Michaelhouse at Cambridge where he took a degree in arts before his ordination as priest. If we take such men as examples, the system of not having seminaries seemed to work; at least in a world where monastic and cathedral and collegiate schools were plentiful. Yet it must be said that John Fisher did not look back upon his own university education with much satisfaction and that this was a motive for the reforms which he brought to the university of Cambridge. It is impossible to judge the system by exceptional people. As late as 1605 Richelieu went off to the country with a private tutor who was a DD from Louvain, studied for three years with him, and then went straight to Rome not only to be ordained priest but to be consecrated a bishop.

The Reformation's most effective criticism, among all its criticisms, was the ignorance of the clergy. The drive for an educated clergy was much more potent and was part of something bigger, a drive towards a more educated everybody. The Protestants were helped in this endeavour because they had at their disposal the resources of the suppressed monasteries, although, as always, governments had more urgent needs than that of education. Their founding of schools and their development of the universities changed for them the conditions under which clergy were trained. It is enough to mention the names of Melanchthon and Sturm. They insisted on more time being taken out of a human life to learn things out of books. They also had a strongly moral idea of education, that the duty of a school was not only to teach children Latin but to teach them how to behave. All this was bound to affect in a marked way the education of priests and pastors.

But already during the fifteenth century the ideas of the Renaissance produced new types of educational foundation for the training of future clergy. The place of honour is held by the still existing Capranica. It was founded at Rome by the cardinal of that name in the year before his death, that is in 1457. Twenty years later there was another college of the same type, at Sigüenza in Spain (refounded 1670).

Since the cry of ignorance was justified, the Catholic reformers were at once as concerned as the Protestant. The famous or notorious *Consilium de emendanda Ecclesia* of Cardinal Contarini and others in 1537 had as one of its first criticisms the ignorance of the clergy and one of its first plans for reform a consideration on how to educate the clergy better. The youngest member of this committee was Reginald Pole, who started the meetings as a layman but was soon both a deacon and a cardinal. It was natural

3

therefore that the Council of Trent when it opened in the winter of 1545–6 should take both the *Consilium* and the training of the clergy into its discussion. In April 1546 they debated it. The bishops proposed colleges to educate boys, the phrase goes, 'in the hope of benefices'. But the decree only extended the decree of the fourth Lateran Council about a cathedral post for education and seems to have been largely a dead letter. The bishops still lived in a fossilized tradition of late medieval education. Despite the universities and the religious orders and the Renaissance and the foundation of Capranica, they still thought in terms of the old cathedral school as the solution to their problems of an educated clergy. And it was this attitude which led to the decision of the Council of Trent.

Almost a year after Reginald Pole arrived back in Queen Mary's England he summoned a synod of the Church of England which met from November 1555 to February 1556. The decrees were published on 10 February 1556 as 'Reformatio Angliae ex decretis Reginaldi Poli, Cardinalis, Sedis Apostolicae Legati'. The most celebrated of its decrees was that which ordered annual processions on St Andrew's Day to commemorate the reconciliation of England with the Church of Rome. Its most important decree contained the word seminary, used for the first time so far as is known in this context; decree 11, 'that in cathedrals a certain number shall be educated from whom persons can be chosen, "tamquam ex seminario"' to rule the churches worthily. The word meant a nursery-garden, but even in classical times was already used metaphorically, in such phrases as the seed-plot of conspiracy. Reginald Pole was evidently not using a word which was familiar; because he twice said 'tamquam ex seminario', 'so to speak out of a seed-plot'. He said that the boys were to be 11 or 12 years old; that they must on admission be able to read and write; that these schools were to be specially for the children of the poor but the children of the rich were not to be barred from attending; that they were to be divided into two classes, one for the older and the other for the younger, but all were to wear the clerical habit and the tonsure and to attend the divine office daily. They are to learn grammar; and then under the chancellor of the cathedral or some other doctor they are to be educated in systematic theology and discipline. Others—that is boys who are not ordinands—may be admitted to these classes.[1]

Less than ten years later the world had lost all sense of innovation, for there was a decree of the Council of Trent *de seminariis*. This was proposed on 10 May 1563 for discussion. It took over Reginald Pole's language. It

---

[1] *Reformatio Angliae ex decretis Reginaldi Poli 1556* (Rome 1562, Aldus Manutius F) section 11.

was agreed with minor alterations on 6 July 1563, and received a final approval as canon 18 on 15 July 1563.[2]

The decree ordered all bishops to found a college which should be a 'perpetual seed-plot (seminary) of ministers of God'. These colleges were to take boys of twelve years or more, and of legitimate birth, and educate them in common in the necessary knowledge of language, liturgy, chanting, calculation, the Bible, ecclesiastical books, homilies of saints, forms of sacraments and rites, and, a clause added afterwards, what pertains to the hearing of confessions. The foundation was for the sons of the poor primarily but did not exclude the sons of the rich. The building was to be conveniently close to the cathedral. The boys were to attend mass every day and to receive the sacrament at least once a month and to make their confession at least once a month. The money for the endowment was to be found by taxing all the diocese including the religious orders (not the mendicants) as well as the bishop, the cathedral chapter, and the prebendaries. If a diocese was too poor to found such a college, the bishops allowed the archbishop to organize a college created by and for two of his suffragans together.

During the discussion the Spanish archbishop of Segovia warmly advocated Pole's plan and said that it was a return to the decree of the Church which was passed by the council of Toledo in 531. But he said that it was important for the bishop alone to have entire control of this institution, and not the bishop in council. Otherwise there appears to have been almost no general discussion of the plan. Two non-placets were pronounced at the actual vote against the draft decree. Both these non-placets were pronounced by French abbots. The abbot of Clairvaux, Jerome de la Souchière, disapproved of the mode of taxation to endow the new institution. No doubt the decree appeared to him an interference with the exemptions of the religious houses. The abbot of Lunéville, Claude de Sainctes, seemed rather to be concerned whether such a decree could fit all the different parts of the Church, and that thus it might make difficulties, and the matter should be referred to provincial councils.[3]

In this epoch-making step, which was to have excellent and disastrous consequences, three innovations are to be observed. The bishop is compelled to found such a college but future clergy are not compelled to attend it. The design is very episcopal—that is, what it sought is the

---

[2] Draft in *Concilii Tridentini Actorum Pars Sexta*, ed. S. Ehses (Freiburg im Breisgau, 1924), 9, p. 483.
[3] *Ibid.*, pp. 523, 596–7, 628–32.

creation of a diocesan clergy—the new seminary is to be another diocesan instrument. And the education is to be imparted in a boarding school. The object of the college is not that of the faculty of theology in a university. It is devoted to applied ends—pastoral care, correct performance of liturgical rites. There is no suggestion, as there came to be in the nineteenth century, that the universities do a bad job in training clergy and that we must provide another and better training.

It was one thing to say that a lot of bishops who were not present should find money to found a college. It was another thing to make them find the money. It was one thing to say that all the cathedral chapters must contribute money; and quite another to force bishops to a fight with their chapters over whether they would give any money and how much. It needed the growing power of Rome in the later Counter-Reformation to achieve anything like what the fathers of the Council of Trent wanted.

The legates of Trent wrote to the Secretary of State in Rome, who was Borromeo, saying that they wanted the diocese of Rome to found such a seminary as an example to everyone but they did not like to say so publicly lest they seem to intrude on the prerogative of the Pope. Borromeo replied at once that the Pope was willing. It took Rome more than eighteen months to open the Roman Seminary. This opened on the evening of 1 February 1565. And by that time other bishops had obeyed the order; Rieti and Larino in 1564, and Milan where Borromeo was now the archbishop. The archdiocese of Milan developed what on paper was an elaborate system. There was the greater seminary for 150 ordinands to receive instruction in languages and then philosophy and theology. There was also a hospice for mature clerics known as La Canonica, where there was simple instruction on cases of conscience, on the Bible, and on the catechism of the Council of Trent. In other parts of the diocese were three junior seminaries, divided according to the range of age; and after the boys or adolescents or adults passed through this seminary, they went on to the *seminarium maius* or to La Canonica.

As the system developed it ran into difficulties which the fathers of Trent had not considered.

First, many dioceses had not the means to found a seminary. While some dioceses successfully founded good places of education, some of those dioceses which thought that they could manage it found that all that they could found was a reach-me-down college which did very poor work. If some very small dioceses started a seminary it might contain only a handful of boys and experience showed that it was a very weak institution. Trent allowed dioceses to club together at need. The seminary of the little diocese of Santa Severina in Southern Italy, which was founded in 1581, was at first designed to serve six dioceses and continued to serve several dioceses far into the eighteenth century.[4] But at its worst a little Italian seminary could consist of three or four or five boys, taught by an ignorant priest, lodged in a miserable house, fed on hardly edible food, and from time to time sent home when the money ran out.

The building was not usually difficult. Parts of the cathedral premises were often underused. Sometimes the bishop's palace was already too large for himself and his staff and his diocesan office. In the diocese of Troia the bishop first (not till 1709) put the college into part of his palace, then built himself a new palace and handed over the old palace to the seminary.[5] In the diocese of Parma it started (1564) in the house of one of the canons, in the diocese of Modena it started in the houses of more than one of the canons and was run by two of the residentiary canons. Sometimes this was very inadequate; at Reggio-Emilia it started in a canon's house but it was regarded as an improvement when it was able to move into part of the bishop's palace. Sometimes it started in the house of one of the parish priests, sometimes a wealthy layman made over one of his houses. In poor dioceses the college buildings could be cramped and miserable. At Imola the seminary started inconveniently in three different houses. One resource was an empty monastery in the cathedral town, for under the law such a building must be used for a religious purpose. At San Severo for example the seminary started (1678) in a convent formerly occupied by the Dominicans and only later was room found for it in part of the bishop's palace. An enormous improvement in buildings for the Italian seminaries was achieved after the suppression of the Jesuits in 1773. Quite a number of seminaries moved into the former Jesuit house. At Florence, which of all places did not start a seminary till 1713, it gained its proper premises only seventy years later, when a Cistercian house became available. A number of seminaries gained rich improvement in their libraries by the suppression of the Jesuit houses.

If a monastery was itself an independent diocese (*abbatia nullius*) it might found its own seminary, but distinct from the monastic buildings. The great house of La Cava near Naples was one such. As the numbers of monks fluctuated or declined, sooner or later the seminary was sure to move into part of the monastic buildings, as happened at La Cava in 1780 and where the seminary is still housed.

---

[4] *Seminaria Ecclesiae catholicae* (Vatican City, 1963), p. 675.
[5] *Seminaria*, p. 670.

A third difficulty was the inability to say at the age of twelve whether a boy whom his parents intended for ordination would in the end be ordained. And since this was soon obvious, and since the best education or sometimes the only such education was to be found in colleges run by the religious orders, parents sent their children to be educated there whether or not they were likely to be ordained. That meant all colleges felt an implicit magnetism to become good schools for everybody and not just good schools for future priests. The seminaries themselves were not exempt from this magnetism. And if they were run by a society with an international reputation for higher education, like the Jesuits, they were the more likely to feel this pull. In one way nothing could be better. You could not get a good seminary unless it educated other people besides ordinands. Therefore the intellectual training of ordinands would be better under those conditions. But men of the Counter-Reformation cared about other things besides the academic—clerical tone, or priestly attitudes, or sobriety for example. They did not think the education of future priests side by side with the secular education of future merchants to be the best system. Various diocesans, starting with Borromeo of Milan, tried to ban entry to anyone who did not intend to seek holy orders. Such a ban was impossible to enforce. No one could possibly say whether or not a boy of twelve or even a boy of seventeen was a bona fide ordinand. Moreover the ordinand received a free education if his parents could not afford to pay for his education. Other boys did not. It was in the financial interest of parents, as well as the educational interest of the boy, to say that their child was intended for holy orders. To prevent such abuse bishops often exacted an undertaking from parents to pay back the money if the boy in the end did not take holy orders. Such an undertaking was impossible to enforce effectively and a bishop behaved with an un-episcopal lack of compassion if he tried to enforce it.

A fourth difficulty was the range of age. Was it easy or even possible to train a priest in the company of noisy boys of twelve? But in the poor dioceses, that had to be attempted. In the less poor dioceses they solved this by dividing seminaries into the *seminarium minus* and the *seminarium maius*, one of which was a school and the other a true seminary. Some dioceses had nothing but a *seminarium minus*. To have nothing but a boys' school in a diocese obeyed the letter of the decree of the Council of Trent but was glaringly in opposition to its spirit. In poor dioceses with difficulties, like Colle di Val d'Elsa, a seminary of 1615 was nothing but a boys school less than a century later.

Once you separate the young from the old, you have an actual choice, which was argued about from the seventeenth century. There were two views:

a. Educate them as ordinands only and admit no others to your college. You have not only to teach them how to conduct services, and how to understand the Bible, and how not to make fools of themselves when preaching, and enough moral theology to be a future confessor, and enough canon law to make sure that they understand what the rules of the game for a parish priest will be, and enough knowledge of chanting and church music so that they are not contemptible among the parishioners. You also have to produce dedicated pastors, who know how to pray, and have truly experienced the worship of God, and will follow high standards in their ministry. Therefore you must have a kind of monastic community in your seminary. They are not under the vows of obedience or poverty but they must learn to obey, and a rule of life. This can only be done when all the members share a common objective. It cannot be done if the college is also giving a higher education to accountants or to merchant bankers. That is the great fault of the universities as places for training clergy, that is why universities are inadequate, and why we must have seminaries.

It is also, said some bishops, a matter of experience that ordinands are unsettled in their vocations by being thrown too much among ordinary youths. 'Experience' said the head of an early American seminary 'showed that many of the seminarians had their vocations shaken by being thrown so much into contact with youth of the world; while scarcely a candidate for the ministry was obtained among those who received their education in the college'.[6]

b. To separate the ordinands from their contemporaries is mistaken. The universities are inadequate, not because they have ordinands and others together but because their arts course is so long that there is no time for theology, and when they come to theology it is of such a high standard and so academic that there is no proper time for the practical training in which they are not interested. But that practical training can be achieved in a different way. The ordinand needs to be among his contemporaries for the sake of understanding the mind of his educated contemporaries and being able in time to interpret his gospel to the more educated of his parishioners. A parish priest is very much in the world. A seminary which is a monastery takes him out of the world and does not fit him for the work ahead because, although it will make a disciplined priest and a priest who

---

[6] Tracy Ellis, in *Seminary Education in a Time of Change* (1965), p. 50; from M. J. Spalding, *Life of Bishop Flaget* (Washington, 1946), p. 153.

will be regular in saying his breviary it may also make a priest remote or even narrow.

From the time of the Sulpicians in the French classical epoch, this argument was won by those who wanted segregation. This was inevitable because the seminary system was devised by bishops for the needs of bishops. Bishops had never been uncritical admirers of universities, great corporations which claimed independence of the bishops. Some bishops wanted seminaries of a high intellectual standard. Gregory Barbarigo at Padua at the end of the seventeenth century turned the seminary at Padua into one of the best places of scientific education in Europe. Some systems, as at Turin, made the seminary one college within the university. But many bishops, and some very good bishops, suspected an excess of intellectualism in their ordinands. They wanted applied theology. And some of them were afraid that an excess of academic theology was bad for applied theology and possibly bad for the soul of the priest.

Even Father Olier, who founded Saint-Sulpice, and made his seminarians attend lectures at the Sorbonne—a custom which was part of the strength of his college—had a strange motive for wanting them to attend lectures at the Sorbonne. He wanted to do good to the Sorbonne. St Vincent de Paul, equally important in the development of the seminary system, had a still stronger touch of the anti-intellectal; he wrote in a letter: 'a general knowledge is enough. Everything the ordinand wants beyond that is to be feared rather than desired'.[7]

Before the French Revolution and its aftermath there were State universities with Catholic theological faculties in several countries. The revolution, or the revolutions of the nineteenth century, abolished many of these theological faculties. Quite often the Catholic bishops were not in the least disturbed. They had their own seminaries in the system ordered by the Council of Trent; and whether or not these seminaries were any good they could control them. Cases were known where the State, after having abolished theological faculties in a Catholic country, offered to restore them, and the Catholic bishops preferred that this should not be done. That shows that the intentions of the bishop's seminary were very different from the intentions of the theological faculty. Nevertheless the argument went on; and it had to go on for financial reasons as much as reasons of pastoral theory. You could not pay a decent staff at a seminary unless you had more pupils than the ordinands. In Victorian England St

---

[7] Spalding, *Life of Bishop Flaget*, p. 40; Vincent, *Works*, ed. Coste, 8, p. 33.

Edmund's Ware and Ushaw were seminaries which also trained lay students, or schools which also trained ordinands whichever way you looked at them. Cardinal Manning thought it a bad system, tried to do something about it, and failed.

Another difficulty was to find an adequate teaching staff. The canon theologian of the cathedral was a strength. But after that whence were the teachers to be found? Much the best resource must be the religious orders. They all had experience of running their own training colleges and some of them included higher education as one of the vocations; especially the Jesuits, who had founded the Roman College in 1551 and the German-icum in 1552. Thus Borromeo of Milan put his system under the control at first of the Jesuits; until later with Jesuit agreement he transferred it to his own new-founded religious order the Oblates of St Ambrose, founded in 1578. But the difficulty of putting a seminary under a religious order was the loss of control of the seminary by the bishop; that it turned the diocesan seminary into the seminary of an extra-diocesan institution, which would be contrary to the scheme imagined by the fathers of Trent. But quite often there was no alternative if the bishops were to find an adequate teaching staff. Bishops were forced to ask a religious order, usually the Jesuits, whose work for seminary education became of ever increasing importance. Sometimes they were Oratorians. In Poland and Eastern Europe they were often the Lazzarists of St Vincent de Paul or the Bartholomites. The Jesuits, who by reason of their educational vocation might have been expected to be the first to be applied to, were hesitant about accepting such a task. Their ethos hardly allowed them to concede authority to the bishop over an institution which they managed, and yet some bishop's authority in a seminary must be conceded.

The clergy did not always welcome a religious order in control of a seminary. At Saintes the bishop brought in the Lazzarists and the students all walked out. Some diocesan clergy disliked the idea that their future curates should be trained by a monastic or quasi-monastic community. Many legacies were bequeathed to seminaries on condition that they were not controlled by a religious order. On occasion the Sulpicians or the Lazzarists or the Oratorians needed to prove that they were not a religious order within the meaning of the law.[8]

Bishops tried to retain their authority over seminaries which they handed over to a religious order. They retained the right of visitation, for example. If the institution ran into financial trouble their support might

---

[8] Degert, *Histoire des séminaires français jusqu'à la Revolution*, 2 edn. (Paris, 1912), 1, pp. 583–4.

be more important to the survival of the institution than the support of the religious order. Here is a strange example. Richelieu became bishop of Luçon in 1607 and entered his diocese in the spring of the following year. He started on the business of reforming his diocese, which needed much reform. He included an examination of all the clergy in post to see that their knowledge was adequate. He then obeyed Trent by founding a diocesan seminary; which in France under the Concordat needed royal approval and under local rights needed the leave of the local Parlement. He bought a house near the cathedral and put in some students with a staff of two teachers. It was a poor diocese, and a small diocese. As with many South Italian dioceses the institution did not prosper, and he could not find adequate teachers. Five years later he was forced to look around for a religious order to take over the teaching and the running of the seminary. He invited the Oratorians and they accepted. But when the Oratorians arrived they could not get the money which they needed out of the chapter of the cathedral. They did not see how they could run an institution which the diocese failed to back in the way that Trent laid down. After eight years of Oratorian rule there was only one professor and soon the institution collapsed. For the bishop had lost interest. He was in Paris and on the way to running Europe rather than the diocese of Luçon.[9] This bishop was untypical. But what happened to his seminary was typical of what happened to quite a number of weaker seminaries; the beginning as an institution run by secular clergy; the failure of that and the need for a religious order to take over; the reluctance of the diocesan bodies to pay the tax to support an institution in which they had now almost no say; and the closure or collapse of the institution.

The Council of Trent laid it down that applicants to the seminary must be legitimate by birth. Therefore it was held by the more rigorous that the bishop could not dispense an illegitimate candidate from this rule. The Spanish bishops were not at all zealous. They preferred the universities and the colleges of the religious orders and hardly started founding seminaries before the seventeenth century. In France the Wars of Religion delayed anything important. In 1612 the archbishop of Rouen founded a seminary and put it under a religious order, the Oratorians. The Oratorian seminaries soon grew like the later Jesuit seminaries to be good places of general education. In France it was St Vincent de Paul and the Lazarists and then the Sulpicians who systematically extended the seminary system in French dioceses; beginning in the diocese of Beauvais in 1628. It did not

[9] Tracy Ellis, pp. 34–5; from L. Lacroix, *Richelieu à Lucon* (Paris, 1890), p. 75.

last. In 1644 there were only four seminaries in all France. Sixteen years later when Vincent died the Lazarists ran some twenty French seminaries. None of them was strong. The Lazarists were even more help to the Polish seminaries where, before the end of the eighteenth century, they ran most of them. France was an example of the way the Trent rule was disregarded because it had to be disregarded if effective training was to be given. In 1642 Father Olier was offered the parish of St-Sulpice and founded a parish seminary—that is, not diocesan except so far as it was part of the parish, and not under the archbishop of Paris for he placed it under the abbot of St Germain des Prés who was of course exempt from the archbishop's control. In due course this seminary won a national reputation and was opened up to all France. Here private enterprise created what was in effect a national seminary of the first rank. By the outbreak of the French Revolution the Sulpicians were running 34 seminaries in France.

The history of the French creation of seminaries was written by Degert in two volumes in 1912. The book was a fundamental advance in the study of the subject. The author was persuaded that the French seminary of the seventeenth century, and its influence, saved the Church at large from extraordinary evils. By 1630 the Catholic revival in France produced lots of nuns, more monks, more educated clergy, better theological faculties, and a stronger demand for seminaries. Bérulle, Condren, Olier, Eudes, Vincent de Paul—the names instantly suggest the idea that the young must be made into better priests. Curiously, what grew into the French seminaries was not the decree of the Council of Trent, nor the Jesuit college extending its mission, but the retreat for priests before ordination. Before they are ordained, get them into quiet, get them to say prayers, teach them a bit about prayer while you have them—eight days of retreat, perhaps, ten days; and gradually the time was extended backwards, a few weeks, then in some dioceses a few months. This made for a wide difference between the French seminary and the Tridentine seminary as it was found, say, in Southern Italy. The basic idea of the Tridentine seminary was, teach poor boys what they will need and that is mainly applied knowledge. The basic idea of the French seminary was, here are some young men about to become clergy, let us teach them how to pray and if possible see that they experience something of God in prayer. So late as 1773 Archbishop de Rohan said, 'The seminaries are useful only because they are a house of retreat before ordination'.[10]

[10] Degert, 2, pp. 3–4.

This started to mean an element of compulsion. Some bishops could easily say, they would ordain no one who would not attend their retreat before ordination. It was no step at all to say they would ordain no one who had not attended a seminary—except that, when they demanded a few months of 'retreat', they were into the problems of staff and buildings and money which would make them hesitant about enforcing such attendance. There was an alarming rumour that Queen Anne of Austria had a wish not to nominate anyone as a bishop unless at some point he had attended a seminary.[11]

In time the one system influenced the other. But we may mark the original difference in the attitude to intellectual labours. The Italian seminaries were not anti-intellectual, but they thought of such ill-prepared persons that they mostly engaged in elementary teaching. The French expected quite well-educated pupils for whom an excess of intellectual endeavour might be a distraction; and some of their founders therefore did not wish their seminarists to spend a lot of time reading for themselves. Naturally much was in common. Give them the knowledge necessary for the job. They must know how to hear confessions, therefore they must know some elementary moral theology. They must be able to chant. They must be able to conduct a ceremony with reverence and dignity. If possible they must know the symbolism of ritual. They must be taught not to store their spare bits of string in the tabernacle. They must be able to preach—and with this last they entered the world of the intellect, with commentaries on the Bible or the Creed or the Fathers. The study of the Bible was devotional rather than academic. Its aim was to help the preacher. No one taught church history, though biographies of saints were read at meals. (Only in the middle of the eighteenth century, in the world of Voltaire and the Encyclopaedists, did the leaders of seminaries realise that their men must know some history.) No one taught canon law. There was no Hebrew and almost no Greek. Normally lectures were dictated, and the students took away what they copied down and learnt it. In the eighteenth century this practice faded out as books were easier to get. But it was still practised sometimes—in an Anglican seminary, which in its origins was influenced by French practice, as late as 1939.

Some of the practical training was very effective: the baptism of a wooden doll, with other students as godparents; listen to a student making an imaginary confession to another student pretending to be his priest and adviser, and discuss afterwards; rehearse the sacrament of holy commun-

[11] Degert, I, pp. 171–2.

ion with pretend elements; administer to a student pretending to be dying, and afterwards discuss; preach to fellow-students and be criticized afterwards, or preach in a country church and be criticized afterwards.

Outside in the world they were regarded as ascetic prisons, full of mortification and servile obedience. In the little seminaries for schoolboys the regimen was often hard and the diet disgusting and there was hardly any heating in winter. But in the seminaries proper there was a decent diet, and a reasonable ration of wine, and normal hours of sleep and recreation, and amateur dramatics. They may have been monastic but they were a sanctuary of quiet, and they had not the espionage system which Borromeo instituted at Milan.

The seminaries produced a new idea: vocation. Formerly no one suggested that a candidate for holy orders needed to be anything but male, of legitimate birth, one who was not a moral scandal, and one who knew enough to do the necessary work in a parish. The idea of vocation existed in that a man or woman might feel a vocation to enter a monastery or nunnery. Luther had talked of everyone's vocation, the sanctity of a shoe-maker's work as well as that of a priest. But from the middle of the seven-teenth century appeared a new idea of vocation. From this moment it was possible to be a male of legitimate birth, and a devout Christian, and one who knows a lot, and is morally to be revered, and has no desire to marry, and yet who has no 'vocation' to be ordained. The seminaries were the principal cause of the new extension of the old idea of vocation. And this was partly because their principal effect was to make the training of the secular clergy resemble much more closely the training of the monk. They reacted against the younger-son-theology of the aristocracy. The elder son must have the estate, the younger must be ordained. Benefices were still conferred on minors, and certainly before ordination. The seminaries reacted against this; though not with a total success; Talleyrand, when a baby, fell off a chest and was maimed and so could not inherit the estate. He was sent to Saint-Sulpice, which he disliked much, and was very clever and, contrary to legend, respected most of the moralities expected of a clergyman—but no one could suppose that he had a 'vocation'.

As they resembled more closely the training of the monk, they were given a habit like a monk. They must all wear the soutane, all day, even when it was hot, even when they went on holiday. Even as candidates they were to be as distinguished from the laity as any monk. It was not just a rule, it became a moral obligation. The seminaries helped to change the customs of the clergy about clerical dress.

The monastic atmosphere also affected the seminary in the realm of mental prayer. No one at the Council of Trent imagined the seminary teaching its pupils advanced methods of contemplation. But the French started with the idea of a retreat. Then more seminaries were run by religious orders, and the house grew more like the house of a religious order. From early in the seventeenth century some seminaries began to teach ordinands methods of mental prayer. The custom of half an hour in the morning, in community, became established. It faded during the later eighteenth century. While it was universal it was often accompanied by a meeting on Sunday where the students reported on their experiences in mental prayer during the week. This system of spiritual direction was also like that of the monk. The seminarist not only had a confessor—twice a week, or once a week—he had a director to whom he should disclose his state of soul, and discuss it, once a month, or once a fortnight, outside the confessional. He was to treat the advice of the director almost as though it was inspired—at least he was to accept it in a reverent and obedient spirit.

Though separated from the world, they were affected by the world. The chief sign is wigs. Wigs and tonsure did not marry. Wigs became the custom of the world. The directors of seminaries banned wigs. For a decade or two they kept them out. But the world won. Similarly with books. Should a seminarist read Rousseau or Voltaire or the Encyclopaedia? He should not. But we find seminarists doing all these things.

The seminaries provided posts and pay for many more teachers of divinity outside the theological faculties. A lot of these were not good teachers. But the nature of the teaching profession is such that some people cannot teach without becoming curious about their subject. On the staffs of the seminaries we find some people who would have been an ornament to a university faculty.

In France, though not in the same way in Italy or Spain, the controversy between Jesuit and Jansenist affected the seminary. If a seminary were run by Jesuits, it was likely to be accused of teaching lax moral theology, because the name Jesuit was now a symbol of that teaching. But French seminaries were not run by Jesuits until after 1682, when they began to accept their management partly as a way of countering Jansenist teaching. The Oratorians won the reputation of being friendly to the Jansenists. They lost several seminaries because the bishop dismissed them after the Pope moved against Jansenism. Some bishops acted in the reverse direction. More often than ridding himself of the staff, the bishop would change the books; ban a text-book suspected of Jansenism, or of laxity, and substitute its opposite. As, by 1750, the battle was over, it became obligatory for seminaries to be strong against Jansenists in the doctrines of grace and justification, which were thought to be too like the Protestant doctrines; it became obligatory to be unlax—that is, severe, on moral issues—when to refuse absolution to penitents, what to say in the confessional, when to refuse communion. Jansenism secretly won in the confessional the battle which it publicly lost in the doctrine of faith. It was also obligatory, because this was France, that they should teach the Gallican articles and the doctrine that the supreme authority in the Church is the General Council and not the Pope. This last did not matter much in the parishes. What mattered was the effect upon ordinary people's practice of three generations of priests who were trained to be rigorous in the confessional.

There is a good deal of evidence of pleasure at what they achieved. The bishop of Cahors founded a seminary in 1643. He could not find staff. He entrusted it to the Lazarists. Nearly thirty years later the seminary had 50–60 students; and at the end of his life the bishop wrote to Vincent de Paul that his seminarists had changed the whole feel of the diocese.[12] In the eighteenth century the chief Italian student of seminaries, Cecconi, expressed the opinion that clergy who have attended a seminary are better clergymen than those who have not. He did not only mean better because they understood their job better. He meant better morally, holier. They had learnt the ways of worship of the Catholic Church and shared in it and knew about prayer and formed the moral ideals of pastoral care.[13] Whether this judgement was true is impossible to test. It was not the opinion of some so-called enlightened Catholics that many of these institutions were worthy of the high object with which they were founded. The best evidence for the French seminaries comes from their behaviour when revolution and poverty and murder fell upon them. On the whole they did well; at times heroically.

At least they were sanctuaries of quiet. A lot of prayers were said. The services in the parishes, especially in the village parishes, were more reverent and more dignified. The altar linen was cleaner, and the tabernacle not used for old wax. The sermons were hardly better, the catechism class was better led. The clergy had a stronger sense of obligation; which meant higher standards to aim at even if they did not achieve any of them.

The Catholic attack against seminaries persisted throughout the eighteenth century. In France its spearhead was the Jansenist newspaper *Nouvelles Ecclésiastiques*, which steadily accused them of breeding the

---

[12] Degert, I, pp. 199 *seq.*
[13] Giovanni di Giovanni, *La Storia dei seminarii chiericali* (Rome, 1747), *passim.*

wrong sort of clergy, and which shrilly charged their teaching staffs with ignorance and superstition. But the criticism that mattered, because it led to an experiment with a different system, happened in Austria.

The Catholic enlightenment was susicious that so many seminaries were run by religious orders. Just as the Curia was suspicious of the Jesuits in the German college at Rome because they were afraid of them trying to form Jesuits rather than secular priests, there was in some areas of the thought of the Catholic enlightenment a more general doubt of that nature. The life of the seminary is formed upon the monastic life; its frequent offices, its regularity of a way of life, its fixed discipline, its ideal of mission, and its cutting itself off from the normal life of the world. Was it certain that this was the best preparation for a parish priest who, whatever else he would have to do, was going to live near the very heart of a poor society and its suffering? And if seminaries were important in the general educational system of the State, was it certain that their syllabuses were the best adapted to educational service to the State as well as to the Church? Since during the later eighteenth century Catholic leaders grew generally critical of monks and the monastic ideal, except so far as they were engaged in education or in nursing care, they naturally were critical of a quasi-monastic ideal when it was applied to train their future parish priests.

The Spanish government was strong about it. Though bishops in Spain had been slow to found seminaries after the Council of Trent, by 1700 they were important in national education. When the Jesuits were expelled from Spain in 1767 it was necessary for government to re-organize the seminaries; and they promptly banned any monks or friars from teaching in them. The plans of the Catholic enlightenment for the reform of the seminaries usually included a wider curriculum, less dogmatic theology and less study of the scholastic philosophy, more study of the Bible and of church history, and of a new subject, which appeared for the first time, 'pastoral theology'. It seemed to have appeared for the first time in the attempted Austrian reforms and was one of the survivors when those reforms failed. Where the Catholic governments could associate seminaries more closely with a university they preferred to do so.

Far the most famous effort was that by the Holy Roman Emperor Joseph II. It was obvious that the Trent rule was a disaster intellectually, at least in some areas and some colleges, because it made for diocesan institutions and therefore often for weak institutions. Teaching ignorance to the ignorant was contrary to the educational ideals of the eighteenth century; and the suppression of the Jesuits, an order which specialized in good higher education, made a sudden gap in teaching power except so far as former Jesuits were allowed to go on doing the same job while they wore a slightly different soutane.

But there was an additional motive. These Catholic rulers wanted reform and enlightenment in the Church. They wanted to restrict papal authority in the Church. They tended to favour Gallican or Febronian ideas of Church and State. Therefore their mode of reforming seminaries had also an intention which was not only that of making better places of education. They sometimes meant, by better places, places where the teachers of canon law strictly limited papal authority and allowed the reforming rights of the Christian sovereign. They tended to identify such teaching as teaching by better informed and better qualified professors. And to achieve their ends they were prepared to take state control over the seminaries, so far as ordering their curriculum and appointing their staff. This was inevitable in countries where the seminaries still represented some of the favoured places of secular as well as religious education. It did not happen only during the eighteenth century. During the Italian Risorgimento it mattered very much to the Italian government what the teachers of South Italian seminaries were teaching about the Pope's power and they were well-prepared to interfere. As they were fighting a civil war in the former kingdom of Naples they needed to control education and that meant interfering in seminaries.

The obvious reform was to suppress the weak little institutions and collect the students in larger ones which would have an adequate teaching staff. Joseph II did this systematically in Austria, merely by state power and without asking the Church. The ordinands were to be educated in what were called general seminaries, which were sited in towns where there was usually also a university. Pavia was one, to which all students from Lombardy were sent. Graz was another. Under the decree of Trent the bishop of the small mountain diocese of Gurk founded a seminary in a small town in Carinthia. In the middle of the eighteenth century it was improved by being moved into Klagenfurt. In 1783 Joseph II abolished it and moved all the students into his general seminary at Graz. Of the two seminaries in Vienna one was abolished and the students from several dioceses around were sent into Vienna. Prague was another general seminary, existing in close connection with the university there.

Belgium was under Austrian rule. Under the system of Trent there was a miserably weak seminary at Malines, another at Bruges which was closed for a long time because of its small numbers, another weak one at Namur, another at Liege, another at Ghent, and the seminary at Tournai was a tiny affair in a village near Cambrai; all an absurd system when the country had a powerful Catholic university at Louvain, and the existence of the magnetic power of a univerity of that calibre in a small country helped to make the seminaries even weaker. Joseph II made general seminaries at Louvain and Luxemburg out of all this. When the famous theological faculty at Louvain strongly resisted the opening of the general seminary, Joseph II simply moved the secular faculties from Louvain to Brussels.

The new system as it existed for the seven years between 1783 and 1790 had the four great general seminaries of Vienna, Budapest, and Pavia for the Italian domains, and Louvain for the Belgian domains; and in addition eight general seminaries of the second rank, at Prague for the Czechs, Olmütz, Graz, Innsbruck, Freiburg im Breisgau, Luxemburg, and two at Lemberg, one for the Latin rite and one for the Uniats with a Greek rite. The State controlled the curriculum and the appointments. No one could be ordained unless he had attended one of these general seminaries.

The plan was opposed by the Cardinal of Vienna on the following grounds: it was a recipe for uniformity in training whereas the diocesan system made for diversity; the association of ordinands with the secular life of undergraduates was not good for ordinands; the old system worked pretty well; the decisions of the Council of Trent must be respected; these bigger institutions would be difficult to keep at a high standard by careful oversight; one could not exclude the bishops from the training of their future priests; the new system would cost a lot of money; the scheme would hurt the religious orders, which were useful to the State in charity and in education; and finally, if all clergy had to have university degrees, there would not be enough clergymen.[14] In 1783 all the bishops complained that they did not know their future clergy. They could not judge either their ability or their morals. To meet this complaint, the course, originally six years, was reduced to five and then the ordinand had to reside at a house in his diocese—at first for a year, later for six months.

In theory it was a better system than anything that had yet existed. The standards of teaching rose dramatically. And yet it did not work for long because it did not persuade either the Church or the public. The bishops might have to endure weak seminaries, but the Trent system gave them ordinands who were under their control and partially even under their oversight. They resented, as an infringement of the bishop's office, the State taking over the training of the clergy. Moreover the old and historic

[14] H. Zschokke, *Die theologische Studien und Anstalten der katholischen Kirche in Österreich* (Vienna, 1894), pp. 394–5.

and natural friction between bishops and university theological faculties increased the vexation. The bishops seldom believed that theological faculties made the best training for their future clergy, for they were designed to do a different sort of job; and Joseph II's system in effect turned the seminaries into a new sort of theological faculty, though with residence and much better catechesis and pastoral training. Moreover the general seminaries naturally attracted teachers who were more liberal or more radical or more Jansenistic or more Febronian than the normal run of seminary teachers, who were the best whom the bishops could find in a dearth of candidates; and this made the general seminaries suspect to a central body of opinion in the Church. The general seminary at Innsbruck fell under particular suspicion. Then there were those who resisted on principle, they thought that the State had no right to interfere in how Christian clergy were trained. Then there were financiers, who did not like so much money going into an expensive new system and who preferred to go on getting clergy on the cheap.

In certain parts of the empire a national or popular resistance to the government in Vienna could focus on these new institutions as a cause of injustice which they could use. In Belgium what was happening at Louvain, in the Tyrol what was happening at Innsbruck, made part of the popular demands for a political decentralizing from the control of Vienna. Croat nationalists were accustomed to a former Jesuit-run seminary at Zagreb which unusually had been founded not by the bishop but by the chapter. They were properly fierce in resenting the order that all their ordinands should train for the priesthood at the Hungarian general seminary in Budapest. Slovene nationalists were accustomed to a former Jesuit seminary at Ljubljana. They were fierce in resenting the order that their ordinands should all go to the Austrian general seminary at Graz. That shows how the old seminary, weak though it might be, was felt by the locals to be local; and therefore was a political and national object as well as a religious object. In British history we may compare the situation of the college at Maynooth in former days.

It was the most interesting experiment in all the history of the training of the clergy, and it would have been good if it could have been given another ten years to find itself. But that was impossible because the French Revolution was already upon Europe. The revived seminary at Bruges became a detention centre for non-juring priests, the revived seminaries at Ghent and Tournai were suppressed, the seminary at Namur was turned into a hospice, and the university of Louvain was shut.

And so when Joseph II died in 1790, his successor at once abandoned the experiment without any qualms. His financiers told him that the cost was astronomical. His political advisers told him that he could not continue in face of the steady opposition of the bishops. Some of the cabinet voted against the revival of bishops' seminaries. But they were reintroduced with provisos—all teachers must be graduates, seminarists must take the final examination before ordination at universities, no philosophy might be taught, and seminaries could only use textbooks approved by the university faculties. The business of transferring back from general seminaries to bishops' seminaries was painful; especially as it happened at a time of European war. Now there really was a shortage of ordinands. In 1821 the Austrian Chancellery asked itself the question whether we need seminaries at all. They answered it thus: in the history of the Church there have been many fine priests and bishops who never attended a seminary. Yet they are useful. Experience shows that the vocation of candidates is neither quite pure nor quite resolute. They have worldly motives mixed with ideals. Their vocation has to be purified and strengthened. Experience shows that this is much easier in a society retired from the world. But bishops must not be allowed to force everyone to undergo this training. Anyway we have neither money nor staff to create a system which will train everyone properly in residential seminaries.[15]

The Catholic seminary of the nineteenth century took less and less notice of the Council of Trent. The attempt in America to found a *seminarium principale*, which led to the establishment of the Catholic University of Washington, rose from most of the same reasons which led Joseph II to want a general seminary. But the philosophy of the seminary until 1965 was still that of withdrawal from society; the monastic pattern; the discipline of prayer and rule of life. In the *aggiornamento* epoch this at last began to be questioned by Catholics concerned with the training of their priests. It also began to be questioned by ordinands, for the nineteen sixties saw an unprecedented unsettlement inside seminaries.

The second Vatican Council had a lot of discussion about seminaries. When it had finished it had turned the whole system, in potentiality, upside down. Because Churches always have to say that they are carrying out better the instructions of the past, and must never say that they are reversing the instructions of the past, the fathers naturally said, in their final decree *Optatam totius*, 'Huius sanctae synodi patres, opus a Concilio Tridentino inchoatum prosequentes', the fathers of the Council have been furthering the work begun by the Council of Trent. That was only

---

[15] Document in Zschokke, p. 462.

true if taken very largely and loosely. What they did in effect was to make a sustained onslaught on the weaknesses generated by the system of the Council of Trent. What they were conscious of was the need to do for their own day what the Council of Trent did in its day for the training of the clergy. But they conceived their task in a very different spirit.

For what Trent had wanted to do was to separate young men from the world. The clerical garb and the tonsure from the age of 12! The Fathers of the second Vatican Council saw that the vision of Trent was defensive; against Protestantism and against the corruptions of society. They saw that what Trent did was to secure a reliable and on the whole an obedient clergy; but also a clergy which was separated from the people, and more and more separated as lay society went its own way. It created disciplined priests. It also created priests with closed minds. Of all this some of the fathers of the second Vatican Council were conscious and said so in no uncertain terms.

The original draft of the decree was meagre, and they refused to put up with it. First, they could only speak in the most general terms, because they agreed that the system for training priests in Africa might differ from the system best for Japan. Therefore each bishops' conference must be allowed to go its own way. Naturally the Curia was given the right of veto on the regulations which each bishops' conference was to propose. But the fathers destroyed the (partly nominal) centralization of Trent. They gave a large liberty to the provinces of the Church. Therefore, since they eschewed detailed general regulation from the centre, that must turn their own decree into the most general of principles. And their decree included, unlike Trent, not a little exhortation. This decentralization was widely welcomed. The missionary bishops regarded it as essential to the proper development of the Church. The German bishops liked it very much. But of course the assent was not universal.

The next thing generally agreed, though after debate, was the insertion of a beautiful passage about the priest's work to which the ordinand looks forward; its Trinitarian context; its share in the Paschal mystery; its place among the sacraments and the hours of prayer; its living after the gospel; its care, especially for the poor and the children and the sick and the sinners and the unbelievers; its love of Mary—this last being added on an amendment from the Polish and the Brazilian bishops. There was also a passage on celibacy, which went through various drafts because its formulation was difficult; and the most important thing about it was the addition of a clause, at the proposal of the ecumenicist Cardinal Bea, that this passage only applies to priests where the rites and laws of their Church insist upon the venerable custom, so making space for Uniats and future united Eastern Orthodox and future united Protestants. The clause showed that celibacy was certainly not indispensable to priesthood. There was also a clause on wholeness of the personality, and psychological balance, and maturity. One of the chief charges made against the old seminary by some fathers was that it did not allow the ordinand to develop sufficiently, not so much as a future priest but as a future mature adult, which was necessary to being a good future priest.

Various proposals were made to prevent the ordination of the personally immature, and especially of persons who took the vow of celibacy when they really had no calling to continence. The most dramatic were proposals to raise the age of permissible ordination above 24, and to make the time as a deacon longer. Neither of these got into the decree, but both were left in the freedom given to the bishops who would ordain.

The next thing generally acceptable was the destruction of the effect of the Trent decree, its most disastrous effect, that each diocese should if possible have its seminary. The fathers now laid it down that if separate dioceses cannot manage to have a seminary, then several dioceses may combine, or there may even be a seminary for the whole region, or even for a single nation. If the result is that the seminary is large, it should be divided into colleges or communities or groups for the sake of fostering the spirit of community. In the debate Cardinal Döpfner spoke strongly against the weakness of having too many little seminaries.

The next thing generally agreed was agreed by silence. There is no mention of the *seminarium minus*. The boys' school ceased to be in effect a seminary. The seminary is still called a *seminarium maius*. But by silence the old idea of Trent to take boys of 12 and make them priests and make them wear clerical habits and tonsures disappeared at last.

Now let us see what was not generally agreed.

Some of the fathers wanted to abolish seminaries altogether. They thought them to make for closed minds and lack of initiative and wanted to get rid of them. These root and branch men were few and had no chance of getting their way.

Without going so far a lot of voices, and probably the majority, wanted more personal initiative; more encouragement of personal initiative; more freshness and originality in the attitudes to the spiritual life; and less emphasis on discipline, and rules, and legality. Therefore they were prepared to use, and successfully got into the decree, attractive language about the nature of the community as a family of friends, having joy in their friendships. This was not a universal wish; because some of the fathers thought that all this new emphasis would weaken the training in discipline which was one of the main gifts of past seminaries, and were suspicious that a friendly community of people with initiative was not compatible with good order. Cardinal Ruffini, who led the party of tradition, was anxious about all this drafting and made his anxieties plain.

The next thing that was got into the decree, but was not universally wanted, was the rule which Trent had significantly not laid down. For the first time in Catholic history it was now, 1965, decreed that an ordinand must attend a seminary before he was ordained. Naturally this new rule was not achieved without opposition. Fifty-two bishops proposed an amendment making it possible for ordinands to be trained outside the seminaries. They failed to carry the amendment. But what their party got into the decree instead were loopholes—not in the stringent rule of compulsion, but in the way it was applied. No rule was laid down for the length of time that an ordinand must spend in the seminary. Nothing excluded the ordinand going out of the seminary to attend a university. Nothing excluded the ordinand from spending most of the time of his training in pastoral work—except that he needed to learn some theology (to which we shall come in a moment), and therefore needed a time with books and lecturers.

The tone of the whole decree was pastoral. What about the intellectual? The authors raised the general standard while they diminished the language requirements—in that, being typical of the entire modern development of modern European education. They said that people who entered the seminaries must have the qualifications which would enable them to enter universities. They must get enough Latin to read documents, but they need no longer have enough Latin to speak or write. Students were encouraged to learn Greek and Hebrew but it was not more than encouragement. Nevertheless all this intellectual expectation was far higher than the universal habits of the old seminaries, though no higher than the habits of the best older seminaries. Most old seminaries, except in Austria and Germany, would have regarded it as an absurd rule that their ordinands should have to have the qualifications to enter a university; even by the low standard of entrance requirement for universities in the modern world.

And now they had a crux of an argument. Ought they to maintain the old tradition and to force all ordinands to learn both philosophy and theology under the guidance of St Thomas Aquinas, even though in most seminaries they did not learn much? The discussion was sharp. Cardinal

Ruffini led a numerous body of protesting bishops who wanted the *philosophia perennis* and Aquinas to be ordered universally in the decree. To the contrary 117 fathers led by the Canadian Cardinal Leger, wanted no philosophical system prescribed, because St Thomas should be taught only so far as he has validity for today. Cardinal Jaeger cried 'Woe to the man of one book! Woe to the Church of one doctor!'

They compromised on philosophy. The decree reads 'innixi patrimonio philosophico perenniter valido' which was Cardinal Leger's proposal— 'relying on the philosophical inheritance so far as it is perennially valid' where the word 'perenniter' hints strongly at Aquinas but does not insist upon him. On theology they said that the teaching must be orientated towards the Bible; and then the Fathers of the Early Church; and then to systematic theology with St Thomas as the master; and then moral theology and liturgy and a knowledge of the Churches separate from Rome, and an introduction to other religions. It must be repeated that even in this intellectual section the emphasis was much upon the pastoral and less upon the academic.[16]

For a millenium and a half the Church did without seminaries, though it had many partial and haphazard substitutes.

The Renaissance gave higher education to the laity and so demanded higher education for the clergy. Trent founded a system to do that. It had modest success. It trained pastors in behaviour. It created some strong institutions and some weak, isolated, ill-equipped and ill-taught institutions. The French classical epoch tried to remedy the low standards as only the religious orders could remedy them. Where the seminaries were not like boarding schools, they were already half-like little monasteries. Now they were more like monasteries, and some imbibed the best side of the monastic ideal. The Catholic Enlightenment did its best. It grouped the weak institutions into bigger units, found better staffs, associated more of the colleges with universities, tried to find less blinkered teachers. The plans collapsed when the old world collapsed in the age of Revolution. In any case, because it depended upon State power and interference, it was already collapsing before the Revolution.

Slowly the new Catholic States of the nineteenth century modified the system because they had to. There had to be seminaries in non-Catholic

---

[16] For the decree 'Optatam totius' cf. J. Neuner, in *Das Zweite Vatikanische Konzil* (Freiburg im Breisgau, 1967), 2, pp. 309 *seq*; L. M. Weber, in *Handbuch der Pastoraltheologie* (Freiburg im Breisgau, 1969), 4, pp. 480 *seq*.

states, and seminaries in the mission field. But a full formal recognition of the changes that were forced waited until 1962–4, when the fathers of the second Vatican Council legislated for far greater variety. Just as it took the Church many decades to put into practice the provisions of the Council of Trent and never succeeded altogether, so it may be many decades before there could be a clear view of the consequences of the Second Vatican Council. Probably it did not make much difference that it made the seminary at last compulsory for the ordinand, for it only made it compulsory for a very short period, and it would be possible to recall the shorter periods of retreat for ordinands or clergy out of which the first French seminaries grew.

Cambridge

ECCLESIASTICAL HIERARCHY IN THE THOUGHT OF PSEUDO-DIONYSIUS*

by GRAHAM GOULD

T HE works of that late fifth- or early sixth-century writer whom we know as Pseudo-Dionysius are among the most difficult and yet also the most influential and compelling of all patristic writings. The whole Dionysian corpus and the many important historical and theological questions which it raises have been the subject of many studies,[1] and it would certainly be untrue to suggest that the *Ecclesiastical Hierarchy*, the subject of this communication, has been wholly neglected; but the work has only recently been made accessible in English,[2] and only one or two recent studies have given serious attention to the central place which the liturgy and its symbolism (the main subject of the work) occupy in Dionysius's theology as a whole.[3] A short study of the *Ecclesiastical Hierarchy* may therefore serve a useful purpose, perhaps at least that of encouraging the reading—now that an English translation *is* available—of what is probably the most accessible and immediately attractive of works which have been described (but who can tell whether such a description is ever accurate?) as 'famous but seldom-read'.[4]

The *Ecclesiastical Hierarchy* includes an extensive discussion of the place of ordained ministry in the Church, but we must approach Dionysius's teaching about the ministry with a more general look at the contents of the work. It is important to stress that for Dionysius 'hierarchy' is not a term to describe the clergy, or even the clergy and laity together in their

---

* I would like to thank the Revd Professor Stuart Hall for his comments during discussion of this communication.

[1] See Paul Rorem, *Biblical and Liturgical Symbols Within the Pseudo-Dionysian Synthesis*, Studies and Texts 71 (Toronto, 1984) for a recent bibliography.

[2] *Pseudo-Dionysius: The Complete Works*, translated by Colm Luibheid, introductions by Paul Rorem, René Roques and others (London, 1987), pp. 195–259. For the text of *EH* see PG 3, cols 369D–565D. All translations in this communication are my own.

[3] See Rorem, *Biblical and Liturgical Symbols*, esp. pp. 27–46. Many discussions of Dionysius's mystical theology make little use of *EH*: see for instance Andrew Louth, *The Origins of the Christian Mystical Tradition from Plato to Denys* (Oxford, 1981), pp. 159–78; C. A. Bernard, 'La Doctrine mystique de Denys L'Aréopagite', *Gregorianum* 68 (1987), pp. 523–66. For commentary on *EH* see Denys Rutledge, *Cosmic Theology: The Ecclesiastical Hierarchy of Pseudo-Denys, an Introduction* (London, 1964), and for a critical review of this work and further discussion of Dionysius's philosophical background, I. P. Sheldon-Williams, 'The *Ecclesiastical Hierarchy* of Pseudo-Dionysius', *DRev* 82 (1964), pp. 293–302, and 83 (1965), pp. 20–31.

[4] Rorem in *Pseudo-Dionysius: The Complete Works*, p. 1.

different grades of ministry and ranks. What Dionysius usually refers to as 'our hierarchy'[5] denotes a spiritual reality, the whole sacramental life of the Church, considered in the light of its ultimate purpose of bringing about perfect union between humanity and God. Thus in the first chapter of the work Dionysius defines the concept of hierarchy in typically compressed and abstract terms: 'Our hierarchy consists of inspired, divine and God-given understanding, activity and perfection.'[6] 'Every hierarchy is the complete expression of sacred realities, the perfect summation of the sacred things of the hierarchy. So our hierarchy is said to be the reality which contains all the sacred things appropriate to it.'[7] And, with reference to the final goal: 'We understand our hierarchy in proportion to our capacity, that is, manifested in a variety of perceptible symbols by which we are hierarchically drawn up, to an extent appropriate to our condition, towards the unity of deification.'[8]

In this last passage the emphasis lies upon the fact that our hierarchy works—brings us to our final goal—by means of symbols available to our senses; a contrast is intended with the celestial world, the world of pure spirits (νόες), whose access to God is direct (although limited) and conceptual rather than mediated through the senses. Nevertheless the goal is the same: 'To speak truly, the thing is one, which all Godlike beings desire, but they do not share in this one and the same thing in the same way.'[9] Dionysius is here attempting to link his understanding of the ecclesiastical hierarchy to the celestial hierarchy which he discussed in his work of that name.[10] As Paul Rorem points out,[11] the parallelism between the hierarchies is sometimes forced; but Dionysius regards the structure of 'our hierarchy' as the normative one, to which that of the celestial hierarchy is made to conform.[12]

The function of the hierarchy is to bring us to a state of deification (θέωσις), that is of 'conformity and union with God as far as

[5] As Rorem, *Biblical and Liturgical Symbols*, p. 28, points out, 'our hierarchy' is Dionysius's usual designation of his subject; the term 'ecclesiastical hierarchy' does not occur outside the title and the heading to chapter one.

[6] *EH* I.i (369D).

[7] I.3 (373C).

[8] I.2 (373A).

[9] *Ibid.* (373B).

[10] *PG* 3, cols 120A–340B. *EH* I.2 (372C) refers explicitly to the previous treatise.

[11] Rorem, *Biblical and Liturgical Symbols*, p. 29.

[12] In *EH* V.1.i–ii (501A, cited by Rorem), Dionysius says that all hierarchies possess sacraments, and applies this even to the celestial hierarchy; see also VI.3.vi (537A–C), where the applicability of the concept of purification (essential in the earthly hierarchy) to celestial beings is discussed.

possible.'[13] This union involves love, knowledge, and an 'inspired sharing in the unity of perfection, in the One himself, as far as possible.'[14] Again Dionysius emphasises the means by which the hierarchy works: it is a gift of divine goodness for the sake of salvation and deification, given to the celestial beings by direct, intellectual illumination, but to us in the form of the variety of symbols contained in the 'divinely-transmitted Scriptures.'[15] It is this emphasis on the importance of symbols which explains Dionysius's concern with the symbolic meaning of the liturgical acts which he describes throughout the remainder of the work.

The first chapter of the *Ecclesiastical Hierarchy* contains one or two passages which are important for Dionysius' understanding of the function of the Church's ministry, although their significance becomes clear only later in the treatise. He comments that the hierarchy 'has one and the same power throughout all its hierarchical reality, namely the hierarch himself', and that 'the being, proportion, and order which he has through the sacred deification which comes upon him from God, are perfected according to divine reality, and deified, and shared with those below him, according to the merit of each.'[16] 'Hierarch' is Dionysius's term for bishop, and this passage, explaining that the hierarchy's 'power', its ability to achieve its spiritual goals, comes from God and is made available through the hierarch who shares it with those below him in the hierarchy, anticipates and explains Dionysius's later descriptions of the bishop as the source and head of the whole sacramental system. 'He who says "hierarch" is designating an inspired and divine man, someone who possesses all sacred knowledge, in whom his whole hierarchy is completely perfected and known.'[17]

In the following three chapters Dionysius describes and interprets different sacraments of the Church in the light of his introduction on the nature of hierarchy. In each case a discussion of the nature of the sacrament is followed by a brief description of the rite itself, then by an interpretation of the symbolism of the different actions. Chapter Two, on baptism, begins by restating the goal of the hierarchy, and explaining that union with God is found only in obedience to his commandments and through training our souls to receive the 'sacred words and actions',[18] that

---

[13] I.3 (376A).
[14] *Ibid.*
[15] I.4 (376B).
[16] I.2 (372C–D).
[17] I.3 (373C).
[18] II.1 (392A).

is the sacraments. Only someone who has 'received inspired existence' can ever 'understand the divine tradition, or put it into practice'.[19] Inspired or divine existence (τὸ ὑπάρχειν ἐνθέως, τὸ εἶναι θείως) is the spiritual gift conveyed by baptism, or divine birth (ἡ θεία γέννησις), which is Dionysius's preferred term for it.[20] 'Let us therefore examine the divine symbols of divine birth.'[21]

Space forbids a detailed examination of Dionysius's understanding of the symbolism of the various sacramental rites, or of the precise role which each of the sacraments plays in the achievement of the goal of the hierarchy, but some comments may be made. In his system there are only three sacraments, for which his usual designation is 'perfector' (τελετή) or 'perfecting action'. The importance of baptism in Dionysius's conception of hierarchy has been noted; the eucharist is seen principally as a sacrament of unity, and Dionysius always uses the traditional term σύναξις, 'gathering' to describe the rite. Every 'sacred perfecting activity', he comments, 'draws our distracted lives into the unity of deification', and offers us communion and union with the One; but it is the σύναξις of which this quality is especially predicated, and whose celebration is necessary for the completion (τελείωσις) of other rites.[22]

The third sacrament is the 'sacrament of ointment' (τελετὴ μύρου). The rite described is the consecration by the hierarch of the chrism or oil which is used in baptism and other ceremonies. Dionysius sees the ritual use of the μύρον as symbolic of the presence and action of Christ in the incarnation and the sacraments. Thus the use of chrism in the τελετή of baptism gives a visitation of the Spirit to the one who is being perfected, and symbolizes the fact that Christ who gives the Spirit was 'himself, as man, sanctified for our sake by the divine Spirit, though unalterable in the substance of his divinity'.[23] Or again, the use of the μύρον in consecrating an altar is tied to a description of Jesus as the true heavenly altar on which all of us are consecrated and offered to God.[24] The appropriateness of the μύρον to symbolize the action of Christ thus seems to rest on the fact that the μύρον both receives sanctification, consecration, and perfection at the hands of the hierarch, and yet is also the instrument of further perfecting acts; Jesus too was sanctified by the Spirit as a man, but is also the source of

---

[19] II.1 (392B).
[20] Ibid.
[21] Ibid.
[22] III.1 (424C–425A).
[23] IV.3.xi (484C). Jesus' baptism is alluded to.
[24] Ibid., xii (484C–85A).

our sanctification.[25] The effect of all these passages is greatly to enhance the significance of the μύρον, which is ranked with the σύναξις in importance, and declared to be a necessary element in nearly all of the perfecting actions of the hierarchy.[26]

Dionysius's treatment of the μύρον is closely related to his understanding of the role of the hierarch or bishop in the sacramental system. The headship which the hierarch enjoys is illustrated in practice by the fact that he alone is responsible for the consecration of the essential μύρον: it is part of his 'perfecting order and power'.[27] Like the μύρον, the hierarch is necessary to the functioning of the whole sacramental system, and Dionysius tends to attribute to the hierarch alone the ministry of perfection which characterizes it.

Dionysius discusses the orders of ministry specifically in chapter five, which begins with another attempt to describe the nature of the hierarchy, this time not in terms of its ultimate goal but of its inherent structure, order, and proportion:

> After the divine sacred actions, it is apropriate to describe the sacerdotal (ἱερατικός) orders themselves, their elections, powers, activities and perfections, and the triad of higher orders which they form, in order to reveal the arrangement of our hierarchy, which entirely rejects and excludes disorder, lack of structure, and confusion, but reveals structure, order and stability in the proportions of its sacred orders.[28]

Dionysius's concern with order and proportion within the hierarchy is a product, of course, of his neo-Platonist understanding of the nature of creation, and of his own special interest in the correlation between the superior, heavenly, and the earthly hierarchies. It is at this point that he introduces one of his excursuses designed to prove that the same structure which he detects in the ecclesiastical hierarchy is present in the celestial one[29]—and he also devotes some attention in passing to the relationship

---

[25] See also *ibid.*, x (484A), where the use of μύρον in the 'perfection of every sacred thing' shows that 'the sanctified Sanctifier' remains the same 'while performing every act of divine goodness'. Also *ibid.*, xii (485A), where the term τελετή is held to designate both 'being sanctified humanly for our sake', and 'perfecting and santifying everything with divine activity', when applied to the μύρον as a symbol (as the context shows) of Jesus.

[26] IV.2 (473A); IV.3.iii (476C–D).

[27] *Ibid.*

[28] V.1.i (500D). 'Perfections' (τελειώσεις) in this context refers to the rite of ordination which Dionysius describes in V.2 (509A–C).

[29] See above, n. 12.

between the Church's hierarchy and the 'hierarchy of the Law', that is of the Old Covenant. The latter made available a real but limited 'perfection', that of 'drawing up to spiritual worship'.[30] Our hierarchy shares with the Law the use of symbols to achieve this drawing up to the divine, but also shares with the celestial hierarchy the possibility of intellectual contemplation (νοερὰ θεωρία).[31] This suggestion of the possibility of direct and immediate access to the divine qualifies Dionysius's earlier statement that our hierarchy, in contrast to the celestial, works exclusively through the medium of perceptible symbols.

To return to the structure of the hierarchy, and hence to Dionysius's teaching on the Church's ministry: 'Our sacred tradition holds that every hierarchical reality is divided into the divine sacraments, those who know and understand them, and those who are being sacredly perfected by them.'[32] In this comment, and in a similar statement which follows shortly afterwards,[33] Dionysius introduces for the first time a general comment on the position of the clergy and laity in the Church's hierarchy. But the triadic structure which Dionysius wishes to impose on every hierarchy, and the fact that he sees the ecclesiastical hierarchy as a structure of sacred actions co-ordinated by reference to a particular goal, rather than as a group of people, demand that the sacraments too be seen as having functions in their own right, separable in theory from those of the clergy who understand and administer them.

In each division of the hierarchy—sacraments, ministers, recipients—Dionysius discerns three different functions or powers (δυνάμεις), those of purification, illumination, and perfection.[34] But the distinction between sacrament and minister proves a difficult one to apply in describing their δυνάμεις. The first function of the sacraments is the 'purification of the unperfected'; the first function of the ministers is 'to purify the unperfected through the sacraments'. The second function of the sacraments is 'the enlightening initiation of the purified'; of the ministers, to 'enlighten the purified'. And the third functions, respectively, 'the perfection of the initiated in understanding of their initiation', and to 'perfect those who share in the divine light in perfect understanding of the

---

[30] V.1.ii (501C).

[31] *Ibid.* (501C–D).

[32] V.1.i (501A).

[33] *Ibid.*, ii (501D): 'There is a threefold division of the hierarchy into the most holy sacred works of the sacraments, the Godlike ministers of the sacred things, and those led by them, in proportion to their capacity, to sacred things.'

[34] *Ibid.*, iii (504A–B).

illumination which they have contemplated'.[35] The close similarities in wording between these definitions of the powers of the sacraments and the clergy suggest that Dionysius failed to distinguish their respective functions very clearly. Schematic definitions can however be misleading; although Dionysius always sees the functions of the clergy as *related* to the administration of the sacraments, or to the preparation of the laity to receive them, he eventually manages to avoid actually equating the ministry of the clergy with their performance of particular rites.

His longest description of the role of the hierarch recalls and elaborates the exulted references to his function and privileges which occur in the introduction to the treatise, and deserves an extended quotation:

> The Origin and Founder of all invisible and visible order causes the rays of divine activity to be given first to those who are more Godlike, and through them (minds more discerning and able to participate in and share the light) he illuminates and manifests himself to those who are below them, in proportion to their powers. It is then for these—the first of those who see God—ungrudgingly to reveal to the second rank, to an extent appropriate to their condition, the divine sights which they behold. To initiate others in the hierarchy belongs to those who have been initiated with perfect understanding into the divine reality of their hierarchy, and have received the sacramental power to initiate. And to share, according to merit, sacred things, belongs to those who are full and understanding participators in the sacerdotal consecration ($\tau\epsilon\lambda\epsilon\iota\omega\sigma\iota\varsigma$).
>
> Now the divine order of hierarchs is the first of the orders which see God. The same order is the beginning and the end, for in it is perfected and fulfilled the whole arrangement of our hierarchy. For, as we see that every hierarchy is summed up in Jesus, nevertheless each has its own inspired hierarch. The power of the order of hierarchs extends through the sacred totality, and performs the mysteries of the hierarchy through all the sacred orders.[36]

The hierarch, as Dionysius says elsewhere, turns temporarily from the communion with God which he enjoys, in order to share his understanding with others.[37]

---

[35] *Ibid.* Of the powers of the sacraments, purification and illumination are associated with baptism, perfection with the $\sigma\acute{\nu}\nu\alpha\xi\iota\varsigma$ and the $\mu\acute{\nu}\rho o\nu$ (504B–C). See Rorem, *Biblical and Liturgical Symbols*, pp. 43–4.

[36] V.3, iv–v (504D–505B).

[37] II.2.viii (397A), II.3.iii (400B), III.3.iii (429B), V.3.vii (513C–D). See S. C. Parsons, 'The

In practical terms, as has been noted, the superior position of the bishop in the ecclesiastical hierarchy is ensured by his control over the sacrament of the μύρον, and also by his unique possession of the power to ordain priests and to consecrate the altar on which the σύναξις is celebrated.[38] The hierarch is specially endowed with the ability to perfect the sacramental actions of the hierarchy.[39] But this 'perfecting' of the sacraments need not be a purely ritual action; it also involves teaching. Dionysius's references to the teaching functions of the hierarch are oblique, but perhaps the clearest is his statement that the hierarch 'initiates others by explaining the meaning of the sacred things, and teaches their proportions and sacred capacities and powers'.[40]

The hierarch's own perfect understanding of sacred reality, which enables him to teach others about the true meaning of the sacraments, is made clear again when Dionysius contrasts his role with that of the priests (ἱερεῖς). Theirs is the second function of the hierarchy, that of illumination, and they, performing their ministry in subjection to that of the hierarchs, 'explain the works of God through the most sacred symbols, and make those who come contemplators of and sharers in the holy sacraments'.[41] Their duty, that is, lies in the day-to-day administration of the sacraments and in the explanation to the people of the meaning of their symbolism. But the priests 'send on to the hierarch those who desire understanding of the sacred actions which they have contemplated'.[42] It is the third function of the hierarchy, to give understanding of what they have seen to those who have already received illumination and contemplation, which belongs exclusively to the hierarch, and is what constitutes his distinctive, perfecting ministry.[43]

"Hierarch" in the Pseudo-Dionysius and its Place in the History of Christian Priesthood', *Studia Patristica*, 18, part 1, ed. E. A. Livingstone (Kalamazoo, 1985), pp. 187–90.

[38] V.1.v (505B–C).
[39] *Ibid.*, vi (505C–D).
[40] *Ibid.* (505D).
[41] *Ibid.*
[42] *Ibid.* (505D–508A).
[43] As these quotations show, Dionysius associates contemplation with the second 'power' of the hierarchy. See also the descriptions of the three δυνάμεις of the laity in V.1.iii (504B), of which the second is 'enlightened contemplation of certain sacred things', and the third, 'the illumination of the sacred enlightenments, of which they have become contemplators, with perfect understanding'. Although he uses 'intellectual contemplation' to designate what the earthly and celestial hierarchies have in common, Dionysius's recognition of the importance of material symbols prevents him from defining contemplation exclusively as an inward disposition of the νοῦς: something which may be called 'contemplation' is associated with simple participation in the sacraments; perfect *understanding* comes later. Dionysius in fact

The role of the deacons (λειτουργοί) is seen as that of purification, necessary before and in preparation for sharing in the sacraments administered by the priests, and involving discerning the faults of those who come, showing them the darkness of their past life and teaching them to turn from it to enlightenment, and purifying them 'with the purifying illuminations and teachings of the Scriptures'.[44] The purifying and teaching ministry which the deacons carry out is represented in the liturgy of baptism by the symbolic actions which the deacons perform of stripping the candidate and turning him round, and in the σύναξις by the fact that the deacons guard the doors of the holy place, to prevent the unpurified from entering.[45]

The ministries of the three orders are thus characterized in slightly different terms, as involving teaching, preparation for and administering of the sacraments, and by this means distinguished from the operations of the sacraments themselves. Dionysius's overriding concern remains however to expound the spiritual significance of the symbolism involved in the Church's different rites, and compared with the detail of chapters two to four of the work, his comments on the clerical orders are compressed and sometimes ambiguous, and usually directed to explaining their role in the sacramental system. The wider concerns of the fifth-century bishop as arbitrator, judge, and philanthropist in his local community, and as a member of the conciliar government of the whole Church, are not mentioned; Dionysius's ideal of ministry is the inspired hierarch, effecting the mysteries of the hierarchy through the lower ministries of enlightening priest and teaching, purifying deacon.[46]

All of this discussion is contained in the introduction to the chapter on the ministry. In the later sections, following the pattern of the work, Dionysius describes the rites of ordination and the meaning of their symbolism. Here he refers to other characteristics of the clergy—their complete devotion to God in purity of mind, their renunciation of all

---

strikes a balance between the sacramental, symbolic and objective, and the purely inward aspects of the spiritual life, by allowing θεωρία a wider range of meaning than it held for, say, Evagrius of Pontus, for whom it is the product of a rigorous purification of the mind and quest for ἀπάθεια, and is not related to the sacraments in the same close way as Dionysius's whole scheme of purification, contemplation and understanding.

[44] V.I.vi (508A–B).

[45] *Ibid.* See also III.2 (425B–C) for role of the deacons at the *synaxis*.

[46] Since it is an important principle that the hierarch's activity extends *throughout* the hierarchy, his role naturally encompasses the purifying and illuminating powers of the lower orders: V.I.vii (508C–D).

desires of the flesh[47]—but also takes the opportunity to refer again to the threefold function of the ministry, and to the perfection or fulfillment of the whole ministry which is the role of the hierarch. The superior position of the hierarch is symbolized by the fact that the Scriptures, the source of all the knowledge of God which he communicates to the hierarchy, are rested on his head during his consecration.[48]

Dionysius's chapter on the laity—'those being perfected'—has rather less to say than those about the clergy or about the particular sacraments. The first and second orders of the laity are, respectively, non-communicants and communicants (whom, as we have seen,[49] Dionysius regarded as contemplatives). The former are described as those who are being formed and strengthened by the teachings of the Scriptures.[50] Here again there is a reference to the teaching ministry of the deacons, for although it is correct to point out[51] that Dionysius attributed great significance to the effect on the non-communicants of the readings from Scripture which they hear before their dismissal from the σύναξις and other rites,[52] it is surely wrong to interpret all his comments on the Scriptures as referring to liturgical actions. Use of the Scriptures in teaching is presupposed.

The rite described in Dionysius's chapter on the laity is the rite of profession of a monk, the third of the lay orders. Dionysius's comments on monks involve a curious inconsistency which bears on his understanding of ministry. He first explains that the monks, whose order enjoys perfect holiness and the possibility of 'contemplating the sacred actions in intellectual contemplation and communion', are 'entrusted to the perfecting powers of the hierarchs', to be perfected in their understanding by their teaching.[53] But almost immediately afterwards he adds that the actual rite of profession is not the province of the hierarch but of the

---

[47] V.3.ii (509D), iv (512A–B).
[48] Ibid., vii–viii (513C–516A).
[49] See above, n. 43, and also the descriptions of the second order of the laity in VI.1.ii (532B–C) and the summary in VI.3.v (536D).
[50] VI.1.i (532A–B).
[51] Rorem, *Biblical and Liturgical Symbols*, pp. 122–5.
[52] IV.3.iii (476D–477A).
[53] VI.1.iii (532D). Here even 'intellectual contemplation' denotes the full understanding of the sacraments communicated by the hierarch, not something acquired by a purely inward process. This is confirmed by III.3.ii (428C), where θεωρία νοητῶν ('contemplation of intelligible reality') refers to the understanding of spiritual truths symbolized by the liturgy, and by *ibid.*, xii (441C–D), where νοητὴ θεωρία refers to spiritual contemplation of the actions of Jesus recalled in the Anaphora.

priest.[54] This unexpected irregularity in Dionysius's system is probably to be explained by his desire to avoid any insinuation (which might be involved if the hierarch performed the rite) that the profession of a monk is an ordination, or confers on him any teaching or other ministry. This can be seen from his explanation of the symbolism of the rite:

> The fact that a monk does not kneel, and does not receive the divinely-given Scriptures on his head, but stands before the priest who speaks the sacred invocation—this shows that the order of monks does not have the duty of leading others, but stands by itself in a solitary and holy station. It follows the sacerdotal orders, and by accompanying them is obediently led by them to a divine under-standing of its own sacredness.[55]

Whatever his precise date, Dionysius lived at a time when the role of the monastery as a source of candidates for the priesthood and episcopate, and of monks in the Church's doctrinal struggles and pastoral ministry, was widely if not universally recognized and applauded.[56] Dionysius how-ever seems never to suggest that professtion as a monk and ordination as a priest or hierarch will often or always be combined in the same person, or that monks, lay or ordained, have a vital role to play in the Church's ministry. In the passage quoted, a leadership role is explicitly denied to them, and elsewhere Dionysius reveals his opposition to any interference by monks with the prerogatives and judgement of the clergy, warning a correspondent of his, a monk Demophilus, against taking it upon himself to reject a penitent sinner and rebuke a priest who was about to admit him to communion, on the pretext that by doing so he was defending the sacred elements from defilement.[57]

It is true that in his description of the rite of profession, Dionysius goes on to say that the life of the monks should be like that of the clerical order, since it 'has much in common with it, and approaches it more nearly than the other orders of those who are being perfected'.[58] Perhaps this indicates

---

[54] *Ibid.* (533A).

[55] VI.3.i (533C).

[56] In Syria, Dionysius's probable place of origin, monks may have played a significant part in the initial conversion of rural areas to Christianity. See Sozomen, *HE* (ed. J. Bidez, *GCS* 50), VI.34, and W. Liebeschuetz, 'Problems Arising from the Conversion of Syria', *SCH* 16, pp. 17–24.

[57] *Letter*, 8 (*PG* 3, cols 1084A–1100D; see especially 1088B–1089B). Dionysius envisages that monks will take part in the same services as other laity (exclusively monastic churches are not discussed); what he objects to is any interference by the monks in the services they attend.

[58] *EH* VI.3.ii (533D–536A).

that Dionysius hesitated to express an unusual attitude to monks, or was reluctant to be seen to devalue their way of life; but more probably, Dionysius means simply that the monks resemble the clergy in their total dedication to service of God, not in the *similarity* of their service. The perfection of the monastic way is seen in its renunciation of everything which distracts from 'understanding the unifying commandments', and its superiority to the other lay orders in the fact that much that is permitted for the ordinary layman is entirely forbidden to the dedicated, or single-minded (ἐνιαῖος) monk, who 'must be made one with the One, and united to the Sacred Monad'.[59] The distinctiveness of the monastic vocation lies in its solitude, and non-involvement in anything likely to distract from the mystical life.[60] Of course many perfectly ordinary things can impede attention to the commandments of God, but perhaps in describing a monk's avoidance of all distraction, and denying him a leadership role like that of the clergy, Dionysius was trying to express, without indulging in explicit criticism, his aversion to the involvement of monks in civil or ecclesiastical politics.[61]

It will always be difficult to do justice to Dionysius, especially in an age when few people can be expected to share the neo-Platonic understanding of an ordered hierarchical spiritual and material cosmos which is the basic presupposition of his account of the ecclesiastical hierarchy. But despite his philosophical views, the difficulties of his overloaded writing, his many compressions, obscurities, and occasional contradictions, it is possible to recognize that we are dealing with a writer of considerable intellectual power, but also of humanity and gentleness. He is rarely polemical in defence of important dogmatic ideas, and never resorts to the aggression and personal defamation of his opponents characteristic of much fourth- and fifth-century theology—even when himself subject to attack.[62] The qualities of the man which—to me at any rate—are aparent in his works make it easier, perhaps, to appropriate, as a valuable ideal and

---

[59] *EH* VI.3.ii (533D). See also VI.1.iii (533A): a monk's life should be ἀμέριστος—undistracted or undivided—and ἐνιαῖος—dedicated, single-minded, or unified.

[60] A monk's dedication to 'unification' does not mean, however, that he possesses a type of perfection qualitatively different from that available to the ordinary layman. He attains intellectual contemplation and perfect holiness not simply through being a monk but through the ministry of the hierarch, and the whole thrust of Dionysius's teaching is that the same perfection is also available, from the same source, to the ordinary (that is, contemplative) communicant.

[61] See also the attitude to the involvement of monks in political affairs expressed in canon 4 of the council of Chalcedon (*HL* 1, pt. ii, p. 779).

[62] For Dionysius's attitude to polemic see *Letter* 7 (1077B–1081C).

a starting point for our own thoughts, if not as a practical blue-print for the ministry and sacramental life of the Church, some of the ideas and goals of the strange spiritual world whose material symbols Dionysius describes for us in the *Ecclesiastical Hierarchy*.

Trinity College, Oxford

PAROCHIAL MINISTRY IN EARLY ANGLO-SAXON ENGLAND: THE ROLE OF MONASTIC COMMUNITIES

by SARAH FOOT

IT was the example of some visiting parochial clergy that first inspired the young Wynfrith, later the missionary Boniface, to adopt the religious life. According to his hagiographer Willibald

> when priests or clerics, travelling abroad, as is the custom in those parts, to preach to the people, came to the town and the house where his father dwelt the child would converse with them on spiritual matters.[1]

As far as one can tell from the available sources, this was the way in which most regular parochial care was effected in the early Anglo-Saxon period; groups of priests or other religious, living in communities, would travel out from their houses into the surrounding *parochiae* to administer the sacraments and preach to the laity.[2] This was, for example, the habit of the Irish episcopal community at Lindisfarne. Bede described how villagers used to gather round any visiting priest, eager to hear the word of life from him

> for the clerics visited the villages for no other reason than to preach, to baptize and to visit the sick, in brief to care for their souls.[3]

Such ministry was not, however, the exclusive prerogative of episcopal establishments. Successive priors at the *monasterium* of Melrose, Boisil and Cuthbert, were in the habit of going out of the minster regularly to preach the way of truth to 'those who had gone astray'.[4] Lay people also sometimes themselves sought the ministrations of holy men. When Willibrord's father, Wilgils, devoted himself to the monastic life, retiring to an oratory dedicated to Saint Andrew on the Humber estuary, he 'did

---

[1] Willibald, *Vita Sancti Bonifatii*, c. 1, ed. Levison, *MGH SRG*, p. 5; transl. C. H. Talbot, *The Anglo-Saxon Missionaries in Germany* (London, 1954), p. 27.

[2] The distinctions between different types of communal religious establishment are discussed at length in my Cambridge University doctoral thesis, 'Anglo-Saxon Minsters AD 597–950: the Religious Life in England before the Benedictine Reform' (in preparation).

[3] Bede, *HE* iii 26, ed. and transl. B. Colgrave and R. A. B. Mynors (Oxford, 1969), p. 310.

[4] *Ibid.*, iv 27, p. 432.

not cease to exhort the crowds who came flocking to him with most sweet instruction in the word of God'.[5] In a period when there were few large centres of population,[6] outside which ecclesiastical settlements were sparsely scattered,[7] and lay access to a church building, or even a standing cross, was severely restricted in rural areas,[8] it can readily be understood why the regular pastoral care of the laity devolved upon peripatetic workers or individual holy men like Wilgils.

The precise nature of the role of early Anglo-Saxon monastic houses in parochial ministry is less immediately obvious than is that of contemporary cathedral communities. The earliest cathedrals were all established for a specifically missionary purpose and continued to minister to the neighbouring laity after the latter's nominal conversion. Local studies have, however, demonstrated in a number of areas the development as early as the seventh century of a system of local minster churches in addition to the cathedrals. These institutions exercised pastoral responsibilities in well-defined *parochiae*, which often corresponded to secular administrative districts.[9] The inmates of these houses provided continuing care for the laity, administering the sacraments, preaching, and offering more basic catechetical teaching, as well as caring for the sick and providing burial for the dead.[10] Their right to receive in return payment such as tithe (church scot) or burial dues (soul-scot) is mentioned in early law codes,[11]

---

[5] Alcuin, *Vita Sancti Willibrordi*, c. 1, *MGH SRM* VII, pp. 81–141, at 116.

[6] For the role of the church in general, and the minsters in particular, in the development of local centres of population see J. Campbell, 'The Church in Anglo-Saxon Towns', *SCH* 16 (1979), pp. 119–35.

[7] The distribution of ecclesiastical sites in the period up to *c*.850 is well-illustrated by Patrick Wormald's map in J. Campbell, ed., *The Anglo-Saxons* (Oxford, 1982), p. 71.

[8] R. Hill, 'Christianity and Geography in Early Northumbria', *SCH* 3 (1966), pp. 126–39.

[9] Notable among such studies is the work of P. H. Hase, 'The Development of the Parish in Hampshire' (unpublished PhD. thesis, University of Cambridge, 1975), and M. J. Franklin, 'Minsters and Parishes: Northamptonshire Studies' (unpublished PhD. thesis, University of Cambridge, 1982). See also J. Blair, ed., *Minsters and Parish Churches. The Local Church in Transition 950–1200* (Oxford, 1988), and C. N. L. Brooke, 'Rural Ecclesiastical Institutions in England: the Search for their Origins', *Settimane*, 28 (Spoleto, 1982), pp. 685–711.

[10] There is also some evidence that parochial workers had to contend with persisting pagan practices throughout the eighth century. See for example the Council of Clofesho, AD 747, c. 3, ed. A. W. Haddan and W. Stubbs, *Councils and Ecclesiastical Documents relating to Great Britain and Ireland*, 3 vols (Oxford, 1869–73), 3, pp. 362–76, at 364, and the report of the 786 Legatine Synods, cc. 3 and 19, ed. Haddan and Stubbs, *Councils*, 3, pp. 447–62, at 449, 458.

[11] Payment of these dues was recommended in early texts, for example tithe is mentioned in Theodore's *Penitential*, II xiv 9–10, ed. Haddan and Stubbs, *Councils*, 3, pp. 176–204, at 203, and by the Legatine Synods of 786, c. 17, *ibid.*, pp. 456–7. Church scot, a fixed render of grain due at Martinmas, was enjoined in the laws of King Ine, cc. 4, 61, ed. F. L. Attenborough, *The Laws of the Earliest English Kings* (Cambridge, 1922), pp. 36–61, at 36, 56.

but payment of these was not made compulsory until the tenth century,[12] when the growth of proprietary churches began to threaten the rights of the old minsters.[13]

Our understanding of the nature of the Anglo-Saxon religious life is at present insufficient for us to be able confidently to distinguish between those houses founded to pursue a purely devotional life and those established to provide for local pastoral needs. Scholars are, however, increasingly presuming that such distinctions are unnecessary and that 'all or most establishments called *monasteria* either performed or supported pastoral work within defined territories'.[14] I should like to test this presumption, not by collecting evidence (either from contemporary sources or from later parish records) for the involvement of individual houses in pastoral activities, but by examining contemporary expressions of the ideals governing the exercise of parochial ministry. If some basic principles underlying the organization of the pastoral cure could be established, which were applicable to the whole of England, it might be easier to place the conclusions reached by local studies in a broader context. The clearest evidence for the organization of the spiritual care of the lay population comes from the period when a system of pastoral care was being developed, between the archbishoprics of Theodore (AD 669–90) and Wulfred (AD 805–832), between the completion of the initial work of conversion and the beginning of the Viking period.

Most statements relating to the principles behind the exercise of parochial ministry are to be found in the edicts of church councils; examination of the ideals expressed in these texts may reveal whether the *monasteria*, as opposed to the cathedral churches, had a recognized role in the cure of souls. It should be stressed that these *monasteria* were not monasteries in the modern sense of the word; the term in the early Anglo-Saxon period encompassed all communal religious institutions from the wealthiest of the royal double houses to the meanest of priests' cells. The Latin term *monasterium*, and its Old English equivalent *mynster*, therefore convey nothing about the nature, status, or regularity of observance of the establishment they describe, they merely indicate that it is occupied by

---

[12] The earliest text to insist on the payment of tithe, church-scot, soul-scot, and plough-alms is King Aethelstan's ordinance of AD 926×*c*.930, prologue, c. 4, ed. D. Whitelock, M. Brett and C. N. L. Brooke, *Councils and Synods with other Documents relating to the English Church, AD 871–1204*, 2 vols (Oxford, 1981), I, pp. 43–7, at 44, 46.

[13] J. Blair, 'Minster Churches in the Landscape', in D. Hooke, ed., *Anglo-Saxon Settlements* (Oxford, 1988), pp. 35–58, at 57.

[14] J. Blair, *Minsters and Parish Churches*, p. 1.

several individuals. No distinctions are made in the terminology used to denote male, female, or double houses, nor can language be used as a means of determining which houses were engaged in external pastoral ministry.[15] Since the word 'monastery' nowadays has connotations of particularly Benedictine regularity, and since in the period before the tenth-century monastic reform it is impossible in England to distinguish between contemplative and active houses, I propose to eschew the word 'monastery' and to encompass the apparent diversity of early Anglo-Saxon religious practice instead in the one word minster, just as contemporary writers did. In this I deliberately depart from the usage of those scholars of the eleventh and twelfth centuries who have adopted the word to describe collegiate communities of priests with parochial responsibility for areas larger than a single village.[16] It remains to be seen whether the early sources relating to the exercise of parochial ministry will reveal clearer distinctions between types of houses, or whether it is to be presumed that all minsters had equal theoretical responsibilities, even if they did not all in practice discharge them to the same extent.

The exegetical writings of Bede provide the fullest available statement of the place of pastoral ministry in the life of early Anglo-Saxon religious. Having lived from the age of seven exclusively in the minster at Jarrow, a house noted for the strictness of its observance,[17] Bede was not typical of religious of his day, but his ideas, coloured by his monastic background, make interesting contrast with the episcopal viewpoint expressed in the conciliar literature.[18] It has been argued that Bede was writing largely for members of the clerical orders rather than for 'monks',[19] but such distinctions cannot easily be sustained in the early period, and do not seem to be drawn intentionally by Bede himself. Alan Thacker has demonstrated the way in which Bede urged all the faithful, without the cloister as well as within,[20] to pursue active virtues as well as

---

[15] This argument, which is based on the careful study of ecclesiastical and secular texts written in England before c.950, is developed more fully in my thesis.

[16] M. J. Franklin, 'The Identification of Minsters in the Midlands', *Anglo-Norman Studies*, 7 (1985), pp. 69–88, at p. 69.

[17] Bede, *HE* v 24, eds. Colgrave and Mynors, p. 566. The nature of the regime followed at Wearmouth and Jarrow is evident from Bede's *Historia Abbatum*, ed. C. Plummer, *Bedae Opera Historica*, 2 vols (Oxford, 1896), 1, pp. 363–87.

[18] Although abbots were present at church councils (for example at Chelsea in 816), the influence of the bishops, and particularly the presiding archbishop, in the drafting of legislation appears to have been paramount. A study of Anglo-Saxon Church councils is being undertaken by C. R. E. Cubitt for a Cambridge University doctoral thesis.

[19] M. T. A. Carroll, *The Venerable Bede: his Spiritual Teachings* (Washington, 1946), p. 251.

[20] Bede, *Homelia*, i 9, ed. D. Hurst, *CC* 122, p. 65.

contemplative devotion.[21] For Bede, perfection could only be achieved through the judicious balancing of the two ideals:

> For neither virtue can be duly completed without the other: if either he who lives a good life neglects the duty of teaching, or a bishop who teaches rightly disdains to practice right behaviour.[22]

The active life could in Bede's view encompass a variety of good works, vigils, fasts, manual labour, meditation on the Scriptures, or preaching,[23] but his writings repeatedly reiterate the paramount importance he placed on preaching and teaching for the salvation of the whole Christian nation. The obligation of preaching he laid not only on those in priestly orders but on all the faithful:

> As pastors are understood not only bishops, priests and deacons but also the rulers of monasteries, also all the faithful who take charge even of small households should rightly be called pastors.[24]

Likening the role of the Church towards the laity to that of a mother nourishing her children,[25] Bede warned against the famine that would ensue if a shortage of preachers deprived the people of their spiritual food.[26] Those who failed to preach but kept to themselves the words of holy teaching would ultimately be held responsible for the condemnation of those people they could have corrected.[27]

In his letter to Bishop Ecgbert of York of 734, Bede attributed the evils in the Church of his own day to a lack of priests and teachers who could preach in the villages, celebrate the holy mysteries, and baptize.[28] His solution to the problem was not only to appoint more bishops and priests, but to employ 'adequate teachers of the salutary life',[29] who could 'teach the truth of the faith and the difference between good and evil'.[30] It is quite clear that Bede considered these *doctores* and *praedicatores*, to be a

---

[21] A. Thacker, 'Bede's Ideal of Reform', in P. Wormald, ed., *Ideal and Reality. Studies in Frankish and Anglo-Saxon Society presented to J. M. Wallace-Hadrill* (Oxford, 1983), pp. 130–53, at 132.

[22] Bede, *Epistola ad Ecgbertum Episcopum*, c. 2, ed. Plummer, 1, pp. 405–23, at 406.

[23] Bede, *In Cantica Canticorum*, IV vi 9, ed. D. Hurst, *CC* 119B, p. 312. Carroll, *The Venerable Bede*, p. 229.

[24] Bede, *Homelia*, i 7, ed. D. Hurst, *CC* 122, p. 49. Thacker, 'Bede's Ideal', p. 131.

[25] Bede, *De Tabernaculo*, I, ed. D. Hurst, *CC* 119A, p. 27.

[26] Bede, *In Marcum*, II viii 6, ed. D. Hurst, *CC* 120, p. 528. Carroll, *The Venerable Bede*, p. 139.

[27] Bede, *Super Parabolas Salomonis*, II xi, *PL* 91, col. 973.

[28] Bede, *Epistola ad Ecgbertum*, c. 5, ed. Plummer, 1, p. 408.

[29] *Ibid.*, c. 15, p. 418.

[30] *Ibid.*, c. 7, p. 410.

separate group from the ordained *sacerdotes*,[31] and there is no reason to assume that Bede intended all the pastoral work to be done by the members of newly created episcopal communities. The minsters also had a recognized role to play. Indeed, the very fact that Bede recommended that existing minsters could be chosen as the sites of his new bishoprics, and a bishop appointed from among the members of such a monastic community, suggests that the exercise of the pastoral cure was not alien to these institutions.[32]

It is now generally agreed amongst historians that early Anglo-Saxon minsters, although many of them were familiar with the teachings of Saint Benedict, did not follow his monastic role exclusively, but instead tended to devise their own systems of regulation.[33] There is therefore no reason to presume that any early minsters would have felt themselves bound by Benedict's insistence on *stabilitas*,[34] and so prohibited from involvement in external ministry. It would appear that a number of those living in religious communities were in clerical orders,[35] but there is no evidence that pastoral work was restricted to priests and deacons. Although ordained priests were essential for administering the mass and other sacraments, the writings of Bede indicate that he at leat recognized the equal role of instituted teachers and preachers, members of minster communities, in pastoral ministry.

Early Anglo-Saxon sources offer no proof that pastoral work was ever done by individuals working alone, independent of any sort of community; if there were single priests ministering in the early Anglo-Saxon period, the sources are silent about their existence. The edicts of church councils repeatedly stress the importance of priests' and monks' ties to their houses of origin, forbidding them to be absent without their superior's permission. At the Council of Hertford in 672/3 it was decreed that *monachi* were not to wander from place to place without their abbot's permission,[36] and that *clerici* were not to leave their own bishop and

---

[31] Thacker, 'Bede's Ideal', p. 131.

[32] Bede, *Epistola ad Ecgbertum*, c. 10, ed. Plummer, 1, p. 413.

[33] E. John, '"Saecularium prioratus" and the Rule of St Benedict', *Révue Bénédictine*, 75 (1965), pp. 212–39; H. Mayr-Harting, *The Venerable Bede, the Rule of St Benedict and Social Class*, Jarrow Lecture 1976 (Jarrow, 1977).

[34] *Rule of Saint Benedict*, cc. 58, 60–1, ed. J. McCann (London, 1952), pp. 130, 136–8.

[35] For example, in addition to the ordained abbots, there were several priests among the inmates of the cell of Lindisfarne described in Aethelwulf's poem, *De Abbatibus*, ed. A. Campbell (Oxford, 1967). This was not of course likely to be the case in the pseudo-minsters established by laymen; for such houses bishops might have to provide priests, see Council of Clofesho, AD 747, c. 5, ed. Haddan and Stubbs, *Councils*, 3, p. 364.

[36] Bede, *HE*, iv 5, c. 4, eds. Colgrave and Mynors, p. 350.

wander about at will.[37] The differentiation made here between monks and clerics apparently distinguishes the members of minsters from cathedral communities, rather than separating the ordained from other religious; the two chapters deal in turn with those under the authority of an abbot and men in a bishop's care. At Hertford and in the late seventh-century law code of King Wihtred of Kent (AD 690–725), members of the laity were also given a responsibility to ensure that wandering religious were returned to their own houses. At Hertford it was decreed that if a cleric was once received by a layman and was then unwilling to return home when summoned 'both the receiver and the received should suffer excommunication',[38] whilst Wihtred's code stipulated:

> if a tonsured man who is under no ecclesiastical authority seeks hospitality he is to be given it once; and it is not to happen that he is harboured longer unless he has permission.[39]

The problems of wandering clergy continued into the eighth century; edicts tackling the problem were agreed at Clofesho in 747,[40] by the legatine synods of 786,[41] and at Chelsea in 816.[42]

Part of the difficulty in controlling the activities of clergy outside their minsters lay in the fact that the size of minster *parochiae* necessitated the frequent absence of those clergy serving the more far-flung areas. In his letter to Bishop Ecgbert, Bede recommended that since the distances in the diocese were too great for a bishop alone to be able to visit them all, he should 'appoint several assistants ... by ordaining priests and instituting teachers, who may devote themselves to preaching the word of God in the various villages and to celebrating the heavenly mysteries'.[43] The need for travel by ministers was also recognized at the Clofesho council in 747, when it was decreed that priests should take care to perform their duties of baptizing, teaching, and visiting 'in the places and districts of the laity assigned to them by the bishops of the province'.[44] That members of communities might often be absent on legitimate business is also indicated by the fourteenth canon of the same council, which ordered that all abbots

---

[37] *Ibid.*, c. 5.
[38] *Ibid.*
[39] Laws of Wihtred, c. 7, ed. Attenborough, *The Laws*, pp. 24–31, at 26.
[40] Council of Clofesho, AD 747, c. 29, ed. Haddan and Stubbs, *Councils*, 3, pp. 374–5.
[41] Legatine Synods, AD 786, c. 6, ed. Haddan and Stubbs, *Councils*, 3, p. 451.
[42] Council of Chelsea, AD 816, c. 5, ed. Haddan and Stubbs, *Councils*, 3, pp. 579–85, at 581.
[43] Bede, *Epistola ad Ecgbertum*, c. 5, ed. Plummer, 1, p. 408.
[44] Council of Clofesho, AD 747, c. 9, ed. Haddan and Stubbs, *Councils*, 3, p. 365.

and priests should on Sundays stay in their minsters and churches, and encourage the laity rather to come to them to receive the sacrament and hear sermons preached.[45]

Contrasting impressions have thus been obtained from the writings of Bede and the edicts of church councils. Bede considered that all those who left the secular world to embrace a religious way of life adopted at the same time an implicit pastoral obligation towards the Christian laity. In his opinion all the minsters had a responsibility to care for the spiritual well-being of their neighbours. However, the directives in canon law relating to parochial ministry refer mostly to the work of priests and to the organization of their ministry by diocesan bishops, apparently ignoring the potential of both other religious and the minsters. This might imply that abbots, or the heads of the minsters, were not involved in the organization of parochial ministry, and that all pastoral workers came automatically under the jurisdiction of their diocesan bishop. Alternatively, the apparent domination of bishops in this sphere might simply reflect the fact that the drafting of canon law was undertaken predominantly by bishops. Although the possible contribution of teachers and preachers was ignored by church councils, it seems inherently unlikely that there was no recognized role outside the minsters for religious who were not ordained. It is also difficult to postulate for the seventh or eighth centuries an adequate supply of trained priests to perform all the necessary pastoral work.

In some respects the importance placed by synods on the central role of bishops in controlling parochial ministry is understandable; only bishops could ordain new priests and appoint workers to specific areas. Repeated references in canon law to the necessity for bishops to test the capabilities of those presenting for ordination reinforce the impression that in the eighth century at least there was widespread concern about the quality of diocesan workers. Bede commented in his letter to Ecgbert on the problems caused by uneducated priests, and by clerics and monks ignorant of the Latin tongue,[46] presenting the problem primarily as one of inadequate education. Yet, when Ecgbert dealt in his *Dialogue* with the qualities desirable in a priest, he dwelt more on the necessity for a candidate to be free from disqualifications such as servility, disability, or having previously committed various crimes or done public penance, and only mentioned in passing that priests should be literate.[47] Eighth-century

[45] Haddan and Stubbs, *Councils*, c, 14, p. 367.
[46] Bede, *Epistola ad Ecgbertum*, c. 5, ed. Plummer, I, p. 409.
[47] Ecgbert, *Dialogus*, c. 15, ed. Haddan and Stubbs, *Councils*, 3, pp. 403–13, at 410.

church councils, however, laid more stress on the appointment of suitably qualified men. At Clofesho in 747, bishops were instructed that they were not to ordain any monk or clerk to the degree of priest until they had investigated the candidate's former life, present manners, and knowledge of the faith, and verified that he had studied sufficiently to be able to preach sound faith, give knowledge of the word, and enjoin penance to others.[48] Similar advice was given at the legatine synods in 786.[49]

Ordination and appointment to a particular office would appear to have been closely connected. One of the objections voiced in Anglo-Saxon texts against the ministry of foreigners, particularly the Irish, was that they were ordained *absolute*, unconditionally, or without any particular charge.[50] The English custom was apparently for the bishop to appoint a priest to work in a specific area when he was ordained. The passage from the 747 Clofesho council instructing priests to perform their duties in the districts of the laity assigned to them has already been quoted,[51] and similar injunctions can be found in the canons of other councils. In 786, priests were enjoined to remain in that *titulus* to which they were consecrated, 'so that none presume to receive a priest or deacon from the title that belongs to another without reasonable cause and commendatory letters'.[52] I understand *titulus* here to refer to the benefice to which a cleric was appointed, and to be a further indication that the ordination of individuals could be directed to meeting the pastoral needs of local areas.[53] Episcopal involvement in parochial ministry could also extend to the foundation of new houses to minister to hitherto unserved areas. For example in Essex, Bishop Cedd established minsters at Bradwell and Tilbury with a multitude of Christ's servants, and 'priests and deacons to assist him in preaching the word of faith and administering baptism'.[54]

Bishops also seem to have controlled all parochial workers within their own districts; individuals were forbidden to exercise any ministry within a diocese without the express permission of the local bishop. Several texts express anxiety about the pastoral activities of priests (or worse, those who by English standards had not been canonically ordained), who worked

---

[48] Council of Clofesho, AD 747, c. 6, ed. Haddan and Stubbs, *Councils*, 3, p. 364.

[49] Legatine Synods, AD 786, c. 6, ed. Haddan and Stubbs, *Councils*, 3, p. 451.

[50] Ecgbert, *Dialogus*, c. 9, ed. Haddan and Stubbs, *Councils*, 3, p. 407. Compare Council of Chelsea, AD 816, c. 5, *ibid.*, p. 581.

[51] See above, n. 44.

[52] Legatine Synods, AD 786, c. 6, Hadden and Stubbs, *Councils*, 3, p. 451.

[53] Du Cange, *Glossarium Mediae et Infimae Latinitatis*, 10 vols (Niort 1884–7), 8, p. 114.

[54] Bede, *HE* iii 22, ed. Colgrave and Mynors, p. 282.

independently of episcopal control. Bishops and clergy when travelling were forbidden to exercise any priestly function without the permission of the bishop in whose diocese they were;[55] no one, bishop or priest, was to invade the *parochia* of another without the permission of its own bishop,[56] and no priest having been ejected by one bishop was permitted to start ministering in the diocese of another until his dispute with his own diocesan were settled.[57] The authority of bishops over parochial clergy was reinforced by secular legislation. King Wihtred's code ordered that

> if a priest . . . neglects the baptism of a sick man, or is too drunk to discharge his duty, he shall abstain from his ministrations pending a decision from the bishop.[58]

The only functions that priests were permitted to exercise without specific episcopal permission were baptism and the visitation of the sick; the 816 Council of Chelsea ordered of priests:

> that no one desires greater business than is allowed him by his bishop excepting only in relation to baptism and the sick; but we charge all priests that they deny nowhere to perform the ministry of baptism, and if anyone do refuse it through negligence, let him cease from his ministry until the time of correction and he be reconciled to his bishop.[59]

The one aspect of the minsters' role that is clearly expressed in canon law is their educational function in training new clergy for pastoral or other work. Although the double house at Whitby was obviously exceptional in training five future bishops during the abbacy of Hild,[60] numerous other bishops were promoted to dioceses from monastic houses.[61] The responsibility of the minsters in educating prospective clergy was overtly expressed at Clofesho in 747,[62] but is presumably also implicit in the canons concerning the quality of candidates for ordination.[63] Those

[55] Council of Hertford, AD 672/3, c. 6, Bede, *HE*, iv 5, ed. Colgrave and Mynors, p. 352.
[56] Council of Chelsea, AD 816, c. 5, ed. Haddan and Stubbs, *Councils*, 3, p. 581.
[57] Ecgbert, *Dialogus*, c. 4, ed. Haddan and Stubbs, *Councils*, 3, p. 405.
[58] Laws of Wihtred, c. 6, ed. Attenborough, *The Laws*, p. 26.
[59] Council of Chelsea, AD 816, c. 11, ed. Haddan and Stubbs, *Councils*, 3, p. 584.
[60] Bede, *HE*, iv 23, ed. Colgrave and Mynors, p. 408.
[61] For example Tatwine, who was a priest at Breedon before he was made archbishop of Canterbury in 731, Bede, *HE* v 23, ed. Colgrave and Mynors, p. 558.
[62] Council of Clofesho, AD 747, c. 7, ed. Haddan and Stubbs, *Councils*, 3, p. 365.
[63] See above.

passages of the councils that dealt specifically with life inside the minsters laid stress on reading and learning as suitable occupations for their inmates.[64]

Although Bede laid an obligation to pastoral ministry on all confessed religious, it has been seen that the edicts of early church councils were concerned exclusively with the pastoral work of priests, controlled by bishops. It is easy to place undue reliance on the writings of Bede, who was not necessarily representative of contemporary ecclesiastical thought, but there are reasons for thinking that the canon law may present only a partial picture. It is for instance inconceivable that any sort of continuity of pastoral care could have been effected without involving the resources of the minsters; as Bede himself commented, dioceses were simply too large and the distances to be travelled too great.[65] It is also difficult to envisage where else parochial clergy could have lived if they were not resident in the minsters, especially in light of the repeated insistence of the church councils that all priests, as well as monks, were to live in communities and not stay outside them for prolonged periods. Ecgbert clearly assumed that all *clerici* lived in minsters, stating in his *Dialogue* that not only *clerici in monasteriis* but also the laity with their wives and families observed Advent and Lenten fasts.[66]

When other sorts of evidence such as charters and later parochial documents are consulted a different picture emerges from that found in the synodal literature, one that is much more in keeping with the ideals presented in Bede's writings. Local studies using these sources, such as those done by Hase and Croom in Hampshire and Shropshire, demonstrate that in these areas from the seventh and eighth centuries, networks of minster foundations can be distinguished, controlling large and well-defined *parochiae*, often coterminous with secular jurisdictional districts; these early minsters frequently correlate with mother churches with wide parochial authority in the eleventh and twelfth centuries.[67]

It is of course possible that the role of minsters in parochial ministry in early Anglo-Saxon England was so obvious to contemporary churchmen as to be self-evident and unnecessary of elaboration. What comments can be found in the sources are frequently incidental. For example, in his

---

[64] Council of Clofesho 747, cc. 7, 20, ed. Haddan and Stubbs, *Councils*, 3, pp. 365, 369.
[65] Bede, *Epistola ad Ecgbertum*, c. 5, ed. Plummer, I, p. 408.
[66] Ecgbert, *Dialogus*, c. 16, ed. Haddan and Stubbs, *Councils*, 3, p. 413.
[67] See P. H. Hase, 'The Mother Churches of Hampshire', in Blair, ed., *Minsters and Parish Churches*, pp. 45–66, and J. Croom, 'The Fragmentation of the Minster *Parochiae* of South-East Shropshire', *ibid.*, pp. 67–81.

Penitential Theodore discussed how anyone wanting to move his minster to another place would need to obtain the consent of the local bishop and the minster brethren, before he mentioned that a priest would have to be released 'for the ministry of the church in the former place'.[68] It might also be that in the silence of the church councils on the role of the minsters we are witnessing the results of a conflict between bishops and abbots in the organization of pastoral work. Abbots were largely successful in preserving their autonomy within their own minsters (at least before 816)[69] but they may have won such concessions as they did achieve at the cost of relinquishing control of their subjects once they were working away from their mother house.

Before these problems can be resolved, more work needs to be done on the nature of the religious life in early Anglo-Saxon England, the role of the minsters in society, and particularly their place in the newly evolving ecclesiastical structure. While it is possible that the validity of the presumption I set out to test, namely that all minster foundations had a public pastoral role, can only be tested effectively through further local studies, the ideas expressed in canon law remain important not only for our understanding of the role of bishops and priests, but also for what they reveal about the broader Church, of which, to most of the laity, a local minster community was the only visible representative.[70]

Newnham College, Cambridge

[68] Theodore, *Penitential*, II vi 7, ed. Haddan and Stubbs, *Councils*, 3, p. 195.

[69] The fourth canon of the council of Chelsea in AD 816 (ed. Haddan and Stubbs, *Councils*, 3, pp. 580–1) gives bishops the right to choose new abbots for minsters. See N. Brooks, *The Early History of the Church of Canterbury. Christ Church from 597 to 1066* (Leicester, 1984), pp. 175–6.

[70] I am grateful to John Blair, Rosamond McKitterick, and Patrick Sims-Williams for their comments on an earlier draft of this paper.

ORDERS AND RANK IN THE CATHEDRAL OF OLD SARUM

by DIANA GREENWAY

IT is a cliché of medieval ecclesiastical history that the clergy was a 'hierarchy'. When we use this term, we may mean 'priestly rule', but more often we are referring to the way in which the clergy was graded in successive ranks, one above another. Most obviously, the clergy was so arranged in the seven steps of holy orders: doorkeeper, reader, exorcist, acolyte, subdeacon, deacon, priest. But simple stratification by orders was only part of a much more complex hierarchical system, in which the major differentiating factor was office. Both elements—orders and office—were the subjects of a considerable literature in the early Middle Ages: side by side with treatises on orders—belonging to the genre *de officiis septem graduum*—is a body of writings concerned to define the functions, relations and grades of ecclesiastical offices—the genre *de ecclesiasticis officiis*.[1] Two related documents telling us of the customs at Old Sarum owe much to tracts of this kind: the *Institutio*, compiled by stages in the later twelfth and early thirteenth centuries, and the *Consuetudinarium* of Richard Poore, written *c*.1215, which greatly expands the *Institutio*.[2]

The rites and ceremonies of the cathedral church, in which the bishop was the central figure, required a large band of priests, deacons, and sub-deacons, as well as numbers of acolytes, young men, and boys. We may see something of the scale of these requirements by looking at the especially important ritual of the episcopal blessing of the holy oils on Maundy Thursday, for which we have a source at either end of the 150 years of Old Sarum's existence as a cathedral. The Sarum Pontifical, an eleventh-century book brought from Sherborne when the cathedral migrated in

---

[1] See Roger E. Reynolds, 'The *De Officiis VII Graduum*: its origins and early medieval development', *Mediaeval Studies*, 34 (1972), pp. 113–51; 'The "Isidorian" *Epistula ad Leudefredum*: an early medieval epitome of clerical duties', *ibid.*, 41 (1979), pp. 252–330; and *The Ordinals of Christ from their Origins to the Twelfth Century* (Beiträge zur Geschichte . . . des Mittelalters 7, 1978).

[2] For the *Institutio*, see D. Greenway, 'The false *Institutio* of St Osmund', in *Tradition and Change: Essays in honour of Marjorie Chibnall* (Cambridge, 1985), pp. 77–101; and for the *Consuetudinarium*, see the critical edition in *The Use of Sarum*, ed. W. H. Frere, 2 vols (Cambridge, 1898), 1 (also printed, from a single MS, *Vetus Registrum Sarisberiense, alius dictum Registrum S. Osmundi Episcopi*, ed. W. H. Rich Jones, 2 vols (RS 78, 1883–4), 1, pp. 1–185).

the 1070s, follows the Romano-Germanic pontifical, requiring a party of twelve priests, seven deacons, seven subdeacons, seven taperers, and two thurifers to assist the bishop.[3] In addition to the thirty-five assistants required in the Pontifical, the *Consuetudinarium* of *c*.1215 mentions three ministers carrying banners, two acolytes with crosses, three boys accompanying the deacon who carried the chrism, and three archdeacons 'cum suis ministris'.[4]

In Old Sarum cathedral's 150 years, the establishment was steadily enlarged. Dr Kathleen Edwards thought that Osmund, who introduced canons at the new cathedral, may have brought the number up to thirty-two or thirty-six before his death in 1099.[5] This may be an over-estimate, although the high output of manuscripts at Salisbury in the late eleventh and early twelfth centuries argues a fair-sized community.[6] It is impossible to be precise about numbers at Old Sarum in the early days, as the members of the community are largely anonymous: the only names we have before 1100 are of four archdeacons and possibly one dean. Bishop Roger extended the choir and capitular buildings in the first decades of the twelfth century, and presumably therefore enlarged the size of the chapter,[7] but for the fifty-year period between 1100 and 1150 we know of only twenty-seven canons and dignitaries by name. By *c*.1150, under Bishop Jocelin, documents relating to the prebends suggest that there were then about forty canons, and the figure was increased in the later twelfth and early thirteenth centuries. By 1226, on the eve of the removal of the cathedral establishment to New Salisbury, there were quite certainly fifty-two canons in possession of individual prebends, as revealed in the taxation list of that year.[8] This figure is exactly double the total number of priests, deacons, and subdeacons required for the

---

[3] BL Cotton MS Tib. C. i fols 42–52ᵛ; cf. *Le pontifical romano-germanique du dixième siècle*, ed. C. Vogel and R. Elze (Studi e Testi 226, 269, 1963–72), 2, pp. 67, 70.

[4] *Cons.*, cap. cxiv, *Use of Sarum*, 1, p. 203. The later Processional has an even greater number of ministers in the Maundy procession, see *Ceremonies and Processions of the Cathedral Church of Salisbury*, ed. C. Wordsworth (Cambridge, 1901), pp. 68–73, and see also T. Bailey, *The Processions of Sarum and the Western Church* (Toronto, 1971).

[5] *VCH Wiltshire*, 3, pp. 156–8.

[6] N. R. Ker, 'The beginnings of Salisbury cathedral library', in *Medieval Learning and Literature: essays presented to R. W. Hunt*, eds J. J. G. Alexander and M. T. Gibson (Oxford, 1976), pp. 23–49. Dr M. T. J. Webber's recent study of Salisbury MSS in the late 11th and early 12th centuries has shed much light on the intellectual interests of the chapter, and it is hoped that this will soon appear in print.

[7] See W. St John Hope, 'The Sarum Consuetudinary and its relation to the Cathedral Church of Old Sarum', *Archaeologia*, 68 (1917), pp. 111–26; also A. W. Clapham, in *Archaeological Journal*, 104 (1948), pp. 140–2.

[8] See the taxation list of 1226, *Registrum S. Osmundi*, 2, pp. 70–5.

Maundy service. Of the fifty-two, four were major dignitaries—dean, precentor, chancellor, treasurer; four were archdeacons—of Dorset, Berkshire, Salisbury and Wiltshire; and two were lesser dignitaries—sub-dean and succentor. Another canon, in possession of a prebend, was the bishop himself. Four more prebends were held by the abbots of Benedict-ine abbeys—Sherborne, Le Bec, Saint-Wandrille, and Montebourg. It is in connection with Sherborne that we find our first reference in *c.*1150 to a vicar at Salisbury.[9] By the last decades of the twelfth century, vicars, who performed the liturgical duties in place of canons, were an established part of the hierarchy. There were also chaplains, some of whom may have officiated at the nave altars and acted as pastors of the town population, and clerks in minor orders. In addition, by the early thirteenth century there were a number of boy assistants.

How was this body of people organized into ranks?

First in status was the bishop. Both his order and his office placed him at the head of the hierarchy. The cathedral church was his church, hous-ing his *cathedra*, which was placed at the east of the choir, very probably in the centre behind the high altar.[10] The bishop, as well as using the cathedral for special pontifical occasions, was the celebrant on major festivals, and played a part in many other services, giving blessings and absolution, saying the Confiteor and collect.[11] At Salisbury, alone among the English cathedrals, the bishop's position was complicated—and enhanced—by the fact that he held a prebend, and so was a member of chapter.[12] The prebend held by the bishops until *c.*1219, when it was exchanged, was that of Major Pars Altaris, consisting of a portion of the oblations of the high altar. Bishop Richard Poore believed that the episcopal prebend dated from Osmund's time,[13] and although a moiety of

---

[9] *Charters and Documents, illustrative of the History of the Cathedral, City, and Diocese of Salisbury in the Twelfth and Thirteenth Centuries*, ed. W. Rich Jones and W. Dunn Macray (RS 97, 1891), pp. 16–17; cf. Greenway, 'Institutio', p. 87.

[10] The central west-facing position was normal Romanesque practice; for Canterbury, see F. Woodman, *The Architectural History of Canterbury Cathedral* (London, 1981), p. 47, citing *The Historical Works of Gervase of Canterbury*, ed. W. Stubbs, 2 vols. (RS 73, 1879–80), I, p. 13. The bishop's throne in Osmund's apse was almost certainly in this position (see *Proceedings of the Society of Antiquaries*, 26 (1914), pp. 100–19 at p. 103), but the excavation of Roger le Poer's square-ended presbytery did not reveal his throne's position (see St John Hope, 'The Sarum Consuetudinary', p. 116).

[11] See *Use of Sarum*, index, pp. 292–3; cf. K. Edwards, *The English Secular Cathedrals in the Middle Ages* (Manchester, 2 edn., 1967), pp. 102–3.

[12] The evidence at Lincoln is inconclusive; see A. H. Thompson, *The English Clergy and their Organization in the Later Middle Ages* (Oxford, 1947), pp. 73–4 and p. 74 n. 1.

[13] *Charters of Salisbury*, p. 95, cited *English Secular Cathedrals*, p. 108.

the high altar oblations was not made a perpetual prebend until the early years of Bishop Jocelin, between 1142 and 1161,[14] it seems likely that this merely formalized and institutionalized an arrangement that had originated through Osmund's regular personal activity in the ministry of the high altar. The bishop's dominant position in the cathedral church was fittingly expressed in his possession of Major Pars Altaris, which is entered first in the mid twelfth-century list giving details of the division of the Daily Psalter. Each prebendary was responsible for saying a portion of the Psalter: the bishop, as prebendary of Major Pars, said Psalms 1–5.[15] In chapter meetings the bishop was the natural president, sitting in the central seat, flanked by dean and precentor.[16]

Next in rank to the bishop were the ten dignitaries. Almost invariably the dignitaries—however many were present—headed witness lists of charters: the four major dignitaries—dean, precentor, chancellor, treasurer—appear in strict order of precedence from the early 1190s, the other dignitaries in their order from at least the second decade of the thirteenth century. By c.1215, when the Consuetudinarium was drawn up, the four majores persone had the four terminal stalls in the Old Sarum choir: on the south, decani side, sat the dean at the west and the chancellor at the east, and on the north, cantoris side, was the precentor at the west and treasurer at the east—the 'four-square' arrangement beloved of ecclesiologists. For reasons that I have given elsewhere,[17] I do not believe that the dominance of these four, and their order of precedence, can date from much earlier than c.1180, although the dean's superiority over the

---

[14] A confirmation charter of Henry II, Salisbury Dean and Chapter Archives IV/C.2/Royal charters/36, copied in Liber Evidenciarum C no. 47, contains a clause omitted from a second, otherwise duplicate, charter, IV/C.2/Royal charters/32, and from the copy in MS 'Register of St Osmund', Trowbridge, Wilts. Record Office, D1/1/1 fo. 22ʳ (printed in *Registrum S. Osmundi*, 1, pp. 203–6). These two charters are listed in *Acta of Henry II and Richard I*, ed. J. C. Holt and Richard Mortimer (List and Index Soc. spec. ser. 21, 1986), no. 262, ii and i respectively (acta nos. 317, 316). I am very grateful to Dr Mortimer for his help on this point.

[15] Printed in *Ceremonies of Salisbury*, pp. 129–32; and W. H. Jones, *Fasti Ecclesiae Sarisberiensis* (Salisbury, 1881), pp. 200–2. The MS list dates from the 15th century, but internal evidence suggests that the division was made in the middle of the 12th, as the ten prebends entered last seem to have been created after c.1150, cf. below n. 27.

[16] *Cons.*, cap. xxxii (*Use of Sarum*, 1, p. 51). Here I agree with Frere, *Use of Sarum*, 1, p. 293, and disagree with Edwards, *English Secular Cathedrals*, pp. 109–10, whose examples of the bishop appearing as a mere prebendary, and not as president, are drawn from the period after the removal to New Salisbury (cf. also Thompson, *English Clergy*, pp. 73–4). For an act of chapter at Old Sarum in 1222 *in presentia episcopi*, see *Registrum S. Osmundi*, p. 18; and cf. *ibid.*, pp. 37, 42, 60. Cf. Lincoln, *Statutes of Lincoln Cathedral*, ed. H. Bradshaw and C. Wordsworth, 3 vols. (Cambridge, 1892–7), 1, p. 107.

[17] Greenway, 'Institutio', pp. 81–6.

cathedral personnel and the precentor's rule over the choir and music were established by the early twelfth century. The dean was first in *dignitas*, a term taken over in the *Consuetudinarium* from a clause in the *Institutio* that dates from *c.*1150.[18] All were required to rise when the dean entered choir or chapter, and when leaving the choir at the west, all bowed to him (on leaving at the east, they bowed to the bishop).[19] Institution of canons belonged to the bishop, but it was the dean's office to assign places in choir and chapter, so that he controlled the hierarchical arrangement.[20] Beneath the four *principales persone* were the four archdeacons—Dorset, Berkshire, Salisbury and Wiltshire—in that order, followed by the subdean and succentor. In choir, Dorset sat next to the dean, Berkshire next to the precentor, Salisbury next to the chancellor and Wiltshire next to the treasurer; the subdean next to Dorset and the succentor next to Berkshire.[21] The seating in chapter also reflected the order of precedence, with the *decani* side dignitaries sitting on the bishop's right, and the *cantoris* side on his left.[22] The importance of the service of the altar, with the bishop as celebrant, is again emphasized here: right and left in chapter only accords with *decani* and *cantoris*, south and north, in choir, if the bishop is facing east, as he would towards the altar.

How was the remainder of the Old Sarum hierarchy arranged? It is quite clear from the *Consuetudinarium*, chapters xii and xxxii, that the canons were ranked in three groups, occupying seats in all three tiers on either choir side. The senior canons—priests, deacons and subdeacons—sat in the *superior gradus*; the junior canons sat below them on the *secunda forma*; and below again, on the *prima forma* were the boy canons, *canonici pueri*. But in all three rows, canons were alongside non-canons. Next to the canons of the upper grade, but inferior in rank, were the priest-vicars (probably including the chaplains) and some deacon-vicars; on the second form, after the junior canons, were the remaining deacons, subdeacons, and clerks in minor orders; and on the first form, next to the boy canons, were the other boys, who served as choristers, readers, thurifers, cross-bearers, taperers and the like.[23] This grading was followed also in chapter, where all had their places, each arranged in order of precedence: the dignitaries and members of the first and second forms were seated, and

---

[18] *Ibid.*, p. 95, cap. 7; *Cons.*, cap. ix (*Use of Sarum*, 1, p. 8); cf. Greenway, 'Institutio', pp. 87–8.
[19] *Cons.*, cap. ix (*Use of Sarum*, 1, p. 8).
[20] *Ibid.*, cap. ii (*Use of Sarum*, 1, p. 2).
[21] *Ibid.*, cap. xii (*Use of Sarum*, 1, p. 13).
[22] *Ibid.*, cap. xxxii (*Use of Sarum*, 1, p. 51).
[23] *Ibid.*, cap. xii, and cf. cap. xxx (*Use of Sarum*, 1, pp. 13, 47–8).

the boys, both canons and non-canons, stood on either side of the pulpit.[24] The distinction of the *superior gradus*, whether canons or not, from the other clergy, was made visible in dress: those of the upper grade wore black almuces, but none of the other clergy were to wear almuces at all by day.[25]

Is it possible to say more about the *Consuetudinarium*'s ranking of canons and vicars by orders? At Salisbury, unlike the other English cathedrals, the prebends themselves were classified as priest-prebends, deacon-prebends, and subdeacon-prebends: of the fifty-two, twenty-two were priest, eighteen deacon, and twelve subdeacon prebends. This classification is found in a list of *c.*1270 and also in Martival's legislation of 1319,[26] but has an earlier origin: it lies behind the order of prebends in both the taxation list of 1226 and the mid twelfth-century list detailing the division of the Daily Psalter between the prebends.[27] The appearance among the canons in the *Consuetudinarium* of boys and juniors demonstrates, however, that canons did not necessarily hold the orders assigned to their prebends. By the later thirteenth century, when there are some details about canons' orders, it is clear that there was no correlation between orders held and the prebendal classification—priests might hold subdeacon prebends, and the pattern of exchanges of prebends reveals transfers downward—from priest to deacon and subdeacon—as well as upward.[28] Was the system devised with vicars in view? Our evidence is very late, but although Martival's code of 1319 required canons to appoint vicars 'in the order which their prebend's *cura* requires',[29] in practice in the 1330s and 1340s not only were many vicars appointed to deacon and

---

[24] *Cons.*, cap. xxxii (*Use of Sarum*, 1, p. 51).

[25] *Ibid.*, cap. xix (*Use of Sarum*, 1, p. 25).

[26] Liber Evid. C no. 461; *Statutes and Customs of the Cathedral Church of the Blessed Virgin Mary of Salisbury*, ed. C. Wordsworth and D. Macleane (London, 1915), pp. 156–9. These late lists were drawn up in connection with residence requirements: the prebends are listed on either choir side in four groups, each group consisting of some priest, some deacon and some subdeacon prebends, and one group from each choir side was required to reside each quarter of the year. Cf. also a list of named canons with their prebends in 1284, Liber Evid. C no. 517, arranged in this way, to be printed as an appendix in my forthcoming *Fasti Ecclesiae Anglicanae 1066–1300*, IV *Salisbury* (Institute of Historical Research, University of London).

[27] The taxation (see above, n. 8), with some disorder towards the end, puts first those prebends that are later called priest-prebends, followed by the deacon prebends and then the subdeacon prebends. The division of the Psalter (see above, n. 15) arranges the first forty-two prebends so that priest prebends are first, followed by deacon and subdeacon prebends.

[28] This statement is based on my forthcoming *Fasti* volume. Cf. *The Registers of Roger Martival, Bishop of Salisbury, 1315–1330*, eds K. Edwards *et al.*, 4 vols (Canterbury and York Society 55–9, 68, 1959–75), 1, pp. 4–5, 14, 19–21, 34, 36, 62.

[29] *Statutes of Salisbury*, pp. 214–15.

subdeacon prebends actually priests, but—more significant—some vicars were in minor orders, acolyte and below.[30]

What, then, was the origin and purpose of the classification? I believe that the system was imposed at the point when the Sarum chapter became fully prebendalized, which seems to have been in the early years of Bishop Jocelin, around 1150. In the simplest terms, my interpretation, which I shall document in my forthcoming *Fasti* volume, is as follows. In Osmund's time (1078–99) the canons of Old Sarum lived a common life, with only a very few, if any, individual prebends; the bishop took a central role in the ministry of the altar as celebrant, pastor, and leader of the community.[31] Under Osmund's successor, Roger le Poer (1106–39), this common life began to break down: the bishop was frequently absent and many more individual prebends were created. It was Bishop Jocelin (1142–84) who legitimized the prebendal system: all canons were put in possession of prebends, the bishop as their head holding Major Pars Altaris. The holder of each prebend was to be responsible for saying a portion of the Daily Psalter, and also for ministering at the altar when required: this might be done in person or by a vicar. In laying down the new system, Jocelin sought to incorporate into it a classification of the prebends that would determine the numbers of priests, deacons, and subdeacons available for services at the high altar. But this requirement—like some others enshrined in cathedral customaries and legislation—was too rigid ever to be workable. Nonetheless, the classification, impracticable though it was, was recorded, copied, and apparently formed the basis of the prebendaries' seating in the Gothic choir-stalls at New Salisbury, and so survived into the modern period.[32]

A final point to consider is the ranking of individuals within the status groups. When looking at the dignitaries, we noted that both their dominance and their order of precedence can be observed in the witness clauses of charters. But it is not possible to discern any such consistency in the attestations of canons and vicars. Canons always attest before vicars, but beyond that, there is no regular order in which the names occur. This does not mean, however, that there was an equality between the members

---

[30] For references to vicars' orders on admission (all priests), see *Hemingby's Register*, ed. H. M. Chew (Wilts. Record Society 18, 1963), pp. 82, 84, 117, 120, 121, 125; and for references to subdeacon's, acolyte's, and other minor orders, see *ibid.*, pp. 91, 92, 107, and cf. p. 93.

[31] Cf. *Willelmi Malmesbiriensis de Gestis Pontificum*, ed. N. E. S. A. Hamilton (RS 52, 1870), pp. 183–4.

[32] *Statutes of Salisbury*, pp. 114–21; *Ceremonies of Salisbury*, pp. 269–73. On the Gothic stalls, see C. W. Tracy, *English Gothic Choir Stalls 1200–1400* (Woodbridge, 1987).

of the different groups in the hierarchy, but that the ordering within the groups in choir and chapter was not applied when attestations were recorded. Certainly each member of the hierarchy had his particular place in choir, in chapter and in processions, and the penalty for gross misconduct was *degradatio*, being deposed from one's stall and placed below the last of the boys.[33] For the purposes of drawing up the table of lections and responsories the canons had their places 'according to the order in which they are written in the *matricula* of the church';[34] in services, lessons and chants were arranged in ascending order of readers and chanters *gradatim* upwards to the *excellentior*.[35] This refers not only to the differentiation between groups, but also to ranking within groups. What factors determined this secondary grading? There are several hints in the *Consuetudinarium* that age was an important criterion. Certainly among the boys of the *prima forma* the order laid down was according to age, and the use of the terms *senior* and *junior* to differentiate the *superior gradus* from the *secunda forma* canons reflects the fact that age entered into the primary classification of priests, deacons, and subdeacons. Canonical age for priests was thirty, deacons twenty-five, and subdeacons twenty,[36] so if the law was observed, the seniors would have been twenty or over. But given the significance of holy orders in the ranking system, it seems possible that within, say, the priestly grade, the date of ordination, rather than the date of birth, was a major consideration. This was the principle behind the seating of priests at councils, as described in the Romano-Germanic pontifical, followed in the Sarum Pontifical,[37] but we cannot tell if this method of arranging individuals was used regularly at Old Sarum. Nor is it clear what part noble birth or education may have played. Within one rank, at least, behaviour was certainly a factor: the *Consuetudinarium* permits deacon-vicars to be admitted to the *superior gradus*, by dispensation, on grounds of age and conduct, 'etate et moribus'.[38] The assessment

---

[33] *Cons.*, cap. xi (*Use of Sarum*, 1, p. 12).

[34] *Ibid.*, caps. xxv, xlvii, xlviii (*Use of Sarum*, 1, pp. 41, 107, 108). For '*matricula*' meaning a list of churches in a diocese, see C. R. Cheney, *English Bishops' Chanceries 1100–1250* (Manchester, 1950), pp. 112–19.

[35] *Cons.*, cap. xlvii (*Use of Sarum*, 1, p. 106).

[36] Gratian c. 5, D 28 (in *Corpus Iuris Canonici*, ed. E. Friedberg, 2 vols. (Leipzig, 1879–81), 1, cols. 101–2), but in the early 12th century it is doubtful if examination was very rigorous, see M. Brett, *The English Church under Henry I* (Oxford, 1975), pp. 121–2.

[37] *Pontifical romano-germanique*, 1, p. 275; BL Cotton MS Tib. C. i fo. 183ᵛ.

[38] *Cons.*, cap. xii (*Use of Sarum*, 1, p. 13); there is, however, no reference to *scientia*, an element linked with age and conduct in Gregory IX's decretal, *X* 1 tit. 14 c. 4 (Friedberg II, cols 126–7).

of these various factors fell to the dean, and ultimately it was his decision that determined the placing of individuals within their groups.

We have been examining an aspect of male culture—the obsessional ranking and grading of groups and individuals within an exclusively masculine community. In such hierarchies, social stratification may exist simultaneously in several spheres of activity, based on different criteria and producing anomalies and contradictions, which are rarely recognized as such, but are absorbed within the system. At Old Sarum, a young canon in minor orders sat in choir in an inferior position to his priest-vicar, while outside, the vicar was in a dependent—almost servile—relationship, acting as messenger for his *dominus*, the canon, and eating at his table.[39] This contradictory situation was produced by the dichotomy between orders and office in determining status, but was probably not recognized as an anomaly by contemporaries. Dramatic and ceremonial role reversal, on the other hand, provides a safety-valve in rigidly organized hierarchies: at Salisbury the nonsense of the 'boy-bishop' ceremonies on Holy Innocents' Day, 28 December, gave just such a temporary release from the tyranny of precedence and protocol. It also underlined the centrality of the bishop in the cathedral: he was the source of both orders and office, and it was from his role in the liturgy, especially at mass and on the pontifical occasions, that the entire ranking system derived and was articulated.

Institute of Historical Research, London

---

[39] *Statutes of Salisbury*, pp. 50, 76; cf. *English Secular Cathedrals*, pp. 270–1.

PRIEST, DEACON AND LAYMAN, FROM ST PETER DAMIAN TO ST FRANCIS

by CHRISTOPHER N. L. BROOKE

FEW incidents in thirteenth-century history have been more often described than the story of the Christmas crib at Greccio.[1] Not long before his death St Francis arranged with a noble layman called John of Greccio to prepare a crib for midnight mass at Christmas, with plenty of hay and real animals, ox and ass, in attendance. Crowds flocked to the place and 'the whole night resounded with jubilation'. Mass was celebrated over the crib. But not by Francis, for he was not a priest but a deacon; and he put on the deacon's vestments, sang the gospel and preached. Strange as it may seem, it is only from this story in the First Life by Thomas of Celano, confirmed by some shreds of other evidence, that we know that Francis was in deacon's orders.[2] No explanation is given, no contemporary commentary expounds the fact. Yet it is abundantly clear that his deacon's orders had some profound significance related to his conception of his Order and its members, and their relations one to another. It is a curious puzzle to discover what it was.

In the early centuries of the Christian era, as the orders of the Church crystallized, to each a special function was attached.[3] Even the doorkeeper, even the exorcist had his own niche, and it was by no means to be taken for granted that he would rise to be a subdeacon, still less that the deacons, who had the administrative and pastoral duties of the Church laid upon them, would ever become priests. In many early monastic communities the monks were not ordained, or anyway not in higher orders; it was the special function of the few priests to celebrate the eucharist for them. The priests had the privilege and duty of celebrating mass; this set them already apart among the clergy, and even the bishop frequently shared in

---

[1] Thomas of Celano, *Vita Prima*, caps 84–7, *Analecta Franciscana*, 10 (Quaracchi, 1926–41), pp. 63–5; trans. R. B. Brooke, *The Coming of the Friars* (London, 1975), pp. 130–1. In all matters related to St Francis, I am deeply indebted to the help of Rosalind Brooke; on the lay brothers in the orders of monks and canons, I have had invaluable help from Giles Constable.

[2] Celano, *Vita Prima*, cap. 86 (p. 64); cf. Julian of Speyer (based on Celano), *Analecta Franciscana*, 10, pp. 335, 361, 369; and later sources, e.g. *ibid.*, p. 492. In Celano, *Vita Secunda*, cap. 219 (*ibid.*, p. 257), St Francis is seen in a vision wearing a purple dalmatic, the deacon's vestment. In *Vita Secunda*, cap. 193 (p. 241), he prefers a small to a large tonsure: see below, p. 85.

[3] See e.g. articles by A. Michel in *Dictionnaire de Théologie Catholique*, 11 (1931), pp. 1193–1405; 13 (1936), pp. 138–61 ('ordre', 'prêtre'); useful references in *ODCC*, 2 edn., p. 1123, cf. p. 1006.

the Latin west the title *sacerdos*. As Melchizedek in the book of Genesis was *rex et sacerdos*, so was Christ in medieval interpretation; and *sacerdos* was a lofty word which would compass a bishop as well as a priest.[4]

What was different in the eleventh and twelfth centuries was that the priesthood became in a special sense separated from the rest of society— especially from lay society—on account of its sublime function, and it came to be the normal ambition of innumerable devout clerks to attain the priesthood. The English monk Eadmer, in his *Historia Novorum*, quoted the words he heard Pope Urban II utter in Rome in 1099. The pope was laying anathemas on all laymen who claimed the right to grant investiture of churches, and on all clergy who made themselves vassals of laymen. It was a heroic effort to disentangle the spiritual and the secular society of his day—a heroic failure we may think it, since full segregation proved impossible; yet a remarkable success too in the effect it had in creating new social orders. Thus Urban:

> it seemed a horrible thing that hands which had been honoured even above anything permitted to the angels, with power to create by their agency the God who is the Creator of all things and to offer Him to God the Father for the redemption and salvation of the whole world—that these hands should be degraded by the ignominy of being made subject to hands which were infected by filthy contagions day and night, stained with rapine and accustomed to the shedding of innocent blood.[5]

Pope Urban's statement, as reported by Eadmer, is a brilliant summary of the platform of the reforming papacy, of the Gregorian reform. The priesthood must be separated from the laity, because theirs is the divine function of celebrating the eucharist, of creating—or helping in the work of creation of—the body and blood of Christ on the altar.[6] As so often in the papal reform, we are not contemplating new doctrine so much as an

---

[4] Genesis 14, vv. 18–20; for his presence in Innocent III's writings, see K. Pennington in *Law, Church and Society: Essays in Honor of Stephan Kuttner*, eds K. Pennington and R. Somerville (Philadelphia, 1977), pp. 54, 64, n. 32. In the next sentence I speak of the ambition to become a priest as normal. It was never universal: among cathedral clergy for example many seem never to have become priests, and though the cathedrals sometimes seem in deliberate reaction against current religious ideals, and many canons perhaps were not especially devout, we have no reason to doubt that many were. For literature, see below, n. 30.

[5] Eadmer, *Historia Novorum*, ed. M. Rule (*RS* 1884), p. 114; trans. in R. W. Southern, *Making of the Middle Ages* (London, 1953), p. 132.

[6] Cf. *MGH Libelli de Lite*, 1 (Hanover, 1891), pp. 223–6 (Humbert, *Adv. Simoniacos*); 348–55 (Manegold of Lautenbach); etc.

inspired effort to put traditional doctrines, ancient statements of law and practice, into effect. Yet there was development of doctrine too.

The chief theologian, or propagandist, of the papal reform was St Peter Damian: his works were to remain immensely popular for many generations and to be more widely distributed than those of any other writer of his age. He combined an exceptional fervour for the ascetic life of the clergy, be it as monks or canons regular, with a deep learning in the Church's law, which added to the authority of his eloquent pen. Here is a characteristic sample.[7]

> Why, o priest, when you should offer yourself sacred, that is as a sacrifice, to God, do you not first refuse to sacrifice yourself as a victim to an evil spirit? For when you fornicate you cut yourself off from Christ's members, and make your body the body of a harlot, as the Apostle bears witness, saying, 'he who is joined to a harlot, is made one body', and again, 'Shall I then take the members of Christ, and make them the members of an harlot?' Far be it. What part therefore have you in the body of Christ, who by luxuriating in seductive flesh have made yourself a member of Antichrist? 'For what fellowship hath light with darkness, or what concord hath Christ with Belial?' Surely you know full well that the Son of God chose the purity of the flesh to that point that he was not born even in pure marriage, but rather from the womb of a virgin? And this too was not sufficient, that she should be a virgin mother only, but the Church's faith is that he too who assumed the role of his father was a virgin too. If therefore our Redeemer so loved the wholeness of flowering purity, that he was born not only of a virgin's womb, but was also handled by a virgin foster father, and this while still he rocked in his cradle—by whom, do you think, will he now wish his body to be handled, when in mighty stature he reigns in heaven? If he wished to be touched with pure hands as he lay in his crib, how great a cleanliness will he wish to be touched with now that he is raised on high in his father's glory?

and he goes on to emphasize the intimate relation of the priest to his church, of which he is husband and sponsor. Any relationship he may

---

[7] Peter Damian, *Opusculum* xvii, c. 3, *PL* 145, cols. 384–5, quoting 1 Cor. 6, vv. 15–16; 2 Cor. 6, vv. 14–15. On Damian and celibacy see C. N. L. Brooke, *The Medieval Idea of Marriage* (Oxford, 1989), chap. 3. On the MSS of his letters and *opuscula*, see *Die Briefe des Petrus Damiani*, ed. K. Reindel, 1 (*MGH, Die briefe der deutschen Kaiserzeit*, IV, 1, Munich, 1983), pp. 33–9.

have with one of his spiritual daughters will be incestuous; and he denounced the fearful error of the Nicolaite heresy which claimed that the clergy could marry. I do not defend this doctrine: it seems to me far-fetched in the extreme. But we must feel its power if we are to understand the region of human experience we are exploring.

Thus the apotheosis of the priesthood is palpably related to the doctrine of the eucharist. The changes and varieties of the tenth, eleventh and twelfth centuries have recently been set in clear focus by Gary Macy in *The theologies of the Eucharist in the early scholastic period*,[8] which showed that the development was not so simple or so monolithic as had been supposed. He distinguishes two new tendencies in particular—new since the tradition which laid emphasis on the role of communion in uniting the believer to God in an act leading to salvation also survived. One tradition was to emphasize the relation of the sacrament to the Church as a whole: it was a corporate act of God's chosen people: Macy calls this the ecclesiastical tradition. It was very powerful in the twelfth century, and has been powerful in the twentieth; but it was rather overshadowed by a rival tradition in the intervening centuries. This tradition was to emphasize the relation of the eucharist to the body of Christ in its mystical sense, and to make the eucharist a part of the heavenly, symbolic world. The eucharist became ever more sublime, but the act of human communion seemed less essential to it.[9] This was one of the trends which made the private mass of the priest—in which no laymen communicated—so widespread and so popular in these centuries. But we must not be too sweeping: there was a wide variety of attitude and practice, and although by the twelfth century frequent communion for the laity was perhaps becoming rare, and the laity were coming to communicate in bread alone, and to be deprived of the chalice, there were still plenty of voices raised to insist that communion was a vital part of the eucharist and of the life of every Christian.[10] One consequence of the mystical approach was to encourage the tendency in eucharistic theology which concentrated on the sacred nature of the host. In the central scene of the Bayeux Tapestry

---

[8] Published Oxford, 1984.

[9] Macy, chap. 3; for the older tradition, see chap. 2. In the early and central Middle Ages, symbols were often seen as deeply inhering in the things they represented: the modern phrase 'mere symbol' would have baffled theologians of that age. A classic example of eleventh-century priestly eucharistic devotion is John of Fécamp's prayer of preparation, later attributed to St Ambrose: A. Wilmart, '*L'Oratio Sancti Ambrosii*, du Missel Romain', *Auteurs spirituels et textes dévots du moyen âge latin* (Paris, 1932), pp. 100–25.

[10] Cf. St Francis, below, p. 84.

Harold swears his oath to Duke William: one hand is over a shrine evidently containing relics, the other over a portable altar covered with little disks, which we may readily interpret as hosts.[11] Of the body of Jesus as he had lived on earth there could be no relics—even though some connoisseurs rejoiced in pieces of his manger and of the loaves with which he fed the five thousand. But the body of Jesus consecrated in the mass was the most powerful relic of all; and the host came to be endowed with all the properties of relics, and to be carried in procession and reserved—not only for the sick, but for special veneration. The full development of this came only in the late middle ages; devotions to the Blessed Sacrament, and all the paraphernalia which came to surround the feast of Corpus Christi— though budding in the thirteenth century—were in full flower and fruit in the fourteenth and even more the fifteenth century. In a similar way the full development of the doctrine of transubstantiation came with Aquinas and Scotus, but the heart of the matter—concentration on the host as an object, and the natural curiosity about its nature, came already in the eleventh century.[12] If the host was a peculiarly sacred object, so were the hands, so was the person, who consecrated it. The eucharist became in a quite special manner the centre of Christian experience, and the priest was sanctified with the bread on his altar.

We might then expect to find in the ordinary terminology of pious writers of the eleventh and twelfth centuries that the priests were set aside from the rest of society as folk with a very special function. The conventional definitions of society, however, made no such distinction.[13] The old threefold categories of those who fight, those who pray and those who work gave the whole clergy a single function, prayer. The more sophisticated lists of the twelfth century distinguished in particular monks, canons, and layfolk—or monks, clerks, and layfolk. But in all sorts of ways the religious impulses of the age tended to obscure these frontiers and create new ones.

The notion that a monk could, indeed, should normally become a priest, was already well established in the tenth century, the same age which (so far as our records inform us) saw the idea first adumbrated that

---

[11] *Bayeux Tapestry*, ed. D. M. Wilson (London, 1986), plates 25–6; for the host as relic, cf. Macy, pp. 81–2.

[12] Macy, chap. 3, esp. pp. 86–93.

[13] For these definitions, see M. D. Chenu, *Nature, Man and Society in the Twelfth Century* (Eng. trans. by J. Taylor and L. K. Little, Chicago, 1968), esp. chap. 6; and for the older ones, G. Duby, *The Three Orders: feudal society imagined* (English trans. by A. Goldhammer, Chicago, 1980).

every priest should normally celebrate mass every day.[14] There was still development ahead: it was only in the twelfth and thirteenth centuries that both practices became the norm. But already in the early eleventh century the beautiful little *Liber Vitae* of New Minster, Winchester, among the Stowe Manuscripts in the British Library, records the orders and status of the monks; and the community with which the book began in 1031 contained 17 priests, 11 deacons (of whom one at least was later a priest), and 6 boys.[15] Bearing in mind that monks were recruited as children, we are shown here a regular *cursus honorum*, which could lead all the seniors, if they survived, into the priesthood. Evidence from other houses suggests that this took another century or two fully to accomplish; but it was clearly well on the way. There are occasional intrusions from another social region in these lists: the *conversi*. Some of these are converts and priests—evidently clergy who became monks in middle life. Others are lay converts, who came from secular life; and these, it seems, remained lay—that is, they were not ordained.[16] But the majority of the monks were priests or on the way to the priesthood.

This practice had a devastating effect on the design of great churches. It is notorious that the eleventh century witnessed the building of vast cathedrals and abbey churches on a scale hardly precedented. All manner of reasons can be advanced for this, and fashion clearly played a leading part. But a major element was the provision of altars for very large communities. Thus if every priest in a monastery reckoned to celebrate mass daily—even allowing that there could be two masses, perhaps even sometimes three, at each altar daily—a very large number of altars was needed. The extreme case is recorded at Cluny in the early eleventh century by Rodulfus Glaber where, 'as we ourselves observed, the number of brethren in that house was so great that it was the custom to celebrate mass without interruption from day-break to dinner-time'.[17] The design

---

[14] See references in C. Brooke and W. Swaan, *The Monastic World* (London, 1974), p. 253, n. 5 to chap. 6; and for daily mass, esp. S. J. P. Van Dijk and J. H. Walker, *The Origins of the Modern Roman Liturgy* (London, 1960), pp. 51 seq.

[15] Brooke and Swaan, p. 88 and plates 142–3, reproduce the relevant folios of BL Stowe MS 944 (for a full edition, see *Liber Vitae: Register and Martyrology of New Minster and Hyde Abbey, Winchester*, ed. W. de Gray Birch (Hampshire Record Society, 1892)).

[16] In the mid and late eleventh century the 'laicus conversus' or 'conversus et laicus' is common (Birch, pp. 36–7). Thereafter, it is frequently noted by the *conversi* that they were or became priests.

[17] Rodulfus Glaber, *Historiarum Libri Quinque*, ed. J. France (OMT, 1989), pp. 236–7. For the growth of altars in Romanesque churches see the numerous plans in K. J. Conant, *Carolingian and Romanesque Architecture, 800–1200* (Harmondsworth, 1959).

of large Romanesque churches allowed for a multiplicity of altars spread about the east end in the transepts; and the pattern of Romanesque triforia suggests that many altars were provided also at first-floor level. If these were not enough, then the nave had to be called into use. The eastern bays of the nave were commonly occupied by part of the monks' choir and the screens which separated it from the nave; and the centre of the nave remained (as all indications serve to remind us) the meeting place of the clerical and lay community, even in a monastic church. But altars could be set by the pillars, as is still evident in the nave of St Albans, or in the aisles, as was to be the practice in Cistercian churches from the 1130s on.[18] To us the eucharist in a great community seems of its nature a common festivity, and if we allow that many priests should participate, it seems natural that they do so by concelebration. Deep in the heart of the religious sentiment of the central middle ages lay the notion that priests were set apart to celebrate, and that each represented his vocation by personally celebrating a private mass each day.

Yet it is also clear that there was much diversity of opinion on the role of the priesthood in Christian society. At the end of the twelfth century many of the evangelical aspirations of the day were summed up in the obscure but deeply influential prophecies of the Cistercian (or ex-Cistercian) abbot Joachim of Fiore.[19] His mind worked inexorably in threes, in three ages and three orders of folk. The first were the married folk, who represented the age of the father, since they were parents too and their special function was to have children. The second was the order of clerks, whose function was not to celebrate the eucharist, which seems to play as little part in his scheme as the hierarchy of the Church itself, but rather to pronounce and preach to the people 'the way of the Lord'.[20] The role of preaching is a crucial element in our story, but must be left for another occasion. To Joachim the function of the monks, who formed the third order, was by contemplation to perceive the Love of God; but the more he talked about the monks the more they seemed—to the wishful thinking of thirteenth-century friars—to resemble the Orders of St Francis and St Dominic.[21]

[18] In Brooke and Swaan, p. 254, chap. 9, n. 5, it is erroneously suggested that the chapel aisles were a later development: those at Rievaulx and Fountains are evidently twelfth century (see C. Brooke, 'St Bernard, the patrons and monastic planning', in *Cistercian Art and Architecture in the British Isles*, eds C. Norton and D. Park (Cambridge, 1986), pp. 11–23 at p. 17 n. 32; cf. also the much later chapels added to the nave at Melrose and on the continent: N. Coldstream, *Cistercian Art*, p. 154).

[19] For what follows, see M. Reeves, *The Influence of Prophecy in the later Middle Ages* (Oxford, 1969), esp. pp. 135–40.

[20] Reeves, p. 136.

[See p. 72 for n. 21]

All these words defining the orders of clergy were used in strangely ambiguous ways. To us the word priest is wholly clear, for it represents an order which was precisely defined. But the vernaculars played tricks with it, and in Old English a *preost* can be a clerk—in any order or none: a priest in our sense was a mass-priest.[22] Granted this, it is not surprising that 'clerk' had many shades of meaning. This is the most general term for a man who was not a layman—and at times, for a clergyman who was not a monk. A simple tonsure, an elementary hair-cut, set the clerk off from the layman.[23] Like the canon, he was expected to be involved in clerical duties in the world; and the clerical order could comprise all the clergy whatever their function. As we read accounts of it we begin to wonder what limits can be set to the clerical order; and when we read about their claims to lead the apostolic life we wonder if monks are not clerks after all.[24] The apostolic life was the supreme goal in twelfth- and thirteenth-century religious aspiration, and it is hardly surprising that many different orders claimed to lead it. To the monks it was palpable that the common life and common property of the first Christian communities described in Acts 4 foreshadowed the monastic order; theirs was the mode of living of the primitive church. Clerks and canons could counter by pointing out the pastoral, active, preaching work of the apostles, and St Francis took one version of Jesus' charge to his disciples and set it in the centre of his Rule. Nothing could be more apostolic than the direct imitation of the Gospel. At first sight these divergent views of the apostolic life seem to justify great diversity of inspiration and practice. But there was a contrary tendency, very well known to all who have studied the religious movements of the twelfth century, towards assimilation between the different modes. A striking example lies in the buildings they lived in. There is an extraordinary uniformity about the monastic complexes which monks and canons of different orders built for themselves in the central middle

---

[21] For the relation of Joachim's prophecies and the mendicants, Reeves, pp. 59–70, 161–273; cf. R. B. Brooke, *Early Franciscan Government* (Cambridge, 1959), pp. 268–72.

[22] T. Northcote Toller and A. Campbell, *Supplement* to J. Bosworth, *Anglo-Saxon Dictionary* (Oxford, 1921), p. 681; cf. the king's priests studied by F. Barlow, *The English Church 1000–1066* (London, 1963), pp. 156–8. For 'maessepreost' see J. Bosworth, *Anglo-Saxon Dictionary* (Oxford, 1898), p. 662; *Supplement*, pp. 628–9; and esp. *Councils and Synods*, 1, pt. 1, eds D. Whitelock *et al.* (Oxford, 1981), pp. 204–5.

[23] On the significance of tonsure in the central Middle Ages, see G. Constable in *Apologiae duae*, ed. R. B. C. Huygens (*CC Cont. Med.*, 62, Turnhout, 1985), esp. pp. 72–5. For Francis and tonsure see below, p. 85.

[24] See e.g. Chenu, chaps. 6 and 7.

ages: church and cloister form the centre of groups of buildings following the same fundamental pattern to a quite remarkable degree.[25] The silent witness of the buildings contradicts the noisy pamphlet wars—or rather, it shows, as we can see time and again in the religious impulses of this age, that though the currents flowed in different channels, yet they often scored a common pattern in different parts of the same landscape.

Into this world something of older traditional views had survived, now beleaguered by the ideals of twelfth-century religion. Little treatises were still copied on the functions of the various orders, and some of them were perhaps read.[26] The seven deacons of the city of Rome had survived into this world, but in the late eleventh century they were claiming to be called cardinal, like the old parish priests of Rome, and to be princes of the Church; and the day was not far distant when they might even cease to be deacons.[27] In Rome the ancient world and the immediate present always lived side by side—only in Rome could perfect early basilicas like San Clemente and Santa Maria in Trastevere be built in the twelfth century;[28] and it was the confident mingling of fashions of very different ages which helped Rome to be conservative and revolutionary at once. More surprising perhaps is the way in which the notion lingered in northern Europe that an archdeacon should be a deacon.[29] This was an ancient office in new dress; in the tenth and eleventh centuries the archdeacon found a new vocation as a diocesan administrator, and in this guise he was imported into England after the Norman Conquest, as the bishop's alter ego in administering his diocese. In the late eleventh and early twelfth centuries church councils were reiterating the rule that archdeacons should be deacons; and there is a good deal of evidence that, for example, English archdeacons in the twelfth century commonly were. Men like Thomas

---

[25] Cf. C. Brooke, 'Reflections on the monastic cloister', in *Romanesque and Gothic: Essays for George Zarnecki* (Woodbridge, 1987), 1, pp. 19–25.

[26] Later examples of this ancient mode are the late tenth century pastoral letter of Ælfric, which includes an account of orders (*Councils and Synods*, 1, pt. 1, pp. 202–5); and the twelfth century tract by Hugh of St Victor, 'De ecclesiasticis ordinibus' incorporated in his *De sacramentis* (PL 176, cols 421–31).

[27] Cf. S. Kuttner, 'Cardinalis: the history of a canonical concept', *Traditio*, 3 (1945), pp. 129–214, at pp. 189–98.

[28] See E. Kitzinger, 'The arts as aspects of a renaissance: Rome and Italy', in *Renaissance and Renewal in the Twelfth Century*, ed. R. L. Benson and G. Constable (Cambridge, Mass., and Oxford, 1982), pp. 637–70, at pp. 641–8; and W. Horn, 'Survival, revival, transformation: the dialectic of development in architecture and other arts', *ibid.*, pp. 711–27, at pp. 719–20.

[29] For what follows, see C. N. L. Brooke, 'The archdeacon and the Norman Conquest', in *Tradition and Change: Essays in honour of Marjorie Chibnall*, eds D. Greenway, C. Holdsworth and J. Sayers (Cambridge, 1985), pp. 1–19, esp. 3–4.

Becket, archdeacon of Canterbury, retained their deacon's orders till they became bishops, when they were hastily ordained to the priesthood before their consecration. Here was a motive for devout clerks to avoid entering the priesthood, in the hope that they might become archdeacons. True, archdeacons were not commonly reckoned devout; but it is noticeable that many canons remained deacons or less.[30] Canons may well have followed a different pattern from the priesthood at large; but it would be absurd to question that some or many of them were devout. Late in the century Peter of Blois, archdeacon of Bath, fervently defended the proposition that an archdeacon should be a deacon—but this was because his bishop took a different view. The archdeacon was second to the bishop in running a diocese, head of all the clergy of his archdeaconry, and he must lead them in other ways too, or so the bishop reckoned. He must be a priest: the tide had turned; and from then on it no longer seemed appropriate that he should be a deacon—and although the reputation of the medieval archdeacon for rapacity and worldliness hardly supported his role as leading priest of a diocese, the decline in the practice of keeping archdeacons in deacons' orders is a piquant illustration of the enhanced role of priesthood among the orders of the Church.

Another ancient practice of a rather different kind which died hard in this epoch was the marriage of the clergy.[31] Among the rank and file of the parish clergy indeed it is likely that the clerical concubine and the clerical family survived over much of England (perhaps over much of Europe) to the Reformation. In England in the early twelfth century there is abundant evidence that many respectable clergy thought they owned their benefices, in this sense at least that they could pass them on to their sons. The hereditary church may well have been encouraged by the increased emphasis on lineage in secular society in the twelfth century: if a lay fee was hereditary, by how much the more—some may have thought—the proprietary church. In St Paul's cathedral we have the edifying picture of hereditary canonries and even hereditary archdeaconries: when, about

---

[30] Calendars and obituaries of cathedrals give some information on the orders of canons, though it is never systematic: see e.g. the St Paul's Obituaries listed by D. E. Greenway in Le Neve, *1066–1300*, I, p. xiv; the Hereford obituary in R. Rawlinson, *The History and Antiquities of . . . Hereford* (London, 1717), pp. (3)–(31), and the Chartres obituaries in *Obituaires de la province de Sens*, ed. A. Molinier and A. Longnon (Paris, 1902–), 2. I have modified the text in the light of discussion with Dr Julia Barrow, to whose advice I am much indebted.

For what follows see Peter of Blois ep. 123, *PL* 207, cols 358–67, cited Brooke, 'The archdeacon', p. 4 n. 11.

[31] See C. Brooke, *Medieval Church and Society* (London, 1971), chap. 4; Brooke, *Marriage*, chap. 3, and refs.

1115, Cyprian archdeacon of Colchester succeeded his father Quintilian, the names suggest an inheritance of learning and scholarly interests as well as of the office.[32] Reformers and bishops and other patrons who wanted the canonries and offices for their own protégés rapidly brought this condition of affairs to an end. In well to do parishes the practice lasted much longer; and in the late twelfth century we see something like a scramble to make religious houses rectors of churches since they at least could not be nests of married clergy and hereditary abuse. But these gifts of rectories of local churches were sometimes made in the face of local juries or the like who clearly thought it the custom that the rector's son and heir should succeed.[33] We can imagine Peter Damian giving witness in such a case. The practice was wrong in law, wrong in theology, blasphemous, he might have said, and insulting to the Holy Family; but it was perfectly respectable custom, reflecting a view very far from Damian's—that priests were not so different from other folk, and could acquire property and found dynasties like other men. Their property was spiritual, like the papal monarchy. But it was property none the less for that.[34] We can understand why the reforming popes were so urgent in their attempts to separate spiritual from temporal possessions, and deny laity and lay courts any say in spiritual property. But we see again the variety of religious sentiment and practice.

In the long run the reformers succeeded in abolishing hereditary benefices and making most of the higher clergy celibate in practice as well as theory. This had one very remarkable effect on European society whose interest has not been fully assimilated by the social historians. We have been taught that lineage, pride in family, and strategies to ensure the enhancement of family estates and family standing, prospered as never before in twelfth-century Europe.[35] For a knight or a secular landowner it mattered who his father was—who his ancestors were. This was not wholly new: family pride has always been possible, and earlier generations had rejoiced in reciting their genealogies real or feigned. But a more

---

[32] Brooke, *Marriage*, p. 87; cf. D. E. Greenway in Le Neve, *1066–1300*, 1, p. 18. Canons could be priests or deacons or less (see n. 30); there was legislation against their marrying in this era, whatever their orders (see Brooke, *Medieval Church and Society*, pp. 74–5 n.).

[33] There are good examples in *English Episcopal Acta*, 6, ed. C. Harper-Bill (forthcoming, 1989). In general, see B. W. Kemp, 'Monastic possession of parish churches in England in the twelfth century', *JEH* 31 (1980), pp. 133–60.

[34] For examples of this highly proprietary attitude to churches, see C. N. L. Brooke and G. Keir, *London 800–1216* (London, 1975), pp. 131–6, esp. 135–6.

[35] A classic statement of these views is in G. Duby, *The Knight, the Lady and the Priest* (Eng. trans., New York and Harmondsworth, 1983–4).

orderly structure of lineage was undoubtedly characteristic of the twelfth century, in secular families and estates. An abbot or bishop was a magnate fully as much as his secular counterpart: in the central event of a secular monarchy, the election or acknowledgement of a new king, spiritual and temporal lords mingled on equal terms: in the eleventh and twelfth centuries at least, it was the archbishop of Canterbury or the archbishop of Mainz who had the first and most crucial voice.[36] The lords spiritual were lords as much as the lords temporal, but their authority depended not at all on their lineage. It was not that the Church was democratic in the modern sense: it has always been exceedingly rare for a peasant to become pope. In some parts of Europe it was common for leading bishops to be brothers or sons of great men, and there was here and there a religious community, especially in Germany, which was the monopoly of a group of noble families.[37] But I deliberately turn to the English evidence since the English was (in the present state of knowledge) the least aristocratic of the regional churches of medieval Europe.[38] Occasionally a royal patron set his heart on promoting a close relation. One of Henry I's favourite nephews, Henry of Blois, enjoyed the see of Winchester with the abbey of Glastonbury *in commendam*, in the jargon of a later age; Henry II's illegitimate son Geoffrey became archbishop of York.[39] But these were exceptional cases, and even the sons of barons were relatively few. None of the archbishops of Canterbury between 1066 and 1200 owed his promotion to his father; none of them was the son of a baron of the first rank.[40] When class distinctions were growing in the secular world, one

[36] Cf. C. Brooke, *The Saxon and Norman Kings* (London, 1963), chap. 2; Brooke, *Europe in the Central Middle Ages* (2 edn., London, 1987), pp. 208–9.

[37] A. Schulte, *Der Adel und die deutsche Kirche im Mittelalter* (Stuttgart, 1910); but cf. now C. Brühl, 'Die Sozialstruktur des deutschen Episkopats im 11. und 12. Jahrhundert', *Le istituzioni ecclesiastiche della 'Societas Christiana' dei secoli XI–XII: diocesi, pievi e parrocchie* (Atti della sesta Settimana . . . Milano . . . 1974, Miscellanea del Centro di Studi Medioevali 8, Milan, 1977), pp. 42–56.

[38] Cf. Brühl, 'Die Sozialstruktur', with R. and C. Brooke in the same volume, 'I vescovi di Inghilterra e Normandia nel secolo XI: contrasti', pp. 536–45, at p. 545 and n. 35 on the English evidence; cf. also B. Guillemain on the French evidence, 'Les origines des évêques en France aux xiᵉ et xiiᵉ siècles', in *Le Istituzioni ecclesiastiche della 'Societas Christiana' dei secoli XI–XII: papato, cardinalato ed episcopato* (Atti della quinta Settimana . . . Mendola, . . . 1971, Miscellanea 7, Milan, 1974), pp. 374–402.

[39] On Henry of Blois see esp. D. Knowles, *Monastic Order in England* (2 edn., Cambridge, 1963), pp. 286–93; Knowles, *The Episcopal Colleagues of Archbishop Thomas Becket* (Cambridge, 1950, corr. repr. 1970), pp. 34–7, 109–11; G. Zarnecki, 'Henry of Blois as a patron of sculpture', in *Art and Patronage in the English Romanesque*, eds S. Macready and F. H. Thompson (London, 1986), pp. 159–77.

[40] Le Neve, *1066–1300*, 2, pp. 1–5; cf. esp. C. R. Cheney, *Hubert Walter* (London, 1967), pp. 16–

distinction alone meant more than lineage: the clerical tonsure, the spiritual office, which might justify the order of priest or bishop.

In other words, the greatest social barrier in this society was between clergy and laymen. It even had something of the character of modern distinctions of race and nationality. When Becket's murderers cut the archbishop to pieces in his own cathedral, they were expressing in brutal form a deeply felt prejudice of caste. Many folk naturally felt quite differently: layman and cleric mingled in the same families, and worked together in the service of king or noble or bishop. The links were as intimate as the frontiers. None the less, the division between cleric and lay was fundamental.

So we turn with a special interest to the ambivalent world of the lay monk. We have encountered lay converts, *conversi*, in Winchester in the mid-eleventh century; and this traditional kind of layman turned monk was common in many parts of Europe at this time. But in the late eleventh century reformed monasteries in various parts of Europe began to acquire a different kind of lay monk, lay brothers who took monastic vows of a kind, but were never expected to enter orders. They first appear in large numbers in the congregation of Hirsau in south Germany in the late eleventh century, and they proliferated in many of the new orders of the twelfth, among the Carthusians, Cistercians, Grandimontines, Premonstratensians, and Gilbertines. Sometimes they were noblemen turned religious, like the eccentric count of Nevers who rebuked Louis VII for playing chess when he might have been making up for his failings as a king.[41] More characteristically, they saved monastic leaders from employing lay servants, who could provide too direct a link between enclosed monks and the wider world. They also provided a vocation for throngs of peasants who could not expect access to traditional monastic communities. They look at first sight democratic in tendency; but the irony is

---

17. Hubert Walter's father was a prosperous baron of the second rank, but in any case Hubert owed his promotion to service to the king.

[41] *Magna Vita S. Hugonis*, ed. and trans. D. L. Douie and D. H. Farmer (Nelson's Medieval Texts, 1961–2; corr. repr. *OMT*, 1985), 2, pp. 55–8; cf. Walter Map, *De nugis curialium*, ed. and trans. M. R. James *et al.* (*OMT*, 1983), pp. 80–1 and n. 2. On the lay brothers see esp. *I laici nella 'Societas Christiana' dei secoli XI e XII*, Atti della terza Settimana . . . Mendola . . . 1965 (Miscellanea del Centro di Studi Medioevali, 5, Milan, 1968), esp. chaps. by J. Leclercq, 'Comment vivaient les frères convers?', pp. 152–76; J. Dubois, 'L'institution des convers au XIIe siècle: forme de vie monastique propre aux laics', pp. 183–261; C. D. Fonseca, 'I conversi nelle comunità canonicali', pp. 262–305. In what follows I am much indebted to Constable in *Apologiae*, pp. 124–30.

that the institution of lay brothers actually sharpened some of the class distinctions of the secular world.

St Gilbert's biographer gives an admirable impression of the philosophy which led the founder of the Gilbertine Order at Sempringham in Lincolnshire to have not one or two, but four groups within his Order.[42] It was founded for women, but from an early date Gilbert formed double communities of women and men—the women dedicated to the Rule of St Benedict, the men, whose original function was to assist the women and act as their chaplains, following the Rule of St Augustine.[43] They were canons, not monks. Gilbert was early advised that his nuns should not have secular women to wait on them. 'He was anxious that (their servants) should not report or perform any worldly deed which might offend the nuns' minds.' So he established a group of lay sisters in his order:

> he preached to them contempt for the world and the abandonment of all property; restraint upon the will and the mortification of the flesh; continual work and infrequent rest; many vigils and little sleep; extended fasting and bad food; rough clothing with no adornment; confinement within the cloister to ensure that they did no evil and periods of silence lest they speak it; constant prayer and meditation to prevent them from thinking what was forbidden.[44]

A pretty tough assignment, it would seem to us, only tolerable on the assumption that they felt fully a part of the Order, sharers in its merits and rewards. After a short interval Gilbert added his fourth estate.

> Now because women's efforts achieve little without help from men [I am quoting his male biographer], he took on men, and put those he kept as servants about his house and on his land in charge of the nuns' external and more arduous tasks; some of them he had raised from childhood at his own expense, others were fugitives from their masters freed in the name of religion, and others again were destitute beggars.

In other words, says our author, he went out into the highways and the hedges and compelled them to come in; and he gave them a way of life identical to that of the lay sisters.[45]

---

[42] *The Book of St Gilbert*, eds R. Foreville and G. Keir (*OMT*, 1987), pp. 30–9, 44–9.

[43] *Ibid.*, pp. 48–9, 52–3.

[44] *Ibid.*, pp. 34–7.

[45] *Ibid.*, pp. 36–9.

In the new orders at large, and especially among the Cistercians, the new type of lay brothers commonly wore beards to distinguish them from the monks, who were clean-shaven, and so they were called *conversi barbati* or *barbati*, the bearded brethren.[46] Some time about the early 1160s, the Cistercian abbot Burchard of Bellevaux wrote a ponderous little treatise on the significance of beards and of shaving, based on many biblical texts morally and allegorically interpreted, and much misplaced learning, the *Apologia de Barbis*. A new edition of this curious work was published in the Corpus Christianorum in 1985 by Professor Huygens, with a learned and entertaining introduction by Giles Constable, making clear many dark places in the history of beards and their significance in the religious life.[47] What emerges first and foremost from Burchard and his commentators is that the beard was preserved as a class distinction. The Cistercian lay brother was clothed like a monk, but his superiors (as the choir monks reckoned themselves) wished to know at a glance with whom they were dealing. In principle indeed, the choir monks and lay brothers were strictly segregated, though not always perhaps quite so much in practice.[48] This is one of the oddest features of the Cistercian way of life, and the texts give us no adequate explanation. The Cistercian church was designed so that the centre of the nave formed a choir for the lay brothers; but they were apparently surrounded by screens sufficiently high to prevent them seeing the choir monks to the east or the little chapels and altars in the aisles all about them.[49] Their domestic quarters lay to the west of the cloister, but in early days they were commonly—perhaps normally— forbidden the use of the cloister itself and provided with a separate lane which enabled them to gain access to and from their own quarters without encountering choir monks.[50] Some mingling could not be avoided, but it was kept to a minimum. It was the same with their way of life: they lived under a rule similar to that of the choir monks, but they were forbidden to cross the frontier; they could not learn letters or be ordained[51]—as had

---

[46] See esp. Constable, pp. 124–8.

[47] *Apologie Duae*.

[48] Constable, p. 129 and n. 416; Leclercq and Dubois in *I laici*, pp. 158–60, 234–5, 245–7. For some evidence qualifying the completeness of the segregation, see my note in *Cistercian Art and Architecture*, p. 17 n. 32.

[49] D. Knowles and J. K. S. St Joseph, *Monastic Sites from the Air* (Cambridge, 1952), pp. xix–xx and *passim*; Brooke and Swaan, *Monastic World*, pp. 139–50, and figs. 11–12; plates 238, 243; Brooke in *Cistercian Art and Architecture*, p. 17 and n. 32.

[50] For the lane, see esp. Dubois in *I laici*, p. 234; Knowles and St Joseph, pp. 89 (Byland), 106–7 (Buildwas).

[51] Cf. Leclercq and Dubois in *I laici*, pp. 160, 255; cf. *Usus conversorum*, ed. P. Guignard, *Les*

79

some at least of the lay *conversi* of the old type. So clearly were lay brothers of inferior social standing that the Cistercian General Chapter actually passed a decree in 1188 forbidding noblemen to become lay brothers.[52]

It has been much disputed whether the Cistercian lay brothers were monks or laymen. Here Constable's learning guides us through a mine-field in the most helpful way.[53] Clearly they were subject to religious vows; they had a simple tonsure; they were celibate; they were not in the full sense laymen. Occasional texts refer to lay brothers in this or that order as monks, just as we encounter bearded choir monks from time to time among the shaven. But it is not normal to call the lay brothers monks, and there is abundant evidence that in the twelfth century they were not normally thought of as monks. Some assimilation took place here and there in the thirteenth century, and in the fourteenth lay brothers almost disappeared. But in their heyday in the twelfth century only a few idealists thought them equal to the choir monks.[54] It is not always easy to see the relationship from the lay brothers' viewpoint, since our commentators were choir monks, and Abbot Burchard's jocular, patronizing tone is only an exaggerated form of the common snobbery which informs the surviving literature. But it is clear that some lay brothers in several orders achieved positions of trust and responsibility and resented their inferior status. So far as we can penetrate the lay brothers' case in these disputes, they are strikingly reminiscent of the arguments between the administrative and academic viewpoint which used to trouble Cambridge colleges thirty years ago. St Gilbert's lay brothers evidently thought he was starry-eyed and unpractical, and were stung by the celebrated scandal of the nun of Watton to accuse him of not keeping nuns and canons sufficiently apart. They were the practical men who knew what was what—and very likely they were often right.

Monuments primitifs de la règle cistercienne (Dijon, 1878), pp. 276–87, at p. 281, no. 5, p. 283, no. 9, p. 285, no. 13; but see esp. edn. of early versions by J. A. Lefèvre in *Collectanea Ordinis Cisterciensium Reformatorum*, 17 (1955), pp. 11–39, 'Les traditions manuscrites des *Usus Conversorum* de Cîteaux', 65–97, 'L'evolution des *Usus Conversorum* de Cîteaux', at pp. 92, 94. The prohibition of learning is in both versions, that against a lay brother becoming a monk only in the later version; but it is clearly of quite early date, since it is in the *statuta* which some have attributed to 1119 and is certainly before 1152 (*ibid.*, p. 69); see also *Les plus anciens textes de Cîteaux*, eds J. de la Croix Bouton and J. P. Van Damme (Achel, 1974), p. 124, no. xxii; and for discussion of date, C. Holdsworth, 'The chronology and character of early Cistercian legislation on art and architecture', in Norton and Park, *Cistercian Art*, pp. 40–55, at pp. 44–52.

[52] Canivez, 1, p. 108; cf. Dubois in *I laici*, p. 261.

[53] Constable, pp. 128–30, esp. p. 128 n. 408; cf. Dubois in *I laici*, pp. 248–60.

[54] Especially among the Grandimontines: Constable, p. 127 and n. 402; and see below.

But they found little sympathy at the papal curia or among the English bishops for the view that laymen should rule clerics, and after a very long-drawn out dispute, they lost their case.[55] The most dramatic of all the many conflicts in the twelfth century between clerics and lay brothers was in the Order of Grandmont. It seems that the founder, in the late eleventh century, had deliberately sought to make the clerks and laymen in his order equal, as part of the extraordinary lessons in humility which mark every aspect of his vocation.[56] I say 'it seems' because the founder, St Stephen, pronounced that 'there is no other rule except the Gospel of Christ' and was reluctant to commit his own rule to writing: he renounced his learning in the most literal manner; his disciples had to reconstruct it from the memory of his teaching after his death.[57] In many ways he anticipated Francis; but even Francis insisted that his rule was written, though as it came to him by divine inspiration its literary form was never sacrosanct till the pope had embalmed it in a bull.[58] No doubt the early constitutions of the Grandimontines are genuine enough, but we can never be sure exactly how and when they were put on parchment, and some of their writings are of the most doubtful authenticity.[59] Still, we may dimly perceive a world in which layman and clerk were equal, and the arrangements of the houses were adapted to fit the needs of the lay brothers as much as of the clerks. After a while the lay brothers naturally took to bossing the clerks; we are told that if the clerks started their services before the lay brothers were ready 'the lay brothers beat them well'.[60] So in this Order it was the clerks, the choir monks, who complained; and in the end the popes of the early thirteenth century laid it down very firmly that the clerical priors had authority; the lay brothers

---

[55] *The Book of St Gilbert*, pp. lv–lxii, lxxxiv–xc, 134–67, 343–4.

[56] See J. Becquet, ed., *Scriptores Ordinis Grandimontensis* (*CC Cont. Med.*, 8, Turnhout, 1968): the early documents give no account of any differences. This was certainly the view of Prior Gerard Iterius (1188–98): see Constable, p. 127 and n. 402, citing Becquet, pp. 397, 431, 473. On Grandmont, the essay of Rose Graham in *English Ecclesiastical Studies* (London, 1929), chap. 9, is still valuable.

[57] Becquet, p. 5 and for the *Regula*, pp. 63–99, esp. p. 65. The *Regula*, c. 24, p. 82, rejects the use of written evidence in lawsuits (cf. c. 31, p. 84).

[58] In the Testament he talks as if every recension of the Rule was the same; cf. *Opuscula*, ed. K. Esser (Grottaferrata, 1976), pp. 439, 442–4; for the surviving texts of the Rule, *ibid.*, pp. 363–404.

[59] See esp. the long tirade attributed to the ex-prior against Henry II after the murder of Thomas Becket: *Materials for the History of Thomas Becket*, eds J. C. Robertson and J. B. Sheppard (London, RS, 1875–85), 7, pp. 450–60, no. 746.

[60] Graham, *Ecclesiastical Studies*, p. 223, citing the poet Guiot de Provins (*Oeuvres*, ed. J. Orr (Manchester, 1915), pp. 56–9, esp. p. 58, ll. 1551–60).

were put in their place. Mary had complained of Martha[61]—in contrast to the Gospel story; and the priors had to do many things forbidden in the rule to exercise their new authority.

For all the many nuances in this story, its tendency is clear: in the religious orders in the twelfth and early thirteenth centuries laymen held a vital role and commanded much respect; but their position was indelibly inferior. Against this St Francis set his face.

Among the first brothers whom Francis gathered in 1209 and 1210 laymen greatly outnumbered clerks.[62] When Pope Innocent III gave verbal approval to the Rule in 1210, he caused all, including Francis, to receive a simple tonsure, and once firmly inside a religious order laymen ceased to be lay in some very obvious senses. But we have seen that in most other orders a class distinction as large as that between lay and cleric in the outer world persisted; and it was this that Francis wished to avoid. The distinction between lay and clerical may have been less fundamental in Italy than north of the Alps—there was a tradition of lay education, of a true mingling of laymen and clergy not nearly so evident in France, for example, or England. It is significant that it was an Englishman educated in Paris, Haymo of Faversham, who destroyed Francis' intention in this region fifteen years or so after his death by introducing a constitution forbidding lay brothers to hold any offices in the Order.[63] To Haymo it must be a clerical organization just like any other Order—he was following closely in the footsteps of the reformers of the Grandimontines, even more closely the arrangements of St Dominic. Dominic, it seems, greatly admired Francis, but was not inspired by his methods of organization.[64] Dominic and his successor placed a general chapter at the head of their Order, which was in effect a representative committee. Francis also collected a general chapter as the supreme organ of his Order, but it was a large, tumultuous, charismatic gathering, a prayer meeting not a parliament.[65] By the same token he was very emphatic that the prayers of

---

[61] What the clerks unctuously observed was that 'they read nowhere that Mary complained of Martha' (Graham, *Ecclesiastical Studies*, p. 223, citing Jacques de Vitry, *Historia Occidentalis*, c. 19: see now *Historia*, ed. J. F. Hinnebusch (Fribourg, 1972), p. 126).

[62] Only one of the first eleven, Sylvester, was a priest; and the *Regula Bullata* of 1223 (c. 7) still envisages that ministers may not be priests.

[63] R. B. Brooke, *Early Franciscan Government* (Cambridge, 1959), pp. 243–5, cf. 197–8; for Dominican influence on Haymo's legislation, see *ibid.*, pp. 239–41.

[64] On the relations between Francis and Dominic, see C. Brooke, *Medieval Church and Society* (London, 1971), pp. 222–6; R. B. Brooke, *The Coming of the Friars* (London, 1975), pp. 95–7.

[65] On the Franciscan general chapter, see R. B. Brooke, *Early Franciscan Government*, e.g. pp. 35–8, 42–3, 130–2, 163–6.

his humble lay brothers were as efficacious as those of the most learned doctors;[66] and he clearly envisaged the main function of the rank and file of the brothers as to live a life which would be an example to their neighbours, not to teach or preach or perform sacraments. His mission was to the humble and the poor, and he reckoned his followers needed to be on their level—simple, ordinary folk like them, if they were really to teach them. It is useless to seek out the rights and wrongs of the difficulties and disputes which followed from this.[67] There is little doubt that he feared that his humble lay brothers would be put in a corner by the clerics, and no doubt at all that this is what happened. The gossip chronicler Salimbene joined the Order in the late 1230s when there were still copious lay brothers; and when he came to write his chronicle fifty years later he looked back with puzzled amusement at the extinct species which he had observed in early days. What good were they? What could they have been for? They were useless for hearing confessions and performing the other pastoral tasks of the friars of his day. They wore long beards, like Armenians and Greeks. At a provincial chapter at Siena, three hundred brothers were present, including an enormous throng of lay brothers. 'They did nothing but eat and sleep'.[68]

Still, there was much talk of the role of the laity in the Church; and in the twelfth and thirteenth centuries much work for lay brothers to perform. In the early thirteenth century it was both natural and extremely difficult to give a lay element in a new religious order a fair share of initiative and authority—while paying due respect to the role of the clergy. The clergy and the sacrament they performed were central to Francis' thinking. 'For St Francis had such reverence and devotion for the body of Christ' wrote his companions,

> that he wished it to be written in the Rule that friars, in the provinces where they were staying, should concern themselves lovingly in this matter and should admonish and preach to the clerks and priests to house Christ's body suitably and in a good place. If they did not do so, he wanted the friars to see to it. At one time he wanted to send some friars through all the provinces with some pyxes, so that wherever

---

[66] *Scripta Leonis*, ed. and trans. R. B. Brooke (*OMT*, 1970), no. 71, pp. 210–13 ('lay' not specified in the context but clearly intended to be included); Celano, *Vita Secunda*, caps 164, 193, and cf. 191, in *Analecta Franciscana*, 10, 225, 241, cf. 239–40; Brooke, *Early Franciscan Government*, pp. 160–1.

[67] See esp. R. B. Brooke, *Early Franciscan Government*, pp. 51–2, 160–1, 243–5.

[68] Salimbene, *Cronica*, ed. O. Holder-Egger (*MGH SRG*, 32, 1905–13), pp. 99–103, esp. p. 102.

they might find Christ's body unlawfully bestowed they might house it honourably in these.[69]

And his reverence was not confined to the sacred elements. In his open letter to all the rulers of the world—to all podestà, consuls, judges, rectors and what have you—after admonishing them to remember that death approaches, he went on 'I firmly advise you, my lords, to set aside every care and business, and gladly receive the most holy body and the most holy blood of our Lord Jesus Christ in his holy commemoration.'[70] And in his Testament, in some respects a very individual document, claiming personal and direct inspiration from God—yet also emphasizing his submission to the Pope and to all the clergy of the world:

> The Lord gave me and gives me such faith in priests, who live according to the model of the holy Roman Church, on account of their order [ordinem: I think he means orders], that even if they should persecute me I wish to run back to them. And if I had as much wisdom as Solomon, and found poor and humble secular priests in the parishes in which they lived, I would not wish to preach against their will. I wish to fear, love and honour them and all others as my masters; and I do not wish to consider sin in them, because I discern in them the son of God and to me they are masters. I do this because in this world I see nothing of the Son of God most high in a tangible sense, except his most holy body and blood, which priests receive and priests alone administer to others. This most holy mystery I wish to honour and venerate above all others and to house in precious pyxes.[71]

It was thus not disrespect for priests which led Francis to people his order with laymen—or rather to accept with gladness the very numerous laymen who aproached him. The union of priests and laity was fundamental to his conception of the Order. But the role of the lay brothers was by no means clearly defined—far less so than in the older Orders which were struggling with lay brothers' rebellions over the generation in which he was born and grew up. It was of the essence that Francis should hold the two elements in his Order together, and this was presumably the reason why he chose to accept deacon's orders but not be a priest. Maybe it was

---

[69] *Scripta Leonis*, no. 80, pp. 226–9.
[70] *Opuscula*, ed. Esser, pp. 274–5 (in defence of its authenticity, see pp. 270–4); trans. R. B. Brooke, *The Coming of The Friars*, p. 127.
[71] *Opuscula*, ed. Esser, pp. 438–9; trans. Brooke, *Coming*, p. 117.

also an act of humility; but if that was the major point, why a deacon? Like the laymen, he could not celebrate mass; but like the clergy, he was in higher orders. Yet he did not want to be given a large tonsure when he was shaved; the simple brothers, who had the small tonsure, should have a share in his head.[72] It was a grand symbolic gesture, we may think, linking him to the two wings of his Order—and in the long run it was entirely fruitless. But like everything he did, it greatly enriched the world he lived in. Clearly he saw the danger of conflict between clergy and laity, and that one of his main duties was to allay it. We may well suppose indeed that he looked beyond his Order to the world about him; to the flourishing, tumultuous, factious Italian city republics at the height of their independent or semi-independent activity. There is a famous story of how he made peace between the bishop and the podestà of Assisi, which has the familiar ring of Don Camillo about it.[73] The pattern of government in the Italian cities over the century or more since Pisa deposed its archbishop from secular rule and established its consuls in the early 1080s had been steadily and firmly secular and anti-clerical—however much some of the cities had to acknowledge the pope and his legates as their overlords. But Pisa had also shown the way in another activity equally characteristic of the Italian city republics: it had set aside a share of its wealth, and in the long run an immense investment, in beautifying the city with lovely churches.[74] The relation of Church and state, of clergy and laity, was exceedingly ambivalent, never more so than in the days of Francis; and he made his Order a microcosm of the world he lived in, and a pattern for the reconciliation of clergy and laity. In that sense the lay element in the Order was fully lay, however it might be modified in the eyes of the Church and in the law of the Church by the tonsure and the vows and the Rule.

Gonville and Caius College, Cambridge

---

[72] Celano, *Vita Secunda*, c. 193, *Analecta Franciscana*, 10, p. 241.
[73] *Scripta Leonis*, c. 44, pp. 166–71.
[74] C. Brooke, *Europe in the Central Middle Ages* (2 edn., London, 1987), pp. 133–5, 142–4 and refs.

VICARS CHORAL AND CHAPLAINS IN
NORTHERN EUROPEAN CATHEDRALS
1100–1250

by JULIA BARROW

THE purpose of this paper[1] is to take a preliminary look at a phenomenon which began to occur over much of northern Europe in the twelfth and early thirteenth centuries: the emergence of vicars choral and chaplains in cathedrals and collegiate churches. Studying the two groups together makes sense since they both acted as replacements for the senior clerics, that is the canons, in the churches where they served. In theory, the vicars chiefly served in choir and the chaplains at altars which had often hitherto been served (we may presume) by canons. In fact it is very difficult to separate vicars from chaplains since the terms were often used interchangeably at the time, and, furthermore, charters establishing these positions often specify that vicars choral would additionally serve altars and that chaplains would also attend the hours. For example, when Bishop Hugh of Wells of Lincoln ordained a chantry at the altar of St Hugh to be served by a priest chaplain and a deacon and subdeacon he laid down that the deacon and subdeacon should be chosen from among the vicars of the choir and subsequent arrangements for this chantry show that the deacons and subdeacons in the choir served for a week at a time.[2] The emergence of vicars choral and chaplains is not of major significance in itself, since these men very rarely rose to positions of any importance, but an explanation of why they were felt to be necessary is essential to a study of clerical ministry in the middle ages. Their employment enabled great churches to provide for a huge increase in private masses and for some experimentation in the pattern of their daily services. The material drawn on for this paper is mostly charter material from about forty churches in Germany, the Low Countries, and England; the virtual omission of France, unavoidable for reasons of time, is unfortunate because developments in France tended to predate developments elsewhere in northern Europe, and means that therefore it is impossible to ask the

---

[1] Research for this paper has been made possible through post-doctoral fellowships generously awarded by the British Academy and the Alexander von Humboldt-Stiftung, Bonn.

[2] C. W. Foster and K. Major, eds, *The Registrum Antiquissimum of the Cathedral Church of Lincoln*, 12 vols (Lincoln Record Society, 1931–73), 2, no. 362. See also F. Israël and W. Möllenberg, eds, *Urkundenbuch des Erzstifts Magdeburg* (Magdeburg, 1937), no. 403, dated 1185.

question 'When do vicars choral and chaplains first appear?' but it is however still possible to ask the questions 'Why do they appear' and 'What conditions permitted them to appear?' and these are, after all, questions of greater importance.

Before we look at the changing liturgical and spiritual requirements and changing economic conditions which lie behind these questions it would be best to begin with a brief summary of the functions fulfilled by cathedral and collegiate churches in the twelfth century. From a liturgical point of view, they existed to say the hours and to say mass, especially for the dead. This constant round of worship meant that continuous residence and a vigorous *esprit de corps* were desirable, though in fact as we know from many sources most secular communities in the early middle ages up to the start of the twelfth century found it hard to maintain a strict communal life for many years at a time. Another function for which cathedrals and collegiate churches, since they were large, were ideally suited, was the veneration of saints. Indeed this was probably one of the reasons why bishops, especially in the Rhineland area, founded so many collegiate churches in their see towns in the tenth and eleventh centuries—Cologne and Liège each eventually had seven of them, Mainz was not far behind with six, and Trier, Utrecht, and Strasbourg had several each.[3] Extra churches meant more patronal festivals, with more processions, and also more clergy to take part in these processions. The clergy attached to minor collegiate churches in the see town were usually forced to take part in the cathedral's patronal festival and clergy from all churches could easily be encouraged, by the endowment of sufficiently lavish feasts, to take part in each others' processions.[4] As a result feast days could be organized on a bigger scale and therefore could attract more of the faithful, and, as a result, more of their oblations.

Big churches were of course ideally suited to the veneration of saints for another, obvious, reason: their architectural layout made the provision

---

[3] Cf. P. Moraw, 'Über Typologie, Chronologie und Geographie der Stiftskirche im deutschen Mittelalter', in *Untersuchungen zu Kloster und Stift*, ed. Max-Planck-Institut für Geschichte (Göttingen, 1980), especially p. 22.

[4] Cf. F. Philippi, ed., *Osnabrücker Urkundenbuch*, 4 vols (Osnabrück, 1892–1902), 1, no. 276 (dated 1147), F. X. Remling, ed., *Urkundenbuch zur Geschichte der Bischöfe zu Speyer*, 2 vols (repr. Aalen, 1970), 1, no. 139, datable c.1220, and D. R Ehmck and W. von Bippen, eds, *Bremisches Urkndenbuch*, 5 vols (Bremen, 1873–1902), 1, no. 167, dated 1231. Alfred Haverkamp has recently suggested that the layout of the city of Trier was partly influenced by liturgical considerations, in particular the organization of processions: '"Heilige Städte" im hohen Mittelalter', in F. Graus, ed., *Mentalitäten im Mittelalter. Methodische und inhaltliche Probleme* (Sigmaringen, 1987).

of numerous altars possible, and this was especially true of churches with large crypts, which were common in Germany, where raised choirs were popular. We hear very little of these altars until they started to be endowed, though the documentation often suggests that they had had a long existence already, as in the case of an anniversary bequest to St Castor's, Coblenz, between 1196 and 1210, where grants are made to the seven altars in the church.[5] One altar whose exact origin we do know is the altar of the four crowned martyrs at Trier cathedral, which was actually established in 1103 or 1104, and which appears from the foundation document and a later one of 1126 to have been in the charge of the *scholasticus*.[6] Perhaps such altars were originally served by individual canons, either those with a special devotion to some saint or those who hoped to gain extra income from the oblations. The *custos* or treasurer of a church would probably have had a deeper interest than any of his colleagues in serving, or supervising, an altar, since he could make good use of the offerings (usually in the form of wax) made by the faithful.[7] The custos had a constant need of wax in order to light the church. A further function of collegiate, and occasionally of cathedral churches, was the provision of parochial duties, but where we find collegiate churches in Germany acting as parish churches it is often as a temporary measure until the acquisition of more endowments made it possible to delegate the work to a parson, leaving two important financial perquisites, the right to invest the parson and hold the archidiaconal visitations, in the hands of the dean and chapter and of the provost respectively. It is only fair to say that some members of collegiate churches took their responsibilities seriously, like Dean Ensfrid of St Andreas, Cologne, who received warm praise from Caesarius of Heisterbach for his devotion to the poor.[8]

Turning from the canons to the vicars and chaplains who deputed for them, it might be best to look at the emergence of each group in turn, and then look at the ways in which their positions were funded. Vicars choral replaced canons in choir, and, as hebdomadaries, at the high altar (the

---

[5] H. Beyer, L. Eltester and A. Goerz, eds, *Urkundenbuch zur Geschichte der jetzt die preußischen Regierungsbezirke Coblenz und Trier bildenden Mittelrheinischen Territorien* (henceforward *UBMRh*), 3 vols (Coblenz, 1860–1874), 2, no. 269.

[6] *Ibid.*, 1, nos. 411, 455.

[7] T. Duchet and A. Giry, eds, *Cartulaires de l'église de Térouane*, Société des Antiquaires de la Morinie (St-Omer, 1881), no. 50, dated 1173; H. A. Erhard, ed., *Regesta Historiae Westfaliae*, 2 vols (Münster, 1847–51), 2, no. 307, datable 1155 × 1159; R. Wilmans *et al.*, eds, *Westfälisches Urkundenbuch*, 3–10 (Münster, 1859–1940), 3, no. 212, dated 1225.

[8] Caesarius of Heisterbach, *Dialogus Miraculorum*, ed. J. Strange, 2 vols (Cologne and Bonn, 1851), 1, Dist. VI, c. 5.

hebdomadary was the canon whose turn it was to officiate at the high altar for a week). The main cause of their appearance on the scene, therefore, as one would expect, is absenteeism on the part of canons, which was usually the result of canons being sucked into more absorbing duties elsewhere, particularly the service of a king or a magnate, or else their having other benefices; pluralism was on the increase in the twelfth century, especially in England. Such absences did not necessarily take them away for more than a few weeks or months at a time, but were sufficient to cause interruptions in the smooth running of the services of the church. By the end of the twelfth century many churches were finding themselves forced to impose strict residence requirements—Liège cathedral and the churches of St Pierre and St Aubain in Namur, for example, all flatly denied prebendal payments to absent canons.[9] But there was one area of northern Europe where absenteeism raised no eyebrows: English cathedrals took it for granted that a high proportion of their canons would be absent. Moreover their requirements for full residence were so lax that canons could be absent for most of the time and still not be penalized (this was especially true of Lichfield and Salisbury),[10] and the penalty inflicted on those who failed to turn up at all was either the deprivation of a small fraction of the prebendal revenue[11] or merely of their share of commons. One of the prebends at Hereford was especially earmarked for absentees, since its holder was precluded from receiving most forms of commons.[12] So the best way to cope with an emptying choir was to insist that the absentees pay for vicars to replace them. Bishop Hugh (St Hugh) of Lincoln allowed his dean and chapter to compel all absentee canons to provide vicars,[13] and in the late twelfth century, Sarum cathedral wrote a letter of advice to a Bishop R. of Bath, saying that they encouraged all their canons to have vicars.[14] Besides

---

[9] S. Bormans and E. Schoolmeesters, eds, *Cartulaire de l'église Saint-Lambert de Liège* (Brussels, 1893), 1, no. 84, dated 1203; E. Poncelet, ed. *Actes des Princes-Evêques de Liège: Hugues de Pierrepont, 1200–1229* (Brussels, 1941), no. 20, dated 1203; J. Barbier, 'Documents extraits du cartulaire du chapitre de Saint-Aubain, à Namur', *Analectes pour servir à l'histoire de la Belgique*, 11 (1874), p. 99, no. 1 (dated December 1207).

[10] For Lichfield, see *VCH Staffordshire*, 3, p. 142; for Salisbury, W. R. H. Jones, ed., *Vetus Registrum Sarisberiense*, 2 vols, *RS* (1883–4), 2, pp. 18, 41–2.

[11] K. Edwards, *The English Secular Cathedrals in the Middle Ages* (2 edn., Manchester, 1967), p. 41.

[12] H. Bradshaw and C. Wordsworth, eds, *Statutes of Lincoln Cathedral*, 3 vols (Cambridge, 1892–1902), 2, p. 58.

[13] *Reg. Ant.*, 1, no. 300.

[14] *Calendar of the Manuscripts of the Dean and Chapter of Wells*, I, Historical Manuscripts Commission (London, 1907), p. 31. In Salisbury's 1219 statutes it was laid down that individual canons had to replace their vicars, when these died, within three months and a day: *Vetus Registrum Sarisberiense*, 2, p. 21.

absenteeism, another feature of this period, particularly in the Low Countries, seems to have been an increasing elaboration of the liturgy. Terwaan introduced extra antiphons and readings of nine lessons in the late twelfth century,[15] and in 1210 Count Philip of Namur insisted that his church of St Aubain, Namur, should celebrate the office of the Virgin Mary on Fridays at mass and all the hours except Matins, Vespers, and Compline, and that every day at each hour one of the penitential psalms shoud be said.[16] Music, too, may have been becoming increasingly elaborate, as the occasional reference to an organist shows,[17] though the demand for highly trained singers as vicars choral would only really have expanded with the vogue for polyphony from the mid thirteenth century onwards. Although the prescriptions for more elaborate liturgical presentation often do not mention vicars, it must have been becoming clear to secular communities already by 1200 that they could, so to speak, perform better in choir if they had some sort of trained auxiliary force; this was even more true of processions, where vicars could play useful subordinate roles, such as thuribles.[18]

The motivations for the introduction of chaplains to serve at altars were somewhat different. The two chief ones seem to have been an anxiety about the number of priests available in the community and an increasing desire to provide fixed daily, or at least weekly, services, at the many side altars in the church. In addition, there was a change in fashion concerning anniversary services. To begin with the availability of priests, therefore, we may note that because of a shortage of documentation there is some difficulty in establishing whether the proportions of priests, deacons, and subdeacons among the canons at any one church remained constant throughout the period 1000–1250. At several churches, however, we can work out the exact proportions of priests, deacons, subdeacons, and acolytes at particular moments, especially in the eleventh century, a

---

[15] *Cartulaires de l'église de Térouane*, nos. 37, 48.

[16] J. Barbier, 'Documents extraits du cartulaire du chapitre de St-Aubain, à Namur, concernant le village de Mellet (Hainaut)', *Analectes pour servir à l'histoire ecclésiastique de Belgique*, 5 (1868), pp. 200–3. In a similar vein, see the statutes drawn up for Le Mans cathedral in 1220: A. Bertrand de Broussillon, ed., *Cartulaire de l'évêché du Mans, 965–1786*, Société des archives historiques du Maine, 9 (Le Mans, 1908), pp. 26–9.

[17] *Urkundenbuch des Erzstifts Magdeburg*, no. 342, dated 1173; *Westf.UB.*, 2, no. 417, concerning the Alter Dom in Münster, dated 1181. An Osnabrück charter of 1217 refers to three specialized singers: F. Philippi, ed., *Osnabrücker Urkundenbuch*, 2, no. 77.

[18] D. R. Ehmck and W. von Bippen, eds, *Bremisches Urkundenbuch*, 1, no. 162, concerning St Willehad's. See also S. Muller and A. C Bouman, eds, *Oorkondenboek van het Sticht Utrecht tot 1301* (Utrecht, 1920), no. 440, of 1163.

period when it was still fashionable to give the grade of ordination when listing clerics as witnesses to charters.[19] Bamberg and Halberstadt cathedrals continued doggedly to do this well into the twelfth century, Tournai until 1220.[20] Where we have figures we see that the proportions of priests, deacons, subdeacons, and acolytes were as nearly as possible identical, and this seems to have been viewed as the ideal.[21] For one church where it is possible to have some idea about the proportions of clerics in the various grades over a longer period, Tournai, Jacques Pycke has shown that in fact the proportion of priests remained fairly stable, at about 20 per cent of canons whose orders are known, except for the twenty-year period 1181–1200, when it fell to 14 per cent;[22] this lower figure coincides with a period in which the proportion of canons whose orders are not known is unusually small, and might possibly reflect something closer to the reality. In the late twelfth century we see all the churches in the Low Countries expressing concern about the number of priests in their communities, and establishing vicarages or chaplaincies for priests to serve the high altar, and quite often stipulating that every second or third prebend falling vacant should be reserved for a priest.[23] This made them unpopular with the papacy, since the popes hoped to further their own candidates, who were unlikely to be priests, let alone residentiaries.[24] This anxiety about the number of priests does not reflect a sudden failure on the part of the canons in the community to seek ordination as priests. In part it means that, in spite of the strict residence requirements which were a feature of these churches,[25] the number of canons with legitimate reasons for

---

[19] K. Janicke, ed., *Urkundenbuch des Hochstifts Hildesheim*, 1 (1896, repr. Osnabrück, 1965), no. 62, dated 1019.

[20] Munich, Bayerisches Hauptstaatsarchiv, Bamberger Urkunde no. 324; A. Brackmann, 'Urkundliche Geschichte des Halberstädter Domkapitels im Mittelalter', *Zeitschrift des Harz-Vereins für Geschichte und Altertumskunde*, 32 (1899), pp. 1–147, here p. 9; J. Pycke, *Le chapitre cathédral Notre-Dame de Tournai de la fin du XIe à la fin du XIIIe siècle* (Louvain and Brussels, 1986), p. 244.

[21] T. J. Lacomblet, ed., *Urkundenbuch für die Geschichte des Niederrheins*, 4 vols (Düsseldorf, 1840–58), 1, no. 187, dated 1052; E. Hautcoeur, ed., *Cartulaire de l'Eglise collégiale de St-Pierre de Lille* (Lille, 1894), no. 1, of the mid-eleventh century; Munich, Bayerisches Hauptstaatsarchiv, Bamberger Urkunde no. 324; for a reference to Arras in 1214, see J. Pycke, *Le chapitre cathédral Notre-Dame de Tournai*, p. 243. An ordination list for the diocese of Hildesheim in 1203 states that 21 acolytes, 3 subdeacons, 4 deacons and 6 priests were ordained at Hildesheim cathedral: *Urkundenbuch des Hochstifts Hildesheim*, 1, no. 582.

[22] J. Pycke, *Notre-Dame*, p. 245.

[23] *Cartulaire de St-Lambert*, 1, no. 84, dated 1203; *Cartulaire de l'Eglise collégiale de St-Pierre de Lille*, no. 80, dated 1205.

[24] *PL* cciv. 721.

[25] See n. 9 above. A similar preoccupation can be seen at Cologne: M. Groten, *Priorenkolleg und*

absence (for example, absence on church business, or illness) made the burden on the other priest-canons, who had to serve the high altar for a week at a time as hebdomadaries, too severe; in part it might be, as we have already seen, owing to the demands of a more complicated liturgy.

The foundation of chaplaincies to serve the side altars seems to have been mostly the work of individual canons, very often dignitaries, acting in an entrepreneurial spirit, and in very much the same way that they might undertake a piece of land reclamation or property speculation for the chapter. A successful chapel, after all, might eventually pay for itself. We thus find the *scholasticus* at Magdeburg endowing vicarages at the altars of St Martin and the Holy Apostles on either side of the choir in 1185,[26] a canon at Münster cathedral endowing the altar of St Mary and St Catherine under the south tower in 1194 and 1204,[27] and the cantor of Münster cathedral endowing the vestments, chalice, and books for the altar of St Peter in 1227.[28] Not all the chapels were in the main cathedral building. Some were adjacent to cloisters or refectories;[29] the richer canons liked having them in their houses,[30] and some canons endowed chapels for hospitals under the general direction of the cathedral.[31] While this boom in the endowments of altars and chapels tells us something about economic changes, it is hard to be sure how much the dedications of the particular altars tell us about twelfth-century piety, especially since it is possible that many of the altars had already long been in existence; the bulk of the dedications, not surprisingly, are to the Virgin Mary, for whom masses might be endowed at altars dedicated to other saints.[32] Individual apostles were also popular dedicatees.

Where we can point to a definite development in popular piety, however, is in the change that is observable in this period in anniversary arrangements for the dead. Such arrangements had always been of

---

Domkapitel von Köln im hohen Mittelalter (Bonn, 1980), p. 221—Groten assumes that this was because of a decline in the number of canons seeking ordination as priests, but it is more likely simply to have been that demand for masses was outstripping the supply of priests.

[26] *Urkundenbuch des Erzstifts Magdeburg*, no. 403.

[27] *Westf. UB*, 2, no. 539; 3, no. 27.

[28] *Ibid.*, 3, no. 239.

[29] *Cartulaire de St-Lambert*, no. 87, dated 1204 and no. 59, dated 1182.

[30] *Cartulaires de l'église de Térouane*, no. 16, dated 1136.

[31] *Cartulaire de St-Lambert*, no. 87, dated 1204; *Monumenta Boica*, ed. Academia Scientiarum Boica, vol. 38, pt. 2 (Munich, 1829), pp. 111–16 (1160), 117–19 (1163), concerning Passau cathedral; W. M. Newman, *Charters of St-Fursy of Péronne* (Cambridge, Mass., 1977), no. 57, dated 1196.

[32] *Westf. UB*, 2, no. 417.

enormous significance, as we know from the number of surviving necrologies, and in communities of secular canons in the empire the endowment of an anniversary distribution seems to have been a condition of becoming a canon; it was a convenient disguise for simony.[33] Important local laymen and women would make a point of providing anniversary bequests too. These arrangements usually took the form of the endowment of a distribution of bread and ale, or bread and wine, money, and sometimes candles, which were paid to those canons present in choir at the mass or service of vigils when the name of the dead canon was read out. All the names of the benefactors whose anniversary it was would be read out together (hence the fact that necrologies are laid out like calendars). Richer benefactors, particularly bishops, were expected to make rather more generous bequests; up to about 1200 all the bishops of Bamberg endowed eight-course feasts.[34] Now, while this system of endowing anniversaries survived much later than the period with which we are dealing, a new system was coming into fashion in the late twelfth century, the foundation of chantries.[35] In these, the duty of holding masses for individuals was often combined with the duty of holding masses for the faithful departed,[36] or sometimes with the duty of providing the necessary month's worth of daily masses which had to be said for deceased members of the community.[37] One of the advantages of chantries was the spiritual privacy which could be obtained, the sense of cutting oneself off from the rest of humanity, which was of especial importance to kings and great magnates, but not to them only; another advantage was that whole families could be remembered together, rather than scattered throughout the year, but of course the main advantage must have been the fact that masses were said daily, not just annually.

The methods of funding vicarages and chaplaincies were extremely

[33] J. Barrow, 'Education and the Recruitment of Cathedral Canons in England and Germany, 1100–1225', to appear in *Viator*, 20 (1989).

[34] E. Freiherr von Guttenberg and A. Wendehorst, eds, *Urbare und Wirtschaftsordnungen des Domstifts zu Bamberg* (Würzburg, 1969), pp. 146–8.

[35] *Bremisches Urkundenbuch*, 1, no. 101, dated 1206; E. Döll, *Die Kollegiatstifte St. Blasius und St. Cyriacus zu Braunschweig* (Braunschweig, 1967); A. de Charmasse, ed., *Cartulaire de l'église d'Autun* (Paris and Autun, 1865), pp. 167–70 (1247); *Cartulaire de l'Eglise collégiale de St-Pierre de Lille*, no. 38 (1183 × 1187) and no. 100 (1212); M. Stimming and P. Acht, eds, *Mainzer Urkundenbuch*, 2 vols in 3 (Darmstadt, 1932–71), 2, pt. 2, no. 653a (1196); *Calendar of the Manuscripts of the Dean and Chapter of Wells*, 1, p. 53.

[36] J. Barbier, 'Documents extraits du cartulaire du chapitre de Saint-Aubain', pp. 102–3, no. 4 (1212).

[37] A whole year's worth of masses for deceased canons at Bremen cathedral: *Bremisches Urkundenbuch*, 1, no. 101 (1206).

diverse. Vicars choral in England received stipends from the canons whom they replaced, and the chapter acted as a whole to enforce this. Otherwise chapters had to search around for suitable parcels of income. One of the means at their disposal was the absorption of smaller, decaying secular communities (much as modern corporations might devour shell companies) to serve as captive supplies of manpower. Thus Autun cathedral made use of the canons of St-Lazare, while Liège cathedral took over St-Materne and the collegiate church of St Fursy, Péronne, took over the small community of St-Léger.[38] A provost of St-Paul, Liège, acquired fifteen benefices to bestow on poor clerks, but this property was alienated through greed or carelessness.[39] The canons of the larger churches were usually in a powerful enough position to insist on strict residence requirements and low incomes for their subordinates. Where powerless communities of this sort were not available, another useful gambit was to divide an existing prebend in half[40] or to make use of prebends which had previously been set aside for schoolboy canons (these were a feature of some Westphalian churches).[41] Furthermore, the prebends set up or set aside as part of confraternity arrangements naturally always had to be served by vicars, sometimes two at once, as in the case of the imperial prebend at Utrecht cathedral.[42] The church of St Pierre, Lille, granted a prebend to the bishop of Terwaan in 1143 on condition that it would be served by a vicar in his place.[43] Several of the English cathedrals made arrangements with abbeys whereby the abbey would turn some of its parish churches into a prebend, which would officially be held by the abbot but would in practice be served by a vicar. An early example is the arrangement between Salisbury cathedral and Sherborne abbey in the 1160s,[44] but the system only really caught on from the 1190s onwards, as various Norman abbeys, Lire,[45] Bec,[46]

---

[38] *Cartulaire de l'église d'Autun*, no. 29, 1195; *Cartulaire de St-Lambert*, 1, nos. 76 (1200), 137 (1223); *Charters of St-Fursy of Péronne*, no. 136.

[39] O. J. Thimister, ed., *Cartulaire ou recueil de chartes et documents inédits de l'eglise collégiale de St-Paul, actuellement Cathédrale de Liège* (Liège, 1878), p. 32 (before 1203).

[40] J. Barbier, 'Extraits du cartulaire du chapitre de St-Aubain, Namur', *Analectes pour servir à l'histoire ecclésiastique de Belgique*, 5 (1868), p. 480; *Cartulaire de St-Lambert*, no. 116 (1215); *Cartulaire de l'Eglise collégiale de St-Pierre de Lille*, no. 44 (1189).

[41] *Westf. UB*, 4, no. 185, and 6, no. 59.

[42] S. Muller and A. C. Bouman, eds, *Oorkondenboek van het Sticht Utrecht tot 1301* (Utrecht, 1920), no. 530 (1196).

[43] *Cartulaire de l'Eglise collégiale de St-Pierre de Lille*, no. 24.

[44] *Vetus Registrum Sarisberiense*, 1, pp. 275–314.

[45] With Hereford in 1195: BL, Add. MS 15668, fol. 50.

[46] Bec made a prebendal arrangement with Wells before 1199: *Calendar of the Manuscripts of the*

Grestain,[47] Montebourg,[48] and Cormeilles,[49] decided to turn their parish churches in England into prebends of the cathedrals of Hereford, Wells, Salisbury, and Chichester, so that the native cathedral could act for them in possible legal disputes.[50] From the point of view of the cathedrals one great advantage of these schemes was the provision of vicars at no extra cost.

When chaplaincies were founded, the basic costs were also rarely met by the community as a whole, but were undertaken by a public-spirited canon or a generous bishop or layman. The new-found ability of canons to endow private chapels in part reflects a growing flexibility in their use of money; where we see canons endowing chaplaincies and altars it is almost invariably with bought, not inherited, property, often a spin-off from property speculations such as urban development, or more intensive agricultural exploitation.[51] Rents, especially of urban property, and tithes were commonly used as the endowments.[52] In Germany in particular it was hard for individual members of a family to alienate inherited property, although anniversary bequests for clerics would be agreed to by the family to ensure their kinsman's entry into a church. When the *scholasticus* of St Marien, Erfurt, wanted to endow a chaplaincy in 1196 with family land, the land had to be bought by the archbishop of Mainz before it was given to St Marien simply in order to remove it completely from the family's control.[53] Now with a developing economy clerics no longer had to rely merely on their families, but could try to acquire their own sources of wealth, with which they could experiment more widely than merely by founding anniversary distributions.

To sum up, therefore, the emergence of vicars choral and chaplains was caused by the shaking up of society and economy which was so marked a feature of the twelfth century. Big churches found that they

Dean and Chapter of Wells, 1, p. 489, and in 1208 with Salisbury: *Vetus Registrum Sarisberiense*, 1, pp. 189–90.

[47] Henry Mayr-Harting, ed., *The Acta of the Bishops of Chichester* (CYS, 1964), pp. 154–5, no. 97, datable 1198 × 1204.

[48] Montebourg made a prebendal arrangement with Salisbury in 1213: *Vetus Registrum Sarisberiense*, 1, pp. 224–6.

[49] Cormeilles made a prebendal arrangement with Hereford between 1216 and 1219: Evreux, Archives-Départementales de l'Eure, H 590, fol. 325ᵛ.

[50] *The Acta of the Bishops of Chichester*, p. 43.

[51] *Cartulaire de St-Lambert*, 1, no. 59 (1182); *UBMRh* 1, no. 455; *Bremisches Urkundenbuch*, 1, nos. 101, 128.

[52] *Westf. UB*, 2, no. 539, 3, no. 27.

[53] *Mainzer Urkundenbuch*, 2, pt 2, no. 653a.

could cope with growing absenteeism on the part of their canons as long as they had suitable replacements; indeed they often found that they could cope better, since they were now free to employ exactly as many priests and well-trained singers as they needed. Individual canons, however, could undertake the endowment of altars as part of their property dealings and have the satisfaction of financial as well as spiritual rewards.

University of Birmingham

RIVALS FOR MINISTRY? ORDINATIONS OF SECULAR AND REGULAR CLERGY IN SOUTHERN ENGLAND *c.*1300–1500

by VIRGINIA DAVIS

AT the beginning of the fourteenth century ecclesiastical recruitment was flourishing in England. Hundreds of men turned up to be ordained at the four Ember seasons each year at which major ordinations were permitted to be held.[1] The majority of these men were secular clergy; only a small proportion were members of religious orders. Of the scores of people in the diocese of Winchester who came at the stipulated time to be ordained to the major orders at this date only about one fifth were members of religious orders and of those, only a handful were mendicants. However, by the end of the century, after the ravages of the Black Death, although the total numbers of men being ordained had declined dramatically a greater percentage of these were regular rather than secular clergy. A similar pattern can be seen all over Southern England. It was a trend which persisted throughout much of the fifteenth century. This paper will investigate the changing patterns of secular and regular ordinations to the priesthood in southern England in the period between 1300 and 1500. In the late fourteenth and fifteenth centuries extensive anti-mendicant feeling was expressed both in late medieval literature and in rivalry between the secular clergy and the friars over the pastoral role of the latter. Was this, in fact, a reflection of a reality which meant that, compared to the position in the early fourteenth century, far more ordained friars were on the streets and in the parishes?

The evidence from episcopal ordination lists for clerical recruitment in this period is extensive but has never been fully exploited. As long ago as 1913 T. F. Tout pointed out the potential of the rich source material[2] but

---

[1] Four days were canonically prescribed for the holding of ordination ceremonies. These were the Saturdays of the weeks following the commemoration of Ash Wednesday, Whit Sunday, the Exultation of the Holy Cross (14 September) and St Lucy's day (13 December); on feast days lesser orders up to and including that of acolyte could be conferred. Men ordained to the minor orders of exorcist, doorkeeper and to the first tonsure were rarely recorded in episcopal registers but most registers record ordination to the rank of acolytes.

[2] 'One is tempted to prepare statistics as to the relative proportion of clerks and regulars but to do so for one diocese would not be very interesting or important. When the work of the Canterbury and York society has gone on a little longer and made more medieval registers accessible in print, an attempt to generalize as to the status of the ordinands in different

99

until recently few have taken up this challenge. The small amount of work which has been completed so far has largely concentrated on isolated local studies.[3] By the early fourteenth century, most bishops' registers included lists of men being ordained as acolytes and to the three major orders of sub-deacon, deacon, and priest in the dioceses. These lists included information as to the candidate's diocese of origin, his title or means of sustenance, his educational qualifications where applicable, and whether he was a member of the secular clergy or a member of a religious order. Not every register contains all this information, the surviving Norwich lists for example do not include details of members of religious orders, or at least fail to distinguish them.[4] More often lists are merely missing or fail to mention the candidate's title in the case of seculars or house in the case of regulars. Recording of educational qualifications is also very uneven, especially in the fourteenth century. These lists have been much under-used as a source of information for the clergy, largely because individual ordination lists are of relatively little value in isolation except for biographical snippets about the ordainees. However, viewed *en masse*, over a substantial chronological period or over a wide geographical area, the lists provide a valuable source of information about the nature of recruitment to the English church in the later middle ages.

The evidence for this paper is drawn from a number of dioceses in southern England but the most detailed material is taken from the diocese of Winchester, England's wealthiest see. For a number of reasons Winchester is a valuable diocese in which to conduct a survey of clerical recruitment. The survival of its ordination lists is high over a lengthy period; the diocese was a populous one, encompassing the counties of Surrey and Hampshire but, unlike a large urban centre such as London, the normal balance of population is not disturbed by a substantial

---

dioceses and at different periods may be commended to students of ecclesiastical antiquities as a useful piece of research, never, so far as I know, systematically attempted.' T. F. Tout, 'Introduction' in *The register of John de Halton, Bishop of Carlisle 1292–1324 (CYS* 12, 1913), 1, p. xxxix.

[3] A brief introduction to the format and content of ordination lists is to be found in R. M. T. Hill, ed., *The rolls and registers of bishop Oliver Sutton*, 7 (Lincoln Record Society, 69, 1969), pp. ix–xi; H. F. Bennett, 'Medieval ordination lists in the English episcopal registers', in J. Conway-Davis, ed., *Studies presented to Sir Hilary Jenkinson* (London, 1957) is the basic article on the subject. Most work has been restricted to particular dioceses, D. Robinson, 'Ordination of secular clergy in the diocese of Coventry and Lichfield 1322–1358', *Archives*, 17 (1985), pp. 3–21; J. F. Williams, 'Ordination in the Norwich diocese during the fifteenth century', *Norfolk Archaeology*, 31 (1957), pp. 347–58.

[4] Williams, 'Ordination in the Norwich diocese', pp. 357–8.

itinerant population. All the major religious orders are represented within the diocese and there are also a number of mendicant houses.[5] Thus evidence from the diocese of Winchester provides a reasonably balanced sample of the trends in ordination in the late middle ages.

The Winchester episcopal registers survive from the episcopate of John of Pontoise (1282–1304) but his register does not include ordination lists. References in later medieval registers show that he did have an ordination register which is no longer extant.[6] The first Winchester episcopal ordination lists therefore appear in the register of his successor Henry Woodlock, bishop 1305–16.[7] Ordinations appear in all the remaining surviving registers for the medieval period except that of Adam Orleton (1333–45). The only major gap is for the early fifteenth century; the register for Cardinal Beaufort, bishop 1405–47 is almost entirely lacking for the period from 1415 and no ordination lists survive for the years 1418–1447.[8]

The body of this paper will be divided into three sections dealing with:

(i) the overall clerical recruitment trends in this period as a whole, fitting them in with English demographic developments of the period;
(ii) the changing ratio of secular and religious being ordained;
(iii) the impact of this changing ratio; in particular how the mendicant orders fared in this period.

(i) *Overall recruitment trends*

During the short episcopate of John Sandale, 1316–19, just under 1000 men were ordained in the diocese of Winchester. Of these 247 were ordained to the priesthood.[9] Ordinations were held regularly all over the diocese in episcopal manor chapels, parish churches, abbey churches and in Winchester cathedral itself. Substantial numbers of candidates presented themselves at each ordination; a total of 260 men turned up to be ordained in December 1317 alone. Seven ordination services were held in that year and in all Bishop Sandale ordained 560 men as acolytes and to the

---

[5] There were Franciscan houses in Winchester and Southampton, Dominicans in Winchester and Guildford; Carmelites in Winchester and Austin Friars in Winchester and Southampton.

[6] The register of Pontoise's successor, Henry Woodlock, records the issue of a certificate of ordination to a John of Monte Hermeri stating that he had been ordained priest in the December in the first year of Pontoise's episcopate.

[7] *Registrum Henrici Woodlock, diocesis Wintoniensis A.D. 1305–1316*, ed. A. W. Goodman, 2 vols (CYS 43, 44, 1940–41).

[8] D. M. Smith, *A guide to bishops' registers* (Royal Historical Society, 1981), p. 207.

[9] 271 men were ordained acolytes, 196 as subdeacons and 234 as deacons, *The registers of John de Sandale and Rigaud de Asserio, Bishops of Winchester*, ed. F. J. Baigent (Hampshire Record Society, 1897).

major orders.[10] Episcopal officials must have been exceedingly busy on the Wednesday and Friday preceding each ordination ceremony, checking candidates' educational qualifications, their title or means of sustenance, and letters dimissory of candidates from outside the diocese.[11]

This healthy situation—perhaps over healthy, for by the early fourteenth century it seems likely that there were too few benefices for this number of qualified men—continued in the years preceding the Black Death. William Edington became bishop in 1346 and the early sections of his register shows substantial numbers proceeding to ordination. A total of 666 were ordained to the major orders between June 1346 and December 1347, 253 of them as priests.[12] Other men were given dimissory letters enabling them to be ordained in dioceses other than their own. Large numbers of acolytes were also being ordained, 123 in 1447 alone, suggesting that, even allowing for a substantial drop-out rate, recruitment would continue well. Estimating the numbers of men ordained as acolytes but not proceeding to the priesthood is complicated by the considerable mobility to be found among the clergy, which means that it is necessary to track men across diocesan boundaries before concluding finally that they did not proceed to the priesthood; missing lists complicate the calculation still further. Nor was this necessarily a failure on their part; many clerics did not feel the need to become priests until elevated to a position requiring sacerdotal orders; it has been shown that 46 per cent of acolytes in the diocese of York did not reach the priesthood.[13] Recent work on the diocese of Coventry and Lichfield suggests, however, that very few men who proceeded to be ordained as subdeacon failed to progress to the priesthood and most in fact did so within three years of becoming subdeacon.[14]

Much has been already written about the impact of the Black Death on

[10] Ordinations in 1317 were held on 26 February in Southampton; 19 March in Merton Abbey conventual church; 2 April at West Ham in the diocese of London; 28 May at St Mary Overy Priory in Southwark; 24 September in York, during a vacancy in the see and by permission of the dean and chapter of the cathedral; 17 December at St Cross in Winchester, *Registers of Sandals*, pp. 171–94.

[11] Relatively little is known of the details of the examination procedure; details of the examiners do not often survive. In March 1316 Bishop Woodlock used as his examiners, Ralph de Caune, the precentor of Winchester cathedral and Master Peter de Worldham, the commissary general of the diocese, *Registrum Woodlock*, 1, p. 668.

[12] F. S. Hockey, ed., *The register of William Edington 1346–66* (Hampshire Record Series 8, 1986–87), 2, pp. 105–28.

[13] J. H. Moran, 'Clerical recruitment in the diocese of York 1340–1530: Data and commentary', *JEH* 34 (1983), pp. 19–54.

[14] Robinson, 'Ordination of the secular clergy in Coventry and Lichfield', p. 7.

the English clergy[15] and it is not the purpose of this paper to detail the extent of the catastrophe. It has been shown elsewhere that Winchester was among the worst hit dioceses; just under half (49 per cent) of all beneficed clergy died.[16] Bishop Edington's register reflects this, showing a sudden dramatic rise in the number of men being instituted to parochial benefices in the period immediately after the onset of plague. Before this date, he instituted about a dozen men a year to benefices within his diocese. In 1349 315 were instituted.[17] The religious houses within the diocese were also badly affected; at least one priory, that of St Mary Magdalen Sandon, lost all its members and other religious houses were severely hit. The drop of population was not reflected in the ordination lists for 1349, and into the early 1350s substantial numbers of men were still being ordained, doubtless to fill the gaps left by mortality among the priesthood.[18] Another indication of the initial impact of plague on the priesthood can also be found in the register, more acolytes are recorded holding benefices than is usual. It is, however, in the generation after the first impact of the plague that its worst effects are felt; by the 1360s only a handful of men, about four a year (1361–5), were recorded as proceeding to the priesthood annually.

This pattern continued for the rest of the century and into the fifteenth century. On average fewer than 30 men were being ordained priests annually in the diocese of Winchester, at best about half of the pre-Black Death figure. If anything the situation worsened as the fifteenth century progressed. In the first ten years of the episcopate of Bishop Waynflete fewer than twelve priests were being ordained annually.[19] Other dioceses show a similar catastrophic drop. In the diocese of Worcester in the early fourteenth century well over a hundred men were being ordained annually; by the end of the century about thirty was the norm.[20] Not only had the overall population dropped, but the attractiveness of a clerical career may well have diminished when there were many more opportunities for young men contemplating a career than had been the case early in the previous century. It has been suggested that the situation at the

---

[15] F. Gasquet, *The Black Death* (1908).

[16] P. Ziegler, *The Black Death* (1969), pp. 148–55.

[17] *Register of Edington*, 1, pp. xii–xiii.

[18] *Ibid.*, pp. 137–61.

[19] Waynflete was bishop of Winchester 1447–86; his unpublished register is in the Hampshire Record Office, 21 M65 A1/13–14.

[20] R. L. Storey reviewing *Calendar of the Register of Henry Wakefield*, ed. M. P. Marret in *EHR* 89 (1974), pp. 378–80.

end of the fourteenth century was further exacerbated by disillusionment with the Church engendered by the papal schism.[21] Yet although the general population had declined substantially, almost the same number of parishes remained to be filled and chantry chapels needed to be served. Union of parishes might alleviate the problem slightly but not entirely, especially in the more widely dispersed rural areas.

In terms of declining recruitment, the worst was over in the diocese of Winchester by the end of the 1450s. Henceforth, recruitment to the priesthood began slowly but steadily to increase; on average 25 men were ordained priests each year in the 1460s and 70s, climbing to over 30 in the 1480s and continuing to rise in the 1490s. The ordination lists in Bishop Fox's register which spans the first quarter of the sixteenth century (1501–28) are too incomplete to enable the figures to be accurately followed further.[22] A similar pattern can be seen in the northern province; work on clerical recruitment in the diocese of York by J. H. Moran demonstrates that the recruitment of priests there showed a dramatic upward swing after c.1460 and remained high well into the sixteenth century.[23] Similarly in Coventry and Lichfield, the last two decades of the fifteenth century saw a return to the pre-plague levels of recruitment among the secular clergy.[24] It is difficult to point with any precision to a reason for this increase. Research on population and mortality in England in the fifteenth century, however, suggests that late medieval population reached its lowest point in the mid-fifteenth century. By the last quarter of the fifteenth century, however, there were signs that the long decline in numbers was slowing and even being reversed. Clerical population seems to have followed similar demographic lines.[25] Agreement of the evidence from a number of major dioceses situated in both provinces, does reinforce suggestions that as far as recruitment was concerned, the English church was in a healthy state in the half century preceding the Reformation.

---

[21] R. L. Storey, 'Recruitment of English clergy in the period of the conciliar movement', *Annuarium Historiae Conciliorum*, 7 (1975), pp. 290–313.

[22] Ordination lists do not survive for every year of Richard Fox's episcopate. In addition a number of the surviving lists are clearly incomplete, Hampshire Record Office 21 M65 A1/17–21.

[23] Moran, 'Clerical recruitment in the diocese of York', pp. 19–54.

[24] R. Swanson, *Church and society in late medieval England* (forthcoming, 1989). I am grateful to Dr Swanson for allowing me to see in advance of publication, the sections of his book relating to ordination and clerical recruitment.

[25] J. C. Hatcher, *Plague, population and the English economy 1348–1530* (London, 1977), esp. pp. 63, 68–9.

(ii) *The ordination of regular and secular clergy*

The episcopal ordination lists are an important source for one particular aspect of clerical demography, the changing ratio of secular clergy and regular clergy being ordained throughout this period. While not all episcopal ordination lists include details concerning the ordination of monks, canons, and friars[26] many do, although it is likely that the regular clergy may be under-recorded.[27] It was usually more important for members of the secular clergy to be ordained to the priesthood than for their regular counterparts. Ordination to the major orders opened the way to being beneficed; it was a necessary part of proceeding in the church hierarchy. This was the case even if patronage opportunities meant that a clerk might well be presented to a benefice before the canonical regulations concerning ordination had been fulfilled. Episcopal registers, especially those of the late thirteenth and early fourteenth century, frequently show acolytes being presented to benefices and then hastening to be ordained to the major orders.[28] Bishops and their household officials were concerned to prevent such a practice developing into a widespread abuse and in this aim they seem to have been reasonably successful. In November 1305 Henry Woodlock issued a mandate to the archdeacon of Winchester requesting that all beneficed persons in his archdeaconry not yet promoted to the priesthood must be cited to attend the forthcoming general ordination.[29]

While secular clergy required a title or guarantee of some form of maintenance before ordination, the same need was not to be found among the members of the religious orders. A convent needed some priests to serve at mass but there was no necessity for all the community to be priests.[30] It was of course easier for members of religious orders to be ordained in that their vow of poverty exempted them from the necessity to demonstrate to the episcopal examiners that they had adequate means

---

[26] Norwich, for example, does not appear to record regulars, Williams, 'Ordination in the Norwich diocese', pp. 357–8.

[27] Registers for some religious houses record ordinations taking place within the house both for some of their members and on occasion for secular clergy, see for example that of Bury St Edmunds Abbey in the fifteenth century, B.L. Add. MS 14848.

[28] In March 1318 for example, Bishop Sandale ordained William de Clyde of the diocese of Durham, rector of the parish of Angreham, as acolyte. The following month, Clyde was ordained as subdeacon, *Sandale's Register*, pp. 195, 200. Of 271 acolytes ordained by Sandale, 11 were already holding parochial benefices and 30 per cent of those ordained as subdeacon during his episcopate were already holding parochial benefices.

[29] *Registrum Henrici Woodlock*, 1, p. 67.

[30] J. G. Greatrex, 'Some statistics of religious motivation', *SCH* 15, pp. 179–86.

of sustenance. This perhaps partly accounts for their omission from the lists of ordained clerics in some episcopal registers.

That it was relatively unimportant for members of religious orders to be ordained as priests can be seen in the pre-Black Death period where relatively few seem to have been ordained. Only about 20 per cent of all ordinands to the priesthood in Winchester were members of a religious order at this date. Of these, approximately 15 per cent were monks or canons and only 4 per cent were mendicants. A number of the ordained monks came from Winchester cathedral and would have had responsibilities for liturgical duties there.

A major change can be seen in the aftermath of the Black Death. For the remainder of the fourteenth century and for a substantial part of the fifteenth, until the 1460s, members of religious orders make up a far greater proportion of the men being ordained to the priesthood. Although the overall totals of ordinees have dropped, regular clergy make up a far more significant element in ordination services. William Wykeham became bishop of Winchester in 1367 and in the first ten years of his episcopate 1368–1377,[31] regular clergy outnumbered secular clergy being ordained in five years—1368, 1369, 1370, 1371, and 1373. Similarly, at the end of Wykeham's episcopate members of religious orders outnumbered seculars in each year from 1399 to 1403. This situation still pertained in the mid-fifteenth century when William Waynflete became bishop in 1447. In the first five years of his episcopate, 1448–52, he ordained a total of 21 men as secular priests, as opposed to 27 men as regular priests. A similar pattern can be seen in other southern English dioceses. In Exeter there is a small but steady increase in the proportion of regular clergy being ordained, from 12 per cent at the beginning of the fourteenth century to between 17 and 25 per cent in the later period. Although no ordination lists are extant for the diocese of London before 1382 the late fourteenth century evidence shows that on average over 40 per cent of priests being ordained were regulars, rising to 50 per cent in the 1420s and 30s. The Canterbury registers demonstrate that only 19 per cent of the priests ordained in Canterbury in 1315 were members of religious orders while in the period of the 1350s to 1370s, they represented 42 per cent of ordained priests. In the mid fifteenth century, they made up over 70 per cent. Monastic recruitment still maintained considerable numerical strength but none the less their numbers were smaller than in the

[31] *Wykeham's Register*, ed. T. F. Kirby (2 vols, Hampshire Record Society, 1896–9).

thirteenth and early fourteenth century.[32] Clearly a greater proportion of monks, canons, and friars were being ordained in this period. It is generally accepted that the Black Death dealt a major blow to the religious orders but in fact it seems also to have instituted a social change within religious houses which has not been widely noticed. When, however, the upturn in recruitment to the priesthood comes in the later fifteenth century, the religious element does not increase commensurately.

(iii) *Anti-mendicant feeling*

The increase in the number of regular clergy being ordained applied both to the monks and canons, and to the mendicant orders. It was, however, the increase in the numbers of ordained mendicants which attracted the adverse attention of many contemporaries. '. . . As thikke as motes in the sonne beem . . .' was Chaucer's comment on the numbers of the friars in England in the late fourteenth century.[33] It was a sentiment echoed by his contemporaries. Langland not only rejected the notion that friars in his day might be of any use to Piers Plowman in his search for Do-best but also complained of their numbers, commenting:

> Moreover the Rules of all Orders of monks and nuns require them to have a fixed number. So the same law applies to Religious as to layfolk—a definite number for a definite class—for everyone, that is, except the Friars. And by common sense it follows that it would be sinful to give you Friars any wages, for heaven knows, your numbers increase beyond all reckoning.[34]

Wyclif and other critics of the mendicant orders likewise complained amongst other things, of their expanding numbers. Grievances relating to the excess numbers and the alleged excesses of the mendicants were to become a standard literary topos of the late middle ages. Complaints covered a range of matters,[35] but one major bone of contention remained

---

[32] It has been estimated that almost half of the total population of the religious houses in England perished in the initial epidemic of the Black Death, D. Knowles, *The Religious Orders in England* (Cambridge, 1955), 2, pp. 256–7.

[33] Geoffrey Chaucer, 'Prologue' to 'The wife of Bath's tale', *Canterbury Tales*, line 868.

[34] 'Monkes and monyals and alle men of religioun her ordre and her reule wil to han a certeyne noumbre. Of lewed and of lered the lawe wol and axeth a certeyn for a certeyne saue oneliche of freres.' *William Langland, The vision of William concerning Piers the Ploughman*, ed. W. W. Skeat (London, 1924), B Passus XX, lines 262–70. The translation in the text is taken from *Piers the Ploughman* trans. J. F. Goodridge (2 edn., London, 1966), p. 252.

[35] An introduction to the subject of anti-mendicant criticism can be found in Knowles, *The Religious Orders in England*, 2, pp. 90–114. The activities of a group of bishops in opposition to

the rivalry between the secular clergy and the mendicants, primarily over the pastoral activities of the latter. Some attempts had been made to reduce such rivalry by the introduction of a licensing system for mendicant preachers. In 1312 Pope Clement V reissued Boniface VII's bull *Super cathedram* which was intended to regularize relationships between bishops and mendicants within their dioceses. It did not solve the problem entirely,[36] and this rivalry remained at the heart of much of the vociferous ill-feeling.

Such ill-feeling does not, however, entirely reflect the numerical reality. There were fewer friars in England after the mid fourteenth century than had been the case fifty years previously. Although recruitment to the four orders of friars was successfully maintained in the aftermath of the plague, they had achieved their maximum number *c.*1320 in the century after their introduction into England and before the Black Death. At this date there were approximately 1700 Franciscans, 1800 Dominicans, 850 Carmelites, and 600 Austin Friars in England.[37] One might expect to see more anti-mendicant feeling at an even earlier date than in fact it becomes widespread.

One explanation for the wave of anti-mendicant feeling in the later middle ages lies in the changing ratio of seculars and regulars being ordained. This meant, among other things, that a far greater number of the mendicant population had been ordained to the priesthood than hitherto had been the case and thus presented a much more serious rivalry to the parish clergy. This pattern of more ordained mendicants can be seen emerging in the decades just prior to the Black Death. When the earliest Franciscans came to England in the early thirteenth century, only one of the nine was a priest and five were described as laymen. This position had changed dramatically by the mid fourteenth century; by that date three-quarters of the Franciscans in one house in Grantham were priests while a study of obituaries of Franciscans in the years 1328–34 shows that of 144 men, 117 were priests and only 9 were described as laymen.[38]

---

the mendicants in the late 1340s and 1350s is dealt with by K. Walsh, *Richard FitzRalph: A fourteenth century scholar and Primate* (Oxford, 1981). See also A. Williams, 'Relations between the mendicant friars and the secular clergy in England in the later fourteenth century', *Duquesne Studies Annuale Medievale*, 11 (1960), pp. 22–95.

[36] The reissue of *Super cathedram* did not finally settle the disputes. At the end of the 1340s and in the early 1350s Archbishop FitzRalph of Armagh was foremost in an effort to counter the friars' attempts to obtain a more favourable interpretation of the bull.

[37] J. C. Russell, 'The clerical population of medieval England', *Traditio*, 2 (1944), pp. 206–11.

[38] A. G. Little, *Studies in English Franciscan history* (Manchester, 1917), p. 116.

The increase in the numbers of mendicant priests can clearly be seen in the ordination lists of the diocese of Winchester. It was a diocese well provided with friaries; the Franciscans and the Austin Friars had houses in Winchester and Southampton, the Dominicans in Winchester and Guildford, and the Carmelites also had a house in Winchester.

The same trend, an increase in the number of regular as opposed to secular clergy, can be seen in southern English dioceses other than Winchester. It is clearly visible in Canterbury and London. Does this trend include a similar increase in the numbers of mendicants? More detailed work using ordination lists will be needed to pursue this point further. The evidence for Winchester over a 200 year period does suggest that mendicant priests were becoming a more significant proportion of the total number of ordained priests. Rivalry for ministry on the streets and in the parishes as expressed in late medieval writings may well be based on a firm numerical foundation.

Westfield College, London

CAREERS AND DISAPPOINTMENTS IN THE LATE-MEDIEVAL CHURCH: SOME ENGLISH EVIDENCE[1]

by A. K. McHARDY

'HE looked up at the pleasant plate-glass in the windows of the house of his friend the dean, and told himself how, in their college days, he and the dean had been quite equal—quite equal, except that by the voices of all qualified judges in the university he, Mr. Crawley, had been acknowledged to be the riper scholar. And now the Mr. Arabin of those days was the Dean of Barchester ... while he, Crawley, was the perpetual curate of Hogglestock.'[2] *The Last Chronicle of Barset* is the story of a model clergyman, 'a hard-working conscientious pastor' and 'still a scholar' long after he had left university, who had never gained lucrative preferment. Yet this novel, as all those in the Barchester sequence, abounds with clerics of modest intellect and minimal spirituality whose benefices afforded extremely comfortable livelihoods. In short, the novel reminds us forcibly that a career in the Church was, in the nineteenth century, a gamble; the greatest rewards did not always go to the most deserving, but to those with the right connections through which they obtained the most lucrative positions.

It is a point which we do well to bear in mind when we consider those underdogs of the medieval Church, the unbeneficed clergy. Before considering the role of the unbeneficed in the ministry of the Church, we should take note of the size of this group. The unbeneficed clergy are important to any examination of the late-medieval Church because they formed such a large proportion of the clerical estate. This assertion is not new. 'The country swarmed with these *clerics*', wrote Augustus Jessopp, more than a century ago.[3] His views were echoed by Bishop John Moorman, whose work on the thirteenth-century Church first appeared in

[1] Thanks are due to the Social Science Research Council and its successor, the Economic and Social Research Council for grants, and to Professor P. L. Payne for advice and encouragement.
[2] Anthony Trollope, *The Last Chronicle of Barset* (London, 1867), chap. 17.
[3] Augustus Jessopp, *The Coming of the Friars* was first published in book form in 1888; this reference is to the 21st impression (London, 1930), p. 83.

1945. Moorman's starting point was the ordination lists surviving from the late thirteenth century. After calculating the average number of ordinations a year, surmising the probable length of a working lifetime, and counting the number of parishes in England, he deduced that the supply of clergy far exceeded the availability of benefices; and he concluded that 'this would allow for something between four and five men in each parish'.[4] the precise distribution of the unbeneficed he could discover only in the small number of parishes for which visitation returns survive, for the problem with the unbeneficed is that they are usually so difficult to pin down.

It is the difficulty of locating the unbeneficed precisely, as a general rule, which makes the clerical poll tax assessments so remarkable and important, for on three occasions in quick succession, 1377, 1379 and 1381, the government levied new forms of taxation on the clergy of England.[5] These subsidies were revolutionary in that they required all the unbeneficed to contribute (if aged over fourteen and not mendicant), since these were taxes on people not property; hence the need for a complete new assessment to be made for each tax. The assessors had to create what was in effect a census of the clerical population on each occasion, and they did this parish by parish. This is not the place for a critique of these documents,[6] but we should note that losses among this material have been very high, and for no diocese is there evidence relating to all three taxes. Despite this, and other difficulties, the clerical poll tax assessments are the best source we have for the unbeneficed clergy of England during the late middle ages.

Let us now examine the thesis that the unbeneficed deserve our attention because of the sheer weight of their numbers. A series of samples from the available tax assessments yields the following results. The diocese of Carlisle consisted of four deaneries, and our sources show that in the late fourteenth century 56 per cent of the clergy there were unbeneficed.[7] In the archdeaconry of Chester, which covered all Cheshire, as well as Lancashire south of the Ribble, we find that no less than 80 per cent of the

---

[4] J. R. H. Moorman, *Church Life in England in the Thirteenth Century* (Cambridge, 1945), p. 53.

[5] A. K. McHardy, *The Church in London 1375–1392* (London Record Society 13, 1977), pp. ix–xiii.

[6] This will be dealt with in *The Clerical Poll-Taxes of the Diocese of Lincoln, 1377–1381* (Lincoln Record Society, forthcoming).

[7] J. L. Kirby, 'Two Tax Accounts of the Diocese of Carlisle 1379–80', *Transactions of the Cumberland and Westmorland Antiquarian and Archaeological Society*, 52 n.s. (1953), pp. 74–81.

clergy were unbeneficed.[8] The Hereford diocese survivals are scrappy, but two sample deaneries show the unbeneficed as being 66 per cent of the secular clerical population.[9] We now move eastwards to the vast diocese of Lincoln. In Lincolnshire the archdeaconry of Stow consisted of four deaneries and lay in the north-west of the county; here the unbeneficed accounted for 55 per cent of the total.[10] From the extensive archdeaconry of Lincoln four deaneries may serve as a sample; they lie in the south-east of the county, and include Holland, a large deanery beside the Wash. Here the unbeneficed averaged 66 per cent of all seculars.[11] Four deaneries in rural Leicestershire yield a result of 62 per cent un-beneficed.[12] In Leicester archdeaconry rural areas were deliberately chosen. In the archdeaconry of Bedford there was no choice; there is only one assessment, and from that the Christianity of Bedford is missing. When sampling four of the other deaneries we find that 75 per cent of the clergy were unbeneficed.[13] A similar result, 72 per cent, is seen in the rural areas of Middlesex.[14] As might be expected, concentrations in towns were heavy, 71 per cent in Stamford,[15] 83 per cent in Lincoln[16] and 82 per cent in London,[17] though the differences in scale were very great; there were thirty-two unbeneficed in Stamford, seventy-seven in Lincoln and 526 in London. (Both the two latter figures exclude the cathedrals and closes.) Thus in the last quarter of the fourteenth century we find that, wherever we look, the majority of the clergy were unbeneficed, the proportion varying between 55 and 83 per cent in this rough sampling. If these results can be criticized it is that the proportion of the unbeneficed they reveal is

[8] M. J. Bennett, 'The Lancashire and Cheshire Clergy 1379', *Transactions of the Historic Society of Lancashire and Cheshire*, 124 (1973), pp. 3, 5.

[9] P. E. Hair, 'Chaplains, Chantries and Chapels of N. W. Herefordshire c.1400', *Transactions of the Woolhope Naturalists' Field Club* (forthcoming) appendix C. I am grateful to Professor Hair for showing me a copy of his article in advance of publication.

[10] This and the next two notes are based on the particulars of account of the abbot of Barlings (Lincs.) collector of the poll tax in 1377 in the archdeaconries of Lincoln, Stow, Leicester and the deanery of Rutland. This is now separated into two documents, PRO, E179/33/5, and E179/35/7. References to these documents will be given to the section numbers in my forthcoming LRS volume: LRS nos. 776–883.

[11] The deaneries sampled were Holland, LRS nos. 126–36, 743–75; Ness, nos. 137–51; Aveland, nos. 682–707; Bolingbroke, nos. 475–94.

[12] Deaneries of Framland, LRS nos. 170–209; Akeley, nos. 210–230; Goodlaxton, nos. 253–91; Gartree, nos. 292–327.

[13] PRO E179/35/24. The deaneries sampled were Clapham, LRS nos. 929–47; Eaton Socon, nos. 948–66; Shefford, nos. 967–95; Dunstable, nos. 996–1017.

[14] *The Church in London*, nos. 217–395.

[15] LRS nos. 152–67.

[16] *Ibid.*, nos. 9–40.

[17] *The Church in London*, nos. 1–117.

too low. Dr Bennett, editor of the Cheshire material, suggests that the assessment was a substantial underestimate,[18] while in the Carlisle deanery of Westmorland, the only individual deanery where the unbeneficed accounted for less than half the clergy, the assessor noted that he had not included married clerks in his list,[19] implying that the total might have been higher had he done so.

There is good reason to believe that the numbers of the unbeneficed revealed by the poll taxes were not unusually high in the later fourteenth century. Recent work by Dr Simon Townley, based on ordination lists of the dioceses of Hereford and Worcester, has reinforced the earlier conclusion of Dr Moorman, in respect of the late thirteenth and early fourteenth centuries. Moreover, a number of pieces of evidence, scattered over the period between the 1220s and 1320s, among them visitation returns, ordinations of vicarages, and diocesan statutes, confirms the view that for parishes to be staffed by a number of clergy was seen as not only normal, but highly desirable. Numbers varied between two and five per parish, much depending on the conscientiousness and competence of the incumbent in maintaining a full complement of parochial staff.[20] It may be said, therefore, that the great numbers of unbeneficed revealed in the later fourteenth century tax assessments were at least equalled, and perhaps considerably exceeded, during the century's early decades.[21]

In the early fifteenth century it seems as though recruitment, and consequently, numbers of the unbeneficed, fell away; the evidence is very incomplete, but every type of information points to the same conclusion.[22] From the later fifteenth century onwards it appears that a national pattern had been replaced by one reflecting a division between north and south. In the north, as represented by York diocese, recruitment to the ranks of the clergy remained high, and indeed, rose, about 1500. By contrast, in the south, for example, London and Salisbury dioceses, the numbers of ordination candidates became markedly lower.[23] The

---

[18] Bennett, 'Lancs. and Cheshire Clergy, p. 3.

[19] J. L. Kirby, 'Two Carlisle Accounts', p. 79.

[20] Simon C. Townley, 'Patronage, Pastoral Provision and the Secular Clergy in the Dioceses of Worcester and Hereford during the Thirteenth Century' (D.Phil. thesis, Oxford, 1985), chap. 4, esp. pp. 222–6 and notes.

[21] Ibid., esp. p. 230; David Robinson, *Beneficed Clergy in Cleveland and the East Riding 1306–1340* (Borthwick Papers no. 37, 1969), p. 8.

[22] R. L. Storey, 'Recruitment of English Clergy in the Period of the Conciliar Movement', *Annuarium Historiae Conciliorum*, 7 (1975), pp. 290–313.

[23] Jo Ann Hoepner Moran, 'Clerical Recruitment in the Diocese of York, 1340–1530: Data and Commentary', *JEH* 34 (1983), pp. 19–54. Storey, 'Recruitment', pp. 130–313; *The*

evidence of taxation assessments supports this division. In the arch-deaconry of Chester there were, in 1541, some 315 unbeneficed clergy, compared with 304 in 1379.[24] For Lincoln diocese we have the valuable assessment made for the subsidy of 1526. This subsidy, printed by H. E. Salter in 1909, covers the entire diocese and presents the same amount of detail as the late fourteenth-century lists. According to this material, the proportion of the unbeneficed among the clergy of Stow had by then fallen from 55 per cent to 42 per cent, in our sample deaneries in the archdeaconry of Lincoln, from 66 per cent to 47 per cent, in the parts of rural Leicestershire from 62 per cent to 50 per cent, and in rural Bedford-shire, from 75 per cent to 44 per cent. In smaller areas of particular inter-est percentages had fallen also: Stamford deanery showed a decline from 71 per cent to 50 per cent (there were eleven of each class in 1526), and the Christianity of Lincoln had gone down from 83 per cent to 66 per cent.[25] The proportion of the unbeneficed, however, was still significant and supports the contention that sheer numbers force consideration of the unbeneficed upon us, however difficult their study may be. To ignore their existence is to produce a gravely distorted picture of the late medieval Church.

From the identification of the great numbers of the unbeneficed, it is not surprising that when we ask questions such as, What were these men doing? Where were they recruited from? What were their incomes? What prospects had they? What were their qualifications? How good were their moral characters? and, above all, What was their contribution to the ministry of the Church? We shall not find a single set of answers. The answers will depend not only on individuals, but also on place, on time, on the distribution of lay wealth, on lines of communication, on jurisidictional boundaries and on settlement patterns which long antedate our period, and also on the physical nature of each region.

A good example of the effects of geography—physical, political and social—on the medieval Church and its unbeneficed clergy may be observed by considering dependent chapels and their ministers. Within the boundaries of one parish there might be a number of subsidiary

---

Register of Thomas Langton Bishop of Salisbury 1465–93, ed. D. P. Wright (CYS, 74, 1985), pp. xii–xiii.

[24] Bennett, 'Lancs. and Cheshire Clergy', p. 6.

[25] *A Subsidy Collected in the Diocese of Lincoln in 1526*, ed. H. E. Salter (Oxford Historical Society 63, 1909), pp. 30–40; 3–6, 56–60, 62–8; 95–103, 110–13, 115–19; 197–200, 202–5, 207–12; 60–1; 80–2.

settlements which could be served by chapels-of-ease which were staffed by chaplains. Much of this has to be inferred; not every dependent vill had a chapel, and chapels, though numerous, are difficult to identify.[26] Moreover, connecting chaplains with the outlying chapels which they served was of no interest to tax collectors at any period, so the names of chaplains were linked to chapelries only in exceptional cases. In some areas, however, large parishes and a high proportion of unbeneficed clergy are too great a coincidence to be ignored. One such area was the archdeaconry of Chester. Here could be found parishes with numerous dependent vills, for example, 44, 36, 32, in Whalley, Great Budworth, and Prestbury, respectively, and in the largest we know that there were six dependent chapelries.[27] A similar situation existed in south Lincolnshire where the draining and settlement of marshy land had resulted in large parishes and new centres of population. Here too, the numbers of the unbeneficed were very great, in Holland deanery 180, representing 86.95 per cent in 1377; the proportion was still as high as 65 per cent in 1526.[28] Undoubtedly many of these, though not all, as will be argued later, were serving chapels away from the parish church. Apart from these substantial areas we can pick out particular parishes where the same situation existed in counties as diverse as Shropshire, Gloucestershire, Worcestershire, and Bedfordshire.[29] In many places in rural England, therefore, it is clear that the ministry of the Church was carried out entirely by unbeneficed clergy. Many people would have seen a beneficed cleric 'in action' only if they travelled to their parish church or to a town.

And perhaps not even then. For one common and widely-recognized function of the unbeneficed was to act as stand-ins for incumbents who were either absent, or incompetent (through having insufficient orders), or incapacitated through illness or age. The insufficiently-qualified incumbent was not a problem frequently encountered in the later middle ages. Presentations to benefices in which the new incumbent was described as being of less than priestly rank—deacon, for example, or the vague terms 'chaplain' or 'clerk'—did occur but their numbers were

---

[26] Dorothy M. Owen, 'Medieval Chapels in Lincolnshire', *Lincolnshire History and Archaeology*, 10 (1975), pp. 15–22.

[27] M. J. Bennett, 'Lancs. and Cheshire Clergy', p. 5.

[28] LRS nos. 126–36, 743–75; *Subsidy Collected in the Diocese of Lincoln*, pp. 62–8.

[29] Clun (Salop) contained eight chapels, Bibury (Gloucs.) and Bromsgrove (Worcs.) three each, Townley, 'Patronage', pp. 229, 232; Eaton Socon (Beds.) contained eight vills besides the main settlement, and probably some contained chapels, for the church was situated in the south-east corner of the parish.

insignificant. Further, the widespread practice of benefice exchanging will sometimes disclose that the man of less than priestly rank at his first presentation had become a priest by the time he acquired his next benefice. As to the numbers of old or infirm incumbents, we have no evidence until the last years of the fifteenth century, and even then such evidence is capable of very diverse interpretations;[30] this is a point to which we must return. It was the non-resident incumbent who is widely held to have provided most opportunities for the less fortunate to act as parochial chaplains. How many parishes were in the hand of non-residents evidently depended on place and, perhaps also, on time. The highest estimate is that one in four parishes was held by a non-resident, while the lowest suggests a rate of one in twenty.[31] It is certainly true that a rich rectory in the patronage of the Crown or of a magnate was the least likely to have its incumbent living and ministering within the parish.[32]

What mattered to the parishioners, of course, was not the reason which made the incumbent a non-functioner, but whether he provided a qualified and suitable substitute. Substitutes were certainly very numerous and the tax assessments of the 1370s enable us to identify large numbers of parochial chaplains. In 1377 the deanery of Rutland had a parochial chaplain in nearly half its parishes: twenty-two out of forty-six. Two years later in the archdeaconry of Bedford, the deanery of Shefford had exactly one third of its parishes, nine out of twenty-seven, served by these chaplains. In Lincolnshire, random sampling of the deaneries of Lawres (archdeaconry of Stow) and Grantham (archdeaconry of Lincoln) shows proportions of about one quarter (seven out of thirty-one) and a fifth (four out of twenty-two) of parishes having parochial chaplains.[33]

In towns the picture was very different. Only four parochial chaplains existed in Lincoln's 31 parishes in 1377, while two years later the 112 parishes of London contained only a single parochial chaplain. The same was true of the archdeaconry of Middlesex: a single parochial chaplain listed in 1381. Although there are difficulties about using this particular

---

[30] For the frequency with which churches were burdened with pensions, compare Kathleen Major, 'Resignation Deeds in the Diocese of Lincoln', *BIHR* 19 (1942–3), pp. 57–65, and Peter Heath, *The English Parish Clergy on the Eve of the Reformation* (London, 1969), pp. 146–7, 183, with *The Register of Thomas Langton*, pp. xx–xxi.

[31] Margaret Bowker, *The Secular Clergy in the Diocese of Lincoln* (Cambridge, 1968), p. 90, for the highest estimate. The lowest arrived at by looking at the non-residence licences relating to the archdeaconries of Lincoln and Stow for the year 1370 recorded in the memoranda of Bishop Buckingham, Lincolnshire Archives Office Register 12.

[32] Bennett, 'Lancs. and Ches. Clergy', p. 5; Margaret Bowker, *Lincoln Clergy*, p. 92.

[33] LRS no. 884–928; 967–93; 776–807; 103–24.

list,[34] the lone parochial chaplain does appear to give credence to the charge that London drained clerical personnel from the surrounding districts. The areas of greatest deprivation, however, seem to have been in those places which apparently lacked any parish minister, having no rector, no vicar, no parochial chaplain. In this respect city centre churches were especially notable. In Lincoln, in 1377, at least 19 out of the 31 parishes had no obvious provision made for the cure of souls. In 1526 the situation was only a little better; at most nine (but probably only seven) churches were occupied by beneficed clergy, while a further nine were served by curates.

It was not that the people of Lincoln were bereft of clergy. As has been observed, late medieval towns had large numbers of clerics, a high proportion of them unbeneficed. It seems likely that we can distinguish the role of the unbeneficed in the towns from that in the countryside. Whereas many country dwellers, perhaps the majority for much of the late middle ages, received their pastoral care from unbeneficed men, town-dwellers had a different relationship with the many chaplains (and smaller number of clerks) in their midst. It looks as though many clergy in urban areas were in the more-or-less direct employment of the laity. Not all the qualities and skills these men provided were necessarily connected with ministry; their duties might be primarily legal, secretarial, administrative, or advisory,[35] and their ranks included a small number of doctors, astrologers, and entertainers.[36] The main occupation of the urban unbeneficed clergy was, however, the performance of rites to speed souls through purgatory after death. Wherever there are collections of wills this practice can be observed: large numbers of men and women made provision for intercessions to be made on their behalf after death. Sometimes the testator left a certain sum of money, sometimes specified the number of Masses to be said, sometimes indicated the length of time a priest would be retained to say a daily Mass. (Very rarely, there was sufficient money to found a perpetual chantry and hence to create one, or

---

[34] The number of chaplains given among the totals were always larger than the numbers listed parish by parish, *The Church in London*, nos. 217, 395.

[35] The most celebrated domestic chaplain, letter-writer and confidant was the Pastons' James Gloys, for over 24 years a member of their household; he obtained a rectory in 1472, the year before his death, Norman Davis, ed., *The Paston Letters* (Oxford World's Classics edn., 1983), p. 10 n. 2.

[36] For examples of doctors and astrologers in aristocratic households, see Colin Richmond, 'Religion and the Fifteenth-Century English Gentleman', in R. B. Dobson, ed., *The Church, Politics and Patronage in the Fifteenth Century* (Gloucester, 1984), p. 200; for John Audley, chaplain and secular musician in Lord Lestrange's household, see below, n. 87.

more, benefices. It must be emphasized that chantry chaplains, that is, those serving perpetual chantries, were beneficed men and, similar as their duties were to those of casual Mass-priests, they lie outside the scope of the present enquiry.) The point need not be laboured for a number of excellent local studies have described this aspect of the late medieval English Church in detail.[37]

What were the implications for the employment of many of the unbeneficed clergy? They were dependent on the ability and willingness of the laity to pay for their ministrations. The concentrations of mass-priests in towns surely reflects, to some extent, urban prosperity. A good example of the correlation between lay wealth and numbers of clergy is provided by London where the richest of the city wards, and hence those with the most chaplains, were Cordwainer, Cheap, and Bridge.[38] It also reflected local loyalties; we know that Norwich contained chantries, both perpetual and short-term, founded by local gentry,[39] and probably other provincial centres attracted similar bequests. This would help to explain the apparent ability of Lincoln, described as a declining town in the later middle ages, to maintain large numbers of unbeneficed clergy. Since the vast majority of the chantries were only temporary, the chaplains who manned them had to be prepared to move to where employment was to be found. Numbers of chaplains in one place could fluctuate wildly in a short time. In 1377, for example, there were 34 chaplains in Boston (Lincs.); in 1381 there were 54, but no explanation for the increase has yet come to light.[40]

Ability to pay for the services of the unbeneficed mass-priests had, of course, to be linked to a desire to do so. The unbeneficed had to attract the goodwill and enthusiasm of the laity who were buying their ministry, so we must enquire how well they were able to retain the loyalty of the laity. The sharp fall in the percentages of the unbeneficed among the clergy of Lincoln diocese between the 1370s and the 1520s might seem to indicate that they were failing to retain the confidence of laymen. Overall numbers of clergy were falling in some areas, but the proportion of the unbeneficed had fallen even more sharply. In part this was because new

---

[37] e.g., N. P. Tanner, *The Church in Late Medieval Norwich 1370–1532* (PIMS, Toronto, 1984); Peter Heath, 'Urban Piety in the Later Middle Ages: the Evidence of Hull Wills', in Dobson, ed., *The Church, Politics and Patronage*, pp. 209–29; Clive Burgess, '"For the Increas of Divine Service": Chantries in the Parish in late Medieval Bristol', *JEH* 36 (1985), pp. 46–65.

[38] A. K. McHardy, 'Ecclesiastics and Economics', *SCH* 24 (1987), p. 135 and n. 24.

[39] N. P. Tanner, *Church in Norwich*, pp. 96–7.

[40] LRS nos. 134, 1399.

benefices had been created by the foundation of perpetual chantries and of secular colleges—perpetual chantries of the grandest type. We have only to look at the list of secular colleges in Knowles and Hadcock, *English Religious Houses* to see that the majority were founded in the fourteenth and fifteenth centuries, the fifteenth century being the age of collegiate foundations *par excellence*. Further, by comparing those two taxes in which the assessors were scrupulous in recording whether the payers were beneficed or not, we can see the rise in the number of beneficed chantry chaplains, that is, those serving perpetual chantries. In 1377 their numbers were negligible; by 1526 they formed a small but recognizable class.[41]

The importance attached by the laity to Masses for the souls of the dead can be illustrated by the foundation of perpetual chantries even though they represent only a small fraction of the total number of chantries.[42] But we know that chantry priests, both beneficed and unbeneficed, played a larger part in church life than acting simply as employees of the departed. Their duties included attendance at parish services, and assisting the parish priest when necessary, for the parish church was the focus of immense loyalty, devotion, and enthuasiasm, as examination of any collection of wills amply demonstrates. How chantry chaplains, who were, of necessity, priests and those in lesser orders, contributed to parish life be seen from parochial accounts from fifteenth-century Bristol;[43] parishioners wanted impressive ceremonial which was to be secured by the participation of several priests in the daily liturgy. At the great festivals and at their own funerals and obits they wanted large gatherings of priests, clerks and assistants, such as cross-bearers and bell ringers, to be present. Bristolians were probably typical; in Norwich John Paston's funeral in 1466 was graced by 38 priests, 39 choirboys and 26 clerks.[44]

A large turn-out of priests and clerks was clearly regarded as desirable, giving an impressive appearance, and during the service producing an impressive volume of sound, though such opportunities for casual clerical employment were almost certainly confined to larger towns.[45] The standard music of the medieval Church was plainsong which required

---

[41] In 1377 Calcewaith and Corringham deaneries (both Lincs.) each had one beneficed chaplain; by 1526 each had nine. In Holland there were three beneficed chaplains in 1377; the number had risen to 34 by 1526.

[42] For the costs of founding perpetual chantries see K. L. Wood-Legh, *Perpetual Chantries in Britain* (Cambridge, 1965), chap. 3, esp. pp. 45–6.

[43] Burgess, 'Bristol Chantries', esp. pp. 54–5.

[44] Richmond, 'Religion and the Gentleman', p. 196.

[45] There is information about London and Bristol; Burgess, 'Bristol Chantries', *passim* for Bristol, and p. 55 n. 50 for references to London material.

only modest expertise and training, its basic requirements being 'a usable voice and a good pair of lungs'.[46] But during the later middle ages a change took place in musical style which created more opportunities for clergy willing and able to acquire higher levels of expertise; this was the growth of polyphony. During the fourteenth and for most of the fifteenth century polyphonic music was written for three voices, and during the fourteenth century at least the ensembles performing it were often small. The foundation charter of the chantry of St Mary and St Katherine at Epworth, Lincolnshire, specified a choir of four clerks: one tenor (*tenorem*), one middle (*medium*), and two singing the third part (*cantum tertium*).[47]

During the fifteenth century the development of polyphony went hand-in-hand with the proliferation of secular colleges and the development of chapels in aristocratic households, led by the chapel royal.[48] The process seems to have accelerated sharply round about 1460, and within the next thirty years the music had become elaborated to five-voice polyphony. At the same time as it became more elaborate in texture, music also increased in compass, from the plainsong range of a ninth, first to two octaves, then, about 1500, to three. The extra octave was accounted for by the use of boys' voices and also, perhaps, by extended use of the bass voice. The need to train singers and especially choirboys—previously choirboys' duties had been 'more ceremonial than musical'[49]—also brought into being the profession of choirmaster. The increasing vogue for polyphony and the consequent rise in the number of practitioners continued in the sixteenth century and reached its apogee in the late 1530s.

These developments undoubtedly affected the unbeneficed clergy—

---

[46] This is the judgement of Dr Roger Bowers in a recent letter to me. The argument in this and the next two paragraphs is based on the work of Dr Bowers published in articles and to be elaborated in his forthcoming book on English choral institutions in the later middle ages. I am most grateful to Dr Bowers for sharing his ideas with me in a long, informative and entertaining letter. Thanks are also due to my colleague Dr Barry Cooper for directing my attention to Dr Bowers' work.

[47] Roger Bowers, 'The Performing ensemble for English church polyphony, c.1320–c.1390', in Stanley Boorman, ed., *Studies in the Performance of Late Medieval Music* (Cambridge, 1983), pp. 161–87; the foundation charter of the Epworth chantry is calendared in C. W. Foster and A. Hamilton Thompson, eds, 'The Chantry Certificates for Lincoln and Lincolnshire', *Associated Architectural and Archaeological Societies' Reports and Papers*, 36 (1921), pp. 246–53.

[48] Roger Bowers, 'Obligation, Agency, and *Laissez-Faire*: The Promotion of Polyphonic Composition for the Church in Fifteenth-Century England', in I. Fenlon, ed., *Music in Medieval and Early Modern Europe* (Cambridge, 1981), pp. 1–19; W. H. Grattan Flood, 'The Beginnings of the Chapel royal', *Music and Letters*, 5 (1924), pp. 85–90.

[49] Roger Bowers, 'The Performing Pitch of English 15th-Century church Polyphony', *Early Music*, 8 (1980), pp. 21–8; the comment on choirboys' duties is on p. 22.

just as they affected beneficed clergy and the religious, who also were prominent in the promotion of new musical style—but did so in ways which are difficult to quantify. New foundations created new benefices but included also provision for unbeneficed clerks and chaplains. These were highly mobile, moving from job to job in search of better pay and more secure provision for their future. At the same time there was some unseemly competition to secure and retain the services of the most gifted musicians.[50] For men in priests' orders a successful period in the chapel royal or in one of the chapel choirs attached to an aristocratic household (whether lay or ecclesiastical) may have been a passport to ecclesiastical preferment and even to higher education.[51]

What this development contributed to the Church's ministry is a debatable point. Not all are of the opinion that with an increase in the musical content of services, 'the glory of the church is increased and the people are aroused to much greater devotion' as Abbot Whethamstede of St. Albans maintained in 1423.[52] 'Frequens cantus in ecclesiis non est fundabilis in scriptura, et ideo non licet sacerdotibus occupari in ecclesiis circa cantum' complained the *Lanterne of Light*.[53] But although Lollards may have been extreme in their opposition to elaborate music—they referred to polyphony as 'knakkyng'[54]—a dislike of intrusive music can be found among the orthodox in any age.

If music did indeed contribute to the Church's ministry, so too, it could be argued, did plays. Perhaps a stronger case could be made for drama as ministry if we remember the openly dramatic elements in the liturgy.[55] Most religious plays were put on by laymen, with the clergy giving advice and often lending or hiring costumes. But parish plays were mounted in nearly a dozen towns in southern England, and all-clergy plays were staged in important ecclesiastical centres. One of these was Lincoln, where the cathedral's play of the Coronation of the Virgin was surely enacted, not by the archdeacons and prebendaries, but by the many

[50] W. H. Grattan Flood, 'Entries Relating to Music in the English Patent Rolls of the Fifteenth Century', *The Music Antiquary*, 4 (1912–13), p. 235.

[51] Grattan Flood in *Music and Letters*, 5 (1924), p. 86.

[52] Quoted by Burgess, 'Bristol Chantries', p. 59.

[53] *The Register of Henry Chichele archbishop of Canterbury 1414–1443*, ed. E. F. Jacob (CYS 47, 1947), 4, pp. 136–7.

[54] Roger Bowers, in Boorman, ed., *Medieval Music*, p. 177 nn. 35, 36.

[55] 'There was an ancient liturgical custom of dressing one of the deacons as an angel on the Feast of the Annunciation in order that he might enter and take the part of Gabriel in the Gospel', Richard Foster and Pamela Tudor-Craig, *The Secret Life of Paintings* (Woodbridge, 1986), p. 97 n. 12.

unbeneficed clergy with which the cathedral teemed during the later middle ages. In London the clerks of St Paul's staged plays, as did the Guild of St Nicholas which was composed of parish clerks. These parish clerks staged their plays in the grounds of Clerkenwell Priory, and their performances were lengthy; in 1384 and 1391 they lasted for five days. Huge crowds attended, composed not only of lords and gentlefolk, but also of undesirables who trampled down crops, broke hedges, and were a sore trial to successive prioresses. One prioress who tried to stop the production of plays on the house's land had her priory set on fire by disappointed drama-lovers.[56]

If drama can indeed be classed as ministry then it was one area in which both laity (men and women) and clergy could take part. With music the situation is less clear. Dr Burgess has found one example of a layman singing the psalms with the chaplains in a Bristol church (All Saints, in 1457).[57] More important were the opportunities offered to those in minor orders, opportunities present before the burgeoning of polyphony, but surely increasing from the later fifteenth century. For some of these tasks—singing antiphons, anthems, psalms, and organ playing—priestly orders were not necessary. Many clerks who earned their livelihood singing in choirs took minor orders but proceeded no further and eventually married; they were lay clerks—a description which in earlier periods would have been a contradiction in terms, but one which existed by the end of the fifteenth century. 'It is at Holy Trinity, Arundel, and St George's Windsor, that the early emergence of the lay clerk can most clearly be traced'.[58]

Most of the unbeneficed, however, were far removed from this state. Since most of them were performing duties which involved the saying of Mass we must suppose that most were priests. Evidence in support of this comes from what appears to be a draft assessment made for the 1381 poll tax. This fragment covers three deaneries in the archdeaconry of Huntingdon (Hitchin, Berkhamsted, and St Neots) and gives the spiritual rank of each man. Analysis yields the following result. The total number listed is 129 men, though damage to the document precludes the descriptions of six. No rank is given for four of the names. Of the

[56] E. K. Chambers, *The Medieval Stage* (Oxford, 1903), 2, chap. xxi; W. O. Hassall, 'Plays at Clerkenwell', *Modern Language Review*, 33 (1938), pp. 564–7.
[57] Burgess, 'Bristol Chantries', p. 54 n. 44.
[58] Roger Bowers in a letter of January 1989; examples of legacies to provide antiphons and anthems may be seen in C. J. Kitching, *London and Middlesex Chantry Certificate 1548* (London Record Society 16, 1980), nos. 4, 16, 57, 98.

remainder, four were accolytes and two had first tonsure. There were 113 priests.[59]

In view of the fact that the unbeneficed were mainly well-qualified men performing duties, whether in parish or chantry, which were identical with those of the beneficed, the question arises as to what was the likelihood of their joining the ranks of those with benefices. The general answer must be that their chances were poor. Sample studies of restricted areas where the necessary combination of sources exist show that the late fourteenth century chaplain had only something like a one-in-ten chance of gaining a benefice. What is more, he would have had to wait a long time for it, ten years certainly from his ordination as priest, and in some cases twenty. Further, the benefice which he finally obtained was likely to be one of low value.[60] This may well represent a point of maximum gloom. Falling recruitment, the creation of new benefices in perpetual chantries and the apparently increasing use of pensions, probably improved promotion prospects over much of the southern province from the later fifteenth century. One measurable result was that the average period between ordination and institution to the first benefice became shorter.[61]

It might be argued that it did not matter if large numbers of the clergy failed to gain benefices. The lot of many incumbents was far from easy. In 1379 eleven London rectors were said to have scarcely enough to live on, while a further twenty-one had incomes of only ten marks a year. Many rural vicars had considerably less.[62] Some benefices were so poor that not even a stipendiary curate would serve them.[63] Even bishops, notoriously hard-hearted towards the low-paid, could be found agreeing that some country vicars were impoverished and that certain urban chantries were inadequately endowed; Bishops Buckingham of Lincoln and Braybrooke of London provide two examples of such episcopal concern.[64] The

---

[59] PRO E179/42/12: LRS nos. 1105–46.

[60] Bennett, 'Lancs. and Cheshire Clergy', pp. 16–17; P. E. H. Hair, 'Mobility of Parochial Clergy in Hereford Diocese c.1400', *Transactions of the Woolhope Naturalists' Field Club*, 43 (1980), pt. II, pp. 170–1.

[61] Bowker, *Lincoln Clergy*, pp. 70, 73.

[62] *Church in London*, nos. 18–111; for Bedfordshire PRO E179/35/24: LRS nos. 929–1041.

[63] This was the case with the parish of St Margaret in Wigford, Lincoln, in 1526, *Subsidy Collected in the Diocese of Lincoln*, p. 80.

[64] e.g., of grant of annuals to Lincolnshire vicars, LAO Reg. 12 fols 98ᵛ (2), 100; and to chaplains of perpetual chantries *ibid.*, fols 96, 100; Rosalind Hill, 'A Chaunterie for Soules', in *The Reign of Richard II*, eds C. M. Barron and F. R. H. Du Boulay (London, 1971), pp. 242–55.

incomes of many west-country incumbents apparently compared un-favourably with those of Bristol Mass-priests.[65]

Money is, of course, not the only consideration. What distinguished the beneficed man was his security of tenure, yet even this might prove insubstantial. Parish benefices were occasionally amalgamated,[66] while perpetual chantries were much less dependable because founders' endow-ments sometimes were or became inadequate. Hence examples could be quoted of chantries which had to be joined,[67] or which lapsed for a time for lack of funds,[68] or, much more common, came into existence but failed, at some time unknown, before the Dissolution.[69]

It could be argued, further, that in practice many of the unbeneficed enjoyed a high degree of security. Employment as a parochial chaplain by a long-standing incumbent could well provide long-term employment, for while the man who had originally employed him remained in-cumbent, a parochial chaplain could not be removed without 'just cause'.[70] Possession of a well-established chapel of ease or 'old retainer' status in a lay household brought similar security. Some chaplains remained in the same place for decades.[71]

Not all were so fortunate. The reason why dependent chapelries are so elusive is that many were only intermittently served. Just how temporary an arrangement could be may be observed in the licence to the inhabitants of 'Herflete' hamlet in the parish of Holbeach, south Lincolnshire, which allowed them to have their chapel served by 'suitable chaplains' for one year; this was in November 1370, and what happened at the end of that period is not known.[72] Parochial chaplains were at the mercy of new incumbents, for if the benefice changed hands the new rector or vicar had no obligation to retain the parochial chaplain whom he found *in situ*.[73] This could be a considerable hazard in the later middle ages when the practice of exchanging benefices was common, and indeed, reached

[65] Burgess, 'Bristol Chantries', p. 50.
[66] The two moieties of Bag Enderby, Lincolns., were joined in 1385, LAO Reg. 12, fols 301–2.
[67] See ref. to Hill, n. 64 above.
[68] Burgess, 'Bristol Chantries', p. 60 n. 76.
[69] Interesting comparisons can be made between the location of beneficed chaplains in 1377 and the existence of chantries as revealed in the chantry certificates of 1548. The printed certificates may be located by reference to Alan Kreider, *English Chantries: The Road to Dissolu-tion* (Cambridge, Mass., 1979), pp. 266–68.
[70] Peter Heath, *The English Parish Clergy*, p. 25.
[71] Bowker, *Lincoln Clergy*, p. 72.
[72] LAO Reg. 12, fol. 95.
[73] Peter Heath, *The English Parish Clergy*, p. 25.

epidemic proportions in the half-century around 1400.[74] All doubtless depended on relations with the incumbent. Robert Syresham, parochial chaplains of Castor, Northamptonshire, was lucky; his rector left him 40s. and a blue gown in his will dated 1373.[75] Richard Coventry, parochial chaplain of Aythorpe Roding in Essex, was less fortunate; his rector not only fell into arrears with payment of his stipend, but had the nerve to borrow money from him as well; or so Richard alleged in the Court of Common Pleas in 1382.[76] Which experience was the more typical cannot be ascertained, though it is perhaps revealing that the post of parochial chaplain was the least popular of the options open to unbeneficed priests,[77] probably because it required the most work. Given a choice, men preferred to act as mass-priests of temporary chantries, a job with inbuilt obsolescence, or as chaplains to fraternities or guilds, many of which were financially precarious.[78]

A confusion in the minds of ordinands concerning the desirability of the various jobs open to the unbeneficed may have been one reason for high recruitment even in those many decades when the possibility of obtaining a benefice was slight. Another reason may have been a blurring of the distinction, especially the financial distinction, between benefices and other posts. A third consideration worthy of exploration is the influence of family. In a number of parishes the fourteenth-century poll tax assessments reveal two, very occasionally three, men with the same surname.[79] Although the number of parishes in which this occurs is minute it does suggest that what drew some men into the Church, even into a certain parish, was a family tradition. The suspicion is reinforced when we find the labels 'senior', 'junior', or 'his brother' attached to names.[80] Most interesting are those few cases in which the incumbent and a chaplain

---

[74] For 'chop-churches', see A. Hamilton Thompson, *The English Clergy and their Organisation in the Later Middle Ages* (Oxford, 1947), pp. 107–108.

[75] LAO Reg. 12, fol. 119.

[76] The case is translated in Edith Rickert, ed., *Chaucer's World* (New York, 1948), p. 381.

[77] Storey, 'Recruitment', pp. 302–3.

[78] e.g., Patricia Basing, *Parish Fraternity Register* (London Record Society 18, 1982), pp. x–xiii, charts the fluctuating fortunes of fraternities in the parish of St Botolph without Aldersgate, London.

[79] There were 30 parishes in Lincoln diocese where family connections seemed to be strong, including Manlake (Lincs.) with three Crakes and Carlton (Beds.) with three Attemors, LRS nos. 855, 943; in Melton Mowbray (Leics.) William and John de Sixtenby were balanced by Walter and Philip Payne, and in Roxton (Beds.) there were William and Richard Golde as well as John and Robert Olyver, *ibid.*, nos. 170, 950.

[80] e.g., Thomas Warde senior and junior in Lockingham, and William Horslay and John Horslay his brother in Long Whatton (both Leics.), *ibid.*, nos. 210, 212.

have the same name or are actually described as brothers,[81] which raises the intriguing thought that some parishes were run partly, or wholly, as small family businesses. This conclusion accords well with the findings of Dr Townley who, working on ordination lists in Hereford and Worcester of the later thirteenth century showed that some incumbents recruited chaplains, a number of whom were relatives, to assist in the ministry of their own parish.[82]

Not all who entered the clerical estate may have hoped or expected to attain a benefice. With the proportion of the unbeneficed being so high the realistic ordinand without money or family connections could hardly have looked for speedy preferment, if indeed he looked for it at all. The office of parish clerk was ancient and honourable, and in the later middle ages the holders of this office, many of whom were married, had probably never aspired to major orders, let alone a benefice. It seems very likely that many who were 'clerks' or 'chaplains' did not make their living primarily as ecclesiastics but rather as notaries, schoolmasters, choristers, or even as members of less likely trades such as blacksmiths[83] or archers.[84]

Some, however, were destined to be disappointed. We know that there were men who were talented and learned, and anxious for promotion which they considered their due, men like 'William Langland' (if not an individual, then surely a recognizable type), Thomas Hoccleve and John Audley. 'Langland', of course, was married so debarred from higher orders and preferment; he was one of a type which became more common in the fifteenth century, though it is to be hoped that not all 'clerks of the second form' of cathedral and collegiate choirs were disgruntled.[85] But

---

[81] e.g., in 1381 Threekingham (Lincs.) was served by Thomas Croke the vicar and John his brother the chaplain, *ibid.*, no. 1338.

[82] Townley, 'Patronage', pp. 230–2.

[83] *The Burgh Court Book of Selkirk 1503–45*, eds J. Imrie, T. I. Rae, W. D. Ritchie (Scottish Record Society 89, 1960, 1969), gives examples of chaplains acting as blacksmiths, John Michelhill, 1531, and ale-conners, Ninian Bryden, 1529, 1, pp. 111–12, 104, as well as notaries and schoolmasters. Inventories of chaplains' goods sometimes mention weapons, e.g. James Jonsone's 'swerd and buklar', 1534, 2, p. 144. I am indebted to Dr Peter Symmons for these references. He also tells me that the priests resident in Selkirk 1503–45 'seemed to have taken part in ridings of the common, and would almost certainly have ridden out armed, in the same way as everyone else'.

[84] John Pekok was contracted to serve as an archer in John Leycestre's company, 23 June 1375, Cheshire Record Office DLT/A11/85. He was described as a chaplain in the will of William Mainwaring 4 Oct. 1393, Manchester, John Rylands Library, Mainwaring charter 173. I am grateful to Dr Philip Morgan for these references and for the gift of xeroxes of the documents.

[85] The 'autobiographical' passage of Piers Ploughman comes from the C-Text, perhaps composed *c.*1390.

Hoccleve spent years as a clerk of the Privy Seal hoping all the while for a benefice to increase his income. After nearly a quarter of a century he lost heart and got married, for love, but as a last resort, and with resignation that this would mean poverty.[86] Audley did achieve a benefice, as chaplain of a perpetual chantry, but only when he was old and infirm. Before then he had spent many years in Lord Lestrange's household, his occupations including playing the organ and harp and singing, but not necessarily in a liturgical context. He hoped for a benefice, but,

> Alas, he ner a parsun or a vecory.[87]

His perpetual chantry came too late for him to have acquired a benefice with cure of souls by exchange—a practice not unknown.[88] As it was, Audley became an embittered man who inveighed against the abuse of simony, which was common, he believed, and against the promotion of kitchen clerks and other undesirables to parish benefices, with disastrous results.[89] The existence of such men as Hoccleve and Audley almost contemporaneously gives the lie to any suggestion that the unbeneficed were intellectual also-rans who deserved ill-rewarded and dead-end jobs.

The attitudes of such men remind us that contemporaries thought that it mattered whether a man got a benefice or not. Nor was it only disappointed candidates who considered the difference important. The evidence of taxation assessments shows that the ecclesiastical establishment regarded the difference as crucial. In 1377 the assessors of the poll tax asked only one question: was the cleric beneficed or not? If the answer was 'Yes', the rate at which he paid was 12d.; if 'No' it was 4d., and the correct amount was noted beside the name of each man. This is what makes this particular tax so useful for our present purposes. In 1381 the injunction that the better off should help the poorer was taken seriously. For Archbishop Sudbury it meant taxing the unbeneficed chaplains within the deanery of Bow at half the rate that he charged those beneficed in perpetual chantries, 3s. 4d. instead of 6s. 8d.[90] In 1526 the Lincoln

---

[86] Thomas Hoccleve, *The Minor Poems*, ed. F. J. Furnivall (EETS, Extra Series 61, 1892), pp. xiv-xv and references.

[87] For Audley's life see Michael Bennett, 'John Audley: Some New Evidence on his Life and Work', *Chaucer Review*, 16 (1982), pp. 344–55. I owe thanks to Dr Philip Morgan for this reference; *The Poems of John Audlay*, ed. E. K. Whiting (EETS, Original Series 184, 1931), p. 15 (Poem 2, l. 148).

[88] *Ibid.*, p. 224. In this last poem (Poem 55, l. 52) Audlay describes himself as deaf, sick, blind and bed-ridden.

[89] *Ibid.*, p. 30 (Poem 2, ll. 560–72).

[90] *Church in London*, nos. 203–15.

assessors collected more detail about the status and occupation of each man but still distinguished rigorously between the beneficed (rectors, vicars, and cantarists) and the rest.

It was concern for the plight of the rest which surely lay behind the growing practice of pensioning off aged clergy,[91] an attempt to ease the 'promotions blockage' caused by 'benefices for life'.[92] By the 1520s pensioners were a recognizable and sizeable group among the un-beneficed. Some may have been aged chaplains, of course, and not all were deserving old people; a minority were ambitious and greedy young men battening on the parishes while awaiting their first benefice.[93] The existence of pensioners was yet another reason why the proportion of the unbeneficed in the clerical population had fallen as promotion prospects improved. Early Tudor historians contemplating the unbeneficed are apt to comment on their numerousness,[94] but to a medievalist the wonder is how, by the 1520s, their numbers had decreased.

In conclusion, how may we assess the contribution of the unbeneficed to the ministry of the Church? It was said earlier that, with so many men involved over so long a period, the results of any enquiry into quality would be various. For example, the excellence and fervour of the chaplains in fifteenth-century Bristol can be contrasted with the laziness and disobedience of those in fourteenth-century Boston.[95] Attempts to assess the morality and conscientiousness of the unbeneficed have also shown widely differing results; certainly no study has been able to prove that they were less laudable than were rectors and vicars.[96] We could take as a yardstick a more positive aspect of their work: effectiveness as missionaries. Any account of the Lollard movement reveals that 'chaplains' included some of the most persuasive communicators, highly

---

[91] Pensioners are identified as such in *Subsidy Collected in the Diocese of Lincoln*, passim.

[92] The problem was not confined to the medieval church; the officers of the Georgian navy were a similarly entrenched class, Michael Lewis, *The Navy of Britain* (London, 1949), pp. 264–77. I owe this reference and helpful comment to Miss P. K. Crimmin.

[93] Bowker, *Lincoln Clergy*, pp. 145–7.

[94] Michael Zell, 'Economic Problems of the Parochial Clergy in the Sixteenth Century', in R. O'Day and F. Heal, eds., *Princes and Paupers in the English Church 1500–1800* (Leicester, 1981), pp. 21–8.

[95] LAO Reg. 12, fol. 312ᵛ.

[96] Bowker, *Lincoln Clergy*, pp. 106–8. A list of those taken in adultery in London between 1401 and 1439 shows the great majority of men being described as 'chaplain', but does not distinguish between the beneficed and unbeneficed, *Calendar of Letter Books of the City of London; Letter Book I*, ed. R. R. Sharpe (London, 1909), pp. 173–87. I owe this reference to Dr C. M. Barron.

effective as preachers and teachers; the names of William Smith and William Swinderby come to mind.[97]

This paper has sought to indicate the importance of the unbeneficed clergy. This was certainly recognized by contemporaries, for example, in the production of self-help manuals for unsupervised chaplains.[98] The unbeneficed clergy were important not only because they were numerous but because they bore the greatest share of the burden of pastoral care in late medieval England. Thus it may be suggested that the fairest assessment of the ministry of the unbeneficed is the character of religious life in general. And much evidence is coming forward to support the view that the Church in late medieval England was in much better heart than was once believed. There was loyalty to old belief and practice,[99] as well as new developments in worship and devotion;[100] there was lively criticism[101]— surely a sign of vitality—and regional diversity.[102] If this new and happier picture of popular religion in late medieval England is accepted, then, I submit that it is the unbeneficed clergy, the workhorses of the medieval Church, who should receive a large share of the credit.

University of Nottingham

---

[97] Anne Hudson, *The Premature Reformation* (Oxford, 1988), p. 553 for references to Smith (of Leicester) and Swinderby.

[98] See article by D. B. Foss, below, pp. 00–00.

[99] This is the overwhelming impression to be gained from reading wills. See above n. 37.

[100] R. W. Pfaff, *New Liturgical Feasts in Later Medieval England* (Oxford, 1970).

[101] From the lollards, from poets, and from the ranks of the clergy, especially from conscientious prelates.

[102] Jonathan Hughes, *Pastors and Visionaries. Religion and Secular Life in Late Medieval Yorkshire* (Woodbridge, 1988).

JOHN MIRK'S *INSTRUCTIONS FOR PARISH PRIESTS*

by DAVID B. FOSS

LITTLE is known of John Mirk. When he wrote *Instructions*, he was, its colophon informs us, a canon regular of Lilleshall priory, Shropshire. Lilleshall was a house of Arroasian canons, a branch of the Augustinian order, so named because its first house was that of St Nicholas, Arras. Lilleshall was founded in 1144–8, and contained some ten canons in 1400.[1]

In accord with the Augustinian order's practice of presenting its own canons to benefices within its extensive patronage, Mirk had exercised a cure of souls, as he tells us in the Preface to the *Festial*,[2] but we do not know when or where. Two manuscripts of his *Manuale Sacerdotum*[3] end with a letter to J. de S., vicar of A., expressing the hope that he will turn the *Manuale* into English. Possibly Mirk had been vicar of A., and J. de S. (who need not himself have been a canon regular) was his successor in that cure. When Mirk speaks of the life and work of the parish priest, it is possible that he does so from long experience.

We learn from the same manuscripts that Mirk subsequently became prior of Lilleshall. When he held this office is not known—no list of priors of the house has survived. The date generally given for Mirk is 'circa 1400'. John Pitaeus, in *Relationum Historicum de Rebus Anglicis* (Paris, 1619) confidently afforded the date 1403, but with no apparent ground for such precision.[4] 'Circa 1400' is based on internal evidence of dialect, reference to Lollards in his sermons in the *Festial*, and his note in the sermon for St Winifred's day that this day 'was not ordeyned by Holy Churche to be halowed'—it was so ordained in 1415. The manuscript of Cotton Claudius A II, which refers to Mirk as already dead, is generally dated between 1425 and 1450.[5]

[1] D. Knowles and R. N. Hadcock, *Medieval Religious Houses in England and Wales* (London, 1971), s.v. Lilleshall.

[2] BL MS Cotton Claudius A. II, fol. 123

[3] BL MS Harleian 5306 and Jesus College, Oxford, MS 1. Harl. gives its author as John *Mireus*, evidently a scribal error for *Mircus*; Jes. Coll. 1 as John *Marcus*, prior of 'Lilyshel'.

[4] M. J. Runn, 'John Mirk's "Festial": a Study of the Medieval English Sermon' (unpublished Leeds M.A. thesis, 1954), p. 3.

[5] By M. F. Wakelin in 'An Edition of John Mirk's "Festial" as it is contained in the Brotherton

Mirk is known as the author of two other works of instruction for parish priests besides his *Instructions for Parish Priests*: the *Manuale Sacerdotum* and the *Festial*. All three were written in response to the need to increase the standards of personal morality, preaching, and pastoral care of the parish clergy. The concern for these matters expressed by the fourth Lateran Council in 1215 was taken up in England by Archbishop John Pecham in his decree *Ignorantia Sacerdotum* of 1281.[6] This directed parish priests to expound to their congregations four times a year the Creed, the Ten Commandments, the two Gospel Precepts, the seven Works of Mercy, the seven Deadly Sins, the seven Virtues, and the seven Sacraments of Grace. Archbishop Thoresby of York issued injunctions in 1357 which required such teaching to be given every Lord's day.[7]

Manuale Sacerdotum is an extended examination of what a priest should be in himself and the work which he should perform. No edition of it has yet been printed. It covers similar ground to *Instructions*, but in Latin, and it is altogether a more elaborate and learned exposition. It exists in five manuscripts. In the Harleian text the author is given as John *Mireus*, and in that in Jesus College, Oxford as John *Marcus*, prior of 'Lilyshel'. Both are undoubtedly Mirk (though Edward Peacock in his Introduction to *Instructions* supposed them to be two different persons), and 'it is very interesting to see one man writing in two completely different styles, though both intended for parish priests'.[8]

The Priests' Manual is divided into five parts. Part I contrasts good priests with bad. The one celebrates Mass daily, and lives soberly in himself, justly towards others, and piously towards God. The worldly priest's devotion is superficial; his interest lies in the value of benefices, not the burden of souls, and he restlessly seeks promotion with the aid of 'master Symon'. There is discussion of the priest's lifestyle and office, of the Mass, and of how the priest's day should be spent.[9]

The Manual assumes that the priest it guides will be unbeneficed rather

---

Collection Manuscript' (unpublished Leeds M.A. thesis, 1960); by Gillis Kristensson in *Instructions for Parish Priests* (Lund, 1974); and by Horstmann in 1881—see ed. Susan Powell, *The Advent and Nativity Sermons from a Fifteenth Century Revision of John Mirk's 'Festial'* (Heidelberg, 1981), pp. 18–19.

[6] Printed in *Wilkins*, 2, pp. 54–7.

[7] H. Maynard Smith, *Pre-Reformation England* (London, 1938), p. 125.

[8] W. A. Pantin, *The English Church in the Fourteenth Century* (Cambridge, 1955), p. 215. The manuscripts are: BL MS Harl. 5306; Bodleian Library, Oxford, MSS 549, 632, Digby MS 75; Jesus College, Oxford, 1.

[9] For a fuller discussion, see Pantin, pp. 215–17.

than incumbent; *Instructions* is similarly targetted at those who are not 'grete clerkes', and ends with 'Still Other Things a *Chaplain* must know'. The Manual betrays a pessimistic estimate of the general standard of clerical morality. It tells of priests who love the tavern more than the Church (*Instructions* likewise finds it necessary to spell out the obvious warning that a priest should not attempt to baptize while drunk),[10] priests who are fornicators and businessmen (i.e. usurers), and of gambling priests whose altar is the gaming table.[11]

Festial is a collection of sermons, compiled with the aim of giving the priest assistance with the work of preaching the Christian faith which it is his duty to carry out. The sermons, in English, are provided for the Sundays and major feastdays of the Christian year. The work exists in twenty-six manuscripts, and underwent nineteen printed editions between 1483 and 1532. Loosely based on *Legenda Aurea*, that massively popular collection of tales of the saints and of demons, generally unlikely and often bizarre, the *Festial* has been criticized for its 'fanciful explanations and sensational anecdotes' and for being 'naïve and lurid'.[12]

The criticism has not been altogether fair. Some of the material (for example the early life of Pontius Pilate, the miracles performed by St John the Apostle, and the horrible death of Nero) stretches human credibility beyond its limit of endurance. But much moral instruction is inculcated by virtue of striking illustrations; generally accurate and helpful explanations are offered of the observances and rituals of the Catholic Church in the course of the Christian year; and extended passages of scripture are related (more in the temporal or 'ordinary time' than in the festal section of the collection), of great benefit to a laity which as yet possessed no English Bible. The enduring impact of Mirk's *Festial* is exemplified in the case of John Minet, tried in York in 1589 for being an 'athiest', heathen, and sorcerer, and for preaching a sermon, which turns

---

[10] Ed. Edward Peacock, *Mirk's Instructions for Parish Priests* (EETS 1868, revised 1902), lines 623–32.

[11] G. R. Owst, *Preaching in Medieval England* (Cambridge, 1926), p. 47, and *Literature and Pulpit in Medieval England* (Cambridge, 1933), pp. 275–7. Owst refers to the Kirkstall MS of *Manuale Sacerdotum* (York Minster MS o.11, especially fols 39ᵛ–40ʳ), and wonders about a link between the Shropshire canons and the Yorkshire Cistercians.

[12] Peter Heath, *The English Parish Clergy on the Eve of the Reformation* (London, 1969), pp. 94–5, 100. See Heath's useful discussion of the *Festial*'s Passiontide and Easter sermons in these pages. See also Pantin, *The English Church*, p. 217; Owst, *Preaching*, p. 245 *passim*; and C. W. Dugmore, *The Mass and the English Reformers* (London, 1958), pp. 67–8, for discussion of the important Corpus Christi sermon.

out to be a late sixteenth century version of Mirk's *Festial* sermon for the Nativity of St John Baptist.[13]

On his own admission, Mirk intended his *Instructions* as a translation and exposition of *pars oculi*, part of the *Oculus*. The *Oculus* referred to is the *Oculus Sacerdotis* of William of Pagula, vicar of Winkfield near Windsor, written *circa* 1320. Pagula's work is an explicit elaboration of Pecham's *Ignorantia Sacerdotum*, conceived in three parts. Part I, or *Pars Oculi*, is the latest section of the book to be written. Its purpose is to assist confessors to examine penitents thoroughly, suggest remedies, and assign penances. The first twelve chapters treat the examination of penitents from different walks of life on their knowledge of the articles of faith, observance of the Ten Commandments, and commission of the seven deadly and seven venial sins. *Pars Oculi* forms the basis of Mirk's instruction on the hearing of confession, by far the single most substantial section of his work, though Pagula's treatment of the subject is subjected to 'appreciable rearrangement'.

Part II, *Dextera Pars*, instructs the priest in the carrying out of his pastoral duties: the ministration of baptism, his duties at confirmation, and the celebration of the Mass and its meaning. He must remind the laity that their tithe obligations must be fulfilled, and that usury and improper conduct in and secular use of churches and cemeteries are strictly forbidden. The material is taken from the collection of canon law the *Decretals*, supplemented by provincial constitutions. A list of thirty-four excommunications is given, followed by a rehearsal of the fourteen articles of the Creed, the seven sacraments, the Ten Commandments, the seven deadly sins, the seven works of mercy, and the seven virtues.

Part III, *Sinistra Pars*, is a study of the seven sacraments. 'Left' and 'right parts' refer to the supposed functions of the individual eyes. The right eye owns a teaching function (morality and instruction), the left eye a preaching function (dogma or speculation). The function of both eyes together, the total seeing, is confession and practice of the faith—this is *Pars Oculi*, the first or greatest or total function of the eyesight, the 'part' or function of the seeing as a whole.[14]

Mirk's work is not a complete or literal translation of Pagula's treatise, either of the three parts in general or of *Pars Oculi* in particular. It in fact

[13] V. M. O'Mara, 'A Middle English Sermon preached by a Sixteenth Century "Atheist": A Preliminary Account', *Notes and Queries*, 232 (1987), pp. 183–4. (I am grateful to Dr W. J. Sheils for this reference.)

[14] L. E. Boyle, 'The *Oculus Sacerdotis* and Some Other Works of William of Pagula', *TRHS* 5th series, 5 (1955).

draws generously on all three parts, though the claim to be an exposition specifically of *Pars Oculi* is justified insofar as Mirk devotes by far the greatest part of his attention to the sacrament of penance, which is *par excellence* the concern of *Pars Oculi*.

Versions of Mirk's *Instructions for Parish Priests* are known in seven manuscripts of which the Douce manuscripts contain the 'Great Sentence' (of excommunication), which was to be read four times a year, but which is not found in the other texts.[15] The text has been edited by Edward Peacock on the basis of the Cotton manuscript, with reference to the two Douce manuscripts. In 1974 Gillis Kristensson prepared a text noting all the manuscripts, but concurred with Pothmann's judgement that Peacock was right to make Cotton Claudius the basis of his edition.[16]

A brief introduction emphasizes the need for priests to live exemplary lives of integrity and moral restraint:[17]

> From nyse iapes and rybawdye
> Thow moste turne away thyn ye;
> . . .
> Thus thys worlde thow moste despyse,
> And holy vertues have in vyse.　　　(lines 61–2, 65–6)

Mirk then outlines what a priest should teach his parishioners about the sacraments of baptism (he offers practical advice to the midwives who will very often be the ministers of the sacrament),[18] confirmation, and matrimony, and the devotion to the Mass which he should encourage. The doctrine of the Real Presence in the Mass is simply and uncompromisingly adumbrated, as indeed is the 'ransom' theory of the Atonement:

> Teche hem thenne wyth gode entent
> To beleve on that sacrament
> That they receyve in forme of bred;
> Hyt ys goddes body that soffered ded
> Vp on the holy rode tre
> To bye owre synnes & make vs fre.　　　(lines 244–9)

---

[15] Descriptions of all the MSS are given by Gillis Kristensson, *Instructions for Parish Priests* (Lund, 1974), Introduction. They are found in BL Cotton MS Claudius AII; MS Royal 17 C XVII: Cambridge University Library, MS Ff 5.48: Bodleian Library, Oxford, MS Tanner 196; MS Greaves 57; MSS Douce 60, 103.

[16] Kristensson, referring to Adolf Pothmann, *Zur Textkritik von John Myrk's 'Pars Oculi'* (1914).

[17] Quotations and references are from Peacock's edition.

[18] D. B. Foss, 'Mirk's "Instructions": Baptismal Discipline in the Age of Faith', *Living Stones*, 1 (1987).

A high view of the sacramental forms enables Mirk to put forward a fantastic set of claims for the benefits which will accrue to faithful parishioners fortunate enough to see a priest pass carrying the reserved sacrament. These include the assurance that sudden death or blindness will not strike that day. Mirk maintains that such teaching was given by St Augustine, a claim he makes also in his Corpus Christi sermon in *Festial*. Perusal of Augustine's known works will of course yield no statement remotely resembling any such claim. Augustinians may naturally suppose their founder to be the originator of dearly-held, longstanding traditions, and similar lists of benefits are found in contemporary French and German texts.[19]

Miscellaneous instructions—keep the church a place of prayer; pay tithe; shun sorcery and usury; a spouse's consent is necessary when vows are made by a married person, unless the vow concerned is that of pilgrimage to Jerusalem, the most solemn and binding of all vows, because it undertakes following in the footsteps which Jesus physically trod—are followed by rhyming versions of the Lord's Prayer, the Creed, and articles of faith which the priest is to teach his parishioners:

> Owre uche dayes bred, we the pray,
> That thow geve vs thys same day;　　　(lines 416–17)
> ...
> Ded and buryed he was also,
> And went to helle to spoyle oure fo;　　　lines 438–9)

Only once in his instruction in the content of the faith does Mirk move from credal dogma to illustrative example, in the case of the most intractable of doctrines, that of the Trinity; the analogy is offered of water, ice, and snow, three things, but essentially the same. He suggests the same analogy in his sermon for Trinity Sunday in *Festial*:

> Se the ensaumpul that I yow schowe
> Of water and ys and eke snowe;
> Here beth thre thynges, as ye may se,
> And yet the thre alle water be.
> Thus the fader and the sone & the holy gost
> Beth on god of myghtes most;
> For thagh they be personus thre,
> In on godhed knyt they be.　　　(lines 472–9)

---

[19] Dugmore, *The Mass and the English Reformers*, p. 70. Bibliothèque Mazarine MS 993, fol. 72 specifies *De Civitate Dei* as the source, a claim already refuted by Jean Gerson (d. 1429).

The third section of the *Instructions* is by far the longest, approximately five-sevenths of the whole. It expounds the priest's duties with regard to administration of the seven sacraments, though only five are dealt with here, there being no discussion of matrimony or orders. The fullest instruction of all concerns the hearing of confessions, which by itself occupies over a thousand lines of verse out of a work consisting of 1934 lines.

In the case of baptism, the priest's duty resides to a large extent in establishing whether baptism of sickly children in emergency was correctly performed by the layperson, usually a midwife, on whom the duty fell, and in putting right any errors or omissions which he might discover. Right administration depends upon use of the Trinitarian formula in the correct order, though syntactical accuracy is not essential—the wrong case endings of Latin words can be safely overlooked.[20] The 'following' is valid

> Yef hyt were hys fulle entent
> To geve the chylde that sacrament   (lines 592–3)

but if the words were in the wrong order,

> Thenne moste thou, to make hyt trewe,
> Say the serves alle anewe   (lines 604–5)

The admonition Mirk thinks it necessary to include that no attempt should be made by a priest to baptize when he is drunk ('But what & thou so dronken be / That thy tonge wole not serve the'), is a sobering reminder that the personal moral standards of the clergy were not always as high as might reasonably be expected.

Confirmation ('bishopping') is of course largely the bishop's responsibility, and not much can be said with regard to the priest's duties in this matter. They do not even include preparatory instruction, since children were confirmed at the age of five, and pressure was exerted on parents and godparents to see that they were brought before the bishop at the due time:

> Also wythynne the fyfthe yere
> Do that they I-bysbede were,
> For tho that bydeth over more,
> The fader & the moder mote rewe hyt sore;
> Out of chyrche schule be put
> Tyl the byschope have bysbede hyt   (lines 157–62)

---

[20] Foss, 'Baptismal Discipline'.

Then comes the long section on the hearing of confession. Except in certain circumstances, a priest should hear the confessions only of his own parishioners. The exceptions are detailed, and include cases where a penitent has reason to fear that his own priest is indiscreet or immoral. Great care must be exercised in the hearing of confession; in particular, the priest must sit very still and quiet so as not to disturb a female penitent:

> Stylle as ston ther thow sytte,
> And kepe the welle that thou ne spytte   (lines 777–8)

until she falters and needs words of encouragement to continue:

> What maner thynge thou art gulty of,
> Telle me boldely & make no scof.
> . . .
> Wonde thow not for no schame,
> Parauentur I haue done the same,
> and fulhelt myche more,
> Yef thow knew alle my sore   (lines 789–96)

The priest's questions to the penitent begin by establishing whether the penitent knows the Lord's Prayer and Hail Mary—in English will do, but they must be quickly learned if they are not known—and believes the articles of faith, including the Real Presence in the Mass. The Ten Commandments are gone through one by one, as are the seven deadly sins. Attention then turns to the venial sins: the sins of the five senses, followed by miscellaneous others—neglecting spiritual and good works, keeping bad company, engaging in domestic conflict, and the like.

The smallest details concerning the sin or sins which have been committed must be ascertained, in order that penance may be assigned in proportion to the gravity of the sin in question; it is worse, for example, if it has been committed on a holy day or in a holy place. The penance given must not be too heavy, or it will be spiritually counterproductive, and it must be private—a married woman's penance should not be apparent to her husband. Specific spiritual remedies—meditation, prayer, service—are recommended against each of the deadly sins. A list is given of the serious sins which are reserved to the bishop:

> A mon that ys a-corset wyth book & belle,
> And eretykes, as I the telle,

> Hym that breketh solempne vow,
> Or chawnge hyt wole, sende hym forth now,
> Clypper of the kynges mynt,
> And hym that lyveth by swerdes dynt... (lines 1659–64)

Its ending ('If he curses any more, send them also to his door') perhaps breathes an exasperated air of 'Serve him right'. The form of absolution is finally given.

After a brief section on the sacrament of Extreme Unction, Mirk comes finally to practical instructions for the saying of Mass. These mainly consist of suggestions for calm, sensible behaviour when things go wrong. When the priest has started the Mass, and finds he has left the things he needs in the vestry, he should go and quietly fetch them, and resume the Mass at the appropriate point:

> Yef hyt befalle, as god hyt scylde,
> That thow of wyt be so wylde,
> That bred or wyn be away
> Consecracyone when thou scholdest say;
> Yef the befalle that ylke cas,
> Lay bred on thy corporas,
> And thagh thow forth I-passet be,
> Begynne agayn, '*Qui pridie*' (lines 1783–90)

If he spills some consecrated wine, that on which it was spilt must be preserved as a relic. Insects which fall into the consecrated wine must be consumed, or extracted and burned if the priest knows he will be sick if he tries to swallow them ('Yef any flye, gnat or coppe / Doun into the chalys droppe...', lines 1825–34).

'Still other things a chaplain must know' concern communion of the sick, to whom ministration should be gentle and generous. Confession before communion is not necessary for the dying—their sickness is penance enough. Assurance should be given to those who wish to communicate, but are too sick to do so, that intention alone is sufficient for the reception of sacramental grace. Woe betide the priest, however, who fails to return the reserved sacrament safely to the church, so that some of it gets lost:

> Yet hyt eten wyth mows or rat,
> ...
> Fowrty dayes for that myschawnce
> Thow schalt be in penaunce (lines 1897–1900)

139

The concluding threat of suspension for malicious celebration may be directed at priests tempted to entertain the simplified ritual forms (without water or light) expressive of a sympathy with the tenets of Lollardy.

The work ends with a brief exhortation to its reader to pray for its author, to read the book and pass it on to others, and to render thanks to the Holy Spirit. Peacock intended that his edition of *Instructions* should be accompanied by an extended commentary, but became convinced that 'the document as it stands speaks clearly to those to whom its voice is audible'.[21] This is a wise omission, since no commentary can do justice to the simplicity yet comprehensiveness of Mirk's 'pastoral poetry'; it would merely cramp, swamp and detract from a delightfully readable text well able to act as its own interpreter.

College of the Resurrection, Mirfield

[21] Peacock, Introduction.

A LAYMAN'S MINISTRY IN THE BYZANTINE CHURCH: THE LIFE OF ATHANASIOS OF THE GREAT METEORON

by D. M. NICOL

THE line between things spiritual and things temporal, between religious and secular, was never very precisely drawn in the Byzantine world. It was not unusual that a man of affairs should be an erudite theologian, that a priest should be a a married man with a family, that a holy man should remain unordained, or that a layman should be appointed as Patriarch of Constantinople. Thirteen of the 122 Byzantine patriarchs were elevated from the laity, four of them in the eighth and ninth centuries. Among them were the Patriarch Tarasios in 784 and his formidably learned nephew Photios in 858. Neither was a priest. Both were high-ranking civil servants and scholars.[1] The popes disapproved of this practice and said so rather forcibly in the case of Photios; but the Byzantines saw nothing odd in it. They continued, from time to time, to appoint a layman rather than a priest to the highest office in their Church. The tenth canon of the Council of Sardica in 343 had recommended that laymen should not be made bishops until they had been ordained and moved up the various rungs of the hierarchical ladder to the top. This, according to the later Greek canonists, required a minimum of seven days on each rung.[2] In later times, Gregory of Cyprus, an admirable lay scholar and theologian, was ordained and elevated to the patriarchal throne in 1283, though he claims in his autobiography that he was 'pushed' on to it against his will.[3] John XIII Glykys, who was made patriarch in 1315, had been a distinguished civil servant with an academic turn of mind and a teacher of philology. The facts of his preferment are outlined by his learned friend Nikephoros Gregoras. Not only was John a

---

[1] L. Bréhier, 'Le recrutement des patriarches de Constantinople pendant la période byzantine', *Actes du VIᵉ Congrès d'Etudes Byzantines* 1 (Paris, 1950), pp. 221–7; *idem*, *Les Institutions de l'Empire byzantin* (*Le monde byzantin*, 2, 2 edn., Paris, 1970), pp. 384–8.

[2] C. J. Hefele, *Histoire des Conciles*, 1 (Paris, 1907), pp. 790–1. S. Gregorii Theologi, *Oratio XLI: in Pentecosten*, PG 36, col. 433C; Theodore Balsamon, in G. A. Rhalles and M. Potles, *Syntagma tōn theiōn kai hierōn kanonōn*, 2, pp. 702–4.

[3] Gregory II of Cyprus, *Autobiography*, with French translation in W. Lameere, *La tradition manuscrite de la correspondance de Grégoire de Chypre* (Brussels-Paris, 1937), p. 187. Cf. A. Papadakis, *Crisis in Byzantium. The* Filioque *Controversy in the Patriarchate of Gregory II of Cyprus (1283–1289)* (New York, 1983), pp. 39, 49.

married man with sons and daughters; he also suffered from an ailment which, his doctors declared, required him to eat meat. He was therefore excused the customary tonsure as a monk before his ordination. A carnivorous monk would not do; a carnivorous patriarch was all right. John's wife, in accordance with the canons, obligingly left him and entered a convent.[4]

By the fourteenth century, however, Byzantine attitudes were changing. The highest office in the Church became a prerogative of monks. That did not mean that the religious had triumphed over the secular. For most Byzantine monks were never ordained. There were, of course, the *hieromonachi* or priest monks, who dispensed the sacraments. But the majority were always laymen, bearing witness to the truth that monasticism was in origin a lay movement. St Antony of Egypt, the first hermit, was never ordained; St Pachomios, founder of the first monastic communities, shunned the idea of ordination; and St Basil submitted to it only with great reluctance. Pachomios advised his monks against it for fear that it might whet their appetites for power and glory. When they had need of the offices of a priest they could always send out for one from the nearest bishop.[5] Their ministry was thus different from that of the priesthood; or so it seems to us. It is indeed hard to find in Byzantine Greek a single word equivalent to that of ministry, certainly in its western and Protestant sense.

It was *de rigeur* in Byzantine literary circles to employ ancient Greek terms wherever possible. The literary word for priest was *hiereus*, as it had been in pagan, Hellenic times. The demotic Greek word was, and still is, *papas*. But no Byzantine writer would have allowed so vulgar a term to sully the Attic purity of his diction. The office performed by the *hiereus*, however, was described as the *leitourgia*, again an ancient Greek word originally meaning 'a burdensome public office discharged by wealthy citizens'. The Christian priest is sometimes called the *leitourgos*; and the word 'liturgy', meaning the office of priest and not simply the communion service, is perhaps as near to the western concept of ministry as we can get. Yet there were other forms of Christian ministry besides the celebration of the liturgy. The emperor himself was in a sense a minister of God.

[4] Nikephoros Gregoras, *Byzantina Historia*, ed. L. Schopen, 1 (Bonn, 1829), pp. 269–70. On his elevation and career, see S. I. Kourousis, *The Learned Oecumenical Patriarch John XIII Glykys* [in Greek] (Athens, 1975).

[5] *S. Pachomii Vitae Graecae*, ed. F. Halkin (Subsidia hagiographica 19, Brussels, 1932), c. 27; A. J. Festugière, *Les Moines d'Orient*, IV/2: *La première Vie grecque de Saint Pachôme* (Paris, 1965), c. 27, pp. 171–2.

The bishops assembled at the Council of Chalcedon in 451 hailed the Emperor Marcian as 'priest and emperor'. The iconoclast Emperor Constantine V scandalized the pope by claiming the same title. Constantine the Great had once described himself as 'Bishop of those outside the Church', whatever he may have meant by that enigmatic phrase. The Emperor of the Romans in Constantinople was hedged about with much divinity. He was acclaimed as *hagios* or holy; he was designated as 'the equal of the Apostles'; he alone was allowed to enter the sanctuary in church and take communion in the manner of a priest. But he remained a layman. One Byzantine canonist in the thirteenth century accorded the emperor all the privileges of a bishop except that of the sacramental office. Theodore Balsamon, a century earlier, had declared that 'the service of the emperor includes the enlightenment and support of both the souls and the bodies (of his subjects); the dignity of the patriarchs is limited to the benefit of souls, and to that only'.[6]

The ministry of the emperor was thus complemented by that of the patriarch. He could never be ordained priest since the office of emperor, always theoretically elective rather than hereditary, was closed to priests, monks, and eunuchs. But many an emperor performed a kind of ministry in the composition of theological and spiritual works. The iconoclast Constantine V wrote no less than thirteen polemical treatises to instruct his people in the truth of what turned out to be heresy. The Emperor Manuel II in the fifteenth century wrote tracts against Latin as well as Muslim theologians. He also composed a discourse on the ethics of marriage, a subject which he understood, having fathered six legitimate children and an unspecified number of others. Many an emperor too sought refuge or comfort in the monastic life when his end seemed near or when circumstances obliged him to abdicate. The Emperor John Cantacuzene relinquished his throne in 1354 and lived out the last thirty years of his life as the much-revered emperor-monk Joasaph. During his long retirement he composed a number of theological works, many of them in support of the doctrine and practice of the hesychast monks whose cause he had championed. It was he who as emperor had presided over the council of bishops in Constantinople in 1351, at which the theology of hesychasm, as formulated by his friend Gregory Palamas, was declared to be fully acceptable to the Orthodox Church.[7]

[6] D. M. Nicol, 'Byzantine political thought', in *The Cambridge History of Medieval Political Thought c.350–c.1450*, ed. J. H. Burns (Cambridge, 1988), pp. 49–79, esp. pp. 70–1.

[7] R. Guilland, 'Les empereurs de Byzance et l'attrait du monastère', in Guilland, *Etudes*

Athanasios of the Great Meteoron was one of these hesychast monks. In the western world the monastic life may not generally be thought of as a form of ministry, except in so far as monks served as educators and teachers of the illiterate. This was a role that Byzantine monks were never called upon to play, since their society had never suffered a corresponding break in the continuity of learning and education from antiquity to the middle ages. Literacy in Byzantium was never a monopoly of clerics. Teaching of the young was usually in the hands of qualified laymen. Many of the great ascetics in the Byzantine Church were well-educated men; but most of them deliberately turned their backs on secular literature, or what they called 'Hellenic' studies, as being irrelevant and possibly dangerous to their true vocation. Monks must be free to devote themselves to prayer and contemplation and to searching the Holy Scriptures in conditions of *apatheia* and *ataraxia*—both ancient Stoic terms meaning absence of passion and distraction. These could best be found in the wildernesses and desert places, in mountain tops or in caves; though some of the great Byzantine monastic houses, such as that of St Theodore of Stoudios in Constantinople, were located in or near the city centres; and the saintly Nicholas Kabasilas in the fourteenth century, himself a layman for most of his life, believed that the life in Christ could just as well be lived in the world, in one's own house, as in the desert.[8]

Yet the Byzantines were always aware that the true meaning of the word monk or *monachos* was a solitary alone with God. The solitary life in the mountains or deserts remained for many the true Christian way to perfection, for which long years of service in a *koinobion* or cenobitic monastery might be the necessary preparation. Hermits or anchorites would, as it were, graduate from the schools of communal monasticism to perfect their *askesis* or training in conditions of total solitude. This may seem a selfish pursuit. Perhaps monks have to be selfish. As St Basil observed: 'The prime purpose of the ascetic life is the salvation of one's own soul'. Or, as an earlier hermit expressed it: 'Unless a man shall say in his heart "Only I and God exist in this world" he shall not find rest'.[9] As

byzantines (Paris, 1959), pp. 33–51; D. M. Nicol, *Church and Society in the Last Centuries of Byzantium* (Cambridge, 1979), pp. 53–4.

[8] Nicholas Kabasilas, *De Vita in Christo*, PG 90, cols. 657D–660A; English translation by C. J. deCatanzaro, *Nicholas Cabasilas. The Life in Christ* (New York, 1974), pp. 173–5.

[9] S. Basilii Magni, *Sermo Asceticus*, PG 31, col. 881B; English translation by W. K. L. Clarke, *The Ascetic Works of Saint Basil* (London, 1925), p. 141. Alonius, in *Apophthegmata Patrum*, PG 45, col. 133A; *The Paradise of the Holy Fathers*, trans. E. A. Wallis Budge, 2 (London, 1907), p. 13.

often as not, the fame and sanctity of such holy men attracted bands of disciples and they would find themselves with the nucleus of a new monastic community on their hands. Such was the origin of most of the great monastic colonies in the mountains and desert places of the Byzantine Empire—Mount Sinai by the Red Sea, Mount Olympos in Bithynia, Mount Athos, the island of Patmos, or the rocks of the Meteora in Thessaly. The anchorite's ministry, in practical terms, was limited to a chosen few, whom he selected, trained, and instructed. But the aura of sanctity surrounding such men was dear to the Byzantine spirit; and their ministry reached a much wider public through the recording of their lives and deeds and miracles. Hagiography had a special place in Byzantine literature. Bishops' sermons were published and no doubt provided edification and instruction. But saints' lives were more edifying still and sometimes more entertaining; and they provided fascinating glimpses of the supernatural powers and graces vouchsafed to holy men. They proved that it was possible for a mere mortal to acquire a measure of divinity, to achieve *theosis* or deification. The ministry of hagiography flourished in Byzantium, not least in the centuries of its decline and fall. Every Christian had access to the divine through touching and kissing the icons in his church or house, for the icon was the medium through which the divine grace of its holy figure flowed, a tangible link between time and eternity, between the temporal and the spiritual. The holy man was a living icon. Though he might shun society and the things of this world, emperors as well as common people sought his advice and company as a purveyor of eternal truths, a medium of divine grace, an oracle; for some had the gift of prophecy among their divinely acquired *charismata*.

Such a one was the Blessed Athanasios of the Meteora, that forest of gigantic rocks that rise precipitously out of the plain of Thessaly in northern Greece. Hermits had loged like seagulls in the caves and crevices of those rocks before Athanasios arrived there; but it was he who founded the first truly aerial monastic community on the very summit of one of the highest of them in the middle of the fourteenth century. He called it 'Meteoron' or 'in the air', and he dedicated it to the Theotokos Meteoritissa, the Meteorite Mother of God. Its chapel, however, perched on the top of the Broad Rock, was devoted to the Metamorphosis or Transfiguration of Christ. Athanasios was a hesychast, trained in the school of St Gregory Palamas. In other words he believed that by ceaseless vigilance, prayer, and contemplation in conditions of *hesychia* or 'stillness' a man could be metamorphosed by the divine light, the uncreated light that had illumined the body of Christ at the Transfiguration. No one could know the essence of God; but the trained hesychast might experience God's 'energies', the electric charges emanating from the Godhead, and he might be momentarily transfigured in body and soul. The mystical experience of the hesychasts was psychosomatic, involving mind, soul, and body. It could be imparted to others only by instruction, *askesis* or training, and example. Nor did it require a priesthood or ministry, since it had nothing to do with the sacraments of the established Church. Yet Athanasios of the Meteoron and his like, though hoping to hide their light under bushels by withdrawing from the world, had a huge following. The doctrine and practice of hesychasm touched a chord in men's hearts in the fourteenth and fifteenth centuries, creating what has been called a 'hesychast international' in the Orthodox Christian world, among Greeks, Slavs, and Russians. The message was propagated by holy men who recognized no national or linguistic boundaries and who were for the most part laymen, not priests or ministers of the word. They were living icons and exemplars of the potential divinity of man.[10]

It would be a mistake to suppose that hagiographies in Byzantium were written with an eye to a market of the credulous and semi-literate. Many of them are highly sophisticated compositions in archaizing Greek which only the well-educated could understand. Some come in two verisons, one for the intellectuals, the other for the average general reader. Such is the case with the Life of Athanasios. The first version is written in literary Greek in the late fourteenth century; the second is a translation into colloquial Greek made by a monk of Athos about 1700. There is also an *Akolouthia* or Office of the Blessed Athanasios composed by a Cretan scholar from Corfu who was also a member of the Aldine Academy in Venice at the turn of the fifteenth century.[11] The sanctity of Athanasios appealed to scholars as well as monks. He was born of prosperous and influential parents in Greece in 1305, though reared and educated by his uncle, who died as a monk. After studying Greek philosophy at

---

[10] On fourteenth-century hesychasm and its influence in and beyond the Byzantine Empire, see J. Meyendorff, *Byzantine Hesychasm: historical, theological and social problems. Collected Studies* (London, 1974); *idem, Byzantium and the Rise of Russia. A Study of Byzantine-Russian relations in the fourteenth century* (Cambridge, 1981), pp. 96–112, 132–44; references in Nicol, *Church and Society in the Last Centuries of Byzantium*, pp. 9 n. 13, 36–42; Joan M. Hussey, *The Orthodox Church in the Byzantine Empire* (Oxford, 1986), pp. 258–60, 286–9. On the term 'Hesychast International', see D. Obolensky, *The Byzantine Commonwealth. Eastern Europe, 500–1453* (London, 1971), p. 302.

[11] For the two versions of the *Life* of Athanasios and the *Akolouthia*, see D. M. Nicol, *Meteora. The Rock Monasteries of Thessaly* (2 edn., London, 1975), pp. 73–6. N. A. Bees, *The Manuscripts of the Meteora* [in Greek] 1 (Athens, 1967), nos. 354, 404.

Thessalonica he felt a call to the monastic life. Being still too young to be received as a novice on Mount Athos, he went on a pilgrimage to Constantinople. There he first met some of the men who were to determine his future, among them Gregory of Sinai and Isidore, later to be patriarch. Gregory was one of the leading exponents of the hesychast technique of prayer and contemplation. He had left his monastery on Mount Sinai to instruct a small Skete or group of anchorites on Mount Athos. Young though he was, Athanasios, or Andronikos as he was then called, followed him to the Holy Mountain in the hope of finding an experienced monk who would accept him as an apprentice.

Athos was a dangerous place to live in the early fourteenth century. Turkish pirates, sailing over from Asia Minor, found it easy to raid and plunder. Gregory of Sinai and his little flock had to take refuge in Thessalonica. Andronikos, however, stayed and moved inland to a spot which his biographer describes as 'the highest and least inviting part of the mountain'. There, he had been told, there lived two monks called Moses and Gregory who had almost reached the peak of spiritual perfection. He was still too young to become a monk. But he persuaded Moses and Gregory to employ him as their handyman and servant, to collect food for them in return for teaching and guidance. It was a hard and genuinely ascetic life. But, as his biographer says, 'by such toils and struggles the Blessed Athanasios, in the words of St Paul, "forgot those things which are behind, and reached forth unto those things which are before"'. In 1335, when he had proved the sincerity and the promise of his calling and had reached the age of thirty, he was tonsured as a novice by his spiritual father Gregory, who then invested him with the 'angelic habit' of a monk with the name of Athanasios.

Turkish pirates continued, however, to plunder the Holy Mountain and monks living beyond the protective walls of the great monasteries were vulnerable. Moses was surprised and captured by one of them, though his great holiness wrought a miracle. He converted his Muslim captor to Christianity. But he had learnt his lesson and he retired behind the walls of the monastery of Iveron, where he died. Gregory and his pupil Athanasios became discouraged. There was no *ataraxia*, no stillness, to be had in such conditions. They elected to leave Mount Athos in search of new spiritual pastures. After some wandering in Macedonia, they moved south to a small town in Thessaly where, they were told, were some enormous rocks set up by the Demiurge at the creation of the world. There was a wilderness totally lacking in comfort and in temptations to vainglory. There was also holy peace and tranquillity to be found, for no one lived among the rocks. Only ravens and vultures nested in them. It seemed that the Demiurge had created ideal conditions for the pursuit of the kind of holiness that Gregory and Athanasios had in mind. They settled in a cave in one of the rocks called Stylos or the Pillar. The biographer of Athanasios is so eager to claim that his hero was the first to found a monastic colony at the Meteora that he conceals the fact that there were already others squatting in caves in nearby rocks, forming a Skete or group of anchorites under the direction of a Protos or spiritual father. They called their colony the 'Thebaid' of Thessaly, for it was consciously modelled on those of the Desert Fathers of Egypt of an earlier age.

The reputation of Gregory the Stylite, as he came to be called, and of his pupil was soon broadcast and people both religious and lay came from far and near to seek his blessing and enjoy the spiritual benefit of his company. After a while he gave permission to Athanasios to find a cave of his own nearby. There he would pursue his solitary prayers and meditations from Monday to Saturday, returning to base, as it were, every Sunday to join in the liturgy and to share a meal with the rest of his brothers before going back to his solitude. His master Gregory was a *hieromonachos*, an ordained monk. Athanasios himself was, and remained, a layman. His biographer commends him for his great humility on this account. But it was his manifest holiness that caused aspiring disciples to come and bother him. To get away from them he climbed up to the top of one of the smaller pillars of rock and there built a hut or *hesychasterion* where his solitary meditations would not be disturbed. To be thus perched with the earth at his feet and nothing but the heavens above his head was wonderfully conducive to the stillness or *hesychia* for which he craved.

Behind his new retreat, however, there loomed up the awe-inspiring cliff of the Broad Rock. On top of that a hesychast could live and pray still further removed from the distractions of this wicked world. The ascent would not be easy, for the flanks of the Broad Rock are precipitous and vertiginously high. It was said that it had been climbed once before by a monk from Athos. Not for nothing were such monks known as 'athletes of the spirit' or *oriebateis*, mountaineers. Gregory the Stylite gave Athanasios leave to try it only on condition that he took one or two other monks with him. They approached the rock from the point at which its height from the ground is no more than 200 feet; and we are told that Athanasios with two companions clambered up by means of rope ladders until they came to a large cave near the top. Here they established their first settlement; and in a smaller crevice above the cave Athanasios decided to build a tiny chapel so that he would not have to come down once a week. He packed one of his monks off to the nearest bishop to be ordained as a priest, much as St Pachomios had advised in the earliest days of monasticism. Bricks and mortar were hauled up from down below; and the cave chapel in which the new priest officiated was dedicated to the Theotokos Meteoritissa. It now houses the relics of its founder Athanasios.

His spiritual father Gregory the Stylite left Thessaly about 1350. He died in Constantinople, having much impressed the patriarch and the emperors with his holiness. It is said that, at the very hour of his death, his disciple, though many miles away, sensed that his master's soul was ascending to heaven and ordered his monks to pray for the repose of their common father. The elder whom Gregory had appointed to succeed him at Stylos did not long survive him. His scorn of the flesh was so great that he left instructions that his corpse was to be thrown to the birds and beasts as an abomination. His obedient monks had therefore left it on a ledge of the cliff to be devoured by vultures and ravens. Athanasios was deeply distressed, especially when a bird flew down beside him holding in its beak a thumb of the late elder; and he took it upon himself to bury the remains of the body, washing it with his own tears. He then climbed back to the home comforts of his own cave on the Broad Rock.

Before long, however, he was minded to complete his ascent to the very summit of the rock. It had and still has a large, flat top and a marvellous view. One side is open to the air, the other is protected from the gales by a natural screen of rock. Trees, shrubs and flowers grow out of it and it is like a roof garden high in the sky. Athanasios had hoped to have it to himself, to perfect his soul in solitude. But, like many a holy hermit before him, he was soon beset by aspiring disciples who yearned for the kind of ministry which he could impart. At first he turned them all away. In the end, however, perhaps because he needed company in the loneliness of his perch in the sky, he permitted fourteen monks to join him and serve under him. The Broad Rock sprouted buildings on its summit. Cells, cloisters and a new chapel were constructed; and the community was dedicated to the Metamorphosis or Transfiguration. The Monastery of the Great Meteoron, as it came to be called, was in the making. If his biographer is to be believed, Athanasios himself had never belonged to a cenobitic community. This was unusual, for it was the general rule that the intending solitary or hesychast must first serve his time as a monk in a monastery before his abbot would allow him to branch out on his own.

It was never Athanasios's intention, however, to found a monastery on his rock. What he had in mind was a Skete or little band of anchorites. In due course he drew up a *typikon*, a charter or list of rules for them.[12] The rules are strict and simple, designed to regulate the affairs of a group of dedicated men, living, as he had lived since his youth, a purely ascetic life under the direction of a spiritual father. He made no provision for the appointment of an abbot. The fact that he was not ordained would not have precluded him from becoming *hegoumenos* or abbot. There were plenty such lay abbots in the Byzantine world. Athanasios wished to be known simply as the Father of the Meteoron. His *typikon* prescribed that his community should be limited to its existing numbers. Its members were enjoined to live together with one mind and one purpose, sharing all food, drink, and clothing equally, and owning no private property. The land in the valley at the foot of the rock was to be tilled and cultivated by the monks themselves. Its proceeds were hauled up to the top in baskets. Any surplus of corn, wine, or oil was not to be marketed. They were not in business as farmers; and anyone found to be in possession of more than three pence would be excommunicated, as St Basil had decreed. The monks found their journey to and from work in the fields to be tiring, not to say startling, since they had to commute either by rope ladders or bundled into nets on the ends of ropes attached to a windlass on the summit of the rock. The journey from top to bottom is somewhat over 200 feet.

That, however, was the purpose of the exercise. Athanasios wished his Skete to be as far removed from the material world as possible. His wish was emphasized in three canons of his *typikon*: no goods from the world below were to be brought into the community; no secular literature was to be imported or studied; no woman was to be allowed to come near the rock nor to be given any food, even though she might be about to die of hunger. The holy horror of the female sex was, of course, common to many of the great ascetics. The same rule had been laid down for Mount Athos in 963; and there it still applies. The biographer of Athanasios praises his misogynism as sure proof of his purity and chastity. 'Not only was he completely free of any emotion or passion with respect to women, he was unmoved even by the word.' If he had to mention the subject, he did so by allegory or by circumlocution, referring to woman as 'the sling' which hurls the stones of sin into the souls of men, or the 'affliction', the powerhouse of passion in those addicted to the flesh. The widow of a local bigwig once thought of asking Athanasios for his blessing. He refused to

---

[12] The text of the *typikon* of Athanasios is included in both versions of his *Life*. Nicol, *Meteora*, pp. 98–100.

see her or to be seen by her and rewarded her curiosity or her piety by shouting at her from a distance and prophesying her imminent death, as he had successfully foretold that of her late husband. She died three months later. This tale is told not to show that Athanasios was a male chauvinist but to prove that he was endowed with the divine gift of prophecy. One has to admit, however, that his ministry did not extend to the gentler sex, for all that he dedicated his aerial community to the Virgin Mother of God as well as to the Transfiguration of her Son.

He died in 1383 at the age of seventy-eight. His biographer concludes by listing his virtues and setting them against the ideals of virtue recommended for the attainment of perfection in the *Scala Paradisi*, the Ladder of Divine Ascent, written by John Klimakos, the sixth-century anchorite of Mount Sinai.[13] The Ladder to Paradise is made up of thirty rungs or grades, each of which represents a particular state of virtue; and its ascent symbolizes the upward progress of the monk towards the ultimate perfection of deification. In later times the Monastery of the Great Meteoron was proud to possess a substantial relic of its saintly author. Athanasios achieved the virtue of total renunciation of the world. He had no known relatives. His father's name was never mentioned. He claimed that his relations and friends were those who shared his way of life. In obedience to his superiors he was an example to all. He was, as a good monk should be, constantly in mind of death and would sit weeping beside the grave that he dug with his own hands near his rock. He loved silence and was seldom caught in the snare of casual conversation. He was always busy and never idle. He had perfect mastery of his appetites, eating the bare minimum of food to sustain life. His anger was reserved for those who disobeyed him. He had no pride or self-esteem and always called himself a common man and a peasant; and he was too humble ever to assume the rank of priest.

Any property that he acquired was never for himself but for the common benefit of his monks or for distribution to the poor. For though he preferred his solitude his sense of duty to his disciples was strong. At the all-night vigils of the great feasts, which he would attend in common with all his monks, when the weakness of the flesh might cause others to doze off, no one ever saw Athanasios nod. He would stand firm and erect like a statue; though sometimes he would be seized by a kind of divine madness and forget the part assigned to him in the service. As for the vigils that he kept alone and in secret, however, no one knows 'save He who

---

[13] The works of John Klimax or Klimakos (Climacus) are in *PG* 88, cols. 596–1209.

knows all things'.But his biographer claims that none of the hesychasts on Mount Athos, whom he had known in person, could aspire to the achievements of Athanasios in the stillness of his own solitude. The portrait of him painted on the north wall of the sanctuary of his church shows him wearing a white habit instead of the usual black of a Greek monk. The artist was trying to convey the impression of Athanasios transfigured, as a hesychast irradiated by the light that shone on Mount Tabor, his garments, as St Mark says, 'exceeding white as snow, so as no fuller on earth can white them'. The proof of his sanctity, if further proof were needed, came two years after his death. His little band of monks, driven to despair by a hard winter, had decided to abandon their rock. Suddenly there welled up from the tomb of their founder 'an inexpressibly sweet fragrance' which lasted until the spring and gave them courage to persevere, knowing that Athanasios was still with them though now released from the bonds of the flesh.

The odour of sanctity emanating from his grave may be taken as the last act of the ministry of the Blessed Athanasios. What sort of ministry was it? Or is ministry the wrong word? The Hon. Robert Curzon, who visited the Meteora monasteries in 1834, and relieved the poor monks of several of their manuscripts which are now in the British Museum, was impressed by the rocks but cynical about their inhabitants. 'It is difficult', he writes,

> to understand by what process of reasoning (these monks) could have persuaded themselves that by living in this useless, inactive way, they were leading holy lives. They wore out the rocks with their knees in prayer; the cliffs resounded with their groans; sometimes they banged their breasts with a big stone, for a change; and some wore iron girdles round their emaciated forms; but they did nothing whatever to benefit their kind.[14]

'They did nothing whatever to benefit their kind'. This is rather redolent of the attitude of some government ministers to the teaching of the humanities in our universities: they are neither relevant nor cost-productive. Two hundred years after the death of the Blessed Athanasios there were fourteen monasteries perched on or in the surrounding rocks of the Meteora. In that sense alone his example and his ministry had borne fruit. He had made the desert fruitful, as St Augustine said of the first

---

[14] R. Curzon, *Visits to Monasteries in the Levant*, ed. with introduction by D. G. Hogarth (London, 1916), pp. 289–90.

hermit, the father of Christian asceticism. The fruits of the hesychast movement of the fourteenth century were certainly exotic by today's standards. But they had a powerful and widespread influence, far beyond what might have been expected from a handful of spiritual athletes on the slopes of Mount Athos and the rocks of the Meteora. There is, alas, no doubt that hesychasm proved to be another stumbling-block between the Catholic and Orthodox Churches. The western church quickly condemned the hesychasts as heretics and the divine light of their vision as dangerous nonsense. For once Edward Gibbon was in agreement with the pope. Gibbon too dismissed the vision of the hesychasts as 'the production of a distempered fancy, the creature of an empty stomach and an empty brain'.[15] The authority of Rome would no doubt have wished to tame St Gregory Palamas or the Blessed Athanasios by making them found an Order of more mundane and manageable monks. The Byzantines were always more attuned to their holy men, more ready to admire their ministry of *theosis* or deification. Part of the strength of the Orthodox Church, as Joan Hussey has recently observed, lay in its ability 'to accept and use the outstanding goodness of a holy man without having to weave sociological theories of explanation'.[16]

Finally, Athanasios and his followers performed a special ministry to Greek Christians in later centuries. In 1393, ten years after his death, the Ottoman Turks descended on Thessaly. Thereafter, for 500 years and more, the monks of the Meteora kept their sanctuary lamps alight on the tops of their rocks as beacons of the Christian faith and tradition above a world controlled by Muslims. They were never such a cosmopolitan community as that on Mount Athos, where Bulgarian, Georgian, Russian, and Serbian monasteries lived side by side with the Greeks; though the first successor of Athanasios as Father of the Meteoron was a Serbian emperor who renounced the world to direct the community on top of the Broad Rock; and the Serbian influence remained strong. In later years, after the Turkish conquest of Constantinople, the Meteora monasteries, like those on Mount Athos, found benefactors and protectors in the Orthodox princes of Moldavia and Wallachia across the Danube. Even the Czars of Russia in their role as defenders of Orthodoxy, took an interest in the welfare of the monks of the Meteora.[17] The benefactions of the high and mighty in these distant Orthodox lands, in the way of landed estates,

[15] E. Gibbon, *Decline and Fall of the Roman Empire*, ed. J. B. Bury, 6 (London, 1898), p. 506.
[16] Hussey, *Orthodox Church in the Byzantine Empire*, p. 365.
[17] Nicol, *Meteora*, pp. 128–31, 168–70.

relics, and treasures, brought to the Meteora a worldliness which would have horrified their first founder. But they helped the monasteries to survive. They were often on hard times. They were saved from destruction on many an occasion simply by being inaccessible. They were thus able to sustain an unbroken if strange and tenuous witness to the Christian faith throughout the centuries of Turkish occupation. That Christianity survived at all in Greece was due in no small measure to the example and the prayers of the monks of the Meteora, secure in their rocky fastnesses. If steadfast witness to the faith is a form of ministry, then Athanasios and his successors were ministers, silently preaching to the world from their rocky pulpits.

King's College, University of London

'EYN MERCKLICH UNDERSCHEYD': CATHOLIC REACTIONS TO LUTHER'S DOCTRINE OF THE PRIESTHOOD OF ALL BELIEVERS, 1520–25

by DAVID BAGCHI

AFTER the great Reformation principles of 'faith alone' and 'Scripture alone', probably the most revolutionary doctrine commonly associated with Martin Luther is that of the priesthood of all believers. It is well known that, as it appears in his address 'to the Christian nobility of the German nation' of 1520, he intended this doctrine to bring down the walls of the new Jericho by striking at the heart of the distinction between clergy and laity on which the medieval Church was based.[1] What is less well known is the reaction to this doctrine of Luther's contemporaries, and in particular his critics. I propose to look at how they regarded the reformer's conception of the universal priesthood, and what they thought its implications were, in the hope of shedding more light on its contemporary significance.

Luther expounded his theory of universal priesthood in other writings, but its exposition in *An den christlichen Adel* was unique. Here it was not intended, as it would be later, as the basis of any practical scheme for re-organizing the ministry.[2] But neither was it any longer serving the relatively innocuous purpose it had in his earlier sermons on baptism, penance, and the mass, as part of a meditation on the true nature of these sacraments.[3] It had now been fashioned into an ecclesiopolitical weapon, showing that the spiritual estate was neither above the temporal estate—nor above being reformed by it. It was this new purpose, rather than any significant change in the content of Luther's teaching, which probably explains why it was only after the publication of *An den christlichen Adel*

---

[1] *An den christlichen Adel deutscher Nation von des christlichen Standes besserung* (1520), in *WA* 6, esp. pp. 406–10.

[2] In 1523, Luther would use the doctrine of the universal priesthood to encourage the evangelicals at Leisnig to appoint their own minister: see *Dass eine christliche Versammlung oder Gemeine Recht und Macht habe, alle Lehre zu urteilen und Lehrer zu berufen, ein- und abzusetzen. Grund und Ursach aus der Schrift* (1523), *WA* 11, pp. 408–16. For a discussion of this treatise in its context, see G. Haendler, *Luther on Ministerial Office and Congregational Function* (Philadelphia, 1981).

[3] *Ein Sermon vom Sakrament der Busse* (1519), *WA* 2, p. 722, line 33, and *Ein Sermon von dem Neuen Testament, das ist von der heiligen Messe* (1520), *WA* 6, p. 370, lines 24–7.

that the doctrine of universal priesthood attracted the attention of Catholic polemicists.

The earliest and the most extensive refutations came from the pens of Thomas Murner, the friar and humanist poet who had (appropriately enough for a Strasbourgeois) earned the nickname 'the goose preacher' after one of his more memorable sermon illustrations,[4] and the canonist Hieronymus Emser, another humanist, who held high office in the court of Albertine Saxony as Duke Georg's private secretary.[5] Their first challenge was to the proof-texts for the universal priesthood which Luther had taken from I Peter and Revelation: 'You are a royal priesthood, a priestly kingdom', and 'You have made them kings and priests'. To Murner, it was all based on a simple misreading: when Peter called the Church a priesthood, he did not mean that all its members were priests, any more than when Germany was described as an empire did it mean that all Germans were emperors and empresses. The 'royal priesthood' of the Church was therefore simply a description of its system of government.[6] Emser's interpretation of the royal priesthood was rather more subtle. Understood literally, he believed, the passage would indeed indicate a priesthood of the baptized. But the Scriptures are never to be understood in their literal sense, for such was the mark of the heretic through the ages.[7] Peter's description of all Christians as priests is figurative. Indeed, they are described in these passages as a 'royal priesthood', as 'kings and priests'. Taken literally it would mean that all Christians were kings too.[8] It was no accident that both men chose to argue that the priesthood of all

---

[4] *An den Grossmechtigsten und Durchlüchtigsten adel tütscher nation das sye den christlichen glauben beschirmen / wyder den zerstorer des glaubens christi / Martinum Luther eine verfierer der einfeltigen christen* ([Strasbourg], 1520). For Murner's background, and an account of his literary activity against Luther, W. Kawerau, *Thomas Murner und die Kirche des Mittelalters*, Schriften des Vereins für Reformationsgeschichte 30 (Halle, 1890), and *idem*, *Thomas Murner und die deutsche Reformation*, SVRG 32 (1891), are still invaluable. More recent studies include J. Schütte, *'Schympf red': Frühformen bürgerlicher Agitation in Thomas Murners "Grossen Lutherischen Narren"* (1522), Germanistische Abhandlungen 41 (Stuttgart, 1973) and J. Beumer, 'Der Minorit Thomas Murner und seine Polemik gegen die deutsche Messe Luthers', *FStn* 54 (1974), pp. 192–96.

[5] *Wider das unchristliche Buch Martini Luthers Augustiners an den Teutschen Adel ausgangen Vorlegung Hieronymi Emser an gemeyne Hochlöbliche Teutsche Nation* (Leipzig, 1521). Emser's life has been documented in G. Kawerau, *Hieronymus Emser. Ein Lebensbild aus der Reformationsgeschichte*, SVRG 61 (1903), now supplemented by H. Smolinsky, *Augustin von Alveldt und Hieronymus Emser. Eine Untersuchung zur Kontroverstheologie der frühen Reformationszeit im Herzogtum Sachsen*, Reformationsgeschichtliche Studien und Texte 122 (Munster, 1983).

[6] Murner, *Tütscher nation*, Ciii[r-v].

[7] Emser, *Vorlegung*, Aiv[r].

[8] *Ibid.*, Ciii[r], Civ[v].

believers implied also the kingship of all subjects. Luther's original treatise had been addressed to Charles V and the imperial nobility. The suspicion that Luther's teaching was as noxious to the temporal order as it was to the spiritual was a valuable *argumentum ad principem*.

Having dealt with Luther's arguments from Scripture, Emser and Murner, after the fashion of these controversies, had next to deal with his arguments from tradition and from reason. Luther had argued that the long-recognized rights of emergency lay baptism and emergency lay absolution suggested that there was no uncrossable gulf between clergy and laity, merely that over the course of time there had emerged a convenient division of labour. The issue of lay absolution was a sensitive one. Although the practice had died out by this time, it had been recognized by canon law, and was still the cause of some equivocation in the Catholic camp.[9] Significantly perhaps, Emser and Murner both ignored Luther's appeal to it. As for lay baptism, they argued that the word which needed to be underlined was 'emergency'. It was to be understood as a gracious concession of priestly powers under extenuating circumstances, not as a right. 'Luther behaves like a naughty child,' declared Emser. 'Give him an inch and he'll take an ell'.[10]

Luther's arguments from reason were dismissed in equally short order. His example of ten princes, all sons of a king, electing one of their number to exercise the royal power to which all were entitled, was impertinent. For Christians are children of God by grace, not by right.[11] The hypothesis of a group of pious Christians left in a desert, who choose a priest from among themselves, proved nothing either. For if they had no duly-ordained priest they would, in Emser's view, have to resign themselves to doing without the sacraments 'like the desert fathers of old'.[12] Murner was surprised by the narrowness of Luther's vision: 'Is God limited to the

---

[9] In his confession manual commonly known as the Sylvestrina, the Dominican Sylvester Prierias came down against it (*Summa summarum* (Strasbourg: J. Grüninger, 1518), *de confessore*, 1, i, fol. 82^{rv}). The Franciscan Caspar Schatzgeyer was firmly opposed to it (*Ecclesiasticorum sacramentorum assertio* (Tübingen, 1530), fols. 86^v–87^r). Henry VIII, on the other hand, accepted it (*Assertio septem sacramentorum adversus Marti. Lutherum, aedita ab invictissimo Angliae et Franciae rege et dom. Hyberniae Henrico eius nominis octavo* (Rome, 1521), Miii^r). For the relevant canon (*De consecratione*, distinctio 4, canon 36) see Gratian 1374. For the history of lay absolution in theory and practice see G. Gromer, *Die Laienbeicht im Mittelalter. Ein Beitrag zu ihrer Geschichte*, Veröffentlichen aus dem Kirchenhistorischen Seminar München 3, no. 7 (Munich, 1909).

[10] Emser, *Vorlegung*, Diii^v–iv^r.

[11] Murner, *Tütscher nation*, Di^v; Emser, *Vorlegung*, Diii^v.

[12] *Ibid.*, Diii^r.

sacrament?' he asked. 'Would he give them nothing that contributed to their souls' salvation simply because there were no priest?'[13]

Luther's intention in using these illustrations had been to show that there was no distinction between clergy and laity as to status (*standt*), but only with regard to function or office (*ampt*). Against this, Murner was able to show quite successfully that the notion of 'office' had only a limited application even in the secular sphere from which it was taken.

> It follows from what he says that there is no estate of the nobility either, but that a prince is chosen simply to exercise an authority, and if he lays aside this office, he becomes again the peasant or citizen he had been before assuming the office. But I know well enough that his assertion that there is no noble estate will displease the aristocracy as much as the spiritual estate is annoyed by the suggestion that everyone is a priest or priestess.[14]

There was, as Emser argued, a real distinction ('eyn mercklich underscheyd') between clergy and laity, not only in function but also in status; indeed, the function follows from the status, not the status from the function.[15] To demonstrate this essential distinction, Emser drew heavily upon the third book of Chrysostom's *De sacerdotio*. As the soul excels the body, so does the priesthood excel the lay estate.[16] The priest has no equal on earth, for he who brings salvation to princes is greater than princes.[17] The role of the laity is entirely subordinate: to provide for the physical needs of priests, and to defend and protect them.[18] Indeed, priests are superior even to heavenly powers, for unto which angel or archangel did God ever promise that whatsoever they bound or loosed on earth would be bound or loosed in heaven? And Scripture refers to priests not as men but as angels (Malachi 2 v.7) or even gods (Psalm 82 vv. 1, 6). In short, concluded Emser, the superiority of priests to people is not just permitted by Christianity, it is its very 'soul and foundation'.[20]

The divine origin of the priesthood was considered unassailable, stemming as it did from the way in which Christ himself differently

---

[13] Murner, *Tütscher nation*, Dii^r.

[14] *Ibid.*, Di^{r-v}.

[15] Emser, *Vorlegung*, Ciii^r.

[16] *Ibid.*, Ei^r. Chrysostom, *De sacerdotio*, III, i (*PG* 48, col. 641).

[17] Emser, *Vorlegung, Ei^v*. Chrysostom, *De sacerdotio*, III, ii (*PG* 48, col. 643).

[18] Emser, *Vorlegung*, Di^r, Eii^r.

[19] *Ibid.*, Ei^r. Chrysostom, *De sacerdotio*, III, v (*PG* 48, col. 643).

[20] Emser, *Vorlegung*, Div^v: 'nicht alleyn Christen, ssonder ouch Sewln unnd fundament der Christenheit gewest'. Compare Murner, *Tütscher nation*, Aiv^v.

treated his apostles and mere followers. But there was of course no explicit record that Christ ordained anyone. And while it was true, as the controversialists often reminded Luther, that Jesus did much that was never committed to writing (with reference to John 21 v. 25), it was not really credible that such a momentous event would have gone un-recorded. The controversialists therefore tried—with some ingenuity and not a little special pleading—to identify this incident in the gospel accounts. Emser suggested that it took place after the resurrection, argu-ing that Jesus' commission to 'Feed my sheep' (John 21 vv. 15–17) was addressed to all the disciples and not to Peter alone, and that they were thereby ordained.[21] This was in fact rather an inept defence, for after Peter's confession at Caesarea Philippi (Matthew 16 vv. 13–19), this passage was the chief Biblical witness for Petrine and papal primacy. It is perhaps not surprising that Emser's fellow-controversialists did not follow his lead. Alternatively, there was the Johannine account of the commissioning of the disciples: 'Receive the Holy Spirit. If you forgive the sins of any, they are forgiven. If you retain the sins of any, they are retained' (John 20 vv. 22–3).[22] But a difficulty also attached to this text, for Luther regarded it as proof that all Christian men and women are priests, because Mary Magdalene was present in the same room and was presum-ably included in the injunction. Partly because of these difficulties, the incident most commonly credited by the controversialists as an ordination was the Last Supper. By commanding those present to perform the sacrifice of the mass, Jesus must incidentally have given them the power to do it by ordaining them.[23]

Murner and Emser had presented the most comprehensive of the early responses to Luther's doctrine of the universal priesthood as developed in *An den christlichen Adel*. They had conceded the propriety of calling all Christians priests only in a remote and extenuated sense, a 'literal' sense, as Emser described it. But they were also quite certain that the 'essential distinction' between clergy and laity, and the superiority of one estate over the other, was a central, irreducible element of Christianity, its 'soul and foundation'. This emphasis was sustained throughout the controversies of the succeeding years, by all the controversialists who addressed the question, including such laymen as Henry VIII of England and Duke Georg of Saxony. The difference between the priest and his people was of

---

[21] Emser, *Vorlegung*, Ei[r].
[22] Murner, *Tütscher nation*, Di[r-v].
[23] Henry, *Assertio*, Riii[v].

159

special importance in the case of the mass. Johannes Cochlaeus insisted that no lay person should so much as hear the canon, for pearls are not to be cast before swine.[24] Indeed, the priesthood was dependent upon the mass in the view of John Fisher, Eustachius Sichem, and Johannes Eck.[25] But it was equally the case that the mass, together with all the other sacraments, depended upon the priesthood. Ordination is the source of grace, remarked Henry: abolish it, and all the sacraments dry up.[26] In contrast with Luther's other revolutionary doctrines, which the controversialists objected to in many cases for pastoral, not ideological, reasons,[27] the special priesthood and the sacramentality of ordination were considered the basis of the faith. It is worth asking why this was such a constant element in their defences of the 'old' religion, and on what sources it was based.

A clue might lie in the influence upon the Catholic controversialists of the writings of Dionysius the Pseudo-Areopagite, mediated through both the standard medieval texts and the Dionysian revival of the later Middle Ages. However equivocal the New Testament may have been on the subject of ministry, the testimony of Pseudo-Dionysius (who was identified with Saint Paul's Athenian disciple by all the controversialists who cited him) was accorded quasi-apostolic status as 'prior et potius' of all authorities after Scripture.[28] For the controversialists, therefore, his

---

[24] Cochlaeus, *Glos und Comment Doc. Johannes Dobneck Cochlaeus von Wendelstein / uff CLIIII Artikeln gezogen uss einem Sermon Doc. Mar. Luterss von der heiliger mess und nüem Testament* (Strasbourg, 1523), Gii[r], Oiii[r], Qiv[r].

[25] Fisher, *Sacri sacerdotii defensio contra Lutherum* (1525), in *Opera omnia* (Würzburg, 1597), col. 1298; Sichem, *Sacramentorum brevis elucidatio* (Antwerp, 1523), Iii[v]; Eck, *Enchiridion locorum communium adversus Lutherum et alios hostes ecclesiae* (1525), edited by P. Fraenkel, Corpus Catholicorum 34 (1979), p. 199.

[26] Henry, *Assertio*, Ri[r]. Compare Powell, *Propugnaculum summi sacerdotii* (London, 1523), fos. 120[r].

[27] Eck, who can hardly be described as moderate, claimed that he fully accepted justification by faith alone. His opposition was prompted solely by the thought that the common people would misunderstand it and neglect virtuous actions. Johannes Fabri (later to become bishop of Vienna) made the extraordinary confession as late as the summer of 1520 that he agreed with almost everything that Luther said, and regretted only that more people were not 'real' Lutherans. (See E. Iserloh's article on Eck and H. Immenkötter's on Fabri in *Katholische Theologen der Reformationszeit 1*, Katholisches Leben und Kirchenreform im Zeitalter der Glaubensspaltung 44 (Münster, 1974) at p. 70 and p. 90.) Another hard-line controversialist, the Louvain theologian Jacobus Latomus, who drew from Luther his most scholarly exposition of *sola gratia-sola fide*, argued only that this doctrine was heretical 'in sensu quem habet et explicat Lutherus', that is, with apparent prejudice to morality. (Latomus, *De quaestionum generibus* (1525), in *Opera omnia* (Louvain: B. Gravius, 1579), fol. 87[v].)

[28] e.g. Eck, *Commentaria de mystica theologica D. Dionysii Areopagitae* (Augsburg, 1519), Avi[v]. Clichtoveus, Cochlaeus, Kretz, Marcello, Fisher, Wimpina, Dietenberger, Campester, Rhadinus and Fabri also explicitly accepted the Pseudo-Areopagite's authenticity.

book on the ecclesiastical hierarchy constituted first-hand evidence from the very infancy of the Church of a threefold ministry,[29] while his *Coelestis hierarchia* helped to explain its theological significance. These books deeply influenced the controversialists, as we can see for example from the third book of Edward Powell's *Propugnaculum*. In the longest section, a defence of the sacramentality of ordination, there is an extended meditation on the necessity to the Church of a divine order of authority and obedience, in which *ordo* and *ordinatio* are interchangeable ideas— 'omnia, quae a deo sunt, ordinata sunt' (Romans 13 v. 1).[30] Such an order, argued Powell, reflects the ranking of the planets, of the metals, of the animal kingdom; as Dionysius showed, it reflects the very order of heaven, of the ranks of angels and the Holy Trinity, which is itself both ordered and the source of all order. The heavenly and ecclesiastical hierarchies consist of a triad of triads, in which each element acts upon the one below it, and is acted upon by the one above it, in purgation, illumination, and perfection.

But each hierarchy also contains its own order, rapt in sweetest contemplation of the Trinity. And this supreme and inerrant Trinity, the fount and origin of all order, disposes its own family and household of angels in a beautiful and decorous order, to which Christ wishes to confirm the Catholic Church which he has redeemed with his own precious blood. He has therefore constituted it in a threefold hierarchy of higher, middle, and lower: that is, of prelates, clergy, and people. The prelates, as supreme, purge their inferiors by correcting faults, illuminate them by teaching the true faith, and perfect them by the example of decent living. The clergy is established as the middle order between prelates and people, so that it first receives purgation, illumination, and perfection from the prelacy, and afterwards diffuses it to the people. The people are the lowest in this subcelestial hierarchy, so that while they receive the hierarchical actions

---

[29] For references to Pseudo-Dionysius's authority on the sacraments and other rites, see Fisher, *Assertionum Regis adversus Lutheri Babylonicam Captivitatem defensio* (1525), in *Opera omnia*, cols 181 and 192; Cochlaeus, *De gratia sacramentorum* (Strasbourg, 1522), Li[r], Liii[v]; Kretz, *Ain Sermon inhaltend etlich spruch der schrifft von dem fegfewr* (No place, 1524), Ai[v]; Clichtoveus, *Antilutherus tres libros complectens* (Paris, 1524), 1, fols 10[r], 53[v]; *De veneratione sanctorum* (Cologne, 1525), Gi[v]; Fabri, *Malleus in haeresim Lutheranam* (1524), in CCath 23/4 (1941/52), pp. 272–6. For his testimony to the sacramentality of ordination, see Fisher, *Defensio sacri sacerdotii*, col. 1239; Emser, *Vorlegung*, Civ[v], Div[r], Kiii[v]; Clichtoveus, *Antilutherus 2*, fol. 63[v]; Marcello, *De authoritate summi Pontificis* (Florence, 1521), fols 39[v]–40[r]; Dietenberger, *Contra temerarium Martini Luteri de votis monasticis iudicium* (Cologne, 1524), 1, Nv[v]ff.

[30] Powell, *Propugnaculum*, III, fol. 154[v]. The quotation is from the Vulgate.

[*operationes*] of prelates and clergy, they cannot themselves act upon one another or upon any below them, nor return it to those above.[31]

Similar Dionysian formulations were expressed by Powell's compatriot John Fisher,[32] by the Italians Archbishop Marcello and Thomas Rhadinus,[33] and by the Frenchmen Jodocus Clichtoveus and Lambertus Campester.[34] In addition, through the writings of many controversialists runs a theme which we might call the beauty of order. Rhadinus asked of Luther's universal priesthood

> What will become of the beauty and ornament of the Church, which consists in the very variety of her orders? 'The queen stands all beautiful within, clothed in varied hues.' [Psalm 45 v. 13] ... And what, pray, will become of the structure of the Church? What of the distinctions within its most beautiful body? What of its admirable form, which is thus extolled in the Song of Solomon: 'How beautiful you are, my friend, how beautiful. How beautiful and how ornate, my beloved.' Abolish the difference and order of the members, and what becomes of the beauty and form of the body?[35]

Both the hierarchism of Pseudo-Dionysius and the theme of *pulcherrimus ordo* serve to show how central to the controversialists' vision of the universe was the idea of an *ordered*—and we remember the double meaning of that word—priesthood and a priestly order.

That the controversialists based their high evaluation of the priesthood on a hierarchical view of the universe is not perhaps very surprising. What is surprising and does require some explanation is the way in which this view of the priesthood existed cheek-by-jowl with an equally positive evaluation of the ecclesiastial functions of secular authority. Again and again, in the lists of theological authorities cited by the controversialists against Luther, one finds the names of kings and emperors.[36] The

31 *Ibid.*, III, fol. 155ᵛ.
32 Fisher, *Defensio sacri sacerdotii*, col. 1248.
33 Marcello, *De authoritate*, fols 39ᵛ–40ʳ; Rhadinus, *Thome Rhadini Todeschi Placentini ord. pre. ad illustriss. et invictis. Principes et populos Germanie in Martinum Lutherum Wittenbergensem or. here. Nationis gloriam violantem: Oratio* (Leipzig, 1520), Hiʳ.
34 Clichtoveus, *Antilutherus*, 2, fols 57ʳ–8ʳ; Campester, *Heptacolon in Summam scripturae sacrilegae Martini Lutheri in Apologia eius contentam* (Paris, 1523), Giiiʳ.
35 Rhadinus, *Oratio*, Hiʳ. See also, for example, Clichtoveus, *Antilutherus*, 2, fols 55ᵛ, 57ʳ, 59ʳ⁻ᵛ; Powell, *Propugnaculum*, fol. 136; Dungersheim, *Multilocus de cocitata seditione ex dictis Lutheri recollectus* (No place, 1525), fol. 10ʳ.
36 Dietenberger, *Widerlegung des Lutherischen buchlins / da er schreibt von menschen leren zu meiden &c.* ([Strasbourg], 1524), Eiʳ; Cochlaeus, *Adversus cucullatum minotaurum Wittenbergensem. De*

Emperor Constantine's initiative in summoning and presiding at Nicaea (the first council of the post-apostolic era), and the Emperor Sigmund's at Constance (the 'German council') were held up as examples for modern Christian rulers much more by the Romanists than by the reformers, notwithstanding Luther's appeal in *An den christlichen Adel*. Certainly there was nothing unusual or innovative in Luther's call for a council convoked by the higher laity, despite Lateran V's very recent declaration that a general council could be summoned by no-one but the pope. And of course the right remained with respect to local councils. When in 1518 Duke Georg of Saxony requested the Leipzig theology faculty to arrange a debate between Luther and Eck to 'discover the truth', they replied without any discernible embarrassment (though with some tactical manoeuvring) that a debate would increase confusion whereas the duke, through his right of summoning a synod of local bishops, abbots, and university representatives, had within his own hands the power of settling the Luther affair once and for all.[37] Most significantly, it is remarkable that no hint of unease was expressed publicly when Georg and Henry VIII turned their hands to writing theological works against Luther. Instead, their fellow controversialists applauded the fact that princes nowadays defended the faith as much by the pen as by the sword.[38] This attribution of what might be called theological competence to secular authorities is all the more startling when one remembers that a constant theme of the Catholic literary response to Luther was that lay people should not be permitted to judge theological issues.[39]

The controversialists insisted on the supernatural character of the priesthood and its elevation above even the highest ranks of the laity. At

---

sacramentorum gratia iterum (Cologne, 1523), edited by J. Schweizer, CCath 3 (1920), p. 17; idem, *Glos und Comment auff den xiii. Artikel von rechtem Mess halten* (Strasbourg, 1523), Bii[r]–iii[r]; Blich, *Verderbe und Schade der Lande und Leuthen* (Leipzig, 1524), Ci[v]; Campester, *Heptacolon*, Eiii[v]. When Cochlaeus came to write his literary biography of Luther in 1547, it is significant that he chose to conclude it with the text of the Edict of Worms and not, for example, the papal bull of excommunication. See Cochlaeus, *Commentaria Iohannis Cochlaei, de actis et scriptis Martini Lutheri* (Mainz, 1549), pp. 327–39.

[37] See the letter from the faculty to the duke of 26 December 1518 (*Akten und Briefe zur Kirchenpolitik Herzog Georgs von Sachsen*, ed. F. Gess, 2 vols (Leipzig, 1905 & 1907), I, no. 63).

[38] See, for example, Ambrosius Pelargus's preface to Dietenberger's *De votis monasticis*, ai[v].

[39] On this see especially Emser, *De disputatione Lipsicensi* (1519), in CCath 4 (1921), p. 41; Murner, *Tütscher nation*, Fi[v]; Dietenberger, *Der leye. Obe der gelaub allein selig macht* (Strasbourg, 1524), Biii[v]–iv[r]; Cochlaeus, *Ein Christliche vermanung der heyligen stat Rom an das Teütschlandt yr Tochter im Christlichen glauben* ([Tübingen, 1924]), Fiv[r]; Fisher, *Adv. Babyl.*, cols 232–54.

the same time, they accorded Christian princes a role and a ministry that went far beyond the purely secular sphere. How are we to explain the coexistence of these two apparently opposing tendencies? Much can be put down to sheer opportunism. The replies to *An den christlichen Adel* show that Catholics were quite as capable as Luther of playing to the stalls and the royal box, as well as to the gallery. Nevertheless, this twofold emphasis was perfectly consistent with their belief in an essential unity which underlay all authority of whatever stripe. They considered, for instance, that the existence of monarchy as the oldest and purest form of secular rule was a sound argument for papal monarchy.[40] The Saxon controversialist Petrus Sylvius wrote a pamphlet (unfortunately never published) in which he argued that any Lutheran who held any public office whatsoever contradicted himself, for Lutheranism and *oberkeyt* were incompatible. 'Lutherans can no more stomach authority,' he wrote later, 'than they can eat fire.'[41] The controversialists also believed in the continuity of all forms of obedience, so that theological heresy and political insurrection were closely identified in their minds. Schism and civil war were simply two sides of the same coin, two manifestations of an essentially spiritual disorder, namely a lack of love.[42] The Peasants' Revolt, they recalled, had followed swiftly on the heels of Wycliffe's teaching, and the Bohemian heresy had ushered in the bloody Hussite wars.[43] Needless to say, when the Peasants' War broke out in 1524, the controversialists considered their warnings against Lutheranism entirely vindicated.

This view of the unity of spiritual and temporal authority allowed the controversialists to explain, in their own appeals to the German nobility, that in attacking one Luther was by definition attacking the other. Only the Italians Prierias, Marlianus, and Modestus, however, argued that this was because imperial power derived from papal power and that to staunch the source would stem the stream. The other controversialists regarded the two powers, if not as equal, then certainly as parallel. There was no question of competition—'the two swords do not clash', wrote

---

[40] For example, Modestus, *Oratio ad Carolem Caesarem* (Strasbourg, 1521), Aiii^v, and Sylvius, *Eyn Missive ader Sendbrieff an die Christliche Versammlunge und ssonderlich an die oberkeit Deutzscher Nation* (No place, 1525), Aiv^r.

[41] Sylvius, *Deutzscher Nation*, Cii^v.

[42] Dungersheim, *Multilocus*, fol. 7: 'Seditionis crimen contra charitatem directe pugnare'; fol. 26: 'Nihil rebuspublicis perniciosius seditione (presertim heretica) esse potest.' Behind this interpretation might have lain Aquinas' classification of the sin against charity into the sin of thought (*discordia*), of word (*contentio*) and of deed (*seditio*). See *Summa theologiae*, IIa IIae, qu. 39.

[43] Cochlaeus, *Christliche vermanung*, Eii^v–iv^r.

Murner.[44] The theory of parallel powers had a distinguished history. It was held by such apologists of royal supremacy as John of Paris and, for a time, Thomas Aquinas;[45] and it is arguable that it contributed to the development of Luther's doctrine of the two kingdoms. But it is extremely surprising that so many of Luther's Catholic opponents adopted it, because it was a theory explicitly condemned by the bull *Unam sanctam* of 1302, which had declared 'de necessitate salutis' the superiority of the clerical over the lay estate, and which had been resurrected as recently as 1516 as part of Leo X's campaign for control of the French church.[46]

It is, as we indicated earlier, sometimes possible to find common ground between Luther and even his staunchest Catholic opponents. They occasionally admitted that their opposition to some doctrines was based more on the manner in which Luther presented them, or on their untoward pastoral consequences, rather than on any fundamental disagreement. With the priesthood of all believers, however, very little basis for agreement can be detected. The doctrine was considered far too serious a threat by the defenders of the Church. But by no means all Luther's Catholic opponents were hostile to the notion of the equivalence of spiritual and temporal *authority*. Exercising a considerable degree of independence, they eschewed dogma in order to present a defence which was both more sensitive to the demands of controversial writing, and at the same time a truer reflection of the relative powers of Church and state at the outbreak of the Reformation.

Centre for Medieval and Renaissance Studies, Oxford

[44] Murner, *Tütscher nation*, Diii^v.
[45] See A. Gewirth, *Marsilius of Padua: The Defender of the Peace*, 2 vols (New York, 1951), 1: *Marsilius of Padua and Medieval Political Philosophy*, p. 9.
[46] For the text of the 1302 bull, see *Decretales*, 1245. It was revived by Leo X's bull *Pastor aeternus gregem*, 19 December 1516 (*Conciliorum Oecumenicorum Decreta*, eds J. Alberigo *et al.* (Bologna, 1973), esp. pp. 643, line 38 and 644, line 6).

CALVIN'S VIEW OF THE MINISTRY OF THE CHURCH*

by GEORGE YULE

CALVIN's view of the ministry is dependent on his view of the Church and his view of the Church is itself controlled by his Christological emphasis. This is not true of Scholastic Calvinism, which before the rise of liberal Protestantism dominated the Calvinist landscape, but is in fact a deviant son of Calvin. The shift was subtle and largely unconscious, so that those brought up in the atmosphere of Scholastic Calvinism felt some unease but could not clearly say why, like Thomas Boston the Scots Minister of Etherick who found he 'had no liking for the conditionality of grace' or Fraser of Brea who 'perceived that our divinity was much altered from what it was in the primitive reformers times.'[1]

The reason was that whereas for Calvin all doctrine was consciously controlled by his understanding of the person of Christ, for the Scholastic Calvinists doctrine was formulated by the exact verbal precepts and prescriptions of the Bible of which the doctrine of Christ was seen to be only one, though admittedly a major one. For Calvin, following Luther, the Bible mediated Christ directly, like the real presence of Christ in the eucharist, for Scholastic Calvinism the Bible was the book of divine truths and propositions. Protestant scholastics, like their mediaeval counterparts, erected a series of truths into a theological system which was equated with the Christian faith, but whereas the mediaeval theologians deduced these truths from the whole history of the Church, the Bible, the Fathers, the decrees of Councils, its traditional thought and practice, and what was revealed by the light of nature, Protestant scholastics said *sola scriptura* — the Bible alone was to be the source from which these truths were to be deduced. Both groups processed the data thus gained by means of Aristotle's logic to produce a highly integrated body of theological axioms. Aristotle's logic held a key place in both systems. Indeed Zanchius, one of the founding fathers of Protestant Scholasticism, claimed that God spoke through Aristotle. 'For this Aristotle,' he wrote, 'or rather God through

* My thanks are due to Professor James Torrance for many helpful insights regarding Calvin and worship.
[1] *Memoirs of the life of Fraser of Brea written by himself* (Aberdeen, 1843), 277–8.

Aristotle presents us with a most useful work, his *Sophistical Refutations*.'[2] By this method one arranged the teachings of the Bible into a series of propositions which then became the deposit of faith so that faith tended to become assent to the propositions of the entire Bible.

Calvin's view of *sola scriptura* was very different. 'We must read Scripture with the intention of finding Christ therein. If we turn aside from this end, however much trouble we take, we shall never attain the knowledge of the truth. We shall be wise without the wisdom of God.'[3] Christ alone is the word of God. The Bible is a mirror in which we see this Word reflected. The mirror is not the same thing as that which it reflects.[4] Calvin, though less so than Luther, realised that what makes the Bible inspired is its subject matter—the incarnate Lord, for it is the witness of apostle and prophet to Christ. Hence Luther could exclude certain books from the canon as they 'talk nothing of Christ'. Calvin believed that all books in fact did speak of Christ and therefore defended the *Song of Solomon* against Castellio because he said it gave an image of Christ and the Church. But he readily admitted that Scripture used the language of accommodation, like a mother using baby talk to a child, and that the apostles were so concerned with the meaning that they were not that particular about dates and chronology.[5] The purpose of the Bible argued Luther was not to give us information historical or scientific but to tell us of the grace of God.[6] The scholastic Protestants totally disagreed. Scripture gave us infallible data that was even more compelling than that derived from our senses or our experience and thus gave precise patterns for the whole life of the Church, so that one could read it off like a text book or if more complex, deduce it from prior deductions by means of a syllogism. So if certain ceremonies were not mentioned in the Bible or could not be logically deduced from it then they must not be used in worship. Calvin's view was different. 'Those ceremonies are permitted in the Church which show forth Christ and do not exclude him.'[7] It was a Christological and not a biblicist touchstone.

Calvin used the Apostles' Creed as the structure for his *Institutes* and

---

[2] Quoted J. P. Donnelly, 'Italian influences on the development of Calvinist Scholasticism', *The Sixteenth Century Journal*, 7 (1975), 85.

[3] *Corpus Reformatorum*, 47. 125.

[4] Calvin, *Institution of the Christian Religion* (henceforth *Institutes*), IV.8.5. See also W. Niesel, *The Theology of Calvin* (London, 1956), pp. 31–3.

[5] Calvin, *Commentary on St John's Gospel*, 3: 12.

[6] Commentary on Genesis, *Luther's Works*, American Ed——n 1, pp. 40–1.

[7] *Institutes*, IV.10.14.

this has obscured this Christological orientation of his whole work despite his many explicit statements. In his comment on Colossians I v. 12 he wrote 'This then is the only way of retaining as well as restoring true doctrine, to place Christ before the view just as he is, with all his blessings that his excellence may be fully perceived.'[8]

The famous lines with which he starts the *Institutes* that 'all true knowledge consists in knowledge of God and of ourselves'[9] is shown in the rest of the work to flow from the incarnation. As true God, Christ reveals the heart and mind of the Father; as true man he reveals man as he is meant to be. The structure of the Apostles' Creed imposed the Trinitarian nature of the Gospel on the structure of the *Institutes* but the whole thrust of the Christological controversies of the Early Church show that the doctrine of the Trinity flows from the incarnation, and Calvin stood in this tradition.

The central core of the *Institutes* is the latter half of book two and the beginning of book three. He summed up his section on the incarnation in a remarkable passage 'We see that all parts of salvation are comprehended in Christ (Acts 4 v. 12). We should take care therefore not to derive the least portion of it from anywhere else.'[10] Not only does Calvin here stress the fact that Christ took to Himself the consequences of our sin, 'if acquittal in his condemnation, ... if reconciliation in his descent into hell', but also, he equally stressed the fact of Christ's obedience on our behalf as man. He is our righteousness. 'If we seek any other gifts of the Spirit they will be found in his anointing.' 'In short since rich store of every kind of merit abounds in him, let us drink our fill from this fountain and no other.'[11] This line of understanding is developed especially in regard to worship.

Christ in his humanity is our high priest. He offered the sacrifice of his own body: he intercedes for his brethren, indeed 'he leads their songs'.[12] This common bond of our humanity means that 'although in ourselves polluted, we are priests in him'.[13] For just as the Jewish high priest entered the holy of holies with the names of the twelve tribes engraved on stones upon his shoulder, 'so that in the person of one man all entered the

---

[8] Calvin, *Commentary on Colossians*, I. 12.
[9] *Institutes*, I. I. I.
[10] *Ibid.*, II. 16. 9.
[11] *Ibid.* Notice how he has transformed the mediaeval doctrine of merit into a Christological statement.
[12] Calvin, *Commentary on Hebrews*, 5. 1–3, 6. 19.
[13] *Institutes*, II. 15. 6.

sanctuary together so our high priest has entered heaven not only for himself but for us'.[14]

This leads Calvin on to the central thrust of book three where he insists that all that Christ did for us would be of no avail unless the Spirit makes Christ present to us and unites us to Him.[15] The work of the Spirit is to create faith in us by means of the Word and Sacraments which unite us to Christ. The Christian hope is that we shall become in ourselves what we already are in Christ, but in the meantime we are led by the Spirit to a life of conformity with Christ, of dying to self and rising to the life of the citizens of heaven.[16] It is in this total Christological setting that Calvin understands the Church and its ministry.

He insisted that there was nothing new in this. When Calvin was temporarily forced into exile by the Genevans in 1539, Cardinal Sadolet, a reforming Catholic, urged the Genevans to return to Rome. When Calvin read his tract he replied immediately and denied all Sadolet's charges of heresy and schism. 'All we have attempted has been to renew the ancient face of the Church.'[17] This renewal was by means of the Christological undergirding of all the life of the Church, and this was to be done by the proclamation of the Word and the administration of the Sacraments by the ministry. Whereas Sadolet had defined the Church as that Body which always and everywhere had been directed by the Spirit of Christ Calvin replied

> What becomes of the Word of the Lord, that clearest of all marks, which the Lord himself in designating the Church so often commends to us? For seeing how dangerous it would be to boast of the Spirit without the Word, Christ declared that the Church is indeed governed by the Holy Spirit, but in order that this government might not be vague and unstable he bound it to the Word. For this reason Christ exclaims that those who are of God hear the Word of God, for his sheep are those who recognise the voice of their Shepherd ... For this reason the Spirit by the mouth of Paul declares (Eph. 2 v. 20) that the Church is built upon the foundation of the apostles and prophets.[18]

---

[14] *Com. on Hebrews*, 6. 19.
[15] *Institutes*, III. 1. 1.
[16] *Ibid.*, 1. 2.
[17] Calvin, 'Letter to Sadolet', in *Calvin's Theological Treatises*, ed. J. K. S. Reid, *Library of Christian Classics*, 22, p. 231.
[18] *Ibid.*, pp. 229–30.

And to strengthen his argument, throughout the work, he endeavours to show that the Reformed Churches conform more closely to the pattern of the early Church.

> I ask you to place before your eyes the ancient form of the Church as their writings prove it to be in the ages of Chrystostom and Basil among the Greeks and of Cyprian, Ambrose and Augustine among the Latins, and to contemplate that which now survives among yourselves.[19]

Calvin stresses the two traditional names for the Church, the Body of Christ and the Mother of the Faithful. Indeed he heads the first chapter of book four, on the Church, 'Of the true Church with which we strive to be at one since it is the mother of all the pious'. She is the mother 'because there is no other means of entry into life, except she should receive and bear us in her womb, feed us at her breast, and then preserve us under her guardianship and guidance until we have put off this mortal flesh.'[20] The means by which the Church nourishes us are the Word and Sacraments through the agency of the ministry. Calvin then argued that magnificent names were given to the Temple in the Old Testament, 'God's Rest', 'His Sanctuary', 'His Habitation' because that is where people heard of the grace of God from the priests.[21]

One of the most remarkable gifts of God to the human race is 'that He deigns to consecrate the mouths and tongues of men to his service making his own voice to be heard in them . . . so that it is foolishness to think that one can gain all that is necessary by private meditation . . .',[22] for Word and Sacrament embrace the whole Gospel. Forgiveness of sin for example is always a mark of the Church. The Keys are given to the Church to impart this blessing which is peculiar to the Church. And this blessing is dispensed by the Word and the Sacraments. As Luther remarked, when one falls into sin one returns to the promise of God given in Baptism and is forgiven.[23] But this is equally true of all other aspects of the Christian life, a growing into conformity with Christ, prayer, love for mankind. Hence the need for the ministry.

But its character is controlled by the fact that the Church is the Body of Christ in whose name and in whose character it stands before God the

---

[19] *Ibid.*, p. 231.
[20] *Institutes*, IV. 1. 4.
[21] 1. 5.
[22] *Ibid.*
[23] On the Babylonish Captivity of the Church, *Luther's Works*, 36.

Father. For in his humanity Christ is our high priest 'so that in him we might be priests offering prayers to the Father thanksgiving and all that we have through his intercession and mediation.'[24] That is, the whole Body of Christ forms the royal priesthood praising God on behalf of all mankind, confessing the sin of all mankind, interceding for the needs of all mankind. This is how Calvin views the priesthood of all believers, whereas the common view is that each individual can perform priestly functions. Consequently he uses the word minister or pastor rather than priest for the ordained ministry because their function is to enable the whole Body of Christ to fulfil its task of priesthood for all mankind.

For Calvin the only essential marks of the Church are the preaching of the Word and the administration of the Sacraments for these alone reveal the saving work of Christ completely. Bucer, Knox and all the Scholastic Calvinists added discipline as a third mark of the Church. Calvin admitted that discipline was very helpful but, nevertheless, 'When the preaching of the Gospel is reverently heard and the sacraments are not neglected, there for the time the face of the Church appears without deception or ambiguity.'[25] 'Even if defects creep into the administration of word and sacrament this ought not to alienate us from its communion.'[26] In this Calvin is completely at one with Luther. 'The Word itself, Baptism and the Lord's Supper are morning stars to which we ever turn out eyes as certain indications of the Sun of grace.'[27]

Following closely Paul's thought in Ephesians 4 Calvin sees the ministry as God's gift to the Church to build up the Church till it reaches a unity of faith, 'unto the measure of the stature of the fulness of Christ'.[28] To achieve this certain functions have to be performed, the essential one of which is this proclamation of the Word and the administration of the sacraments, for from this all else flows. By this means Christ rules in the Church by his grace and each member serves the other according to the gifts given by Christ.[29]

This was the essential work of the pastor or minister or bishops. (Calvin thought that the words were synonyms.[30]) Whereas the Biblical and Scholastic Calvinists from this premise then sought to construct from the

[24] 1536 edition of the *Institutes*, 1. 68.
[25] *Institutes*, IV. 1. 10.
[26] *Ibid.*, 1. 12.
[27] *WA* 42, p. 185.
[28] *Institutes*, IV. 1. 5.
[29] *C.R.* 10b; 52. 147. See also Niesel, *Theology of Calvin*, pp. 199 *seq*.
[30] *Institutes*, IV. 3. 5.

Bible the specific ministries that they thought could be found there, Calvin too went to the Bible but not by means of extrapolating specific offices but by seeing what functions had to be fulfilled by these ministries in order to ensure the Gospel of Christ was proclaimed and the Church built up in that faith.

Consequently Calvin is quite flexible about the form the function might take in the Church provided that it is performed. The function of doctor was there to ensure that the Church's doctrine was true to the Bible but in the last edition of the *Institutes* in one passage he speaks of doctors and pastors as one,[31] while in Geneva he simply took over the existing overseers of the poor and the sick as the deacons, whereas the Scholastic Calvinists in Britain insisted on creating a separate new order to follow the biblical precedent. Again where the Scholastics strongly condemned episcopacy as such Calvin wrote to the King of Poland allowing not only bishops but an archbishop provided the abuses of the system then present were not followed.[32]

In the first edition of the *Institutes* Calvin had only two orders of ministry, pastors and deacons, one to proclaim the Gospel the other to nurture the fruits of this proclamation. But after his stay in Strasbourg he developed the fourfold order which was embodied in Geneva in the Ecclesiastical Ordinances of 1541.

> There are four orders that our Lord instituted for the government of his Church: first the pastors, then the teachers, after them the elders and fourthly deacons. Therefore if we would have the Church well ordered and maintain it in its entirety we must observe that form of rule.[33]

In effect what this does is to break his former two orders each into two; teachers to ensure sound doctrine and to train future pastors; elders to govern the Church by pastoral care, and deacons specifically to care for those in need.

Bucer in Strasbourg had already instituted the office of elder and Calvin took it over. Calvin certainly conceived it as a pastoral office, for after the Ecclesiastical Ordinances of 1541 set out the types of misdemeanours of which the elders should take notice they conclude with, 'yet this should all be done with such moderation that there be no rigour

---

[31] *Ibid.*, 4. 1.
[32] *Letters of John Calvin*, ed. Bonnet (Philadelphia, 1858), 3, p. 111.
[33] 'Draft Ecclesiastical Ordinances', 1541. In *Calvin's Theological Treatises*, p. 58.

by which anyone may be injured, for even the corrections are only medicine for bringing back sinners to our Lord.'[34]

Certainly, as R. M. Kingdon has shown, the Consistory of elders had many of the characteristics of a family guidance bureau and the majority of cases dealt with family or neighbourhood quarrels, and most individuals brought before the Consistory were merely given an admonition, while the commonest penalty was exclusion from one Communion.[35]

There were also cases of people adhering to the old faith, of others who 'dogmatised against received doctrine', and of others who absented themselves from church. 'The Ordinances for the supervision of country churches' list such ethical issues as blasphemies, drunkenness, dissolute songs, games and dances, usury, brawling, and fornication,[36] while more serious crimes against civil order were both punished with excommunication and the offender sent to the civil magistrate to receive a civil punishment.

However right the intention to bring about a real amendment of life, the fact that this discipline was tied to exclusion from communion, partly in order to keep the sacrament from being profaned, led to moralism and legalism. Calvin saw much less clearly than Luther that we do not do God's will until we delight to do it. Consequently the Consistory was quite unable to deal with the basis of sin, and tended throughout its history in most countries to deal only with its public consequences, most commonly sexual misdemeanours, drunkenness and brawling, or those who broke specific laws of the Church such as the shopkeepers of Edinburgh who opened their stalls 'on the filthy feast of Yule'.[37] This issue was hotly debated in the Westminster Assembly and the Long Parliament. Whitelocke saw the problem when he said in Parliament that to debar sinners from communion meant that they were deprived of their greatest help to repentance.[38] The 'fencing of the Table', as it came to be called in Scotland, created serious pastoral problems and often caused tension and division in the local communities while it as frequently engendered despair or self-righteousness rather than repentance.

The office of deacon was primarily to assist and organize Christian compassion for the Church, for compassion was seen as an essential aspect

[34] *Calvin's Theological Treatises*, p. 71.
[35] R. M. Kingdon, 'Was the Protestant Reformation a Revolution: The Case of Geneva', *idem*, ed. *Transition and Revolution* (Minneapolis, 1974), pp. 53–107.
[36] *Calvin's Theological Treatises*, pp. 80–2.
[37] W. M. McMilla, *Worship of the Scots Reformed Church*, pp. 304–5.
[38] George Yule, *Puritans in Politics* (Sutton Courtnay, 1981), p. 347.

of 'growing into the mature manhood of Christ'. The Draft Ecclesiastical Ordinances of 1541 state 'There were always two kinds in the ancient Church, the one deputed to receive, dispense and hold goods for the poor . . ., the other to be kind and care for the sick and administer allowances to the poor. This custom we follow again now for we have procurators and hospitallers.'[39]

In his attempt to rethink this office of deacon Calvin differs both from the mediaeval practice and from the theory of the Scholastic Calvinists. He accused the Catholics of not having the order at all but only a pretence.

> It is however more than absurd for the papists to maintain that in their appointment of deacons they carry out Paul's instructions. For first why do they appoint deacons only to carry a chalice in processions to impress the ignorant with all sorts of ridiculous exhibitions? And they do not even keep to that for not a single man has been made deacon for the last five hundred years except with the intention that he should be promoted to the priesthood almost immediately. What shameless hypocrisy is it to boast of advancing to the higher rank, men who have ministered well as deacons when in fact they have never fulfilled one single duty of the diaconate.[40]

Calvin saw the office of deacon as assisting a part of the worship of the Church. The sacrifice of praise and thanksgiving which the sacrifice of Christ re-presented in the eucharist should call forth has its counterpart in care for 'one of the least of these my brethren' in the body of Christ as a continuation of the liturgy.[41] And it is significant that it could be a deacon who was to assist the minister in the communion service.[42] This care for those in need was emphasized further in that the Ordinances laid down the sick, the prisoners, and especially those in irons, should be regularly visited in order to be consoled.[43]

Calvin seems to have been indifferent as to whether the diaconate and also the eldership was a lay or clerical office. Not the Scholastics, for them both were clerical offices. Calvin's intention to rethink the whole idea of the ministry in the light of the incarnation was remarkable, and even though the actual results fall far short of the intention these results were far from negligible. The emphasis on the central nature of Word and

---

[39] *Calvin's Theological Treatises*, p. 64.
[40] Calvin, *Commentary on First Timothy*, 3. 13.
[41] Elsie McKee, *John Calvin on the Deacons and Liturgical Alms Giving*.
[42] *Calvin's Theological Treatises*, p. 67.
[43] *Ibid.*

sacrament led to far more people reading the Bible, receiving the sacraments and on occasion being edified by sermons.

The effect on civic leaders alone was enormous. On Sundays and Wednesdays many would hear expository sermons from Calvin himself in Geneva, as they did in Zurich from Zwingli and from numerous ministers on Sundays and at the weekly or monthly lectures in the market towns of Britain,[44] a tradition that continued right into the early years of this century. The effect of many Fast Sermons preached before the Long Parliament can be documented.[45] Nevertheless the Christological emphasis of Calvin in the hands of the Scholastic Calvinist preachers tended to slide back into an emphasis on legal repentance which in turn led to legalism and moralism of the eighteenth-century rationalist or to the importance of one's own experience for the evangelical.

Mount Waverley, Victoria

[44] Patrick Collinson, *The Religion of Protestants* (Oxford, 1982). See index *sub* Preaching, Sermons.
[45] George Yule, *Puritans in Politics*, pp. 106 *seq*.

RICHARD HOOKER ON THE LAWFUL
MINISTRY OF BISHOPS AND KINGS

by ARTHUR STEPHEN McGRADE

THE part of Hooker's *Of the Laws of Ecclesiastical Polity* most attractively relevant to the theme of this conference is Book V, the first spiritually constructive exposition of the religion of the *Book of Common Prayer*. Hooker's edifying account of the public duties of religion in the first seventy-five chapters of Book V and of the ordained ministry in the concluding six chapters can readily be appreciated today on its merits, leaving aside the fact that the religion of the Prayer Book was legally prescribed for all English Christians when Hooker wrote. It is on this currently unattractive fact of legal prescription that I want to concentrate, however, for it sets the historical context for the public devotional theology of Book V. To understand Hooker's justificatory account of this fact is to become clearer about an essential difference between what is going on today when people minister and are ministered to in accordance with Anglican religious forms and what Hooker, at least, held to be going on when these forms were used in the sixteenth century.

In attempting to show the 'lawfulness' of certain forms of coercive authority in matters of religion, Hooker perforce sought grounds of legitimacy outside the legal system he was defending. It would hence be natural in terms of current political theory to take Hooker's 'lawfulness' as a metaphor. We might then read him as trying to 'legitimate' the supreme power of the crown in the English Church in Book VIII of the *Laws* without ourselves much respecting the legal root sense of the term 'legitimate'. There are at least two good reasons, however, for bearing this root sense in mind when discussing Hooker. One is that Hooker's own distinctively rich idea of lawfulness might help us to see more clearly both the similarities and the differences among the various sorts of norms involved in any serious project of legitimation. Here the much admired survey of laws and their several kinds in general in Book I is a provocative resource for political theory as well as a literary classic.

A second reason for bearing in mind the legal ancestry of the term 'legitimation' when considering Hooker is that legality in the narrow sense was the chief characteristic Hooker sought to build into the political institutions whose lawfulness in the broader sense he had set out to establish. Hooker was a nomocrat. If he did not believe that episcopal and royal authority operating in accordance with detailed, communally endorsed positive law was the only defensible system of public power, he clearly preferred it to any other currently available, and he clearly wished to represent the Elizabethan establishment as just such a system. For Hooker, then, the ministry of bishops and kings was a lawful ministry in the broad sense of being theologically, morally, psychologically, and socially well grounded largely because it was lawful in the narrower, internal sense of an appropriately regulated, orderly operation. This was his conception of the Elizabethan fact of legal prescription in religion.

There is nothing novel in suggesting that Hooker, following a venerable English tradition, exalted the rule of law, but the point is no longer uncontroversial. Hooker's emphasis on law is liable to be overlooked or undervalued if his work is read simply as window-dressing for an essentially arbitrary power-structure, as seems implied in recent anti-hagiographical studies.[1] There is, however, a newly available body of manuscript material which significantly confirms the nomo-cratic or republican character of the *Laws*. This is what I want to report on here. The present paper is thus the corroboration of a cliché, but a contested cliché and one which may deserve corroborating anyway, on its merits.

Before considering the new material, we may do well to recall a few of the passages from Book VIII which support the traditional approving view:[2]

> The axiomes of our regall governement are these, *Lex facit Regem*. The *Kings* graunt of any favour made contrary to law is voyd. *Rex nihil potest, nisi quod jure potest* (VIII. 3. 3, K 2. 13; 3: 342).

> Wherefore in regard of *Ecclesiasticall* lawes we willingly embrace that of *Ambrose Imperator bonus intra Ecclesiam, non supra Ecclesiam est. Kings* have dominion to exercise in *Ecclesiasticall* causes but according to the lawes of the *Church* ... [F]or the received lawes and liberties of the

[1] W. D. J. Cargill Thompson, 'The Philosopher of the Politic Society: Richard Hooker as a Political Thinker', in W. Speed Hill, *Studies in Richard Hooker*, pp. 3–76; reprinted in Cargill Thompson, *Studies in the Reformation*, ed. C. W. Dugmore (London, 1980). Robert Eccleshall, 'Richard Hooker and the Peculiarities of the English: The Reception of the *Ecclesiastical Polity* in the Seventeenth and Eighteenth Centuries', *History of Political Thought*, 2 (1981), pp. 63–117.
[2] Parenthetical references are to the newly discovered autograph notes and to book, chapter, and section of the *Laws*, followed by volume and page of *The Folger Library Edition of the Works of Richard Hooker*, W. Speed Hill, general editor (Cambridge, Mass. and London, 1977–). Where the Folger numbering of sections within chapters differs from Keble's, both numbers are given, Keble's indicated with a K.

Church, the *King* hath supreme authoritie and power but against them none (VIII. 3. 3, K 2. 17; 3: 347).

[W]ith respect to the state and according to the nature of this Kingdome ... it standeth for an axiome ... *The King is major singulis universis minor* (VIII. 3. 2, K 2. 7; 3: 336–7).

The entire communitie giveth generall order by law how all thinges publiquely are to be done and the *King* as the head thereof the highest in authoritie over all causeth according to the same lawe every particular to be framed and ordered thereby (VIII. 8. 9, 3: 434).

To an American raised on John Locke and the division of the legislative from a supposedly subordinate executive power, this last passage is downright inspirational. To be sure, when it comes to religion, what 'the whole communitie' 'giveth order for' by law in the United States is that there shall be no established religion. Still, the notion that establishment by the whole community in law is what would make the enforcement of religion politically legitimate (not necessarily theologically correct) seems to me a happy one. Although, however, the distinctly republican side of Hooker's Anglicanism is well represented in this and other passages in the *Laws*, there is still room for uncertainty about its importance. After all, Hooker says other things about the crown's power which tend to exalt rather than subordinate it. Like earlier apologists for the supremacy, for example, he accepts Old Testament kingship as a model for the authority of English monarchs. It is indeed a *royal* supremacy that he defends in Book VIII. Furthermore, although his declaration that the king only has supreme power 'for' the 'received lawes ... of the *Church*' is a ringing one, he says very little about what the received laws of the Church in fact are. Finally, although he enunciates the principle that the king is 'less than' the community taken as a whole, his discussion at the end of Book VIII of the problem of correcting an erring supreme ruler leaves us with only the negative conclusion that a king is not subject to the ordinary processes of ecclesiastical discipline appropriate for the parishioners of a local church. But how, if at all, *is* one to correct a bad king? One would like to hear more on this question. More generally, one would welcome confirmation that the republican passages in the *Laws* are to be taken at least at face value.

A fair measure of such confirmation is provided in a batch of Hooker's working notes for Books VI and VIII of the *Laws* discovered among Archbishop Ussher's papers at Trinity College, Dublin in 1974 and published for the first time in volume 3 of the Folger edition of Hooker's works.[3] There are at least five ways in which this material accentuates Hooker's concern to establish the rule of law as an essential characteristic—indeed, *the* essential characteristic—of the regime he had set out to defend.

First, the notes largely *consist* of law—transcriptions by Hooker of more than a hundred passages from a daunting variety of legal sources: Bracton, the Roman civil law, the body of canon law, medieval English ecclesiastical law, the contemporary French jurisconsult René Choppin, Christopher Saint German, Sir Robert Brooke, and a group of Pythagorean treatises on law and justice from the Hellenistic period. All in all, impressive testimony to the seriousness with which this former Master of the Temple took law in the narrow sense of the term.[4]

A second way in which the Dublin notes emphasize the narrowly legal and republican aspect of Hooker's legitimation project is by redrawing the division between two important chapters of Book VIII in such a way as to highlight the role of law and community as *restraints* on 'supreme' royal power and to make less prominent the appeal to Old Testament monarchy as a model for early modern England. We can now see that Hooker intended to follow up his long discussion of 'the distinction of the church and the commonwealth in a christian kingdome' in chapter 1 of Book VIII[5] with a very short and pointed chapter saying what the power of ecclesiastical dominion is. This was in turn to be followed by another long chapter declaring by what right, after what sort, in what measure, by what rule, with what conveniency, and according unto what example or pattern Christian kings may have such dominion. In recent editions of Book VIII, the last item in the preceding list—'according unto what example or pattern'—has been printed as a separate chapter—chapter 3—while in all previous editions Hooker's involved discussions of the earlier topics listed were added on to his statement of what the power of dominion is. As a result, Hooker's resort to Old Testament kingship as a confirming example of the sort of power Christian rulers *may* have has sometimes been given the prominence appropriate to an independent

---

[3] Autograph Notes; 3, pp. 463–523. Hooker's notes for a response to the attack on his position on predestination in the *Christian Letter* of 1599 are printed on pp. 523–38 and also in 4, pp. 83–97, with commentary at 4, pp. 234–9.

[4] Comparatively few studies of Hooker consider him in a narrowly legal context. Exceptions are Paul Forte, 'Richard Hooker's Theory of Law', *Journal of Medieval and Renaissance Studies*, 12 (1982), pp. 133–53, and C. M. A. McCauliff, 'Law as a Principle of Reform: Reflections from Sixteenth-Century England', *Rutgers Law Review*, 40 (1988), pp. 429–65.

[5] Hooker considered this informative title for cap. 1 in his Autograph Notes, 3, p. 495.

principal argument. At the other end of this material, Hooker's incisive initial statement of the essential nature of supreme ecclesiastical power has been absorbed into his treatment of the right, the sort, etc. of a king's possession of such power. When that initial statement is given its proper, independent place, one notices with some surprise that fully a third of the chapter is devoted to three 'exceptions' to supreme ecclesiastical power (VIII. 2. 1, K 2. 3; 3: 332–3). No king is supreme in relation to God. Where the law gives dominion, the king has it from and according to law. Finally, while a king's power is greater than that of any part of the society he rules, it is not greater than the power of 'all the states' of the society conjoined. We are here offered a valuable hermeneutic clue to reading the rest of the book, for each of these qualifications or restraints on supposedly supreme power turns out to play an important role in subsequent parts of the argument. While the importance of one or another of these limitations of supremacy has previously been recognized, the recovery of Hooker's own division of chapters makes his republican intentions evident at the outset.

A third confirmation of Hooker's republicanism is provided by an uncharacteristically indignant comment on a passage he transcribed in the Dublin notes from Thomas Stapleton's *Principiorum Doctrinalium Fidei Demonstratio Methodica* of 1578. Stapleton was the most learned Roman Catholic controversialist of the later sixteenth century, but in Hooker's view he was guilty of a 'calumnious untruth' in imputing to the Elizabethan establishment the thesis that kings as such have supreme power in matters of religion (Autograph Notes, 3: 496–7). The correct view, according to Hooker, is that the 'original subject' of political power is the community and that communities are not logically required to grant their rulers any one kind or degree of power. This reflection on Stapleton in the Dublin notes is thus an early expression of the communitarian or conciliarist ideas evident in chapters 3 and 6 of Book VIII and in the Lockeian passage on the legislative authority of the whole community which I have quoted above.[6] Seen in direct relation to Stapleton, the contrast between the descending conception of political authority, which Hooker rejects, and the ascending conception, which he vigorously develops, is very clear.

The fourth and most striking way in which the Dublin notes fill out the picture of Hooker as an advocate of the rule of law is by revealing his intention to add a substantial discussion of English ecclesiastical law to his treatment of public spiritual discipline in Book VI. Working at least partly in response to a question raised by Edwin Sandys about the

[6] See above, p. 179.

distinction between secular and spiritual cases in the dual system of courts inherited from the medieval period,[7] Hooker collected relevant passages amounting to eighteen pages in the Folger edition from such sources as Bracton, Lyndwood's compilation of English synodal and archiepiscopal legislation, and the constitutions of the thirteenth-century papal legates Otho and Ottobono. He organized this material under four heads (Autograph Notes, 3: 471–90):

1 What causes particularly are spirituall.
2 The forme and maner of proceding in them.
3 The punishments necessary in spiritual processe.
4 The care which justice hath alwayes had to . . . uphold ecclesiast-icall jurisdiction and courts (Autograph Notes, 3: 472).

The body of ecclesiastical law Hooker planned to expound in Book VI was not, to be sure, markedly communal in origin. The legatine constitutions of Otho and Ottobono did not claim authority as being made by representatives of 'the entire communitie' in anything like a Lockeian sense of representation, nor were the people of England much involved in establishing the constitutions of the medieval synods of archbishops of Canterbury. Yet, whatever the origin of this legislation, Hooker must have intended to defend its current validity on the basis of its acceptance by the community. Such a defence would have given substance to the ringing but dangling endorsement of Ambrose we noted earlier, 'for the received lawes and liberties of the *Church*, the *King* hath supreme authoritie and power but against them none' (VIII. 3. 3, K 2. 17; 3: 347). A discussion in Book VI based on the working notes would have provided some specification of what the received laws of the Church actually were, and this would have meant, for Hooker, that the religious life of the nation was to that extent not subject to the personal wishes of those in power.

The fifth and final point in this series of republican evidences from the Dublin notes concerns the final chapter of Book VIII, Hooker's discussion of the crown's exemption from the ordinary processes of ecclesiastical censure. As it stands, the chapter is somewhat disappointing. In it Hooker explains away, as in various respects extraordinary, such incidents as Ambrose's excommunication of the emperor Theodosius the Great after

---

[7] Sandys was commenting on an early draft of Book VI of the *Laws*. His and George Cranmer's comments on this draft are published in vol. 3 of the Folger edition, pp. 107–40. Sandys's question is at pp. 130–2.

the massacre at Thessalonica. Now one may perfectly well agree that these incidents were extraordinary, but that makes it all the more pertinent to ask: what is to be done when one's rulers are extraordinarily malfeasant? The Dublin notes do not, alas, give a Hookerian solution to this problem, but they do confirm Hooker's intention, announced at the beginning of the chapter, to discuss the problem in some detail, giving arguments on both sides of the question, whether it is necessary that there be someone in every body politic exempt from all processes of legal correction. If he had fulfilled this intention on the scale suggested by the list of seven arguments for sovereign incorrigibility given in the notes (3: 503–4), he would not have solved this most radical of all problems in constitutional theory, but he would have raised the problem more forcefully than any of his compatriots and would have left it for the country to solve at a time when the practical urgency of the problem was not very great. Sadly, his statement of the issues, if he completed it, has not survived. Tragically, when the issues became urgent, they were not resolved short of civil war.

The surviving version of Book VIII was not published until 1648, nearly fifty years after Hooker's death. One cannot help wondering what effect this legitimation of an internally legitimate royal religious supremacy would have had on the conflicts over royal absolutism in that half-century, had it been available. But this is not the place for political speculation. Instead, I would like to conclude with a few words about the implications of Hooker's way of legitimating political authority for the theme of this conference, Christian ministry. What do Hooker's deepening of the traditional English emphasis on the rule of law and his location of ultimate legislative authority in the community imply for the ministry of bishops, the ministry of kings, and the ministry of Christians generally?

Hooker devoted an entire book of the *Laws* to the ministry of bishops. I do not think his account of episcopacy in Book VII has been well appreciated, but this is not the place to go into that, either. The point about episcopal ministry I would offer from the material discussed in this paper is simply that Hooker's planned attempt to reinvigorate the complex structure of traditional ecclesiastical law would have had a tendency to make the authority of ecclesiastics—including, but not only, bishops—both more effective and less authoritarian. There are many who would doubt that the system of church law Hooker meant to defend had the virtues he presumably planned to ascribe to it, but almost any system of justice, when consistently applied, lessens the extent to which the power exercised by some persons over others is a personal power. So I would suggest that Hooker's legalism was to some extent responsive to reformist outcries over the supposedly inevitable tyranny implicit in any hierarchically organized structure of ministry.

The obvious question to ask about the ministry of kings on Hooker's principles is: whose ministers are they? Hooker affirms the (more precisely, a) traditional medieval view of the crown as a power delegated by God, but curiously enough he brings this formula forward in a reference to Bracton, the source of his and Sir Edward Coke's favourite aphorisms about the king's subordination to law (VIII. 3. 1, K 2. 5; 3: 335). The king *is* God's minister on Hooker's principles, but only insofar as he operates lawfully. But further, when the whole community is the continuing, as well as the original, source of law, then the king can exercise ministerial power on God's behalf only insofar as he is empowered to do so by the community.

What, then, of the community? What sort of ministry does it have? What is the ministerial calling of all Christians in the context of Hooker's idea of lawfulness? This is a question which would reward fuller discussion. I believe that the proper basis for any such discussion would be a recognition of community itself as an exceptionally important part of human and Christian purpose for Hooker. I don't mean to suggest that Hooker wished to preserve a tranquil outward appearance of community at whatever individual spiritual cost, but I think that his very broad notion of church membership is a very important part of his overall position. As far as I know, Hooker does not directly discuss the mission of Christians to non-Christians, but within the bounds of Christendom, it seems fair to say, ministry for Hooker is not so much a work wrought by good Christians on the rest of us as it is a matter of living *with* one another as best we can, jointly seeking and accepting union with God through participation in Jesus Christ. This may strain some aspects of the traditional notion of ministry, but I think it captures an essential part of Hooker's own ministry as a legitimating agent for the English Church of his day.

University of Connecticut

SHEPHERDS, SHEEPDOGS, AND HIRELINGS: THE PASTORAL MINISTRY IN POST-REFORMATION ENGLAND

by PATRICK COLLINSON

I

THE categories of shepherd and hireling are conventional elements of what may be called biblical and ecclesiastical pastoral, the legacy of John's Gospel chapter 10 and the basis of a perennial polemical dichotomy. Preaching at Manchester in 1582 on a text redolent of arable husbandry (Luke 10 v. 2—'the harvest truly is great but the labourers are few') the vicar of Warrington strayed out of the cornfield into this pastoral vein: 'Wee must understand that our Savior speaketh not of false Hierlings but of true Pastoures, not of those which beare an ydle name and title of Pastoures.'[1] John 10 had inspired a literary motif running back to Chaucer and Langland which, in what Sir Philip Sidney called 'the old rustic language' of Spenser's *Shepheardes Calendar* (1579), revived in the May eclogue. 'Piers', a good (and, according to Spenser's commentator 'E.K.', protestant) pastor rebukes 'Palinode' (a papist, or at least a traditional clerical type) for condoning the Maytime sports of the country people, and in the person of Palinode all hirelings:

> Well is it seene, theyr sheepe bene not their owne,
> That letten them runne at randon alone.
> But they bene hyred for little pay
> Of other, that caren as little as they,
> What fallen the flocke, so they han the fleece,
> And get all the gayne, paying but a peece.

Long before the Reformation, it was a commonplace that there were two kinds of priests, good and bad. For hirelings in the post-Reformation Church read double-beneficed men, non-residents, scandalous ministers and, above all, non-preachers.[2] We shall not assume that two clearly cut categories really existed, only that they made a convenient rhetorical and

---

[1] Simon Harward, *Two godlie and learned sermons, preached at Manchester in Lancashire* (London, 1582), Sig. Ciiij.

[2] See the categories employed in the puritan 'Survey of the Ministry' carried out in various counties in 1584 and 1586. (*The Seconde Parte of a Register*, ed. Albert Peel (Cambridge, 1915), pp. 88–184).

polemical device. Robert Carr, an Elizabethan curate of Maidstone, was variously esteemed according to some inconsistent evidence given under oath, in court. Some had seen him leaving the pub the worse for wear and testified that he was a gamester who played at tables for his dinner or the price of a pint of wine, using 'hot and lowd speaches touching misreckoning', that once when he had gone from the sign of the Star to the King's Meadow to play at bowls he had been too drunk to stand and cast his bowl: a hireling if ever there was one. But others reported that Mr Carr was of good name and fame for both doctrine and living, and 'a good preacher'. Mr Clark, minister of a Romney Marsh parish, was sorely abused by one of his parishioners who railed on him, accusing him of coming in at the window and starving souls. That is evidence of one layman's familiarity with John 10, where the hireling climbs up 'some other way'; but not necessarily of Mr Clark's character and professional standing, since the man who defamed him had been disappointed in failing to secure a profitable lease of some tithes.[3]

Our subject is that portion of the ministry conventionally deemed to be not only good but 'godly', that is, the 'godly preaching ministry', a dominant and even normative model in the post-Reformation Church of England. By the 1570s it was usual for Kentish clergy to call themselves 'minister and preacher of the word', while in Surrey 'minister of the word' was the style used in almost all clergy wills by 1600.[4] The common currency of these terms accompanied the creeping 'graduatisation' of the parish clergy, the process of converting it into a more or less learned profession described by Dr Rosemary O'Day.[5] A secondary consequence of this development was to convert Puritanism from a stridently alien and minority tendency into the dominant religious culture of the Jacobean Church.[6] Dr Helen Hajzyk found that in early seventeenth-century Lincolnshire those professionally competent parsons who set themselves against the godly model, on some such ideological basis as the ideas of Richard Hooker or 'Arminianism', made up a tiny minority of scarcely

---

[3] Cathedral Archives and Library Canterbury (hereafter CALC), MSS X. 11. 2, fols 218–28, X. 11. 9, fol. 103.

[4] Patrick Collinson, 'Cranbrook and the Fletchers: Popular and Unpopular Religion in the Kentish Weald', in Collinson, *Godly People: Essays on English Protestantism and Puritanism* (London, 1983), p. 415; R. A. Christophers, 'Social and Educational Background of the Surrey Clergy, 1520–1620' (unpublished London PhD. thesis, 1975), pp. 86–7.

[5] Rosemary O'Day, *The English Clergy: the Emergence and Consolidation of a Profession 1558–1642* (Leicester, 1979).

[6] Patrick Collinson, *The Religion of Protestants: the Church in English Society 1559–1625* (Oxford, 1982).

half a dozen.[7] So this is some indication of what we shall understand by 'shepherd'.

The further difference implied in my title between shepherd and sheepdog is less canonical, if only on account of certain basic differences in the practice of animal husbandry between the biblical Near East and the Christian West. But it was present in the Church nevertheless, as a tension between pastoral care and a coercive discipline with punitive overtones. When Martin Luther defined the Church as the sheep who hear their shepherd's whistle[8] this was an echo of Psalm 23, where the flock is not driven but led. The Old and New Testaments are silent on the subject of sheepdogs. So when protestant controversialists sharpened their pens against the Romish Wolf who menaces the sheep and from whose approach the careless hireling flees, their pastoral borrowed from the more secular metaphors of the hunting field.[9] But Isaiah 56 v. 10 complains of dumb dogs that cannot bark, a text which was often invoked in the denunciation of non-preaching hirelings. The text presumably refers to watchdogs. But the function of sheepdogs too, in pastoral literature, was to bark in urgent warning at the approach of the wolf. The funerary brass of Bishop Henry Robinson of Carlisle, designed in about 1610 by Richard Haydocke, shows such a dog standing stoutly between the wolf and the flock which he refuses to desert, clearly the sheep's faithful friend.[10] And in the September eclogue of *The Shepheardes Calender* we meet Roffyn's vigilant and vocal Lowder: 'Never had a shepheard so kene a kurre, / That watcheth, and if but a leafe sturre.' 'Roffyn' was evidently meant for Spenser's employer, Bishop Young of Rochester. Perhaps

---

[7] Helena Hajzyk, 'The Church in Lincolnshire c.1595–c.1640' (unpublished Cambridge PhD. thesis, 1980), pp. 301–2. One of this minority, George Buddle, published *A short and plaine discourse fully containing the whole doctrine of evangelicall fastes* (London, 1609), a not conspicuously evangelical work which is concerned with fasting at Lent and other appropriate seasons of the Kalender, and which pays tribute to 'that good *Hooker*', 'worthy *Hooker*' (Sigs. A2ᵛ–3).

[8] *Luther's Meditations on the Gospels*, ed. Roland H. Bainton (London, 1963), pp. 98–9. Luther was preaching on John 10 vv. 1–18.

[9] (William Turner and John Bale), *The huntyng and fynding out of the romyshe foxe* (Basyll, 1543, i.e. Antwerp, 1544); William Turner, *The huntyng of the Romyshe vuolfe* (Emden, 1555(?)); (William Turner), *The hunting of the fox and the wolfe, because they make havocke of the sheepe of Christ* (London, 1565). Instructing the people that it was not for them to decide whether or not to deliver the fleece (rents, tithes and other duties) to their masters, Thomas Lever said: 'It is magistrates dutyes, to consyder and note, whether they be theeves, or shepheardes, dogges, or wolfes that taketh the fleese.' (*A sermon preached before the kynges maiestie* (1550), ed. E. Arber, *Thomas Lever, M.A., Sermons*, English Reprints (London, 1870), p. 86.)

[10] For Haydocke, see Karl Josef Höltgen, 'The Reformation of Images and Some Jacobean Writers on Art', in *Functions of Literature: Essays Presented to Erwin Wolff on his Sixtieth Birthday* (Tübingen, 1984), pp. 138–46; Lucy Gent, *Picture and Poetry 1560–1620* (London, 1981).

'Lowder' was his chancellor, or generally symbolic of the corrective, even punitive apparatus of the ecclesiastical courts.

Such 'keen curs' 'with wide open throte' remind us that the pastoral ministry could itself be intrusively aggressive as well as protective. Addressing his fellow clergy in Somerset in 1615, Samuel Crooke insisted that it was their proper role as ministers to preside over a 'reformation of manners' (an early use of an expression which was to have a great future), to 'rise up first in the Lord's quarrel', attacking 'the troops of armed and audacious enemies, I meane sinners'. Here were the beginnings of that new symbiosis of spiritual and secular government summed up in the slogan 'magistracy and ministry' and celebrated by Samuel Ward of Ipswich when he spoke of 'these two opticke peeces', 'guardians and tutors of the rest'. Another preacher invoked the sword of the magistracy and the bow of the ministry.[11]

However we cannot state it as a simple and exhaustive fact that the ministry became in this period a crudely coercive instrument of so-called 'social control', all bark and bite. The formal record of the church courts gives one impression, the stray correspondence which accompanied court proceedings but survives more scantily, sometimes stuck between the leaves of act books, another. In one such note Robert Abbot of Cranbrook asked the court at Canterbury to spare one of his more timid parishioners the trauma of public penance: 'I would willingly winne him by more gentle courses if I may.'[12] And the parsons of the twin parishes of Toynton in Rutland wrote to ask that a poor labourer might be relieved of his formal excommunication: 'Who is so pore that he is not able eyther to paye the charges or sustaine the cost that he shall be at in the iourney.'[13] In Durham diocese the clergy were presumably no slower than elsewhere to condemn incontinence. But at Hurworth the rector took the lead in organizing public relief for the mother of a bastard, while in Durham city the curates regularly stood as godfathers to illegitimate children.[14]

[11] Samuel Crooke, *The ministeriall husbandry and building* (London, 1615), Sigs. A2ᵛ–3; Samuel Ward, *Jethros Iustice of Peace* (London, 1618), Sig. A3ᵛ; Alexander Grosse, *Deaths deliverance and Eliahs fiery chariot* (London, 1632), p. 24.

[12] Collinson, 'Cranbrook and the Fletchers', p. 427.

[13] Francis Parker, rector of Toynton St Peter and Lawrence Freeman, rector of Toynton All Saints (to the surrogate at Stamford?), c.1607, Lincoln Archives Office, MS COR/M/2, no. 32.

[14] Jane Freeman, 'The Parish Ministry in the Diocese of Durham, c.1570–1640' (unpublished Durham PhD. thesis, 1979), p. 387.

II

So much for shepherds, hirelings, and sheepdogs, the first and ornamental part of my title. What follows takes a more direct path to the subject, but not a very hopeful one, since I shall propose that it is more difficult to write about the pastoral ministry in this period than at almost any other time in the history of the English Church and churches, whether medieval or modern. And that is because of a credibility gap standing between what the ministry was supposed to have consisted of according to nearly all public discussion of the matter at the time and what we know, or may think that we know, it must really have entailed, although that reality is seen through a glass, somewhat darkly. To anticipate much of what follows: public and what we may call abstracted accounts of the ministry in the later sixteenth and early seventeenth centuries (the period in question is roughly 1570 to 1640) were restricted to a remarkable extent to one function and one function only, that of preaching, or preaching and catechizing: a bias built into these sources themselves, since often they consist of sermons delivered, for example, at ordinations, or prove as books to have been derived from courses of sermons. Sometimes contemporary commentators, especially those reacting against the prevalent Calvinism of the English Church in a more or less Arminian direction, objected to this unbalanced obsession with the pulpit, as if the human body had been reduced to a single organ and that organ the ear. Yet it is sufficiently remarkable that those who insisted that prayer rather than preaching was what the ministry was about should have been so many lone voices crying in the wind. I doubt whether Matthew 21 v. 13 ('mine house shall be called the house of prayer') was much preached upon between 1598, when John Howson took it as his text at Paul's Cross, and 1633, when Walter Balcanquall handled it in the presence of Charles I and asked: can there be too much preaching? 'Yes, there may be too much of any thing.'[15] But where were these and similar complaints expressed? In sermons.

Of course we know that the life of a clergyman, even if he called himself 'preacher of the word', consisted of more than preaching. In an often quoted account of his burdens, John Favour, vicar of Halifax, explained that his controversial writings were squeezed into a routine which otherwise included not only preaching on Sundays and lecturing on every other

---

[15] John Howson, *A second sermon, preached at Paules Crosse, the 21. of May, 1598* (London, 1598); Walter Balcanquall, *The honour of christian churches; and the necessitie of frequenting of divine service and publike prayers in them* (London, 1633), p. 23.

day of the week but also 'exercising justice in the commonwealth' and the 'practising of Physick and Chirurgerie'.[16] There was also a living to be made, collecting tithe and sometimes suing for it, working the glebe and seeking out those supplementary pieces of by-employment and enterprise which earned Ralph Josselin a little more than his 'living' and which made the difference between Micawberish misery and happiness.[17] To dwell only on those ways of spending time which may be deemed professional: we know that they included above all the conduct of common prayer and the administration of the sacraments, weddings, churching women, baptizing babies, catechizing children, visiting the sick, burying the dead, reproving the wicked and comforting bruised consciences. The minister had a role to play with other parish officers in reporting offences and offenders to higher authority, administering and certifying acts of penance, denouncing excommunicates. He and the material resources at his disposal were involved in parochial charity. Time was spent in study (the night time in Favour's case) and in the company of other clergy, for the purpose of what is now called in universities career development.

One may well imagine that of all these many activities the most significant in the estimation of the laity had to do with the occasional offices, which in anthropological language is to say those rites of passage which are the punctuation marks of all our life-cycles. These occasions, invested as they were with the inevitability of life and death and the capacity to make and break, resolve and dissolve the bonds of human society, brought the parish clergy into the most meaningful and certainly the most earthbound of their involvements with their flocks. These offices, as well as the sacramental office of ministering communion, interlocked with what John Bossy has identified as the primary social task entrusted to the parish priest or his equivalent throughout the rural parishes of Europe between the fourteenth and seventeenth centuries, that of a settler of conflicts, the principal instrument of what Bossy has elsewhere called the social miracle.[18]

Many of these scenes from clerical life are under-explored, some are unexplored and a few are almost unexplorable. Almost to excess we have

---

[16] John Favour, *Antiquitie triumphing over novelties* (London, 1619), Epistle.

[17] *The Diary of Ralph Josselin 1616–1683*, ed. Alan Macfarlane (Oxford, 1976); Alan Macfarlane, *The Family Life of Ralph Josselin A Seventeenth-Century Clergyman: an Essay in Historical Anthropology* (Cambridge, 1970).

[18] John Bossy, 'Blood and Baptism: Community and Christianity in Western Europe from the Fourteenth to the Sixteenth Centuries', *SCH* 10, p. 139; John Bossy, *Christianity in the West 1400–1700* (Oxford, 1985), chapter 4.

studied the formation of the clergy, their recruitment through the multiple processes of higher education, ordination, patronage, and preferment, their incomes and livelihood, their quality in terms of residence, moral behaviour and, above all, capacity to preach: which makes the point that academic studies of the post-Reformation clergy reflect the limited concerns of contemporary comment on the subject, as well as the original sources which, as it were, deep-freeze those concerns. These studies embody the static qualities and methods of administrative and prosopographical history and they tell us very little about activity, what the clergy did in a day, a week, or a year. So from a very substantial body of scholarly literature we do not learn about such matters as whether baptism was administered (as the Prayer Book directs) in a congregational context, at the time of common prayer, or more privately at other times, and at which times; whether the clergy visited the sick and dying according to commonly recognized rules and at prescribed times, and what rules and times; or how their pastoral visits to other parishioners interacted with habits and rhythms of hospitality and according to what social conventions; and what, in the absence of a sacramental economy of supreme unction and auricular confession, was said on such occasions. Would the threatened visit of the minister lead to an onslaught on house-hold dirt, as in modern Scotland? I have already had my say elsewhere about the failure of historians to consider the English clergy in this period as a social and collegiate group or 'tribe' (to use a contemporary expression), sharing each other's company not only at synods and what George Herbert called 'clergy councels', but at combination lectures, funeral sermons and the concomitant dinners which invariably accompanied these events; or simply over business at market or travelling to and from market. It was emphatically not the case that every parish was a desert island and its incumbent Robinson Crusoe in a Geneva gown.[19]

Some of the neglected corners of the clerical life will not remain in shadow for much longer. Dr Ralph Houlbrooke and Mr Christopher Marsh are about to tell us only a little less about the terminal pastoral ministry than Professor McManners knows about deathbeds in eighteenth-century France.[20] Did ministers attend the dying to minister

---

[19] See my *Religion of Protestants*, pp. 114–30. See also my 'Lectures by Combination: Structures and Characteristics of Church Life in 17th-Century England', in *Godly People*, pp. 467–98 and Ann Hughes, 'Thomas Dugard and his Circle in the 1630s—a "Parliamentary-Puritan" Connexion?', *HJ* 29 (1986), pp. 771–93.

[20] J. McManners, *Death and the Enlightenment: Changing Attitudes to Death in Eighteenth-Century France* (Oxford, 1981), chapter 8. I am indebted to Dr Houlbrooke for an unpublished

the sacrament, or to pray, or to exhort? or to write the will? And was exhortation significantly related to will-making, and with what motives? We shall soon know.

Other subjects are capable of recovery from sources which are still too little used, but which are also somewhat limited and deceptive in their utility. The occasional offices are illuminated from the church courts both by instance causes between parties and by office causes, which is to say, quasi-criminal prosecutions. Cases detailing a state of hostility between parson and parishioners contain the bias of untypicality which made them criminal, or actionable, in the first place. But normality can sometimes be inferred from abnormality. The vicar of Selling in Kent offended when he conducted the ceremony of 'churching' from his own seat without calling the woman who was to give thanks up to the communion table. The Prayer Book rubric will tell us that that is what he should have done, for it directs the women to kneel 'in some convenient place nigh unto the place where the table standeth', with the vicar standing by. But only the kind of evidence given in this case informs us that in this parish at least churchings were conducted immediately after morning prayer. When the vicar of Wye refused to church women who came to the ceremony wearing kerchiefs 'as the custome hath bene in tymes past', when failed to meet the dead corpse at the church gate or stile, and when he remained seated throughout the marriage service except to rise to ask who gave the bride in marriage, failing to put the ring on her finger, we can infer normal practice which may not be otherwise recorded. The last detail, for example, confirms that marriages took place, in this parish at least, inside the church (the rubric requiring that 'the persons to be married shall come into the body of the church') and not, as we sometimes assume to have been the case, at the church door.[21]

But depositions in matrimonial causes usually concern marriages which failed to take place, and so they tell us less about weddings, when the minister was present, than about betrothals, from which he was normally absent.[22] Actionable slander not infrequently happened around

---

seminar paper on deathbeds, part of a study in progress on death in early modern England; and to Mr Christopher Marsh of Churchill College, Cambridge for sight of a so far unpublished paper on will-making.

[21] CALC, MSS X. 10. 19, fols 229ᵛ–44ᵛ, X. 11. 1, fols 225ᵛ–31ᵛ.

[22] This reflects a mass of evidence in the series of deposition books from the Canterbury courts in CALC. This material has been extensively investigated in work so far unpublished by Miss Diana O'Hara.

a child-bed, among a group of gossips, not at christenings, which women, mothers at least, seem not to have attended. It was an unexpected bonus for the historian when the tittle-tattle at a confinement in Canterbury in 1579 turned to the subject of the vicar of St George's, Mr Saunders, and to the offence which he had occasioned by rebuking the women of the parish for taking their prayer books with them to church in order to follow the service in the somewhat private manner of the old religion.[23] These sources often reveal the parson in Professor Bossy's role of peace-making among quarrelsome neighbours, sitting, as it might be, in a great seat in the church or even on an alebench. But such episodes appear as snapshots, frozen in a moment of time. Outside the record left by a very few diarists it is difficult to reconstruct regular rhythms of activity, or to answer the question once put by a child within my hearing of a certain rhinoceros in the Zoo: 'But what does he do *all day?*'

Yet it is unlikely that these rhythms were a matter of idiosyncratic whim or circumstance. Social pressures, collegial and professional, tended towards a regularity of practice. The Dedham ministers, meeting in monthly conference on the Suffolk-Essex border in the 1580s, sought a common mind on such matters as 'the right use of the lordes daie', the baptism of children born to pregnant brides, and whether all their parishes should administer communion on the same day. Richard Parker, vicar of Dedham and clerk of the conference, wanted to know 'whether a pastor were bound by virtue of his office to visit every particular family in his charge notwithstanding his public teaching; so that if he do it not he omittes a duty'. In response he received a variety of conflicting advice. Yet the point is that the Dedham ministers in principle accepted that they should follow a more or less consistent practice, even if this was made up of case law of their own devising.[24] Much standard pastoral technique must have been acquired in the informal apprenticeship schemes or mini-seminaries conducted in their households by such celebrated divines and preachers as Bernard Gilpin, Richard Greenham, John Cotton, and Richard Blackerby.[25] But whatever Elizabethan and Jacobean clerics learned from their colleagues or mentors it was not a lore recorded in instructive manuals for the ministry since there were no such manuals, in stark contrast to the fourteenth and fifteenth centuries when there was

---

[23] CALC, MS X. 10. 17, fols. 185-8^r.

[24] *The Presbyterian Movement in the Reign of Queen Elizabeth as Illustrated by the Minute Book of the Dedham Classis, 1582-1589*, ed. R. G. Usher, *C3Ser* 8 (1905), pp. 27, 29, 39, 41, 47, 48, 49-50, 55-6, 71, 72, 73.

[25] This is still a neglected topic. But see my *Religion of Protestants*, pp. 118-19.

an abundance of more or less technical literature bearing such titles as *Oculus Sacerdotis* and the related *Pupilla Oculi*, the *Memoriale Presbiterorum* and John Mirk's *Instructiones*, which remained in print up to the 1530s.[26]

III

It is an'exaggeration to say that no such written advice was supplied to the post-Reformation clergy. There was an Elizabethan and Jacobean literature of exhortation on the ministerial office which bears the same sort of relation to the real circumstances of clerical life as domestic conduct literature, books like Gouge's *Of domesticall duties* or Whateley's *Bride bush*, seems to have borne to marriage and parenthood in the same period.[27] But if anything the scene set by these texts is rather less satisfactory, since Gouge and Whateley dealt with many aspects of family life and in principle with the whole of it, whereas books which profess to be about the ministry have nothing to say about most aspects of their subject, as viewed with any descriptive objectivity. So we can say that the first great age of print saw less matter published on many facets of this subject (of all subjects) than on bee-keeping, or the management of great horses, or the husbandry of hops.

So far I have taken up a prejudicial position against such titles as John Holme's *The burthen of the ministerie* (1592), William Perkins's *Of the calling of the ministerie* (1605), Samuel Crooke's *The ministeriall husbandry and building* (1615), or George Downame's sermon of 1608, *Commending the ministerie*. But let us by all means hear what these teachers have to say. Downame declares that 'the principall burden and chiefe worke of the Ministery . . . is the preaching, that is the expounding and applying of the word to the diverse uses of doctrine, confutation, instruction and reproofe.' So far he says no more than the Council of Trent which defined preaching as '*munus praecipuum*'. But Downame comes close to making it *munus solum*. On the subject of 'the Leiturgie or publike service of God in the Congregation', he found space for just 165 words; on the administra-

---

26 W. A. Pantin, *The English Church in the Fourteenth Century* (Cambridge, 1955), chapter 9, 'Manuals of Instruction for Parish Priests'; see above, pp. 00–00.

27 Patrick Collinson, 'The Protestant Family' in my *The Birthpangs of Protestant England: Religious and Cultural Change in the Sixteenth and Seventeenth Centuries* (London, 1988); Kathleen M. Davies, 'Continuity and Change in Literary Advice on Marriage', in *Marriage and Society: Studies in the Social History of Marriage*, ed. R. B. Outhwaite (London, 1981), pp. 58–80.

tion of the sacraments, for 140 words.[28] And on other duties there were no words at all. Charles Richardson, preacher at St Katherine's by the Tower, laid down in *A workeman that needeth not to be ashamed . . . A sermon describing the duty of a godly minister* (1616) that the function consisted first in private study, second in frequent prayer, and third 'in diligent preaching of God's word'. Only the last of these was a public action and no other public action was mentioned.[29]

Other treatments of the subject are indicative of their contents by their very titles: for example, Stephen Egerton's *The boring of the ear* (1623) and Samuel Hieron's university discourse *The spiritual fishing* (1618), which contains this metaphorical conceit, worthy of Archdeacon Paley himself: 'For as the fishes skippe and play and take their pleasure in the sea, and are unwillingly taken in the net, and labour to get out, and being in the boate would faine, if they could, leape backe into the sea; so naturally we take pleasure in our sinfull wayes'; it being God's contrary purpose 'by man to catch man, and by his ministerie to bring soules into his kingdome.' 'Fishes do die if they be taken; wee can not escape eternall death if we be not caught.'[30] The argument for a preaching ministry consisted in the stark fact that there was no salvation to be had without it. Downame declares: 'The necessitie is that without it ordinarily men cannot attain to salvation, no nor yet to any degree of salvation.' So Edward Dering spoke exaltedly of 'the minister by whom the people do beleeve'.[31] This reminds us that the difference between the pre- and post-Reformation churches lay not so much in the emphasis put upon preaching as in its motive and object. William of Pagula told fourteenth-century priests that 'all their work should be in preaching and teaching', but not because that was the only way that souls could be redeemed.[32]

One of the most substantial treatments of the ministry published within our period was *The faithfull shepherd* by Richard Bernard, some time a radical Puritan plucked back from the brink of Separatism and

---

[28] George Downame, *Two sermons, the one commending the ministerie in generall: the other defending the office of bishops in particular* (London, 1608), pp. 17–18, 25–6, 35–6.

[29] Charles Richardson, *A workeman that needeth not to be ashamed: or the faithfull steward of Gods house. A sermon describing the duety of a godly minister, both in his doctrine and in his life* (London, 1616), p. 12.

[30] Samuel Hieron, *The spirituall fishing. A sermon preached in Cambridge* (London, 1618), pp. 14–16, 22. See also Jerome Phillips, *The fisher-man. A sermon preached at a synode held at Southwell in Nottinghamshire* (London, 1623).

[31] Downame, *Two sermons*, p. 27; Dering quoted in Patrick Collinson, 'A Mirror of Elizabethan Puritanism: The Life and Letters of "Godly Master Dering"', in *Godly People*, p. 299.

[32] Pantin, *The English Church in the Fourteenth Century*, pp. 198–9.

transported by the great and the good of the Jacobean Church from Nottinghamshire to Batcombe in Somerset.[33] An outsider to this discussion might suppose that a book 355 pages in length and with such a title, written for the benefit of ordinands, 'to further young divines in the studie of divinitie', might deal in a fully-rounded fashion with a whole range of professional and practical skills. Not so. After some preliminary, defensive discussion of the ministry as a worthy calling which gentlemen ought not to despise, distinguishing between the worthy and the unworthy who secured livings 'not to feed Christes flock but only to maintaine themselves with the fleece', the entire contents were devoted to the minister as preacher. Chapter two 'of a mans fitness to the ministerie' proves to be about his fitness for the pulpit: 'It is fit that there be a comely bodily presence of a Minister, standing up in the face of the Congregation, and in the place of God ... a comely countenance, sober, grave, modest, ... a seemly gesture, stable and upright.' There is a long taxonomical chapter dealing with pastoral sociology and psychology and distinguishing between six kinds of people in a typical congregation. But they are defined exclusively in respect of their various responses to the word preached. Book Three has for its subject 'The Public Assembly', but includes nothing about the liturgy and sacraments, or rather only this: 'The Minister and man of God well prepared, the godly order of Divine Service, so called, as it is by the Church appoynted, without giving of offence observed, and as the custome is, after a Psalm sung; then may he ascend up into the Pulpit.' Once there we reach Book Four, 'The Method to be Observed in Preaching', which runs to 200 pages, or almost two-thirds of the entire text.[34] If Bernard's treatise be taken as representative of early seventeenth-century treatments of its subject this literature contrasts not only with the pastoral science associated with what may be called the seminarian approach to priesthood and ministry in more recent times but with what was available for the instruction of apprentice priests up to the 1530s. And what is more, as an ideal it must surely have conflicted with much early seventeenth-century reality.

The exception which may seem to prove the rule is George Herbert's *Priest to the Temple*, the book more familiarly known from its sub-title as *The Countrey Parson*. Here we find distinct chapters on 'The Parson's

---

[33] Collinson, *Religion of Protestants*, pp. 85–6, 133–4.
[34] Richard Bernard, *The faithfull shepherd: wholy in a manner transposed and made anew, and very much inlarged both with precepts and examples, to further young divines in the studie of divinitie. With the shepherds practise in the end* (London, 1621), pp. 3, 35–6, 98 *seq*, 131–2, 159–355.

Charity' and 'The Parson in Circuit', that is, as parochial visitor. 'The Countrey Parson upon the afternoons in the weekdays, takes occasion sometimes to visite in person, now one quarter of his Parish, now another', for there he finds his flock 'most naturally as they are, wallowing in the midst of their affairs'. Sunday afternoons were to be spent 'either in reconciling neighbours that are at variance, or in visiting the sick, or in exhortations to some of his flock by themselves.' Further passages follow on 'The Parson Comforting', 'The Parson in Sacraments', 'The Parson Blessing'.[35] It is clear that here is a different set of values from those of Bernard, in conventional perspective Anglican rather than puritan or 'godly' values. There is a conspicuous contrast between Herbert's condescension to country habits and customs, 'if they be good and harmlesse', and the contempt expressed for these things by such a Puritan as George Gifford, author of *The countrie divinitie* (1581), or by the Northamptonshire preachers Robert Bolton and Joseph Bentham with their caustic denunciation of so-called 'good fellowship'.[36] Herbert's parson 'condescends even to the knowledge of tillage, and pastorage, . . . because people by what they understand, are best led to what they understand not.'[37]

But some words of caution are necessary before we conclude that Herbert furnished what was otherwise lacking from the resources of the early Stuart Church: an instructional manual for an Anglican priesthood. For one thing *The Countrey Parson* is not an instructional manual of any kind but a piece of expanded character literature, as its title proclaims, 'The Countrey Parson, His *Character*'. It is an example of that subtle parody of the Theophrastan character, the idealized and edifying character: written indeed for Herbert's own edification, 'a Mark to aim at' in his ministry at Bemerton and not published until twenty years after the author's premature death.[38] Like the poems comprising *The Temple*

---

[35] *The Works of George Herbert*, ed. F. E. Hutchinson (Oxford, 1941), pp. 244–5, 247–9, 236, 249–50, 257–9, 285–6.

[36] I am indebted to Dr Eamon Duffy for making this point quite forcefully in discussion. The antagonism of Bolton and Bentham for commonplace neighbourly values (which may be less familiar than Gifford's writings) can be sampled in Bolton's *Some general directions for a comfortable walking with God* (London, 1638) and Bentham's *The saints societie* (London, 1636). This piece of Bentham's invective (pp. 167–8) is not untypical: 'The pretty lispings and stammerings, the falls and stumblings, the unmannerly roguing, or whoring this man, that woman: the pretty pronunciation of this or that oath of their children shall not be forgotten: and then from these merrie Colloquies rake into the dunghill puddles of the true, or fained miscarriage of their neighbours, good or bad . . .'

[37] *Works of Herbert*, p. 228.

[38] However Benjamin Boyce in *The Theophrastan Character in England to 1642* (London, 1967), describes Herbert's treatise as a conduct book rather than a 'character' and suggests that the

(which however were published immediately after the poet's decease by Nicholas Ferrar and which were in their fifth edition by 1638) these were evidently somewhat 'private ejaculations'. We have also to note that Herbert's stress on preaching, if somewhat differently premissed, is not much less than we find among his 'godly' contemporaries. The difference, as I have suggested elsewhere, was that between 'godliness' and 'holiness' and it was not an enormous difference.[39] Nor should we expect any absolute difference in a Calvinist (of a kind) like Herbert, who could write of God's providence in predestination:

> Wherefore if thou canst fail,
> then can thy truth, and I.

So, says Herbert, 'The Country Parson preacheth constantly, the pulpit is his joy and his throne.' Even his pastoral visits are directed particularly towards those 'whom his sermons cannot, or doe not reach'. Herbert indeed differs from the godly school in nowhere suggesting that sermons are a unique instrumentality for the conversion of souls, so standing in a succession which, as Peter Lake has demonstrated, was not so much Arminian as Hookerian[40]—and both pre-protestant and a-protestant. But he was typical and wholly of his time in the didactic assumptions which govern every line of *The Countrey Parson*, including the first two lines: 'A Pastor is the Deputy of Christ for the reducing of Man to the Obedience of God.' As Stanley Fish has argued, *The Temple* was not only metaphorically architectonic (which is sufficiently obvious) and protestant (something insisted upon since Joesph Summers wrote on Herbert and Barbara Lewalski published her *Protestant Poetics*) but in form a kind of catechism with a close affinity to that fundamentally Pauline and protestant concept of edification explored by John Coolidge, in which the essentiality of preaching is seen to consist in the fabrication of a living temple out of lively stones.[41]

---

word in the title was intended to have 'the ordinary, non-technical meaning' (p. 197). See also Heinz Bergner, ed., *English Character Writing* (Tübingen, 1971) and J. W. Smeed, *The Theophrastan Character: the History of a Literary Genre* (Oxford, 1985).

[39] Collinson, *Religion of Protestants*, p. 110.

[40] Peter Lake, *Anglicans and Puritans? Presbyterian and English Conformist Thought from Whitgift to Hooker* (London, 1988), chapter 4, 'Richard Hooker'.

[41] Stanley Fish, *The Living Temple: George Herbert and Catechising* (Berkeley, 1978); Joseph H. Summers, *George Herbert, His Religion and Art* (London and Cambridge, Mass., 1954); Barbara K. Lewalski, *Protestant Poetics and the Seventeenth-Century Religious Lyric* (Princeton, 1979); John S. Coolidge, *The Pauline Renaissance in England: Puritanism and the Bible* (Oxford, 1970).

IV

I have already disclosed my scepticism about the 'mark to aim at', whether of Herbert or of his more puritanical contemporaries, if it is to be taken as a decriptive account of how, in fact, the bulk of the early seventeenth-century clergy understood and acted out their role. Such scepticism is as much in order as when historians reading domestic conduct books doubt whether they provide a realistic description of early modern family life. To say no more, the transcendent totalitarianism of the theory necessarily overlooks the phenomenon known to sociologists as 'routinization'. Parochial circumstances must have imposed a certain constraining routine on all but the most exceptionally inspired of ministers.

However, before that argument is extended it is necessary to examine with an equally critical scepticism the suggestions of some recent historians that the model of the godly preaching ministry, far from representing the only legitimate expression of valid pastoral care, was utterly antipathetic to many of the social and cultural contexts in which it asserted itself, and perhaps to all save certain favourable urban contexts. Consequently it was bound to fail, since protestant preaching was intellectualy over-demanding, morally and culturally oppressive, and instrumentally unrelated to the real needs of ordinary people. These were better served by sacraments and sacramentals working on the traditional principle of *ex opere operato*, not to say by magic, and performed by a kind of folk or at least folksy clergy cut from the same homespun as their parishioners.[42]

Perhaps the most extreme statement of this prejudice (for I am not sure that it is much more respectable than a prejudice) was made by Christopher Haigh when he pronounced this verdict on evidence of the failure of the quintessentially godly Richard Greenham to cut much ice in his parish of Dry Drayton: 'If Richard Greenham, of all men, in Cambridgeshire of all counties, could not make committed Protestants of more than a tiny handful of his parishioners, then nobody could and the task was impossible. In Elizabethan conditions ... the English people *could not* [Haigh's italics] be made Protestants.'[43] But how reliable is the evidence of

---

[42] This view is explicit in the writings of Dr Christopher Haigh and implicit in the work of a number of other recent historians. The ultimate indebtedness of this negative assessment of the protestant ministry to the rich and subtle learning of Keith Thomas in *Religion and the Decline of Magic* (London, 1971) is, of course, very considerable. See Haigh, 'Introduction', 'The Recent Historiography of the English Reformation' and 'Anticlericalism and the English Reformation', all in *The English Reformation Revised*, ed. Christopher Haigh (Cambridge, 1987).

[43] Christopher Haigh, 'The Church of England, the Catholics and the People', in *The Reign of Elizabeth I*, ed. Christopher Haigh (London, 1984), p. 213.

Greenham's failure? It occurs in what is, in effect, his obituary and consists of these few words in explanation of his withdrawal to London: 'The causes of his Removal were partly the untractableness and unteachableness of that people amongst whom he had taken such exceeding great pains.' The author's motive was to explain why his hero deserted a parochial charge for a more lucrative and comfortable post in London as a lecturer or 'doctor', and this he did partly by reference to an untractable people but also by informing the reader that Greenham had built up a nation-wide practice in the resolving of afflicted consciences which required a London base.[44] Whether the people of Dry Drayton were really so unresponsive will remain uncertain until Dr Kenneth Parker and Mr Eric Carlson tell us more about this deeply agricultural and thoroughly closed little community on the edge of the fen.[45] (One recalls Thomas Settle's complaint against the inhabitants of Mildenhall 'being frozen in their dregges, which seeme to have made their large Fen their God'.[46]) It is certainly possible and Greenham himself taught as a general principle that 'Ministers should most frequent those places where God hath made their Ministerie most fruitfull: they should heerein be like the covetous man, that where they have once found the sweetnesse of gaining of soules, thither they should be most desirous to resort.'[47] Compatability was all. It was Dry Drayton's misfortune, perhaps, to be so close to that powerhouse of militantly evangelical Protestantism which was Cambridge University, as it was Greenham's to be stuck with Dry Drayton: two incompatibles who were probably wise to part, with Greenham shaking the dust (or washing the mud) off his feet. But as the basis for a comprehensive indictment of the supposed failure of the godly preaching ministry in its entirety the case is evidentially almost worthless.

That the preacher was liable to fail in his object was a commonplace, the commonplace of the Parable of the Sower on which George Gifford preached in Essex and William Harrison in Lancashire.[48] The parable

---

44 Samuel Clarke, *The Lives of Thirty-Two English Divines* (London, 1677), p. 15.
45 Dr Parker is preparing an edition of John Rylands University Library Manchester, Rylands English MS 524, containing a collection of Greenham's casuistry compiled by Arthur Hildersham (?). Mr Carlson is engaged in a reconstitution of the population and society of Dry Drayton.
46 Thomas Settle, *A catechisme* (London, 1585), Epistle.
47 Richard Greenham, *Grave counsels and godly observations* in *Workes* (London, 1612), p. 24.
48 George Gifford, *A sermon on the parable of the sower* (London, 1582); William Harrison, *The difference of hearers. Or an exposition of the parable of the sower. Delivered in certaine sermons at Hyton in Lancashire* (London, 1614). On Harrison's sermon, see Christopher Haigh, 'Puritan Evangelism in the Reign of Elizabeth I', *EHR* 92 (1977), pp. 30–58.

finds fault with the unsuitable soils on which most of the seed fell, rather
than with the seed or the sower. Already in Edward VI's reign Latimer's
court preaching had made this point: there was no fault in preaching, 'The
lack is in the people, that have stony hearts and thorny hearts.'[49] But the
great John Dod was only one of many Jacobean commentators to blame
the sower as well, complaining that 'most ministers in England usually
shoot over the heads of their hearers'. Richard Bernard insisted that the
minister must take stock of his people, 'what sort of people as they bee'.
'For as they bee, so must hee deale with them.' 'He that is a Pastour must
informe the ignorant, urge men of knowledge to sanctification, reclaim
the vicious, encourage the vertuous, convince the erroneous, strengthen
the weak, recall the back-slider, resolve such as doubt, confirme the
resolved, and comfort the afflicted.'[50] Elizabethan and Jacobean preachers
cannot be accused of underestimating the complexity of this task and it is
unreasonable to make a wholly negative assessment of the didactic
instincts and methods of the Church in this period. Such a basic device as
dividing the biblical text into verses implies a realistic sense of how
uneducated or poorly educated minds work. As Dr Peter Jensen has
remarked of this innovation, it imparted to the Bible 'an oracular, aphor-
istic nature'. 'The text was to be absorbed piece by piece, word by word.'
Whatever its theological consequences, which those nostalgic for a more
humanistic, less sententious Protestantism may regard as deplorable, this
was not necessarily a mistaken pedagogical method.[51]

Dr Jensen has remarked that those who listened to sermons and read
their bibles 'did so with faculties trained by catechisms'. We should only
write off the effectiveness of the instructive ministry when we have carefully considered the almost universal practice of the catechism and found
it wanting. Catechizing, according to Herbert, was the first point in the
parson's repertoire and without it the other two, the infusion of saving
knowledge and the building up of knowledge into a spiritual temple, were
not attainable. '*Socrates* did thus in Philosophy.'[52] Richard Bernard, who
was the author of two catechisms and of a treatise on the subject,[53] wrote

---

[49] *Sermons by Hugh Latimer*, ed. G. E. Corrie (Cambridge, 1844), p. 155.
[50] Dod quoted in Collinson, *Religion of Protestants*, p. 231; Bernard, *The faithfull shepherd*, pp. 98, 107.
[51] Peter F. Jensen, 'The Life of Faith in the Teaching of Elizabethan Protestants' (unpublished Oxford D.Phil. thesis, 1979), p. 29.
[52] *Works of Herbert*, p. 256.
[53] Richard Bernard, *Two twinnes or two parts of one portion of Scripture. I is of catechising. II of the Ministers maintenance* (London, 1613); *A double catechisme* (Cambridge, 1607); *The common catechisme* (London, 1630); *Good Christian looke to thy creede* (London, 1630).

in *The faithfull shepherd*: 'Experience shewes how little profit comes by preaching, where catechizing is neglected.'[54] The more obscure Richard Kilby, a curate of Derby who was often too ill or too disorganized to preach and who used a catechizing method instead, turned necessity into a virtue and advocated the more extensive and creative use of that medium. The common sort were 'very grossely ignorant', but also 'much neglected', since most sermons were unfit for their 'lowe and small capacities'. 'For ought I know', Kilby went on, such persons had a greater appetite for the things of God than many of higher degree and greater understanding, but they needed to be plainly and briefly taught. Instead of which the often interminable sermon left them wondering: 'When will yonder man have done?'[55]

Both Dr Jensen and Dr Ian Green[56] have seen the flood of published catechisms as evidence in itself for a perception of pastoral failure, a response to the spectacle of nominal Protestantism and to a kind of crisis in the presentation of the protestant doctrines of faith and assurance.[57] But in view of the volume of that flood we should perhaps stress the perception and response to failure rather than failure itself. Dr Green counts an astonishing total of 350 catechitical titles printed in the century from 1549 to 1646, and this is far from a complete tally of all catechisms published, let alone unpublished. Some were best-sellers: the More-Dering catechism, over forty editions, Paget-Openshawe, at least thirty-one, Perkins over thirty, Egerton forty-three by 1635 (the earliest surviving edition being the sixteenth), Ball thirty-three by 1645. Some of the titles are indicative of the degree of condescension implicit in the enterprise of exploring the mysteries of religion plainly and economically. In the preface to his catechism, Francis Inman wrote of 'poore servants and laborers, . . . aged persons of weake and decaied memories'. 'Yet all

---

[54] Bernard, *The faithfull shepherd*, p. 100. Perkins's editor William Crashawe expressed himself in similar terms in what was evidently a commonplace, declaring that catechizing was 'the life of preaching and such a meanes of knowledge as without it all preaching is to little purpose'. (Quoted, Ian Green, '"For Children in Yeeres and Children in Understanding": the Emergence of the English Catechism under Elizabeth and the Early Stuarts', *JEH* 37 (1986), p. 417.)

[55] Richard Kilby, *Hallelu-iah: Praise ye the Lord for the unburthening of a loaden conscience* (Cambridge, 1618), pp. 82–3. For more about Kilby, see pp. 00–00.

[56] Jensen, 'The Life of Faith', pp. 174–228; Green, 'The Emergence of the English Catechism', pp. 397–425.

[57] See as examples of pessimistic pastoral perception Jeremy Corderoy, *A short dialogue, wherein is proved that no man can be saved without good workes* (Oxford, 1604) and Timothy Rogers, *The righteous mans evidence for Heaven. Or, A treatise shewing how every one while he lives here may certainly know what shall become of him after his departure out of this life* (London, 1619).

these have immortall soules ... Of these care must be had.' William Crashawe's 'North Country Catechism' was called 'milke for babes', Samuel Hieron's west country catechism was 'short for memory, plaine for capacity'.[58]

Bernard's method was admirable and perhaps influential. (We are told that 'diverse painfull and profitable labourers in the Lordes vineyard had their first *initiation* and *direction* from and under him.'[59]) This was his advice: Let the people learne word for word, by rote. 'Interrupt not beginners with interpretations ... Goe not beyond their conceits; stay somewhat for an answer but not too long; if one know not, help him and encourage him by commending his willingnesse ... Teach with cheerful countenance, familiary and lovingly.' With exquisite tact William Lyford told his people: 'You first directed and taught me, how to teach you.'[60]

V

There can be no attempt made on this occasion to measure the degree of success eventually obtained towards the middle decades of the seventeenth century by these and more advanced methods of indoctrination, such as the almost universal practice of sermon repetition.[61] In the *longue durée* of the English reformation process it would be premature to draw up a balance sheet much earlier than 1640. It may be that many, even most people beneath a certain economic and social level, or below a certain age, remained resistant. The teachers and preachers often said so, but from polemical and rhetorical motives which limit the value of their testimony. No doubt Protestantism in its didactic and demanding presentation was selective and divisive, like education and literacy sowing the seeds of a kind of sectarianism. But to acknowledge that this was not a religion for all should not blind our eyes to its attractiveness for some, like the women at Wye in Kent who on summer evenings came to the house of the curate Mr Gulliforde at eight or nine of the clock until late, 'as yt is sayd, at prayer'; or the 'divers gentlewomen' of that part of Kent who dined with

[58] Francis Inman, *A light unto the unlearned* (London, 1622), Epistle; William Crashawe, *Milke for babes. Or, a North-country catechisme made plaine and easie, to the capacity of the simplest* (London, 1628); Samuel Hieron, *The doctrine of the beginning of Christ* (13 edn., London, 1626).

[59] Preface by John Conant to Bernard's posthumously published *Thesaurus Biblicus* (London, 1644), Sig. A3ᵛ.

[60] Bernard, *The faithfull shepherd*, pp. 102–3; Lyford quoted by Green, 'The Emergence of the English Catechism', p. 415.

[61] Patrick Collinson, 'The English Conventicle', *SCH* 23, pp. 240–4.

Mr Gulliforde after his Thursday lectures, paying two shillings and sixpence each for the privilege.[62]

That the religious and even the theological concerns of country and small town clergy were capable of being communicated to some at least of their hearers is suggested by the affair of the Lincolnshire minister William Williams, rector of two rural parishes near Sleaford. This case is the discovery of Dr Helena Hajzyk.[63] Williams was a proto-Arminian who imported into deepest Lincolnshire the anti-Calvinist doctrines taught in Cambridge by Peter Baro and refuted in the Lambeth Articles of 1595. For these opinions, and specifically for a provocative visitation sermon preached at Sleaford in June 1598, Williams was denounced to Bishop Chaderton by his fellow clergy. Dr Hajzyk is fascinated, as well she may be, by the light cast by the cause papers surviving with exceptional richness from this prosecution on Williams's dealings with other ministers of the district, not only at sermons and other clerical gatherings but 'sitting in Sleaford market place upon a seate there', or riding to and from Sleaford and Lincoln. She plausibly suggests that this fierce controversy was the reason not only why Bishop Barlow later refused to sanction a combination lecture at Sleaford but why in 1614 Bishop Neile's visitors reported that at the visitation dinner held in the town there was no talk at all of divinity matters.[64]

But of equal interest in the Sleaford affair is evidence of the intelligent response to Williams's heresies of some of the more substantial townspeople. In August 1598 there was a meeting held in a chamber of the Angel Inn and attended not only by the clergy but by two local gentlemen, a 71-year old mercer, a 33-year old ironmonger, and three self-styled yeomen, aged 44, 38 and 34, including the landlord, George Gladwin. On

---

[62] CALC, MS X. 11. 1, fols 229^r, 230^r.

[63] Hajzyk, 'The Church in Lincolnshire', pp. 225–42. The episcopal hearings into the Williams case are documented in Lincoln Archives Office, MS Cj/12 (Episcopal Court Book 1598–1600) with the cause papers in Box 80/7.

[64] Hajzyk, 'The Church in Lincolnshire', pp. 270–1. For the report of Bishop Neile's visitors, see my 'Lectures by Combination', p. 483, and references there. How exceptional the doctrinal storm in the little *pays* of Sleaford may have been remains uncertain. In 1595 Bishop Fletcher of London reported the clergy of Colchester and Maldon as 'at war with themselves, as well in matter of popular quarrels as points of doctrine'. (*H.M.C. Cal. Hatfield MSS* 5, p. 394.) See also Peter Gunter's *A sermon preached in the countie of Suffolke before the clergie and laytie for the discoverie and confutation of certaine strange, pernicious and hereticall positions publickly delivered herd and mainteyned touching justification by a certaine factious preacher of Wickham Market in the said countie, by which divers, especially of the vulgar, farre and neare, were greatly seduced* (London, 1615). Dr Freeman writes of the diocese of Durham in the 1620s and 1630s: 'The unity in which they had previously lived . . . was destroyed by doctrinal argument.' ('The Parish Ministry', pp. 408–17.)

this occasion the company heard Williams affirm baptismal regeneration (which the wife of one the gentlemen present, Mrs Burton, said he had also taught in two christening sermons which she had heard); and that 'an elected man might fall away from grace totallie', as David did 'in his adulterie and murder'. Everyone knew that the word 'totally' was of crucial significance. The ironmonger, William Barrow, who had often heard Williams 'speake somewhat disdainfullie of God's predestination', told him that no learned man in England was of his opinion, that is, that the elect can fall irrevocably from grace. Williams responded: 'Yea, that there were, for my lord grace of Canterbury was of his opinion.' Everyone present remembered this dramatic and scandalous claim, which related to Williams's direct dealings with Archbishop Whitgift and a number of ranking Cambridge theologians and heads of houses. William Burton of Aldingham put an anxious question: 'Are we not to believe that there ys predestination?' Both Mrs Burton and William Scochie reported that it was generally thought and by some uttered that if Mr Williams were not punished his hearers would have to conclude that his doctrine was right and true. One wonders how many converts to 'Arminianism' Williams made, for he was not punished but managed to have his case transferred to the Court of Arches which left him unmolested and free to preach in and around Sleaford for another forty years.

How 'general' was the concern about predestination voiced by Mrs Burton? How widespread interest in the proposition that baptized children dying before actual sin were regenerated, leading Williams's hearers to believe, or so complained the bishop, that the sacraments confer grace *de facto*? Perhaps quite general, surprisingly widespread, although a majority of the inhabitants of Sleaford below the rank of iron-monger may have cared little for such niceties. It may be that the intensification of the debate about the terms and title-deeds of salvation, together with rising professional standards and collegial pressures, had the effect of spiritually disfranchising the majority. Of the famous Northamptonshire preacher Robert Bolton it was said that 'he prepared nothing for his people but what might have served a very learned Auditory'.[65] (And yet Bolton's published sermons are fine examples of the so-called 'plain style'.) 'Christian Reader', explained the Leicestershire minister Anthony Cade in introducing a published sermon: 'the

---

[65] This was affirmed by Nicholas Estwick in Bolton's funeral sermon. See *The life and death of M. Bolton*, published with *Mr Boltons last and learned worke of the foure last things* (London, 1639), pp. 18–19.

concourse of many learned Ministers at our Ordinary Monthly Lecture
... whereunto now also resorted ... many learned iuditious gentlemen
required matter of more then ordinary worth and learning. To satisfie
whome, if I have layd the grounds of my Sermon more Schoole-like then
thou thinkest fitte for the Country, beare with mee ...'[66] But most
Elizabethan and Jacobean sermons were doubtless more 'fit for the
country' than for publication and those which were published may give a
false impression of the typical level of learned sophistication at which
such discourses were pitched.

Nor should we underestimate the sensitivity of the palates of country
sermon-tasters. In the early 1580s the Kentish village of Egerton, a religiously serious community on the northern edge of the Weald,[67] was
subjected to the irregular ministrations of a hedge priest called Edward
Hudson. The inhabitants could easily distinguish between the real
MacCoy and the incoherent tale-telling which was Hudson's idea of a
sermon. When Hudson expounded the text 'God so loved the world' and
went on about kissing and cuddling and 'thank God all love was not lost',
assuring the congregation that he would not fob them off with stories of
St Francis or of a 'roasted horse', they smelt a rat. John Wythers, a fifty-
year old weaver, Simon Wolton, a thirty-nine year old clothier, Ralph
Elston, a forty-five year old butcher and a young farmer Robert Spycer,
were all contemptuous of Hudson's 'fryvolous tales', his 'fond speeches
tending to no man's edification', the butcher reporting that 'the sobrest
sort of the auditory ... were much offended at his so light and undiscreet
toyes then uttered', when, said another parishioner, 'godly preaching and
good informacion to the edification of Gods people ought to be in the fear
of God reverently to be done'. Spycer said that Hudson's speeches were
applied 'to no purpose at all'. The butcher knew that Hudson was speaking
out of turn when he claimed that whenever he was at a deathbed 'he could
have an ayme which way that party should go'. Wolton the clothier was
offended in conscience when Hudson taught that the people would be
saved whether they had communion or not. And even if the parishioners
sympathized with Hudson's nonconformity they knew it was an offence
against decorum to refer to the surplice as a 'whore's weed'.[68] At

---

[66] Anthony Cade, *Saint Paules agonie. A sermon preached at Leicester at the ordinary monthly lecture* (London, 1618), Epistle.

[67] For some evidence of Egerton's religious environment, see R. J. Acheson, 'Sion's Saint: John Turner of Sutton Valence', *Archaeologia Cantiana*, 99 (1983), pp. 183–97.

[68] CALC, MS X. 10. 20, fols 148ᵛ–62ᵛ, 211ᵛ–20ʳ. However Mr Hudson's sermon was perhaps not such an incoherent rigmarole as it was represented by his hearers. He seems to have been

Hawkhurst in the same county a sixty-year old miller, a forty-seven year old clothier, and a young husbandman were all sufficiently alert after an hour-long sermon on the gospel for the day to know that their curate was digressing from his text in making a gratuitous attack on the sexual mores of the rich, which a local worthy interpreted as a personal attack upon himself. They were able to give an exact account in court of the words in question.[69]

VI

So much for preaching. But what are we to say of the bulk of the minister's vocation, that nine-tenths of the iceberg below the surface of the evidence which was the non-preaching ministry, or at least the ministry when not engaged in preaching? It is a paradox that we are able to say least about that function which competed with preaching as the bread and butter of the job, the reading of common prayer and the conduct of public worship: and it must be a paradox since if we count up the time spent on this activity by a normally conscientious incumbent in a full year, morning and evening prayers, Wednesdays and Fridays and holy days as well as Sundays, the common prayers and readings, litany and ante-communion, we are talking about not less than five hundred hours, in a lifetime's ministry perhaps twenty thousand hours. But this is not a paradox confined to the sixteenth and seventeenth centuries. From the early nineteenth-century Somerset diary of William Holland it is difficult to say much about Holland's inner disposition to what he called 'the Duty', that is, the duty of conducting divine worship in his two parishes. On Sunday, 8 September 1805 the church at Overstowey was 'uncommonly full'. But what Holland found memorable about that day was the unusual quantity of wasps' nests encountered along the road to Overstowey. 'They were burnt out and smoking and the places startled the horse several times.'[70] It is tempting but would be unwise to conclude that

---

quoting from Sir Thomas More's *Dialogue Concerning Heresies* which includes the story of St Francis reacting to the sight of a young man kissing a girl by going down on his knees to thank God 'that charyte was not yet gone out of this wretched worlde'. Or did More and Hudson share a common source? (*The Complete Works of St. Thomas More*, 6, pt. ii, ed. Thomas M. C. Lawler, Germain Marc'Hadour and Richard C. Marius (New Haven, 1981), p. 287.)

[69] CALC, MS X. 10. 11, fols 185ᵛ–8ᵛ.

[70] *Paupers and Pig Killers: the Diary of William Holland A Somerset Parson 1799–1818*, ed. Jack Ayres (London, 1986 edn.), p. 118.

'the Duty' was for Holland as much a routine as his regular Saturday night chore of winding up all the clocks before retiring to bed. But what if it was? Historians (unlike anthropologists) are not best qualified to evaluate routine.

It is not difficult to find Elizabethans of the godly school who took a wholly negative view of liturgy. John Field, the voice of radical Elizabethan Puritanism, can speak for all when he complained not only of certain 'popish dregs' in the Prayer Book service but of its inordinate length, 'the quantity of thinges appointed to be reade, saide, songe or gone over', which was 'tedious'.[71] A Norfolk minister claimed to have read the appointed service with all the prayers and chapters, except, he disarmingly explained, when 'by reason of preaching I omitted them'. Radical puritan practice seems to have discarded nearly everything, Venite, Te Deum, Creed, and Litany, retaining only the lessons, a few prayers, and the psalm, on which the Prayer Book was silent but which was now *de rigueur*.[72]

We are talking about a small minority of incorrigibly puritan parishes. A more widespread and moderate practice was to read the whole service according to law but to omit certain objectionable ceremonies. In 1605 the vicar of Loughborough reported that kneeling at the communion, the sign of the cross in baptism and the surplice had been disused in the town 'all her Majesty's reign'.[73] At Loughborough it was the people who insisted on these omissions, just as in parishes of a different temper there were popular pressures to have the entire service as printed, whether we attribute that preference to 'Prayer Book Anglicans' or to 'church papists'.[74]

[71] 'Articles presented by a preacher of London called John Feld', PRO SP 12/164/11; another version in Dr Williams's Library, MS Morrice B II, fols. 94–6, calendared in *The Seconde Parte of a Register*, 1, pp. 284–6 as 'Mr Feilde and Mr Egerton their tolleration'.

[72] *A parte of a register* (Middelburg, 1593?), p. 317. See my *The Elizabethan Puritan Movement* (London and Berkeley, 1967), pp. 356–71 and, more fully, my unpublished London PhD. thesis, 'The Puritan Classical Movement in the Reign of Elizabeth I' (1957), pp. 716–54.

[73] John Browne vicar of Loughborough to the chancellor of Lincoln Diocese, 22 July 1605; Lincoln Archives Office, MS COR/M/2, no. 8.

[74] Miss Judith Maltby has investigated a number of these cases from East Anglia and Huntingdonshire, evidently favouring the 'Prayer Book Anglican' thesis. (Information communicated in Oxford at a Colloquium for Local Reformation Studies, April 1980.) The case of Mr Gulliforde vicar of Wye in Kent, referred to twice above (pp. 192, 203) appears to have been of the same order, with parishioners objecting to various pieces of 'puritan' practice, especially in the administration of the occasional offices. Since Wye probably had more recusants than any other parish in East Kent I tend to be strengthened in a rather different estimate of these complaints as indicative of the habits of church papists.

However, conformity, whether partial or complete, by the emphasis placed on legal compliance does not in itself suggest much positive enthusiasm for the liturgy. Elizabethan apologists for the *status quo* of the religious settlement defended ceremony and liturgical practice as things merely indifferent. In Peter Lake's phrase, 'they were there because they were there'.[75] Dr Jane Freeman found that in the diocese of Durham service books virtually disappeared from clerical inventories in this period, in marked contrast to the libraries of pre-Reformation clerics in which they predominated.[76] It appears that few Elizabethan and Jacobean clergy would have listed liturgy among their hobbies or private enthusiasms, or have joined the Henry Bradshaw Society. It was in pronounced and polemical reaction to this apparent contempt for the very principle as well as what Dom Gregory Dix called the shape of the liturgy that Hooker and Howson, and presently Andrewes and Buckeridge, began to insist on the supreme value of worship and prayer as the essential content of public religion, reflecting that churches were properly '*oratoria*', not '*auditoria*'. Hooker gloried in the length of liturgical services and even commended the Roman Church for regarding public prayer as 'a duty entire in itself'.[77] In 1598 Howson proclaimed at Paul's Cross that 'of all religious actions, prayer is reckoned the first and the chiefe', bitterly complaining that 'all the service of God is reduced to hearing of sermons'. In 1633 Walter Balcanquall spoke of a generation of fools who would run miles to hear a sermon 'but for the publike prayers of the Church, they will hardly crosse the street'.[78] But this was reactive and no more part of the main stream than Field's extreme Puritanism. Perhaps less so.

Communion presents an even greater problem, and mystery. Leaving aside the voice of rabid radicalism ('Do they make so much a do for chewinge a peece of bread and drinkinge a cupp of wine?')[79] the generality of godly practice looks 'low', in the terms of modern churchmanship, but perhaps deceptively so. Dr Jeremy Boulton has established that in some of the larger London parishes communion was offered to householders no more than the canonical minimum of three times a year and perhaps only once, round about Easter, when the sacrament was almost universally

[75] Lake, *Anglicans and Puritans*, p. 164.
[76] Freeman, 'The Parish Ministry', p. 55.
[77] Lake, *Anglicans and Puritans?* chapter 4, 'Richard Hooker'.
[78] Howson, *A second sermon*, pp. 39, 43–4; Balcanquall, *The honour of christian churches*, p. 22.
[79] This was said in Barnstaple in the early 1580s by one of the supporters and offsiders of the radical minister Eusebius Paget, and in defiance of a faction of the town who had demanded the communion on Christmas Day. (Dr Williams's Library, MS Morrice B II, fol. 69ᵛ.)

received. But there were more select monthly communions for the parish élites, the members of what were now normally closed vestries.[80] That looks more like a social perk than extraordinary devotion on the part of the vestrymen. But it is very difficult to appreciate the spirit and motivation with which the sacrament was both administered and received: again the problem of routine. John Randall of the London parish of St Andrew Hubbert always preached on the subject of the Lord's supper before his monthly administration of it, and the gist of his doctrine was this: 'Nothing concerns your spirituall state more than the reverent and worthy receiving of this sacrament, no dutie more necessarie to be taught, no greater danger then the prophanation and abuse of it.'[81] That was the voice of the moderate puritan tradition, not of sacramental 'Anglicanism'. Writing of the later seventeenth century, Dr Donald Spaeth suggests that reluctance to receive or to receive more than very occasionally may have implied not disrespect for the sacrament but the reverse: an almost superstitious dread of receiving unworthily, induced by the prohibitive tone of the Prayer Book prefaces and rubrics. That too was the legacy of Protestantism, even of Puritanism.[82]

And so, it may be, with the Prayer Book forms in the perception of the godly ministry. We cannot be sure that they were simply dismissed as a meaningless waste of time. This was a religious culture which took such a grave view of the language of vain and casual swearing that it became a scandal throughout Kent when it was rumoured that the bishop of Dover had said in public hearing 'By God's Soul!'[83] Is is likely that this tradition was indifferent to the language of solemn invocation in the public assembly? To deplore, with the New Testament, 'vain repetitions' was not to despise all repetitions whatsoever. But the devotional mood and temperature of the typical Elizabethan congregation and its president remains an impenetrable subject. Bowing at the name of Jesus and the sign of the cross were widely rejected as popish superstitions. But did English Protestants, like continental Calvinists, remove their hats every time God was named? We know all too little about hat drill in church. Standing to

---

[80] Jeremy Boulton, 'The Limits of Formal Religion: Administration of Holy Communion in Late Elizabethan and Early Stuart London', *London Journal*, 10 (1984), pp. 135–54.

[81] John Randall, *Three and twentie sermons, or, catechisticall lectures upon the sacrament of the Lords Supper. Preached monthly before the communion* (London, 1630), pp. 3, 5.

[82] Donald A. Spaeth, 'Common Prayer? Popular Observance of the Anglican Liturgy in Restoration Wiltshire', in *Parish Church and People: Local Studies in Lay Religion 1350–1750*, ed. Susan Wright (London, 1988), pp. 125–51.

[83] CALC, MS X. 10. 13, fols 24 *seq*.

recite the Creed was spoken of in the House of Commons as if it was a rare innovation.[84] Kneeling for prayer on entering one's pew may have been conventional practice, then as now.[85] Yet some denounced it, together with 'putting the hat and hand before the face to pray', declaring that such 'private praying' was a sin. That was not to despise prayer but to insist on the fully corporate nature of common prayer, 'the worship of God in hand'.[86] So much for puritan 'individualism'. When Herbert spoke of the parson in prayer as 'truly touched and amazed with the Majesty of God before whom he then presents himself' and with himself the whole congregation, this was not a narrowly Anglican in the sense of anti-puritan sentiment, any more than Hooker went against contemporary standards of 'godliness' in insisting that the people should not repeat the prayers 'as Parrats' but as a reasonable service.

VII

It remains to discuss the ministry in what, in the categories of the seminary, is taken to be the essentials of 'pastoralia', beyond and outside the public assembly and devoted situationally and clinically to the cure of souls. Mr Mark Byford has recently drawn our attention[87] to an Essex incumbent who can serve to epitomize an alternative and, as it appears, older and more traditional model of the pastoral ministry than the 'godly' school so far discussed, practical, compassionate, and devoted to the unbroken continuum of the christian community. The question is whether or how far this tradition was suppressed by the superimposition of the godly preaching model. This incumbent, appropriately named Sheppard, was vicar of the obscure village of Heydon for forty-five years, as it happens the most critical forty-five years in the long history of the English Reformation and perhaps in the entire history of English

---

[84] Collinson, *Religion of Protestants*, p. ix n. 2.

[85] Gratia Johnson, household servant of Henry Hayward, butcher of Herne in Kent, gave evidence in July 1606 in the case of Butler contra Crumpe of how on a certain Sunday she 'made bold' to sit at the end of the pew in Herne church where Mother Crumpe and Butler's wife usually sat when Mother Crumpe came into church (late!) 'and sat her downe uppon her knees in the same pewe . . . and when she arose from her kneeling she the said Susan Crompe set her selfe downe uppon the seat . . .' (CALC, MS X. 11. 10, fol. 8ʳ.)

[86] John Angier, *An helpe to better hearts, for better times. Indeavoured in severall sermons preached in the year, 1638* (London, 1647), p. 75.

[87] Mark Byford's paper on William Sheppard of Heydon was communicated at the Colloquium for Local Reformation Studies held at Sheffield in April 1988 and will form part of his forthcoming Oxford doctoral dissertation on the Church and religion in Elizabethan Essex. I am most grateful to Mr Byford for allowing me to use his material on Sheppard.

Christianity, since they began in 1541, with the late Henrician catholic reaction in full swing, and ended in 1586 on the eve of that event which, politically speaking, ensured the survival of Protestantism, the execution of Mary Queen of Scots. Sheppard, who was born in the days of Henry VII, that Indian Summer of the old religion, and lived to hear about the Spanish Armada, was already middle-aged when he came to Heydon as an ex-monk of the Augustinian Priory of Leeds in Kent. If we knew less than we do about this old Henrician it would be easy to dismiss him as one of those dumb dogs and hirelings who continued for too long to obstruct the onward march of protestant evangelism. In fact, or so Mr Byford suggests on the basis of Sheppard's own record of his achievements, he, and perhaps others like him whose lifespan encompassed 'a series of conforming experiences', helped to ease the transition from the old religious world to a measure of adaptation to the new. 'Silent conformity need not have been the product of indifference.'

Yet the continuities of Sheppard's ministry are more in evidence than the discontinuities and he does seem to have embodied a number of old rather than new pastoral values. Indeed the motivation behind the chronicle of 'beneficiall good deeds' which he recorded in the parish register[88] speaks of a religion of 'good works', the old religion. Sheppard's good deeds included regular repairs and improvements to the church fabric over and above his legal responsibility for the upkeep of the chancel, many acts of charity including the provision of generous dowries for the girls of the village, and the making over of all his glebe land to the poorer inhabitants, together with the provision of causeways, bridges, fences, and drainage ditches.[89] He also extended the village hall with the intention of promoting good fellowship among all his neighbours. The total value of these various bequests was £134 15s. 4d., a quarter of his entire income as vicar of Heydon, and that before rather than after tax. Forty years after his death, Sheppard was still remembered as 'a liberall man and good to the poore'. He was a preacher but his one surviving sermon suggests that he confined himself to short homilies of a traditional kind, punctuated with many 'now good neybors' and 'therefore good neybors'.[90]

---

[88] Sheppard's 'Epitome' occupies fols 100ʳ–3ʳ of the parish register of Heydon, Essex Record Office, MS D/P 135/1/1.

[89] A similar pattern of charity is inferred in the will of John Gylderde, parson of Runwell, Essex, another celibate, made on 5 June 1551. The residue of Gylderde's estate was left to provide dowries for the poor maidens of the village and for 'mending of the most noisome highways about Runwell'. (Greater London Central Record Office, MS DL/C/357, fols 36–7. I owe this reference to Mr Brett Usher.)

[90] This sermon, also entered in the parish register (fol. 57) proved a calamity for Sheppard, since

Sheppard may remind us a little of a more famous contemporary, himself initially ambivalent in his response to enforced religious change, the sainted apostle of the North, Bernard Gilpin. According to his biographer, Gilpin overflowed with charitable works, both casually spontaneous and as it were programmed, in the Sheppard style. He also conducted on a more heroic scale a notable ministry of reconciliation and extended hospitality to his parishioners at Houghton-le-Spring not only at Christmas, which was usual, but on every Sunday from Michaelmas to Easter.[91]

This kind of ministry, with its hallmark of active, practical, reconciling love must always have been somewhat exceptional, but as 'a mark to aim at' it is echoed in Herbert's *Countrey Parson*. And the question stands, was it temporarily thrust aside in the interim by the alien and less benign programme of the impatient godly ministry? Dr Haigh thinks so, characterizing the post-Reformation Church as 'a more obviously repressive institution', served by university-trained professionals, more clericalist than the old priesthood and determined to replace meaningful ritual with incomprehensible Bible-reading and 'tedious sermons to pewbound parishioners'. This figure was 'naturally less popular than his priestly predecessor'.[92] Possibly so. Dr Freeman found that in the diocese of Durham there were a hundred more tithe disputes in the five years 1595 to 1600 than there had been in 1577–82 and more than twice as many between 1629 and 1634. But for this trend there may have been more than one reason and Dr Freeman is too cautious to attribute the inflation in tithe litigation to personal or professional unpopularity.[93] More or less popularity cannot be so easily measured. On the one hand we hear the voice of the vicar of Gateshead, writing his will in 1571 and committing his 'deare and loving flocke' to 'the great Shepherd Jesus Christ . . . Fare well once agayne my deare and loving flocke';[94] or, sixty years later, Robert Abbot of Cranbrook in Kent, rejoicing with Pauline fulsomeness in his 'deare and loving parishioners . . . my ioy and my

---

in it he was moved by the occasion of the festival of Christ's circumcision and naming as Jesus to exhort his parishioners, in 1581 of all years, to 'studye to be . . . true Jesuytts'.

[91] George Carleton, *The Life and Death of Bernard Gilpin* (London, 1727 edn.), pp. 29–31, 43–4, 91–2. Gilpin's confessional ambivalence, of which there is some evidence in the *Life*, is discussed by David Marcombe, 'Bernard Gilpin: Anatomy of an Elizabethan Legend', *Northern History*, 16 (1980).

[92] Haigh, 'Anticlericalism and the English Reformation', *The English Reformation Revised*, pp. 73–4.

[93] Freeman, 'The Parish Ministry', pp. 429, 438–9.

[94] *Ibid.*, pp. 418–19.

crowne!'[95] On the other we hear the bitter recriminations of the rector of the Leicestershire village of Belleau who said that it ought to be called 'Helloe'.[96] No general conclusions are possible on the basis of this teeming and inconsistent evidence.

Nor can we jump to conclusions about discontinuity in traditional pastoral routines from the failure of godly ministers, one-eyed in their obsession with preaching, to mention them. Many recorded lives of ministers in the godly tradition suggest that Herbert's practice of door to door visitation was not as 'Anglican' and exceptional as it may seem.[97] However, if we may presume to confront these elusive topics of popularity, compatibility and effectiveness we must face one clear and easily established fact, not so far mentioned. William Sheppard, who gave away a quarter of his modest substance, was an unreconstructed lifelong celibate. Gilpin, who spent three quarters of his large income on his school and seminary at Houghton and other charities, commended the married state to the clergy—but was himself unmarried, or he could hardly have been as generous as he was. Herbert regarded virginity as a higher state than matrimony and wrote that the country parson was 'rather unmarryed than marryed'; although he was himself, like St Peter, a married man. Apart from other, theological considerations, for it or against it, a married clergy was in practice hard to reconcile with the proverb quoted in the Royal Injunctions of 1559: 'the goods of the Church are called the goods of the poor'. And to be sure, all that the Injunctions required by way of christian charity was that non-resident incumbents worth no less than £20 a year should distribute a fortieth part of their income to the poor of the parish, which could be as little as eight shillings. And the Canons of 1604, all 141 of them, were utterly silent on the use of ecclesiastical revenues for charitable purposes. The Elizabethan Mr Quiverfull could barely afford to be as generous as the law required, let alone to emulate the example of the solitary Sheppard of Heydon. This the many critics of clerical marriage, sounding off in the public bar, knew very well.[98]

Perhaps the partner of the parson's great double bed offered some pastoral compensation. We know all too little about what clergy wives of

---

[95] Collinson, 'Cranbrook and the Fletchers', p. 427.

[96] Thomas Ballow rector of Belleau ('alias Helloe') to the surrogate of Stamford, 24 August 1609; Lincoln Archives Office MS COR/M/2, no. 39.

[97] For example, the godly Richard Rothwell's daily routine was said to have consisted of mornings spent in study and afternoons 'going through his Parish and conferring with his people'. (Clarke, *Lives of Thirty-Two English Divines*, p. 70.)

[98] Collinson, *Religion of Protestants*, p. 106; Collinson, *Birthpangs of Protestant England*, pp. 67–8.

this period did or were expected to do in a pastoral way. Perhaps they were for ever diving in and out of cottage doors with baskets on their arms. But at Norton in County Durham the vicar's wife was sheepdog as much as co-pastor. She made it her business to interrogate unmarried mothers in order to identify the fathers of bastard children, which was to take upon herself the office normally assigned to the midwife.[99] And a fleeting snapshot of Mrs Plat, the wife of an Elizabethan vicar of Graveney near Faversham in Kent, is a little daunting. She had taken up residence in the 'cheefest pewe in all the church', historically the property of Judge Martyn and his wife, her former seat being thought 'a blemishe to the church and not thought fyt for any the meanest of the parishioners there to syt, muche lesse for the ministers wife'.[100]

But one source in particular suggests that we should not simply assume that the godly preaching ministry neglected such perennial mainstays of the pastoral function as visitation, reconciliation, and even generous charity. I refer to the compilation of the *Lives* of notable divines in the puritan tradition derived from funeral sermons and put together in the later seventeenth century by Samuel Clarke.[101] Richard Greenham may have been as unsuccessful in converting his parishioners to his own form of religious faith as his obituarist suggests, but according to the same narrative it was not for want of charity. Not only was he generous with his own resources. He persuaded the wealthier villagers to set up and stock a common granary for the poor. He was also said to have worked hard at reconciling his neighbours and acquaintances, preventing them going to law. William Bradshaw was exercised by the condition of the prisoners kept on the galleys at Chatham. The Suffolk saint John Carter was said to have been 'very diligent in visiting the sick, especially the poorer sort', and to have given more than the total annual revenue of his vicarage to the poor. (Perhaps he had private means.) Part of the folklore relating to John Dod was that when the poor came to buy butter or cheese he commanded his dairy maid to take no money from them. William Whateley, the 'roaring boy' of Banbury, was nevertheless 'a great Peace-maker amongst any of his flock that were at variance'.[102] There is no indication in these sources that the idealized role of the post-Reformation ministry differed

[99] Freeman, 'The Parish Ministry', p. 384.

[100] CALC, MS X. 11. 9, fol. 18ʳ.

[101] Patrick Collinson, '"A Magazine of Religious Patterns": An Erasmian Topic Transposed in English Protestantism', in *Godly People*, pp. 499–526.

[102] Clarke, *Lives of Thirty-Two English Divines*, pp. 13, 59, 133–4, 171; Samuel Clarke, *The Lives and Deaths of Eminent Persons* (London, 1675), p. 461.

in any substantial respect from the standards of a century before, or indeed from those of Chaucer's parson, who was 'a shepherde and noghte a mercenarie', loth to sue for his tithes but ever ready to give to his parishioners from his own small substance.[103] Or, as one of William Sheppard's parishioners reported, years after his death: he 'did not seek to increase his lyvinge by that which to others pertayned'.[104]

VIII

So was there nothing new under the sun? There was. Apart from the critical factor of clerical marriage and clerical progeny there was the sacrament of penance, or rather the absence of that sacrament and of the compulsory practice of making and hearing confessions. Other reformation changes made a deal of difference, not least the eradication of the mass and of the concomitant doctrine and practice of propitiatory masses for souls in Purgatory. But in relation to the pastoral ministry in the narrower sense, nothing can have made a greater negative impact than the lapse of the universal obligation to confess to a priest, as the condition both of receiving the sacrament and of remaining an acceptable part of what was still a compulsory christian society.

To be sure, the post-Reformation Church had its surrogates for sacramental confession, even in the absence of that comprehensive 'discipline' which presbyterian Puritans so ardently desired. The social rationale of the sacrament was partly met by the obligation of parishioners to reconcile themselves to their neighbours before presuming to receive, together with the matching responsibility of the ministry to take an active and even intrusive role in reconciling the irreconcileable and to repel from the sacrament those who remained obstinately unreconciled. There is so much direct evidence from the church courts of clergy performing this function, especially with the approach of the obligatory Easter communion, that we are probably entitled to regard it as a normal and nearly universal office. And in some places the parson's peace-making role was formalized as an accepted extra-curial mechanism for ending quarrels. At Gilpin's Houghton, for example, but after Gilpin's time, it was agreed that all controversies should be formally referred to the arbitration of some of the chief inhabitants and of the parson who was to be universal 'umpire'. (But later it was acknowledged that this 'pious order' had lapsed into

---

[103] *The Works of Geoffrey Chaucer*, ed. F. N. Robinson (Oxford, 1957 edn.), pp. 21–2.
[104] Ex inf. Mark Byford.

disuse.[105]) Jane Freeman brings a challenging charge against the post-Reformation clergy as fallible peace-makers when she suggests that every one of the thousands of defamation suits heard in the courts represented another small failure in the ministry of reconciliation.[106] But defamation suits were themselves part of a delicate mechanism made up of informal and formal procedures for damage limitation in social relations which invites a sensitive anthropological as well as legal-historical investigation.[107]

The passing of confession also displaced into the presentment of offenders to the courts and the forms of public penance often enforced against those convicted. These too were last resorts for conscientious clergy anxious to induce christian and moral behaviour by 'gentler' means stopping short of total social humiliation.[108]

As John Bossy has taught us, confession and absolution were both public and private business.[109] As private business, the sacrament was replaced by that form of casuistry dispensed in the reformed Church of England and called the healing of wounded consciences. Of this ministry there is abundant testimony, not only in Clarkeian hagiography but in the correspondence passing between divines and their lay 'patients', as often as not female,[110] and in such sources as the record kept by Arthur Hildersham of the sayings and resolutions of Richard Greenham, in which literary continuity is provided by the repetitive formulae 'To one that would know . . . hee gave this advice', 'When one complained to him . . . he said', 'Unto one that was troubled with unbeleef, he gave this counsaile . . .'[111]

But none of this was a sufficient substitute for the old sacrament and discipline of penance, or so many Protestants themselves said. If we refer

---

[105] Freeman, 'The Parish Ministry', pp. 378–9.
[106] *Ibid.*, p. 377.
[107] J. Sharpe, *Defamation and Sexual Slander in Early Modern England: the Church Courts at York*, Borthwick Papers 58 (York, 1980); J. Sharpe, '"Such Disagreement betwyx Neighbours": Litigation and Human Relations in Early Modern England', in *Disputes and Settlements: Law and Human Relations in the West*, ed. John Bossy (Cambridge, 1983); Martin Ingram, *Church Courts, Sex and Marriage in England, 1570–1640* (Cambridge, 1987), pp. 292–319.
[108] This follows the suggestions of Ingram, *Church Courts*.
[109] John Bossy, 'The Social History of Confession in the Age of the Reformation', *TRHS* 5th ser., 25 (1975), pp. 21–38.
[110] Patrick Collinson, 'The Role of Women in the English Reformation Illustrated by the Life and Friendships of Anne Locke', in *Godly People*, pp. 273–87. I hope to publish more extensively on this theme under the title '"Not Sexual in the Ordinary Sense": Women, Men and Religious Transactions'.
[111] John Rylands University Library of Manchester, Rylands English MS 524.

back to those pre-Reformation manuals for parish priests we find that they imply by their literary organization that sacramental penance was what nineteenth-century Anglo-Catholics would later insist that it was, the mainspring of the priesthood. The *Oculus Sacerdotis* of William of Pagula begins with a manual for confessors sufficiently comprehensive to include advice for expectant and nursing mothers. The *Memoriale Presbiterorum* is nothing more nor less than a manual for those hearing confessions. For example, it warns those dealing in this capacity with sailors that 'pen can scarcely suffice to write the sins in which they are involved'.[112]

I do not know how closely acquainted Elizabethan and Jacobean ministers were with the sins of sailors, the special case of ships' chaplains aside. It was as if the great unwashed public said to them: don't call us, we will call you. The difference was critical and perhaps critically damaging. A succession of protestant and even puritan writers complained that the loss of the ordinary penitential function had had the effect of tying one of the reformed minister's hands behind his back. Not that they had any ambition to bring back the popish claim to bind and loose with all the abuse inseparable from it. But to abandon the practice of one christian making confession to another was to throw the baby out with the bath water. Latimer had complained in the time of Edward VI: 'But to speak of right and true confession, I would to God it were kept in England; for it is a good thing.'[113] Nor was this merely the backward-looking opinion of a proto-Protestant born in the year of the battle of Bosworth. The Elizabethan puritan ideologue Thomas Cartwright taught that it was as lawful and convenient to make one's confession to any other man as unto a priest. Yet 'there is none so meete for thy purpose in the behalfe as thine own Curate . . . For he is appointed of God to be heardman of thy soul.'[114] And William Perkins later taught that since it was incumbent upon the minister to confess to God not only his own sins but the sins of his people, his people must first confess their sins to him. 'The want of this is a great fault in our churches' and it made ministers 'accessories to the sinnes of their people'. Perkins went on to condemn auricular confession as a spiritual confidence trick, 'a rack to the consciences of poore Christians'. But he commended the more informal practice of opening one's estate to the pastor, unburdening the conscience and craving his assistance and

---

[112] Pantin, *English Church in the Fourteenth Century*, pp. 197, 209.

[113] *Sermons and Remains of Hugh Latimer*, ed. G. E. Corrie, PS (Cambridge, 1845), p. 180.

[114] Thomas Cartwright, *Two very godly and comfortable letters* (1589), in *Cartwrightiana*, eds Albert Peel and Leland H. Carlson, Elizabethan Nonconformist Texts 1 (London, 1951), pp. 88–105.

prayers. 'And the want of it is the cause why a Minister cannot discerne the estate even of his own flocke, nor can complaine to God of their pollutions and confesse their sinnes so particularly as would be good both for him and them.'[115]

In effect Cartwright and Perkins were complaining of the neglect of one essential part of Calvinist discipline, and one committed as much to the eldership and consistory as to the minister alone. But in England the discipline remained in most respects a pipe dream and these pleas were so much hot air escaping between the formalized censures of the church courts on the one hand (what the Separatist John Robinson called 'rattles')[116] and the voluntary resolution of afflicted consciences practised on the other by such physicians of the soul as Greenham. Later the attempt by Laudians to reinstate universal auricular confession along lines closer to Roman practice were no more successful. Anthony Sparrow's words published in 1637, 'he that assents to the Church of England . . . cannot deny the Priest the power of remitting sinnes', were a 'popish' provocation.[117] Anglican rather than Calvinist discipline was closer to coercive social control than to the genuinely pastoral and restorative cure of souls. It was capable of imposing conformity but not of completing and complementing the preacher's work of conversion. For the converted, the logic of conscientious voluntarism tended towards sectarianism and separatism, something as remote as possible from the intentions of the godly ministry and from the fully parochial establishment of religion which has been assumed as the basic 'given' throughout this paper.

Historians are rightly suspicious of mono-causal explanations. If we wanted to explain why the Church of England as a pastoral agency eventually found itself ministering to a largish sect rather than to a nation we should have to scan several centuries and a great many distinct factors including, at theological root and so far as this period is concerned, Calvinism in all its implications. But the loss of confession on the catholic model without the gain of effective protestant discipline would be high on the list if we had to opt for a single explanation. As Dr Spaeth has pointed out, in the late seventeenth century it was left to individuals and self-selecting groups to decide on the basis of general exhortation whether they were morally fit, or could be bothered, to conduct themselves as

---

[115] William Perkins, *Of the calling of the ministerie, two treatises, discribing the duties and dignities of their calling, delivered publickly in the Universitie of Cambridge* (London, 1605), pp. 28–9.

[116] John Robinson, *Works*, ed. R. Ashton (1851), 2, p. 60.

[117] Anthony Sparrow, *A sermon concerning confession of sinnes, and the power of absolution* (London, 1637), p. 17. Sparrow's sermon was reprinted in 1704.

fully communicant members of the Church or not. How they responded to that challenge, and to the Gospel itself, depended upon the preacher, the effectiveness of his sermon and the response of the hearers, that variety of soils on which English exponents of the Parable of the Sower had so often commented.[118]

The Parable of the Sower was not a suitable foundation on which to erect a national Church. Richard Hooker provided a more plausible basis for what Dr Lake has called a 'broad-bottomed' christian community, but Hooker's motivation was itself polemical and so in a sense sectarian, part of the problem rather than a solution.[119] And in any case Hooker and the Hookerians were not much read or listened to. In the past I have been reluctant to agree with Dr Christopher Hill that a voluntarist plurality and diversity of religious belief, including what Newman in the nineteenth century called 'Nothingarians', was implicit and imprinted in Protestantism in its Lutheran title-deeds, since these consequences were so clearly at variance with everything for which the protestant ministry stood. But I suppose that the *longue durée* of the Reformation proves Dr Hill to have been right after all. The pastoral ministry in post-Reformation England was a long-term failure, the religious plurality and secularity of modern Britain its ultimate consequence and legacy.

Trinity College, Cambridge

---

[118] Spaeth, 'Common Prayer?', pp. 125–51.
[119] How polemical is shown by the judicious Hooker's autograph notes on the margins of the book written against him, *A christian letter*: 'How this asse runneth kicking up his heels as if a summerfly had stung him.' (*Richard Hooker's Of the Laws of Ecclesiastical Polity: Attack and Response*, ed. John E. Booty, *Folger Library Edition of the Work of Richard Hooker*, 4 (Cambridge, Mass., 1982), p. 42.)

RICHARD KILBY: A STUDY IN PERSONAL AND PROFESSIONAL FAILURE

by PETER LAKE

THE image of the minister of the word current amongst English evangelical protestants and puritans was both exalted and ambiguous. Ministers were 'the lord's ambassadors, the salt of the earth, the light of the world, the dispensers of God's mysteries, the builders of God's church and the chariot and horsemen . . . of a Christian kingdom.'[1] However, the qualities and qualifications necessary successfully to fulfill that role were onerous in the extreme. To be a true minister it was necessary firstly and essentially to preach, which in turn entailed the mastering a large range of scholarly skills, involving knowledge of the original languages, of logic, rhetoric, church history, and theology. But it was necessary also for a true minister to be personally godly, first because he had to lead his flock toward a Christian life not merely through exhortation but also through example and, second, because his own spiritual condition, the integrity of his calling both as a Christian and as a minister, vitally effected the efficacy of his ministry. After all, the deeper his own understanding of the word—always as much a function of spiritual insight as formal learning—and the more completely his own character had been made over by the sanctifying activity of the Holy Spirit, the more effectively he could communicate his saving message to his flock.[2]

Perhaps the clearest picture of the successful integration of these disparate elements into successful public ministries can be found in the series of godly lives of famous puritan divines collected by Samuel Clarke in the 1650s and 1660s. Amongst other things these lives often represent a

---

[1] Robert Some, *A godly treatise of the church* (London, 1582), sig. A4[v].

[2] J. Morgan, *Godly Learning* (Cambridge, 1986), chapters 5–7; for a list of the learned skills necessary for the ministry drawn up by Laurence Chaderton, see P. Lake, *Moderate puritans and the Elizabethan church* (Cambridge, 1982), pp. 36–7; on the need for personal godliness, see R. Bernard, *The faithful shepherd* (London, 1621), pp. 73–8. 'For he stands in God's room and speaks for God, is the instrument appointed by Christ to publish the gospel, the word of grace and to guide the people in the way of grace. It is therefore necessary that he be endued with grace and with the gifts of God's most holy spirit . . . He must have the spirit of illumination to see into the mysteries of God's word farther than nature or art can teach.' He must have 'the gift of supplication and prayer' of 'inward sanctification' and of 'outward reformation and holy conversation'.

retrospective view of successfully completed processes of upward social mobility. In the lives there is a basic congruence established between the doctrine of election and the process of clerical recruitment and advancement. On the one hand the individual is plucked by the arbitrary will and grace of God out of the unregenerate mass of humanity, to enjoy in this life a gradual process of sanctification and a consequent sense of assurance about his or her own salvation. On the other, a young scholar is plucked from often humble and unenlightened origins by the impersonal forces of social mobility, acting here through the agency of the university and its patronage networks. Here his painfully acquired academic skills are given a potent ideological rationale as the necessary tools for the interpretation of God's word and he is recruited into a new peer group, that of the university-educated ministry. This represented a classic instance of the career open to talents, since a minister's success as a preacher was in theory entirely a function of the academic and spiritual qualities he brought to his work. Thus provided with a glistening new self image the aspirant minister was given the opportunity to forge a career. In the *Lives* we are given examples of this process in successful operation. Often the decision . to take up the ministry is tied up with a personal conversion experience undergone at university. From the university the young scholar then goes out into the Church and there spiritual and modest material success mirror one another. The minister's personal godliness serves to underwrite the efficacy of his public ministry. Often as not he gains the love and esteem of the local godly community and enjoys the patronage and even the friendship of the local gentleman. He is nearly always married, with a household run as a 'little church', often serving as a sort of seminary for other young would-be ministers from the university.[3]

That then was the ideal. But ideal or not, there were enough clerical careers that approximated to it in their rough outlines to make it seem to aspirant ministers both attainable and desirable. There were, however, snags. Apart from the inherent difficulties of striking the right balance between charisma and learning, spiritual enthusiasm and admonitory

[3] For lives centred around university conversions see those of John Preston and John Cotton in S. Clarke, *A general martyrology* (London, 1677) and that of Thomas Goodwin at the front of volume 5 of *The works of Thomas Goodwin* (London, 1681–1704). On this phenomenon, see P. Seaver, *Wallington's world* (London, 1985), pp. 14–15; for a typical ministerial success story, see the life of Samuel Fairclough in S. Clarke, *The lives of sundry eminent persons* (London, 1683); on the seminaries for aspiring ministers held in the households of established divines, see in particular the life of Richard Blackerby in S. Clarke, *Eminent persons*; on the running of the household as a little church, see the lives of John Cotton, John Carter and Thomas Gataker in S. Clarke, *Martyrology*.

rigour, the demands of the godly and the expectations of authority, there were other practical obstacles. By the early seventeenth century more and more formally qualified candidates were chasing a limited number of decent livings.[4] There were, therefore, more than enough reasons for a career to miscarry. In the present paper I want to examine just one such career, using as a source the two accounts Richard Kilby produced of his own personal and professional failures; accounts intended as a sort of negative godly life, a cautionary tale through which Kilby could transcend his own private crisis by making it the public grounds of others' success.[5]

In retrospect Kilby concluded that he had entered the ministry for the wrong reasons, for, as he put it, 'worldly gain and glory'.[6] Coming to the university relatively poor he needed to find friends. This he managed but his lack of funds caused him to steal from and cheat his 'good friends' and contemporaries. Nevertheless the university and his place in it allowed him to project a positive, even assertive image of himself. 'My study was to make a great show of little learning and therefore I sought after fine choice words. When I disputed with any I was desirous to dismay them with reproaches instead of reasons and to that end I had a written phrase book stuffed with daunting and biting speeches.' Commenting retrospectively on his university days Kilby remarked that 'pride and envy are properties of the devil; and of all other sins most ready to wait upon scholars. Therefore take great heed of them; if you be proud you are Lucifer high in your own conceit and therefore shall be brought low, even down into hell. If you envy the learning, estimation and prosperity of others you are Satan, an enemy to the gifts of God's grace.'[7]

Having to make his way in the world on the basis of his wits and his education Kilby took the conventional path for young scholars in his position and became first a schoolmaster and then a minister. On his own

---

[4] For figures on employment opportunities for ministers, see I. Green, 'Career prospects and clerical conformity in the early Stuart church', *P & P* 90 (1981). Green's figures are intended as a corrective to those of M. H. Curtis and present a fairly optimistic picture of the number of openings relative to the numbers of graduates entering the ministry. The point being made here is that to pursue the vision of the ministry described in the lives required a certain level of prosperity and esteem, required, that is, a good living and that by the early seventeenth century the pressure on good livings from formally well qualified candidates was increasing. See R. O'Day, *The English clergy* (Leicester, 1979).

[5] Richard Kilby, *The burthen of a loaden conscience or the misery of sin* (Cambridge, 1608); this was followed by *Hallelujah praise the lord for the unburthening of a loaded conscience* (Cambridge, 1618). I should like to thank Patrick Collinson for drawing these fascinating volumes to my attention.

[6] *Burthen*, p. 88.

[7] *Ibid.*, pp. 59, 82.

account Kilby laboured long and hard to master the scholarly techniques which men like Laurence Chaderton and other leading lights in the puritan movement considered essential for the learned minister. He was forced

> to toil myself night and day else that lowest degree of sufficiency which by God's mercy I have I should never have had. I had been forced to renew my knowledge of logic, the art of understanding again and again and yet am far short of perfection. He that is ignorant in this art I cannot devise how he may be an understanding minister. In the latin tongue I was not very perfect yet somewhat ready. But to get a little smack in that learned language the Greek mine eyes have foregone much sleep and been made to smart very often. Into the language of Chanaan, the Hebrew, I have so little sight as may be; yet it cost me some labour and expense withal. By these pains I have obtained (God being merciful unto me) this profit; I can make shift to understand many learned authors that have written books very helpful for him which studieth divinity.[8]

Kilby then, had clearly bought into the image of the learned divine current in his college, Emmanuel, and attributed no little importance to the skills he had so painfully acquired there. And yet even he was forced to admit that when he first arrived in a rural parish those same skills were not of immediate relevance. He soon found that, instead of a second sermon on the sabbath, a question and answer session with some of the better informed members of the congregation concerning some 'three or four questions touching the foundations of religion' had more value. Kilby would then make their 'short answers plain' and prove 'them out of the bible in half an hours space'. Here, he claimed, was a lesson for all aspiring ministers.

> I humbly advise all young preachers that they will not imagine they can build Jerusalem suddenly for sudden buildings will soon fall down. I marvel how it cometh to pass that in some places even where learned preachers have killed themselves with sore labours the greater number of people are grossly ignorant . . . The common sort is much neglected for neither matter of doctrine nor manner of speech is fitted unto their low and small capacity. Most people for some three quarters of an hour if they understand the words and perceive the

[8] *Burthen*, p. 84; *Hallelujah*, pp. 127–8.

matter concerning their salvation to be plainly proved out of the book of God (which for ought I know is of greater reverence with them then with many of higher degree and greater understanding) I say if they be plainly and briefly taught out of God's book they will give very diligent ear. But if the preacher confound their understanding or be longer than ordinary they leave all and think thus when will yonder man have done; he hath no reason to make an end.[9]

Thus not only was the gloss removed from Kilby's university-produced self image by his own mediocre academic performance, the very logic of his situation as a rural minister called into question the value of his training for the immediate task of bringing the saving word of God to his simple flock as they sat slumped before him in their pews. Even if we take similar ministerial jeremiads with a pinch of salt, and make due allowance for the exceptional situation confronted by those Lancashire ministers whose pastoral failure has been so sharply pointed out by Dr Haigh, it seems very unlikely that Kilby's experience here was unique or even unusual.[10]

But Kilby had sources of worry greater than these. The image of the godly minister against which he felt compelled to measure his own performance did not only emphasize the minister's formal qualifications, it also stressed the quality and authenticity of his own calling as a Christian and a minister. As we have seen, Kilby felt he had entered the ministry for all the wrong reasons. Just as at university Kilby had exploited his sharp tongue to impress his contemporaries so now as a minister he used his position to cut a dash in front of his parishioners. In his earlier days that impulse had led Kilby to espouse formally puritan opinions. In his first job, in 1598, he had got into trouble over a sermon on the succession. Elsewhere he implied that the rebukes he had delivered to his flock at that time had been less than moderate and had consequently led not to repentance and reconciliation but to contention and strife. He was, he admitted, 'of a froward disposition apt to displease and disquiet everyone'. He had preached 'with a kind of furiousness, the common behaviour of such as are tumultuously, confusedly and rawly prepared'. He acknowledged that he was of a malicious caste of mind. 'It is an hellish property of

---

[9] *Ibid.*, pp. 81–2.

[10] C. A. Haigh, 'Puritan evangelism in the reign of Elizabeth I', *EHR* 92 (1977). It is perhaps worth pointing out that Kilby's point, stressing as it does the readiness of the people to respond to a simple exposition of central truths straight from the bible, does not square with Dr Haigh's perhaps overly pessimistic view of popular imperviousness to all sorts of protestant preaching.

mine to occasion speech of any in place where they are likely to be ill spoken of whereby I set them as a mark for others to shoot at.' Too often such impulses had marred his performances in the pulpit and elsewhere. In the arbitration of 'question touching goods between party and party' 'I have oftentimes been very partial . . . because I have been ill conceited of the one or well opinioned of the other or thought to be the gainer by the business.'[11]

Kilby, it seems, was less than pleased with his performance as a minister. But given the integral relationship established in puritan theory between the spiritual standing of the minister and the success of his public ministry it is scarcely surprising that Kilby's sense of failure generated a full-scale spiritual crisis of the classic puritan sort. He started to think that he was damned, that his failings as a minister betokened a reprobate heart.

> I took upon me to preach neither understanding the word of God nor endued with the power of godliness therefore I have endangered the salvation of many people . . . The word of God is in itself most pure and wholesome but my preaching hath defiled it with ignorance and with the wicked infection of pride, envy, wrath, covetousness and all sins, every vice upon occasion putting itself into my sermons. Moreover if I preached anything according to the word of god I utterly unpreached and denied it in my life and conversation . . . I cannot say upon my conscience that in all this time wherein I have taken upon me to be a minister I have done my duty so much as to the saving of one soul . . . It had been better for me to have gotten my living by begging from door to door; yea less had been my sin if I had lived by stealing and robbing, for he that is a minister and doth not discharge his duty is a thief and a robber in the highest degree because he robbeth God of his people and robbeth people of their salvation. How is it possible for me to escape the vengeance of hell fire?[12]

I want now to focus on the extent to which this personal and professional crisis was conditioned and exacerbated, if not caused, by his lowly status in the ecclesiastical pecking order. Kilby's career is an almost classic example of the sort of circumstances which Mark Curtis years ago identified as producing the alienated intellectuals of the puritan movement. A victim of the increasing numbers of graduates becoming clergymen Kilby never obtained a proper living. He held, instead, three

---

[11] *Hallelujah*, pp. 36–7, 54, 79; *Burthen*, pp. 48, 61.
[12] *Burthen*, pp. 87–8.

curacies; one in Kent, which he lost due to the hostile attentions of Bishop Barlow, and two in Derbyshire, the first of which he obtained through the good offices of an old friend at Emmanuel and John Cotton. In the crudest terms, then, Kilby never made it; moreover his lack of material success contributed directly to his other spiritual failures and failings.[13]

To begin with the tightness of the job market put pressure on Kilby, pressure which in turn produced sinful thoughts and aspirations. As Kilby confessed,

> I was never content with that which God gave me but continually dis-liked my state murmuring and casting out complaints, envying the prosperity of others judging them not so worthy of it as myself; yea wishing in my heart that I had their goods. Being promised a living which I could not have till the death of him that had it and hath it I often desired to hear of his death. Wherefore by the just judgement of God he is likely to hear of my death. When I had heard that such and such were in possibility of preferment or had obtained it I fretted and fumed at it because I would have had it myself.[14]

Once installed as a curate, lack of funds may well have helped to prompt his propensity to seek personal gain and play favourites in the arbitration of disputes. Similarly, Kilby's straightened circumstances may well have contributed to his failure to marry. This was a source of constant regret to him since he was tortured by the lusts of the flesh. These were a most unsuitable affliction for a minister of the word, of course, and Kilby counselled his readers not

> to muse of women or let your eyes be delighted in beholding their beauty and fineness; give no regard to their coy behaviour, tripping and dancing. Take no pleasure in hearing their delicate talking, sweet singing and amorous playing; for the devil is ready when you are any-way touched with the delight of women presently to kindle his fire in your heart. Be not much familiar with any woman, specially alone;

---

[13] M. H. Curtis, 'The alienated intellectuals of early Stuart England', *P & P* 23 (1961), reprinted in T. H. Aston, ed., *Crisis in Europe* (London, 1965); for details of Kilby's career see *Hallelujah*, pp. 34–44. He went first to Gloucester Hall in Oxford, then spent 'not so long' at Emmanuel Cambridge 'but to that college I am singularly bound'. He became a minister in 1596, having been ordained by Bishop Young of Rochester and been granted a preaching licence by Whit-gift. He became curate to the parson of Southfleet in Kent, only to be put out by Bishop Barlowe. Thence he went to a curateship in the parish of St Alkmunds in Derby, gained through connections made at Emmanuel. He left there and ended his days (in 1617) as curate of All Hallows also in Derby.

[14] *Burthen*, p. 72.

for it will cause danger to you and suspicion to others. If you see a woman to be very fellowly judge her not for she may be good but be you a stranger unto her lest Satan make you nought. Do not dally, jest or play with women lest it happen to you as to the fly that playeth about the candle till she have spoiled her flying.

The remedy for such temptations and dalliances lay, of course, in marriage but Kilby never succeeded in finding a wife. 'I had been a married man and freed from the flames of lust but that I gave ear to those that disliked the party whom I had good cause to like and to love . . . I was accursed and therefore unstedfast in all good courses.' Kilby thus continued to be afflicted with unclean thoughts and these led him into the sin of envy at other men's success in the marriage stakes. 'When I saw a man have a wife of good condition I coud find in my heart to wish him dead and myself married to his wife. And when one married a wife whom I liked I stomached it much because I had her not.'[15]

Again his relative poverty made the establishment of the social distance between himself and his flock, which on the puritan view was so essential for a minister, difficult to sustain. 'Your conversation' Kilby told other would be ministers,

> must be every way square to your profession; for you cannot so much as speak a word in jest but it shall be heeded and considered. Yea if there be any ill word spoken in your hearing people will mark how you take it . . . When I as a curate entered into a charge of souls the people at the first had such a reverent opinion of me by reason of mine earnest plainess in preaching that they were very careful lest I should see any fault in their behaviour; but afterwards when they perceived that the practice of my life was not according to my preaching they grew in a manner careless what they said or what they did; whereas if I had not lost that first reputation I think in my conscience that many yea most of them would have amended their ways.

Here the key was the maintenance of distance. 'A minister ought to be grave and mild. Gravity without mildness is surliness, mildness without gravity is lightness. Jocund, jesting and scoffing behaviour doth not become a minister for he is the true messenger of God and weighty is his message.' 'It is' claimed Kilby,

---

[15] *Burthen*, pp. 55–8, 72.

a true saying that too much familiarity breeds contempt and so I have always found it. Therefore use to retire yourself and be no common company keeper; for howsoever you may preserve your personal reputation yet the power of your office, which is much grounded upon a reverent estimation, will be by company keeping many ways diminished; the appearance of any vice in a minister doth disable his ministry; specially pride and covetousness.[16]

And yet covetousness was a particular threat to the impecunious. Ministers, he claimed, should be careful to live within their means, otherwise, falling into debt, they would become 'engaged' to creditors with disastrous consequences for the impartiality of their position in the parish. 'Who hath more cause to keep himself free than a minister. For if he be engaged to any the devil will tempt him to sooth them in their sins or at least to be tongue tied and not reprove them for their faults. Alas! in what wretched state are many curates? For they are driven to seek their commodities where they can find them.' Again, Kilby complained, 'another inconvenience on a hinderly minister is that he cannot be beneficial to the poor; which is a very special point in a minister; for how can it appear that he is zealous to feed men's souls that hath no care to comfort their bodies.'[17]

All in all a shortage of funds rendered it almost impossible for Kilby to cut the right sort of godly, grave, yet charitable and approachable figure so necessary for an effective ministry of the word. Single and relatively impecunious, Kilby's lodgings were poor. Having once found comfortable quarters with a kindly family he was forced to move when he changed jobs and stayed from then on in an ale-house. This rendered Kilby both as a minister and as an ordinary Christian singularly exposed to what Kilby termed 'company'. This was particularly worrying at moments of spiritual crisis for, lamented Kilby, frequent and passionate prayer was central to all true piety and for that solitude was essential. However, Kilby's lowly status made privacy something that he found difficult to afford. 'The stairs to my chamber' he wrote, 'are the coming up into three other chambers, so oft as I heard the noise of any bodies feet coming up the stairs I was very fearful that some or other were coming unto me and as glad as if I heard them go by the door to any of the other chambers.'[18]

This image of Kilby crouching in his room, jumping at every footfall

---

[16] *Ibid.*, pp. 93–5.
[17] *Ibid.*, pp. 95–6.
[18] *Hallelujah*, pp. 76, 138–9, 113.

on the stairs, hugging his spiritual crisis to himself as some final validation of his apartness from the world as a minister and an elect saint is striking enough. However, often as not, as is clear from other passages, his exposure to the delights and distractions of company led to spiritual defeat and forgetfulness. Hence, Kilby noted on one day 'at evening prayer I read and preached again. Afterward being very much wearied I had a mind to go and refresh myself in company (the bane of sabbath day keeping) and went first to one house and then to another, ending the day very heathenishly.' On another day, having presided at a burial Kilby 'went into the town where being in company I forgot God and what any man perceived in my behaviour I know not. Thence I came home and after some idle communication with some which I found in the house coming into my chamber my spirit was so ashamed to speak unto God that I went prayerless to bed.' On a third occasion Kilby noted 'I was drawn to a feast and so into much sin; for no sauce is so common at a feast as sin. Sin maketh all the company merry. Satan also hath his factors who begin some one or other ungodly kind of merriment.' On his own account, at least, Kilby was 'naturally such a one, yea worse than the worst of them that are so disposed' and he devoted one of his extended prayers (reproduced in his books) to a petition for divine aid in resisting his proneness to 'accompanying and talking'.[19]

Kilby came to the conclusion that 'if I could in company be mindfull of God and shun the displeasing of his majesty I were in a very fair forward-ness of reformation', but his attempts to keep this resolution continued to be dogged by temptation and failure. That he met with any success at all in finally freeing himself from the toils of Satan and the world Kilby came to attribute to physical affliction. He had for years suffered from the stone, and it was the resulting pain and despair in the face of an imminent death that forced his thoughts back to God and plunged him into despair and distress every time he lapsed into company again and forgot his repeated resolutions to repent and reform. We are back with Kilby, cowering in his room, creased with pain, desperately bargaining with God for spiritual solace and physical relief, and hoping all the time that each set of footsteps he hears on the stairs keeps on going.[20]

---

[19] *Hallelujah*, pp. 81, 85, 83, 110.
[20] *Ibid.*, p. 42; the complaint had always been with him ('Gravel hath bred in me from my youth and oftentimes I was pained with it'), but it became more serious and then excruciating in the period between July 1612 and November 1613; *ibid.*, pp. 109–10, 122–3. 'I am fully persuaded that had not this disease come upon me yea and prevailed more and more even to the putting of me quite out of all hope of a recovery I should never have been divorced and

In all this Kilby's prime concern was with his fate in the next world, as an individual Christian and sinner. His was the typical puritan quest for a lively sense of a true saving faith, an assurance of salvation. However, he included enough incidental detail in his two books to allow us to see how that private spiritual quest and crisis interacted with and was compounded by his sense of his public, professional failure as a minister. In the process it has become clear that there was much in Kilby's situation in common with the forces which, on Professor Curtis's account, produced the alienated intellectuals of the puritan movement. Perhaps I can conclude, therefore, with a discussion of Kilby's somewhat ambiguous relationship with 'puritanism'. Did Kilby's less than happy socio-economic position produce the sort of radical disaffection posited by Curtis? If anything, Kilby's failure led him to turn away from puritanism, defined either as a series of gestures of disaffection towards the structure of the Church or of radical commitment to a public reformation of morals. He associated his earlier puritan phase, with its intemperate attacks on the sins of his parishioners, its pronouncements on affairs of state, its tendency to play favourites within the parish, with his old corrupt impulse to exploit the ministry for personal glory or gain. Now, however, Kilby counselled moderation and restraint. He had learned their value from bitter experience. 'The best way for a preacher's self and the most likely to prevail in persuading his hearers is, if I be not much deceived, grave, mild and treatable speech.' 'If you be assured that any one doth amiss in your parish tell him his fault secretly and very kindly beseeching him in Christ's behalf to turn unto God. Whosoever fall out do not you appear to be adversary to any one nor to uphold the party against him. It will hinder your ministry and peradventure put you into more trouble then you can imagine.' Similarly, his experiences over the succession sermon led him to advise his readers not to meddle 'with state matters above your calling; for it is a piece of a rebellious nature to call the doings of higher powers into question ...' The minister was similarly to draw a veil over the shortcomings of his colleagues in the ministry. 'Although any other minister seem faulty and have an ill report yet do not endure to speak or hear any evil of him ... Do not envy nor despise any minister whomsoever nor meddle with any man's charge but your own.'[21]

---

separated from the love of this world.' For an example of Kilby bargaining with God for both physical and spiritual relief in return for repentance, see *ibid.*, pp. 104, 108–9, 48–68.
[21] *Hallelujah*, p. 79; *Burthen*, pp. 97, 40.

Kilby's disaffection with an aggressively zealous puritanism had roots other than his youthful excesses. He himself had not always fared well at the hands of the self-styled godly. In a sermon preached in Derby in 1611 against the evils of popery he had argued that 'though the papists be our dangerous enemies as well as being full of malice and treason yet we ought to be rather angry with our sins than with them' for it was our sins not the papists that would lose us the favour of God and allow 'the mystery of iniquity to prevail against us'. That together with a slip of the tongue in pronouncing the king's full title in his prayer before the sermon had been enough for some 'men professing great preciseness of conscience' to report him for popery. Similarly the confessions and revelations contained in his first book had not gone down well 'with many precise folk that know not other men's hearts howsoever they know their own'.[22]

Kilby, however, was no aggressively conformist renegade from the puritan cause. He retained a reputation for familiarity with precisians strong enough to gain a rebuke for it from 'a learned friend of mine'. Elsewhere, enjoining his readers to give thanks to God before every meal, he warned them that such behaviour might win them the reputation of 'a precise foolish body'. Such slights were to be expected and ignored. 'If you for serving God be ill thought of a blessed soul are you. It is a great favour of God if he vouchsafe to give you the grace to suffer any wrong for his sake.' On this view, the appellation 'puritan' was a mark of distinction bestowed by the ungodly on the godly, to be worn almost with pride.[23]

It is true that he lamented the bitterness of the divide between puritans and conformists, claiming that it gave advantage only to 'popery and prophaneness'.

> Is it not a lamentable case that some appear to have almost no con-
> science but against ceremonies, others none but for ceremonies? The
> precisian doth (in my conscience not without cause) cry out against
> the ignorant, idle and prophane ministers. But where is the fault? the
> coast had been well cleared by this time of the day had not Satan
> caused church government to be both by way of soberness and in the
> fashion of madness very fiercely assailed. But to what end. To reform
> the church not to deform it?

Kilby was no presbyterian then, but if he felt the government of the Church to be essentially sound he remained prepared to condemn abuses.

[22] *Hallelujah*, pp. 37–43.
[23] *Ibid.*, p. 87; *Burthen*, p. 22.

He denounced what he took to be the corruption and ineffectiveness of the Church courts where the 'punishment of fornication and adultery is little else but large fees. A filthy gain fie upon it'. Again, discussing the sign of the cross used in baptism, while he denied ever having disobediently omitted to use it himself he did unequivocally denounce it as a popish abuse.[24]

More important for Kilby than the external structures of the government or liturgy of the Church was the spirit with which they were administered. The crucial question was not whether episcopacy was legal or not, but whether a particular 'lord bishop' seek his own worldly commodity' or 'the edifying of his diocese and the glory of Jesus Christ'. Again, Kilby remarked darkly

> touching the ministry ... I humbly pray great scholars and all that seek after riches and advancement in the church to ponder these my words. The gospel of the son of God must and will throw down pride and covetousness before it work a universal good in this kingdom. Those two great sins cannot be upheld anyway but only by popery for they must be accompanied with a superstitious conceit that pomp is religion; which when all have said what they can say the gospel will not endure.[25]

And so we return to sin and in particular the sins of pride and covetousness. Kilby's own failure, personal, pastoral, and professional, he attributed to these, just as he saw them behind his own early fractiously puritan phase, behind presbyterian schemes for further reformation, and behind conformist careerism. Interestingly from the point of view of the Curtis thesis, his underemployment in the Jacobean Church had not led him into a radical puritan rejection of that Church, but had rather prompted a revulsion at such self-serving and aggrandizing gestures. Kilby remained committed to the puritan vision of the minister, which linked so closely the state of a man's ministry with the state of his soul. Perhaps the existence of paradigmatic success stories, like those retold by Clarke, in which ministers of the same background and attitude as himself achieved an enviable mixture of personal happiness, social status, and ideological purity rendered his own failure the more unpalatable and inexplicable. Either way, confronted with the failures and frustrations of his life as a minister, he blamed neither the structure of the Church nor

[24] *Hallelujah*, pp. 87–9, 120–1.
[25] *Ibid.*, pp. 89–90.

the monopoly of the best jobs by corrupt conformists; instead he blamed himself. The result was not radical puritan activism but rather moderate puritan quietism, as Kilby internalized his failure as a minister and came to experience it as a deep crisis of faith; a crisis experienced and handled within the terms laid down by a classically puritan style of religious subjectivity, centred on the search for a settled sense of assurance that one was saved, a sense sought through a continuous process of covenanting with God and the self in pursuit of true repentance and a personal reformation of manners.[26]

Despite his in many ways perfect replication of the characteristics laid down by Curtis for alienated puritan intellectuals Kilby can scarcely be taken to provide confirmation for the Curtis thesis. And yet it is worth remembering that viewed as a bare statistic, without the inner light provided by Kilby's books, Kilby would be just another graduate, entering the ministry and not quite making it, further evidence of the attractiveness of the ministry as a career and of the conformist solidity of the early Stuart Church.[27] Indeed, in one sense Kilby's career does show that jobs could be found in the Jacobean Church for graduates, who, inspired by a very exalted, puritan view of the ministry, were willing both to accept relatively poor terms of employment and to conform to the rites and ceremonies of the Church. And yet in Kilby's case that was scarcely all there was to it. Here, at least, the awesome demands placed on the individual by the very image of the ministry that attracted him in the first place—combined with material circumstances that made it all but impossible to meet those demands successfully—produced a genuine spiritual crisis. This is not to argue that behind every impecunious or frustrated curate or schoolmaster waiting for a living lurked another Richard Kilby.[28] But it is perhaps worth remembering that in the vast

---

[26] Thus he felt that he had refused God's 'preferred grace' by 'taking upon thee to be a preacher of my righteousness and denying the power thereof'. (*Hallelujah*, p. 92.) His status as a minister served simply to render already serious faults the more unforgiveable—'of all counterfeits' he observed, 'the most incurable is a counterfeit preacher of thy righteousness'. (*Ibid.*, p. 75.)

[27] Very much the line taken by Green ('Career prospects and clerical conformity') who largely ignores questions of ideology or the subjective apprehension of individual career trajectories.

[28] Some sense of the range of individual experience that can lie behind careers, which, taken at face value, for statistical purposes, might appear almost identical can be gained by comparing Kilby with Dr Hughes' account of Thomas Dugard. Dugard was a schoolmaster for fifteen years before he became a minister in 1648—a classic victim of the crush of qualified applicants for clerical employment during this period—except that his job at Warwick school was well paid, brought him into frequent contact with local godly notables, up to and including Lord Brooke, as well as the leading members of the local puritan clergy. Through friendship

number of cases we are denied any such insight into the interior life of such lowly ministers, and that, as Kilby's case shows, beneath the seemingly calm surface of the Jacobean Church might lurk all sorts of resentment, fear, and loathing. The likes of Kilby might not be a cause of the English civil war, as Curtis claimed, but Kilby's experiences and the light they throw on the personal costs of puritan clericalism and the drive toward a largely graduate clergy retain, I think, some claim on our attention.

Royal Holloway and Bedford New College, London

---

networks of this sort he was able to enjoy the benefits of learned and godly conversation and even to try out his gifts in the pulpit, long before he was ordained. For Dugard, see A. L. Hughes, 'Thomas Dugard and his circle in the 1630s—a 'parliamentary-puritan' connexion?' *HJ* 24 (1986).

PETTY BABYLONS, GODLY PROPHETS, PETTY PASTORS AND LITTLE CHURCHES: THE WORK OF HEALING BABEL

by D. J. LAMBURN

ON 14 February 1608, William Crashaw, who three years earlier had been vicar of St John's Church in Beverley, preached a sermon at St Paul's Cross.[1] He took as his text a verse from Jeremiah—'We would have cured Babel but she would not be healed; let us forsake her, and go every one to his own country.'[2] Yet Crashaw was no schismatic. His own career, beginning with his fellowship at St John's College, Cambridge, had always been within the mainstream of the Established Church. In his will he set out the positions he had held as 'the unworthy and unprofitable servant of God'. He had been 'Preacher of God's word first at Bridlington then at Beverley in Yorkshire. Afterwards at the Temple since then pastor of the Church at Agnes Burton in the diocese of York, now Pastor of that too great parish of White Chapel in the suburbs of London.'[3] There was much else besides; he had been one of the official editors of William Perkins, a writer of numerous works, whose sermons and catechisms were much sought after, one of the founders and shareholders in the New Virginia Company, with good connections at Court.[4] At Paul's Cross Crashaw condemned Brownists 'who forsake our Church, and cut off themselves and separate themselves to a faction, and fashion, or as they call it, into a covenant or communion of their own devising', just as much as those who 'be such as refuse public places in the Church, and commonwealth, and retire themselves into private and discontented courses and will not be employed for the public'.[5] In common with mainstream puritans he deeply disapproved of schismatics and was not above attacking them with the same vehemence

---

[1] William Crashaw, *A Sermon Preached at the Crosse, 14th February 1607* (second impression reviewed by the author, H. L[ownes] and F. M. Lownes, 1609). Dates in the text are given new style. All spellings in quotations have been modernized; names have been standardized.

[2] The text is from Jeremiah 51 v. 9, Geneva Bible.

[3] His will was proved at the Prerogative Court of Canterbury on 16 October 1626, Prob. 11/149 f. 97. A transcript appears in P. J. Wallis, *William Crashawe, the Sheffield Puritan*, reprinted with addenda and Index from Transactions of the Hunter Archaeological Society, Vol. 8 parts 2–5 (1960–63), 1, pp. 5–13.

[4] See Wallis, *William Crashaw*, pp. 15–26 and 27–51, and the *DNB*.

[5] Crashaw, *Sermon at the Crosse*, pp. 26 and 34.

he normally reserved for papists. It is 'unthankful' he wrote, to desert our Church. 'There is indeed a true ministry of the word amongst us ... We have the word truly preached.'[6] When Crashaw referred to the forsaking of Babel he had something very different in mind, for the solution this early seventeenth-century cleric offered concerned the Church's ministry.

It is not without significance that he did not explicitly define what he meant in urging his hearers and readers to forsake Babel. Yet from all his works it is clear what he intended. The spectre of separation from the Church of England posed a threat to the unity, identity, interests, and respectability of protestants. But above all it was popery which Crashaw believed constituted the major threat and which necessitated protestant unity. He saw his life's work as attacking popery, on a pastoral, academic, and polemical level. He made his views clear in the profession of his faith in his will:

> I account popery (as now it is) the heap and chaos of all heresies and the channel whereinto the foulest impieties and heresies that have been in the christian world have run and closely emptied themselves. I believe the Pope's seal and power to be the power of the great antichrist and the doctrine of the Pope (as now it is) to be the doctrine of antichrist yea that doctrine of devils prophesied of by the Apostle and that the true and absolute Papist so living and dying debars himself of salvation for ought that we know and I believe that I am bound to separate myself from that synagogue of Rome if I will be saved.[7]

But if Rome and its doctrine constituted the great Babel or Babylon, physical separation from which was essential, there were other evils, 'petty Babylons', from which separation was required and for which healing was not only possible but was a positive duty to be attempted by all of the godly;

> There is also a mystical Babylon and that is the kingdom of sin ... We endeavour to heal it and make it a paradise ... but when all is done that can be, it cannot be healed, but it is still a very Babel of confusion and disorder, a miserable world, a vale of tears, and a sea of trouble and turmoil to whosoever hath the sweetest portion of it.[8]

[6] Crashaw, *Sermon at the Crosse*, p. 29.
[7] Wallis, *William Crashaw*, pp. 5–6.
[8] Crashaw, *Sermon at the Crosse*, p. 167.

Some of Crashaw's 'petty Babylons', 'sprigs of that cursed root' [popery] affected the Church directly. One such concerned the position and status of the ministry. In his preface to the First Treatise of William Perkins's *Of the Calling of the Ministerie*, which he dedicated to Sir Edward Cooke, he wrote, 'if all our great ones did use and esteem good ministers as you do, we should soon pull the ministry from under that foot of contempt, with which this prófane age doth daily tread upon it'.[9] Comparing the ministers of the English Church with that of Rome he said, 'Contrariwise, our Church ... by avoiding this Scylla, have fallen into Charybdis, by avoiding one extremity, have fallen into the other, and by taking too much dignity and authority from our ministry, and by laying too much poverty, contempt and baseness upon it.'[10] For Crashaw the importance of this matter was simple. One of the principal offices of the minister was to advise the king, the nobles, and the magistrates, as well as the least and poorest soul in his parish. Yet by 'that great Sacrilege and Church-robbing committed by impropriations, (in which at this day almost half of this kingdom is) whereby it comes to pass (above any other one means) that an ignorant and unteaching ministry is set over a great part of our people; which is the source and fountain of all other evils in our church'.[11] Such poverty brought the ministry into contempt: it prevented it from exercising the influence it ought to enjoy. Writing in the *Epistle Dedicatorie* to Perkins's Second Treatise *Of the Calling of the Ministerie* he said,

> I fear none but the very hand of God, can wipe out this stain from our church; the baseness of the general body of our ministry, whence is it, but either from the unworthiness, or poverty thereof: and this unworthiness, whence is it, but from the poverty, and base mainten- ance of our ministry which was once robbed by abbies and after worse by some in our own state ... our whole duty is still required then why should not our whole due be paid ... hath not God ordained ... that those which teach the gospel shall live of the gospel? But alas, how shall the ministry of England live of the gospel, when my small experience can show, that in one corner of one county of this kingdom, [and in his marginal note he makes it clear that he is referring to the East Riding of Yorkshire] wherein there are some 105

---

[9] Crashaw, *Epistle Dedicatory* to First Treatise of William Perkins, *Of the Calling of the Ministerie*, 1606 (3 impression, Thomas Creede for William Welby), p. 9.
[10] *Ibid.*, p. 10.
[11] Crashaw, *Sermon at the Crosse*, p. 168.

parishes, or parochial chapels, almost a hundred of them, (if not a full 100) are impropriate.

He went to on to show how in some parishes but £4 per annum was left as the yearly living for the minister whilst the impropriators had up to £300. Crashaw, who often made references to his own experiences, had been better off than many of his colleagues, receiving from the town governors of Beverley a salary of £32 10s. per annum, but he continued by making a specific reference to his former living:

> Yea there is one worth £400 per annum where there were but £8 left for the minister, until of late with much ado, £10 more was obtained for a preacher . . . in that parish where there are 2,000 communicants. Of all the rest, the crown hath some £100 rent, or not so much, and the remainder of £280 (being a rich living for a worthy learned minister, a competent living for two or more than some seven painful and able ministers have) I know not what becomes of it, unless it goes to the feeding of kites and cormorants.[12]

But if the baseness of the body of the ministry was a petty Babylon in itself, there were others, springing from it, which had serious effects upon society. There were 'the ungodly plays and interludes [which] so rise in this nation; what are they but a bastard of Babylon, a daughter of error and confusion, a hellish device (the devil's own recreation to mock at holy things) . . . they grow worse, and worse; for now they bring religion and holy things upon the stage'.[13] There was 'this horrible abuse of the sabbath day . . . in some places by fairs and markets, by May games and morris dancers, by wakes and feasts: in all places (almost) by buying and selling, and bargaining: in this city, by carriages in and out, by selling business in the morning and after dinner: by playing in the streets and in the fields'.[14] There was poison of 'self love, ambition, pride, vain glory, hypocrisy, high conceits of a man's self'; expenditure on lavish goods, bribery, fashion in women's dress; drunkenness, which 'abuse grows so enormous, as it creeps into the courts, and all company's of worth . . . to the dishonour of our nation, and shame of our religion'; swearing, 'we shall find but few righteous ones among the many millions of professed sons of christianity'.[15] There was 'the ignorance or the unlearnedness of our gentry and

---

[12] Crashaw, *Epistle Dedicatorie* to second Treatise of Perkins *Of the Calling of the Ministerie*. It is not paginated.

[13] Crashaw, *Sermon at the Crosse*, pp. 169–70.

[14] *Ibid.*, p. 171.

[15] Crashaw, *The Parable of Poyson*, 1618 (Thomas Snodham for Richard Moore), pp. 8–25.

nobility'; the beggary of the poor, 'poverty may be a cross, but it is no curse; but beggary is a fearful curse. The daily cries in our streets, cry for yet further reformation'.[16] Such petty babylons and poisons were sins, whose importance Crashaw expressed simply but graphically. 'Take heed of giving ill example by thy sins, for thats worse than to mingle poison for mens bodies . . . for those that either instil false opinions by persuasions, or teach false doctrines by writing, and preaching, or teach men to sin by evil and lewd example, these are the great poisoners of the world, for these kill men's souls.'[17] It 'creeps as a canker through our whole state, from the foot to the head. But let us take heed: for it will eat out the heart and life of a state'.[18]

It went without saying that such ills were intolerable. Reformation had to be attempted. But by whom and how? It was in the stress he put on the personnel he saw as responsible for this further reformation that he expanded upon the views of Chaderton, his former teacher William Perkins, and the mainstream of puritan teaching. The healing of Babel was not confined solely to the ministry, nor, in association with it, to the magistrate, be he the King, a noble, a member of the gentry, or governor of a town. Perhaps influenced by his pastoral experience, he saw it as the work of a godly alliance. 'The curing and converting of the soul hath God delegated to his Prophets, being men like ourselves.'[19] But in addition, by means which he was to set out for his hearers and readers, 'one private man [may] further the salvation of another. Thus every good man is as it were a little pastor to his neighbour: and happy were it for the church of God, if all private persons would perform these duties one to another'.[20] Moreover, whilst it was important for men 'to meet together duly with the congregation in time and place appointed',[21] it was in the household that more could be done:

> those that be the heirs of Abraham's faith will distribute their love to every one, and care for the soul of their meanest servants, and take order in their families . . . and their very kitchen boys and horse boys, may learn to know the God of their salvation; and that so he may be able to say with a good conscience, I found my family a confused

---

[16] Crashaw, *Epistle Dedicatorie*.
[17] Crashaw, *Poyson*, p. 37.
[18] Crashaw, *Sermon at the Crosse*, p. 172.
[19] *Ibid.*, p. 1.
[20] *Ibid.*, p. 13.
[21] Crashaw, *Milke for Babes, or a North-Countrie Catechisme* (6th impression, Nicholas Okes, 1633), p. 6.

Babel of disorder and profaneness, but I have heartily endeavoured to make it a little church.[22]

Compared to Crashaw, William Perkins had a much higher view of the office of the minister. He saw his function being 'to declare unto a man his righteousness. And this is the peculiar office of a minister of God, and this is the height and excellency of his office'.[23] Ministers were unique in their titles, rareness and office, in the blessing God gave to their labours, in their commission and authority. He was a messenger, an interpreter, 'one that is able to deliver aright the reconciliation made betwixt God and man', 'inwardly taught by the spiritual schoolmaster, the Holy Ghost', being 'even the high commissioners of God ... to redeem souls from the power of hell, and the devil's claws'.[24] It was Christ 'who giveth to his church ministers which preach the gospel ... Christ giveth protection and defence, unto his ministers when they are faithful ... this showeth the dignity of this calling ... Christ honoureth it'.[25] Even ministers endowed with small measure of gifts may be able to do great service unto God in his church, 'and at this day many men of smaller gifts in the ministry, do more further the increase of the Gospel ... than those that are enriched with far greater gifts of knowledge both in tongues and arts'.[26]

On the other hand Crashaw, with his practical experience of life in parishes in Bridlington, Beverley, Burton Agnes, and London took a more pragmatic view of the minister's role. Where Perkins recommended a minister to deliver his testimony 'in a plain, easy, and familiar kind of speech',[27] Crashaw was more concerned with practicalities and example. The minister was like a physician healing the poison of the world—'the godly and learned minister is the man of God, by him appointed to correct, make, mix, temper, and apply this heavenly physic that must save the poor and poisoned soul'.[28] It was his property 'to wish above all things the spiritual good of them with whom he lives: the wicked man seeks the spiritual hurt of man; the natural man the carnal good: but the holy man their spiritual and eternal good'. Elsewhere he wrote,

[22] Crashaw, *Sermon at the Crosse*, p. 15.
[23] Perkins, *Of the Calling of the Ministerie*, p. 9.
[24] *Ibid.*, pp. 1–4 and 14.
[25] Perkins, *A Godly and learned Exposition of the three first Chapters of the Revelation* (3 edn., Adam Fflip, 1606), p. 58.
[26] Perkins, *A godly and learned Exposition*, p. 184.
[27] *Ibid.*, p. 19.
[28] Crashaw, *Poyson*, p. 84.

see what a good neighbour, a holy man is: he comes, he dwells, he sojourns in no place, but he seeks the good of it ... Thus the whole shire and parish shall fare the better by one good man dwelling among them. He comes no where but presently he considers what that people want, what is their disease, what he may do to heal them, or in any way to help them: he comes no where but he leaves behind him signs of his goodness, monuments of his holiness, and a sweet savour of his virtues.[29]

This pastoral care was vital. It was not only the great and powerful ones who were aimed at;

The godly and conscionable minister, must here learn to have care of the least and poorest soul in his parish, considering it as dear and precious as the best ... as precious blood was shed to save it, as for the greatest man on earth. Therefore let them not be like those proud spirits, and carnal minded men, that think ordinary parishes not worthy of them and therefore will preach no where but at the Court, or in great and solemn assemblies: nor like those, who in their parish, will be acquainted with none, converse with none, visit none, but the rich and mighty; but as for the poor, they may live and die as they can for them ... He that looks for Paul's reward, at God's hand, must thus behave himself to God's people, remembering his account is not for trifles, but for souls and to that God who hath told us aforehand, every soul is mine.[30]

It was because of this practical experience that Crashaw called for a godly partnership to cure Babel, extending ministerial powers and duties to laymen;

Who they be that would have cured Babel: the text saith we would, that is not the prophets alone, or the people alone, or the princes alone, but we, that is all together ... where we may learn, that how-soever properly, and peculiarly, and more principally it is the office of the minister: yet it belongs also to every Christian, to perform the duties of holy and spiritual edification to them with whom he lives for their spiritual good.[31]

[29] Crashaw, *Sermon at the Crosse*, pp. 9 and 10.
[30] *Ibid.*, pp. 13 and 14.
[31] *Ibid.*, pp. 10 and 11.

It was this more than anything else which distinguished his teaching from that of Perkins, who had said that 'in want of godly ministers, I confess that godly christian men may help one another in the performance of these duties . . . but it is the proper function of a godly minister to do it'.[32] But for Crashaw there was no question of the laity performing such duties out of mere necessity. By the time of his preaching there were more godly ministers around. He was at pains to acknowledge the advances which had been made and the successes which had been achieved. But his own experience in the field (for him a battlefield) showed the necessity for widening God's army to bring into the fight those outside the ministry. In part it reflected disillusionment. It was all to the good to aim for the conversion of important men but there were too many disappointments, too much still to do;

> The Israelites aimed not at the converison of the great ones, and men of state only, but even at all the people of Babel. Whereby, it is apparent they fought not for themselves: for then they would have fished for the great ones only or especially (as do the jesuits, and craftier sorts of friars at this day); but they fought for the salvation of souls, which they knew to be all alike before God.[33]

Crashaw recognized the importance of influencing the officers of state;

> Well knew David, that if once the King would abandon his idolatry, and embrace the truth, easily would the people be induced to follow him: so where ever is true reformation either of errors in doctrine, or corruption in manners, it must begin at the highest; else it would be to little purpose ... even so in our state, how shall popery be extinguished? How shall vain swearing, wantonness, profaning of the sabbath, bribery, and other the sins of this age be reformed in the body of the people, if they be suffered to harbour in the Court, and to creep into the King's privy chamber?[34]

It was precisely because of such developments that Crashaw recommended the course he did. Babel would not be healed. 'O deaf adders, that stop their ears against the voice of the best and wisest charmers.' The work was discouraging to ministers of the word. 'Ministers and prophets of the Lord, find oftentimes so little profit of their great labours, that they cry

---

[32] Perkins, *Of the Calling of the Ministerie*, p. 9.
[33] Crashaw, *Sermon at the Cross*, p. 13.
[34] *Ibid.*, p. 16.

out: I have laboured in vain, and spent my strength in vain.' But hope remained if ministers did not work alone. 'We must here learn, not to be discouraged in our courses of seeking men's conversions; private men to practice the duties of admonition, exhortation etc unto their neighbours that be out of the way: nor ministers to preach the word, with all diligence. For howsoever thy labour may be lost to some; yet know, thy labour is never lost before God.'[35] Petty pastors, supplementing the work of the minister, in their own little churches, constituted an option not to be ignored.

If necessity caused Crashaw to look to laymen to join with ordained ministers to perform God's work he was happy to offer practical advice on how they should go about their godly task. The joint enterprise of healing Babel permeated all aspects of life and was to be undertaken using two principal weapons and applied in four main ways. The two main weapons were preaching and the Bible. Crashaw had no argument with Perkins's view of the minister as a messenger, preaching God's word as God's word, neither adding to it nor taking anything away from it, as evidence and demonstration of the spirit of God.[36] Consequently the preaching of the word and the hearing of it were the principal parts of piety and God's service and one of man's main duties on the sabbath.[37] 'Seest thou a minister that receives the fleece but feeds not the flock? The cause is he is an unsanctified man.'[38] But Crashaw did not see this duty as confined to the minister alone, nor as one to be performed solely as part of public worship in the church. The teaching of God's word could be done by those in business or trade. He quoted as an example Daniel 'who after he had done the business for which the king sent for him, then fell he to the business of God'.[39] His petty pastors, the heads of households, in their little churches, their families, could do the same. The marginal note on Genesis 17 v. 23 in the Geneva Bible taught that 'masters in their houses ought to be as preachers to their families, that from the highest to the lowest they may obey the will of God'. In his catechism, *Milke for Babes*, he wrote of the duty of the head of the family. Not only was he to call to mind what had been spoken in the church and apply it to himself and his

---

[35] *Ibid.*, pp. 21 and 22.
[36] Perkins, *Of the Calling of the Ministerie*, p. 2.
[37] Crashaw, *Poyson*, p. 64.
[38] Crashaw, *A Sermon preached in London before the right honourable the Lord Lavvarre, Lord Governour and Captaine Generall of Virginea* . . . (1610, London, William Hall for William Welby) (not paginated).
[39] Crashaw, *Sermon at the Crosse*, p. 16.

house, but like the appointed minister he was 'to retire himself every day into secret and there betwixt God and himself, first, to lay open his heart, and confess his sins. Secondly, to call on God, and give him thanks for his mercies. Thirdly to read God's word'. Above all he was to instruct his family and house in religion.[40] The daily reading of the Bible served to sanctify. 'God's law and word is plain both in the Old and New Testament, that every one as well laity as clergy, read the Book of God, and search the scriptures daily.'[41] Those who would cure their own souls or help cure others were to be diligent readers of the scriptures. When the gospel was read and heard preached it was to be believed, retained, and applied, for 'faith brings Christ to us, and holiness keeps him to us and us to him'.[42] The stress Crashaw placed on the role of the household in religious life was aimed at supplementing the work of the Church. 'More shame for the great men of this age, both in city and country, (who though they be great and daily plot to be greater, yet keep they not so great houses and families as Abraham did).'[43] So many servants rarely came to church that the household and family worship was the only opportunity they had to hear God's word. 'The good-father of the family must learn here, not himself, and his wife only, but to see that his children and servants and those not some of the chief, but all, even the meanest may know and fear God.'[44]

But preaching and words were not the only means of healing Babel. 'Words are cheap. But gave they Babel nothing but sweet words?'[45] All good means were to be used. Three such were capable of exploitation by all classes of the laity; the fourth depended on the magistrate. Instruction, example, and prayer were the chief methods to be employed. 'By continual instruction, laying open their errors, discovering their impieties, and laying before them the excellency of true religion.' Such instruction was to be undertaken both in the churches and in homes and business. No opportunity was to be ignored. 'By their continual example, practising their own religion before their very faces, not fearing the scorns and rebukes, no not the contrary laws made purposely against them.' Finally, they were to endeavour to heal Babel by prayers, both in public and private worship. If Rome, the great Babylon, was to be forsaken, prayers

---

[40] Crashaw, *Milk for Babes*, p. 7.
[41] Crashaw, *Poyson*, p. 65.
[42] *Ibid.*, pp. 59–60.
[43] Crashaw, *Sermon at the Crosse*, p. 15.
[44] *Ibid.*, p. 14.
[45] *Ibid.*, p. 12.

for the salvation of Catholics were still to be undertaken. Public and private prayer was to be offered as the cure for all Babel's ills. 'Whatever the hardship, nor must we forsake them in prayer.'[46] These were the means Crashaw urged upon his hearers and readers as the ways whereby private men could work to cure Babel, to achieve the salvation of others, to further reform in the Church, working as petty pastors in their little churches.

But in another way the magistrate was still required to assist in this godly work. It was not simply that the magistrate should set the example for others of lesser degree to follow. Certainly, kings, men of the Court, and judges had their role to play in this regard. Crashaw gave thanks that

> God hath moved the hearts of our honourable, and reverend judges
> . . . to begin a blessed reformation . . . by coming in into the great
> cities and towns of the kingdom, on the Saturdays, and keeping care-
> fully the Lord's days . . . not preferring their own profit, nor ease,
> before the honour and service of God.[47]

He was aware that men of high calling in both magistracy and ministry had their own sins and must be careful of giving an ill example. But above all the magistrate was required to provide good execution of the laws;

> Now therefore you honourable magistrates and judges of this nation
> set your shoulders to the work of your God, rouse up your spirits to
> execute the good laws yourselves and your forefathers have enacted:
> our laws are enough and good enough, they want nothing but execu-
> tion, and that belongs to you.[48]

'Be well advised,' he preached to the Lord Governor of Virginia, 'in making laws, but being made, let them be obeyed, and let none stand for scarecrows . . . and you will teach us in England to know (who almost have forgot it) what an excellent thing execution of laws is in a common-wealth.'[49] Duty required them to act in time. Throughout there was a sense that time was running out, both for individuals and for the nation. It was not that God would desert his people but that if Babel was not cured speedily 'God will take the matter into his own hands, and some way or another will get himself glory upon us.'[50]

---

[46] *Ibid.*, pp. 12, 13 and 23.
[47] Crashaw, *Poyson*, p. 80.
[48] Crashaw, *Sermon at the Crosse*, p. 165.
[49] Crashaw, *Sermon Preached before Lord Lavvarre*.
[50] Crashaw, *Sermon at the Crosse*, p. 173.

In part it was this sense of urgency which led Crashaw to stress the role of his petty pastors and little churches. They were not, as for Cartwright, mere nurseries for the Church.[51] They had a role to play in their own right. At no time was there any sense of the dangers inherent in this, that individualist anarchy could develop or that traditional communities of the Established Church and parish could be threatened. The Church and its minister remained of vital importance. 'Despise not then the church of God, nor the congregation of his saints, run not with the schismatics into corners and conventicles.'[52] Godly expediency demanded the use of all methods to heal Babel. God had provided many helps to further his work; to take hold and make use of them brought blessing upon the individual, the Church, and the nation.

University of York

[51] A. Peel and L. H. Carlson, eds., *Cartwrightiana* (1951), p. 159.
[52] Crashaw, *Poyson*, pp. 80–1. For a discussion of the significance of private household meetings leading to the breakdown of established forms of religion see Christopher Hill, *Society & Puritanism in Pre-Revolutionary England* (London, 1986), esp. chapters 12–15, and Patrick Collinson, *The Religion of Protestants* (Oxford, 1985), pp. 249–52.

'REFORMED PASTORS' AND *BONS CURÉS*: THE CHANGING ROLE OF THE PARISH CLERGY IN EARLY MODERN EUROPE

by IAN GREEN

O VER the last half century, a number of sociologists on both sides of the Atlantic have tried to define the contemporary role of the ministry. Among the ideas which emerged from their work, three are relevant for our purpose here. The first was that a number of roles which well-intentioned if not always well-qualified clergy had tried to play in the past had been lost or were being lost to rival professions, few of whose members were in holy orders: doctors and psychiatrists, marriage guidance counsellors and social caseworkers, solicitors and schoolteachers. Sociologists detected a sense of what was called 'role uncertainty' among the English clergy, and a feeling that in future they should be trained in new skills such as counselling.[1] Allied to this disquiet was another concern, that the administrative and organizational side of the minister's work was threatening to swamp the more important traditional roles of priest, pastor, and preacher.[2] A third suggestion was that in an increasingly secular society the status of the ministry was declining. For centuries, it was argued, the clergy had enjoyed a unique place in society because of their sacerdotal functions and special skills, but this was now changing: the value of the Christian ministry in the eyes of the laity was falling behind that of more 'useful' professions such as medicine and the law.[3]

Now there are various reasons why we might be cautious about accepting these conclusions or trying to apply them historically, not least the

[1] The preparation of this paper would not have been possible without grants from the Research Fund committee and much help from the Librarians of the Queen's University of Belfast, to whom I should like to extend my deep gratitude. For America, see the work of the Lynds summarized and revised in T. Caplow, ed., *All Faithful People: Change and Continuity in Middletown's Religion* (Minneapolis, 1983), pp. 39–42, and the comments in H. R. Niebuhr, D. D. Williams and J. M. Gustafson, *The Purpose of the Church and its Ministry* (New York, 1956), pp. 31, 48–53. For England, see the works cited by R. Towler, 'The Social Status of the Anglican Minister' in R. Robertson, ed., *Sociology of Religion* (Harmondsworth, 1969), pp. 443–50, and A. Russell, *The Clerical Profession* (London, 1980), pt. 3.

[2] S. Blizzard, 'The Minister's Dilemma', *The Christian Century*, 73 (1956), pp. 508–10, and other work summarized by P. E. Johnson, *Psychology of Religion* (Nashville, 1959), at pp. 260–6, 286–7; S. Ranson, A. Bryman, B. Hinings, *Clergy, Ministers and Priests* (London, 1977), cap. 4.

[3] As previous notes, and B. Wilson, *Religion in Secular Society* (Harmondsworth, 1966), cap. 5.

common experience of the last sixty years that by the time historians have grasped ideas in a related discipline they are often on the point of being replaced. Thus the idea of secularization or dechristianization has proved very attractive to historians working on the eighteenth and nineteenth centuries, but already in the late 1960s too simple or deterministic a use of such terms was being attacked by sociologists like David Martin, who suggested that what was being described as secularization was in reality a number of discrete elements 'loosely put together into an intellectual hold-all'.[4] Historians who use this term today usually do so with the mental caveat that there has never been a period when the great majority of the people can be demonstrated convincingly to have been devout Christians, or when there has been general agreement about what constitutes the sacred or what separates it from the secular.

A similar fate threatens the notion of the rise of the professions, for, as Wilfrid Prest pointed out recently, while historians were discovering the joys of a comparative, functionalist approach and of concepts like professionalization, the sociologists themselves were becoming increasingly aware of their shortcomings. The term 'profession' is far from being a neutral value-free description of an objective phenomenon, and the notion of 'professionalization' has Whiggish overtones.[5] Given the number of characteristics that have been suggested as quintessential to a profession, it is perhaps not surprising that five scholars who have written about the 'professionalization' of the English clergy have come to very different conclusions about the nature and chronology of that process. Rosemary O'Day dates the rise of the clerical profession, in terms of uniform procedures for training and admission, distinct function, separate career-structure, and a sense of esprit de corps, to the late sixteenth and the early seventeenth centuries; Geoffrey Holmes sees the late seventeenth and early eighteenth centuries as a period of transition for the professions in general, if not so much the clergy in particular; Anthony Russell, detecting a shift from 'high-status occupational roles' to a wider and more utilitarian set of functions, points to the late eighteenth and nineteenth centuries; while Brian Heeney, focusing on the new doctrinal, liturgical, and pastoral emphases emanating from the Oxford and other movements, and Alan Haig, adopting an institutional and

---

[4] Quoted by Peter Burke in 'Religion and Secularization', *New Cambridge Modern History XIII Companion Volume* (Cambridge, 1979), p. 294; see pp. 292–5 for further discussion of this point.

[5] W. Prest, 'Why the History of the Professions is not Written', in G. R. Rubin and D. Sugarman, eds, *Law, Economy and Society, 1750–1914* (Abingdon, 1984), pp. 300–30.

prosopographical approach, both settle for the reign of Victoria as the crucial period of development.[6] Suitably refined or qualified, the concept of professionalization may still prove to be of value, though there remain some who doubt whether the Christian ministry, whose special powers are ascribed rather than achieved, can ever be fitted satisfactorily into a category of the professions.[7] Meanwhile the very differences between the conclusions drawn in recent years suggest that it may still be useful here to pose some questions about the ministry, starting from a sociological standpoint. In particular, in what period, if any, did the roles of the parish clergy become as varied as some of these accounts suggest? and at what stage, if any, did the status of the ministry reach the peak from which it is thought to have declined recently? At this point, I should stress that the focus here will be on full-time beneficed parish clergy, excluding plural-ists who spent little time in the parish, and clergy without parish duties such as chaplains, in addition to, on the Protestant side, nonconformist ministers and, on the Catholic, monks and friars with only limited parish responsibilities.[8]

At first sight, the answer to the questions just posed would seem to be the seventeenth century for some Protestant parish clergies in Western Europe, and the eighteenth century for some Catholic ones: it was in the early modern period that the mould of the medieval clergy was broken. The effect of both Reformation and Counter-Reformation was in differ-ent ways to strengthen the idea that the clergy formed a separate estate. Protestant reformers following Luther may have argued that all men were priests, but this did not mean that all men were equal. In the Bible there were prophets, apostles, evangelists, pastors, and doctors who were in one way or another set apart from the rest; and in all the major Protestant

---

[6] R. O'Day, *The English Clergy: The Emergence and Consolidation of a Profession 1558–1642* (Leicester, 1979), but see also 'The Anatomy of a Profession: The Clergy of the Church of England' in W. Prest, ed., *The Professions in Early Modern England* (London, 1987), pp. 25–63; G. Holmes, *Augustan England: Professions, State and Society, 1680–1730* (London, 1982), caps. 1, 4; Russell, *Clerical Profession*, pts 1–2; B. Heeney, *A Different Kind of Gentlemen: Parish Clergy as Professional Men in Early and Mid-Victorian England* (Ohio, 1975); and A. Haig, *The Victorian Clergy* (Beckenham, 1984).

[7] Towler, 'Social Status', pp. 447–9, and below n. 50.

[8] These exclusions are bound to lead to anomalies, for example where Protestant noncon-formist clergy performed a similar or even a complementary function to established clergy—see W. J. Sheils, 'Oliver Heywood and his Congregation', *SCH* 23 (1986), pp. 276–7; or where regulars provided an unusually high proportion of the Catholic parish clergy, as in parts of Central Europe: R. J. W. Evans, *The Making of the Habsburg Monarchy 1550–1700* (Oxford, 1979), pp. 123–33, 185–6; but this paper is already too broad, and lines have to be drawn somewhere.

churches it was stressed that only those who had been called and ordained to the ministry could preach and perform the sacraments.[9] Indeed, in the eyes of many reformers, the act of preaching, of being the channel through which the Holy Ghost called the faithful to salvation, took on an almost mystical significance comparable to that felt by Catholic priests for the miracle of the mass. Similarly, although Protestant theologians had a different view of the doctrine of the sacraments, it would be wrong to think that they downgraded them or those who performed them. Correct performance of the sacraments was, like preaching, one of the marks of the true church, and Protestant clergy of all persuasions went to great lengths to persuade their congregations to participate.[10] As for the Counter-Reformation, it responded to the challenges thrown down by late medieval heretics, sixteenth-century reformers, and an increasingly literate and critical laity by trying to accentuate the separateness of the priesthood. This was done partly by reasserting the priest's distinctive powers of mediation, absolution, performing the sacraments, and so on, and by stressing such attributes or characteristics as vocation, celibacy, special title, dress and appearance, and the ability to read Latin. It was also achieved by trying to enhance older roles such as teacher and confessor and by an attempt to tighten up the institutional machinery which was supposed to ensure that the priest's duties were properly performed.[11]

Furthermore, although there were clearly major differences of emphasis and attitude between a 'reformed pastor' and a *bon curé* there were other ways in which the two were remarkably similar. In both cases, a number of the older priestly and pastoral tasks were still needed and performed: leading the faithful in prayer and worship, comforting the sick and bereaved, and guiding parishioners through spiritual or other crises.[12] Moreover, in both cases new tasks, or to be more precise new emphases and techniques, had been added, of which the best example is the clergy-

---

[9] J. L. Ainslie, *The Doctrines of Ministerial Order in the Reformed Churches of the Sixteenth and Seventeenth Centuries* (Edinburgh, 1940), pp. 5–13; J.-J. von Allmen, *Le Saint Ministère selon la Conviction et la Volonté des Réformés du XVIe Siècle* (Neuchatel, 1968), cap. 2.

[10] Ainslie, *Doctrines*, pp. 40–56; Allmen, *Saint Ministère*, cap. 6; P. E. Hughes, *Theology of the English Reformers* (London, 1965), cap. 5. See also S. Hieron, *The Dignitie of Preaching* (London, 1615), and the discussion of preaching by Patrick Collinson in his contribution to this volume at pp. 185–220.

[11] *Canons and Decrees of the Council of Trent*, ed. H. J. Schroeder (London, 1960), pp. 25, 105–6, 110, 152–3, 173, 175–6, 195–8, 246–8; for examples of national or regional statements, see P. Broutin, *La Réforme pastorale en France au XVIIe Siècle*, 2 vols (Tournai, 1956), 1, *passim* and 2, pp. 3–34; J. Ferté, *La Vie Religieuse dans les Campagnes Parisiennes (1622–1695)* (Paris, 1962), pp. 26–7.

[12] J. T. McNeill, *A History of the Cure of Souls* (London, 1952), caps. 8–12.

man's role as religious instructor. In John Bossy's view, the educational function of images, symbols, and traditional rites was undermined by the Christian humanists' preoccupation with the correct interpretation and effective dissemination of the message contained in the scriptures. Once Erasmus had rendered the start of St John's gospel as *In principio erat sermo*, it became, he says, 'the office of the "ecclesiast" (hitherto priest) to retransmit' the scriptural message 'by the eloquence of his *sermo*, delivered as a living word to the *ecclesia* (assembly, congregation)'.[13] Preaching was only one task now expected of all parish clergy; catechizing was another, and Profesor Bossy has also pointed out the unwitting consensus that rapidly emerged between Reformation and Counter-Reformation authorities on the duty of the parish clergy to catechize. Scores and in some cases hundreds of different catechisms were produced by each major denomination reflecting the value placed on this exercise. As Bossy says 'the carrying to the masses of these pedagogical versions of Christianity probably had in the long run more considerable effects than any other innovation of the sixteenth century'.[14]

There had been some formal religious instruction in late medieval parishes, but if we could compute the number of sermons or the amount of catechetical instruction in the fifteenth century and compare it with an equivalent figure for the seventeenth or eighteenth, the result would almost certainly be a dramatic increase.[15] Admittedly the records of preaching or catechizing in, say, eighteenth-century England and France are often of an indirect or negative kind—the absence of reports of failure to perform these tasks, or the huge number of copies of catechisms printed. But if we add in the role of clergymen in elementary education, the core of which was often scriptural or moral, all the indicators are that the parish clergy were at least outwardly taking the role of instructor more seriously than before.[16] If religious leaders after 1520 were trying to purify

---

[13] J. A. Bossy, *Christianity in the West 1400–1700* (Oxford, 1985), p. 98.

[14] *Ibid.*, pp. 118–20; on catechizing in general, see the works cited by J.-C. Dhotel, *Les Origines du Catéchisme Moderne* (Paris, 1967), p. 10 n. 6; E. Germain, *Langages de la Foi* (Paris, 1972); and 'Transmettre La Foi: XVIe–XXe siècles', *Actes du 109e Congrès National des Sociétés Savantes, Dijon 1984* (Paris, 1984), pt. 1.

[15] In England, for example, P. Tudor, 'Religious Instruction for Children and Adolescents in the Early English Reformation', *JEH* 35 (1984), pp. 391–413; I. M. Green, '"For Children in Yeeres and Children in Understanding": The Emergence of the English Catechism under Elizabeth and the Early Stuarts', *ibid.*, 37 (1986), pp. 397–425; F. C. Mather, 'Georgian Churchmanship Reconsidered', *ibid.*, 36 (1985), pp. 279–80; *Wiltshire Returns to the Bishop's Visitation Queries of 1783*, ed. M. Ransome (Wiltshire Record Society, 27, 1971), *passim*.

[16] R. Gawthrop and G. Strauss, 'Protestantism and Literacy in Early Modern Germany', *P & P* 104 (1984), pp. 31–55; E. Johansson, 'The History of Literacy in Sweden', in H. J. Graff, ed.,

Western Christianity of pagan elements at the same time as downgrading the collective and demanding much more of the individual believer in the way of understanding and action, then the parish clergy were crucial agents in seeking to effect those changes; and the type of cleric this called for was one who not only shared his leaders' aspirations but also had a much higher standard of education than before. In the late middle ages there had been a growing number of men holding parish posts who had received more than just the bare minimum of education, but by the eighteenth century this small minority had become a sizeable majority as first the Protestant and then the Catholic parish clergy came to be recruited largely from those who had attended a university, academy, or seminary.[17]

What would also have undergone a fairly sharp rise in many western churches, both Catholic and Protestant, would have been the number of occasions on which the parish clergy would have been expected to perform some administrative task, either for the church hierarchy or for the state: recording births, marriages, and deaths in a parish register, or sending off a list of names of heads of households; helping to administer poor relief or some other form of charity, or to organize local road repairs or health precautions during the plague; informing their charges of some new government decree or important piece of news, whether good or bad; exhorting their flocks to obedience, or acting as an agent of the ecclesiastical courts or secular authorities, for example in inspecting the schools; and so on.[18] The fact that the clergy were increasingly called on to perform such tasks may have been partly a reflection of the additional problems brought about by population pressure and by confessional and other forms of strife, and partly a reflection of the well-attested efforts of many contemporary governments to increase their authority at this time,

---

Literacy and Social Development in the West: A Reader (Cambridge, 1981), pp. 151–82; P. K. Orpen, 'Schoolmastering as a Profession in the Seventeenth Century', *History of Education*, 6 (1977), pp. 183–94; J. Scotland, *The History of Scottish Education*, 2 vols (London, 1969), 1, pp. 114–16; T. C. Smout, *A History of the Scottish People 1560–1830* (London, 1972), pp. 81–4; J. Delumeau, *Le Catholicisme entre Luther et Voltaire* (Paris, 1971), pp. 288–92.

[17] On the education and training of the clergy, see below pp. 264–70; for late medieval graduates, S. Karant-Nunn, 'Luther's Pastors: The Reformation in the Ernbestine Countryside', *Transactions of the American Philosophical Society*, 69 (1979), pp. 14–16; and M. Bowker, *The Secular Clergy in the Diocese of Lincoln 1495–1520* (Cambridge, 1958), pp. 44–8, 78–9.

[18] See below pp. 257–8 for Sweden and France. For Germany see the diary of a country minister in late eighteenth-century Baden: A. Schmitthenner, *Das Tagebuch meines Urgrossvaters* (Freiburg, 1922); and for England, C. Hill, *Society and Puritanism in Pre-Revolutionary England* (London, 1966), pp. 32–43, and Russell, *Clerical Profession*, caps. 10–14.

to cope with pressures both domestic and international. Indeed, another of the major changes that Professor Bossy has ascribed to the sixteenth and seventeenth centuries was the way in which the leaders of most Churches gave much greater support to the secular arm than had often been the case in the past.[19]

The growing administrative burden of the parish clergy may also have owed something to the fact that the typical incumbent was better educated, and in some countries more likely to have been recruited from the middling or lower middling ranks of society than before.[20] The social standing of the clergy may have been raised further by the fact that, though there was clearly great variation between regions and to some extent between periods, the clergy do in many areas appear to have been able to abandon manual labour on the glebe and to enjoy a modicum of financial security if not of comfort by the seventeenth or eighteenth centuries.[21] I am not sure if this, together with their role as agents of a Church demanding greater uniformity of conduct and as agents of a state making greater demands on its subjects, made them as a body into the

[19] H. Kamen, European Society 1500–1700 (London, 1984); H. J. Cohn, ed., Government in Reformation Europe (London, 1971); J. H. Shennan, The Origins of the Modern European State (London, 1974); Bossy, Christianity, pp. 153–61.

[20] On social origins see I. M. Green, 'Career Prospects and Clerical Conformity in the Early Stuart Church', P & P 90 (1981), pp. 73–8; M. Fulbrook, Piety and Politics: Religion and the Rise of Absolutism in England, Wurttemberg and Prussia (Cambridge, 1983), pp. 79–80, 86; M. Roberts, Gustavus Adolphus: A History of Sweden 1611–32, 2 vols (London, 1953–8), 1, p. 391 n. 1; L. Pérouas, 'Le Nombre des Vocations Sacerdotales Est-il un Critère Valable en Sociologie Religieuse aux XVIIe et XVIIIe Siècles?', Actes du Congrès National des Sociétés Savantes. Poitiers 1962 (1963), p. 37; A. Viala, 'Suggestions Nouvelles pour une Histoire Sociale du Clergé aux Temps Modernes', Etudes d'Histoire du Droit Canonique Dédiées à G. Le bras, 2 vols (Paris, 1965), 2, pp. 1471–81; A. Molinier, 'Curés et Paroissiens de la Contre-Réforme', in J. Delumeau, ed., Histoire Vécue du Peuple Chrétien, 2 vols (Toulouse, 1979), 2, p. 70, and L. Pérouas, 'Clergé et Peuple Creusois du XVe au XXe siècle', ibid., 2, pp. 136–7; P. T. Hoffman, Church and Community in the Diocese of Lyon 1500–1789 (New Haven, 1984), pp. 156–8.

[21] Comments on clerical standards of living are bound to be impressionistic in the absence of comparative studies over different periods and different areas, but see the following: J.-F. Bergier, 'Salaires des Pasteurs de Genève au XVIe Siècle', Mélanges D'Histoire du XVIe Siècle Offerts à Henri Meylan (Geneva, 1970), pp. 159–78; F. W. Brooks, 'The Social Position of the Parson in the Sixteenth Century', Journal of the British Archaeological Association, 10 (1945–7), pp. 23–37; Green, 'Career Prospects', pp. 78–88, and 'The first years of Queen Anne's Bounty', in R. O'Day and F. Heal, eds., Princes and Paupers in the English Church, 1500–1800 (Leicester, 1981), pp. 231–54; O'Day, 'Anatomy', pp. 53–6; Roberts, Gustavus Adolphus, 1, pp. 392–4; Delumeau, Catholicisme (Paris, 1971), pp. 211–13, 273–4; Ferté, Vie Religieuse, pp. 43, 48; Hoffman, Church and Community, pp. 159–60; W. R. Foster, The Church before the Covenants (Edinburgh, 1975), cap. 8, and Bishop and Presbytery (London, 1958), pp. 108–10; but cf. Fulbrook, Piety, pp. 84–6 (as opposed to 77–9) and E. Sagarra, A Social History of Germany 1648–1914 (London, 1977), p. 117.

champions of privilege and tradition that Hugh McLeod and others seem
to regard as the norm for the European clergy on the eve of the French
Revolution. But arguably it made them rather different from Chaucer's
'poure Persoun' or from those priests attached to local churches in
Domesday Book whose lands had put them on a par with many peasants.[22]

Indeed, one might go further and suggest that the position of the clergy
was almost bound to have changed as the structure of society became
more complex.[23] The aristocracy, for example, may have been changing
from an order based on its function as an hereditary military élite to a
wider group which performed a variety of services for the state, including
some which required much higher standards of education than before.[24]
By the same token, might not the second of the three medieval orders—
those who prayed—have undergone a similar change, from performing a
few functions requiring a limited range of skills to being a service group
with higher qualifications and broader skills than before? In this context,
it is interesting to note that in sixteenth-century Strasbourg the new
clergy were treated by the city fathers not as a separate caste but as *diener*
or *kirchendiener* (servants of the Church, though servants of some importance, it may be added); and in early seventeenth-century Sweden,
Gustavus Adolphus referred to his parish clergy approvingly as 'the
tribunes of the people'.[25] In eighteenth-century Germany a clergyman like
Herder may have resented being treated as a member of a service group,
but a few *curés* in contemporary France actually welcomed it in that it
made them appear useful as citizens as well as priests.[26]

Another broader process one might consider here was the social and

---

[22] H. McLeod, *Religion and the People of Western Europe 1789–1970* (Oxford, 1981); W. Doyle,
The Old European Order 1660–1800 (Oxford, 1978), pp. 156–61; R. Lennard, *Rural England
1086–1135* (Oxford, 1959), p. 307.

[23] R. Mousnier, *Social Hierarchies: 1450 to the Present Day* (London, 1973); see also the articles by
Wrightson, Thompson and Mettam in *History Today*, 37 (1987) and the references therein,
and K. Wrightson, 'The Social Order of Early Modern England: Three Approaches' in
L. Bonfield, R. Smith and Wrightson, eds., *The World We Have Gained* (Oxford, 1986), cap. 7.

[24] As previous note, and J. H. Hexter, 'The Education of the Aristocracy in the Renaissance', in
Reappraisals in History (London, 1961); L. Stone, 'The Educational Revolution in England,
1540–1640', *P & P* 28 (1966), pp. 57–70; R. Mousnier, *The Institutions of France under the
Absolute Monarchy, 1598–1789: Society and the State* (Chicago/London, 1979), caps. 1, 4, 5;
I. A. A. Thompson, 'Neo-noble Nobility: Concepts of *Hidalguia* in Early Modern Castile',
European History Quarterly, 15 (1985).

[25] R. Bornfert, *La Réforme Pastorale du Culte à Strasbourg au XVIe siècle* (Studies in Medieval and
Reformation Thought 28, Leiden, 1981), p. 419; Roberts, *Gustavus Adolphus*, 1, p. 394.

[26] W. H. Bruford, *Germany in the Eighteenth Century* (Cambridge, 1965), p. 255; W. H. Williams,
'Voltaire and the Utility of the Lower Clergy', *Studies on Voltaire and the Eighteenth Century*, 58
(1967), pp. 1869–91.

cultural polarization that some historians have suggested resulted from the growing economic and educational gap between rich and poor in the sixteenth and seventeenth centuries.[27] Such a process might, as has been suggested for England and France, have led the clergy to try to hang on to the coat-tails of the patrician élite as it attacked the rowdy or semi-pagan aspects of popular culture and popular religion, and withdrew into a distinct culture of its own; or it could—less commonly, but perhaps in Sweden and parts of Spain and Italy—have encouraged some of the poorer incumbents and curates to throw in their lot with their ill-educated and hard-pressed parishioners; or it might have left them in limbo or with a role to play as bridge-builders between the two halves of society.[28] But even if one accepts the idea of polarization only with some qualifications, it is evident that such a process was bound to have had some impact on the position and role of the parish clergy.

If we follow this line of argument, we could point to various examples of 'new' clergies which seem to fit the bill, for example that of rural Sweden under Gustavus Adolphus. In remote communities, says Michael Roberts, 'the priest was not merely their spiritual pastor; he was doctor, magistrate, schoolmaster, oracle and lawgiver. The vicarage was the natural resort of the unfortunate, as it was the obvious hospice of the traveller'. Such a minister was probably himself the son of a clergyman, since about half of the Swedish clergy came from clerical homes at the time, and though modest in his educational achievements and his standard of life, he had a sufficiently high estimate of his own worth and enough support from his parishioners to stand up against the crown and the nobility when he felt the occasion merited it.[29] As an example of a Catholic country, let us take France. By the mid-eighteenth century, the parish priest was likely to be better born and better educated than in the sixteenth century, and, according to Olwen Hufton, 'was arguably the most overworked individual in Old Regime France'. In addition to being responsible for the spiritual well-being of his flock, the catechetical

---

[27] P. Burke, *Popular Culture in Early Modern Europe* (London, 1978); K. Thomas, *Religion and the Decline of Magic* (Harmondsworth, 1971), pp. 797–8.

[28] K. Wrightson, *English Society 1580–1680* (London, 1982), pp. 13–14, 222–8; E. P. Thompson, 'Patrician Society, Plebeian Culture', *Journal of Social History*, 7 (1974), pp. 382–405; R. Muchembled, *Popular Culture and Elite Culture in France 1400–1750*, tr. L. Cochrane (Baton Rouge/London, 1985), pp. 208–23; Hoffman, *Church and Community*, caps. 3–4. For Sweden see next note, for Catalonia and Sicily n. 96; the idea of bridge-building is taken a stage further, below pp. 277–85.

[29] Roberts, *Gustavus Adolphus*, 1, p. 392, and cf. p. 395, and cap. 7 *passim*; see also M. Roberts, ed., *Sweden's Age of Greatness 1632–1718* (London, 1973), pp. 115–19, 132–73.

instruction of the young, and the administration of the sacraments, he was also used by the government as an unpaid civil servant and policeman. He had, by law, to register every birth, marriage, and death; he had, when asked, to give the *intendant* information about the wealth of his parishioners and the state of the roads; he was the middleman between parish and government, whether it was passing government decrees downwards, or pleading the case of his parishioners with the higher powers. He supervised the conduct of the mid-wife, the schoolteacher, and the tavern-keeper, and, says Professor Hufton, his influence 'intruded into almost every aspect of parish life'.[30] If one needed a confirmation of these developments in Western Europe, one might point to the church reforms carried out in Russia by Peter the Great as part of his efforts to bring his country up to date with the west. Borrowing from Swedish and German *kirchenordnungen*, Peter tried to persuade his clergy to carry on with their traditional duties but at the same time to improve their standard of education, to preach and catechize, and to become a service group with special administrative and policing duties.[31]

The idea of a different type of clergyman with a different set of values or duties also seems to be reflected in the literature of the period. The *Reformed Pastor* who forms part of my title was reminded by Richard Baxter of his need to possess or acquire certain skills:

> O what qualifications are necessary for a man who hath such a charge upon him as we have! ... How many obscure texts of Scripture to be expounded! How many duties to be performed, wherein ourselves and others may miscarry, if in the matter, and manner, and end, we be not well informed! ... what men should we be in skill, resolution, and unwearied diligence who have all this to do? ... O, therefore, brethren, lose no time! Study, and pray, and confer, and practise; for in these four ways your abilities must be increased.[32]

---

[30] O. Hufton, 'The French Church', in W. H. Callahan and D. Higgs, eds., *Church and Society in Catholic Europe of the Eighteenth Century* (Cambridge, 1979), p. 24; see also T. Tackett, *Priest and Parish in Eighteenth-Century France* (Princeton, 1977), pp. 155–66, and Molinier, 'Curés', pp. 73–4, 77–8, 86–7.

[31] Peter's actions are well described in J. Cracraft, *The Church Reform of Peter the Great* (London, 1971) and G. L. Freeze, *The Russian Levites: Parish Clergy in the Eighteenth Century* (Cambridge, Mass., 1977).

[32] R. Baxter, *Gildas Salvianus. The Reformed Pastor* (London, 1655), cap. 1, section 1: 5; it is interesting that Baxter devotes two-fifths of his text to catechizing and household instruction and very little to preaching compared to Bernard: see Collinson, above pp. 195–6.

Another work first published in the 1650s though written in the 1630s was George Herbert's *A Priest to the Temple* which provided a wide-ranging survey of the ways in which the country parson could set an example to his flock. Herbert may have had a higher concept of the dignity of the priestly office than Puritan authors, but his vision of the different skills needed by the pastor and the variety of tasks he had to perform was much the same as theirs.[33]

Indeed, if one compares the handbooks of Baxter and Herbert with some of those written for Catholic priests in France at the same time, one will find differences of emphasis and to some extent of technique, but a similar preoccupation not only with the importance of inner purity, zeal, and an edifying life-style, but also with the range of tasks to be accomplished. The idea of the *bon curé* (or *bon prêtre*) which forms the second part of my title can be found in differing forms in French literature and synodal statements throughout the early modern period, but one version of it is striking both for its content and for the time at which it appears—in the mid-eighteenth century—by which time most French parish priests had attended a seminary and many were from the middling or lower middling ranks of urban society. In the writings of the Abbé de Saint-Pierre and later Voltaire and Rousseau, we find the picture of a priest who was well educated, preferred to live not with the idle upper clergy in the towns but in the countryside, where he taught not rigid dogma but a simple religion of morality to his equally simple flock. He was the tutor of society who both served his king and brought enlightened ideals to the people.[34] It was not too far a step from this notion to that of the 'citizen priest', who was not the sort of priest envisaged by the Tridentine decrees—clearly separated from lay society by his ordination and special functions—but someone who without forgoing his priestly duties could play a useful role in society and take the oath to the new constitution of 1791.[35]

There are other ways in which one might argue that by the late eighteenth century a type of parish clergy had emerged which had a

---

[33] G. Herbert, *A Priest to the Temple Or The Countrey Parson* (1652), caps. 4–5 and *passim*.

[34] Broutin, *Réforme Pastorale*, 1, pp. 44–5, 227–30, and pt. 3 *passim*; A. Playoust-Chaussis, *La Vie Religieuse dans le Diocèse de Boulogne au XVIIIᵉ Siècle* (Arras, 1976), pp. 177–8; P. Sage, *Le Bon Prêtre' dans la Littérature Française* (Geneva, 1951); Williams, 'Voltaire', art. cit.; and see M.-L. Fracard, 'Le Recrutement du Clergé Séculier dans la Région Niortaise au XVIIIe Siècle', *Revue d'Histoire de L'Eglise de France*, 57 (1971), pp. 262–4.

[35] T. Tackett, 'The Citizen Priests: Politics and Ideology among the Parish Clergy of the Eighteenth Century', *Studies in Eighteenth-Century Culture*, 7 (1978), pp. 307–28.

clearer perception of its collective identity and a moderately high estimate of its importance. One could point to the labels some of them used to describe themselves. Bishop Jewel described the Elizabethan clergy as 'the eyes of Christ, the pillars of the church, the interpreters of God's will, the watchmen of the Lord's tower, the leaders of Christ's sheep, the salt of the earth, the light of the world', and on another occasion as nurses and pilots (marine, not aerial).[36] Among the Protestant clergy of the late sixteenth century one can find well over a score of such titles derived from the scriptures, of which the more obvious included prophets, apostles, evangelists, stewards, and so on, and the more esoteric included angels and—shades of James I—gods.[37] By the seventeenth century, the euphoria or the sense of urgency in justifying themselves seems to have passed, and Protestant clergymen settled for more modest but still distinctive titles such as (to use the English equivalents) minister, preacher or servant of God's word, shepherd or pastor, presbyter or divine.[38] As marks of a growing separateness, one could also point to the larger number of books owned or borrowed by Catholic and Protestant clergy, the redesigning of their houses to include a small study, the distinctive style in which they dressed, and the way in which some of them permitted their features to be reproduced in their publications. Indeed, the distinctiveness of the appearance and life-style of some of the clergy made it easier to satirize them in the popular prints of the day.[39] Nudged in that direction

[36] J. Jewel, *The Works* (Parker Society, 4 vols, Cambridge, 1845–50), 2, pp. 1130, 1022.

[37] P. Gerard, *A Preparation to the Most Holie Ministerie* (London, 1593), pp. 36–8; G. Bucanus, *Institutions of Christian Religion* (London, 1606), pp. 562–4.

[38] Richard Rogers, Samuel Smith and Lewis Thomas are referred to as 'preacher' on the title-pages of some of their printed works; Thomas Shephard and Samuel How are referred to as 'pastor' in their *The Sincere Convert* (London, 1648) and *The Sufficiencie of the Spirits Teaching* (London, 1655); some British authors, even episcopalians, used the term 'presbyter', as in the catechism published in Edinburgh in 1712 by T.M. ('a suffering presbyter of the Church of Scotland') and the *Primitive Catechism* published by Daniel Whiston ('a presbyter of the Church of England') in London in 1718. For the German 'pfarrer', 'praedicant' and other terms, see B. Vogler, *Le Clergé Protestant Rhénan au Siècle de la Réforme (1555–1619)* (Paris, 1976), p. 121.

[39] See n. 21 above; also Luciano Allegra, *Ricerche sulla Cultura del Clero in Piemonte. Le Biblioteche Parrocchiali nell' Archidiocesi di Torine, sec XVII–XVIII* (Turin, 1978); L. Pérouas, *La Diocèse de la Rochelle de 1648 à 1724* (Paris, 1964), pp. 203, 263–4; D. Julia, 'Le Prêtre au XVIIIe Siècle', *Recherches de Science Religieuse*, 58 (1970), pp. 521–34; Tackett, *Priest and Parish*, pp. 89–92; J. H. Pruett, *The Parish Clergy under the Later Stuarts* (Urbana, 1978), pp. 45–6 and cap. 5; O. Chadwick, *The Popes and European Revolution* (Oxford, 1981), pp. 103–9, 118; in England, not only fashionable Anglican authors like Andrewes but also nonconformist authors such as Richard Baxter, John Bunyan and Matthew Henry had their features reproduced in their works. For satirical prints, see J. Miller, *Religion in the Popular Prints 1600–1832* (Cambridge, 1986).

by the sociologists' findings with which we began, we might go further and suggest that the intrusion of administrative chores into the life of the clergy, though on occasions a source of grievance, was not yet sufficient to prevent a number of eighteenth-century clergy in England and France finding time to go hunting, pursue botanical interests, or engage in other scholarly or gentlemanly pursuits.[40] It might be the case that in the next two centuries the parish clergy would be laden down with further responsibilities, such as Sunday Schools, Mothers' Unions, and fundraising, leaving them little time for such tasks, and turning them (to use Brian Heeney's phrase) into a different *kind* of gentleman, distinguished less by his origins, education and life-style than by his functions.[41] But it could be argued that these were merely variations on a theme, and were to some extent cancelled out by the loss of 'secular' tasks to a regular civil service; it could still be maintained that it was in the period from the mid-sixteenth to the mid-eighteenth century that the major break with the late medieval model of the priesthood occurred.

At this point, however, I must admit that I am not fully convinced by this argument, though to prevent the charge that it has been set up as a straw man, I should add that some of the changes already sketched in, for example the increased emphasis on instruction and the heavier administrative burden, do seem to me to be reasonably certain and significant, as do one or two other changes to be mentioned later. The nub of the matter is that if, like Jean Delumeau, Louis Pérouas, Pierre Chaunu, Robert Muchembled, John Bossy and others, we are to attribute to the early modern clergy such a key role in inculcating the ideas of the Reformation and Counter-Reformation,[42] we must try to obtain as clear an impression of the parish clergy as possible; and my own impression, for what it is worth, is that at a number of points we are running the risk of stereotyping them. I am not sure if they were as well educated or as well trained for the tasks they were asked to perform as is implied, or if they were as willing to impart the new ideas to their parishioners as obediently as is assumed, or if indeed their role or even their message was in practice all that different from their medieval counterparts. I also suspect that there

---

[40] Russell, *Clerical Profession*, pp. 33–4; Tackett, *Priest and Parish*, pp. 74–5, 88–91, 167–8; Ferté, *Vie Religieuse*, pp. 179, 191–4; T.-J. Schmitt, *L'Organisation Ecclesiastique et la Pratique Religieuse dans l'Archidiaconé d'Autun de 1655 à 1750* (Autun, 1957), pp. 129–30; Chadwick, *Popes*, p. 108; Gilbert White, *The Natural History of Selborne* (London, 1788–9).

[41] Heeney, *Different Kind*, cap. 2.

[42] Delumeau, *Catholicisme*; Pérouas, *La Rochelle*; Muchembled, *Popular Culture*; Bossy, *Christianity*; and P. Chaunu, *Le Temps des Réformes* (Paris, 1975).

may be too many differences between Churches, not just between Catholic and Protestant, but between different Catholic Churches and different Protestant ones, to sustain broad comparisons for very long.[43] In particular, there is a risk that we may assume the moderately well-documented French clergy to be typical of the Catholic experience when it was not, and although no-one in their right mind would say that the English Church was typical of Protestantism, the well-known insularity of Anglo-Saxon scholars may push them further in that direction than they should go. I also suspect that certain parts of the argument for change, for example the notion of a considerably enhanced social status by the eighteenth century, are highly selective in their use of evidence, and may perhaps be an unnecessary diversion from the direct route to understanding how the early modern clergy fared.[44]

The root of all our problems is, of course, the limited and lopsided nature of the sources. On certain crucial areas, such as the minister's sense of inner calling or his concept of the pastoral role, we know little beyond the earnest injunctions of pious authors and zealous diarists, backed up by the occasional testimonial or application for a bursary. On other matters, such as what the authorities thought the minister should be doing or where he was born or who his patron was, we are better informed but have few means of checking what effect these had on his performance.[45] As a result, we are never likely to be in a position to make an informed comparison between the day-to-day practice of the parish clergy in medieval and modern times. If one is tempted to draw a sharp contrast between a late medieval priest with little but the sacraments to perform and a 'reformed pastor' or *bon curé* with a much wider range of tasks, one could well be guilty of taking a blinkered view of the former's work and an unduly optimistic view of the latter's readiness to perform the tasks set

---

[43] The differences I am thinking of are not simply matters of the ratio of clergy to parishioners, the background and education of ordinands or the size and value of livings to which they were appointed, but also matters such as the extent of stratification between upper and lower clergy and the strength of rivals such as regulars or nonconformist preachers.

[44] While social standing might have been important to the self-confidence and thus the performance of the clergy (unless humility triumphed over worldliness), the laity were surely just as likely to be offended by a rise in clerical standards as impressed by them to the point of listening more carefully to what the minister said.

[45] See above nn. 9–12, 20, and below pp. 265, 271–3. Preliminary attempts to assess calling and the concept of the ministry can be found in Vogler, *Clergé Protestant*, pp. 52–3, 117–34; T. E. Weir, 'Pastoral Care in the Church of Scotland in the Seventeenth Century' (unpublished University of Edinburgh Ph.D. thesis, 1960); and F. Bussby, 'A History and Source Book for the Training for the Ministry in the Church of England, 1511–1717' (unpublished University of Durham M.Litt. thesis, 1952), cap. 6.

him. On the basis of what is known about the late middle ages, one would clearly be unwise to understimate the role of the medieval priest as pastor, teacher, legal adviser, physician, or agent of the local seigneur or some higher authority in matters of taxation and propaganda.[46] The sources for the early modern period are not much fuller. The offical records of the Church confirm that certain minimum requirements were usually being met by the seventeenth or eighteenth century: the eucharist and other sacraments or ceremonies were being performed regularly; sermons, of a sort, were delivered; catechizing was performed, though with what degree of zeal or skill is unknown; charities were kept up, and most clergy by then were avoiding the charges of immorality or drunkenness that were still not uncommon in the early seventeenth century.[47] But again we cannot be certain if much more than the minimum was performed, or in what spirit or with what degree of insight it was done. As for tasks which were recommended but not necessarily the subject of official enquiry, such as visiting each household in the parish, there is often a resounding silence. As Professor Collinson reminds us in this volume, it is hard to know what the rhinoceros in the zoo does all day long when our back is turned![48]

To put the opposite case to that of major change for a moment, one could argue that the changes in the role of the ministry between 1520 and 1750 may have been smaller than the changes between the seventh century and the twelfth, when the clergy had had to make the transition from converting adult pagans scattered widely across the countryside to dealing with a population that had been nominally Christian for some time and was at last settled into manageable parish units.[49] The changes may also have been smaller than between 1750 and 1950, though I suspect that some of the major developments in this latter period were not just those pursued by the sociologists, some of which may prove to have been

---

[46] Bossy, *Western Christianity*, p. 66; P. Heath, *Church and Realm 1272–1461* (London, 1988); A. K. McHardy, 'Liturgy and Propaganda in the Diocese of Lincoln during the Hundred Years War', *SCH* 18 (1982), pp. 215–27, and 'Clerical Taxation in Fifteenth-Century England: the Clergy as Agents of the Crown', in R. Dobson, ed., *The Church, Politics and Patronage in the Fifteenth Century* (Gloucester, 1984), pp. 168–92.

[47] L. Binz, *Vie Réligieuse et Réforme Ecclésiastique dans le Diocèse de Genève ... (1378–1450)* (Mémoires et Documents Publiés par la Société d'Histoire et d'Archéologie de Genève 41, Geneva, 1973), pp. 358–72; Hoffman, *Church and Community*, pp. 19–20, 50, 98–100.

[48] Above p. 193.

[49] P. Riché, 'La Pastorale Populaire en Occident VIe—XIe Siècles', reprinted in *Instruction et Vie Réligieuse dans le Haut Moyen Age* (London, 1981), pp. 195–221; B. Hamilton, *Religion in the Medieval West* (London, 1986), pp. 70–3, 108–11, 133–41.

based on false comparisons or on an ill-fated attempt to treat the ministry as one among many professions,[50] but a much larger complex of changes—including developments in theology and liturgical practice, changing attitudes towards church membership and religious pluralism. In some ways the late modern clergy were actually reverting to the early medieval pattern, of acting as witnesses of their faith to large numbers of non-believers at the same time as ministering to small but faithful flocks of committed Christians.

If we start again from the premise that the role of the parish clergy was unlikely to have been exactly that laid down in the ordinals, decrees, or injunctions of the sixteenth century, but was to a greater or lesser extent affected by the circumstances in which the theory was put into practice, we are, I think, in a better position to assess the nature and extent of change in that role. Thus, if we look at the institutional framework within which the clergy were trained and deployed, at the sort of men who offered themselves for ordination, and at the types of situation and lay attitudes they faced in the parish, what we find is a partly reformed ministry being asked to operate in largely unreformed structures. We also find the local clergy having to take the initiative in meeting the needs of their flocks, if necessary by modifying or supplementing the official formularies, and in so doing creating a perspective which on some issues was typical neither of the authorities nor of the uneducated masses.

The educated élites who drew up the ecclesiastical ordinances or canons of the early modern period hoped that the parish clergy would soon be able to understand and teach the essential doctrines of their Church, which meant that the rank and file had to be given the sort of education that the officers had already received, or something approximating to it.[51] However, it proved very difficult to translate this ideal into practice, and in too many cases the provision of clerical training was ill planned or badly funded, and was either left unfinished or was under-

---

[50] It is not so much that most clergy have lost the social status of gentleman or the roles of doctor, counsellor, etc., as that most probably never had them; and by the nature of both their calling (inner and outer) and the difficulty of assessing the quality of their 'work', especially the sacerdotal, it is hard to see how they can be compared with occupations now widely accepted as professions. Moreover given a sense of vocation among clergy, the questionnaires used by some of the sociologists mentioned in n. 2 above were bound to produce answers that gave administrative chores a very low priority.

[51] The best general introductions to training schemes are L.-E. Halkin, 'La Formation du Clergé Catholique après le Concile de Trente', in D. Baker, ed., *Miscellanea Historiae Ecclesiasticae*, 3 (Louvain, 1970), pp. 109–25; H. Meylan, 'Le Recrutement et la Formation des Pasteurs dans les Eglises Réformées du XVIe Siècle', *ibid.*, pp. 127–50; and Vogler, *Clergé Protestant*, cap. 1.

mined by traditions and vested interests which could not be swept aside overnight.

Protestant and Catholic authorities were in theory anxious to provide opportunities for the sons of the poor to enter the ministry,[52] but during both primary education and training the practice often fell well short of the theory. Some Churches set up a system of bursaries or scholarships for talented boys who were thinking of entering the ministry, though shortage of funds meant that these were nearly always in short supply, and sometimes were awarded through connections rather than on merit alone; other Churches provided free education, but asked parents to reimburse the costs if their son dropped out of the course, a system which put unfair pressure on adolescent boys to complete.[53] Either way, many a budding ordinand had to rely on his parents for at least part of the cost of his education, if not the fees and lodging, then other expenses such as books, clothes, or the sums demanded by the authorities before ordination,[54] so that in practice only a boy whose parents lived near a school, could manage without his labour, and could afford to pay something towards his expenses was likely to secure enough education to be considered for the ministry.

Two results followed. Few ordinands came from the poorest sections of society: a small minority came from the nobility, but most came from the middling or lower middling groups of society, especially in the towns and larger villages, or from the richer peasants in the countryside.[55] Secondly, there was an onus on all but the richest students to spend as little money and as little time as possible on their education. Most ordinands received their early education at the hands of the local minister or schoolmaster, and were probably fortunate if he was attuned to the latest ideas on pedagogy or enjoyed the task; thereafter much depended on what was available

---

[52] For example, M. Brecht, 'Herkunft und Ausbildung der Protestantischen Geistlichen des Herzogtums Wurttemberg im 16 Jahrhundert', *Zeitschrift für Kirkengeschichte*, 80 (1949), p. 170; Karant-Nunn, 'Luther's Pastors', p. 13; Ferté, *Vie Religieuse*, p. 148.

[53] Meylan, 'Recrutement', pp. 131, 134; Vogler, *Clergé Protestant*, pp. 50–3; Foster, *Bishop and Presbytery*, pp. 89–93; Ferté, *Vie Religieuse*, pp. 160–9; A. Schaer, *Le Clergé Paroissial Catholique en Haute Alsace sous l'Ancien Régime (1648–1789)* (Paris, 1966), p. 130; Fracard, 'Recrutement', pp. 245–55; Chadwick, *Popes*, p. 117.

[54] e.g., Tackett, *Priest and Parish*, pp. 54–71, 79, and Pruett, *Parish Clergy*, p. 35; funds could be eked out by acting as servant to richer students: *ibid.*, pp. 39–40, and Bruford, *Germany*, pp. 247–8. On sums demanded before ordination see below n. 76.

[55] See above n. 20, and Meylan, 'Recrutement', pp. 144–7; Vogler, 'Formation et Recrutement du Clergé Protestant', in *Misc. Hist. Eccles.*, 3, p. 219; D. Julia, 'Le Clergé Paroissial dans le Diocèse de Reims à la Fin du XVIIIe Siècle', *Revue d'Histoire Moderne et Contemporaine*, 13 (1966), pp. 206–9; Playoust-Chaussis, *Vie Religieuse*, pp. 150–2, 286.

locally by way of secondary education, which could be of a high standard or relatively poor.[56] Further education was often kept to the minimum an ordinand could get away with. In some Protestant states a minority of clergy had not attended university at all, and of the majority who had a number for one reason or another did not stay long enough to take a degree.[57] In most Catholic countries, even in the eighteenth century, graduates were still in a minority among the parish clergy, since the better-connected graduate secured an administrative post or a benefice in the upper ranks of the Church. As for the majority, while some spent a few years at a local college or monastic school, others still received most of their preparation at the hand of the local priest, first in his school and then, having taken minor orders, as an assistant living in his house. In either case, such ordinands might spend as little as a few months or at most a year or two at a seminary immediately prior to ordination.[58]

On paper, then, the early modern clergy were better qualified than their medieval counterparts, but in the case of many ministers it is open to question whether the imprint of such a relatively short stint of study at university or seminary was all that deep or permanent compared to the impressions left by the local priest or schoolteacher who had shaped their adolescent minds, perhaps in a relatively traditional manner since humanist ideals were not always translated into practice.[59] Moreover, as we shall see shortly, the best qualified ordinands tended to move to the more

---

[56] Two recent surveys have useful bibliographies: G. Mialeret and J. Vial, eds., *Histoire Mondiale de L'Education*, 4 vols (Paris, 1981), 2, pt. 2, and J. Bowen, *A History of Western Education*, 3 vols (London, 1972–81), 3, caps. 4–5. For regional variation, see R. Chartier, D. Julia and M.-M. Compère, eds., *L'Education en France du XVIe au XVIIIe Siècle* (Paris, 1978), pp. 23–5, and compare Hoffman, *Church and Community*, pp. 112–14 and Tackett, *Priest and Parish*, pp. 72–4.

[57] Vogler, *Clergé Protestant*, pp. 46–57; Pruett, *Parish Clergy*, pp. 42–5, but see J. C. Shuler, 'The Pastoral and Ecclesiastical Administration of the Diocese of Durham 1721–1771' (unpublished University of Durham Ph.D. thesis, 1976), cap. 6; Roberts, *Gustavus Adolphus*, 1, pp. 470–6, and 'The Swedish Church', in *Sweden's Age of Greatness*, pp. 147–8.

[58] In eighteenth-century France graduates comprised as little as a sixth of the parish clergy in more remote dioceses and perhaps a half nearer university cities: Tackett, *Priest and Parish*, p. 76 n. 14. See also *ibid.*, pp. 72–5; Schaer, *Clergé Paroissial*, p. 122; J.-P. Gutton, 'Notes sur le Recrutement du Clergé Séculier dans l'Archidiocèse de la Région Lyonnaise', *Bulletin du Centre D'Histoire Economique et Sociale de la Région Lyonnaise*, 2 (1974), p. 19; and Chadwick, *Popes*, p. 118. For graduates securing higher office, see R. L. Kagan, 'Universities in Castile 1500–1700', *P & P* 49 (1970), pp. 51–2, 59, 62; Hoffman, *Church and Community*, pp. 10–14; M. C. Perronet, *Les Evêques de L'Ancienne France* (Lille, 1977), pp. 4–15.

[59] Karant-Nunn, 'Luther's Pastors', pp. 19–20; Pruett, *Parish Clergy*, pp. 44–5; Roberts, *Gustavus Adolphus*, 1, p. 391; and see below pp. 278–80. C. Webster, 'The Curriculum of the Grammar Schools and Universities 1500–1660: A Critical Review of the Literature', *History of Education*, 4 (1975), pp. 56–8.

prosperous areas of a country, and the less qualified to go back to the less advanced regions in which they were born. There was therefore a very real risk that the parishes that were most in need of evangelization or purification were the ones that were least likely to receive the sort of clergy who might have been in sympathy with or well equipped to achieve those ends.[60]

Lack of funds and planning led to other problems in the provision of training. In some cases it led to delays: in the smaller Protestant states of Germany and in Sweden, such provision was not made until the seventeenth century, while in most parts of Catholic Europe the availability of seminary training was not widespread until the late seventeenth or eighteenth centuries or even later.[61] In other countries, provision was made sooner but often not without creating tension: between the old cathedral schools or theology faculties and the new institutions; between a bishop and the members of an order such as the Jesuits and Sulpicians who wanted to set up a diocesan seminary which would be outside his jurisdiction; between different orders competing to set up a seminary in a desirable location.[62] Once some sort of general provision had been made and tensions resolved to a greater or lesser degree, this did not mean that the method of moulding a priest was uniform. Further education for the most part continued to be dominated by the classical studies and the scholastic approach which had dominated earlier centuries, but there were differences of emphasis between one university or gymnasium or consistory and another, and there were certainly differences of curriculum between the seminaries run by different orders.[63] The co-existence of old and new institutions could also lead to the production of clergy with not only different styles and standards of education, but also to some extent with different perceptions of the task of the Church, especially where the instructors were members of a religious order.[64] Moreover, there are too

---

[60] See below p. 273.

[61] Vogler, *Clergé Protestant*, p. 72; Halkin, 'Formation', pp. 109–25; A. Dégert, *Histoire des Séminaires Français jusqu'à la Révolution*, 2 vols (Paris, 1912); Sagarra, *Social History*, p. 122; Chadwick, *Popes*, pp. 112–14; Callahan and Higgs, *Church and Society*, pp. 56, 131.

[62] Meylan, 'Recrutement', pp. 132–3; C. A. Tukker, 'The Recruitment and Training of Protestant Ministers in the Netherlands in the Sixteenth Century', *Misc. Hist. Eccles.*, 3, pp. 202–13; Halkin, 'Formation', pp. 120, 122, 124; Dégert, *Histoire des Séminaires*, 1, pp. 117–254; Broutin, *Réforme Pastorale*, 2, pp. 117–254, 507–40; Ferté, *Vie Religieuse*, pp. 152–4, 157–9.

[63] Webster, 'Curriculum', pp. 58–60; Green, 'Career Prospects', pp. 109–10; Kagan, 'Universities', p. 54; Roberts, *Gustavus Adolphus*, 1, pp. 454–5; and see previous note.

[64] J. Verger, 'Les Universités à l'Epoque Moderne', in *Histoire Mondiale*, 2, p. 249; Roberts, *Gustavus Adolphus*, 1, pp. 455, 474–5; Kagan, 'Universities', p. 59; R. Briggs, 'The Catholic Puritans: Jansenists and Rigorists in France', in D. Pennington and K. Thomas, eds., *Puritans and Revolutionaries* (Oxford, 1978), pp. 345–7; Peronnet, *Evêques*, pp. 44–56.

many reports of institutions in which either the standards of teaching were poor—usually in the more backward areas—or a devout atmosphere had been weakened by the admission of youths not destined for the ministry, for us to be confident that the training received by the early modern clergy was as uniformly good as that of sixteenth-century Geneva or eighteenth-century Padua.[65]

The rigour with which academic standards were tested also varied: some examination questions were rigorous, others fairly predictable; and as late as the eighteenth century there are still many cases of unsuccessful candidates being passed soon afterwards by a more indulgent examiner, or of rules being bent in order that a patron's wish should not be opposed or an isolated parish be left any longer without a shepherd.[66] Again what this means is that we should not too readily assume that the strike-force of Reformation and Counter-Reformation was a completely uniform body: the academic qualifications possessed by the parish clergy as a whole may have been higher than in the fifteenth century—in some parts of Protestant Europe and some Catholic cities it was much higher; but there were still wide variations in standards between the best and the worst. This was implicitly recognized in Protestant efforts to provide in-service training or handbooks on how to preach or be a good pastor, and in efforts to provide better clergy for the 'dark corners' of the land.[67] It can also be recognized in the Catholic Church's increasing reliance in the seventeenth and eighteenth centuries on retreats and conferences for existing clergy and on missions by regulars to make good the continuing reluctance of the secular clergy to preach to their flocks.[68]

The amount of practical as opposed to academic preparation for the

---

[65] A. D. Ortiz, *The Golden Age of Spain 1516–1659*, tr. J. Casey (London, 1971), pp. 123–4; Kagan, 'Universities', pp. 49–50, 54, 56–7; G. N. Clark, *The Seventeenth Century* (Oxford, 1960), pp. 291–3; Verger, 'Universités', pp. 256–9, 259–66; Scotland, *History of Scottish Education*, 1, pp. 151–8; C. Bourgeaud, *Histoire de l'Université de Genève: 1. l'Académie de Calvin, 1559–1798* (Geneva, 1900); P.-F. Geisendorf, *L'Université de Genève* (Geneva, 1959); Chadwick, *Popes*, pp. 114–15, 118–22, 129–31.

[66] *Ibid.*, pp. 124–33; Verger, 'Universités', p. 251; Bruford, *Germany*, p. 252; Pruett, *Parish Clergy*, p. 51.

[67] e.g., R. Peters, 'The Training of the "Unlearned" Clergy in England during the 1580s', in *Misc. Hist. Eccles.*, 3, pp. 184–97; T. Wood, ed., *Five Pastorals* (London, 1961); J. R. H. Moorman, ed., *The Curate of Souls* (London, 1958); C. Hill, 'Puritans and "the Dark Corners of the Land"', *TRHS* 5 ser., 13 (1963), pp. 77–102; and see below n. 111.

[68] Ortiz, *Golden Age*, pp. 201, 208, 213–14; H. Kamen, *Spain in the Later Seventeenth Century 1665–1700* (London, 1980), p. 298; Schaer, *Clergé Paroissial*, pp. 138–41; Hoffman, *Church and Community*, pp. 77–9; Delumeau, *Catholicisme*, pp. 271–2, 278–80; and see Callahan and Higgs, *Church and Society*, pp. 30, 32, 43, 47, 56, 72, 74, 112, 133–5, 147–8, 154.

ministry that was provided also varied from institution to institution; however, at its best the practical element was narrowly conceived and at its worst almost non-existent. In the better Protestant and Catholic institutions, training was usually limited to ensuring that ordinands could read the Bible in the original languages and preach sound doctrine, or could administer the sacraments correctly and sing in tune.[69] Beyond some fairly general advice in manuals, however, there appears to have been little in the way of practical advice or training on how to conduct a catechism class, comfort bereaved relations at a funeral, or fill in a parish register correctly. The French seminary at which ordinands were given a wooden doll on which to practice baptizing was probably exceptional.[70] At its worst, the training was more relevant to polemics and oratory, as in England where most ordinands studied grammar, logic, and rhetoric but not necessarily Greek or Hebrew and only incidentally hermeneutics or divinity.[71]

The list of criticisms should not be taken as implying that all such training was flawed: some Protestant institutions produced parish clergy capable of excelling at such functions as preaching and handling troubled consciences, and some Catholic Churches produced men who were both pious and gifted priests. But even at its best the training provided reflected the priorities of the church leadership more than the realities of parish life; it reflected the hope that the preaching of sermons or the purification of church ritual would transform the attitudes of the laity. Less attention was paid to preparation for other duties, and it is hard to think of any Church that produced a ministry that was thoroughly prepared for the full range of tasks it was being expected to perform by the authorities and by their congregations.

There may have been an assumption that any shortcomings in this preparation would be made up by another legacy from the past: the period of a few months, or more commonly several years, during which many young ordinands acted as assistant to an experienced minister before, if they were lucky, obtaining a benefice of their own.[72] This particular scene

---

[69] e.g., Foster, *Bishop and Presbytery*, pp. 89–96; Roberts, *Gustavus Adolphus*, 1, pp. 454–6; Tackett, *Priest and Parish*, pp. 81–2.

[70] Ferté, *Vie Religieuse*, p. 158.

[71] Green, 'Career Prospects', pp. 109–10. For attempts to increase the study of theology, see O'Day, *English Clergy*, pp. 132–4, 139–40, and C. M. Dent, *Protestant Reformers in Elizabethan Oxford* (Oxford, 1983), pp. 165–66.

[72] Brecht, 'Herkunft', p. 171; O'Day, *English Clergy*, pp. 7–16, 177; Pruett, *Parish Clergy*, pp. 52–7, 69–71, 96–7; Foster, *Church before the Covenants*, pp. 135–8; Schmitt, *L'Organisation Ecclésiastique*, p. 156; Tackett, *Priest and Parish*, pp. 98–102.

from clerical life does not seem to have been written into the trades description of the ministry, perhaps because many of those who had drafted that description had themselves by-passed this stage (or had relatives who wished to by-pass it). Moreover, though a period of probably reluctant apprenticeship was a fairly widespread phenomenon, it did not guarantee that an ordinand's training would be rounded out properly. The sort of careful supervision which some Puritan pastors provided in England was probably not the norm. If the incumbent was jealous of his position, he could perform the more important functions himself, and leave only the drudgery to his curate. On the other hand, if he was an absentee, or there was a shortage of ministers in the area, a young minister could be thrown in at the deep end with little or no supervision.[73] It is interesting that the testimonials given in Scotland to a young 'expectant' who was seeking a post in another presbytery might stress his good character, sound learning and zeal, but said little or nothing of his ability as a catechist, celebrant, or comforter. This may have been because the man in question had had limited experience of these tasks, or because the referees did not consider it merited much space compared to his ability at 'interpreting the Sacred Scriptures, and ... sustaining publick disputes upon the controversies in religione'.[74] Either way, the omission is instructive.

As in the centuries before the Reformation and Counter-Reformation, a curate or *vicaire* received little in the way of remuneration. Given the modest level of clerical income in general, this was not by itself surprising; but in practice what it meant was that the period during which a young priest was straining to keep body and soul together, or was reliant on his family's resources, was extended once again. The need to serve as curate could delay by up to ten years the point at which the typical young priest could hope to repay the efforts of parents who by that stage might very well themselves be in some need of support.[75] Curates were usually either deacons or priests, and at the point at which they were admitted to the priesthood, there were further expenses in the form of fees and also, in many Churches—some Protestant as well as Catholic, a financial bond or proof of independent means, as a guarantee that the new priest would not

[73] P. Collinson, *The Religion of Protestants: The Church in English Society 1559–1625* (Oxford, 1982), pp. 118–19; Foster, *Church before the Covenants*, p. 138; Ferté, *Vie Religieuse*, p. 60; Playoust-Chaussis, *Vie Religieuse*, pp. 163–4.

[74] Foster, *Church before the Covenants*, pp. 136–7.

[75] See above n. 72, and J. McManners, *French Ecclesiastical Society under the Ancien Régime* (Manchester, 1960), p. 138.

become a burden on the diocese.[76] The motives of those parents who were prepared to meet or to guarantee the costs of this long process of education, apprenticeship and ordination may have been piety or a desire for reflected prestige, especially among those parents who felt that their current position as merchants or minor officials lacked it. In other cases, as among gentry looking for a career for a younger son, there may also have been some confidence that in the end he would obtain financial security or even a modest profit of a more honourable and less risky kind than that obtained in trade or industry.[77] But whatever the motive, the impact on the attitude of the young minister was likely to be to push him towards viewing a benefice as an office like that of a tax-collector or minor law officer for which he had been trained and to which he could reasonably aspire.[78] It should be added that this did not necessarily mean that he did not also see it as a vocation: he would have known that many of the livings to which he aspired were not going to make him wealthy, and the sons, brothers, or nephews of existing clergy, who formed a substantial element of both Protestant and Catholic parish clergies, would have been under no illusion of the need for a strong sense of calling to help cope with the everyday problems of being a minister. As Pierre du Moulin wrote to his sons, 'Vous savez que la pauvreté et le mépris, et la haine des adversaires, sont attachés à cette vocation', though assured of the honour of such a task—'si sainte et si salutaire', and one performed by Christ himself—at least one son followed him into the ministry.[79]

When we reach the point at which this new minister was seeking an appropriate post in the Church, we come across a further example of how inherited structures could hinder improved performance: the system of allocation was either haphazard or worse. The patronage system and the principles of operation inherited from the past meant that the most promising ordinands were not necessarily dispatched to the parishes which needed them most. In few parts of early modern Europe had the

---

[76] The amount of the bond could vary even within one Church and one diocese: Viala, 'Suggestions', pp. 1474–6; Y.-M. Le Pennec, 'Le Recrutement des Prêtres dans le Diocèse de Coutances au XVIIIe Siècle', *Revue du Département de la Manche*, 12 (1970), p. 195; Fracard, 'Recrutement', p. 246.

[77] See above nn. 20, 55, and Green, 'Career Prospects', pp. 71–88.

[78] Pérouas, 'Le Nombre des Vocations Sacerdotales', p. 38.

[79] Fracard, 'Recrutement', pp. 244, 256, 264; B. Vogler, 'Recrutement et Carrière des Pasteurs Strasbourgeois au XVIe Siècle', *Revue d'Histoire et de Philosophie Religieuse*, 48 (1968), pp. 159–60; Roberts, *Gustavus Adolphus*, 1, p. 391; O'Day, *Parish Clergy*, pp. 161–2; Green, 'Career Prospects', pp. 76–8; Pruett, *Parish Clergy*, pp. 35–7; Tackett, *Priest and Parish*, p. 55. Du Moulin is cited by Meylan, 'Recrutement, pp. 148–9.

major changes in doctrine or practice associated with the sixteenth century been matched by a major change in the pattern of patronage. In Catholic countries, the top posts tended to be in crown hands, but the vast majority of appointments to parish livings were controlled either by the nobility or, more commonly, by bishops, deans and chapters, and heads of religious houses who were by and large drawn from the nobility or educated élite. In Protestant countries which had experienced a 'magisterial' reformation, such patronage tended to lie more with the princes, nobility, urban patriciates, or parish elders than with the clergy. In neither case was much attention given, except perhaps in a negative sense, to the views of the average parishioner, who might well be looking for different qualities in a pastor than his social superiors.[80] The result was that in all too many cases promotion to the best livings, in the sense of the most prestigious, congenial, or profitable posts, was decided not on the grounds of education or proven pastoral ability, but on the basis of birth or connection. Indeed, when those with the best academic qualifications were appointed, it was often the case that their route to those qualifications had been smoothed by the fact that they were the sons of the better born or better placed members of their Church.[81] And even appointment to less prestigious or well-endowed livings could depend on who the candidate (or his father) knew, or whether he spoke the local dialect or with a comprehensible accent. Such arrangements should not be condemned out of hand: the nomination of someone who was known to the patron or parish elders and who spoke the local dialect would ensure him at least some support when he embarked on the difficult first steps of his ministry.[82] However, for the disappointed members of the clerical proletariat, the result may have confirmed them in their belief that the patronage system did not put the highest premium on pastoral quality alone.[83]

---

[80] McManners, *French Ecclesiastical Society*, pp. 138–9; Ferté, *Vie Religieuse*, pp. 19, 40–1; Playoust-Chaussis, *Vie Religieuse*, pp. 156–8; Chadwick, *Popes*, pp. 130, 154; Vogler, *Clergé Protestant*, pp. 79–84; O'Day, *English Clergy*, caps. 6–9; Foster, *Church before the Covenants*, pp. 138–9.

[81] Brecht, 'Herkunft', pp. 174–5; Pruett, *Parish Clergy*, cap. 2; Hoffman, *Church and Community*, pp. 10–14.

[82] Green, 'Career Prospects', pp. 89–92; but more local men were recruited in the remote diocese of Durham than in the county of Surrey: J. Freeman, 'The Parish Ministry in the Diocese of Durham, c.1570–1640' (unpublished University of Durham Ph.D. thesis, 1979), cap. 1; R. A. Christophers, 'Social and Educational Background of the Surrey Clergy, 1520–1620' (unpublished University of London Ph.D. thesis, 1975), cap. 2.

[83] For a disappointed place-seeker, see J. H. Pruett, 'A Late Stuart Leicestershire Parson: the Reverend Humphrey Michel', *Leicestershire Archaeological and Historical Society Transactions*, 54 (1978–9), pp. 26–38.

Other features of the parish structure that the leaders of neither the Reformation nor the Counter-Reformation tackled were the unequal size of parishes and the unequal distribution of resources between them, both problems being exacerbated by the shift of population to new centres. The result was a system shot through with anomalies which made it very difficult for the early modern clergy to function as effectively as they might have done. So great were the problems of serving the huge or impoverished parishes of the Highlands of Scotland, the arid areas of Southern Portugal, and parts of Spain, Austria, and Poland that it proved very hard to find priests to serve them, certainly not priests of any calibre.[84] The problems of serving urban parishes swollen by regular floods of immigrants during Europe's 'iron century' and later were different but could be just as bad from a pastoral point of view.[85] Meanwhile in parishes with smaller but more stable populations, especially in or near a university city, incumbents could find a much more manageable unit, and one which was more rewarding both from a pastoral and a financial standpoint. Common to both Protestant and Catholic countries was a pattern whereby the better qualified men were presented to livings nearer to the capital or major cities, and with some exceptions the less well qualified to livings further away.[86] Nor can these inequalities be lightly dismissed as unfortunate aberrations. The success with which the parish clergy played their appointed role as bearers of the Reformation or Counter-Reformation must have been strongly affected for better or worse by the size and the equipment of the stage upon which they were called upon to act. There is clear evidence by the seventeenth and eighteenth centuries, if not earlier, of regional variations in the extent of lay commitment to the official Church, and among the reasons for this may well have been a shortage of suitably qualified, conscientious clergy. Indeed, the process was probably circular: if an area did not attract or was not allocated decent clergy, had few schools (and those of poor quality) and provided few recruits for the ministry, then there would be few local men to attract back to the region, and so on. In this way, regional variations could be reinforced and prove very hard to break down in the nineteenth century.[87]

[84] Smout, *Scottish People*, pp. 70–3; Callahan and Higgs, *Church and Society*, pp. 37–8, 41–2, 54–55, 89–91, 123, 131.

[85] e.g., Vienna, *ibid.*, pp. 90–1, and Madrid: Kamen, *Spain*, p. 299.

[86] See above notes 58, 82, 84; Tukker, 'Recruitment', pp. 201–3; Ferté, *Vie Religieuse*, pp. 42–3, 186–7; Chadwick, *Popes*, pp. 99–100; Callahan and Higgs, *Church and Society*, pp. 3–8.

[87] Delumeau, *Catholicisme*, p. 218–23 (citing the work of Pérouas in particular); Callahan and Higgs, *Church and Society*, p. 25; McLeod, *Religion and People*, pp. 2–3, 5–10; B. I. Coleman, *The Church of England in the Mid-Nineteenth Century* (London, 1980), pp. 8–25.

IAN GREEN

Before we turn to more positive aspects of the minister's work, it is necessary to point out one further constraint under which he laboured: the ambivalent attitude of the laity towards him. The ambiguity of this relationship is as old as the priesthood itself: fallen man cannot do without a priest, but he frequently has difficulty dealing with the one he's got. Whether the alterations in the education and role of the clergy meant that the early modern period was one of growing anticlericalism it is hard to gauge.[88] The steady demand for the rites of passage and the relatively low levels of illegitimacy among the laity, together with support for devotional practices in many Catholic countries and the desire for sermons, strength of pietism, and the vast market for religious books in some Protestant ones suggest that this can be viewed as an age of faith, or at least of outward conformity.[89] For all the changes in official doctrine or in the training of the parish clergy, it is possible that the prime task of the early modern clergy in the eyes of their parishioners, and so to some extent in their own eyes as well, remained much the same as before: to provide the rites of passage, to comfort those in distress, to be a good neighbour, and to settle conflicts when called upon to do so. Most laymen may have exhibited a degree of what one recent survey of the English scene calls 'unspectacular orthodoxy'; and in many parts of Europe only a minority of parishes with a resident minister or an acceptable deputy seem to have experienced serious conflict.[90]

On the other hand, it is possible to detect a number of ways in which the clergy were regarded as open to criticism. The gentleman resident in a village might resent greater demands being placed upon him in terms of religious knowledge or practice, especially if they came from an incumbent not of blue blood; the merchant, yeoman, or rich peasant might be as well-to-do and as well-born as the minister but resent his superior education or special exemptions; while the artisan or labourer

[88] For England, compare P. Heath, *The English Parish Clergy on the Eve of the Reformation* (London, 1969), pp. 10, 106–7, 133–4, 152–3, and C. Haigh, 'Anticlericalism and the English Reformation', *History*, 68 (1983), pp. 391–407, with O'Day, *English Clergy*, caps. 14–15, and E. J. Evans, 'Some Reasons for the Growth of English Rural Anti-Clericalism', *P & P* 66 (1975), pp. 84–109. On Germany, see R. W. Scribner, *Popular Culture and Popular Movements in Reformation Germany* (London, 1987), cap. 11.
[89] C. Larner, *Witchcraft and Religion: The Politics of Popular Belief* (Oxford, 1984), cap. 2 ('Pre-Industrial Europe: The Age of Faith'); J. A. Sharpe, *Early Modern England: A Social History 1550–1760* (London, 1987), pp. 44–5; Kamen, *Spain*, pp. 297–300; Callahan and Higgs, *Church and Society*, pp. 7–8 and cap. 10.
[90] M. J. Ingram, *Church Courts, Sex and Marriage in England, 1570–1640* (Cambridge, 1988), p. 123 and cap. 3; see also Spufford, *Contrasting Communities*, cap. 13, and next note.

might object to his paternalism in thwarting the time-honoured customs associated with certain church ceremonies or to any pretensions in his life-style.[91] Relations between laity and clergy could also deteriorate where, as in the Middle Ages, there were allegations of clerical neglect or quarrels over parish finances, or where the Church was a major local land-owner, as in Burgundy and parts of Southern France, Italy, and Portugal (the parish clergy did not as a rule share the profits from this land-owning, but they could be exposed to anti-seigneurial feeling directed at those who did). Relations could deteriorate quite rapidly, especially if the authorities were being particularly insistent upon uniformity of behaviour by the laity, or if there was an alternative form of priesthood or magic readily available.[92] In this sense, a minister always had to tread warily if he wished to achieve the ideals laid down in the ordinal.

Let us turn finally to look at the ministry as seen from the practising clergyman's point of view. There are two changes we might expect to find: a growing sense of esprit de corps among the parish clergy, and an increasingly political outlook. The fact that the majority of the parish clergy appear to have come from similar backgrounds, indeed were often interrelated, the fact that they had undergone a similar if not identical process of education and training, followed the same pattern of apprenticeship and benefice-hunting, and if successful of trying to cope with often similar pastoral or administrative problems—all this may have stimulated a stronger sense of common identity or purpose than in the later middle ages. Moreover, although the lower clergy in many states were less well represented in the synods, convocations, or other representative bodies than the bishops or capitular clergy, there were still occasions on which they met and could exchange ideas, at a conference or retreat in a Catholic country, or at a consistory or visitation in a Protestant one.[93] However, the idea of a stronger clerical ethos should perhaps be treated with caution. We may see signs of it in early seventeenth-century

---

[91] e.g., Tackett, *Priest and Parish*, cap. 7; D. Spaeth, 'Parsons and Parishioners: Lay-Clerical Conflicts and Popular Piety in Wiltshire Villages, 1660–1740' (unpublished Brown University Ph.D. thesis, 1985), *passim*. Of course, many other variables come into play when one tries to assess lay-clerical relations in a parish.

[92] Binz, *Vie Religieuse*, p. 444; Hoffman, *Church and Community*, p. 140 and caps. 4–5; Fulbrook, *Piety and Politics*, pp. 85–6; Callahan and Higgs, *Church and Society*, pp. 5–6, 15, 25, 50–1, 68–72; M. Spufford, *Contrasting Communities: English Villagers in the Sixteenth and Seventeenth Centuries* (Cambridge, 1974), pt. 3; Thomas, *Religion and the Decline of Magic*, *passim*; and G. Strauss, 'Success and Failure in the German Reformation', *P & P* 67 (1975), pp. 30–63.

[93] e.g., O'Day, *English Clergy*, cap. 12; Tackett, *Priest and Parish*, pp. 225–9; and see above nn. 39, 68, 79.

Sweden (though less so a century later) or in late eighteenth-century France (in some regions),[94] but was it a permanent feature of clerical life elsewhere or merely a response to an immedite threat—from the state, the papacy, the local bishop or synod, the laity or whoever? If so, that response probably varied from one period to another, according to the strength and direction from which the threat was perceived to be coming. It could also have varied according to the degree of stratification between the different grades of clergy. The best educated ministers might well have one foot on a higher rung of the ecclesiastical ladder, such as a canonry or royal chaplaincy, and so be more likely to sympathize with the higher clergy than fellow incumbents on some matters. On the other hand it is doubtful if the clerical proletariat of assistants and unbeneficed clergy shared all the views of their more fortunate brethren who had secured a benefice. And were the occasional brief meetings of parish incumbents sufficient to develop or sustain a strong sense of identify or a corporate plan of action?[95]

On a few occasions the parish clergy's reaction to events was apparently political. If one thinks of the clashes between Remonstrant and Counter-Remonstrant clergy in Holland, between the parish clergy and the upper orders in Sweden, between Puritan and Laudian clergy in England in the 1630s and early 1640s, or between Jansenists, rigorists, and Jesuits in seventeenth-century France, or if one considers the part played by some of the lesser clergy in the Catholic League in France and in revolts in Catalonia, Sicily, France, and Scotland in the 1640s and '50s,[96] one can readily see that the parish clergy did not always fit into the mould of obedient servants of the state Church. But these conflicts involved an interpenetration of ecclesiastical and secular issues at a number of points, and it might be unwise to try to detect a common theme in all of them

---

[94] Roberts, 'The Swedish Church', pp. 164–5; Tackett, *Priest and Parish* caps. 9–10, and *Religion Revolution and Regional Culture in Eighteenth-Century France* (Princeton, 1986), *passim*.

[95] For the complexity of ecclesiastical relations in France from 1650 to 1800, see R. M. Golden *The Godly Rebellion: Parisian Curés and the Religious Fronde, 1652–1662* (Chapel Hill, 1981); B. R Kreiser, *Miracles, Convulsions and Religious Politics in Early Eighteenth-Century Paris* (Princeton, 1978); McManners, *French Ecclesiastical Society*; and previous note.

[96] J. den Tex, *Oldenbarnevelt*, 2 vols (Cambridge, 1973), 2, cap. 10; N. Tyacke, *Anti-Calvinists The Rise of English Arminianism c.1590–1640* (Oxford, 1987); A. Whiteman, 'Church and State', in F. L. Carsten, ed., *New Cambridge Modern History: 5. 1648–88* (Cambridge, 1964) pp. 132–6; J. H. Elliott, *The Revolt of the Catalans* (Cambridge, 1963), pp. 34, 289–90, 422 427, 444–5, 486–7; H. G. Koenigsberger, *Estates and Revolutions* (Ithaca, 1971), pp. 262, 271–2; Golden, *Godly Rebellion*, *passim*; Scotland: D. Stevenson, *The Scottish Revolution 1637–44* (Newton Abbot, 1973) and *Revolution and Counter-Revolution in Scotland 1644–1651* (London 1977); F. D. Dow, *Cromwellian Scotland 1651–1660* (Edinburgh, 1979).

such as the politicization of the parish clergy. In some cases the conflict was due to a theological difference being politicized by the laity rather than the clergy, as in seventeenth-century Holland, England, and to some extent France;[97] while in the eighteenth century conflicts were more likely to be between different groups of churchmen, as in England over convocation or in France over Richerism or clerical income, than between clergy and laity.[98]

The most that these conflicts may suggest is that on a limited number of occasions certain sections of the early modern parish clergy felt sufficiently confident of their role as leaders against Antichrist, heresy, or manifest wrong for them to take action against the expressed wishes of the authorities. But few such groups sustained this position for long, and in those cases where there was an element of popular protest which the clergy proved unable to control, as in England and Sweden, the result may have been to persuade those ministers, or their successors, that in this world obedience to the authorities ordained by God was not only lawful but essential.[99] The notion of the late eighteenth-century parish clergy as the champions of a hierarchical society has some validity if seen in theological as well as socio-political terms, but the idea of a politicized body may need qualifying on the score that in most areas the process either was incomplete or had not even begun.[100]

Two much clearer and more important examples of the way in which the ministry evolved are provided by looking at the kind of pastoral initiative that emerged at parish level: the clergy's efforts to act as a medium between official and popular views; and their attempts to provide forms of instruction better suited to a particular parish's needs than those produced by the authorities. A great deal of work on the early

---

[97] Den Tex, Oldenbarnevelt, 2, cap. 12; H. R. Trevor-Roper, Catholics, Anglicans and Puritans: Seventeenth Century Essays (London, 1987), pp. 40–119; Briggs, 'Catholic Puritans', pp. 338–43; J. McManners, 'Religion and the Relations of Church and State', in J. S. Bromley, ed., New Cambridge Modern History: 6. 1688–1725 (Cambridge, 1971), pp. 132–4.

[98] G. V. Bennett, The Tory Crisis in Church and State 1688–1730 (Oxford, 1975), pt. 1; E. Préclin, Les Jansénistes du XVIIIe Siècle et la Constitution Civile du Clergé (Paris, 1929), and see works cited by Tackett in n. 94 above.

[99] G. S. Abernathy, 'The English Presbyterians and the Stuart Restoration, 1648–1663', Transactions of the American Philosophical Society, 55 (Philadelphia, 1965); J. Spurr, 'Anglican Apologetic and the Restoration Church' (unpublished Oxford University D.Phil. thesis, 1985); J. Buckroyd, Church and State in Scotland 1660–1681 (Edinburgh, 1980).

[100] The proportion of the French parish clergy who initially backed the Revolution and the Civil Constitution was just over a half (Tackett, Religion, Revolution and Regional Culture, p. 41), but in other countries, including England, the proportion of politically active clergy may have been much smaller.

modern period in the 1960s and '70s detected a growing confrontation between those, especially learned clerics, who wished to suppress forms of popular culture and popular religion which were deemed misguided or even dangerous, and those who tried to defend them.[101] More recently, doubts have been expressed about the extent and the precise nature of such a rift. Was there a single 'popular religion' or a complex of religious cultures, varying in time, place, and level? Do we risk downgrading or underestimating those cultures by regarding them as 'traditional', or by isolating them as 'religious' when they might have been part of much broader attempts to create an individual or collective identity? How far was the flow of ideas one-way, downwards from the élite or outwards from the centre, or how far was there a two-way flow between educated and uneducated, centre and periphery, for example in the case of church music?[102] Rather than expect uniformity of action or reaction, should we not expect to uncover more individuals like Mennochio or Hans Keil who found their own highly individual balance between competing ideas? To put it more succinctly we could ask, with Professor Collinson, how many people in Elizabethan England went to both a sermon *and* a dance?[103]

One consequence of these doubts is that we may need to view the clergy not as unthinking agents of a paternalistic élite, but individuals who in their own minds combined elements of the old with elements of the new, for example in their attitudes towards spirits and 'magic', astrology and healing, or literature and popular entertainments.[104] Such men may have wittingly or unwittingly built bridges between potentially diverging points of view. One thinks of work on the mass in sixteenth-

---

[101] For a recent survey see K. von Greyerz, ed., *Religion and Society in Early Modern Europe 1500–1800* (London, 1984), pp. 1–14.

[102] N. Z. Davis, 'Some Tasks and Themes in the Study of Popular Religion', in C. Trinkaus and H. A. Oberman, eds, *The Pursuit of Holiness in Late Medieval and Renaissance Religion* (Leiden, 1974), pp. 307–36, and 'From "Popular Religion" to Religious Cultures', in S. Ozment, ed., *Reformation Europe: A Guide to Research* (St Louis, 1982), pp. 321–41; M. Venard, 'Popular Religion in the Eighteenth Century', in Calahan and Higgs, *Church and Society*, pp. 138–42. Church music awaits a full comparative study.

[103] C. Ginzburg, *The Cheese and the Worms: The Cosmos of a Sixteenth-Century Miller*, tr. J. and A. Tedeschi (London, 1980); D. Sabean, *Power in the Blood: Popular Culture and Village Discourse in Early Modern Germany* (Cambridge, 1984), cap. 2; P. Collinson, *From Iconoclasm to Iconophobia: the Cultural Impact of the Second English Reformation* (Reading, 1986), p. 7.

[104] Thomas, *Religion and the Decline of Magic*, pp. 328–30, 438–9, 450–3, 523–4; 533–4, 559–80, 601–2, 707–9, 797; A. Macfarlane, *The Family Life of Ralph Josselin* (Cambridge, 1970), pp. 189–96; M. MacDonald, *Mystical Bedlam: Madness, Anxiety and Healing in Seventeenth-Century England* (Cambridge, 1981), cap. 2 and *passim*; A. Sinfield, *Literature in Protestant England* (London, 1983), caps. 3–6; I. M. Green, 'The Persecution of "Scandalous" and "Malignant" Parish Clergy during the English Civil War', *EHR* 94 (1979), pp. 521–2.

and seventeenth-century Germany suggesting that some priests managed to accommodate elements of popular belief and folklore into the official liturgy, of work on early modern France and Spain suggesting that some local priests were reluctant to attack practices or organizations which were the object of official disapproval but seemed not without devout intent to their pastors, or of the negotiations which took place between centre and region over the canonization of saints after the Counter-Reformation.[105] In the case of Protestant Churches, one can think of cases of ministers having to come to terms with the local customs that accompanied weddings, funerals, and church festivals, or with parishioners' reluctance to accept new ideas, for example that a mastery of the catechism was a necessary qualification for those who wanted to get married or act as a godparent.[106]

Quite how or why these adjustments to the official ideal were made or justified is not always clear (indeed, on closer inspection of the sort of elementary instruction contained in catechisms and simple devotional works the need for adjustment may prove to have been less than has some-times been imagined). It is tempting to dismiss many of these examples as indications of faint-heartedness on the part of incumbents or curates who to make life bearable tried to find a middle position between what the authorities said should happen and what their parishioners were prepared to accept, but the situation may often have been less clear-cut than this suggests. Some of those many ordinands who went back to the area in which they had grown up may have been reluctant to force change on villagers who included a number of their own relations or supporters. Conversely, an outsider might have been cautious of upsetting local feel-ings by too vigorous an enforcement of new ideas from 'outside' as soon as he arrived, and thereafter had lost the initiative. In this context it is inter-esting to note the reasons given by the majority of the *curés* in the relatively well-provided diocese of Reims in 1774 for evading a straight answer to an official questionnaire on the character and conduct of their parishioners: the incumbent had only recently arrived; he was too young

---

[105] Scribner, *Popular Culture*, cap. 2, and see the essays by Hörger and Burke in Greyerz, *Religion and Society*; W. A. Christian, *Local Religion in Sixteenth-Century Spain* (Princeton, 1981); Tackett, *Priest and Parish*, pp. 208–15; Briggs, 'Catholic Puritans', pp. 350–4.

[106] On the survival of older attitudes and customs in England, see J. R. Gillis, *For Better, For Worse: British Marriages 1600 to the Present* (Oxford, 1985), pt. 1; Spaeth, 'Parsons and Parishioners', caps. 3–4; B. Bushaway, *By Rite: Custom, Ceremony and Community in England 1700–1800* (London, 1982); J. Obelkevich, *Religion and Rural Society: South Lindsey 1825–1875* (Oxford, 1975), cap. 6.

to judge; he did not wish to break the secrecy of the confessional, or commit parishioners' sins to paper; he did not want to bring odium on the ministry. The most that some *curés* would concede was that the faults of their flock were 'much as elsewhere'.[107]

Perhaps some of the clergy also had difficulty in determining exactly where their parishioners were going wrong. Their training does not seem to have prepared them thoroughly for the task of distinguishing between outward conformity and inward religiosity, and in many parishes they probably found parishioners with a basic knowledge of the Lord's Prayer, Creed, commandments, and sacraments that was adequate for their everyday needs (albeit much less than the zealots wanted).[108] Departures from the official line were more likely to be unwitting deviations than deliberate defections, and if recent scholars are right to suggest that lay opinion tended to reinterpret the religion of the educated élite in terms of its own mental vocabulary of words, images, and categories,[109] then it is at least possible that those parish clergy who had grown up with much the same vocabulary were able to recognize that this was what was going on. As recently as the 1970s William Christian noted that the priests of central Spain spoke to him of local devotions 'with a bemused tolerance, occasionally wondering out loud about "pagan superstition"'. But when asked about the shrines of their home villages, 'the same priests speak with tenderness, excitement and pride'. As Dr Christian observes, 'For them the religion learned at home . . . transcends the doctrinal attitudes learned in the seminary, which they may apply elsewhere'.[110]

The authorities of the early modern period seem to have been aware of the risk that even better trained parish clergy, once they had become isolated in their parishes, might go native: the regular enquiries made by archdeacons, rural deans, or other officials, the books that the authorities recommended their clergy to buy and read, the pastoral letters they circulated, the regular repetition of the need to suppress certain 'pagan' or impious practices, and the conferences and retreats they organized—all point to this conclusion.[111] It is also interesting that where assessments of

---

[107] D. Julia, 'Le Clergé Paroissial du Diocèse de Reims à la Fin du XVIIIe Siècle', [pt. 1], *Etudes Ardennaises*, 49 (1967), pp. 26–8.

[108] *Ibid.*, [pt. 2], 55 (1968), pp. 52–4; Green, 'Emergence of the English Catechism', pp. 413–14; Kamen, *Spain*, pp. 299–300.

[109] Davis, 'From "Popular Religion"', pp. 327, 330–1; and see M. Aston, *Lollards and Reformers: Images and Literacy in Late Medieval Religion* (London, 1984).

[110] Christian, *Local Religion*, p. 20; and cf. Sabean, *Power in the Blood*, p. 199.

[111] Hoffman, *Church and Community*, pp. 50–2, 99–103, 109–10; Schaer, *Clergé Paroissial*, pp. 158–9, 165; Playoust-Chaussis, 'Vie Religieuse', pp. 167–8; Pérouas, *La Rochelle*,

parish clergy have been drawn up by contemporary authorities or present-day historians the typical incumbent is described as being of moderate education and showing a degree of orthodoxy and commitment or optimism somewhere between the zeal of a small minority at one end and the apathy or ignorance of a small minority at the other.[112] Much of our limited knowledge of parish religion comes from the pens of zealots who condemned the ignorance of the laity and the lack of commitment of their fellow clergy; but their standards of what could be learnt or taught may have been unrealistic, and their testimony flawed.

Other clerical initiatives were more dynamic, and though perhaps more typical of the minority of zealots in the parish clergy seem to have been readily copied by their less confident brethren. In particular I am thinking here of the way in which forms of religious instruction developed in England between the late sixteenth and the early eighteenth centuries, though there are parallels in other countries. In England, as I hope to show on another occasion, there were changes in the type of sermon preached, in the type of bibles published and the aids to biblical study produced, in the forms of catechisms used and in the type of religious publications aimed at the less educated as well as the moderately educated by their clerical authors, and in nearly all these cases the initiative came not from the authorities but from the parish clergy.[113] What seems to have become the fairly standard form of sermon by the later Elizabethan period—a carefully structured and applied analysis of a particular text for an hour or more—was increasingly supplemented by other types, such as shorter, pithier sermons with a less rigid structure and using simpler everyday language and images, and catechetical sermons on a phrase covered in that day's catechizing. The clergy also played a part in the campaign to ensure that bibles of the right size and price and printed in the right kind of typeface were on sale to the public; and they took part in the process of making available a variety of concordances, thesauruses, dictionaries, summaries, and commentaries of varying lengths and standards of difficulty. What is interesting about the shorter bibles and the more elementary aids to bible study is which

pp. 249–56; Broutin, *Réforme Pastorale*, pt. 3; Hufton, *Bayeux*, p. 35; Pruett, *Parish Clergy*, p. 46; Moorman, *Curate of Souls*, caps. 1, 3, 5; and see above, n. 68.

[112] I. M. Green, *The Re-establishment of the Church of England 1660–1663* (Oxford, 1978), pp. 170–7; Julia, 'Clergé Paroissial du Diocèse de Reims' [pt. 2], pp. 54–7.

[113] Much of this paragraph is based on material that will be discussed in my *Religious Instruction in England c.1540–1740* (forthcoming).

aspects of official teaching it was thought wise to stress and which to leave out.

As for catechisms, as in Germany, Scotland, France, and elsewhere, what is revealing is the number of individual efforts produced by clergy on the spot, trying to find a form that suited the needs of their particular congregation at a given time.[114] So far I have tracked down over six hundred question-and-answer catechisms produced in England from the 1540s to the 1730s (using a more liberal definition the total would be nearer seven hundred).[115] This series of individual efforts is characterized by trends towards shorter questions and answers, and more explanations of technical terms, and by experiments with form designed to ensure that the catechism was not simply learnt but understood as well. As on the continent, there were also catechisms for different age and ability groups; there was a shift from catechisms designed to guard against error to ones aimed to defeat ignorance; after an early concentration on decalogue, creed, Lord's Prayer, and sacraments, there were experiments with different material, or with the use of scripture or history. The number and variety of new forms is a tacit admission that many sixteenth-century authorities had aimed too high, and that the parish clergy had to rectify this mistake by producing something more suited to the specific needs of their flocks. Not all new forms were written by the parish clergy, but most of those that were reprinted regularly had been prepared by churchmen with some experience of parish conditions. In many churches, the history of catechizing is the story of the parish clergy at the sharp end of their ministry.[116]

It is also interesting to note changes in the other types of popular religious work written by the English clergy, above all the types that borrowed techniques and subjects from the popular press of the day: broadsides, religious verse for children and adults, sometimes set to well-known tunes, short treatises with catchy titles and lurid woodcuts on the cover, dreadful-warning stories and uplifting moral tales, open letters, improving thoughts and epigrams, and (what to our eyes may seem a contradiction in terms) religious jokebooks! On the basis of a sample of several hundred popular religious works of the period, it can be shown

---

[114] See above n. 14; also G. Strauss, *Luther's House of Learning: Indoctrination of the Young in the German Reformation* (London, 1978), and J. R. Armogathe, 'Catéchisme et Enseignement Populaire en France', *Actes du Colloque d'Aix 1969* (Paris, 1973).

[115] These will be listed in Appendix 1 of my *Religious Instruction*.

[116] Green, 'Emergence of the English Catechism', pp. 401–25; B. Plongeron, *La Vie Quotidienne du Clergé Français au XVIIIe Siècle* (Paris, 1974), pp. 235–9.

that the lower or lower-middling end of the market represented by works such as these was growing apace during the seventeenth century.[117] Above these were the better known works of Bishop Bayly, Jeremy Taylor, and Richard Allestree; these were larger and more expensive, and their authors used more demanding vocabulary and syntax than many of the cheaper works.[118] But analysis of the same sample suggests that these larger works dealt with much more than holy living and holy dying: there was a relative decline of works of a more technical kind, such as on assurance, but long before the rise of Laudianism, a steady rise had begun in the numbers of handbooks designed to help the laity prepare for holy communion and in the numbers of devotional manuals or handbooks to explain the liturgy. How far the clerical authors of these and other works were leading the laity or being led by them it is hard to tell, and in a sense is irrelevant here; the point is that the changes in the type of works published suggests the existence of a number of experienced parish clergy who, with the support of enterprising publishers, were perfectly capable of taking their own line in recognizing the laity's needs and meeting them.

A similar conclusion might in varying degrees be possible for other countries, both Catholic and Protestant, at this time, for in a number of Churches we find similar developments. Visual and dramatic methods are revived or revised to supplement the written or spoken word; sermons are found to be of limited use in edifying the people unless a solid basis has been laid through catechizing; preachers are reminded regularly not to use technical or affected language but simple terms that all could under-stand; if existing forms of instruction were too hard, then simpler hand-books were composed or other types of instruction devised; and the simpler the forms became, with an emphasis on Decalogue, Creed, and Lord's Prayer, the closer Protestant forms came to Catholic (with some obvious differences, of course), and the more they resembled the instruc-tion of the late middle ages.[119] During the early modern period an increas-ing number of levels of instruction were developed, from the most

---

[117] The sample will form Appendix 2 of *Religious Instruction*; see also M. Spufford, *Small Books and Pleasant Histories* (London, 1981), cap. 8, and R. Chartier, *The Cultural Uses of Print in Early Modern France* (Princeton, 1987), caps. 2, 5.

[118] C. J. Stranks, *Anglican Devotion: Studies in the Spiritual Life of the Church of England* (London, 1961), pp. 35–95. For some preliminary remarks about size and difficulty of books, see I. M. Green, 'Bunyan in Context: the Changing Face of Protestantism in Seventeenth-Century England' (forthcoming).

[119] Ortiz, *Golden Age*, pp. 213–14; J.-J. von Allmen, *L'Eglise et ses Fonctions d'après Jean-Frédéric Osterwald* (Neuchatel, 1947), pp. 78–9; Weir, 'Pastoral Care', p. 80; Ferté, 'Vie Religieuse', p. 189; Schaer, *Clergé Paroissial*, p. 165; and see previous notes.

elementary forms ('milk for babes') through an increasing variety of intermediate forms ('meat for men') to the most advanced tier (for those capable of handling the deepest mysteries of the faith);[120] but most of the clerical energy went into the elementary and intermediate levels. Although there was a strong vein of élitism and paternalism in the outlook of the better educated clergy on many matters, at least some of those with practical experience with a congregation seem to have learnt to temper their enthusiasm for education in general with a realization of the needs of their flocks in particular.[121]

In acting as a medium the parish clergy may also, though this is more speculative, have acted as a filter, preventing certain ideas put forward by the better educated sections of society from reaching their rural congregations lest they should be confused or harmed by them.[122] The extent to which the lower clergy were aware of which idea was flavour of the month—pietism, scholasticism, rationalism, or whatever—presumably depended on how good the lines of communication were between the intellectual or spiritual leaders of the day and the parish clergy; it seems likely that there were better channels of communication in countries like France, England, Scotland, and parts of central Europe than in others.[123] But even where communication was reasonably good, it is open to question as to how soon or how far the parish clergy decided to transmit these ideas to their congregations. My own work on elementary religious instruction in England suggests that the bitter debate between Calvinists and non-Calvinists did not percolate through very much to the lower levels of religious education, the reason most often given being that such things were too hard for the uneducated or too disturbing.[124] For much the same reasons, the spirit of rationality and the new forms of textual criticism of the bible that we find in works aimed at the better educated Englishmen in the late seventeenth and early eighteenth centuries do not

---

[120] Green, 'Emergence of the English Catechism', pp. 408–10.
[121] See, for instance, the many efforts by English and Scottish Presbyterian clergy to make the Westminster Shorter Catechism easier for their catechumens to grasp; also Gawthrop and Strauss, 'Protestantism and Literacy'; Johansson, 'Literacy in Sweden'; and Chartier, L'Education en France, pp. 64–5.
[122] The filter may have worked in the other direction too, in that some of the clergy may have concealed evidence of unconventional local ideas or practices from the authorities.
[123] The impression is based on the higher proportion of graduates in the parish clergy, and the greater availability of information through booksellers, lending libraries, newspapers and societies.
[124] Green, 'Emergence of the English Catechism', p. 404 and n. 32. See also H. C. Porter, Reformation and Reaction in Tudor Cambridge (Cambridge, 1958), pp. 398–403.

seem to appear much in elementary catechisms or in sermons given to rural congregations, at least by the middle of the eighteenth century.[125] And in France there are grounds for thinking that it took some time for the ideas of Jansenist and rigorist bishops and seminary teachers to percolate down to the localities, and that when they did they met with such resistance that they 'disintegrated at parish level'.[126] There are, of course, examples to the contrary: in Geneva, Scotland, and the Netherlands, and among English Presbyterians scholastic Calvinist views on double predestination were probably inculcated with as much rigour as any deviant views were condemned. But even there there are some indications of clerical awareness that there might be pastoral drawbacks in this teaching.[127]

If we try to bring together the threads of this very broad enquiry, three points emerge. The first is that in many ways the ministry had not changed dramatically between 1500 and 1800. Clergy may have been forced to undertake some new tasks, but the essential duties of performing the sacraments and rites of passage and helping those in need remained much the same. Ministers were in general better educated but not necessarily better trained for their work. They may have been drawn from somewhat higher social strata than before, but the methods of appointment to livings still reflected the hierarchical attitudes of the age. There remained sources of tension, between upper and lower clergy over remuneration, and between clergy and laity over the abandonment of old practices or over tithes or neglect; but as yet there were relatively few challenges from the laity to the essential functions of the clergy. In general the clergy were conformable, though individually or in groups they proved willing to take steps to adapt the theory of the ministry or the official doctrine of the Church to local circumstances.

The second conclusion is that there was probably a much greater diversity of parish clergies by the mid-eighteenth century. It might be unwise to imagine that a priest in medieval Sicily was performing exactly the same role as one in Scotland, but there was almost certainly greater uniformity in 1500 than in 1800. We are only just beginning to understand the number of variables that could have affected attitude and

---

[125] The samples upon which I base these remarks stop in the 1730s: see my *Religious Instruction*.
[126] Briggs, 'Catholic Puritans', p. 351.
[127] See J. K. Cameron, 'The Church of Scotland in the Age of Reason', *Studies on Voltaire and the Eighteenth Century* 58 (1967), pp. 1941–7; and the debate among English and Scottish Presbyterians in the late 1730s provoked by James Strong's revision of the Westminster Shorter Catechism.

performance, leading to contrasts not only between Protestant and Catholic, but also between different Churches within that major divide and between different regions within each Church. This is not the place to attempt a full list of the variables, and in any case there are still too many unanswered or even unasked questions to attempt to construct a worthwhile typology, for example about the way in which the ministry was depicted in the more elementary forms of instruction described above, about ministers' attitudes to their vocation and their task as reflected in court records, sermons, and biographical material, about the extent to which comparative studies might throw light on the way geographical and social background affected a minister's preconceptions, about the effect on his ministry of the existence of rival holy men in the area, and so on. But as a possible typology to be tested at some date, one might ask why the early modern ministry appears to have enjoyed greater success in Catholic Spain, Lutheran Sweden, and Calvinist Scotland than in the more moderate churches of England, France, and parts of Germany.

The third conclusion to some extent cuts across this and supports the first. Changes in population distribution, social relations and political ideology can have a considerable bearing upon the context in which Christian worship takes place and upon the attitudes of those who take part. But such changes, whether in the dark ages, the sixteenth century, or the last two hundred years, are never more than part of the story. At its core the Christian ministry has probably always been much the same, even if in its externals it is always adapting to new circumstances. In the writings of men like Pierre du Moulin and Richard Baxter one can sense the pride in being one of those who through the ages have been entrusted with such a task, and one can hear the despair when a minister felt he was failing his flock, or his flock was failing Christ. Between the sense of duty and divine mission implicit in Baxter's 'Oh what a charge it is that we have undertaken!' and the sense of human fallibility in his 'If we cannot do all, let us do what we can',[128] there is never likely to be an easy or a lasting balance.

Queen's University, Belfast

---

[128] Baxter, *Reformed Pastor*, cap. 2, sections 3: 4 and 3: 1; for du Moulin see above p. 24.

PRIEST AND LAYMAN IN A MINORITY CHURCH: THE ROMAN CATHOLIC CHURCH IN THE NORTHERN NETHERLANDS 1592–1686

by MATHIEU G. SPIERTZ

Church strategy

IN 1572, when the provinces of Holland and Zeeland were almost completely overrun by the 'Geuzen', Pope Gregory XIII (1572–1585) succeeded to the Holy See. In 1578 this Pope forbade the Roman Catholics in the rebellious provinces to give any civil or military service to the rebels' authority—on penalty of excommunication—and identified Catholicism with being faithful to the Spanish cause. When this Pope died in 1585, there was reasonable hope held in Rome that the recapture of the Northern Netherlands—and hence the restoration of Catholicism—would soon be realized, as Parma's campaign was succeeding in the South of the Netherlands and one town after another fell into his hands.

During the pontificates of Sixtus V (1585–1590) and Clement VIII (1592–1605) it gradually became clear to the Holy See that in the Northern Netherlands an independent state under Calvinist authority might be in the making. In these provinces the episcopal sees, set up in 1559, were either vacant or deserted since the bishops lived in exile. In spite of requests by Philip II the Holy See postponed the appointment of new bishops. However, in 1592 Clement VIII appointed an administrator, a 'vicar apostolic', who, in the name of the Pope, was to administer all the provinces where Calvinism had gained the upper hand, notably the area north of the great rivers in the present-day Netherlands. This vicar apostolic Sasbout Vosmeer (1592–1614) was consecrated in 1602 and given the title of archbishop of Philippi *in partibus infidelium*.

All five vicars apostolic who, during the seventeenth century, administered their territory in the name of the Pope and not by virtue of their own authority, aspired to become archbishop of Utrecht. All cherished the hope that the Holy See would end the missionary status to which the Northern Netherlands church had been reduced. Sasbout Vosmeer, Philippus Rovenius (1614–1651) and Jacobus de la Torre (1651–1661) believed that the kings of Spain would be able to achieve this. In 1672 during the French occupation of parts of the Republic Johannes van

Neercassel (1663–1686) was to make a formal appeal to Louis XIV about this. Later, in 1701, Petrus Codde (1688–1702) tried to achieve the same object by writing a very elaborate report of the Dutch Mission and taking it to Rome himself.[1]

The status and appearance of the Catholic Church in the Republic changed dramatically after 1580. Until that year it had been the Established Church to which everyone belonged automatically by birth. Thereafter it was no longer tolerated and became a minority Church in a diaspora situation. It was to develop more and more into a Church of volunteers. Owing to the attraction of Protestantism or to the pressure of persecution only staunch Catholics stayed members. A number of causes of the steady decline of Catholicism can be mentioned: systematic repression of all visible expressions of the Catholic faith, massive exile of notable priests, and a chronic shortage, until about 1638, of priests trained in the spirit of Trent. Much to their regret Vosmeer and Rovenius were forced to keep priests of the old persuasion in service.

Apart from these factors the following is also important. Until about 1650 two other major groups—apart from the Catholics and the Protestants—existed. The first group consisted of the 'Mennonites'; the second was formed by those who, in the first decades of the seventeenth century, had not yet decided which Church to join. During the first quarter of the century the Church had been abandoned on a large scale and secularism was rampant. This may have been true of the Republic before 1580, but it grew stronger after 1580 when Catholic pastoral care ceased and the Reformed Church had too few pastors. These two Churches probably did not have many committed members during the first decades of the seventeenth century.[2]

The Catholic revival produced by the spirit of the Council of Trent first became apparent in two centres in Holland: in Delft where Vosmeer worked around 1580, and in Haarlem where the cathedral chapter, founded in 1578, remained active. Around 1590 Utrecht became the third centre, and in 1607 Oldenzaal, which was in Spanish hands until 1626, emerged as a fourth stronghold of missionary activities.

The ambulant mission, which was mainly carried out by regular clergy

---

[1] M. G. Spiertz, *L'église Catholique des Provinces-Unies et le Saint-Siège pendant la deuxième moitié du XVII siècle* (Louvain, 1975), pp. 8–23, 119, 154.

[2] M. G. Spiertz, 'De ontwikkelingsgang van de katholieke Missie in Friesland', *Archief voor de Geschiedenis van de katholieke kerk in Nederland* (= *AGKKN*), 21 (1979), pp. 290–1. "Godsdienstig leven van de katholieken in de 17de eeuw', *Algemene Geschiedenis der Nederlanden*, D. P. Blok *et al.*, eds., 8 (Bussum, 1979), p. 346.

travelling from region to region, was slowly but surely reshaped into organized pastoral care by archpriests. Rovenius entrusted the pastoral care for the faithful in the entire district specifically to the archpriests. The presence of many a Catholic enclave in Calvinist regions was due to the industry of regular clergy. However, the eventual religious hue of the regions was determined by the organization in the centres.[3]

It should be realized that both in Amsterdam and other towns, including Utrecht, a degree of toleration by the magistrate could be detected around the middle of the seventeenth century. In other parts of the Republic Catholics were, for longer or shorter periods, hindered in the practice of their religion until 1678 and, in the North, until well into the nineties. By paying what were often huge sums of recognition money to officers of the law they managed to buy a freedom throughout the Republic which elsewhere in Europe was hardly ever granted to a Church not in line with the Established Church.[4]

To fight the shortage of secular priests trained in the spirit of Trent, Vosmeer founded the College of SS Willibrord and Boniface in Cologne, where future clergy for the archdiocese of Utrecht were to be trained. The college was also known as 'Collegium Alticollense' or 'De Hoge Heuvel', because it had its origin in 1613 in a former inn of that name in the Budengasse. The college was a sort of mixture of a junior and senior seminary. During the first years of this Cologne seminary all, or nearly all, lessons were taught by the resident teachers. Later the students attended the 'gymnasium' or the university departments in the city. From the very beginning plans existed to transfer the college to Louvain. Vosmeer had kept this right of transfer for himself and his successors because, when the college in Cologne was founded, Catholics from the Republic were not allowed to study in Louvain. The transfer plans were again discussed in 1616, 1643, 1652, and 1662. In 1670, while Neercassel was in office, the students moved to Louvain. They remained in the Papal College until 1683. In that year the Cologne College was officially founded in Louvain in a house that, from then on, was to be known under its original Cologne name 'De Hoge Heuvel'.[5]

In 1617, during the Twelve Years' Truce (1609–1621) Rovenius opened a college called 'Collegium Pulcheriae Mariae Virginis' for future

[3] L. J. Rogier, *Geschiedenis van het katholicisme in Noord-Nederland in de 16e en de 17e eeuw* (Amsterdam, 1947²), 2, pp. 352–4.

[4] W. Nijenhuis, 'Religiegeschiedenis 1621–1648, kerk in het meervoud', *Algemene Geschiedenis der Nederlanden*, 6, pp. 397–9.

[5] K. H. M. Mars, 'Seger Stevens Sueck', *AGKKN* 18 (1976), pp. 143–7.

priests for the dioceses of Haarlem, Friesland, and Groningen. The Haarlem chapter was determined to help the dioceses lacking priests. The students attended the courses of philosophy and theology of Louvain University where they also took their degrees. In the college they received their spiritual guidance and their practical spiritual education. Through the foundation of the 'Pulcheria', named after a statue of the Holy Virgin over the front entrance, Rovenius and the chapter were able to provide Noord-Hòlland with an uninterrupted supply of priests.

After 1660 the dioceses of Friesland and Groningen also saw the number of priests rise steadily. Grammar school boys who wished to join the Haarlem clergy could go to Louvain and to Trinity College there which offered arts studies in the university.[6] Some secular priests received their education neither in 'De Hoge Heuvel' at Cologne nor the 'Pulcheria' in Louvain. Some of them were trained in the Propaganda Fide College in Rome, in Douai, and in the Oratoire de France colleges, founded in Paris in 1609. An Oratoire college was founded in Louvain with the help of Rovenius.[7]

In 1629 Fabius a Lagonissa, nuncio in Brussels, who supervised the Dutch Mission on behalf of the 'Congregatio de Propaganda Fide', reported that Rovenius had consecrated 300 portable altars and 250 chalices. Lagonissa saw in these figures that the number of priests and Catholic lay people in the Mission was increasing. Reports sent to Rome between 1625 and 1650 show that 1,501 portable altars and 1,178 chalices in total had been consecrated. The portable altars were built inside wooden cases which could easily be transported. They were hidden in many hide-outs. The chalices were made mainly of tin.

Since the 1630s great efforts had been made by priests who tried, in the spirit of the Council of Trent, to win back the ground that had been lost or was lying fallow. They found the ministers of the Reformed Church to be extremely tough opponents. Soon after they first arrived in the Republic in 1594 the Jesuits saw the Northern Netherlands Church as purely missionary territory where they could, without the secular clergy's consent, freely dispense their pastoral care by virtue of papal prerogatives. The number of Jesuits, four at first, grew to eighty in 1667 in spite of all

---

[6] L. J. Rogier, *Geschiedenis*, 2, pp. 98–9.
[7] The sources of the consulted reports of the Dutch Mission are mentioned in: M. G. Spiertz en J. A. M. M. Janssen, *Gids voor de studie van Reformatie en Katholieke Herleving in Nederland 1520–1650*, Archiefdienst Nederlandse Hervormde Kerk (Den Haag, 1982), pp. 113–21. The results of the mission-reports of 1656 and 1701 can be found in L. J. Rogier, *Geschiedenis*, 2, pp. 362–7, 392–9, 424, 435–9, 471–7.

Table 1   *The numbers of missionaries, both secular and regular,*
working in the Holland Mission, as mentioned in the respective annual
mission reports

	Secular priests	Regular priests	Total
1602	70	—	70
1605	—	—	0
1613	—	—	0
1614	—	—	0
1616	200	15	215
1617	250	23/24	273/4
1619	200	31	231
1622	200	32/33	232/3
1626	—	—	0
1629	250	70	320
1631	246	97	343
1635	300	121	421
1638	350	132	482
1640	—	—	0
1645	300	140/142	440/442
1656	311	132	443
1701	340	126	466

the agreements Vosmeer and Rovenius had reached with the provincial
superiors in this respect. Against all protests by the vicars apostolic they
claimed the freedom of movement and freedom of initiative granted to
them by Rome. All vicars apostolic had the experience of a number of
Jesuits who simply ignored their jurisdiction, until Rome resolved the
problem in 1671 and gave Neercassel adequate authority over all regular
clergy, including the Jesuits, whose total number was then fixed at sixty-
five.[8]

The vicars apostolic and the Haarlem Chapter quite deliberately
guided the spirituality of the secular clergy towards the national saints.
Thus they continued the pastoral policy of Vosmeer who had rediscovered
in Willibrord the man who brought the faith to the Netherlands. This

[8] M. G. Spiertz, *L'église*, p. 113.

Table 2 *Regular clergy in the Holland Mission**

	1616	1617	1619	1622	1631	1635	1638	1645	1656	1701
Jesuits	15	16/17	20	22	53	65	70	62	68	59
Franciscans	—	7	7	5	18	25	24	25	33	30
Dominicans	—	—	—	5/6	14	18	20	26	14	16
Capucins	—	—	—	—	8	8	8	7/8	1	—
Norbertins	—	—	—	—	—	—	—	—	—	4
Augustinians	—	—	—	—	4	5	10	12	7	7
Carmelites	—	—	—	—	—	—	—	2/3	4	6
Benedictines	—	—	—	—	—	—	—	5	1	2
Bernardins	—	—	—	—	—	—	—	1	1	—
Bogards	—	—	—	—	—	—	—	—	1	1
Sacred Cross	—	—	—	—	—	—	—	—	1	1
Regular Canons	—	—	—	—	—	—	—	—	1	1

* No regular clergy were recorded in the reports for 1602, 1605, 1613, 1614, 1626, and 1640 (see Table 1).

devotion to national saints may be seen as a distinctive feature of the spirituality of the Catholic Reformation in the Northern Netherlands.

In their disputes with the Protestants the vicars apostolic looked for examples in their immediate surroundings which could not fail to appeal to the Catholics. Just as Rovenius had done, Neercassel also turned to the grandmasters of disputation, notably to Cardinal Jacques-Davy Duperron. He stated that whoever condemned the Catholic Church as 'the whore of Babylon' who had seduced the whole world with her doctrine, slandered all great men who had held the faith of the Catholic Church in the Netherlands. Such a slanderer would have to call Boniface, Suitbert, Werenfrid, and the other apostles of the land 'Willibrord the idolator, Boniface the follower of the Antichrist, Suitbert the betrayer of Christ, Werenfrid the superstitious'. The saints from the Netherlands can be found on the calendar that the Haarlem chapter together with Rovenius drew up for the diocese of Haarlem. All holy-days, fast days, and days of abstinence, as well as all days on which indulgences could be won, were to be found on the calendar. Apart from those already mentioned other national saints to attract support were Wulfran, Egbert, Gangulf, Engelmund, Odulf, Adelbert, Willibald, Jeroèn, Bavo, the Ewald brothers, Wilfrid, and Lebuin.[9]

The priests

During the first phase of the reorganization of Catholic pastoral care all of the missionaries were confronted with an extremely aggressive policy of persecution by the authorities. According to Willibrord van der Heyden no Jesuit had worked in Friesland for longer than four years. They were recalled mainly to monasteries in the Southern Netherlands to recuperate. Only a few of St Ignatius' followers, who worked in Friesland before 1638, managed to stay out of prison. The Greyfriars, too, together with the Jesuits, deserve credit for their pioneering spirit and great courage during the first stage of the revival. They departed for the Republic with a personal mission from Pope Urbanus VIII to go and preach the Catholic faith, if need be, at the risk of their own lives.

All meetings which Catholics held to practise their religion were forbidden. Infringement would cost the owner of the house where the

[9] P. P. V. van Moorsel, 'De devotie tot St. Willibrord in Nederland van ongeveer 1580 tot ongeveer 1750', *Ons Geestelijk Erf*, 32 (1958), pp. 128–9. Bevestigingh in 't Geloof en Troost in Vervolgingh, door Jan Baptist, priester van 't Oratorie Jesu Christi (Brussel, 1670), p. 64.

meeting took place a fine of a hundred gold 'riders'. Everyone present would forfeit twenty-five gold 'riders' and, possibly, his outer garments. The priest ran the risk of being flogged. Hiding a priest carried a fine of fifty gold 'riders'; a second and third offence would cost a hundred, or a hundred and fifty. In the last case the offender could also be sent into exile. The priest who had been caught saying mass suffered this punishment, and he also forfeited all income and pensions he had received up to that time.

The new style missionaries, who attempted to improve the neglected areas in the spirit of the Council of Trent, found themselves in a tight situation. They represented a Church which was socially in its infancy, was not accepted, and was even outside the law. They probably succeeded in expressing the Catholic faith in such a new way that, unlike their old-style predecessors, they were able to show their audiences that 'clericalism' was alien to them. Such a missionary could not fail to feel that his office lacked every attractive side of human existence. He was often a tramp, a fugitive, a hunted refugee, who could only see his people safely in the dead of night. These missionaries turned out to be prepared to be in contact with ordinary people, and—in both adverse and favourable times—by their fortitude they presented the faithful with a strict system of certainties within which they could feel secure in the face of God.

There is little doubt that the missionaries managed to inspire their flock by their ministry to the sick and the dying, who were often plague victims. If it was too hazardous to visit the sick in the daytime, this was done in the night. In 1656 the friar Arnoldus Peerkens, who held the Overijssel post of Kuinder, had had a great many plague victims among his parishioners. According to his notes he was unable—much to his regret—to accompany the dead to their resting-place or to comfort the bereaved families. On such occasions he was closely watched. In spite of the dangerous circumstances he would try to give some comfort to the bereaved family. As soon as he possibly could, he would come to celebrate mass in the dead person's parish, or in the immediate vicinity, in order to commemorate the dead.

Mathias Chinay, OFM, of the mission post of Bolsward, wrote to his superior in 1685 that he could not go out on the street during the daytime. If the occasion offered itself, he would bring the faithful together in the night, so that they could use the cover of darkness in order to come and go. He would assemble the faithful of the several villages around Bolsward in the middle of the night between Saturday and Sunday, now here, now there. He also visited the sick, taught the catechism for about ten minutes, and celebrated the eucharist with them after that. Then he returned to Bolsward where, if at all possible, he celebrated the eucharist for the second time with his parishioners between five and six in the morning. In the course of the Sunday morning he taught the catechism to the children. While Chinay was writing this report in 1685, the priests in Bolsward were persecuted severely and Catholics were fined heavily if their meetings became public. A situation aggravated by the revocation of the Edict of Nantes in that year, and the expulsion of the Huguenots from France.[10]

In many districts the Reformed Church had managed to arrange that all newly born babies, including Catholics, were to be baptized by their ministers. Heavy fines were given to those who refused. This threat of heavy fines meant a special problem for poor Catholics. If a child had been baptized by a Protestant minister, there was no need for re-baptism by a priest. Both Rovenius and Neercassel held baptism in the Reformed Church to be valid, but not to be permissible. If Catholic parents of a child baptized by a Protestant minister later asked the missionary priest for the anointing or for other Catholic rituals, priests were allowed to undertake them.

Marriages by Protestant ministers also produced many problems for the Catholic priests. One could get married either before the magistrate, or the Protestant minister in the Reformed Church. A wedding in the Reformed Church was free; there was a charge for a civil wedding before the magistrate, which meant quite a financial burden for the average Catholic who was not well off. In Overijssel, Catholics were not allowed to be married before a registrar, even as late as 1794, so those who refused marriage by a Protestant minister were faced with the prospect of their children being illegitimate in the eyes of the law.[11]

The regular missionaries, Greyfriars and Jesuits, usually had a great deal of understanding for the often impoverished and simple Catholics who had to practise their religion under difficult circumstances. As a rule couples who had been married in a Reformed Church were not given such heavy penances as those required by Neercassel. He had insisted that these Catholic couples should not be admitted to holy communion for six months, but he did give permission for their marriage to be blessed by a

[10] M. G. Spiertz, 'De ontwikkelingsgang', pp. 278–81. *Groot Placaatboek*, Cornelis Cau, ed., 1 (The Hague, 1658), cols 203–9.
[11] M. G. Spiertz, 'Pastorale problemen in de Noordnederlandse katholieke kerk van de zeventiende eeuw', *Kleio*, 20 (1979), pp. 126–32.

priest. The regular clergy were afraid that the vicar apostolic's strict policy would have a negative effect and turn newly-weds away from the Catholic Church and maybe towards the Reformed Church.

There was also a difference in spirituality between secular and regular clergy. By and large the regular clergy had less rigorous rules for the receiving of the sacraments than did the secular clergy. In contrast with the rather strict rules promulgated by the secular clergy, mostly educated in Louvain, they considered Holy Communion as a means of making progress rather than as a kind of reward for perfection achieved. This view could pave the way towards an opportunist way of life which, in the eyes of the stricter secular clergy, was made easier by laxity over the hearing of confessions.

It may be said that the regular clergy were less keen on a 'voluntary' church which was to make more demands on its membership than was usual in the broad popular church. They preferred the popular church strategy where human failures were looked upon in a milder way. They obviously had more understanding of the heavy pressure that was put upon their faithful. The majority of the secular clergy, however, required each Catholic to state his or her position unequivocally. One was either a Catholic or one was a Calvinist. They rejected any form of ambiguity: one could not receive one sacrament in one Church and another sacrament in the other.

In their secret churches the regular clergy, mainly coming from the Southern Netherlands where the Catholic reformation had taken place, quite emphatically stimulated the veneration of saints which they had learned and practised in their youth in the parish churches in their home villages and in their monasteries. In the sermons and from the attitudes of the secular clergy they noticed the lack of the easy-going and somewhat nonchalant nature of the baroque Catholicism that they had known. They found the faith of a great many secular clergy cold and puritan. The cool soberness of the secret churches which were served by the North Netherlands secular clergy impressed them as rather Calvinistic. In the secret churches of the regular clergy, however, the cult of the saints, the fraternities, and processions were amply indulged.

In the Holland Mission two completely—or virtually completely—different types of pastoral care were practised towards the Catholics. That of the Greyfriars and the Jesuits had its roots in Christian Humanism; the other, that of the secular clergy, had its roots in a strict Augustinianism. The Catholics had, in large numbers, opted either for one strategy or another; certainly from the moment when Neercassel and Petrus Codde, together with the priests who, in their spirit, had been trained in Louvain, introduced a much more severe church discipline. Towards the end of the 1680s a clear shift in allegiance became apparent, away from the secret churches served by the secular clergy and towards those served by the regular clergy.[12]

The laity

In view of the great shortage of priests, Vosmeer, soon after 1660, had appealed to the laity to serve as 'lectores' and to read litanies, a homily, and prayers in the vernacular during the Sunday meetings. Next to the 'lectores' the vicar apostolic had also appointed 'directores' and 'cursores'. The 'directores' were lay people who looked after priests and the poor; the 'cursores' were to take care of the safety of both priests and the faithful and to keep watch during the nightly services.

Since a great many Catholics were unable to observe their Sunday obligation, the schoolmaster Heyman Jacobsz had, at the end of the sixteenth century, compiled a pious book in which he had assigned the prayers by which the Sunday should be revered in detail. For centuries to come this book, called 'de Sondaghs-Schole' (the Sunday School), written for those who had to go without mass, was to be an integral part of the domestic libraries of Catholics in the Republic. According to Andreas Tiara, secular missionary in the post of Hemelum (Friesland) between 1660 and 1666, the faithful in Hindelopen—which was part of his territory—assembled on Sundays and feast-days, even if there were no priest to say Mass for them. In that case one of the Catholics, who had been authorized, read a homily to them from 'de Sondaghs-Schole'. Before and after the reading the congregation sang hymns, and the service ended with a collection for the poor.[13]

It is clear that the missionaries were quite dependent on those staunch Catholics who were aware of their responsibility to their priests and for their fellow Catholics. Often they formed a small group in each post or missionary unit. The missionaries' pastoral care was mainly directed towards them. They were the ones who ran the risk of persecution, fines, or even imprisonment; they brought non-Catholics to the services; they

---

[12] Willem Frijhoff, 'Vraagtekens bij het vroegmoderne kersteningsoffensief', *Religieuze volks-kultuur*, Gerard Rooyakkers and Theo van der Zee, eds. (Nijmegen, 1986), pp. 81–6. M. G. Spiertz, 'Godsdienstig leven', pp. 351–3.

[13] *Ibid.*, pp. 348–50.

had often, during discussions or in giving neighbourly help, been the first to show a good many people the way to the Roman Catholic Church.

In a number of villages and towns loyal Catholics are known to have played an important role in the outlining of the boundaries of the missionary posts as pastoral units. Together they looked for opportunities to celebrate mass with adjacent villages. The loyal Catholics in these villages, which were to merge into one post, also considered it their duty to provide a living for the priest. Their influence was, quite often, considerable in other matters. When a new missionary was to be appointed, for instance, they sometimes wanted a say in the appointment.

Convinced Catholics were aware of their concern, their responsibility for, and their solidarity with the Catholic faith, with their fellow Catholics, and with the priest who worked amongst them. Often people were only admitted to the secret nightly services at their invitation. These leading members in fact selected the Catholics. The rather large category of Catholics, who turned to the Church only on important moments of their lives for the sake of the 'rites of passage', the sacraments of baptism, marriage, and, in danger of death, of confession and the last rites, were distanced in times of persecution and then no longer invited. These fringe Catholics were, in the eyes of the missionaries, still members of the Church, but hardly practised their religion and had only a smattering of their faith. In the long run they were out of place in the voluntary church. They were called 'Nominal Catholics' by the missionaries. Around the middle of the seventeenth century they and the Church were to part for good.[14]

Among the leading members were many spinsters and widows. In Catholic literary language and in more pious conversation they were known as 'spiritual maidens'. In Protestant circles they were, rather unflatteringly, called 'kloppen', a vulgar nickname for a 'horsey' type of woman or 'virago'. These were women who wanted to stay virgins outside the protective surroundings of the convents, for these institutions had either been closed, or were doomed to shrink to extinction because no new novices were allowed. In Catholic circles the nickname 'kloppen' was softened to its diminutive 'klopjes', a name which was in general use during the eighteenth century.

The 'klopjes' did not take solemn vows, mostly only a simple vow of chastity and not even that was standard procedure. In spite of the absence of vows it was assumed that the 'klopjes' were to obey their confessor. In

---

[14] M. G. Spiertz, 'De ontwikkelingsgang', pp. 284–5, 291.

the Greyfriars' posts they would follow the Franciscan rules, in the Black-friars', the third rule of that order.

The 'klopjes' resembled the 'beguines' in three ways. As a rule they formed communities, had the general meeting as their rule of order, and worked each for their own livelihood. They differed from the 'beguines' at least in two respects. They had no part in any sort of communal property, nor did they wear any sort of uniform. The 'klopjes' wore simple, dark clothes. 'Beguines' were found in Delft, where they had their own chaplain and, in the 'Begijnhof' itself, a complete community of 'klopjes' lived, who also had their own priest. This was so in 1637, and as late as 1656.[15]

The best-known association of virgins was 'Den Hoeck' in Haarlem, begun in 1583. The association spread in the town district, 'Den Hoeck'. When in 1601 'klopjes's' homes were raided in Delft, Den Haag, and in 1602 in 'Den Hoeck' in Haarlem, the bailiff could not find and arrest Vosmeer. In 'Den Hoeck' a considerable quantity of church vestments and utensils were found which were, amid loud cheers, taken to the town hall on carts. The 'klopjes' stayed free but shaken. After a few months had passed peace returned to the association, and everything returned to normal.

Towards the end of the Truce (1609–1621) attitudes towards the Catholics hardened again. Old posters were re-issued and severe measures were taken against the Jesuits in particular. In 1628 the South Holland Synod expressed its dismay about the growing number of 'klopjes'. Papists (priests) and 'klopsusteren' were said to be active in lay clothes and, in particular, were trying to lure children to take part in their 'superstitious practices'. The first poster of the States General is dated as late as 1641. In it was mentioned a certain kind of female known as 'Klopsusteren' or 'Kloppen', who were thought to be quite dangerous and who could lure the children especially, but also adults, to the 'papist superstitions'. At last in 1655 the States General issued a ban by poster on any money or goods being bequeathed to 'klopjes'. The defence in law on the part of the Catholics was that virgins could, at any given moment, enter a lawful marriage and therefore were entitled to receive their heritage. A great many law suits were fought over this.

[15] E. M. R. Schulte-van Kessel, *Geest en Vlees in godsdienst en wetenschap* (The Hague, 1980), pp. 51–7, 76–7, 101–6. E. B. F. Pey, 'De manuscripten van Trijn Jans Olij als bron voor een prosopografisch onderzoek naar de klopjes van 'De Hoek' te Haarlem van 1583–1650', *AGKKN* 28 (1986), pp. 138–43.

There were strong protests, too, against the teaching activities under-taken by 'klopjes'. They taught children the first steps in reading, writing, arithmetic, singing, and perhaps, the beginnings of latin, which was also done in a 'kleyne school'. Some of them showed real pedagogical and didactic talents. This was the case in Amsterdam, for instance, where some Reformed christians found no problems in having their children educated by them.

From an investigation by the Hof van Holland in 1643 in Gouda it appeared that each priest had his own district with his own group of 'klopjes'. The secular priest Wilem de Swaen had as many as fifty or sixty 'klopjes' and the Franciscan O. Simpernel had thirty. For fifteen years Jesuit 'klopjes' ran a girls' boarding school. They, too, formed a small asso-ciation. In Culemborg also the Jesuit 'klopjes' had a girls' boarding school, which, at certain times, had up to thirty pupils.[16]

In 1663 Neercassel mentions associations of virgins in Delft, Gouda, Rotterdam, and Utrecht. In Amsterdam, where the Begijnhof continued to exist, and the beguines' association kept going, the 'klopjes' lived all over the town, and they belonged to different posts. Data about the numbers and the spread of the spiritual virgins in the Holland Mission is scarce and should be treated as only approximate. It is assumed that in the latter half of the seventeenth century the Holland Mission can have had as many as 3,500 'klopjes'. Each missionary, either regular or secular, had the help of a few 'klopjes' for his pastoral work.

The social background of the 'klopjes' varied. There were rich women among them from the nobility or the middle class, who provided the room for the secret churches and who paid the heavy fines if the priests were caught while exercising their spiritual duties. They looked after the lodging and the livelihood of the priest, who was not well off as a rule. The typical 'klopje', however, earned her keep by sewing, spinning, lace-making, or by teaching these crafts in what were known as the shop-schools.

But there were also 'klopjes' who worked as servants or nurses. They, too, were indispensable in the posts, not only to notify people where and when mass was to be said, but also as vergers, altar servers, and choristers. Visiting the faithful, especially the sick, and taking care of the poor and the aged were among the duties of 'klopjes'. Religious education was close to their hearts; they often assembled the faithful on Sundays from far and wide, even if there was no priest to say mass. If a church room was

[16] E. E. A. J. M. Theissing, *Over klopjes en kwezels* (Utrecht, 1935), pp. 39–62, 184–99.

available, sometimes in the private property of a well-to-do 'klopje', they read the lessons during mass or the vesper services on Sundays and Holy days, and took care of the liturgical singing, sometimes accompanied by the violin or organ.[17]

At the very moment when the disorganized Catholic Church in the Republic suffered the heaviest blows and the established Reformed Church was given a great many real opportunities, the 'klopjes' began to assist in the restoration of a new infrastructure in the Holland Mission, however primitive. They took part in the care of the poor, began religious instruction to both children and adults, and turned out to be 'pastoral workers' *avant la lettre*. In remote areas especially the 'klopjes' slowed down the Calvinization process and even checked its progress in a few places. It was the Protestant contemporaries' complaint that these women 'with a thousand false practices made the weak of heart waver again'.[18]

Catholic University, Nijmegen

---

[17] E. M. R. Schulte-van Kessel, *Geest en Vlees*, pp. 53–6.
[18] I. H. van Eeghen, 'De eigendom van de Katholieke kerken in Amsterdam ten tijde van de Republiek', *Haarlemse Bijdragen*, 64 (1957), p. 269.

PASTORAL OFFICE AND THE GENERAL PRIESTHOOD IN THE GREAT AWAKENING

by w. r. ward

WHATEVER Luther may have said about the priesthood of all believers, it took more than a century and a half for the idea to receive full-scale treatment, and Spener, who achieved this during his time as Senior of Frankfurt (1660–86), approached the goal indirectly through editing Arndt's sermons (1675). To catch the public eye he republished the introduction separately later in the year under the title *Pia Desideria, or heartfelt desires for an improvement of the true evangelical church pleasing to God, with some Christian proposals to that end.*[1] With a dedication to all the overseers and pastors of the evangelical church it was now a deliberately programmatic writing. In this tract Spener castigated every class of society for their responsibility for the lamentable state of the Church, making suggestions for improved clerical training and preaching, which might have been made at any period of Church history. The real sting came in an explicit appeal to Luther on how best to realize the priesthood of all believers. To spread the word of God more richly among the people there should be private gatherings under clerical leadership for the exchange of views and Bible study; more radically, there should be private gatherings for the exercise of the obligations of the general spritual priesthood. The faithful should teach, warn, convert, edify each other. These gatherings should be cells for the renewal of the Church. They would also enable Spener, the expert catechist, to drive home his conviction that Christianity was a way of life, learnt by doing.

The general, or as Spener preferred to call it, the spiritual priesthood, was part of a programme of church renewal. There was nothing anti-clerical about it; the faithful of whatever order were to take a more exalted view of their vocation than hitherto, and live accordingly. But in Spener's later works, *Das geistliche Priestertum* (1677) and *Die allgemeine Gottesgelehrtheit* (1680) the tone began to change. The basic definitions of the spiritual priesthood conferred by Christ upon his followers still

---

[1] This tract was reprinted in the Olms edition of *Philipp Jakob Spener. Schriften*, 1 (Hildesheim, 1979), and was translated into English by Theodore G. Tappert (Philadelphia, 1964).

stood,[2] but the language was already one of rights; men had the right to test the doctrine of their preachers, and women most emphatically had the right to participate in these priestly offices [reference to Joel 2 vv. 28–9].[3] The upper classes had appropriated all the rights in the Church at the expense of the third estate.[4] Spener's *collegium pietatis* or class-meeting in Frankfurt had begun as an élite society, much like the groups already gathered by Jean de Labadie, but speedily it was joined by artisans and servants of both sexes; like Wesley later, Spener was surprised at the knowledge possessed by simple men, and had now no doubt that the work of the Holy Spirit was not circumscribed by boundaries of class or education.[5]

All this Spener sought to argue from the Fathers; from the young Luther who in the preface to the *Deutsche Messe* of 1526 had called for the formation of a gathering of earnest Christians much like Spener's *collegium pietatis* or Wesley's select bands;[6] from other pillars of the Lutheran tradition, especially from his own old stamping-ground in Strasbourg;[7] and not least from the very title-deed of Lutheran Orthodoxy, the Formula of Concord.[8] Yet the dominant view in Lutheran Orthodoxy had staked everything on the Pastoral Office (*Amt* in German). 'Without the Pastoral Office is there no salvation'. 'Pastors stand in a single succession to the prophets and apostles; they are to reveal the will and counsel of God

[2] 'What is the spiritual priesthood? It is the right which our Saviour Jesus Christ earned for all men, to which he anointed all his faithful through the Holy Spirit, by virtue of which they may and they ought to bring suitable sacrifices to God, to pray for themselves and others, and edify each other and their neighbours . . . From whom comes this spiritual priesthood? From Jesus Christ, the true high-priesthood according to the order of Melchizedek 1) which as he has no successor in his priesthood, but remains eternally the sole high-priest; also has 2) made his Christians to be priests 3) before his father to whom sacrifices have their sanctity solely from his son and are made acceptable to God'. *Das Geistliche Priestertum* is included in *Spener Schriften* 1. The copy here used is in P. J. Spener, *Drey erbauliche Schriften*, ed. J. G. Pritius (Frankfurt, 1717), pp. 14–15.

[3] *Ibid.*, pp. 42, 74, 76. For Spener's change of tone, see Paul Grunberg, *Philipp Jakob Spener* (Göttingen, 1893–1906), 2, p. 171.

[4] *Ibid.*, 2, p. 119.

[5] Johannes Wallmann, 'Geistliche Erneuerung der Kirche nach Philipp Jakob Spener', *Pietismus und Neuzeit*, 12 (1986), p. 29.

[6] Spener held more clearly than Wesley that membership of these groups implied not withdrawal from the world but acceptance of responsibility for it. J. O. Rüttgardt, *Heiliges Leben in der Welt. Grundzüge Christlicher Sittlichkeit nach P. J. Spener* (Bielefeld, 1978), pp. 146–7.

[7] Spener, *Drey erbauliche Schriften: Das Geistliche Priestertum*, Appendix; Martin Brecht, *Martin Luther* (Stuttgart, 1981–7), 1, pp. 276, 354 *seq.*; 2, pp. 20, 36–8, 249–53; *Luther's Works*, American ed. by J. Pelikan and H. T. Lehmann, 55 (Philadelphia, 1965), pp. 63–4.

[8] P. J. Spener, *Die allgemeine Gottesgelehrtheit aller glaubigen Christen und rechtschaffenen Theologen* (Frankfurt, 1680), pp. 335–6. This work is to be reprinted in *Spener Schriften*, 3.

to men'. To deny that the ministry so-to-speak turned on the tap was to deny the *sola fide*, *sola gratia*. Even Valentin Ernst Löscher who sought in the hostile climate of the next generation to maintain the notion that theology derived its intellectual and scientific character as an essential function of church office, would concede no more than that 'Theologia ideo intendit pietatem, sed non includit'.[9] Moreover, Spener's precedents in the Lutheran tradition included nothing on the scale on which he came to treat the priesthood of all believers. He put a minority theme in a major key.

Spener's programme evoked a vivid response, soon followed by a violent reaction; both owed much to the special situation of Frankfurt in the ecclesiastical geography of the Empire. A few years ago the Evangelical Church of the Rhineland published a learned analysis of the religious psychology of their own congregations, the leading feature of which was independence, an independence exemplified especially in lay emancipation and immediacy of religious experience.[10] The first of these characteristics was greatly strengthened by the experiences of the seventeenth century; the second by the revivals which followed. The Lutheran Church in Julich, Cleves, and Berg had never had the sympathetic backing of the state which Lutheran Churches still thought they needed, and the intrusion into the area of both the Reformed House of Brandenburg and the Lutheran house of Pfalz-Neuburg added to its troubles. The latter house brought in the church order of Pfalz-Zweibrücken which was a kind of Melancthonian middle way between the Saxon order and the Reformed order in the Palatinate; Lutheran in doctrine, this order never introduced the Formula of Conford. On the morrow of these changes, the house of Pfalz-Neuburg turned Catholic, with the result that the Lower Rhine Lutheran Churches lost their old synodical constitution without ever

---

[9] Cf. The Swabian Confession Art. VII: 'To attain such faith and give it to us men, God has established the Pastoral Office or spoken word;... nor is there any other means, nor method, neither way nor bridge to receive faith' (T. Harnack, *Die Grundbekenntnisse der Evangelisch-Lutherischen Kirche* (Dorpat, 1845)). For a liberal commentary on the development of Lutheran clericalism see Paul Drews, *Der evangelische Geistliche in der deutschen Vergangenheit* (Jena, 1905), pp. 24, 40–4, 51. On Löscher see Martin Greschat, *Zwischen Tradition und neuem Anfang. Valentin Ernst Löscher und der Ausgang der lutherischen Orthodoxie* (Witten, 1971), pp. 137–42: Emanuel Hirsch, *Geschichte der neurn evangelischen Theologie* (5 edn., Gütersloh, 1975), 2, pp. 202–5: Moritz von Engelhardt, *Valentin Ernst Löscher, nach seinem Leben und Wirken* (Stuttgart, 1856), pp. 74, 107. On the Lutheran ministry in general, see Wilhelm Pauck, 'The ministry in the time of the continental Reformation' in *The Ministry in Historical Perspectives*, eds H. Richard Niebuhr and Daniel D. Williams (New York, 1956), pp. 110–48.

[10] Ottfried Kietzig, *Die kirchliche Frömmigkeit in den evangelischen Gemeinden des Niederrheins* (Düsseldorf, 1971), pp. 5, 22, 64.

gaining an effective monarchical consistorial constitution. Self-help must be the order of the day, and it comes as no surprise that Johannes Scheibler (1627–89), superintendent of the Church in Berg, turned to Spener for assistance, nor that a Church with no convenient access to a place of ministerial training turned first to Giessen, the earliest university in which Pietists set the tone, and then on a big scale to Halle, for their clergy. Meanwhile the self-help had made these Churches more like their Reformed neighbours.

Frankfurt belonged to the Upper Rhine area where the Reformation had been introduced from above. French intervention and dynastic conversions to Rome had brought the Counter-Reformation up to the left bank of the Rhine, but they had created problems for princes and clergy more than ordinary congregations. Despite sharp opposition in doctrine, the Churches of the upper Rhine, evangelical and Reformed, were alike in owing their origin to princely initiative, and in undergoing a powerful Melancthonian influence; they had begun gradually to approximate to each other in constitution, and in the nineteenth century were to accept union schemes relatively willingly. The Lutheran Churches of this area embodied many features which in Saxony were regarded as Reformed. In Strasbourg, for example, the Church exercised church discipline through elders, and maintained public catechizings, public confirmation, communion without confession, and baptism without exorcism. What irked Spener was that established status undermined the exercise of discipline; his remedy was to revive internal sanctions by using semi-reformed methods not unfamiliar in the Upper Rhine.

Through his godmother and original sponsor, the widowed Countess Agathe von Rappoltstein, née Countess of Solms-Laubach, Spener also enjoyed entrée to a quite different milieu, that network of counts stretching away to Lusatia and Silesia who were to form the backbone of the Pietist party. And this group were among those who put Spener in the way of appointment in 1686 as court chaplain to the Elector of Saxony, in effect Primate of Lutheran Germany.[11] In the race for this dignity Spener pipped Johann Benedict Carpzov, a Leipzig theologian of formidable polemical violence. But the storm which now descended upon him, led by Carpzov with the predictable argument that Spener's friends substituted piety for faith, owed less to personalities than to the fact that the Saxon

---

[11] On the churches of the Upper and Lower Rhine areas, see Max Goebel, *Geschichte der christlichen Lebens in der rheinisch-westphalischen evangelischen Kirche* (Coblenz, 1849–52), 2, pp. 438–9, 459–60, 511–25.

Church embodied a Lutheranism very different from that of the Rhine Churches, and saw its metier in protecting the gospel from what it regarded as Reformed contamination. What became the Pietist party was the wretched remnant left at the end of a fearful battering, gathered under the liberal protection of the Reformed Elector of Brandenburg.[12] That shrewd old warrior Hobbes would have been delighted by this contract between the leaders of an individualist piety and a despotism on the make, concluded to mutual advantage.

Everything seemed to go wrong with the revived priesthood of all believers. Spener was a churchman to the core; but his right-hand man, Johann Jakob Schütz, took up with Labadism and led a separation, part of which confirmed the worst fears of the Orthodox by ending up in Penn's Quaker colony in America. Spener, again, had spoken up for women, but the distaff side did not respond with tact. Spener did not expect unusual or extravagant phenomena in his class meeting at Frankfurt, and did not get them. Ecstatic phenomena, mostly among women and nothing to do with Pietism, had been fairly common in seventeenth-century Germany. But when the Orthodox mounted their horrendous assault on the Pietists, a number of spectacular cases, mostly of ecstatic pietist servant-girls, cropped up in central and northern Germany. Revelations to order were, of course, grist to the Orthodox mill, and of Magdalena of Quedlinburg it was unkindly reported that 'she is so much on heat [*brunstig*] that she can scarcely bear the name of Jesus or the memory of his love and grace; as soon as she speaks or thinks of them she goes into convulsions'.

Unlike Luther, Spener was very interested in dreams and visions—and it is notable that pietists who dropped out of the ministry often took up medicine with what might now be called a psychiatric bent—and his main contribution to theological discussion consisted of thousands of pages of expert opinions on particular cases and issues such as these. Spener was not prepared to deny that God might possibly have fresh revelation in store through these unlikely channels; though the scriptural warnings against false prophets in the last days were still to be heeded. He would not accept a simple alternative that unusual religious phenomena must be of God or of the devil, and put forward other possibilities including disturbances in the unconscious, some of which might be evidence of sickness, some beyond understanding. In many of the personal cases Spener had to judge, he declared clearly against the divine origin of the visions; but in others he abstained from judgment on the grounds that he simply did not know.

[12] There is a narrative of the conflict in Grünberg, *Spener*, 1, pp. 214–56.

This modesty, which has lately earned him the title of 'the father of theological pluralism', disappointed friends as well as enemies. In the current view, it was the job of a theologian to know. Spener might be thought not so much to be coordinating the general priesthood with the Pastoral Office, as downgrading the Pastoral Office.[13]

The Orthodox might, finally, think that Spener had given the game away in the vocabulary he used. In his programmatic writings Spener talked indeed of regeneration, but the key-word was 'spirit'. What the evangelical church lacked was not pure doctrine in preaching and liturgy, but spirit. Spiritual poverty characterized the official Church and clergy, the habitual Christianity of the pew, the dead technicalities of the polemical theologians. Almost immediately after his call to Saxony, Spener preached in Leipzig on 'The Office of the Holy Spirit in the work of our salvation'. Spener was not merely inviting the charge that he was a Quaker, but, consciously or unconsciously, was putting himself in that line of writers known in the German tradition as spiritualistic. With this there were two immediate snags. Proclaiming in 1520 that 'all Christians are truly of the spiritual order, and there is no distinction among them simply on account of office', Luther had set himself and his fellow pastors a problem of conscience. Could they exercise their office representatively? Luther sought to solve his own problem by appeal to his academic office and for the candidate for the parish by a call from the congregation in due form. Still, the nagging question remained, not whether the individual was worthy of his office, but whether the office was justified at all. This dilemma had plagued the spiritualistic tradition.[14] Not all the anxious resigned, but in 1698, in Spener's own lifetime, Gottfried Arnold, less than a year after his call to a chair at Giessen, resoundingly did so, forsaking the academic Babel on the grounds that it was ruinous to the 'tender life of Christ within'.[15] Still worse, at the very moment when Spener replied to a polemic which equated Pietism with Quakerism by a piece of contemporary church history which sought to establish the churchmanship of Pietists, Arnold produced a series of historical works culminating in his enormous *Impartial History of Churches and Heretics*, a

---

[13] Albrecht Ritschl, *Geschichte des Pietismus* (Bonn, 1880–86; repr. Berlin, 1966), 2, pp. 183–90; Wallmann, 'Geistliche Erneuerung', *Pietismus und Neuzeit*, 12, pp. 32–7.

[14] Rudolf Mohr, 'Die Krise des Amtverstandnisses im Spiritualismus und Pietismus', in *Traditio-Krisis-Renovatio aus theologischer Sicht. Festschrift Winfried Zeller*, eds B. Jaspert and R. Mohr (Marburg, 1976), pp. 143–71.

[15] Rüdiger Mack, *Pietismus und Frühaufklärung an der Universität Giessen und in Hessen-Darmstadt* (Giessen, 1984), p. 86.

work damned by the Orthodox as the worst book ever written and lauded by Thomasius as the best book since the gospels. Arnold would have no truck with a conventional church history intent on elucidating God's providential care of the true church of the author's choice. He did not think that Christianity had ever quite maintained its apostolic level, but the fall had come in the time of Constantine. Christianity had then made its choice between the only two options ever open to it, accepting decline or accepting persecution. The result was that the 'true active believer had no longer any place in it and religion was established in fixed concepts and terms grasped by the intellect, and in outward confessions and other *opera operata'*. These concepts established who was orthodox, whether the orthodox were genuine Christians or not. The history of the true church was now hidden and invisible, sustained by witnesses who accepted persecution; and very often they were those who had figured in church histories hitherto as heretics.[16] Antichrist, indeed, was to be found as often among the Protestants as among the papists. In the long run Arnold contributed enormously to transferring church history from the history of Providence to that of ordinary sinful humanity where we now expect to find it; and quite immediately he showed that Spener's attempt to revive lay vocations raised the modern question whether it is possible to have Christianity without the Church.

The opening of this question, the last thing that Spener desired, did not, however, constitute a knock-out blow for the Orthodox. For in all the areas requiring urgent attention by the Lutheran Churches, Christianity would have to survive without the Church or not at all. There were 20,000 Swedes exiled to Siberia after Charles XIII's disastrous Pultava campaign; there were many times that number of Germans in America, by 1776 about 200,000; there were many times this number again of Protestants abandoned by the Westphalia settlement in the great triangle bounded by Salzburg, Transylvania, and Poland, most of them without a Church, and all of them subject to the most savage pressure of the Counter-Reformation. And then there were the endless mission-fields of the world, many still untouched even by the Catholics. Orthodoxy did a little. New Sweden on the Delaware had ended a brief and inglorious existence in 1655, but the Swedish Lutheran church continued to supply

[16] The vast and often contentious literature about Arnold is summarized in Klaus Wetzel, *Theologische Kirchengeschichtsschreibung im deutschen Protestantismus, 1660–1760* (Giessen/Basel, 1983), pp. 175–209. See also Jürgen Büchsel, *Gottfried Arnold—sein Verständnis von Kirche und Wiedergeburt* (Witten, 1970): J. F. G. Goeters, 'Gottfried Arnolds Anschauung von der Kirchengeschichte in ihrem Werdegang' in *Traditio-Krisis-Renovatio*, pp. 241–57.

clergy and other assistance right down to the time of American independ-ence; and the Church in the Netherlands did a good deal for New Amster-dam and other parts. By contrast, the informal devotions intended by Spener to supplement the parish round proved extraordinarily successful among church-less Protestants outside the Westphalia ring-fence in keeping the flame of Christian piety alight and in generating a new phenomenon which required a new word, viz. revival. Even in Hungary where Protestant church-systems did exist, the real progress was made by the so-called 'widowed congregations' which had no pastor. The great missionary to the Protestants of Salzburg and Austria was the ex-miner of Hallein, Joseph Schaitberger;[17] Lutheran Orthodox in views, he did a noble work in the most reduced circumstances, despite clerical dis-couragement, and with no ecclesiastical recognition.

Everywhere else the back-up to what was accomplished by the priest-hood of all believers was supplied by the charitable institutions at Halle which were organs of neither Church nor state. In America Halle and the Moravians, who reckoned, at any rate, to be an interconfessional religious society, competed to provide assistance, and the fact that the Pastoral Office was eventually established among Lutherans in America was due to the labours of Henry Melchior Mühlenberg, who started life in the service of Zinzendorf's family, but was despatched by Halle to save the German Americans from the ravages of the Count. He succeeded in getting Swedes and Germans to form a Lutheran Church in America, an achievement which owed nothing to authority in Church or state. *Amt*, the Pastoral Office, had been saved in spite of itself.[18] It was the same story with foreign missions where there was no question either of a call by a congregation to a pastor, or of any 'sending' by the Church; Halle, the Moravians, and, much later, the *Deutsche Christentumsgesellschaft*[19] made a start on the basis of private enterprise with whatever assistance could be found. The pressure exerted on the German Pietists was such that the radicals were always tempted to withdraw altogether from ordinary social relations to a hermit-like existence, and very many did not marry; but

---

[17] On Schaitberger see my paper, '"An Awakened Christianity". The Austrian Protestants and their neighbours', *JEH* 40 (1989), pp. 53–73.

[18] For Mühlenberg see *The Journals of Henry Melchior Mühlenberg*, trans. by T. G. Tappert and John W. Doberstein (Philadelphia, 1942–58): *Die Korrespondenz Heinrich Melchior Mühlenbergs aus der Anfangszeit des deutschen Luthertums in Nordamerika*, ed. Kurt Aland (In progress, Berlin/ New York, 1986–).

[19] On which see Ernst Staehlin, *Die Christentumsgesellschaft in der Zeit der Aufklärung und der beginnenden Erweckung* (Basel, 1970).

others rediscovered a dynamic aspect to the life of the Christian community altogether neglected in Orthodoxy. This dynamic aspect was to spring further surprises in the Lower Rhine area to which Spener had spoken directly in his Frankfurt days.

On the problems of the Lower Rhine we have touched already; they were compounded by the gathering momentum of emigration, the rapid growth of certain industrial towns, especially Essen, and the indigenous mysticism of some of the artisans. In this milieu where mysticism and the desire for dynamism went hand in hand the curious idea took root among Pietists most at risk to French and Catholic aggression that monasticism had been a kind of revival movement, that had the monasteries remained true to their ideals, the Reformers would not have turned against them. Gerhard Tersteegen (1697–1769) who combined a Reformed heritage with Quietism and with an authentic power of exegetical imagination that is still hard to resist, formed a 'Brotherhood of the common life' in his youth, his followers formed *Pilgerhütten* up and down the Lower Rhine, and it was out of this German milieu in exile that the Protestant monastery at Ephrata in Pennsylvania was formed. Tersteegen in the Pietist manner spent twenty years writing a collection of *Select lives of holy souls* (1733–53); but the holy souls were all Catholic, and mostly hermits and members of religious orders of Counter-Reformation provenance.[20] It was a paradox when a radical Protestant insistence on the priesthood of all believers and an Arnoldian distaste for ecclesiastical pretension issued in veneration of a Catholic élite; but the logic of the process was as clear as the spiritual gifts which set it in motion.

Tersteegen's confessional neutrality was of course only possible to a Protestant of a special kind, and he made it clear that he had no desire to be anything but a Protestant, and a Reformed Protestant at that. Much of his work in realizing the general priesthood was done through the conventicles which the Reformed communities in the Lower Rhine had to hand as Spener did not. Tersteegen respected the officers of the Chuch, especially its pastors, though like Wesley he preferred those who did the job they were appointed for. He never wanted to found a separate sect, yet in practice he did not attend church or partake of the sacraments. He did not despise external props to the inner life, but hankered after the early

---

[20] Winfried Zeller, 'Die kirchengeschichtliche Sicht des Mönchtums im Protestantismus, insbesondere bei Gerhard Tersteegen' in his *Theologie und Frömmigkeit. Gesammelte Aufsätze*, ed. B. Jaspert (Marburg, 1971–8), 2, pp. 185–200. For the view of Tersteegen as a Protestant Carmelite see Giovanna della Croce, *Gerhard Tersteegen: Neubelebung der Mystik als Ansatz einer kommenden spiritualität* (Bern, 1979).

congregation at Jerusalem which held all things in common, and had not yet turned the lovefeast into a sacramental occasion for compulsion and polemic. And through force of personality, through his preaching, pastoral care, and genuine interest in healing, Tersteegen worked revival in Reformed communities which were moving in that direction under an impetus of their own. Nor was it long before ecclesiastical barriers, particularly against his hymns, began to crumble, so that posthumously he began to reach a larger public.[21] What then was it that had begun to happen in the Reformed world?

The Reformed tradition began promisingly with the assertion that Christ had instituted not one but four kinds of office for the government of the Church, pastors, teachers, elders, and deacons,[22] with a great hostility to the idea of ordination and inherited talk of clergy and laity. The Scots reformers would not use the word 'clergy' except when referring to the Roman Catholic priesthood,[23] and late in the seventeenth century Voetius in the Netherlands could still speak of 'populus seu plebs ecclesiastica, quos in Papatu vocant laicos', insisting that there was no distinction in Scripture between clergy and laity, only between elders and people.[24] But punditry had long since set in in the Reformed world. The later Helvetic Confession (1566) held that ministerial power in the Church was like empire (*imperio similior*) and included the power of the keys.[25] The Westminster Confession (1647) proclaimed that Christ had given the Church 'the ministry, oracles and ordinances of God . . . to the end of the world', and that the latter were in the hands of the former, 'lawfully ordained'. *The Form of Church Government* (1645) despatched other New Testament gifts and offices in short order: 'apostles, evangelists and prophets . . . are ceased'. The *Larger Catechism* (1648) was even firmer: 'Q. 156. *Is the word of God to be read by all?* A. Although all are not permitted to read the word publicly to the congregation, yet all sorts of

---

[21] Cornelis Pieter van Andel, *Gerhard Tersteegen. Leben und Werk-sein Platz in der Kirchengeschichte* (Düsseldorf, 1973, original Dutch ed., Wageningen, 1961), esp. pp. 75, 160–6, 169.

[22] *Ordonnances Ecclésiastiques* (Geneva, 1561), no. 2. The Reformed confessions from the West are conveniently collected by W. Niesel in *Bekenntnisschriften und Kirchenordnungen der nach Gottes Wort reformierte Kirche* (Munich, 5 vols, n.d., 1937 &c.). Here 1, p. 43 [for the circumstances in which this collection was produced, see Klaus Scholder, *The Churches and the Third Reich* (London, 1987), 1, pp. 296–7]. See also C. Fabricius, *Corpus Confessionum. Die Bekenntnisse der Christenheit* (18 parts Berlin/Leipzig, 1928–44).

[23] Duncan Shaw, 'The Inauguration of Ministers in Scotland, 1560–1620', *Records of the Scottish Church History Society*, 16 (1966), pp. 35–8.

[24] Gisbertus Voetius, *Politicae Ecclesiasticae* (Amsterdam, 1663–9), 1, pp. 12, 27; 2, pp. 8–12.

[25] Niesel, *Bekenntnisschriften*, 4, p. 256.

people are bound to read it apart by themselves, and with their families: to which end the holy scriptures are to be translated out of the original into vulgar languages', provided, in the view of the Kirk, that vulgar language was not Gaelic.[26] The Dutch adorned the cake with the thinnest of icing. In 1643 Appolonius explained that the Church was 'mixtae naturae, partim quasi aristocratica, partim quasi democratica', and there was no mistaking the balance between the two; the aristocratic part consisted of the offices through which the lordship of Christ was exercised in the Church, the democratic part consisted of the fraternal fellowship of believers. Voetius wrote with Hobbesian directness. There were two material parts to the institutional Church, rulers and ruled; the former were ministers and elders, the latter the people.[27] It is no wonder that the leaders of the Dutch pietist movement were all clergy.

Elsewhere office could not fail to be magnified by the fact that, in Bern for example, the pastor was and is an official of the state, paid by the state, who cannot enter a pastoral appointment until he has taken an oath before a state official. As recently as 1959 the *Konsekrator* received the ordinands' vows, laid his hands on them, but omitted to go through the necessary legal requirements for the holding of church office, with the result that every candidate had to be put through the entire ordination ceremony again. The official commentary says that whether the *Konsekrator*'s omission was due to his having Catholic ordination in mind, or congregationalist indifference to the wider Church, or to simple forgetfulness, is not known. This, after the explanation that *Konsekration* is not ordination, simply an acceptance of the duties of office, and that the laying on of hands, though problematical from a Reformed standpoint, is acceptable as a long-standing custom, is very striking; small wonder that the commentary having discussed lay service in terms of organists, sacristans, and grave-diggers, is constrained to admit that the Swiss reformers expelled hierarchy with one boot and the priesthood of all believers with the other.[28]

---

[26] These texts are conveniently gathered in *The Confession of Faith; the Larger and Shorter Catechisms with the Scripture proofs at large* ... republished by the Free Presbyterian Church of Scotland (n. pl., 1976), pp. 108, 113, 248–9, 398. An official Gaelic Bible was not available in the Highlands till the early nineteenth century (J. MacInnes, *The Evangelical Movement in the Highlands of Scotland, 1688–1800* (Aberdeen, 1951), pp. 4, 62). Marilyn J. Westerkamp demonstrates that the Westminster Confession could be made by the Scots-Irish into an instrument of revival, and of self-assertion against English assimilation in Ulster, Scotland and America, but not that it led to 'the triumph of the laity'. *Triumph of the Laity* (New York, 1988).

[27] Enno Conring, *Kirche und Staat nach der Lehre der niederländischen Calvinisten in der ersten Hälfte des 17. Jahrhunderts* (Neukirchen-Vluyn, 1965), p. 103; Voetius, *Politicae Ecclesiasticae*, I, p. 12.

[28] On this paragraph see Kurt Guggisberg, *Bernische Kirchenkunde* (Bern, 1968), pp. 24, 89–90,

But though new presbyter might be old priest writ large, his rule might be modified or even challenged by reference to other things in the Reformed tradition. Worship must be tested by scripture, not least by the injunction of 1 Cor. 14 v. 1 to 'follow after charity, and desire spiritual gifts, but rather that ye may prophesy'. In Dutch circles this was understood to mean the exposition and practical application of scripture by pastors and members of congregations jointly; comparing the various scripture texts used in public sermons during the week gave these meetings the name of *collatio scripturaria*. This was the order of the Dutch congregation in London in 1550; the Walloon congregation of the same period had the custom of a portion of scripture expounded by the pastor and discussed and questioned by the congregation. The idea was taken up by Dutch national synods later in the sixteenth century, but it had always been in part an instrument of control and could not survive the rigours of etablishment. Voetius, exponent as he was of the *praxis pietatis* and *theologia affectiva*, explained that these prophesyings were not an indispensable function of the Church, and should take place not as a public exercise of the whole congregation, but in private gatherings consisting entirely of speaking participants or of a select group of non-speaking hearers. Even then the presidency or leading exposition of scripture should be reserved for a theologically trained man.[29] Conventicles, indeed, came to be associated with rigorists who could not bear the lax discipline of a national establishment, and were constantly tempted to move off into separation.

These devices for the development of spiritual gifts were nevertheless important in the Reformed communities scattered along and outside the borders of the Netherlands, communities which came to have a powerful effect upon the Netherlands themselves. Voetianism and Coccejanism, the two great schools of Dutch Reformed Orthodoxy, each contributed

---

109, 244. Wernle justly comments that old customs died very hard in the Swiss churches, even in the case of the sacraments which they did not take over from Catholicism (which of course included ordination). P. Wernle, *Der schweizerische Protestantismus im XVIII. Jahrhundert* (Tübingen, 1923–5), 1, p. 65.

[29] The institution is decribed in *Joannis a Lasco Opera tam edita quam inedita*, ed. A. Kuyper (Amsterdam, 1866), 2, pp. 101–5 [French version in *Toute la Forme et Manière du Ministère ecclésiastique, en l'Église des estrangers, dressée a Londres en Angletcrre*, tr. by Giles Clematius (n. pl., 1556)]: *Original Letters relative to the English Reformation*, ed. by Hastings Robinson (Cambridge, 1846–7), 2, pp. 575: W. D. Robson Scott, 'Josua Maler's Visit to England in 1551', *Modern Language Review*, 45 (1950), p. 351. For modern comment: Ritschl, *Geschichte des Pietismus*, 1, pp. 120–1: J. Lindeboom, *Austin Friars. A History of the Dutch Reformed Church in London, 1550–1950* (The Hague, 1950), pp. 24–7: Andrew Pettegree, *Foreign Protestant Communities in sixteenth-century London* (Oxford, 1986), pp. 63–4.

something to the later growth of pietism and revival, the former being a main channel of the affective side of English Puritanism, and encouraging preaching like that of the young Daniel Rowland in Wales,[30] while Coccejanism with its covenant theology encouraged the kind of historical reconsideration that we have observed in Arnold. What made the issue between the two schools so intractable was that the Voetians were strong in the lower middle class and in politics were devotees of the Orange family and central government; while the Coccejans moved in the world of wealth and scholarship and stood for the Patriot opposition to Orange power. That political issue could never be resolved in the Netherlands to the complete advantage of either party, but was not a problem in Bremen, East Friesland, and the Lower Rhine. Bremen, a town of strict Voetian ethos, was not merely the birthplace of Coccejus, it was a great stronghold of Coccejan theology. Of Theodor Untereyck (1635–93), a Coccejan who in his early days in Bremen ran into great trouble with the clergy of the town both on doctrinal grounds and because he held class-meetings during the time other men held church services, it was said in his funeral oration that 'what Spener is in the Lutheran church, Untereyck is in the Reformed'; and with equal justice it could have been said that Untereyck was the source of many of Spener's ideas.[31] He had a powerful influence on the publicists of the New Birth like Reitz, maintained active contact with the Quakers, and was father-in-God to various second-generation pietists, the most important of whom was Friedrich Adolf Lampe (1683–1729). Lampe united in his own education the traditions of Bremen, Franeker (the principal Coccejan faculty in the Netherlands), Utrecht, and the Lower Rhine, and was developing Pietism in the direction of what was to become revival. He himself became a Netherlands figure in 1720 when he was called back to a chair at Utrecht; his catechisms left their mark on the whole Rhine valley, even on Switzerland.[32] Thus in the early

---

[30] A Dutch pastor at Middleburg told his English colleague in 1681, 'Before the Belgick Churches were pester'd with the Dogmes of Cocceius, the ministry of the Word was exceeding successfull, many Hearers would weep at Sermons, proud sinners would quake and tremble at the word preached, multitudes were converted and reformed . . .' (G. F. Nuttall, 'English Dissenters in the Netherlands, 1640–1689', *Nederlands Archief voor Kerkgeschiednis*, 59 (1979), pp. 37–8). Cf Eifion Evans, *Daniel Rowland and the Great Evangelical Awakening in Wales* (Edinburgh, 1985), pp. 39, 43; Martin H. Prozesky, 'The Emergence of Dutch Pietism', *JEH* 28 (1977), pp. 29–37: F. Ernest Stoeffler, *The Rise of Evangelical Pietism* (Leiden, 1971), *passim*.

[31] Gottfried Mai, *Die niederdeutsche Reformbewegung*, Hospitium Ecclesiae Bd. 12 (Bremen, 1979), pp. 110–11: Heiner Faulenbach, 'Die Anfänge des Pietismus bei den Reformierten in Deutschland', *Pietismus und Neuzeit*, 4 (1977–78), pp. 205–9.

[32] On Lampe see Heinrich Heppe, *Geschichte des Pietismus und der Mystik in der Reformierten Kirche, namentlich der Niederlande* (Leiden, 1879), pp. 236–40: Ritschl, *Geschichte des Pietismus*, I,

eighteenth century in the Reformed Rhineland, as in Reformed New England, the necessities of the Churches were driving some of the ministry towards revivalism; Theodorus Jacobus Frelinghuysen (1692–1747), pastor of a village near Emden, became indeed the earliest of the revivalists in the American Middle Colonies, a decade before the revival in New England;[33] and among the chief weapons of the proto-revivalists were those conventicles which had appealed to Spener as means of realizing the general priesthood. The experience of the torch-bearers inside the Reformed Churches was here much the same as that of Tersteegen outside.

The punditry which the Reformed tradition embodied in its fully developed shape might also be challenged from within. 'We know not what you mean by your popish term of laymen' declared Elizabethan separatists; 'May any person preach who hath no office to do so?' asked John Penry, hot for the conversion of Wales, and the answer was a foregone conclusion: 'Yes, that he may'.[34] These assumptions did not necessarily imply a low view of the Pastoral Office and harmonized with the idea that both the call to the office and its exercise must take place within the covenanted circle of visible saints. As John Cotton put it to the church at Salem, Mass., in 1636: 'if you should come to crave baptism for your children, or the Lord's Supper for yourselves, of a minister whom you have not called over you, he hath no power, and therefore he cannot dispense an act of power.'[35] It was the covenanted congregation which

---

pp. 427–54: Mai, *Niederdeutsche Reformbewegung*, pp. 252–301: Gerrit Snijders, *Friedrich Adolf Lampe, ein deutsche reformierte Theologe in Holland* (Bremen, 1961): W. Hollweg, *Geschichte des älteren Pietismus in den Reformieten Gemeinden Ostfrieslands* (Aurich, 1978), pp. 151–3.

[33] James Tanis, *Dutch Calvinistic Pietism in the Middle Colonies. A Study in the Life and Theology of Theodorus Jacobus Frelinghuysen* (The Hague, 1967). The attempt by Herman Hermelink III to argue that, despite the contemporary estimates of Gilbert Tennent and Jonathan Edwards, Frelinghuysen was not a revivalist at all, actually shows that Frelinghuysen was a revivalist who approximated more nearly to the Voetian stamp than those who came later. 'Another Look at Frelinghuysen and his "Awakening"', *Church History*, 37 (1968), pp. 423–88.

[34] Cf. 'The Apostle inseparablie coupleth the gathering together of the saints with the work of the ministerie'. John Penry, *Three Treatises concerning Wales*, ed. D. Williams (Cardiff, 1960), p. 81.

[35] *John Cotton on the Churches of New England*, ed. Larzer Ziff (Cambridge, Mass., 1968), pp. 43–4. Cf. 82–3, 98–9. Cotton would not baptize his child Seaborn, born on the Atlantic passage, 'at sea (not for want of fresh water, for, he held, sea water would have served:) 1. because he had no settled congregation there; 2. because a minister hath no power to give the seals but in his own congregation'. E. S.Morgan, *Visible Saints. The History of a Puritan Idea* (New York, 1963), p. 97. See also the New England 'Platform of Church Discipline' (1649). Cotton Mather, *Magnalia Christi Americana* (3 ed., Hartford, Conn., 1852: repr. Edinburgh, 1979), 2, pp. 220–1.

made the ministry, not the reverse. A question from the church at Salem evoked the resolution that 'such as had been ministers in England were lawful ministers by the call of the people there, notwithstanding their acceptance of the call of the bishops &c. (for which they humbled themselves, acknowledging it their sin &c.) but being come hither, they accounted themselves no ministers, until they were called to another church, and that, upon election, they were ministers before they were solemnly ordained'.[36] And as congregational theory came to be worked out in England the whole issue of ministry was bound up with the cultivation of spiritual gifts in the congregation, the issue which so exercised Spener. If a congregation was to find ministerial gifts in its circle it must encourage them without applying opprobrious names such as 'lay-preaching';[37] and when it had sought out a pastor for itself the essence of the act of ordination (whether or not accompanied by the laying on of hands) was prayer, and this also was a collective act of the church: 'By this it appeareth that the people may perform the substantial act of Ordination, viz. Prayer'.[38] John Winthrop noted that under Cotton's approach 'more were converted and added to that church, than to all the other churches in the bay'.[39] Thus while the Quakers sought to escape priesthood by abolishing the Pastoral Office, the Congregationalists, having reshaped the Office in the context of the spiritual life of the congregation, felt able to include in their covenants far-reaching professions of 'obedience to our Pastors & governors over us in ye Lord'.

America was ruthlessly to expose the hazards of this synthesis.[40] Congregationalism became for a time the state Church in Massachusetts; a polity in which only freemen could vote and hold office, only church

---

[36] John Winthrop, *The History of New England*, ed. J. Savage (Boston, 1825–6), 1, pp. 217.

[37] John Owen preserved a nice balance: 'Spiritual gifts of themselves make no man actually a minister, yet no man can be made a minister according to the mind of Christ who is not a partaker of them . . . if the Lord Christ at any time or in any place cease to give out spiritual gifts unto men . . . then and in that place the ministry itself must cease'. *Two Discourses concerning the Holy Spirit and his work* (London, 1693), p. 232.

[38] This theme is worked out in inimitable style under the heading 'The principle of fellowship' by Dr G. F. Nuttall in *Visible Saints. The Congregational Way* (Oxford, 1957), pp. 85–95. I am indebted to Dr Nuttall for much advice on the congregational doctrine of the ministry.

[39] John Winthrop, *Journal, 1630–1649*, ed. James K. Hosmer (New York, 1908), 1, p. 116.

[40] An admirable account of the evolution of the ministry in New England is given in David D. Hall, *The Faithful Shepherd* (Chapel Hill, N.C., 1972). The constitutional documents are collected in Williston Walker, *The Creeds and Platforms of Congregationalism* (New York, 1893). Much information about the constitution and English background of the American churches is given in Jon Butler, 'Power, Authority and the Origins of the American Denominational Order. The English Churches in the Delaware Valley', *Transactions of the American Philosophical Society*, 68 (1978), 2, pp. 1–81.

members could become freemen, and only those able to satisfy the clergy of a work of grace in their soul could become church members. This rule of saints proved extraordinarily difficult to perpetuate in practice. Within the first generation ministers discovered that if they admitted children of church members who could not testify to the work of grace within, they would destroy the pure church; but if they did not admit them, a political system already very oligarchic would become impossible to sustain. Temporary relief was sought in the adoption of the Half-way Covenant in 1662. Under this arrangement ministers might admit to the Church the children of members who professed a belief in Christian principles and wished to affiliate. Without proof of conversion they could not take communion and enjoy the full privileges of membership; but at least they could vote. The Congregationalists now reaped the full embarrassment of trying to make a religious establishment from a polity designed to withdraw the saints from the parish. The second problem, there from the first generation, was exacerbated by the record growth of a population which doubled every twenty-five years up to the Revolution. Immigrants poured in from Germany, Switzerland, France, Sweden, and elsewhere. Some brought a pastor with them; most brought nothing, not even the language of the country; none could be fitted into the American establishments. And the dire poverty of many of the immigrants differed in two ways from its European counterpart. The new populations were far more mobile than was usual in Europe, and their mobility was taking them into areas where not merely the kingdom of God but the kingdom of this world had to be built from the bottom upwards. None of the European Churches was used to this situation; and the Congregationalists had two particular problems. The need for basic social construction contained an implicit challenge to their attitude towards the righteousness of works; and a church polity conceived in terms of pastoral relationships was ill at ease in circumstances the overwhelming requirement of which was evangelism.

Thomas Hooker, minister of Hartford, Conn., who had served in the Netherlands, spoke for many of the early settlers in finding those provinces 'wonderfully ticklish and miserable',[41] and the ministry viewed their predicament as one characterized by disorder, social and ecclesiastical, of the lamentable Dutch kind, of which they had hoped Congregational discipline would afford a cure. But discipline there must be. Hooker was adept at lobbying his elders as a church within a church;[42] Samuel

[41] Mather, *Magnalia Christi Americana*, 1, p. 340.
[42] *Ibid.*, p. 349.

Stone gave a Yankee version of Appollonius, describing the Congregational polity as 'a speaking *Aristocracy* in the face of a silent *Democracy*'.[43]
Others pleaded for Presbyterianism, and thanked God they had escaped
'that *sink* of all errors, QUAKERISM'.[44] They managed to shed their
ruling elders, exalted ministerial status, pushed an associational life with a
view to setting bounds to local licence, and altogether changed the
character of ordination ceremonies. Ministers now came to be ordained
by other ministers rather than by the congregation, to claim that their
office was conveyed in ordination rather than congregational election;
and the quantities of mutton, beef, rum, and wine ordered to celebrate
these occasions are much more reminiscent of the beanfeasts required on
entrance to an Old World guild than the congregational prayer of New
World theory.[45] This programme of aggrandizing the Pastoral Office and
shaking loose its roots in the gifts and graces of the congregation was not
necessarily bloodless; in Cotton Mather whom the *Oxford English Dictionary* credits with the first use of the word 'revival' in the modern sense, an
intensely renewed chiliasm, a ravishing vision of the heavenly joy awaiting the pure in heart, provided its own emotional dynamite.[46] But clerical
bullying, remarkably ineffective in the Old World could not possibly
work in the New.[47]

An alternative strategy was to abandon the pure church, a policy associated with that powerful character, Solomon Stoddard.[48] Called to
Northampton, Mass., in 1670, he married Esther Mather, his predecessor's widow, added twelve children to her three, and created
an unrivalled network of family influences right through the Connecticut valley. Moreover, in a record which puts the protracted meetings

---

[43] *Ibid.*, p. 437.

[44] *Ibid.*, pp. 453, 492.

[45] These developments are a main theme of J. W. T. Youngs, Jnr., *God's Messengers. Religious
Leadership in Colonial New England* (Baltimore, 1976), esp. pp. 30–9, 64–78. See also
G. Selement, *Keepers of the Vineyard, The Puritan Ministry and Collective Culture in Colonial New
England* (Lanham, 1984).

[46] This is one of the themes of Robert Middlekauf, *The Mathers. Three Generations of Puritan Intellectuals, 1596–1728* (New York, 1971).

[47] David Harlan argues that the whole mechanism of ministerial authority was much more frail
than recent scholars have tended to suggest. (*The Clergy and the Great Awakening in New
England* (Ann Arbor, 1980), pp. 13–30). When Mather came to recommend religious
societies, they were not Spener's *ecclesiolae* designed to optimize the general priesthood, but
societies for the reformation of manners on the English pattern, designed to add lay pressure
to that of the clergy in social regulation. James W. Jones, *The Shattered Synthesis. New England
Puritanism before the Great Awakening* (New Haven, 1973), pp. 85–6.

[48] Stoddard is justly prominent in the literature. See e.g. Jones, *Shattered Synthesis*, pp. 104–28:
Perry Miller, 'Solomon Stoddard', *Harvard Theological Review*, 34 (1941), pp. 277–320.

of nineteenth-century revivalists in the shade, he did not miss a Sunday sermon or weeknight lecture for illness for the next 59 years. He extended the Halfway Covenant by admitting all respectable baptized persons to church membership. Having got his flock in, Stoddard relied on a combination of powerful preaching for conversion and the converting effect of the communion ordinance itself. This system Stoddard built up throughout the Connecticut valley in opposition to the Boston policies of the Mathers, and it brought him a series of harvests of souls; the largest fell to his former assistant and successor at Northampton, his grandson Jonathan Edwards.

The experience of the Connecticut valley shows clearly enough why, when revival finally broke out on a large scale, it was more warmly received by the ministers of the Standing Order than by official clergy anywhere else, and why in 1740 Whitefield was given a hero's welcome, notwithstanding his episcopal ordination and his notoriously lax views on church order. The upshot of the Great Awakening from the standpoint of our theme was curiously contradictory. The Standing Order paid a high price for past punditry in a great outburst of attacks on unconverted ministers and in demands for the exercise of the general priesthood in itinerant and unordained preaching. The New England establishment was irrevocably broken, and a hundred separatist congregations formed in the 'forties. Yet on another view things changed extraordinarily little. The leadership even of the radical movements was predominantly in ministerial hands, and Gilbert Tennent who had begun with a sharp blast against unconverted ministers became apprehensive of spiritual gifts when they turned up in the shape of Zinzendorf. Still more striking was the case of the Revd James Davenport of Long Island, himself a Yale graduate, who came close to claiming the immediate direction of the Holy Spirit. This claim appeared to the authorities of Connecticut and Massachusetts evidence of mental illness. The high point of Davenport's demonstrations came in the famous bonfire at New London on which were cast 'a Quantity of Books . . . all suppos'd by them to be tinctured with Arminianism & opposed to the work of God's Spirit in ye Land'. This theatrical assault on one of the bases of professional clerical punditry is a striking index of the real state of affairs. William Tennent's famous Log College for the training of revival preachers had offered a recognizably Presbyterian education on an economical basis;[49] 'the Shepherd's Tent'

---

[49] See the old classic, Archibald Alexander, *The Log College* (Philadelphia, 1851: repr. London, 1968).

founded by Davenport and Allen, who had been suspended from the ministry for declaring that in the work of conversion the reading of the Bible, unless it was accompanied by the immediate operation of the Holy Spirit, was of no more use than reading an old almanac, was a much more down-market institution, and one dedicated to attaining the immediate gifts of inspiration rather than to any educational process.[50] Founded at a favourable moment when Harvard and Yale were drained of students, The Shepherd's Tent was put down by legal proceedings against its leaders. Princeton was begun on a conservative basis by the New Side Presbyterians in 1747; but it was a long time before the heirs of the revivalists ventured to create their own foundations at Brown, Dartmouth, and Rutgers (to use their modern names), and then on much the same basis as the old New England colleges. Punditry had reasserted itself.[51]

It was the same story with church order. The Separates continued to insist that their members improve the gifts with which the Spirit had endowed them, but they imposed the controls of Scripture, a ministry, and the advice of neighbouring congregations. Many of the Separates had parted company with their parish churches because of the lax discipline prevailing. As that discipline was tightened, many returned to their original home. Most of the rest were picked up by the Baptists who now became a force in New England for the first time,[52] and whose polity came off the same Reformed stem as that of the Standing Order. They too played their part in pruning back the more inconvenient claims to spiritual gifts. There were Separates who claimed the ultimate spiritual gifts of sinlessness and immortality, but the church of Isaac Backus, the great New England Baptist leader, separated from the Easton Baptists because they condoned perfectionism, spiritual wifery, and baptism by 'unordained itinerants'. Punditry, however chastened, was back, and Calvinist New England was Calvinist New England still. It was not for

---

[50] Richard Warch, 'The Shepherd's Tent. Education and Enthusiasm in the Great Awakening', *American Quarterly*, 30 (1978), pp. 177–98.

[51] The most recent and spirited account of Davenport is given in Clarke Garret, *Spirit Possession and Popular Religion. From the Camisards to the Shakers* (Baltimore, 1987), pp. 119–126.

[52] W. G. McLoughlin, *New England Dissent, 1630–1833* (Cambridge, Mass., 1971), I, pp. 329–488: *The Diary of Isaac Backus*, ed. W. G. McLoughlin (Providence, 1979), 1, p. 570; 2, p. 703. Backus (*ibid.*, 1, pp. 74, 101) would not allow the power of ordination to be separated from the power of election. Cf. his *Discourse Showing the Nature and Necessity of an Internal Call to Preach the Everlasting Gospel* (1754) in *Isaac Backus on Church, State and Calvinism. Pamphlets, 1754–1789*, ed. W. G. McLoughlin (Cambridge, Mass., 1968); D. S. Lovejoy, *Religious Enthusiasm in the New World* (Cambridge, Mass., 1985), pp. 183–4.

another generation, after the excitements of the American Revolution, and after the back lands of Maine, Vermont, New Hampshire, and Massachusetts had filled up with settlers that high pressure revival could produce new religions with an almost Californian fertility.[53] In old New England, as Wesley was to note with some acerbity, revival had been killed stone dead for fifty years.

Dissenters in Old England and New pursued similar fashions[54] in dissimilar contexts, and reacted to revival in similar ways. The spiritual heart of English dissent never ceased to beat in spite of Restoration persecution and many political disappointments thereafter; and there were dissenters who adapted themselves to a colder climate by hotter preaching, and deliberate evangelism.[55] In the eighteenth century a generous man like Doddridge could sympathize with much in the revival and in Enlightenment too. But there were always others who were conscious that they had an order and a discipline to maintain, even if the church established did not. These stiffer brethren[56] had torpedoed the Happy Union attempted in 1691, and doubtless their successors contributed to that long series of cases down the century where Methodists were refused communion or other friendly relations,[57] a series much longer than that of the obnoxious parish priests of legend. Of course, if the sacraments were an ordinance of a covenanted fellowship, many Methodists were not eligible, and Wesley's creation of an interdenominational religious society did not constitute a moral claim on their behalf. And even those who were sympathetic, like Isaac Watts and Philip Doddridge, had quite clear reservations.[58] Of course the leading Methodists were Anglicans, the Wesleys were Arminians and sometimes incautious advocates of Christian

---

[53] This subject is vividly recreated by Stephen A. Marini, *Radical Sects of Revolutionary New England* (Cambridge, Mass., 1982).

[54] Pretty constantly keeping an eye on each other. Cf. Thomas Harmer, *Remarks on the antient and present state of the Congregational churches of Norfolk and Suffolk* (1777) in his *Miscellaneous Works* (London, 1823), pp. 137–220: Hall, *Faithful Shepherd*, pp. 221, 223–6.

[55] W. R. Ward, 'The relations of Enlightenment and religious revival in Central Europe and the English-speaking world' in *Reform and Reformation. England and the Continent c.1500–c.1750*, ed. Derek Baker (Oxford, 1979), pp. 294–7.

[56] How the various nuances were to be recognized in the eighteenth century is attractively described by Isaac Watts in *Posthumous Works* (London, 1779), 2, pp. 158–62.

[57] 'Mr Harmer... thinks... that the spirit of the Methodists is hurtful to the peace and order of our settled churches. Dr Wood, who had large experience of Methodists was very clear... that very few of that people could walk comfortably and usefully with our churches'. John Browne, *History of Congregationalism and Memorials of the churches in Norfolk and Suffolk* (London, 1877), p. 199.

[58] G. F. Nuttall, 'Methodism and the older Dissent. Some perspectives', *United Reformed Church Historical Journal*, 2 (1981), 272–74.

perfection, and, in his early years of field-preaching, John Wesley, with a fine sense of impartiality, balanced the irritation he gave the bishops by interfering in other men's parishes by the irritation he gave nonconformists by rebaptizing dissenters.[59] And the constitutional structure in Whitefield's Tabernacles in England or the building he created in Philadelphia were hardly churches according to the English Reformed understanding.[60]

What finally of the relations between the Pastoral Office and the general priesthood among religious communities created during the revival, taking as examples the Methodists and the Moravians? The Methodists, it must be said, muddied the waters very considerably.[61] Methodism in Wesley's lifetime might be thought to be an improved model of what Spener had sought, with class-meetings and love-feasts providing for the improvement of the spiritual gifts of the society members, with band-meetings for the élite, and with what Wesley called the prophetic office, the right of laymen to preach, being usefully directed to evangelistic purposes for which Spener had not clearly provided. And underlying the whole were the regular ordinances of church or chapel of which Methodists were required to partake. But when, by a chapter of accidents in the generation after Wesley's death, Methodism became, not one but several, churches, Wesley's sons developed nearly the worst possible ecclesiology. At a time when other communities were seeking to realize the New Testament office of evangelist, Wesleyan Methodism turned its evangelists into pastors, and claimed for pastors an authority which ensured that, however the priesthood of all believers might be realized in Methodist practice, it would not be recognized in church government. Christ had filled the whole Pastoral Office and transmitted his authority to his ministers, in this case embodied in the Conference. The pastor wholly given up to the work,

---

[59] *The Journal of John Wesley*, ed. N. Curnock (2 edn., London, 1938), 2, p. 135. The circumlocution Wesley uses in two later cases (*ibid.*, 5, p. 195; 7, p. 132) suggests that these ex-Baptist candidates may never have received believers' Baptism. 'Mr. Wesley ... maintained with jealousy his high-church professions, and kept at a suspicious distance from Dissenters'. D. Bogue and J. bennett, *The History of the Dissenters from the Revolution to the year 1808* (2 edn., London, 1833), 2, p. 25.

[60] *Ibid.*, 2, pp. 48–9.

[61] For a fuller treatment of the following see my two papers: 'The Legacy of John Wesley: The Pastoral Office in Britain and America' in *Statesmen, Scholars and Merchants. Essays in Eighteenth-Century History presented to Dame Lucy Sutherland*, eds A. Whiteman, J. S. Bromley and P. G. M. Dickson (Oxford, 1973), 323–50; and 'Die Methodistische Kirchen' forthcoming in the *Theologische Realenzyclopaedie*.

must feed and also rule the flock; his authority, which included ordination, legislation, the power of admission into the church, and of reproof, exhortation, and excision from it, was *sui generis*, and could not be shared with those who were not pastors, even if, like local preachers or classleaders, they performed valuable spiritual functions. The passage of time, the diplomacy necessary to achieve Methodist Union in 1933, and the long-term pressure of Protestant examples which now seem to be fading from the Methodist official mind, eventually softened this to a statement in the Deed of Union that the ministry exercised no priesthood different in kind from that of other members of the Church. Moreover, as if there were a legalistic device for realizing the priesthood of all believers, the Deed of Union wrote the obituary of the class-meeting by extolling its merits in an amazing hortatory passage which was entirely out of place in a constitutional document and could be guaranteed never to be read by anyone likely to be influenced by it.[62]

The position with the Moravians was perhaps a little happier but even more confused. At the root of the difficulty was the disparity between Zinzendorf's original intention of creating a philadelphian *Schlossecclesiola* on his estate and the tenacious desire of the Moravians refugees who began to settle it to maintain dimly recollected traditions of the old Bohemian Brethren.[63] Zinzendorf believed he could provide for both by creating a movement within the evangelical church of the sort he thought Luther had provided for in the Preface to the *Deutsche Messe*.[64] Like Wesley, he was hamstrung by the inability of the Protestant establishments to cope with missionary situations beyond their borders, and for

---

[62] H. Spencer and E. Finch, *The Constitutional Practice and Discipline of the Methodist Church* (5 edn., London, 1969), pp. 289, 291.

[63] On this see my paper on 'The Renewed Unity of the Brethren. Ancient church, new sect, or interconfessional movement?' in *Bulletin of the John Rylands Library of the University of Manchester*, 70 (1988), pp. 77–92. Part of the difficulty was that the old Bohemian Brethren had more than once been forced to improvise in life-and-death emergencies. See David Cranz, *The Ancient and Modern History of the Brethren*, tr. B. Latrobe (London, 1780), pp. 26–8. Cf. *Primitive Church government . . . or the Unity of the Brethren in Bohemia* (n. pl., 1703). The old Brethren held that the ministry was not one of the essentials of Christianity, but was necessary because it mediated the Word of God, held the keys, and dispensed the sacraments, all of which were essentials. *Church constitutions of the Bohemian and Moravian Brethren*, ed. and trans. B. Seifferth (London, 1866), pp. 102–3.

[64] *Luther's Works*, American edn. 53, p. 62. In the 'forties Zinzendorf affirmed his Lutheran orthodoxy by getting the Brethren to receive the Confessio Augustana Invariata (*Twentyone Discourses or Dissertations upon the Augsburg Confession*, trans. F. Okeley (London, 1753), pp. ii, xxix, 250–1) while admitting that 'a hierarchical state in the church was perhaps never absolutely necessary'. *An account of the Doctrine, Manners, Liturgy and Ideas of the Unitas Fratrum*. Presented to the House of Commons in 1749 (London, 1749), p. 66.

many years threatened with the loss of his base in Saxony and vociferously denounced by the watchmen on the Lutheran ramparts. Zinzendorf's response was to secure episcopal consecration for David Nitschman from Jablonski, the last remaining bishop in the old Moravian line, the authority to be exercised solely in the New World where there was then no Lutheran jurisdiction and where it was important (in Cranz's words) to have a status 'which the most rigid Episcopalian in the English colonies must acknowledge'.[65] Three years later Zinzendorf himself received consecration by the same route, also as a missionary bishop, the pair numbering themselves 63 and 64 in the old Moravian succession. Before this, however, Zinzendorf had braved family opposition to acquire Lutheran ordination in bizarre (and as Ritschl insisted, illicit)[66] circumstances, in what must have been have been one of the more hilarious ordination examinations of modern times.[67]

Aiming to obtain his orders from the Swedish Lutheran Church still entrenched on the south side of the Baltic at Stralsund, Zinzendorf obtained himself employment as a tutor in a merchant's household there under an assumed name. He also preached incognito on the grounds that though the Superintendent knew who he was, it was 'not necessary for the people to know, and the effect of the sermons on their hearts was thus much more innocent and reliable'.[68] The first crisis of the examination would have sunk many candidates; required to preach a sermon, the Count was about to step into the pulpit when the examiner, white as death, came after him to say that he had given him the wrong gospel text. Zinzendorf coped with aplomb, but the examination continued severe. One of the examiners took occasion to deliver an attack on Zinzendorf which clearly embarrassed the candidate who was still incognito. When the examiners began to twig the situation 'the Superintendent asked him with these words "I ask you before God, are you not the Count himself?"'

---

[65] *The Ancient and Modern History of the Brethren*, p. 196.

[66] 'The examination [which] followed [was conducted] not by the whole Ministerium in Stralsund, nor by the college of three pastors, but, since Zinzendorf must expect opposition in either case, by two pastors one of whom was the Superintendent'. *Geschichte des Pietismus*, 3, p. 276.

[67] A good (and respectful) modern account of this episode is given by E. Beyreuther, *Zinzendorf und die Christenheit* (Marburg-an-der-Lahn, 1961), pp. 75–81. See also A. G. Spangenberg, *Leben des Herrn. Nicolaus Ludwig Grafen . . . von Zinzendorf* (Barby, 1773–5), pp. 826–46: Cranz, *Ancient and Modern History of the Brethren*, pp. 177–9: *Büdingische Sammlung* (Büdingen, 1742–5), 3, pp. 670–7: J. G. Carpzov, *Religions-untersuchung der Böhmisch- und Mährischen Brüder . . .* (Leipzig, 1742), pp. 454–9: J. P. S. Winckler, *Des Herrn Grafen Ludwig von Zinzendorfs Unternehmungen in Religions-sachen* (Leipzig, 1740), pp. 73–83, 95.

[68] *Büdingische Sammlung*. Biographical footnote to vol. 1 Preface (no pagination).

He replied: "Yes, I am" and, undoing his coat, showed them upon his waistcoat the star and order of the cross, but begged them to keep quiet about his person, and to pay him no compliments. This they promised and faithfully performed'. At the next examination the Count began with name-dropping about his influence with the Cardinal de Noailles, Primate of France, and ended with his drawing his sword and promising 'never more, life-long, to wear it again. The Superintendent still [had] it in his keeping'. The Count's examiners who were men of repute ended by giving him a good testimonial, which predictably proved entirely unconvincing to his Orthodox and Hallesian enemies.[69] By this strange route Lutheran ordination and Moravian episcopacy were grafted on to what all insisted was the Renewed Unity of the Brethren, and already by the time Moravian doctrine was received in England it was a high one: 'Why does the Holy Ghost consecrate the Bishops? Because he has consecrated Jesus. Who outwardly [appoints to church office?] The Elders and Bishops. What is holy Ordination? A gift [of the Holy Spirit] through the laying on of hands'.[70]

This story is a confused one, but it may serve a purpose by showing how much more confused is the contemporary situation. The majority parties among the Churches insist on maintaining a corporative attitude towards their professional ministries, apparently oblivious of the fact that the rest of the world manages its affairs much better by contracts of service, and making up its mind what it wants from is employees. The ecumenical movement now seems clearly dedicated to making catholics of us all. And what of non-stipendiary ministries? Anglican bishops and Baptist congregations alike combine to use this device to close their mind to the general priesthood, and to create the impression, much as the pre-Reformation Church created the impression that the Christian life *par*

---

[69] Winckler, a Hallesian, found the Count's professions of loyalty to the Lutheran Church hypocritical (*Des Herrn Grafen . . . von Zinzendorfs Unternehmungen*, pp. 71–81). Certainly he made the curious promise to avoid the sham church in public. N. L. von Zinzendorf, *Die Gegenwärtige Gestalt des Kreuz-Reichs Jesu in seiner Unschuld . . .* (Frankfurt/Leipzig, 1745), pp. 133–4.

[70] *A Manual of Doctrine* [translated and published by James Hutton] (London, 1742), nos 113, 1140, 1179. Cf. Fabricius, *Corpus Confessionum*, 10, pp. 4, 32–3. Spangenberg came as close as he could to treating ordination as a sacrament (A. G. Spangenberg, *Apologetische Schluss-Schrift* (Leipzig/Görlitz, 1752), pp. 427–8), but stressed that Moravian bishops, priests and deacons were all 'under the conference of elders appointed by the synod, to whom the superintendency and counselling of the whole Unity is committed' (*A Concise Historical Account of the Present Constitution of the Unitas Fratrum . . .*, trans. B. Latrobe (London, 1775), pp. 43, 46). In the next century Edmund de Schweinitz maintained that 'episcopacy is essential to [the] existence' of the Unity. *The Moravian Episcopate* (n. pl. or d.), p. 4.

excellence was the regular life, that the Christian vocation *par excellence* is that of ordained ministry. Churches which stoop to this kind of thing deserve all they get. It is characteristic of the present day that the spiritual gift currently in greatest demand, viz. healing, is the one about the eliciting and development of which least is known. Yet so far has the history of the Church parted company from the pursuit of spiritual gifts that there are even those who would confine healing services to the eucharist. For clergy of this ilk the Pastoral Office has clearly swallowed up the General Priesthood. They are the true Levites, not the eternally nonconformist priesthood after the order of Melchizedek.

Petersfield

A DESCRIPTION OF THE QUALIFICATIONS NECESSARY TO A GOSPEL MINISTER— QUAKER MINISTRY IN THE EIGHTEENTH CENTURY

by DAVID J. HALL

I
N 1750 Samuel Bownas, then aged about seventy-four, published *A Description of the Qualifications necessary to A Gospel Minister*, a manual of advice to ministers and elders in the Religious Society of Friends.[1] In 1738 the church discipline of the Society was codified and made available to Friends' meetings, first in manuscript form and then from 1783 in print, providing rules and advice covering aspects of Quaker life from administration at national level to personal conduct.[2]

In the earliest days of the Society the appearance in print of such advice would have been considered superfluous. A Friend received his call to minister directly from the Spirit once he was in a receptive state as a result of turning to the light, then found the direction of his particular ministry. This call bore no relation to the education or status of the recipient, it was not recognized by any external rite, it could be of short duration, and it could take varied forms.[3] There soon came to be definitions of some aspects of ministry and as early as 1653 all Friends' meetings were enjoined by William Dewsbury to ensure that they had:

> one or two who are most grown in the power and life, in the pure discerning in the truth, to take care and charge over the flock of God in that place.[4]

Thus it was the Spirit working in the meeting for church affairs that discerned the actual or latent gift of an individual member ('The least

[1] Samuel Bownas, *A Description of the Qualifications Necessary to a Gospel Minister, containing Advice to Ministers and Elders, how to conduct themselves in their Conversations, and various Services according to their Gifts in the Church of Christ* (London, 1750).

[2] *Christian and Brotherly Advices Given forth from time to time by the Yearly Meeting in London* (unpublished manuscript, 1738); *Extracts from the Minutes and Advices of the Yearly Meeting of Friends held in London* (London, 1783). For the early history of the books of discipline see David J. Hall, 'Christian and Brotherly Advices', *The Friends' Quarterly*, 22 (1981), pp. 506–15.

[3] A helpful recent discussion of the early development of Quaker ministry is in Donald S. Nesti, *Grace and faith: the means to salvation* (Pittsburgh, 1975), pp. 285–307.

[4] William Dewsbury, *The Faithful Testimony of that Antient Servant of the Lord and Minister of the everlasting Gospel William Dewsbery . . .* (London [1689]), p. 1.

member' wrote Fox, 'hath an office and is serviceable') and by recognition of it, in some cases through specific appointment, fostered that gift so that it could be effectually exercised, recognizing always that 'there are diversities of gifts but the same spirit', a theme which finds abundant expression in Bownas's *Description*.

Before going further it will be useful to explain that the primary meeting for church affairs was not the local congregation but the area monthly meeting. Monthly meetings were grouped in county quarterly meetings which in turn were grouped into the Yearly Meeting held in London. Beginning with the local congregation the structure of the Society consisted of geographically widening tiers until the Yearly Meeting was reached. There was no authoritarian government from above nor was authority vested in any one individual locally. The basis of church government was essentially to 'let all things be done decently and in good order'.[5] Ministry in any of its forms was open equally to women and men. It was entirely in keeping with the acceptance of the diversity of gifts for a particular individual to serve in several forms of ministry, though in the eighteenth century it was likely that service in any one would be undertaken for a lengthy period.

It will now be useful to identify four different types of ministry as they were later distinguished in four different offices:

ministers whose gift in the ministry of the word, or preaching was acknowledged or recorded by their monthly meetings;

elders whose function was to counsel ministers and whose responsibilities were primarily to the right conduct of meetings for worship;

overseers whose responsibilities were to the ministry of pastoral care;

clerks whose business it was to discern the growth of unity or 'the sense of the meeting' in meetings for church affairs and to encapsulate that sense in a minute drawn up, amended as necessary, and approved at the time.

This paper will outline the development of the appointments of ministers, elders and overseers in the Society of Friends in the eighteenth century, looking at the corporate understanding of their roles at national level expressed in the books of discipline. Then, looking at the advice offered by Bownas and at his own experiences,[6] it will attempt to examine

---

[5] I Corinthians 14 v. 40.

[6] *An Account of the Life, Travels, and Christian Experiences in the Work of the Ministry of Samuel Bownas* (London, 1756).

the practical basis of the ministry. While looking at the sources of the authority of Friends' ministry in this brief study no attention can be paid to the content of spoken ministry though a number of examples have been published.[7] Nor will there be any further reference to Robert Barclay's *Apology*, the most sustained exposition of Quaker theology, where the tenth of his fifteen propositions 'Of the ministry' is particularly relevant.[8] The *Apology* was first published in English in 1678. Although at least nine further editions were published in the British Isles in the eighteenth century it is not at all clear how far the work, despite steady and considerable sales, really influenced Friends or was read by them.

Ministers

The call to the preaching ministry first prompted the individual to serve in the local meeting but for some another aspect followed, a call to travel in the ministry. This, continuing the tradition of the 'Valiant Sixty' of Fox's time, could involve extensive and prolonged travel by the standards of the time, sometimes for years overseas, preventing the minister from following a normal livelihood and possibly causing great strain to a family remaining at home. The work of travelling ministers, pastoral as well as preaching, prevented the isolation of local congregations and helped in the process of binding the Society together as a national church and in spreading as well as encouraging Quakerism overseas particularly in North America. Bownas quotes the apostate Friend George Keith as having proposed, as a means to prevent the growth of Quakerism:

> the making of a law to restrain Friends from travelling, save to their own meetings; for, he said, it was the travelling preachers that kept the Quakers up so strong in countenance.[9]

At the same time the authority inherent in their form of ministry was prophetic, not administrative, and these ministers made less tangible

---

[7] For example: *Scripture Truths Demonstrated in Thirty-Two Sermons or Declarations of Mr Stephen Crisp* . . . (London, 1707); *Sermons preached by Samuel Fothergill, taken down in Shorthand* . . . (Dublin, 1783); *Twelve Discourses by the late Thomas Letchworth* (London, 1787). See also for an account of the style of ministry Lucia K. Beamish, *Quaker Ministry 1691 to 1834* (Oxford, 1967).

[8] Robert Barclay, *An Apology for the True Christian Divinity as the same is held forth, and preached by the people, Called, in Scorn, Quakers* . . . (Aberdeen, 1678).

[9] Bownas, *Life*, p. 107. Rufus M. Jones, *The Later Periods of Quakerism*, 2 vols (London, 1921), 1, chapter 7 gives a number of examples of Friends in the travelling ministry.

contributions to the practicalities of running the Society. Other forms of ministry, eldership, oversight, or clerkship made use of different gifts and ensured continuity within meetings. Ministers and elders were called to visit Friends and their families in their homes. This sometimes became an intensive exercise, Samuel Fothergill as an elderly man undertook 127 such visits in the company of Samuel Emlen in the space of twenty-eight days in 1769 just to families in Gracechurch Street Monthly Meeting in London.[10] John Rutty took the view that: 'We visitors are preachers *ad hominem*, a more awful office than that of public ministers' and he obviously devoted a good deal of time as an elder to this service, writing of it in 1756 as: 'a new operation in our spiritual campaign, and of signal service in these dreary times.'[11]

The *Christian and Brotherly Advices* of 1738 was not a newly prepared text but a collection of passages that already existed. The earlier passages in the collection had already been issued by the Yearly Meeting to monthly meetings as need arose. Formal rulings and definitions were only prepared when necessary and a situation might be accepted for a long period in the Society before there was any need for regulations. The first printed book of discipline repeated many of the entries from the 1738 manuscript. Whereas in 1738 'preacher' or 'public Friend' were used for ministers, and the terms minister and elder seem to have been used almost interchangeably, by 1783 there were sections entitled 'Ministers and Elders' and 'Meetings of Ministers and Elders'. The repetition of earlier entries concerning problems suggests that many remained constant for much of the century.

The heading in 1738 chiefly concerned with ministers is 'Concerning Preachers'.[12] The earliest entries are about unsatisfactory preaching as in this extract from 1689:

> A concern coming upon Friends of this meeting concerning several persons both men and women who go rambling idly up and down the counties under pretence of preaching truth, who are out of the unity of Friends in their own county, whose conversations and examples are not savoury as becomes the truth: Friends in the several counties should beware of such, and give no encouragement nor countenance

[10] George Crosfield, *Memoirs of the life and gospel labours of Samuel Fothergill* . . . (Liverpool, 1843), pp. 478–9.

[11] John Rutty, *A Spiritual Diary and Soliloquies*, 2 vols (London, 1776), 1, pp. 111, 113.

[12] A number of copies of this manuscript exist in libraries, Quaker archives and record offices. Given possible variations in pagination page references have not been provided here.

to them, but warn them to return and settle in their places and honest employments, and seek unity with their own meetings.

In 1698 it was recommended that in cases where Friends were dissatisfied 'with any that take upon them to preach' the local 'faithful approved ministers and elders' should admonish them. By 1720 it was:

> ... tenderly recommended to the monthly and quarterly meetings to see that Friends who travel in the work of the ministry, do go in the unity of the meetings to which they belong, and with certificates therefrom.

The practice was earlier. When Samuel Bownas first felt that he must travel in the ministry he spoke to his master (he was still an apprentice) who told him to speak to some of the elders in the meeting because he would need a certificate to show that they supported the journey.[13] On a later visit to the meeting in Worcester he also experienced the need for a certificate:

> an ancient Friend examined me very closely, after meeting was over, from whence I came, and for a certificate ... My certificate being at my quarters in my saddlebag, he could not then see it ... my landlord William Pardoe, a brave sensible elder, advised me not to be uneasy at the old Friend's examining so, for, said he, he does so to every stranger. We went to meeting in the afternoon ... but the old Friend, after the meeting, was upon me in the same strain to see my certificate, but I had it not then about me either, at which he seemed displeased: I made no reply, but told him, I was very willing he should see it; but my landlord took him up, and told him, he thought the young man had already shown us his best certificate in both the meetings.

Eventually the old Friend[14] saw the certificate at Pardoe's home and was satisfied.[15]

Those who were accepted as ministers were advised in 1728:

> against all indecent postures and gestures, uintelligible tones and sounds, misquotations and misapplications of scripture which renders such a ministry contemptible.[16]

---

[13] Bownas, *Life*, p. 10.

[14] The old Friend was Edward Bourne, identified by Henry J. Cadbury in *George Fox's 'Book of Miracles'* (Cambridge, 1948), p. 47 n. 4.

[15] Bownas, *Life*, pp. 17–18. A similar, earlier example at Doncaster is recorded on p. 13.

[16] Under 'Morning Meeting of Ministers and Elders'. Significantly 'and Elders' is a later addition in the manuscript heading.

In 1731 'an Epistle of advice to ministring Friends that travel' was issued. It reminded those who heard ministry to adopt a receptive, not a critical attitude. Also taken up in that epistle was the problem of long absences on travel in the ministry, ministers were urged once their travels were done to return home to take care of their business, household, and family. The advices to ministers and elders issued in 1775 (replacing a set of 1702) were printed in the 1783 book of extracts.[17] They cover various practical points about ministry as well as offering suggestions on general behaviour. They provide a concise statement of what was expected of ministers and of what was to be avoided by them, often confirming the validity of the observations made in the contemporary biographies. Ministers were urged to read the scriptures frequently. The concluding paragraph warned against rhetoric and prayer offered simply for the sake of speaking, against lengthy and repetitious prayer and running 'from supplication into declaration, as though the Lord wanted information'.

Elders

A passage in 1720 recommending 'the elders of the church, both ministers and others' to care for those inexperienced in the ministry shows the emerging distinction between the ministers and the elders. An entry in 1727 can be taken as making formal provision for the appointment of separate elders:

> This meeting desires all monthly meetings to appoint serious discreet and judicious Friends, who are not ministers, tenderly to encourage and help young ministers and advise others . . . And where there are meetings of ministring Friends, such Friends so chosen be admitted as members of such meetings . . .

A further extract in 1735 makes specific reference to the elders in the London monthly meetings who are to be members of the important Morning Meeting, a weekly meeting of ministers concerned with arrangements for Quaker publications as well as public ministry. In 1761 it was felt necessary to say that age or wealth should not be considerations in the appointment of elders, those nominated 'being of clean hands' were to 'comfort the feeble minded and reprove the unruly with proper weight'. Much of the role of the elders in the eighteenth century, at least as it emerges from the books of discipline, was to nurture younger or less

---

[17] *Extracts*, pp. 149–50.

experienced ministers.[18] This meant of course that elders had to be able to discern when a minister's call was genuine and to dissuade those would-be ministers who were deluding themselves. John Griffith, a Friend actively involved in the movement of the 1760s for the revival of the Quaker discipline, wrote of true and false ministry in a 1764 work exhorting Friends to maintain their traditional standards. He suggests that the encouragement of beginners in the ministry is important:

> The main point, in my apprehension, is to be able to form a true judgement of the source or spring from whence ministry proceeds; and if found to be right in the ground a great deal of tenderness is to be used, and much childish weakness is to be patiently borne with. For, although some through fear, and a deep sense of the weight of so important an undertaking, may (at first) speak very stammeringly, and with considerable perturbation, yet the sweet efficacy of the quickening powerful Spirit, which is felt with them in their service (by those who are circumcised in heart and ear) far exceeds the finest eloquence without it.[19]

In 1754 a Yearly Meeting of Ministers and Elders was established. This was asked in 1758 to consider the answers returned to the queries sent down by the main Yearly Meeting to quarterly meetings of ministers and elders and to report on the answers to Yearly Meeting. By the 1770s there was some appearance of laxness among the elders and in 1772 it was suggested that monthly meetings should make more appointments.

Overseers

Under the heading 'Monthly Meetings' a passage in the 1783 *Extracts* referred for the first time to the appointment of overseers, though it dated from 1752 when it was part of the written epistle from the Yearly Meeting:

> we desire, pursuant to former advices, that meetings would appoint suitable friends as overseers of the flock . . .[20]

This passage goes on to refer to the choice of elders or overseers and it cannot be said at this point that the two functions are clearly separate. The

---

[18] The classic account of the elders in the eighteenth century suggests that they neglected this aspect, see Jones, *Later Periods*, 1; pp. 125–7.

[19] John Griffith, *Some Brief Remarks upon Sundry Important Subjects* . . . (London, 1765), p. 71.

[20] *Extracts*, p. 159.

term overseer had been used towards the end of the seventeenth century and a number of appointments were certainly made well before 1752.[21] The necessary moral qualifications of elders and overseers were outlined in a minute of 1715, they were to be 'free from covetousness, over-reaching, oppression and extortion' but their role was only defined there by the quotation of I Peter 5 vv. 2–3. A study of the records of a selection of local meetings could usefully supplement this scanty central informa-tion and help to ascertain the actual role of the early overseers. An entry under 'Correspondents' in the 1783 *Extracts* refers to action to be taken by elders and overseers in London jointly.[22] The separate nature of the two functions was finally clarified in 1789, suggesting that some genuine confusion had arisen in the mid-century:

> This meeting [the Yearly Meeting] is of the judgement that the offices of elder and overseer are distinct, and do not coincide in one person, unless appointed to each; and that overseers, under that appointment only, are not entitled to sit in meetings of ministers and elders.[23]

This passage also provides the information that there must have been occasions where individuals did serve in both roles at the same time.

Clerks

There is little reference to clerks in the books of discipline though from early times each kind of meeting must have had someone to assume the responsibilities concerned, indeed the role must have been an important one, undertaken perhaps by an elder. The procedure for appointing a clerk to the Yearly Meeting was laid down in 1733 'in order to prevent debate ... respecting the choice of a Clerk'. Many instructions in the *Christian and Brotherly Advices* required material to be prepared in writing but no mention is made of how this was to be organized. Curiously little attention seems to have been paid to the history of Quaker clerkship and there appears to be scope for further investigation in local records.[24]

---

[21] W. C. Braithwaite, *The Second Period of Quakerism* (London, 1919, 2 edn., Cambridge, 1961), p. 504 cites Chesterfield 1607, Oxfordshire 1701. Harold W. Brace, ed., *The First Minute Book of the Gainsborough Monthly Meeting of the Society of Friends*, 3 vols (Lincoln Record Society, 1949), 2, p. 125 cites Gainsborough Monthly Meeting, 1703.

[22] *Extracts*, p. 37.

[23] *Extracts from the Minutes and Advices of the Yearly Meeting of Friends* ... (2 edn., London, 1802), p. 109.

[24] Jones, *Later Periods*, 1, pp. 183–7 describes the office of clerk but says nothing of its history and development.

Quaker Ministry in the Eighteenth Century

Samuel Bownas

Bownas has been chosen as an example of an individual minister both on account of his *Description* and his own life and travels, surely one of the most straightforward and persuasive in the genre. Other individuals or their biographers were sometimes less forthcoming, though in a more extensive study attention would certainly be given to John Churchman, Samuel Fothergill, John Griffith, Catherine Phillips, John Rutty, and the anti-establishment views of James Jenkins later in the century.[25]

In his preface to Bownas's *Life* Joseph Besse described it as:

> a plain man's plain and undisguised account of his own progress in religion: an artless narrative of his sincere and hearty endeavours, as much as in him lay, to promote the doctrine of the Gospel of Christ in the earth.

Besse notes that Bownas's 'literary accomplishments were but small, extending little farther than to enable him to read the Scriptures in his mother tongue'. After his death the testimony from his monthly and quarterly meetings recorded that:

> It pleased the Lord to endue him with a large gift in the ministry, in which he was a faithful labourer ... he had a gift of utterance superior to many, sound in judgement and doctrine ...[26]

The *Description* gave 'Directions which may be as waymarks to such who are called into the work of the ministry and to the elders of the church'. The author specifically disclaimed its suitability for general circulation.[27] It was the only published manual on the subject in the eighteenth century though more concise advice was also available, officially in the 1783 *Extracts* and in works such as Rachel Chandler's brief *A letter ... to Ministers and Elders* (London, 1766). Individual ministers were no doubt well read in the stream of published spiritual autobiographies and biographical accounts of ministers.[28]

Bownas's own life contained the basic components of many ministers' careers; he began as a youth careless of religion, was converted from his

---

[25] For the latter see J. William Frost, ed., *The Records and Recollections of James Jenkins* (New York, 1984).

[26] Bownas, *Life*, pp. iii, vi–vii.

[27] Bownas, *Description*, p. iii.

[28] On journals see Howard H. Brinton, *Quaker Journals* (Wallingford, Pennsylvania, 1972) and Edward H. Milligan, '"Saw dead dog in Went" some reflections on the writing of journals', *The Friends' Quarterly*, 24 (1986), pp. 83–91.

nominal Quakerism, went on to consider speaking in meeting, feared that his call might not be genuine, and found that there were times when he should have spoken but held back as well as those when he dried up in the course of ministry and had to sit down. He was called to travel extensively in the ministry, he experienced periods of despair and he went on to make prolonged trips to North America. The *Description* is not therefore a piece of theorizing, though Bownas avoids giving precise examples from his own life. In his opening remarks he stresses the need for the sanctification of the spirit as a preliminary to being ready to offer vocal ministry and for personal humility. In his main text he explains that the divine inspiration cannot be received by a would-be minister in an unreformed state. He expects the first stirrings of the Spirit to cause uneasiness and melancholy in those who do not recognize them while those moved to pray and repent may find new life. Reminding the reader of the story of St Paul's conversion he points out that the gap between these first stirrings and the call to minister can be so short that onlookers well acquainted with the minister's previous state may initially suspect his authority. This echoed his personal experience when three weeks after his conversion he resisted the call to speak, partly because many of the companions of his unregenerate days were in the meeting too. Denying the call cost him much anguish and at the next meeting he had to speak. In the first few years of his ministry he spoke little. After about two years he felt the desire to travel in the ministry for the first time.

Bownas goes on in the *Description* to discuss 'the necessity of divine inspiration to the being of a gospel minister' defining it as 'an inbreathing of the divine Word into our minds giving a true understanding of divine things'. In the meeting for worship he waits for this inspiration as 'the foundation and spring of all right ministry, devotion and worship of the true God'.[29] The authority thus claimed by the minister is considerable but Bownas recognizes too the risk of self-deception. He feels, and this point deserves emphasis, that the congregation will be able to detect ministry arising from the imagination rather than inspiration. Next he examines the gift of ministry quoting I Corinthians 12 vv. 4–6 as a framework. Practical advise is given on delivery, speed, and length of vocal ministry, and the new minister is reminded to consider his own gift and not to try to model himself on others. The minister is urged to stand as soon as he feels compelled to speak and not to sit mulling over or expanding his message. The advice that he may have to be silent in some meetings

---

[29] Bownas, *Description*, pp. 23, 26.

relates to an experience in North America when Bownas was surprised to find himself compelled to be silent at a number of meetings. Eventually he and his companion:

> saw clearly the reason why we were so shut up in silence; some of them [the local ministers] were got into an extreme in preaching and praying, and would continue meetings to an unseasonable length, as likewise in their preaching and praying at table . . .

Revisiting later he found that 'they now saw it their place not to preach in every meeting, but to wait for the constraint of the divine work before they spoke'.[30]

Having discussed the diversity of gifts Bownas identifies the different forms that the vocal ministry can take; for example, parables, allegories, narrations of God's dealings with his people in past ages, recounting the goodness of God in our own lives, showing the encouragement to be derived from others' blessings, and expounding particular texts. He recounts elsewhere that these words came to him in a period of doubt when visiting a meeting:

> Thou runs, and God has not sent thee; thou speaks, but God don't speak by thee; therefore thou shalt not profit the people.[31]

A warning against using quotations extends even to scripture though he had earlier urged careful reading of the Bible:

> the danger of borrowing may lie as near, respecting the scriptures of the Old and New Testament, with any other books that may affect our minds . . . For it is no more lawful for us to preach what we have read, because we have read it, than it is for us to preach what we have heard because we have heard it.

The passage goes on to state the Quietist view of ministry which appears to devalue completely experience, scripture and education in the preparation of the minister:

> Now a spiritual minister is, and ought every day to be like blank paper, when he comes into the assembly of the Lord's people, not depending on any former openings or experience, either of his own or others, that he hath heard or read; but his only and sole dependence must be on the gift of the Spirit, to give, and bring to

---

[30] Bownas, *Life*, pp. 98–9, 100.
[31] *Ibid.*, p. 14.

his understanding matter suitable to the present state of the assembly before him.[32]

An entry in the *Christian and Brotherly Advices* had explained the ground of the ministry in similar terms:

... we exhort Friends to be very careful to observe the hours appointed for religious worship, & that when together they labour to feel their minds abstracted from visible objects into a true stillness & nothingness of self, wherein the teachings of the Holy Spirit are witnessed by humble and contrite souls: in such a waiting state you will have a true relish & savour of the ministry of those who are rightly concerned by the same spirit to labour in word and doctrine among you.

After establishing the principle of ministry Bownas offers more practical information. In his fifth chapter he advises those travelling in the ministry. The young minister has to accept that notwithstanding his sense of his calling a certificate from the monthly meeting is necessary and that there can be circumstances in which a monthly meeting may not consider him ready. We have seen already how the Yearly Meeting had to legislate for difficulties with travelling ministers and it is clear that the need for corporate discipline might seem at variance with the high claims for the minister's authority. Bownas goes on to provide general advice on the demeanour of the minister along the lines of the advice offered to Friends generally in the *Christian and Brotherly Advices* though he takes into account the greater public scrutiny to which ministers were exposed.

In his introduction to the *Life* Besse gave his view of Bownas's authority as a minister:

The motives inducing him to undertake the office of a *Preacher*, appear to have been perfectly consonant to the precepts of Holy Writ, and to the practice of Christ and his Apostles, *viz.*

1st. A *clear*, *cogent* and *convincing evidence* of a divine call, and heavenly impulse thereunto.

2dly. An indispensable sense of his duty necessarily obliging him to yield obedience to that call. And

3dly. The sweet returns of inward peace and divine consolations accompanying his obedience there, did greatly conduce to his confirmation and perseverance in the way of his duty.[33]

---

[32] Bownas, *Description*, pp. 58–9.
[33] Bownas, *Life*, pp. iii–iv.

In this brief account it has not been possible to do justice to either Bownas's *Life* or the *Description* which together are major sources for any study of the Quaker ministry in the eighteenth century. Nor has it been possible, though this has also to do with the nature of the evidence, to produce as clear an account of the history of the development of the other recognized channels of ministry (eldership, oversight, and clerkship) to be placed alongside the amply documented history of the preaching ministry. It is important to remember that in the Society of Friends the ministry took a variety of forms.[34]

University of Cambridge

[34] I am most grateful to Edward H. Milligan for his comments on a draft of this paper.

PIETY AMONG 'THE SOCIETY OF PEOPLE': THE WITNESS OF PRIMITIVE METHODIST LOCAL PREACHERS IN THE NORTH MIDLANDS, 1812–1862

by WAYNE J. JOHNSON

THE chief business of Primitive Methodism,' wrote the editor of the denominational magazine, 'is to cultivate personal religion, and to seek the salvation of souls.'[1] Although statements at the national level seldom made their way unhampered down to the lay-dominated local circuit, nevertheless, this was one directive which was generally pursued by a substantial number of its local preachers. Indeed, this search for personal holiness, as well as the seeking of it in others seems to have been the two main strands tying Primitive Methodism together. A frustrated Primitive Methodist, however, wrote, 'Have we shown to the poor and needy that the gospel . . . teaches us to regard their temporal as well as their spiritual wants?'[2] Just here lay the source of much of what has concerned historians interested in interpreting the nature and influence of Primitive Methodism. Indeed, when taken together, these two comments have, coincidentally, established the parameters of debate within which the study of Primitive Methodism has been conducted.

A popular religious movement, predominantly of the labouring poor, Primitive Methodism was borne out of the main Methodist body by those calling for greater democracy and revivalist initiative at the local level. It originated and flourished in the rather diverse and diffuse early nineteenth century North Midlands landscape; in the factory towns, isolated agricultural hamlets, and industrial villages of North Staffordshire, South Cheshire, and West Derbyshire. Active where Church of England provision was weak and where official Wesleyanism had failed to reach, Primitive Methodism established societies among the miners, potters, and farm labourers, in the cottages, barns, and later, chapels of the North Midlands.[3]

Although Primitive Methodism has been described both as 'the Society

---

[1] *Primitive Methodist Magazine* (1849), p. iii.
[2] *Ibid.* (1848), p. 2.
[3] For the origins of Primitive Methodism, see J. S. Werner, *The Primitive Methodist Connexion: Its Background and Early History* (Wisconsin, 1984).

of People' and as a religion of predominantly lay piety, existing histories have, ironically, tended to present the movement almost exclusively within an ecclesiastical and institutional framework; the effect has been to construct a shell around members, thus isolating them from their own landscape, culture, and community. When studies do focus on 'people', they tend to be accounts of the lives and views of the leadership or of the more famous itinerant preachers. Yet the great majority of Primitive Methodist evangelists were both local and unordained lay preachers. For example, in 1837, in the six circuits of the North Midlands (Tunstall, Ramsor, Burland, Macclesfield, Belper, and Winster), there were 358 local preachers to 21 'travelling' preachers.[4] Consequently, it was local preachers who carried out the bulk of the preaching. As William Garner, the notable preacher and chronicler of the 'primitive' in Primitive Methodism pointed out, that without local preachers:

> many preaching places would have to be entirely withdrawn, congregations would be dissatisfied, societies would dissolve, revenue would fall off, the itinerant ministry could not be supported, and the community would have to be contracted and reorganised.[5]

As such, local preachers must be viewed both as the indispensable staple of the movement, and as the real guardians of the true message of Primitive Methodism. Despite this, the testimony of the local preacher at the circuit level is seldom heard and is largely unknown to the historian.

Even when historians do mention local preachers, it tends to be for the wrong reasons. Thus, the most famous Primitive Methodist local preacher in Tunstall was Joseph Capper, whose fame has been earned entirely due to his political activity during the Chartist agitation. Taking him as being typical, labour historians have then studied the influence of Primitive Methodism on national and regional politics; that Primitive Methodism served in turn as a conservative force,[6] as an influence on the later organization, leadership, and oratory of the trade-union movement,[7] as the agent of a 'chiliasm of despair' following political agitation,[8] and more

---

[4] *P.M.M.* (1837), pp. 248, 254: a notable exception to the institutional histories is D. Valenze, *Prophetic Sons and Daughters: Female Preaching and Popular Religion in Industrial England* (Princeton, 1985).

[5] *P.M.M.* (1861), p. 34.

[6] E. Halevy, *History of the English People in the Nineteenth Century*, I (London, 1960), p. 458.

[7] R. F. Wearmouth, *Methodism and The Working Class Movements of England, 1800–50* (London, 1937), p. 167.

[8] E. P. Thompson, *The Making of the English Working Class* (Harmondsworth, 1968), p. 427.

recently, as a 'safety valve' allowing for the expenditure of energies of a more radical kind.[9] The overall effect, however, is to dim the essential Primitive Methodist spiritual message.

This interpretation can partly be explained by the fact that although the line between ministry and laity in Primitive Methodism was thin, nevertheless, a fundamental distinction can be made, between the spiritual territory of itinerant preachers who 'lived of the gospel' and the temporal sphere of those lay members of the circuit committees and quarter-day boards who 'lived of the world'. Local preachers, many of whom also served as class leaders, were not inclined to perceive of the world in the same way as the travelling preacher. Unsure of the true extent of the ecclesiastical authority of the itinerants, and yet elevated, at least spiritually, above the everyday-worldly 'business' of the committees, local preachers were caught between the two. It is the significance of this which has been misinterpreted by labour historians. They have mistakenly defined the polarity of 'religious–secular' as a political one. But politics was not so deeply ingrained in the spiritual fabric of Primitive Methodism, for Capper was the isolated exception rather than the rule.

Local preachers, as opposed to itinerants, resided permanently in their respective localities, and were therefore, rooted in the immediate, localized culture that surrounded them. Whereas travelling preachers were 'entirely released from secular vocations', local preachers were unpaid volunteers, 'who toiled through the week at the plough, the forge, the bench, in the mine, and at the market'; as miners, potters, and agricultural labourers.[10] They were, therefore, actual participants in the 'world'. As a result, the story of local preachers emerges from the more immediate context of the day-to-day, face-to-face relationships within the community, and the ensuing contact and conflict. Accordingly, for them, the more pertinent dichotomy was between 'Christian and non-Christian', 'sacred and profane'. Attempting to analyse, albeit tentatively, the more relevant questions of personal faith, morality and experience might go some of the way in unravelling that 'all-embracing fabric of meaning' that was the world of the Primitive Methodist labouring poor.[11]

The spiritual message of Primitive Methodism was its primary appeal, for not only did it offer a comprehensive, but simple view of the world, it

---

[9] A. D. Gilbert, 'Methodism, Dissent and political stability in early Industrial England', *JRH* 10 (1978–9): for a useful synthesis, see H. McLeod, *Religion and the Working Class in Nineteenth-Century Britain* (London, 1984).

[10] J. Ritson, *The Romance of Primitive Methodism* (London, 1910), p. 176.

[11] P. L. Berger, *The Social Reality of Religion* (London, 1967), p. 54.

also enhanced the movement's contemporary reputation as a lay body. With an in-built message of spiritual emancipation, Primitive Methodists believed that everyone was a sinner, but 'all' could be saved if they repented of their sins. 'Repentance of sins towards God' and 'faith in our Lord Jesus Christ' would ensure 'God's forgiveness of sins', 'purification from all unrighteousness' and 'everlasting life'.[12] When set in their own words, the belief of local preachers does not readily transfer into political terms. Labour historians should not impose secular motives on those whose lives were fired by religious beliefs. The dutiful local preachers did not directly seek political changes, indeed, they believed politics to be a diversion, 'to draw the mind from converting work'.[13] Moreover, they saw the political system as created by man, and, considering man's tendency towards evil, therefore corruptible. Indeed, the perceptions of the majority of local preachers extended much further than that. There has been a tendency by labour historians to forget that, first and foremost, Primitive Methodists believed in God. They also genuinely believed that if sinners died un-pardoned and unsanctified, it was impossible for them to escape the pun-ishment and eternal damnation of hell. And if the obvious pain and dislocation suffered by John Silvester of Checkley, Cheshire (b. 1774), who as part of a large, poor family, was forced to leave home as a child to procure his own maintenance on a farm, was real, then the fear of hell was no less palpable.[14] Deeply impressed with those solemn realities, most local preachers, like Job Shenton of Tunstall (b. 1810), possessed a burning zeal for the conversion of sinners to God. It became their sole concern in life to preach the gospel of salvation to as many sinners as possible, to seek the spiritual regeneration of the individual, with the accompanying levels of personal morality. A local preacher for thirty years, Shenton, who may serve as a more vocal and more typical representative of a Tunstall evangel-ist than Capper, felt 'the latent and pent-up feelings of his soul...rose, and were like "fire in his bones"; he could not but exhort and warn'.[15] It was said of John Brown of Newcastle-under-Lyme (b. 1810), a local preacher for twenty-two years, that when he preached, 'all the faculties of his mind and energies of his body seemed called into action'. Under his addresses, 'none were drowsy', and 'many were the shouts of exulting joy, as he expatiated on the love of God to a fallen world'.[16]

[12] *P.M.M.* (1861), p. 104.
[13] *Ibid.* (1834), p. 436.
[14] *Ibid.* (1869), p. 96.
[15] *Ibid.* (1864), p. 675.
[16] *Ibid.* (1850), p. 75.

One prevailing myth is the view that the 'morals and manners' of all those labouring people who became Primitive Methodists 'were of course brutal and vicious', that they were larger-than-life reprobates prior to their conversion, to be plucked from the gaping jaws of hell.[17] Whilst many were 'vile sinners', an equal number were, from their youth, trained up in the principles of religion, were 'steady, moral and peaceable in their conduct' and were 'free from those gross immoralities into which so many people unhappily fell'.[18] Someone like Ephraim Sadler of Burland (b. 1773) who, blessed with pious parents became subject to powerful and serious spiritual impressions at an early age, impressions which 'grew with his growth and strengthened with his strength'.[19] These were people who developed early a general appetite for theological understanding, who were aware of the necessary theological prerequisites and commitments, and for whom conversion was to become something like an inevitable step in a process well begun. This was true even though the constraints of a limited education reduced their capacity for academic theological understanding. But then these Primitive Methodists were educated in the rough college of life. Even though some like Michael Tunnicliff of Tunstall (b. 1818) 'sat up nights, praying, studying and reading', before the next day's address, sermons ultimately owed more to the local preacher's 'intimate knowledge of human nature, and to the close acquaintance with the daily life of the common people, derived from life-long association with them'.[20] Besides which, because they were from the same background as their 'uncultivated hearers ... the plain, rustic, but sensible local preacher was as intelligible as ... the most refined pulpit orator'.[21]

'Society', wrote the Baptist preacher, Robert Hall, 'is the atmosphere of souls, and we necessarily imbibe from it something which is either infectious or salubrious.'[22] There is every reason to believe that Primitive Methodist local preachers, who accommodated their belief in the existence of a supernatural world to a framework of popular revivalism, sincerely perceived the life in the world as a constant spiritual battle between God and Satan, ably encapsulated in the hymn;

> Apollyon's armies we must fight,
> And put the troops of hell to flight,

---

[17] S. Smiles, *Josiah Wedgwood* (London, 1894), p. 12.
[18] *P.M.M.* (1861), p. 266.
[19] *Ibid.* (1853), p. 330.
[20] *Ibid.* (1860), p. 266; Ritson, p. 187.
[21] *P.M.M.* (1861), p. 34.
[22] *Ibid.* (1849), p. 240.

To gain that heav'nly land;
Come on ye soldiers in the rear,
Be stout and bold, and never fear,
Come join the conqu'ring band.[23]

This spiritual war was with 'the ale-house and the denizens of Satan's strongholds', which the Primitive Methodists believed to be energized by evil spirits.[24] There is no space here to deal with the popular culture of the day, suffice to say local preachers perceived the role of such evil and sinful amusements as bull and bear-baiting, cock-fighting, dog-fighting, gambling, boxing, and dancing, as leading to the immediate physical, moral, and above all spiritual degeneration of its participants.[25] People were not (at this stage) interested in the ultimate destiny of their souls, or in the future of their 'class', whatever that might mean; theirs was a 'now' world of hard work and equally hard and cruel recreation.

The nature of this challenge was not entirely new. The traditional culture had been consistently opposed and criticized by seventeenth-century Puritans, who more politely conceived of the 'world' as 'out there'. The censure was repeated by eighteenth-century Methodists, but the confrontation entered its most intense phase with early nineteenth-century Primitive Methodism. Moreover, where the Primitive Methodist challenge was new was in the fact that the vile 'practices of the world' and the ensuing conflict occurred within the same societal context.

The nature and extent of this cultural conflict was the struggle for allegiance in which the publican and the local preacher, both inhabitants of the same community, both evangelistic, symbolized the two opposing forces. The publican was the villain, Apollyon, the 'demon of spiritual doubt' and the profit-minded sponsor of Satan, all rolled into one.[26] The local preacher, for his part, was the carrier of the armour of God. Whilst the former provided for the present excesses of the labouring poor, the local preacher spoke of things pertaining to the Kingdom of God. And the setting of the conflict was the open space between their divergent 'domains' of chapel and public-house.

One episode may serve as an example. It is a scene described by a

[23] G. Herod, *Biographical Sketches of Some of those Preachers Whose Labours Contributed to the Origination and Early Extension of the Primitive Methodist Church* (London, 1855), Hymn 20; for Primitive Methodism and popular religion see W. R. Ward, 'The Religion of the People and the Problem of Control, 1790–1830', *SCH* 8.

[24] Thompson, pp. 451–2.

[25] J. G. Rule, *The Labouring Classes in Early Industrial England, 1750–1850* (London, 1986), p. 220.

[26] John Bunyan, *Pilgrim's Progress* (Harmondsworth, 1965), pp. 90–4.

preacher in the Macclesfield circuit. The report gives a vivid account of the 'work of God' in the cotton village of Bollington, three miles north of Macclesfield, in Cheshire. As a result of the 'unremitting efforts of the itinerant and local preachers and members', the whole village 'appeared more or less affected . . . and many sinners were inquiring what they must do to be saved?' Included among them were 'a host of long continued and confirmed drunkards'. The revival had developed to such a level that publicans 'felt concerned for their interest and wondered what could have caused many of their best customers too have forsaken them'. The preacher then went on to describe one particular incident:

> One day, when one of the newly converted drunkards was passing a public house, in which he had spent many pounds and had been an occasional assistant at public festivals, several of his old companions invited him to turn in, and drink with them in token of old friend-ship: but he promptly refused. They then asked him to sing them a song, (for he had been one of their chief singers), and immediately he sung the words,
>
> > My old companions, fare you well,
> > I will not go with you to hell,
> > I mean with Jesus Christ to dwell,
> > Will you go? Will you go?

That encounter reveals much about the new convert's intense perception of the serious life to which he was devoting himself and the cynical one from which he was withdrawing. It reveals the convert's rejection not only of the transient joys of the traditional culture, but also an acceptance of the voluntary separation from his old boon companions, who tied him to the old life. It also epitomizes, in 'Will you go?' the overriding evangelism of the Primitive Methodists. But it also symbolizes, above all, two halves of the same community perpetually opposed.[27]

The Primitive Methodist message, however powerful, needed a frame-work, a setting. The established view is that Primitive Methodism waged war against the existing popular culture, with the intention of providing an alternative, 'to remodel traditional patterns of recreation'.[28] The most famous and often-quoted means was the camp meeting, the staple of early Primitive Methodism, such as the one in Penkhull, on Sunday 3 August

[27] *P.M.M.* (1845), p. 219; (1846), p. 222.
[28] B. Harrison, 'Religion and Recreation in Nineteenth-Century England', *P & P* 38 (1967), p. 99.

1845, held 'with a design to counteract the evil tendencies of the village wake'; a carnival in which all the 'vulgar amusements' were concentrated.[29] What is not stressed, however, is the significance of the 'prayer meeting' for which there was no counterpart in the traditional culture. Indeed, the prayer meeting displayed a depth of both individual spirituality and communal feeling which would have received contempt, ridicule, and scorn from the 'formal' and ignorant traditional culture.

More popular than both camp meetings and prayer meetings, however, was the lovefeast, where even the name aroused hostility. From an entry in a journal, there is a description of an attempted disruption of a stormy lovefeast, held at Hanley on Sunday, 26 July 1829. Often conducted by local preachers, indeed dominated by lay participation, lovefeasts consisted of exhorting, praying, and singing. The effect of speaking at the Hanley lovefeast was such that 'several were so overpowered with the love of God that their bodily powers were affected much ... souls were crying for mercy that it was no longer possible for the speakers to be heard'. There being 'more noise than the people of Hanley were accustomed to, hundreds collected at the door, using violent means to enter, while several stones were thrown through the windows'. After the meeting broke up, the congregation was followed through the street by the 'mob', who 'shouted at them, pulled at their clothes and stoned them'. What was displayed by this pronounced 'persecution' was a brutal reaction to the religious counter-culture, a response behind which lay incomprehension, unease, ignorance, and probably fear. Yet for the Primitive Methodists, the lovefeast provided 'a mighty outpouring of the Spirit'.[30]

As with the wakes and public-houses for their respective constituency, so too camp and prayer meetings and love-feasts set the boundaries, outside the home (which could be controlled) and the work-place (which could not), where members could circulate: thus serving as a cohesive bond. They also provided the settings within which the Primitive Methodist 'message' could be conveyed, and the more sober truths of grace be publicized, by local preachers. These occasions and activities were all part of a rich and vibrant chapel life in which the local preachers, class leaders, and committees were charged with attempting to combat and replace the corrupt temptations of the traditional way of life, symbolized

---

[29] *P.M.M.* (1846), p. 99; Rule, p. 215.
[30] *P.M.M.* (1830), p. 185; on persecution see J. Walsh, 'Methodism and the Mob in the Eighteenth Century', *SCH* 8.

by excess, violence, and contest, for patterns of strict piety and personal morality concomitant to a christian life.

Though the ideologies of the cultural and spiritual antagonists were clearly defined, many exhorters and hearers drifted into Primitive Methodism, and just as easily slipped back out. Accordingly, the focus here is both on those local preachers and members who chose to make a commitment for life with Primitive Methodism, and those whose high ideals were shipwrecked on the rocks of intemperance and sloth. Pages of the *Primitive Methodist Magazine*, however, only provide examples of the 'perseverance of the saints'. One will suffice. That of Elijah Colclough of Talk-o'-th'-Hill (b. 1796), a neighbourhood of 'darkness, ignorance and vice, for religious means were scanty and religious influences seldom experienced'. Unchecked by parental restraint, Elijah took a prominent part in the leading vices of his day. His 'unbridled propensities and passions had full sway and he grew up in sin, becoming addicted to drunkenness'. A man of strong constitution, he had a stout and robust frame, and an indomitable spirit, and he obtained a 'rank of importance' in that 'unholy and brutal pursuit', boxing. Elijah continued 'in his course of wickedness' until 1813. Then, like many of his contemporaries, he became convinced of his sin; realizing that the course he was pursuing was offering him no solid joy, was dishonourable to himself, and insulting to God. He found that the gospel as preached by Primitive Methodist local preachers 'came unto him not in word only, but in power'. As a result, he was led, through divine grace, to 'a more ennobling enterprise'.[31]

Was it a complete success? Whilst the *Magazine* paraded the triumph of faith, circuit records are most illuminating as they reveal the 'self-imposition' of a system of strict discipline and social control (rather than one imposed from above by social superiors). Of all the occasions for expulsion or censure, drunkenness appears to have been the most frequent. Adultery and indebtedness were other persistent problems. In the Congleton quarter-day commitee meeting of 15 September 1851, it was resolved that the local preacher 'brother Charles Foster (of Canal Street) be put off the plan and out of the society for lying, drunkenness and getting into debt'. In the committee's attempts to 'shut out' the corrupt morality of the time, such a catalogue of offences could not have received any less. However, just as it is a mistake to assume that all Primitive Methodists were, prior to their conversion, vile reprobates, it is equally fallacious to expect all converts to have led a blameless life after

---

[31] *P.M.M.* (1859), p. 9.

their conversion. Primitive Methodist local preachers were not stained-glass window saints, but men.[32]

The one recurring problem which the lay committees sought vigorously to control within their own circuits was the lack of discipline, and in particular, the neglecting of appointments by local preachers. The importance of their task was set down as early as 1825, in an 'Address to Local Preachers' on a Belper circuit preachers' plan. It stated:

> Remember, Brethren, it is upon your faithfulness, zeal, and united efforts that the prosperity of God's cause in this circuit, in a very great measure depends. If you neglect your appointments, you miss your reward, injure your souls, grieve your brethren, stab the cause of God, expose the members to reproach, and strengthen the hands of the enemy.[33]

This call was echoed right through to 1846: 'You are accountable, not only to . . . your circuit, but to Him for the performance or nonperformance of your duty.'[34] Circuit records are once again most enlightening. Of the noted minutes of the Nantwich circuit quarterly meetings for the period 1838–45, one quarter of the minutes were devoted to censuring local preachers for the neglecting of appointments. The usual punishment for failure to keep an appointment was the 'sinking of a figure' in the league-table of the preaching plan. The remainder of the minutes were devoted to a highly successful campaign of organization, such as the setting up of camp meetings, which reflected the growing view that revivalism, rather than being inspired by God, could now be humanly stage-managed.[35]

Whatever one may say, and many historians have said it, that in its inculcation of a sense of self-discipline and duty, Primitive Methodism unintentionally imposed habits of time-keeping concomitant to factory production, accompanied by the withering of traditional patterns of behaviour, the above evidence does not wholly support this hypothesis. This can partly be explained by the fact that even though the distinction in Primitive Methodism between itinerant and local preachers was sometimes blurred, preaching plans however, reveal that itinerant preachers were frequently given both the honour of administering the sacraments as

---

[32] Cheshire Record Office, Quarterly Meeting Minute Book, Congleton Circuit, 1844–56, E.M.C. 5/9/1.

[33] *P.M.M.* (1825), p. 270.

[34] *Ibid.* (1846), p. 398.

[35] C.R.O., Quarterly Meeting Minute Book, Nantwich Circuit, 1838–45, E.M.C. 2/11/1.

well as preaching to the more successful congregations. Not only did local preachers do formidably more preaching on Sundays, they were often instructed to preach invariably on week-nights to the smaller and often more remote congregations.[36] James Clifton of Englesea Brook (b. 1780) a local preacher for fifty-two years, was indefatigable in his labours, often walking up to twenty-four miles on the sabbath to preach three times. He would then set off for home late in the evening, after a prayer meeting, taking rests along the way. Often reaching his cottage after sunrise on the Monday morning, Clifton would then change his clothes, and go to his employment. Not only did this style of life eventually alienate some local preachers, but many regarded themselves as being increasingly 'taken for granted' by the committees. It was also, in effect, part of the consequence of the 'institution' strangling lay initiative. Maybe this was reflected in the withering of the earlier missionary zeal by many local preachers, rather than the backsliding into the slothful ways of the old life.[37]

The more dutiful local preachers, however, could expect, as a final testimony, and a 'precious heirloom to posterity', an obituary in the denominational magazine: the purpose being to 'stimulate every reader to be prepared for the final summons'.[38] In testimony to one Primitive Methodist, the *Magazine* stated, 'once more has the grave closed over the mortal remains of a servant of God, whose glorified spirit is now before the throne, exulting in its happy exemption from all the trials which are our lot in this vale of tears'.[39] Primitive Methodism has been described by one historian as providing only 'consolation' to its audience, in preparing them for the next world, and by another to have reflected only the 'aspirations' of its members.[40] There is every reason to suggest that it provided both, and often to the same individual. Primitive Methodism possessed a genius for myriad ambiguity. As an indigenous religious movement of the labouring poor with local preachers in the vanguard, Primitive Methodism grasped, as few religious groups seldom did, the tragic nature of life for its members. Whilst on the one hand it represented a protest against the sin and excess of the 'half-pagan popular culture' of the labouring poor, which had dominated the cultural landscape of the North Midlands,

[36] C.R.O., Sandbach circuit plan, July–October 1857, Burland circuit plan, April–July 1845; Tunstall circuit plan, April–July 1846.
[37] *P.M.M.* (1867), p. 28.
[38] *Ibid.* (1861), p. i.
[39] *Ibid.*, p. 66.
[40] Thompson, pp. 417–19; A. D. Gilbert, *Religion and Society in Industrial England, 1740–1914* (London, 1976), p. 83.

it was also an appeal to a common cultural understanding of the basic vicissitudes of life. *Primitive Methodist Magazine* obituaries reveal a touching catalogue of the premature deaths of local preachers by disease and industrial accident: events all too frequent in a world of factory production and agricultural capitalism. But this very tragedy was a common bond which local preachers shared with their 'uncultivated hearers' whom they lived among. Because he was a participant in the despair and suffering as well as the aspirations and hopes of the families, fellow workers, and neighbours, the local preacher, in coming to terms with his own existence, was in the best position to interpret for his contemporaries (and for the benefit of the historian), the harsh realities of their world, and, as a response, they were able to give purpose and direction. Out of this suffering came a vision, an aggressive and ultimately optimistic sense of destiny, blossoming from confident faith in Providence, in which every life, no matter how ordinary, had a place in God's ultimate plan for the destiny of mankind. In effect, Primitive Methodist local preachers provided for their members an eschatology of faith: their quest for holiness, both in themselves and in their audience, gave them self-respect in the face of the agonies of their own 'now' world, since their salvationism offered them an all-embracing vision of the world to come. Contrary to the more secular interpretations which, in effect, have presented Primitive Methodism as an intermediary stage on the path towards social idealism, this faith in God was the real 'subjective world view' of Primitive Methodist local preachers; a system of belief more pertinent to the early nineteenth-century industrializing North Midlands.[41]

A Primitive Methodist for thirty-three years, Ephraim Sadler spent the last sixteen years of his life in 'a continued scene of affliction'. Towards the end, when reflecting on all that had gone before, and thinking of the better world that was to come (and, being imbued with the Primitive Methodist culture), he felt he could not express himself better than to quote a hymn:

> Jesus, my all to heaven is gone,
> He whom I fix'd my hopes upon,
> His track I see, and I'll pursue,
> The narrow way, till him I view.[42]

---

[41] On subjective world view see, P. L. Berger, *The Social Reality*.
[42] *P.M.M.* (1853), p. 330.

His faith had provided Sadler with both the dignity to live with that which he could neither understand nor change, and the firm assurance that his suffering was something which he would one day rise above.

In 1861, as the Connexion approached its jubilee, the occasion provoked a time of celebration and foreboding. Celebration in the knowledge that thousands had been diverted away from the dominant culture (there were 6,616 Primitive Methodist members in the North Midlands by 1862 in contrast to 200 in 1812),[43] as an alternative to which, members could seek sanctuary, albeit for the fleeting present, in a more warm community of mutual responsibility, devoted to strict models of personal moral conduct, values, and beliefs: the mandate for which came from the anticipation of the perfect world beyond. Yet there was foreboding in the fact that so much more remained to be done. Here lay the problem: that of perpetuating the energies of revivalism beyond one generation. And in summing up the role and past achievements of the 'heroic' local preachers in all of this, and in looking beyond the transient present to an inherited destiny, the editors of the *Magazine* profoundly stated what Primitive Methodism had really been about: 'they were friends and sojourners . . . through time towards an incomprehensible eternity'.[44]

A poem by Joseph Hutchinson of Ramsor circuit, entitled 'Lines on the death of a local preacher', sums up aptly much of what has been discussed, and must serve as a conclusion. It stands alone as a product of the 'world' of Primitive Methodism, and therefore needs no comment.

> Noble warrior, hard thou toil'd'st
> In the vineyard of thy Lord;
> All thy foes thou nobly fac'd'st
> With the spirit's two-edg'd sword.
>
> Now, the victory's achiev'd,
> Accomplish'd now thy warfare is;
> Thro' blood divine thou hast receiv'd
> Thy rich and fair inheritance.
>
> In this wilderness thou suffer'd,
> For thy Lord and Master's sake;
> But the crown of glory offer'd,
> Amends doth for thy suff'ring make.

[43] *Minutary Records: Being Rules, Regulations, and Reports, Made and Published by the Primitive Methodists*, vols 1–5.
[44] *P.M.M.* (1861), p. iii.

All thy foes are truly vanquish'd,
All thy sufferings now are o'er;
Gainer thou—for sin relinquish'd,
Heaven is thine for evermore.

Jordan's waves did but befriend thee,
Tho' they lash'd the peaceful shore;
The billows foam'd, but 'twas to land thee
Where death is felt and fear'd no more.

Landed safe in heaven's harbour,
Is the soul, that better part;
The body too, now rests from labour,
A stranger now to every smart.

We awhile are left hard toiling,
Yet again we hope to meet,
Where free from every foe's annoying,
In heaven above we shall thee greet.[45]

University of Keele

[45] *P.M.M.* (1835), p. 440.

MINISTERING TO THE MINISTERS:
THE DISCIPLINE OF RECALCITRANT CLERGY IN THE DIOCESE OF LINCOLN
1830–1845

by FRANCES KNIGHT

B Y 1830, the effectiveness of the Church of England's ministry was believed to have become seriously compromised, because it still possessed no adequate means for disciplining its clergy. It had long been recognized that the Church's structure, and in particular the strength of the parson's freehold, made it impossible for it to exercise the same sort of authority over its ministers as the dissenting bodies, or even the Church of Scotland. The view that the inadequacy of disciplinary measures was detrimental to the standing of the Established Church was in fact shared both by those hostile to and those supportive of it. On the one hand, John Wade's *Extraordinary Black Book*, published in 1831 and intended as an indictment of corruption, rapacity, and jobbery within the Establishment, made the exposure of abuses in Church discipline one of its principal objectives.[1] Not unnaturally, loyal churchmen also expressed considerable anxiety at the spectacle of bishops almost powerless in the face of clerical malefactors within their dioceses. Throughout the 1830s, the correspondence of clergy and the speeches of senior Anglicans in Parliament reflect an urgent desire that appropriate measures be swiftly introduced in order to combat cases of clerical irregularity.

It was not however until 1840 that the Church Discipline Act finally made its way on to the Statute Book. The measure had been conceived as far back as 1832, in the Report of the Royal Commission on Ecclesiastical Courts. Several abortive attempts were made at passing a Bill between 1836–9, and their failure resulted in its being entirely redrafted. The earlier Bills owed their unpopularity to the emphasis which they placed on the Court of Arches and the Court of Chancery as having exclusive jurisdiction in clergy discipline cases. Although this would have resulted in a simplification of an extremely archaic and complex judicature, it encountered opposition in both Houses. Bishop Henry Phillpotts of Exeter, in particular, argued that it represented a tremendous erosion of

---

[1] John Wade, *Extraordinary Black Book* (London, 1831), p. 8.

the rights of individual bishops within their dioceses,[2] and for once it was difficult to disagree with him. The text of the 1840 Bill, in which even Phillpotts described himself as able 'entirely and heartily to concur',[3] provided for the establishment of a radically different framework for the correction of wayward clergymen. The diocesan bishop, rather than the archbishops' courts, was confirmed as the source of jurisdiction, and provision was made for the investigation of alleged offenders within their own locality.[4] It can be argued that this decision in favour of the administration of discipline by relatively simple procedures conducted on the spot made an invaluable, if little recognized, contribution to the Church of England's ministry to its own ministers.

The 1840 Church Discipline Act was the first legislative measure to be devoted to the matter of clergy discipline since the time of Henry VII. Despite its undoubted limitations, it has provided the underpinning for all subsequent related measures.[5] Yet it has attracted little attention from scholars.[6] The purpose of this paper is therefore to demonstrate, by use of examples drawn from the diocese of Lincoln, the methods adopted by its bishop, John Kaye,[7] for disciplining recalcitrant clergy in the years immediately before and the years immediately after the passing of the Act.

For this purpose, 'recalcitrant' is defined as describing those clerics whose offences took one of two forms. The first category encountered episcopal censure because of their failure to conform with the theological and ministerial standards of traditional high church orthodoxy—a creed which was typified, incidentally, by Bishop Kaye and his archdeacons.[8] Their offences might take the form of attendance at dissenters' meetings,

---

[2] Hansard's *Parliamentary Debates*: Third Series Vol. 47 cols 1029–30; 1314–30.

[3] Hansard's *Parliamentary Debates*: Third Series Vol. 55 col. 74.

[4] 3 & 4 Vict. c. 86, *An Act for Better Enforcing Church Discipline*, 7 August 1840.

[5] Report of the Commission on Ec lesiastical Courts: *The Ecclesiastical Courts: Principles of Reconstruction* (London, 1954), p. 28.

[6] It is only mentioned in passing by G. F. A. Best in *Temporal Pillars* (Cambridge, 1964), p. 399.

[7] John Kaye, 1783–1853. The son of a Hammersmith linen draper, he entered Christ's College Cambridge in 1800 and remained there until 1830, by which time he was Master, and had occupied other important posts in the university. Kaye's assiduity and ability attracted favourable notice from Lord Liverpool, who raised him to the episcopate—first Bristol (1820) and then Lincoln (1827). Kaye remained at Lincoln until his death. When he arrived in the diocese, it was still the largest in the country—stretching from Grimsby to Eton—but during his episcopate it was transformed into a smaller, more manageable unit. The diocese of Lincoln during John Kaye's episcopate is the subject of the doctoral research upon which I am currently engaged.

[8] For an invaluable discussion of this type of pre-Tractarian high church orthodoxy see Peter B. Nockles, 'Continuity and Change in Anglican High Churchmanship in Britain 1792–1850' (unpublished Oxford D.Phil. thesis, 1982).

the adoption of itinerant styles of ministry, or of diverse departures from the rubrics of the Book of Common Prayer. The second type of offender had engaged in a mode of life deemed unsuitable for a clergyman. For example habitual drunkenness, sexual misdemeanours, or debt, behaviour which hardly surprisingly was often accompanied by a gross neglect of duty. This paper will not, therefore, be concerned with the twin evils of pluralism and non-residence; the single major blot upon the clergy's ministerial effectiveness at this time which was dealt with by separate legislation,[9] and is too large a question to be considered here.

Throughout the period under discussion it was not of course resort to the law, but to the stern verbal or written rebuke which remained the chief weapon in the episcopal armoury. Cheap to administer and relatively free from constraining legal ramifications, it could prove singularly effective. Often the simple fact of knowing that his conduct had been noted and disapproved was all that was necessary to put an erring clerk back upon a safer course. This was however less likely to be true when a man's offences were theological rather than moral, and when principle, rather than passion was at stake. John Missing of Fawley in Buckinghamshire, whom Kaye refused to licence to a curacy on the grounds that, in addition to 'mutilating the ritual', he had expounded Bunyan's *Pilgrim's Progress*, had baptized in the chancel and not at the font, and prevented the Church catechism being taught at the Sunday school, complained of victimization. 'I might have been a fox hunter or a gambler—I might have frequented the theatre or the race course and no offence would have been taken.'[10] These protests, however, failed to elicit a sympathetic response from the bishop, who always remained hostile to departures from the Book of Common Prayer, whatever their motivation.

A characteristic of misdemeanours which originated in conscience was that the miscreant himself was often willing to disclose his difficulties to the bishop, and thus invite him to give judgement upon them. In 1831, William Start of Claybrooke in Leicestershire wrote to Kaye concerning the doubts which made it impossible for him to give his unfeigned assent to the Prayer Book. He could not bring himself to use the absolution in the service of visitation for the sick, or read the burial service over persons of bad character. He could not baptize according to the prescribed form, or read the prayer for Parliament. Because he felt unable to conduct burials, perform baptisms, or read prayers whilst Parliament was sitting, his

---

[9] Of greatest significance being the Plurality Act 1838.
[10] Lincolnshire Archives Office (LAO) Cor B5/19/2 & 3 Missing to Kaye, 20 April 1837.

ministry had become more or less confined to preaching occasionally for others. 'It has occurred to me however that if you knew my scruples you might not approve of my occupying any of your pulpits.'[11] Kaye's reply reveals an appreciation of the candour of Start's communication. But his inability to sign a declaration promising to conform to the liturgy of the Church of England made it illegal for him to preach in the diocese.[12]

Another evangelical, C. W. Eyre, rector of Carlton in Nottingham-shire, was equally candid with the bishop. He had been invited to take the chair at a meeting of the Wesleyan Missionary Society at Stokenham near Retford. At first he had thought it appropriate to decline, on the basis that to do otherwise might be contrary to the order and discipline of the Church. But he began to doubt if he was in fact assisting the Church 'In thus refusing the right hand of fellowship publically held out by an influ-ential and I trust sincere body of Christians, from whom I must ever feel that the Church was more estranged, than they from the Church.'[13] Kaye responded that although he disapproved strongly of a clergyman presid-ing at a meeting of a dissenting society, to do so was not an offence against church discipline. Under no circumstances, however, was Eyre to join in worship with the Wesleyans, for this would undoubtedly constitute a serious breach.[14] Eyre meekly promised to obey the bishop's strictures—although to have done so must surely have placed considerable difficulties in the way of his chairmanship of the Missionary Society.

Tractarian sympathizers, and converts to Rome, were as likely to attract unfavourable notice from the bishop as were fervent evangelicals. The most notorious conversion in the diocese of Lincoln during the period under review was that of Bernard Smith of Leadenham.[15] Richard Waldo Sibthorp, despite being a native of Lincolnshire and spending much of his ministry there, was in fact serving in Ryde, Isle of Wight, at the time of his secession in 1841.[16] In Smith's case, as in those of more obscure clergy, Kaye was simply presented with a *fait accompli*, and could

---

[11] LAO, Cor B5/5/5/1 Start to Kaye, 28 June 1831.

[12] LAO, Cor B5/5/5/1 Kaye to Start, 30 June 1831.

[13] LAO, Cor B5/8/22 Eyre to Kaye, ? May 1841.

[14] LAO, Cor B5/8/22 Kaye to Eyre, 28 June 1841.

[15] Bernard Smith, 1815–1903. He seceded in 1842, attracting notoriety because of rumours that he had been advised by Newman to keep his conversion secret and retain his living.

[16] Richard Waldo Sibthorp, 1792–1879. A member of a distinguished Lincolnshire family, he appeared to find little peace within either the Anglican or the Roman Communion. Kaye readmitted Sibthorp to Anglican orders in 1847, but he seceded again in 1865. Both Smith and Sibthorp are treated, if somewhat hagiographically, by R. D. Middleton, *Magdalen Studies* (London, 1936), pp. 195–267.

do little more than register his sorrow at what had taken place. When W. G. Penny resigned from the perpetual curacies of Ashendon and Dorton in Buckinghamshire in 1844, Kaye expressed his deep regret at the delusion under which he believed Penny to have acted, 'In exchanging a pure for a less pure branch of the Catholic Church.'[17] But he respected Penny's openness in making known his change of opinion. Kaye consistently held to the view that those who found the Anglican position untenable should depart swiftly from its communion. In reality, the number of men in the Lincoln diocese who had come under the influence of the Oxford Movement by 1845 appears to have been extremely small. Amongst those that did, Kaye placed a strict emphasis upon the maintenance of outward conformity. The effect of this policy appears now almost comic, as archdeacons and increasingly rural deans ordered hapless incumbents to trim off lace, remove lights, and in one case cover a stone altar with wood and place it on a frame—thus making it into an honest table.[18]

It was becoming increasingly apparent that although the bishop, his archdeacons, and the rural deans could offer rebuke, minor departures from the rubrics were very much a matter safer left to individual conscience. At least one of the archdeacons, Charles Goddard of Lincoln, would certainly have disapproved if the bishop had attempted to offer anything more than a reprimand. As he put it in a Charge to his clergy: 'The bishop indeed may, even as now circumstanced, admonish, censure, arbitrate, as in the early church ... but if he should proceed further he would find himself involved in difficulties practically insurmountable.'[19] Neither was excommunication, theoretically the final spiritual sanction available to the bishop, regarded by Goddard as an appropriate option. In an Established Church coextensive with the country, containing many lax members and surrounded by dissent, he concluded that excommunication would be largely devoid of the force which it would have possessed amongst the first Christians. Goddard was no doubt wise in maintaining this pragmatic approach. At least one of his colleagues would have disagreed with him, however. In 1841, George Wilkins, archdeacon of Nottingham, wrote to Kaye begging him and his episcopal brethren to adopt a more public stance in checking what he described as the 'furious

---

[17] LAO, Cor B5/3/3/5 Kaye to Penny, 7 November 1844.
[18] LAO, Cor B5/3/20/3 Archdeacon Hill to Kaye, 10 September 1845 with respect to Medmenham church.
[19] Charles Goddard, *A Charge Delivered to the Clergy of the Archdeaconry of Lincoln* (London, 1839).

career of the sectarian clergy'. Wilkins particularly objected to the practice prevalent among a handful of Nottinghamshire clergy like C. W. Eyre of engaging in itinerant preaching and taking an active part in Wesleyan missionary societies. He blamed an influx of Church Pastoral Aid curates for the behaviour, and lamented that it made 'episcopacy only a form, and church discipline of no force'. The bishops, he argued, must compel their clergy to take the via media—or to depart.[20]

If archdeacons differed about the extent to which individual conscience should be permitted to govern the religious behaviour of the clergy, they and most of the lower clergy too, were unanimous in concluding that a far greater threat was posed to the Church by the wayward and notorious men within her ranks. Lord Sidney Godolphin Osborne, rector of Stoke Poges, expressed the mood well in 1841. 'Puseyism and Noetism are bad enough, but neither do in my opinion the mischief that the ill conduct of the clergy do when that conduct is allowed to pass unnoticed.'[21] Yet as with those who offended for conscience's sake, before the passing of the 1840 Act resort to written or verbal censure was in practical terms virtually the sole disciplinary strategy at the bishop's disposal. Although theoretically it would have been possible for Kaye to bring legal proceedings, experience taught him that the expenses entailed therein would be too great to bear. It must be remembered that prelates at this date were expected to meet all professional expenses from their stipend, making involvement in protracted and costly legal disputes a constant source of anxiety for bishops and archdeacons alike.[22] Thus in 1833, when serious charges were brought against John Bewicke, rector of Hallaton and vicar of Loddington in Leicestershire, Kaye was forced to admit that although deeply grieved by Bewicke's behaviour, he possessed no powers of suspension. In order for this to be effected, he explained, it would be necessary to institute a suit in the Ecclesiastical Court. A similar suit had cost him and his predecessor (George Pelham) £1500, an expense which he could not afford to incur a second time. The only alternative would be for the churchwardens to institute a suit, but he perceived that the chances of persuading the parish to meet an expense of this nature were extremely remote.[23]

The breaches of discipline with which Bewicke was charged were both

[20] LAO, Cor B5/8/19 Wilkins to Kaye, 29 June 1841.
[21] LAO, Cor B5/3/12/4 Godolphin Osborne to Kaye, 8 April 1841.
[22] LAO, Cor B5/19/2 & 3 Archdeacon Hill to Kaye, n.d.
[23] LAO, Cor B5/5/1/2 Kaye to Thomas Vowe, 7 January, 28 February 1833.

rubrical and moral. He was alleged never to wear black gown or bands, and despite excellent health never to kneel and seldom to preach. Furthermore, he·had formed a connection with a Mrs Hickman, who had been observed climbing into his bedroom window by means of a ladder. As a result of his preoccupation with her, he had neglected to do duty on a Sunday and on Ash Wednesday, and in a parish of eight hundred only seven or eight attended the church.[24] As Bewicke appeared impervious to the bishop's admonishment, and was not disposed to resign his living, virtually the only strategy left to Kaye was to demand that he appoint a curate for Hallaton, and relinquish the performance of any duty there himself. A curate was already employed in his other parish of Loddington, and the bishop demanded that his stipend be raised in accordance with the law.[25] Bewicke cooperated, and although he retained his incumbencies until his death in 1843, he does not appear to have performed any spiritual functions after Kaye's intervention. In the years before 1840, this pattern of persuading the miscreant to appoint a curate and withdraw from residence is well attested. Similar strategies were adopted by the bishop on the advice of his archdeacons in the cases of the rector of Beauchampton, Buckinghamshire, who assaulted a tithe payer in 1833[26] and the vicar of Selstone, Nottinghamshire, who in 1839 was reported to have been in a constant state of intoxication for the previous eight months.[27]

What difference, then, did the passing of the Clergy Discipline Act make to the bishop's exercise of his powers? The case of John Willis, rector of Haddenham with Cuddington in Buckinghamshire, does throw some light on the question. When Willis' misdemeanours first became apparent, in the mid 1830s, a curate was appointed by the bishop to perform his duties in the manner described above.[28] But when he offended again in 1843, the provisions of the new legislation were utilized to their fullest extent. A commission of enquiry, consisting of two rural deans and two well respected local incumbents, was granted powers to examine upon oath Willis, his accusers, and the witnesses. Initially, an attempt was made to enhance the atmosphere of legal gravity by holding the proceedings in the Magistrate's Chamber at Aylesbury, but this was

---

[24] LAO, Cor B5/5/1/2 Vowe to Kaye, 4 January, 25 February 1833; Archdeacon T. K. Bonney to Kaye, 3 April 1833.
[25] LAO, Cor B5/5/1/2 Kaye to Bewicke, 4 April 1833.
[26] LAO, Cor B5/3/10/2 Archdeacon Hill to Kaye, 26 June 1833 and following.
[27] LAO, Cor B5/8/7/3 Archdeacon Wilkins to Kaye, 10 May 1839.
[28] LAO, Cor B5/3/14/1 G. Cracroft to Kaye, 27 May 1835.

abandoned, probably for fear of incurring unnecessary expense.[29] Willis was found guilty of having frequented a brothel in Aylesbury and of having been intoxicated in the pulpit and later in a hayrick. A charge of his having been thrown out of an inn in High Wycombe was dropped on the grounds that the only person who could have formally identified him could not be found in order for a notice to be served upon her.[30] Willis pleaded guilty to the charges. A full report was transmitted to Bishop Kaye. After consultation with John Haggard, his lawyer at Doctor's Commons, Kaye took the course which Haggard regarded as safest, and suspended Willis from his benefice for one year.[31]

Despite following the provisions of the Church Discipline Act to the letter, it transpired that Kaye was only empowered to take this very moderate sanction against one who had been a considerable force for evil upon a large and important parish for at least fifteen years. It was alleged by Benjamin Harrison, the rural dean, that Willis enjoyed a private income of £800 in addition to his preferment which was worth £370.[32] In such circumstances, it was hardly surprising that the twelve month break from his clerical labours which the punishment afforded was greeted by Willis with considerable equanimity. In the letter he wrote to acknowledge his sentence, he praised Kaye for blending mildness with wisdom, and promised that he would abide cheerfully by his decision.[33]

Because the concept of the parson's freehold emerged unblemished from the Act, a year or so of suspension appears to have been the gravest penalty which the bishop could inflict under it. In reality, the procedures Kaye adopted under the Act differed little from the pre-1840 strategy of demanding that the offender go out of residence and appoint a curate. Indeed, it could be argued that the public attention which would surround the summoning of a commission of enquiry, as required by the Act, would inflict greater damage upon the Church than the quieter, more private proceedings of the old days.[34] It is also apparent that once it became necessary to adopt quasi-legal forms of cross-examination, it became correspondingly harder to obtain sufficient evidence for an indictment. It has already been noted that the charge of unruly behaviour at High Wycombe had to be dropped against Willis because the woman in

---

[29] LAO, Cor B5/19/11 Benjamin Harrison to Kaye, 23 December 1843.
[30] LAO, Cor B5/19/11 Harrison to Kaye, 3 February 1844.
[31] LAO, Cor B5/3/14/1 Robert Swan to Kaye, 24 March 1845.
[32] LAO, Cor B5/19/11 Harrison to Kaye, 29 September 1843.
[33] LAO, Cor B5/19/11 Willis to Kaye, 5 April 1844.
[34] LAO, Cor B5/19/11 Paul Wilmot to Kaye, 30 October 1843.

whose company he had allegedly been at the time could not be found to identify him. Yet the rest of the evidence suggests that he was as guilty of this misdemeanour as he was of the others with which he was charged. The case of Henry Dashwood, vicar of West Wycombe, illustrates the point well. In November 1844, John Pigott the rural dean recommended to the bishop that a commission of enquiry be issued to investigate allegations that Dashwood had been heard to 'damn the Church', had boxed with prize fighters, had been intoxicated in public, and had breakfasted with women at a statute fair.[35] The bishop assented to the investigation, but by the following March, it had to be abandoned. The accused was a baronet whose father owned most of the parish and whose brother was MP for Wycombe. Almost all of those witnesses who could have given evidence against him were tenants of the family estate, and were afraid to do so.[36] Haggard the lawyer counselled Kaye against proceeding any further on such slender testimony.[37] Once more, he had to resort to the time honoured method of delivering a stern lecture to the miscreant upon the necessity of his living up to his sacred calling.[38] The well tried technique had the most desirable effect, however, for the following month Dashwood resigned his living.[39]

So far these observations about the Church Discipline Act have been somewhat negative. How then is the assertion, made earlier, that the Act made an invaluable contribution to the Church of England's ministry to its own ministers to be sustained? It can be argued that its benefits lay in the emphasis which the Act placed upon the responsibility of incumbents within the offender's own locality, and of rural deans in particular, to take the initiative in resolving disciplinary problems. The office of rural dean was revived in the diocese during the period under discussion—initially in the Lincoln archdeaconry. By 1840, rural deans were active in all parts of the diocese, and their role in the pastoral care of the clergy was becoming extremely important. Even before the passing of the Church Discipline Act, it had become quite common for informal commissions of rural deans, or of incumbents chaired by a rural dean, to be formed in order to give judgement in disputes between clergymen, or to investigate allegations made against them. It is significant that sometimes requests for the formation of such commissions would come from the bishop, but at other

---

[35] LAO, Cor B5/3/16/2 J. R. Pigott to Kaye, 4 and 12 November 1844.
[36] LAO, Cor B5/3/16/2 B. G. Parker to J. R. Pigott, 26 November 1844.
[37] LAO, Cor B5/3/16/2 Haggard to Kaye, 4 December 1844.
[38] LAO, Cor B5/3/16/2 Kaye to Dashwood, 12 March 1845.
[39] LAO, Cor B5/3/16/2 Dashwood to Kaye, 9 April 1845.

times from the clergy themselves.[40] As one of them remarked, 'They (the rural deans) can ascertain more of the truth of the question in an hour than the correspondence of many days can draw forth.'[41]

This pointed strongly to the need for the development of a locally based tier of the diocesan hierarchy, as the most effective means of promoting good order. The revival of the rural deaneries afforded an unparalleled opportunity for making use of those incumbents who were known to be conscientious and reliable. Their first hand knowledge of people and places enabled them to mitigate the perceived remoteness of the archdeacons and the bishops. Their presence was particularly valuable in those areas where a high proportion of incumbents were almost permanently out of residence, and many parishes were therefore in the hands of a body of transitory curates. Investigation of rural deans within the Leicester archdeaconry reveals that they provided an important thread of continuity. Of the ten appointed in 1838–9, a decade later one had died and one had resigned, but the other eight remained in office. Random sampling amongst incumbents who were not selected as rural deans suggests that only 57 per cent were still in office after a decade in the Leicester archdeaconry.[42] Thus the most significant clauses of the Church Discipline Act were those which gave legal sanction to the rural dean's role within the investigative process. The measure was far superior to the expensive and chaotic muddle of discipline as it had been administered in the ecclesiastical courts, which it superseded.

Christ's College, Cambridge

---

[40] LAO, Cor B5/19/15 George Watson to Kaye, 28 December 1835 and Cor B5/19/7 William Pym to Kaye, 26 March 1840.
[41] *Ibid.*
[42] This figure is based on a sample of forty Leicestershire incumbents from four deanerie between the period 1841–51. The information is extracted from the *Clergy List*, and does no take into account those incumbents who were non-resident for part or all of the period.

'NOT A LITTLE HOLY CLUB':
LAY AND CLERICAL LEADERSHIP IN AUSTRALIAN ANGLICAN EVANGELICALISM
1788–1988

by STUART PIGGIN

EVANGELICALISM is a good branch of Christianity in which to study lay ministry.[1] *Australian* evangelicalism is a good branch of evangelicalism for such a study.[2] *Sydney* and *Melbourne* evangelicalism are good branches of Australian evangelicalism on which to make this study. And *Anglican* evangelicalism is a good branch of Sydney and Melbourne evangelicalism on which to focus the study.

Surely, having sorted through all those branches, little more is left than an insignificant antipodean twig, hardly sufficient to stoke for long the fires of ecclesiastical history. There is, however, enough fuel here to heat the secular historians, if only because they were believers once:

> The religious in Australia may have been incredibly hypocritical . . .
> but they have defended their patches well enough and exercised some
> power, especially in cultural and educational matters. And that has
> been particularly true of Anglicanism in Sydney.[3]

There is something to be explained here. Sydney evangelicalism, probably since Bishop Barker (1854–82) and certainly since Archbishop Mowll (1933–58), has been predominantly Anglican, clergy-led, and therefore parish-based. Melbourne evangelicalism has not been dominated by Anglicanism, and has been largely lay-led and therefore non-parochial; its

[1] Evangelicalism honours tasks which the laity are equipped to perform, especially evangelism and social engineering. It is a supra-denominational movement and establishes cross-denominational institutions which are more attractive to laity than to clergy who need to succeed within denominational structures. In many evangelical institutions women and youth, to whom traditionally ordination has been closed, are principal agents or objects.

[2] In some ways Australia is propitious soil for evangelicalism. In traditional stereotyping Australians value the practical above the theoretical, and therefore activity above doctrine. They are not rabidly anticlerical, but they are more so than the English. The mobility of Australian society and its democratic spirit favour individualism rather than the covenantal community so conducive to clerical power. For the most part Australian churches are organized on a regional or state basis; such decentralization allows greater scope for the initiative of laity as well as the lower clergy.

[3] Jill Roe, 'Theosophy and the Ascendency', in J. Davidson, ed., *The Sydney-Melbourne Book* (Sydney, 1985), p. 215.

power base is the non-denominational evangelical institution. Accordingly, Sydney has been able to produce areas characterized by genuine evangelical sub-cultures. Modern Melbourne evangelicalism seems to be far more committed to permeating the mainstream culture. Hence Australian evangelicalism is an interesting laboratory for testing, on a diocesan scale, two different types of leadership. The same test cannot be carried out in England because dioceses, thanks to the establishment-generated need for comprehensiveness, are not monochrome as they often are in Australia.[4] Furthermore, Australian bishops have had more power over their dioceses than their English counterparts, limited by the long accretion of local customs and rights. In Australia, the absence of the parliamentary framework, in which English evangelicals had always thought about the Church of England, allowed dioceses to adopt extreme positions and defend them politically. This explains why the Anglican Church League, established in 1909, has succeeded in holding the fort of Sydney evangelicalism against all comers.[5] Ironically, the non-establishment of Australian evangelicalism resulted in its thorough politicization.

Australians have a sense of belonging to a state or region first and to a nation second. Strong national leadership therefore has been difficult and there has been little sense of national purpose or of national destiny. Rather, as one evangelical minister of religion, admittedly of the mid nineteenth-century nonconformist liberal school, said, things happen in Australia because of 'so many casual or concurring incidents'.[6] This hardly represents a robust evangelical providential view of history, but it is a divine scheme which has allowed everyone an opportunity, even the laity![7] It is to the role of regionalism in the development of Australian lay evangelicalism that I wish to address this paper. It is a bold thesis, not my own,[8] which questions the received scholarly judgment of the role of

---

[4] On the development of Adelaide as a monochrome Anglo-Catholic diocese, see D. Hilliard, 'The Transformation of South Australian Anglicanism, c.1880–1930', *JRH* 14 (1986) pp. 38–56.

[5] S. E. Judd, '"Defenders of their Faith": Power and Party in the Anglican Diocese of Sydney 1903–1938' (unpublished Ph.D. thesis, University of Sydney, 1984); D. W. B. Robinson, 'The Origins of the Anglican Church League', Second Moore College Library Lecture, Sydney, 1976.

[6] J. West, *History of Tasmania* (Launceston, 1852), p. 31.

[7] Not that most Australians have seen it that way. Few settlers felt that they had come to Australia in obedience to a divine plan, and few have felt any sense of mission, national or otherwise.

[8] The argument that evangelicalism has been dominant, and not domineering, in the fashioning of Australian life, and that it cannot be understood without the regional factor, has been pressed on me by Canon Len Abbott of Sydney. I am grateful for all the energy he has

religion in Australia. This scholarship, if secular, is overwhelmingly negative,[9] and, if religious, largely ignores the role of the laity.[10] And regionalism as a factor in the history of Australian religion has never been systematically explicated even if it has not been ignored.[11]

The thesis of this paper is not primarily about the impact of the admittedly distinctive cultures of Australian cities on the evangelicalism in those cities.[12] It is rather about the dialectic set up when the Church in the diocese of Sydney provoked a different response or reaction in other dioceses. It is about the dynamic set up within the inner history of Australian evangelicalism, which like all evangelicalism is reactive primarily, not to social forces, but to religious factors.[13]

---

expended in communicating his very deep vision of Australian religious history to me. Margaret Lamb, my research assistant, has been a faster learner of the Abbott thesis than I. Much of the illustrative detail of this paper has been gathered by her.

[9] T. Inglis Moore: Australian society has always been 'fundamentally irreligious, loosely pagan'; Tom Collins: A metaphysical question seems to slip out of the average Australian's mind 'like a wet melon seed'; D. H. Lawrence took six weeks in Australia to arrive at the firm conclusion that 'Australians have no inside life of any sort: just a long lapse and drift'; T. L. Suttor, the Catholic historian, 'My theme is of an absence, a vacuum'; he speaks of the 'great Australian tragedy, the refusal to explore God'; O'Farrell: 'What is most significant historically about Australian religion is its weakness'; he speaks of Christianity's 'tenuous and intermittent hold on the minds and hearts of the Australian people', its 'peripheral or subordinate relation to their main concerns'; John Barrett on the position of the churches in Australia's past: 'There is little drama here for the historian'; J. D. Bollen: 'Religion has not taken a spectacular part in our past . . . has not determined the life of a people . . . fairly unobtrusive'; McLeod, in his preface to *The Pattern of Australian Culture* (1963), says 'Religion because it cannot be regarded as a cultural force in Australia . . . has been omitted'; J. Alex Allan, *Men and Manners in Australia* (1945), p. 163: 'it must be said, for better or worse, that [the Australian] is not a "religious" type as far as dogma is concerned'; Russel Ward concludes that part of the Australian stereotype is an aversion to religion—The 'typical Australian' is a 'hard case', 'sceptical about the value of religion'; Manning Clark characterizes Australia as 'The Kingdom of nothingness'.

[10] K. S. Inglis, 'Colonial Religion', *Quadrant*, 21 (December 1977), pp. 65–72, stresses the importance of studying the laity, the forgotten factor in Church History.

[11] '. . . . there is a striking difference between Sydney and Melbourne right across the religious board . . . Religious life in Melbourne has always been more urbane, more ecumenical, more catholic in its social vision, more Tory in its conservatism, whereas Sydney has been more assertive.' R. Campbell, 'The character of Australian Religion', *Meanjin Quarterly*, 36 (1977), pp. 183 *seq.* The regional differences have been discussed by M. Roe, *Quest for Authority in Eastern Australia, 1835–1851* (Melbourne, 1965), and J. Barrett, *That Better Country: The Religious Aspect of Life in Eastern Australia, 1835–1850* (Melbourne, 1966).

[12] Michael Hogan argues that Sydney's culture explains its distinctive evangelicalism as well as its distinctive Roman Catholicism, Presbyterianism, and Methodism. Sydney is the 'maverick' in matters intellectual, sporting, political, and religious. See his review of Stephen Judd and Kenneth Cable, *Sydney Anglicans* (Sydney, 1987) in the *Journal of the Royal Australian Historical Society* (1988), pp. 84–6.

[13] This claim is based on the sociological work of the Australian academic, Hans Mol, a

I

The first Christianity introduced to Australia, by chaplains and missionaries, was the vital religion of the Evangelical Revival.[14] It was also anti-establishment, and in the period from 1788 to 1836 the Church of England was transformed from a quasi-establishment to a denomination, albeit the biggest and most influential. The British governing classes tried to use the Church as an instrument to assist them in subjecting Australia to British interests. But most of the chaplains and free settlers were of a different social class from the early governors and did not sympathize with their imperialistic ambitions. No doubt a military establishment was the most irksome form which the establishment could take, and the first generation of Church of England evangelicals were anti-establishment. They did not favour the Church and Schools Corporation set up by Archdeacon Scott in 1825 since Scott understood the Church as a state department. Nonconformists did not like it either as it was a Church of England monopoly. The combination of Evangelical Anglicanism with nonconformity explains the non-establishment in Australia of the Church of England, which always threatened or was believed to threaten an imposed external prelacy, with, after 1833, overtones of Rome as well as privilege. That the Protestant ascendency, reinforced in its Protestantism by Keble's Assize sermon,[15] was not prepared to express itself through the traditional institutions of the establishment is evidenced by the failure of powerful New South Wales laymen to co-operate with William Grant Broughton who became bishop of Australia in 1836. In 1849 he sailed from Sydney for the last time, in deep depression over his recalcitrant laity.[16]

II

But to see most clearly what the Protestant free settlers wanted it is best to look at events in the new colonies. Melbourne settled in 1834, Adelaide

---

confessed evangelical. See his *Meaning and Place: An Introduction to the Social Scientific Study of Religion* (New York, 1983); *Faith and Fragility* (Burlington, Ontario, 1985); *The Faith of Australians* (Sydney, 1985).

[14] Not all were impressed with its vitality. In 1825 Archdeacon Scott wrote to the Bishop of London: 'I have a difficult task to perform, too, amongst the clergy, many of them altho' good and excellent men, have been bred up with those peculiar notions of gloominess and what they call 'real piety' that their flocks are much affected by it as by the various sectaries which are here.' Bonwick Transcriptions, Box 53, 44271/1 1512.

[15] Anglican evangelicals joined the nonconformists to establish a Reformation Society in New South Wales in 1836.

[16] Stephen Judd and Kenneth Cable, *Sydney Anglicans* (Sydney, 1987), p. 67.

in 1836, and Brisbane in 1859[17] were Puritan counters to Sydney, not spin-offs.[18] Free settlers and evangelical ministers of religion, especially in South Australia and Melbourne, denounced the establishment and prelacy, the convict system, state aid for religion and schools, and corruption in public life. They stood for and eventually secured self-government, universal free education, a social welfare system, and self-defence.[19] These were all at heart evangelical achievements,[20] as indeed was the renovation of the convict colonies, itself something of a social miracle. To accord such powers of social engineering to evangelical forces is to rewrite Australian history. Historians, however, may have failed to see the formative power of evangelicalism because they have either not studied evangelicalism or, if they have, they have studied clerical evangelicalism. Lay evangelicalism may have influenced our institutions decisively: Congregationalism is such a spent force religiously in Australia because it has been so successful politically and ecclesiastically.[21]

The new states, set on nation-building, needed to cultivate godly laymen to pay for their anti-establishment programme. It is a hypothesis worth testing that whereas evangelicalism in Sydney was dependent on the support of the middle and working classes—there were significant working-class parishes in the centre of Sydney—the other states or dioceses were able to draw on the larger munificence of the wealthy mercantile classes and the squattocracy.[22] Christian philanthropy in New South Wales is less evident, especially among the Anglicans.[23]

Understanding the evangelical emphasis on nation-building and social

[17] Tasmania had been separated from New South Wales in 1825 and Western Australia was settled in 1827.

[18] Queensland began as a separate colony in 1859 with the determination not to be the waste paper basket for 'England's sweepings', a resolve aided by the Revd John Dunmore Lang who was always on the lookout to establish a Presbyterian eden in Australia.

[19] J. D. Lang was obsessed with the need for a white Protestant citadel in the South Seas.

[20] I. D. Pike, *Paradise of Dissent* (Melbourne, 1967) documents the nonconformist role in the establishment of civil liberties in South Australia.

[21] D. H. Borchardt, *Australians: A Guide to Sources* (Broadway, 1987), p. 349.

[22] In Victoria, Ormond, Cato, Grimwade, and the Evangelical Trust founded by Lee Neil, W. M. Buntine, and the Griffiths; in South Australia the Elders, Smiths, Hughes's, Coltons, and the Angas's. The Victorian country diocese of Bendigo did not have a strong squattocracy because of the operation of the Land Acts. It may be no accident that evangelicalism flourished there as well as in Sydney until the early decades of the present century.

[23] The New South Wales Methodists, however, had George Allen, the 'lay bishop', and Ebenezer Vickery who purchased the Lyceum Theatre for the Wesleyan Methodist Central Mission, the Presbyterians had J. A. Brown who is said to have endowed so many churches in the Hunter Valley that he threatened their spiritual vitality, and the Baptists had G. E. Ardill.

achievement has been befuddled by the anachronistic perspectives of many historians who have worked on this period, say from 1836 to 1870. First it is necessary to realise that we are speaking here about an evangelical achievement. Evangelism and the apologetic defence of fundamentals were not then the distinguishing hallmarks of evangelicalism. The fundamentals were not then under attack, and the task was not therefore to defend or propagate the fundamentals, but to apply them to society. It is this application which has been scorned by a number of historians. Gillman has observed that nineteenth-century Australian Christianity was unrelentingly and mercilessly moralizing.[24] But the moralizing was perceived to be a route to social respectability or improvement which had long been accepted as a good fruit of evangelical religion,[25] and a fairly important fruit one would have thought in an erstwhile gaol or frontier community. While no form of Christianity appealed to convicts, evangelicalism appealed to emancipated convicts because it was a ladder back to social respectability. So, in 1852, John West, Congregationalist minister at Launceston, published his *History of Tasmania* for a new generation 'not inferior in virtue and intelligence' and who, he was confident, would not be interested in a history of vice, but only in 'the instructive and inspiriting events of the past'.[26] Nor was it ever the case that evangelicals, born of a reaction to the arid moralizing of the eighteenth century, identified religion completely with morality. The discontinuity between the two in evangelical preaching is evidenced by Governor Phillip's charge to his chaplain Richard Johnson, before the first fleet even set sail, to 'begin with moral subjects',[27] since he had already begun without them!

Manning Clark, Australia's best-known historian, is also saddened by the moral constructs of the evangelicals. According to Clark, Christianity is an ephemeral Anglo-Saxon tribal religion transmitted to Australia with the first fleet, and which most Australians discarded during the First World War. Its chief value now is to provide this prophet and rhetorician with a high-sounding vocabulary for his new truth: religion in Australia, has been a force for philistinism, provincialism, and puritanism.[28] More

---

[24] Ian Gillman, *Many Faiths, One Nation* (Sydney, 1984), pp. 33–5.

[25] S. Piggin, *Making Evangelical Missionaries* (Appleford, Oxford, 1984), pp. 40–4, 129–32; Boyd Hilton, *The Age of Atonement: The Influence of Evangelicalism on Social and Economic Thought, 1795–1865* (Oxford, 1988), p. 379.

[26] Volume I, p. 3.

[27] M. L. Loane, *Hewn from the Rock: Origins and Traditions of the Church in Sydney* (Sydney, 1975), p. 3.

[28] M. Clark, 'Faith', in P. Coleman, ed., *Australian Civilization* (Melbourne, 1962), p. 79; Hilton, p. 379.

a

than most historians, Clark wears his heart on his sleeve as he writes history in his own image: he is the failed Puritan who projects his troubled faith onto his characters.[29]

Of much greater historical penetration is the contention of Richard Ely that 'civic', as distinct from 'corporate', Protestantism dominated the Australian churches in the nineteenth century. Whereas corporate Protestantism stresses the separation of the faithful remnant from a disobedient nation and supports the welfare role of the Church, civic Protestants, whilst sometimes favouring the separation of Church and State, always favour the unity of nation and religion, and support the welfare role of the State.[30] Civic protestants appear to endorse uncritically current social trends. Most Australian evangelicals were of humble social origins. Hence they were sensitive to charges of uncouthness, prized education, and had great faith in human progress, an attitude justified by their experience in Australia which was soon a propitious environment for white settlers. They honoured the man who had been overseas for his education, regarded everything in print as gospel, and were therefore of a receptive rather than a critical disposition. This produced an evangelicalism which was inclusive, not narrow or defensive. The nonconformists of the nineteenth century did not defend the faith as twentieth-century evangelical clerical Sydney Anglicans do with incomparable pugnacity.

In mid-century, Robert Lowe, a barrister in the House of Commons following a colourful career in New South Wales, prevailed on Lord Melbourne to appoint evangelical bishops to Sydney and Melbourne. English evangelicals were aware that Broughton's high-Church views had met with consistent opposition from Sydney laity, and, by the time of Broughton's death, were convinced that evangelicalism might be permanently institutionalized in colonial Anglicanism.[31] Barker's episcopate has been judged as having been very successful in establishing the strong clergy-led evangelicalism which characterizes Sydney to this day. Barker was a preacher and missionary, less a Calvinist than Marsden and the first generation of evangelicals in Australia and less a politician than Broughton. His style of evangelicalism was much to the laity's liking, and he established Sydney Anglicanism on broad-based popular support. He set up effective parishes, the Church Society to secure from Anglican laity

[29] John Carroll, 'Manning Clark's Vision Splendid', *Quadrant*, October 1982.
[30] S. Piggin, 'Towards a bicentennial history of Australian Evangelicalism', *JRH* 15 (1988), pp. 20–37; R. Ely, 'The Forgotten Nationalism: Australian Civic Protestantism in the Second World War', *Journal of Australian Studies*, 20 (1987), pp. 59–67.
[31] Judd and Cable, p. 69.

the funds to open new churches, Moore Theological College, the Lay Readers' Association, and the St Andrew's Cathedral Chapter.

Barker kept a low profile and nurtured his evangelical clergy, thus avoiding a show-down and a schism between Church and society, with his laity and low-Church clergy siding with the latter.[32] But there were signs of strains to come. His clergy increasingly shared the views of the laity: they were religiously conservative and politically liberal. Some of them shared their pulpits with nonconformists. A significant number of them were from parts of Ireland where Protestants were in a minority. They came to form the nucleus of the extreme low Church party for which Sydney was to become proverbial.[33] Yet, apart from minor disagreements over education and synodical structure, there was peace under Barker between bishop, clergy, and influential laity. The greatest achievement of this unity of purpose was the 1866 Enabling Act which allowed each diocese in New South Wales to control its own properties. The diocese, not the provincial or general synod, was the sovereign body, allowing Sydney to resist takeovers either from the bush dioceses in the nineteenth century or high-Church dioceses in the twentieth. The sovereign diocesan synods also allowed the lower clergy and laity a strong voice in the government of the Church and from the beginning were well attended by clergy and laity.[34] This was a form of Church administration which concentrated on internal rather than community issues. The present character of Sydney evangelicalism—clergy-led and concerned with the Church first and the community second—was beginning to take shape.

In Melbourne, Bishop Perry found the going tougher. He, too, had his fair share of Irish clergy, crediting them with zeal and 'more or less of a wrong-headedness'.[35] He never managed to start an evangelical training college in his diocese. He sent his men for training to Moore College in Sydney.[36] For this he was constantly criticized, especially by William Wilson, Professor of Mathematics at the University of Melbourne.[37] Perry was the stern academic who lacked Barker's rapport with men, and he provoked opposition from his strong laity. Loane writes that Perry's 'great

---

[32] 'Barker saw Australia as a mission field which required parish clergy to be able evangelical missionaries', Judd, p. 42.

[33] E. D. Daw, 'Hulton Smyth King: The Curate of Fenagh and Wells', *Church of England Historical Society Journal*, 15 (1970), pp. 94–9.

[34] Judd and Cable, p. 92.

[35] Daw, p. 94.

[36] Judd and Cable, p. 75.

[37] A. de Q. Robin, *Charles Perry, Bishop of Melbourne: The Challenges of a Colonial Episcopate, 1847–76* (Nedlands, 1967), pp. 128–30.

insight was the importance of the laity in church affairs whether on a parochial or a diocesan level'.[38] It was, perhaps, an insight forced upon him by the quality and independence of the Melbourne laity. The superiority of Melbourne to Sydney in the quality of its laymen is explained by the fact that following the gold rushes of the 1850s Melbourne became the financial capital of Australia. Its population outstripped that of Sydney, and the first federal parliament met there. It was the place to be for those at the top. Stuart Barton Babbage, who has been Dean of both St Andrew's Cathedral, Sydney, and St Paul's Cathedral, Melbourne, draws this significant distinction between them:

> The Cathedral in Melbourne has played a role in the life of the community in a way that the Cathedral in Sydney has never done. This is reflected in the composition of the Chapter. The Lay Canons of St. Paul's Cathedral have always been men of the highest eminence; the Lay Canons of St. Andrew's Cathedral, by contrast, have generally been worthy rather than distinguished.[39]

III

In the period from 1870 to 1919 the evangelical diocese of Sydney became increasingly isolated among Australian dioceses and inward-looking on social issues. There was a conspicuous net inflow of strong evangelical clergy to the diocese. Melbourne went pluralistic, and evangelical enterprise passed to laymen who, untroubled by denominational boundaries, sensitive to the power of nonconformity which was stronger in Melbourne than in Sydney, and increasingly disappointed in their parochial experience, channelled enthusiasm into non-denominational conventions and evangelistic campaigns.

In 1872 four Australian dioceses were evangelical: Melbourne, Sydney, and two other New South Wales dioceses, Bathurst and Goulburn. By 1915 there were still four evangelical dioceses, but Bathurst and Goulburn had seceded from the evangelical camp to be replaced by Bendigo and Gippsland, two Victorian dioceses. James Moorhouse, who succeeded Perry as archbishop of Melbourne,[40] eroded the conservatism of the Perry tradition. Melbourne went liberal evangelical and pluralistic, and though the dioceses of Bendigo and Gippsland slowed that erosion, they too were

---

[38] M. Loane, *Hewn from the Rock*, p. 112.
[39] As yet unpublished autobiography, manuscript, pp. 120 *seq*.
[40] 1876–86.

to become pluralistic.[41] Sydney was isolated in New South Wales, and, as a monochrome evangelical diocese, isolated in Australia. Sydney turned in on itself; its synods of the 1880s became energetic legislative bodies, signalling 'the increased administrative and legislative oversight of the diocese by the laity and clergymen of synod'.[42] Synods of the 1890s during the episcopate of the retiring William Saumarez Smith were uncomfortable with debates on issues of society and economics and contented themselves with an emphasis on churchmanship.[43] Social comment was now the preserve of a handful of prominent if isolated clergymen, especially F. B. Boyce and R. B. S. Hammond. The services of prominent Sydney laymen were confiscated for the Church. For the most part, Sydney evangelicalism was pietist, adventist, and, because of the party concern for churchmanship, politicized. The lineaments of the proverbial Sydney Church of England sub-culture were deeply etched by the end of this period.

Therefore, if a male Christian wanted to amount to something in Anglican circles, it was more natural to become a clergyman in Sydney and easier to remain a layman in Melbourne. Some important Sydney clergy went from Sydney to Victoria, such as H. Langley who was influential in the formation in 1910 of Ridley College, a Melbourne Anglican theological college. But the traffic of clergy was mainly the other way: Nathaniel Jones, S. Kirkby, R. B. S. Hammond, R. C. M. Long, J. B. Montgomery, R. J. Hewett and William Langley were all Victorian men whose great contribution was made in Sydney when Moore College was evangelically soft under D. J. Davies, principal until 1935. This clergy drain was much regretted by increasingly beleaguered Melbourne laity, and Archbishop Mowll of Sydney and the Church Missionary Society were to be charged with stealing the best men from Melbourne.[44] The Victorian bishops, however, did not want them, and they, consistent with the evangelical ethic, preferred to serve where their usefulness would be maximized.

Whereas the evangelical clergy in Sydney assumed control of the Church of England, evangelical laity in Melbourne, discouraged by a growing army of non-evangelical parish clergy, assumed control of the evangelical movement. Melbourne lay evangelicals often took the

[41] Judd and Cable, p. 213.
[42] Ibid., p. 143.
[43] Ibid., pp. 148 seq.
[44] Archdeacon J. Moroney interviewed by Margaret Lamb, 17 November 1986.

initiative in inviting leading evangelists to Australia from Britain and America. The Grubb mission of 1891 had a much greater impact on Melbourne than on Sydney.[45] Along with Adelaide, Melbourne witnessed the full flowering of the evangelical revival. The 1902 revival in Australia, characterized by contemporaries as a 'remarkable religious awakening' and 'the big revival', was the culmination of a prayer movement which originated in Melbourne. 2,100 home circles of prayer, attended by 40,000 people, met every Tuesday evening for seven weeks before Torrey and Alexander arrived in Melbourne in April 1902. Why was Melbourne then apparently so open to the Gospel? Dr Warren, a leading Melbourne layman, suggested that, while money and pleasure were the greatest forces in Melbourne society, the people were 'educated, earnest, and energetic; they appreciate what is good, and are responsive and gracious'. He added:

> In such a community there is ample room for aggressive Gospel effort, and no spirit-filled man need wait long for a respectful bearing from a responsive and devout congregation. An evidence of this is supplied by the keen and generous response to appeals on behalf of the heathen both in men and money; today many an Australian name is found on the martyr-roll of China.[46]

Melbourne evangelicalism's acceptance of lay mercantile leadership, with a corresponding non-theological pietism, spawned not only revival but also the convention movement. During Torrey's 1908 mission to Melbourne, H. P. Smith, manager of the Coffee Palace, was converted, and thereafter his considerable administrative gifts were channelled into a variety of evangelistic activities. One such was the Melbourne Gospel Crusade. To provide its converts with good Bible teaching he established the Upwey Convention which later moved to Belgrave Heights. It developed into the largest convention in Australia. Of such laymen as H. P. Smith, Leonard Buck, himself an outstanding layman, reminisced: 'there were strong lay businessmen who were leading men in the formation of evangelical movements and who led them as consecrated businessmen'.[47] By the 1920s, when theological liberalism was in full cry, the convention movement was a well-oiled machine. All the key evangelicals were connected with it, and lifelong friendships across denominational boundaries were formed. Predating the liberal onslaught, it was the best

---

[45] Judd and Cable, p. 150.
[46] *Ibid.*, p. 201.
[47] L. Buck, interviewed by Margaret Lamb, 15 November 1986.

antidote to it, involving its members in the positive pursuit of spiritual renewal, rather than the negative pursuit of the modernists' jugular. It has been argued that the joint influence of Upwey, including the Upwey Extension Movement (for unlike New South Wales, the Victorian convention movement was decentralized with branches throughout the state), and the Melbourne Bible Institute (the largest Bible College in Australia) have had more impact on evangelical life in Victoria than any other factors.[48]

IV

The period from 1920 to 1949 represents the fundamentalist decades of world evangelicalism. In Sydney, clerical Presbyterianism, Methodism, and Congregationalism surrendered to the forces of modernism brilliantly led by a Presbyterian divinity professor, Samuel Angus. The Baptist ministry was saved by G. H. Morling, foundation principal of the Baptist Theological College, and a close personal friend of Archbishop Mowll. The forces of Sydney evangelical Anglicanism, deftly marshalled by the conservative evangelical triumvirate of D. J. Knox, R. B. Robinson, and H. S. Begbie,[49] responded to Angus by deposing the liberal evangelicals in their own Church. The conservative evangelicals, initially nurtured by Nathaniel Jones, Principal of Moore College, and kept in the wings for a generation under the liberal evangelical triumvirate of Archbishop Wright, Dean A. E. Talbot of Sydney, and Principal D. J. Davies, took over the Anglican Church League and succeeded in having Mowll elected to Sydney.

Melbourne might have gone the same way. In the 1920s Archbishop Lees and Dean Aickin of Melbourne were both liberal evangelicals. The Anglican Church League of Melbourne formed in 1929, however, was like similar bodies in dioceses other than Sydney,[50] almost exclusively a lay organization, whereas Sydney's ACL was dominated by clergy.[51] In Melbourne the chief concentration was on protecting the laity rather than the clergy from liberal contamination. This was the life-work of the evangelical colossus, C. H. Nash.

---

[48] R. Pocklington, Melbourne Director of Open Air Campaigners, interviewed by Margaret Lamb, 19 May 1988.
[49] The most mundane explanation of the success of conservative evangelicalism in Sydney is not the inherent supremacy of its churchmanship, but rather that it was an administrative success.
[50] The Church of England League of Tasmania, established in 1922, and the Church of England Defence Association of Queensland (1927).
[51] Judd, pp. 185 seq.

Nash had studied at Corpus Christi College, Cambridge, and Ridley Hall. He was ordained to the priesthood in 1893 and in 1900 became incumbent of Hawthorn in Melbourne. In 1902 he founded the Parker Union, a fellowship of evangelical clergy. In 1907 he was required to resign by Archbishop Lowther Clarke from the Anglican ministry because of 'indiscretion'. He ran a boy's school in Kew and then became pastor of the Prahran Independent Church which had been established by laymen. In fact, it was the laity who were the making of Nash. In 1920 at the age of fifty-four he was invited to become foundation principal of the Melbourne Bible Institute. By his own assessment a failure because he had not himself become a missionary, Nash sent over a thousand students into the mission field and other ministries, and supported a group of young laymen who established a new missionary society, the Borneo Evangelical Mission. Nash's leadership was comprehensive: he seemed to have more than a finger in every evangelical pie: he was a Council member of the China Inland Mission, President of the Bible Union of Australia (of which he was founder in 1923), a popular convention speaker, the teacher of the City Men's Bible Class, a founder member of Campaigners for Christ, and a committee member of the Church Missionary Society, helping to form its League of Youth.[52]

Nash inspired his lay following with more than a passion to defend the faith from modernist attack. Melbourne businessman, Leonard Buck, said 'C. H. Nash . . . taught us a lot about leadership and the place of laymen in it'.[53] The young laity gave him his platform, which was a happy arrangement since he did not like to listen to other speakers. To his numerous disciples, he was 'The Chief'. Frequently the young laymen were streets ahead of the clergy who 'approved' programmes after the event. Nash particularly interested himself in the CMS League of Youth, formed in Melbourne in 1928. Max Warren said: 'From the League of Youth in Australia and New Zealand has come a stream of recruits for missionary service which has no parallel in the church life of those countries.'[54] All this resulted in a mini-revival in the 1930s. The laity who studied under Nash in the City Men's Bible Class had 'fire in their bellies'. Nash taught laymen such as Buck the importance of not being 'a little holy club'. Together with George Hall, who was to become a Baptist pastor, Buck formed Campaigners for Christ, the work of which was to take it beyond

[52] On Nash, see *Australian Dictionary of Biography* (Melbourne, 1986), 10, pp. 665 *seq.*
[53] L. Buck, interviewed by Margaret Lamb, 15 November 1986.
[54] G. Cutler, *The Torch* (Lilydale, 1976), p. 7.

379

Australia to New Guinea, Singapore, and Vietnam. It was a student of Nash, Charles Sandland, who took on the Methodist Master of Queen's College in the University of Melbourne, Raynor Johnson, and won. Johnson had denied the virgin birth in a book entitled *A Religious Outlook for Modern Man*. At the Methodist Conference Sandland was comprehensively defeated, but shortly afterwards 'the back room boys got at the Master of Queen's and he resigned'.[55]

In Sydney the name equal in stature to Melbourne's Nash was H. W. K. Mowll. He was elected archbishop of Sydney in 1933 at the height of the Modernist controversy, due to the clear understanding of a distinction between liberal and conservative evangelicalism. He was nominated by H. S. Begbie, and supported by D. J. Knox and R. B. Robinson. Not a fundamentalist sectarian, Mowll refused to allow the Bible Churchmen's Missionary Society to be established in Australia. His first priority was training evangelical clergy at Moore Theological College under T. C. Hammond, appointed in 1935, and placing them in strategic parishes. The celebrated author of *In Understanding be Men*, T. C. Hammond *was* a fundamentalist sectarian with a mind like a rapier and a tongue like a whip'. Mowll further consolidated the conservative evangelical control of the diocese by appointing R. B. Robinson as General Secretary of the Home Mission Society in 1935 and S. M. Johnstone as Diocesan Registrar in 1936. D. J. Knox did not need a special diocesan appointment: he was the brains behind the Anglican Church League. The remainder of the Anglican Church responded to this conservative evangelical takeover by further isolating the diocese of Sydney. In 1935 Mowll was snubbed for the primacy; Archbishop Henry Le Fanu of Perth was elected instead, a slight which Mowll and Sydney evangelicals felt deeply.[56] Sydney, too, was out of step in its resistance to any constitution which centralized the Australian Church. Neither their clergy, nor their lay supporters thought that a strongly centralized denomination under tight episcopal control was healthy.

V

If Melbourne enjoyed more of the fires of revivalism at the turn of the century and again in the mini-youth revival of the 1930s, it was Sydney's turn in the 1950s. The only decade of equipoise in Australia's twentieth-

---

[55] C. Sandland, interviewed by Margaret Lamb, 20 March 1987.
[56] Judd and Cable, p. 251.

century history, the 1950s, with its balance of individual rights and community responsibilities, was a triumph of the civic evangelicalism central to the aspiration of generations of Australian evangelicals. In the 1950s Moore College saw something of a theological revolution from subjective pietism to that objective evangelicalism which is Sydney's distinctive contribution to the history of scholastic Calvinism. Nourished by the experience of its missionaries in the East African and Pakistan revivals, a number of Sydney clergy forged a unity of Keswick-inspired spirituality with Reformed theology and the fires of revival began to smoulder in a number of Sydney parishes.[57] A. Begbie, B. Gook, G. Rees, and G. Delbridge worked hard on parish missions. Student members of the Inter-Varsity Fellowship conducted meetings in churches. Attendance at churches grew, sometimes remarkably so; membership of the mainstream churches generally rose throughout Australia in the 1950s and peaked in the next decade.[58]

In Melbourne in the 1950s only the League of Youth seemed to exhibit the spirit evident more generally in Sydney. The main clerical brotherhood in Melbourne Anglicanism was then Anglo-Catholic; evangelical clergy seemed to keep to themselves, nervous of being labelled 'party men'. Frank Woods, archbishop of Melbourne from 1957 to 1977, endeavoured to break down the isolation of parties by the doubtful means of placing evangelical curates with Anglo-Catholic incumbents.

The 1959 Billy Graham Crusade made a much bigger impact on Sydney than on Melbourne, though it was more marked in both centres than the organization had witnessed anywhere else hitherto.

	Melbourne	*Sydney*
Weekly prayer meetings	500	5,000
counsellors trained	5,000	9,000
attendance	750,000	1,000,000
enquirers	28,000	57,000[59]

In the 1960s the Biblicism, revivalism, and holiness emphasis of previous decades in Sydney were eclipsed as scholasticism and anti-authoritarianism

---

[57] Piggin, 'Towards a bicentennial history of Australian Evangelicalism', p. 30.

[58] W. W. Phillips, 'Religion', in W. Vamplew, ed., *Australians: Historical Statistics* (Broadway, 1987), pp. 428–35.

[59] S. B. Babbage and I. Siggins, *Light beneath the Cross: The Story of Billy Graham's Crusade in Australia* (Melbourne, 1960), pp. 14–36.

were consolidated in parishes by the new breed of Moore College graduates. The isolation of Sydney from the rest of the Australian Church increased as liturgical experimentation made it untenable to maintain that evangelical meant 'Prayer Book Anglican'. Marcus Loane was appointed archbishop of Sydney in 1966, the same year as Martin Lloyd-Jones called evangelicals out of the Church of England to establish a new evangelical denomination. To John Stott, whose word was law in Sydney, Lloyd-Jones' proposal was abhorrent: with Marcus Loane, Stott had established in 1963 the Evangelical Fellowship of Anglican Churches.[60] Today, however, some of Sydney's anti-erastian clericals are making the same suggestion. It is a logical conclusion of 200 years of accumulating clericalism in the evangelical mould.

Today there is a new opportunity to revive clerical Melbourne Anglican evangelicalism under evangelical Archbishop David Penman. Anglicanism is no longer scorned by nonconformists, a legacy of the work of the convention movement and C. H. Nash. The doctrine of Melbourne Anglican evangelicals is purer than that of the other denominations which have succumbed to either emotional pentecostalism or liberalism. Melbourne evangelicalism, less clerical than Sydney, is more determined to be socially relevant. It is lay initiative, however, which continues to be the hallmark of Melbourne evangelicalism. Outstanding Melbourne lay leaders include businessman, Len Buck, and lawyers, Harold McCracken and Brian Bayston. Three who have risen to prominent international leadership are Stacey Woods, from 1947 Secretary of the International Fellowship of Evangelical Students, David Cummings, International President of the Wycliffe Bible Translators, and Alan Kerr, International Chairman of Scripture Union. Melbourne evangelicals have recently developed non-ecclesiastical enterprises such as God Squad, STEER Incorporated, Christian Leaders Training College, Prison Fellowship.

All these Melbourne developments are not those which Sydney Anglicans, in their strength, have felt compelled to contemplate. They are contemplating more dramatic things. Cut off from the rest of the Australian Church, Sydney's scholastic theologians are looking increasingly to an international network: in Vancouver, Regent's College; in the United States, Gordon Conwell Seminary, founded by Australia's own Stuart Barton Babbage; and to a decreasing extent, John Stott in the

[60] In Sydney EFAC and the Evangelical Alliance have not been strongly promoted, but among Melbourne evangelicals they have been looked on as essential to the consolidation of evangelical ministries.

United Kingdom. This trend, it is feared by the laity, will increase the tendency of some Sydney clergy to cultivate theological precision rather than practice. Then there is a tendency to take over evangelical institutions which hitherto have been non-denominational. The Katoomba Easter Convention has been captured by the champions of propositional Christianity who have turned it into something of a Moore College convention. For the most part Moore College Anglicans adopt the stance of J. I. Packer in his *Keep in Step with the Spirit*, where he roasts Keswick spirituality. The chairman, a Sydney Anglican cleric, claims that he will not share the platform with anyone who 'does not hold to the historic evangelical position relating to the trustworthiness of the Scriptures'. The old Keswick emphases of exclusive concentration on practical holiness, the need to reflect the motto 'all one in Christ Jesus' in a wider selection of speakers, and the desire to allow laymen to contribute, are being stoutly defended by such stalwarts as Arthur Deane, a Baptist minister,[61] but voices like his are being drowned by the rising chorus of Anglican triumphalism. With a taste for the dramatic, some of the most successful of the Anglican clerics are threatening to establish a new denomination, untrammelled by bishops and ordained women. In the past evangelicalism has rarely challenged church order which has been the principal reason why it has been able to engross power and stamp its character on the whole diocese. Yet Sydney evangelical Anglicanism is now more clerical than ever, and its unique brand of Richerism has long portended revolution.

University of Wollongong

---

[61] Correspondence between Arthur Deane and John Dykes, Secretary of the Katoomba Christian Convention, 1987.

PASTORAL PERFECTION:
CARDINAL MANNING AND THE
SECULAR CLERGY

by PETER DOYLE

TOWARDS the end of his life Cardinal Manning made some notes on what he called, 'Hindrances to the Spread of Catholicism in England'.[1] High on his list was the state of the English diocesan clergy: they were, he felt, neither cultured nor 'civil', in that they were unprepared to play a part in public life and did not understand English institutions and the outlook of the educated Englishman. One might in passing wonder how the Cardinal squared this criticism with his desire that the seminaries which trained these priests should remain secluded from the world and that Catholics should not be allowed to attend the English universities. But he felt that a stronger failing in the clergy was the low opinion which they had of their own calling and the low esteem in which many of the faithful held them. They were regarded as no more than parochial hacks, not expected to raise their sights beyond the roofs of the slums which they served. They were, according to Manning, compared unfavourably with the regular clergy: as preachers, confessors, directors of souls, judges of vocations, and even advisers in worldly matters, they were held in less esteem. Lay people were too fond of saying, 'He is only a secular priest'; this judgement had been passed so often that the parochial clergy had come to believe it themselves, and when they were exhorted to higher things too often replied, 'I am only a secular'.[2]

It was not that Manning saw nothing to praise in his priests: they were, indeed, 'exemplary and highly meritorious' for extreme devotion to duty. Most of them had been trained at St Edmund's, Ware, in a system of 'humble and unworldly goodness'.[3] But they remained 'cowed, discouraged, depressed, weakened' by the belief that they need not aim any higher; only the Religious were expected to aim at perfection. Indeed, this had become so strong a tradition that Manning felt it was taken as opposition to the Regulars even to speak of perfection anywhere but in the

[1] E. D. Purcell, *Life of Cardinal Manning, Archbishop of Westminster*, 2 vols (London, 1896, repr. New York, 1973), 2, pp. 773–92.
[2] *Ibid.*, pp. 784–5.
[3] *Ibid.*

Religious Orders![4] It may be that Manning's diagnosis was at fault in all this, and that he was as guilty of misjudging his priests as those lay people who could only recognize priestly holiness if it was packaged in a religious habit. What, after all, was the criterion of priestly holiness? Earlier in the century one of the Vicars Apostolic had responded angrily to a suggestion from Rome that his clergy lacked spirituality: 'Do you wish to know if we are in earnest here? Then count our dead missioners.'[5] The ideal of the priest dying through devotion to duty was long-lived: ten 'martyrs of charity' had died in Liverpool in 1847, and three more as a result of working in a fever hospital between 1862 and 1866. Devotion to duty on such a level must have been motivated by a deep belief in the importance of salvation and by 'more than ordinary devotion to God'.[6] Manning was not good at recognizing values different from his own, and both he and Wiseman had been at fault in mistaking caution for lack of zeal, and the old English spirituality as 'cold and Anglican'.[7]

Whatever the reason, even if it were only to cut the Regulars (especially the Benedictines and the Jesuits) down to size, Manning set out to build up the secular clergy. This involved improving their self-esteem: they certainly felt that the Regulars regarded themselves as better educated and better trained and that many of the better-off laity shared this view. They felt, too, that they did the more unrewarding and unnoticed work, while the Regulars did 'the more showy work connected with the reception of converts and the like'.[8] Manning laboured to create the correct image, that of a body of men called to the highest possible vocation, a vocation which demanded perfection and which was inherently superior to the vocation of a Religious. Ordination to the priesthood was indeed a sign of perfection already reached; as he put it, the priesthood is a sign *perfectionis jam adeptae* while the imperfect enter Religious Orders *ad perfectionem acquirendam*.[9] No doubt Manning would have fully supported Faber's view, expressed over thirty years before, that the Seculars were superior to the Regulars because they had been

---

[4] Letter to Bishop Ullathorne, in C. Butler, *The Life and Times of Bishop Ullathorne*, 2 vols (London, 1926), 2, p. 153.

[5] G. P. Connolly, 'The Secular Missioner of the North', *North West Catholic History*, 10 (1983), p. 23.

[6] *Ibid.*, p. 27. For the Liverpool priests, T. Burke, *Catholic History of Liverpool* (Liverpool, 1910), pp. 63, 86–7.

[7] Manning to Talbot, in Butler, 1, pp. 358–9.

[8] B. Ward, *The Sequel to Catholic Emancipation*, 2 vols (London, 1915), 1, pp. 138–9.

[9] Purcell, 2, p. 787.

instituted by Christ himself: they were the life of the Church, whereas the Regulars were only its ornament.[10]

In the 1860s Manning had discussed the matter with Bishop Ullathorne of Birmingham, a Benedictine himself but equally concerned about the status of the secular clergy. The very name 'secular' was, according to Ullathorne, part of the problem, for it misled people into thinking that the parochial clergy were worldly, less spiritual, whereas it just meant that they worked in the world but were not of it. They should be known as the Pastoral Order, of which Christ himself was the founder, and they should have their vocation spelled out in spiritual laws and customs as the Regular Orders had. Various attempts had been made to put this into practice with what he called 'select bodies of the clergy in individual dioceses', but the result had always been the setting up of new Religious Institutes which then separated themselves from the rest of the clergy.[11] Manning himself had done this with his Oblates of St Charles, providing diocesan clergy with the advantages of rule and community, but it could only be a partial solution and was of no help to the many priests serving in isolated country parishes.

Manning adopted the title 'Pastoral Clergy' as his own, and later wrote to Ullathorne inviting him to give the opening address at the Provincial Council in 1873, at which the 'pastoral clergy' should be the chief, if not the only, matter for discussion.[12] While he was preparing his discourse, Ullathorne wrote to a friend that his main theme would be the sanctity of the priesthood. He thought it remarkable that both Aquinas and Suarez 'decide that more sanctity is required in the pastoral clergy than in mere Religious'; he added, however, that the perils facing the pastoral clergy were greater, and so the degree of sanctity required was 'rarely attained'.[13]

The whole of his long discourse was taken up with the sanctity required of the pastoral clergy and to make the point that 'Perfection is not an ivy that grows only on monastic walls'.[14] He claimed that the first demand to be holy arose from the 'purity, the sanctity and excelling dignity of the sacrifice of the Mass'. The second arose from the fact that

[10] Faber's sermon at the consecration of Bishop Goss of Liverpool, *Tablet*, 1 Oct., 10 Dec., 1853.

[11] Butler, 2, pp. 152–3.

[12] *Ibid.*, p. 153.

[13] W. B. Ullathorne, *Letters of Archbishop Ullathorne*, ed. A. T. Drane (London, 1892), p. 343.

[14] W. B. Ullathorne, *Ecclesiastical Discourses* (London, 1876), pp. 115–46, at p. 135.

priests offer that sacrifice 'in the power of Christ and in the name of the Church which is His body'. The third demand on them to be holy was that they 'represent Christ to the people, and are the channels to them of His light and grace'. The priest thus has power over the mystical body of Christ and over 'His very Body and Blood'.[15] Ullathorne wished to remove three misconceptions which he claimed were having a 'retarding influence' on too many priests. The first of these has already been mentioned: the idea that the title 'secular' meant that the clergy were not called to a holy, interior life and could 'walk more freely in the secular path'. The second arose from the narrow way in which Moral Theology concentrated on sin, which led to a legalist spirit of 'What am I bound to do?', instead of helping the priest to guide others in the paths of perfection: duty dominated the priest's mind instead of generosity and charity. The final misconception arose from the failure to make clear what the Church taught about the nature of priesthood and what the great theologians had said about priestly holiness. Ullathorne quoted at length from Aquinas, Gerson, Suarez, Borromeo and others; for example, from Aquinas, 'For the rightful execution of Orders common goodness will not suffice, but an excelling goodness is required'.[16]

It is interesting that in addition to his principal aim of improving the image of the clergy Ullathorne added a contemporary reason for 'exalting the prerogatives of the Catholic priesthood'. In a clear attack on Anglican ritualists he maintained that an increasing number of men were claiming the 'sacerdotal office that their fathers rejected'; they had no claim to it by descent or tradition, nor did they have power 'over the sacrifice'; their claims were also spurious because they did not have that 'law of sacerdotal purity that devotes the priest to the virginal victim'.[17]

When it came to it, the Fourth Provincial Council, under Manning's presidency, devoted only four of its eleven substantive decrees to the priesthood: they dealt with the Seminaries, the Obligations on those charged with the Care of Souls, the Priestly Life, and the Regulation of Presbyteries.[18] The decrees were not meant to be theological treatises. That on Presbyteries, for example, was concerned with the rules necessary to allow priests to live communally in peace, and to avoid obvious causes of scandal or dangers to celibacy; that on Seminaries stressed the need to

---

[15] Ullathorne, *Ecclesiastical Discourses*, p. 127.
[16] *Ibid.*, pp. 129–40.
[17] *Ibid.*, p. 120.
[18] *Decreta Quatuor Conciliorum Provincialium Westmonasteriensium 1852–1873* (London, n.d.), pp. 214–39.

educate young clerics-to-be apart, to avoid the *pestifer spiritus* of a love of liberty and to test the candidates' piety, obedience, and self-denial from the earliest years. But the decree on the Priestly Life set out to give legislative backing to Manning's concerns about the secular clergy, and in doing so summarized the theological ideas which both Manning and Ullathorne felt supported their case.

The decree said that while all the faithful were called to be holy, priests must ascend to the very height of sanctity. It quoted Aquinas's warning about the serious nature of this obligation in words very similar to those used in the ordination service: 'Those who undertake the ministry of divine things acquire a regal dignity and must be perfect in every virtue'. Priests had to bear in mind that holiness in them was pre-supposed; the degree of holiness must be nothing less than a resemblance to the High Priesthood of Christ. The priesthood had been established to be in men's eyes a living reflection of the life of Jesus, labouring in lonely places, in poverty, and in the face of human opposition. The decree went on to say that the dignity of the priest rested on a double title: first, he was the companion of Jesus and had accepted a share in the divine mission; second, he had jurisdiction over the real and the mystical body of Christ.[19]

The rest of the decree dealt with a variety of related topics: the need for the priest to be able to guide some of the faithful to perfection, and the obligation to preach which was his principal task—an interesting point in an age which put such a stress on the sacraments. Finally, it was acknowledged that the life of a priest was hard, but he was given many helps towards acquiring the necessary perfection; in particular, in England, there was the fact that missioners largely served the poor, and were themselves poor and reliant on alms; they were daily engaged in tasks which demanded self-denial and enabled them to offer themselves as a daily sacrifice to God.[20]

We do not know how far these decrees were drafted by Manning himself, but it would be strange if he did not have a major hand in them, perhaps with help from Ullathorne. What is clear is that he did not think they were sufficient by themselves to create a new image for the pastoral clergy or to improve their self-esteem. Perhaps this was a realistic appraisal of the likely impact of such legislation: even if the clergy took notice of it, it would be most unlikely that lay people would do so. Moreover, the decrees could not be used to make comparisons between the two sets of

---

[19] *Ibid.*, pp. 234–6.
[20] *Ibid.*, pp. 237–8.

clergy and to establish the pastoral priest as at least theoretically superior: and this, for Manning, was fundamental. To continue his campaign he planned a trilogy of books on the subject. The Regulars, he wrote to Ulla-thorne, had 'authors, friends, preachers, books, prestige, tradition' always working for them. The 'humble, hard-worked, hard-working, self-denying, unpretending, self-depressing' pastoral clergy needed to be 'encouraged, cheered and told of their high and happy state'.[21] No doubt he was also influenced by the long-running and often bitter quarrels between the older Orders and the English bishops, and especially by his strong dislike of the Jesuits—a 'mysterious permission of God for the chastisement of England'—in wanting to cut the Regulars down to size.[22] For his part, Ullathorne hoped that the Roman Decree published in favour of the bishops in 1881 would give the religious orders and especially the Jesuits 'a more modest estimation of their position'.[23]

The first of the trilogy was *The Eternal Priesthood*, published in 1883 and regarded by many as Manning's spiritual masterpiece; even a Jesuit reviewer called it a 'beautiful little treatise'.[24] This was followed by *The Pastoral Office*, completed in the same year. This was much more con-troversial, and Manning sent it to a number of people for comment before publication. Ullathorne was one of these: he recommended a number of changes, feeling that otherwise the book would be taken as just another of the Cardinal's attacks on the Regulars; he also felt that the book was too harsh on bishops in former times who had lived worldly lives: this could easily awaken scandal in lay people. He was, overall, doubtful about the value of the book for readers not versed in theology. Manning humbly accepted all of Ullathorne's suggested changes, admitting that people thought he was prejudiced against the Regulars. In the end he even agreed to Ullathorne's suggestion not to publish the book, but to have a number of copies printed for private circulation.[25]

The third part of the trilogy, 'The Rights and Dignity of the Priest-hood', did not get beyond the manuscript stage. According to Leslie, Manning gave it to an American archbishop who was to publish it after his death, but the manuscript disappeared while the archbishop was crossing the Atlantic![26]

---

[21] Shane Leslie, *Henry Edward Manning: His Life and Labours* (London, 1921), pp. 342–3.
[22] *Ibid.*, p. 295.
[23] Butler, 2, p. 189. For the decree *Romanos Pontifices* see *Decreta*, pp. 345–65.
[24] Review in *The Month*, 49 (1883), pp. 571–3. See also Leslie, p. 339.
[25] Butler, 2, pp. 154–6; Leslie, pp. 341–3.
[26] Leslie, p. 343.

It is in *The Eternal Priesthood* that we have the most balanced account of Manning's views on the priesthood.[27] The plan of the book is straight-forward. The first three chapters deal with the nature of the Christian priesthood, and the next three with the holiness demanded of the priest. The remainder of the book, fourteen chapters, deals with more practical matters: the helps at a priest's disposal, the dangers he faces, preaching, and other similar topics. Two of these later chapters, on 'The Priest's House' and 'The Priest's Life', are almost entirely repeats of the relevant decrees of the Provincial Council of 1873. The whole book is clearly written, with a number of striking aphorisms dear to the giver of clerical retreats, for example, 'if we lose the seed-time, we lose the harvest', and, 'a small mission becomes a Sleepy Hollow, and the priest too often a harm-less lotus-eater'.[28]

Manning was not an original thinker, and one gets the impression that he was more at home writing the later, more practical, chapters than in dealing with the deeper theological issues. His basic theological method was to rely heavily on quotations from the Fathers and scholastic theo-logians, especially Aquinas, with reference to the Pauline epistles as appropriate. Some contemporaries thought that his grasp of scholasticism was not very deep: as Wilfrid Ward said, he championed it as an inspiring idea and it became one of his catchphrases, but he had not been able to read enough of it to avoid being 'densely ignorant' of particular issues.[29] A quotation or two from Aquinas was usually considered enough to prove a point.

On the nature of Christian priesthood Manning stresses that there is only one priesthood, and that is Christ's. Those ordained are not priests because they represent Christ, but because they are, in Aquinas's term, 'configured' to Christ's priesthood and are made one with him. One sacri-fice redeemed the world and is continually offered in heaven and on earth: in heaven by Christ, on earth 'by the multitude and succession of priests who are one with Him as partakers of His priesthood'. But priests are con-figured to Christ not just as Priest but also as Victim: when the priest offers Christ to the Father he is also offering himself, and this must be in a spirit of complete self-sacrifice. The sacramental character of ordination con-sists in this configuration to Christ and participation in his priesthood.[30]

[27] H. E. Manning, *The Eternal Priesthood* (London, 1883). I have used the 21st ed of 1936. Refer-ences will be to *E.P.*

[28] *E.P.*, pp. 83–4, 120.

[29] M. Ward, *The Wilfrid Wards and the Transition* (London, 1934), pp. 209–10.

[30] *E.P.*, pp. 3–11.

In going on to talk of the priest's powers Manning takes up the point made by Ullathorne in 1873: the priest has a two-fold jurisdiction or power over the natural and mystical body of Christ. The priest is truly 'the guardian of his Lord . . . no relation more intimate, close and ceaseless can be conceived'. The living contact in the Mass between Christ and the priest is as real, according to Manning, as that between Christ and the apostles at the Last Supper. The power of the priests mean that they are 'fellow-builders with God in edifying the Church' and in raising 'the temple of the Holy Ghost' upon the foundation which Christ laid.[31]

In these early chapters Manning was concerned to show that the priest shared in a network of relationships as partaker in Christ's priesthood, as custodian of his sacramental presence, and as pastor of the people committed to his charge. Each of these relationships, he went on to demonstrate, bound the priest to holiness, indeed to perfection. Manning was quite uncompromising about this: it was, after all, the main plank in his campaign to raise the image of the secular clergy. Referring to Moses and the burning bush he claimed that 'an unholy man if he seeks the priesthood is seeking eternal death'. Again, he wrote that it was theologically certain that interior spiritual perfection was a prerequisite to receiving orders, quoting Alphonsus Liguori in support; sanctifying grace alone was not sufficient, still less a 'professional' holiness.[32]

Manning was obviously fully aware that in practice priests were not perfect; to insist on perfection before ordination would have been the shortest route to handing over the whole English mission to the Regulars for lack of any alternative. So what did he mean by perfection in this context? It was not actual sinlessness, but freedom from the power of sin. It meant that a person would rather die than commit a mortal sin, and would rather suffer any pain or loss than commit a wilful venial sin. There was a positive side to it as well: 'a glad and deliberate choice of a life in the spirit of povety, humility, labour and the Cross'. It implied a preference for suffering in order to be like Christ. Finally, the priest was bound to exercise this perfection, and this involved, firstly, that he should show perfect charity in his own life, and, secondly, that he should diffuse this charity by 'impressing the same law of charity upon others'. After ordination the priest was bound to persevere by all means possible in this life of loving perfection. Manning was predictably outspoken in his condemnation of sinful, worldly, or lax priests.[33]

[31] E.P., pp. 12–25.
[32] Ibid., pp. 26, 41, 42.
[33] Ibid., pp. 41, 47–8, 71–3.

The pastoral relationship to his people was one of the factors binding the priest to holiness. It also created, according to Manning, 'a mutual relation of authority and submission'; where there is no authority there can be no duty to submit. The priest's authority, therefore, arose from his pastoral care; to the extent that he carried out that care faithfully then he could expect the people to submit to his authority. The Provincial Council had not dealt with this, but it had stressed that the priest only had a right to the financial support of his people if he carried out his duties as missioner and preached the gospel to them 'in season and out'.[34] In practice, however, a priest's authority might well rest on other grounds, and be exercised and accepted without reference to his zeal or personal holiness.

There was, first of all, the priest's canonical position. He was in charge of his mission, responsible only to his bishop and not needing to consult anyone in his day-to-day administration. In his 'Hindrances' Manning recognized that this could be dangerous: the priest was not used to being criticized, and could easily develop 'officialism'—a dependence on official powers instead of on subjective fitness. This, according to Manning, could lead even good priests to 'swagger': they thought to magnify their office, but only succeeded in belittling themselves.[35]

A second source of authority in practice was the fact that the priest was the sole dispenser of the sacraments. This was most important in a sacramentalist age, particularly in connection with the sacrament of penance. The efficacy of the sacraments was wholly independent of the personal holiness of the priest, and all the stress was on their *ex opere operato* effect and the correct carrying out of the rubrics. Again, in the 'Hindrances' Manning pointed to an obvious danger: the priest could easily become a 'Sacrament-monger', neglecting his own and his people's spiritual development, and administering the sacraments exactly but mechanically. He added that the objective efficacy of the sacraments was not intended to dispense with the subjective fitness of either priest or recipient.[36]

A third source of authority in practice may be mentioned here: the reputation of the priest as 'holy man', a bringer of peace and healing— what Connolly has called in a stimulating article, 'an objective bearer of holiness'.[37] In such a priest there could well be much of the true spirituality

---

[34] *Ibid.*, p. 35; *Decreta*, p. 225.
[35] Purcell, 2, pp. 782–3; also, *E.P.*, p. 17. The missions in England were not canonical parishes, but in practice the priest's position was the same.
[36] Purcell, 2, p. 782.
[37] G. P. Connolly, 'The Priest as Holy Man in the Ghetto', in *SCH* 19, pp. 191–206.

and self-sacrifice which Manning demanded; indeed, his reputation would depend to some extent on the people's recognition of such qualities in 'their' priest. But it appears that there could also be elements of superstition in such cases, and some danger of the priest's being diverted into non-spiritual activities.

The theology of the priesthood and the sanctity required for ordination were central to Manning's aims in writing the book, but there is much else in it and, as has been suggested, he was happier handling this other material. It is non-controversial, and while there is little that is original the chapters are infused with an understanding of the pastoral priest's life, with its hardships and rewards. There are moving passages on the comfort and confidence which a priest should draw from his service to the poor, the sick, and the dying.[38] To uphold him in this service he has the friendship of Jesus, who is 'unchangeable in love, pity and forgiveness', and who each evening will absolve the priest from the 'failures and inconsistencies' of the day's work. This friendship of a priest with his Lord is beyond all other friendships in 'conscious nearness and conscious intimacy'.[39] It is kept alive by the priest's prayers and devotions, especially, of course, his daily offering of the Mass—'the mystery of Christ's personal nearness'. Union with Christ in communion is almost a physical union: 'we are made flesh of His flesh and bone of His bone'.[40] Manning stresses time and again that no matter how hard the task facing the priest may be and how strong the temptation to settle for the easy minimum, the graces which he can expect are beyond measure.[41] There was, one feels, more in these parts of the book to encourage the ordinary priest than in the theological discussion of the perfection required of him.

There are several references to the poor, all in this context of the priest's spiritual service. We are told that in England especially the priest and the poor 'are bound together by a mutual dependence and with a primitive charity'. As for many Catholic writers in the nineteenth century, for Manning the poor are the special friends of Jesus. Parts of the Provincial Council's decrees on the poor are incorporated in the book.[42] There is no hint at all of an interest in social issues, despite the part this played in Manning's own ministry. In his eyes the priest had one prime function, to help his people to become holy. If he was also a leader of his people, an

38 *E.P.*, cap. XVII.
39 *Ibid.*, pp. 168–70.
40 *Ibid.*, pp. 91–2.
41 *Ibid.*, pp. 88–9, 106, 110.
42 *Ibid.*, pp. 118–19, 238, 267.

agent of social improvement or even an agent of social control, that was no more than coincidental.

Much more surprising is another omission: there is no treatment of celibacy in the book. Indeed, there are very few references to it at all, and those only in the context of the dangers facing the priest; for example, the regulations about the presence of women in presbyteries. As we have seen, Ullathorne had spoken of the 'law of sacerdotal purity' as one of the marks of the truly Catholic priest, but it was not a point taken up by Manning. There is just one reference to the liberty which sets the priest free from 'all inordinate friendships and all undue attachments'.[43]

On other topics Manning's views are predictable. The priest's relationship to the Church, for example, should be marked by obedience. Even if a rule or injunction is needless or comes from an ill-informed authority, the duty of obedience remains; those who criticize authority are not docile. *Sentire cum Ecclesia* means to believe, hope, love, and therefore obey with the Church. A priest must be a 'man of many obediences'.[44] One of these obediences must be a 'deference to theologians', to replace the reliance on private judgement which had become law three hundred years before and which had 'infected the atmosphere' which the Church had to breathe.[45] Manning insisted that the priest must continue to study and always have books to hand, but in an age of what he called 'unlimited intellectual liberty' he warned the priest to be on the defensive against the 'restless sea of human intellect casting up mire and darkness'. He thought that the habit of intellectual independence was too easily formed; priests had no hesitation in reading what was forbidden by the Index, and they believed that 'as in philosophy there is no heresy, so there need be no fear'. The whole Christian world was running fast to a 'liberty which ends in license'.[46] In general terms, the world was an evil place of temptation, as it was in the Provincial Council's decrees on the seminaries. According to Manning it had grown steadily worse since the sixteenth century, for 'spurious reformation has generated revolution and revolution has desecrated the sovereignties and states of Christendom'; but faithful priests could rest in the peace of knowing they were on God's side.[47]

Almost fifty years later, Manning's successor Cardinal Bourne wrote a preface to a book on the secular clergy. In this he attacked the Regulars

---

[43] *Ibid.*, p. 160.
[44] *Ibid.*, pp. 211–12.
[45] *Ibid.*, p. 216.
[46] *Ibid.*, pp. 206, 218–19.
[47] *Ibid.*, p. 117. *Decreta*, pp. 218–19.

and their supporters for holding the seculars in such low esteem. The book itself contained two strongly worded chapters on the sanctity required of the secular priest; the author used many of the same quotations that Manning had used, and referred to his book with great approval.[48] It would seem that Manning had failed to cut the Regulars down to size and to reduce their popularity. His arguments may have convinced some people of the theologically higher standing of the secular priesthood, but had that been the real issue? After all, most of the Regulars whom he had had in mind had been priests as well as Religious, and so could claim the dignity he was upholding. Perhaps he had been nearer the mark in his 'Hindrances' in concentrating on the *ne colto ne civile* state of the clergy, on the inappropriateness of much of their preaching and on the need to 'get out of the sacristy'. Attention to a proper reform of the seminaries might have borne richer fruit.[49]

Whether he had had any greater success in his other aim, of raising the self-esteem of the secular clergy, is impossible to assess. His image of the priestly ideal, demanding a level of asceticism similar to his own and such a commitment to sanctity, could have been as psychologically depressing for some as it was encouraging for others. Yet his book remained a classic, and was used in English seminaries until its high clerical tone and image of the priest as set apart and superior to everybody else in the Church (except the bishops, of course) were no longer acceptable to post Vatican II ears.

Bedford College of Higher Education

---

[48] E. J. Mahoney, *The Secular Priesthood* (London, 1930), chaps. 8 and 9, and pp. 233–9.
[49] Purcell, 2, pp. 773–81. See also P. Doyle, 'The Education and Training of Roman Catholic Priests in Nineteenth-Century England', *JEH* 35 (1984), pp. 208–19.

PRINCIPAL WHEN PASTOR:
P. T. FORSYTH, 1876–1901

by CLYDE BINFIELD

W HAT marks a minister? Such a one, for example, as this, formed within Scottish Congregationalism but formative for and proved by English Congregationalism. Born 1848, died 1921. Born under Russell, died under Lloyd George. Or, from Palmerston to Asquith with Gladstone as the longest fact of political life. Born Aberdeen, died Hampstead. Born a postman's son, died a college principal, lives a theologian. Formed educationally by Aberdeen, London and Göttingen and indirectly by Manchester and Cambridge. Culturally Pre-Raphaelite, a man for Rossetti and Holman Hunt and also G. F. Watts, for Ruskin and Giotto, for Wagner as for Hegel. Peter Taylor Forsyth, set apart by ordination in 1876; twenty-eight years, therefore, in preparation for ministry, twenty-five years in congregational ministry, twenty years in training Congregational ministers.

The spoken word dies with the memory of its last hearer. Forsyth's word lives chiefly through what he wrote in that last twenty years and since ministerial training was then more academic than practical, a matter therefore of words and Word for the wordy, he is remembered accordingly, a mass of contrary evidence notwithstanding: remote and mannered, grandly, unforgettably different on both counts.

Such a man must first be seen in denominational perspective. Forsyth has best been seen as the preacher's theologian, a phrase describing as much his medium as his message.[1] However 'academic' the training the Congregational college principal trained preachers. That 'difficult' style of Forsyth's was to be communicated in a pulpit or at a lecturer's desk. It was best not read and it was never found difficult by his students.[2] Again, the Congregational college principal had a role in his denomination which was quite different from any role played in the Established Church by that much newer animal, the Anglican college principal. He was a representative figure, almost uniquely so, a bishop indeed, a key man at

---

[1] D. G. Miller, ed., *P. T. Forsyth: The Man, The Preacher's Theologian, Prophet for the Twentieth Century. A Contemporary Reassessment* (Pittsburgh, 1981).

[2] Thus his pupil, H. F. Lovell Cocks, *Expository Times*, April 1953, p. 195, and in Miller, pp. 71–2.

ordinations, called frequently to arbitrate in Congregational disputes, preaching at the solider special occasions. He was a minister of and for ministers. His was ministry writ large.

But what was such ministry? In the half-century after Forsyth's death the phrase 'Ministry of Word and Sacraments' became a Congregational cliché. The Congregational minister broke the Word as he broke the bread. He poured the wine as he sprinkled the water. He re-presented the ordinances for God's people consciously gathered in responsive obedience. There was nothing chance or haphazard about this relationship of stated ministry to duly constituted church. It was brought about by a call, with the Church—as gathered in that place—as intermediary, at once caller and sharer in call. The mutuality of minister and people validated that call, subject only to the constraints (but also, therefore, the generosities) of the voluntary principle. That is all. There was no parson's freehold. There were seldom any endowments. Given human nature, it was hard for such a minister truly to be a *pastor*, though that word was in vogue. He might easily be a slave. He was most naturally a managing director for God's entrepreneurs, staving off hell's bankruptcy, leader yet servant in a relationship built ideally on trust, frankness, honesty, manliness but formed inevitably by the limitations of personality and the facts of social and economic life. Moreover, though founded on call this relationship apparently owed as much to skills in calling: to the vocal more than to vocation.

Forsyth as minister expressed all this. 'You have called and I have answered gladly', he told the church at Cheetham Hill, Manchester, in his induction sermon in 1885. 'But it is not your call that has made me a minister. I was a minister before any congregation called me. My election is of God.' And he went on to stress the sacraments: communion and baptism—and the Word, that 'distinctly Protestant Sacrament'.[3]

The Forsythian elements are all there, as they were throughout his ministry, though their emphasis changed: the Congregational dynamic of call and response; the perfect freedom in service; the Calvinistic resonance ('My election is of God'); the disciplined churchmanship; the high role of ministry, which was the consequence of such things. Above all there is the sense of time captured in that vital act for each Christian—election, that point at which eternity meets time.

Forsyth's sense of time sprang from his apprehension of the revelation of God in history. That revelation was recorded in the Bible. It was experi-

---

[3] Quoted in W. L. Bradley, *P. T. Forsyth: The Man and his Work* (London, 1952), p. 38.

enced by each Christian. The record was preserved and the experience communicated through the Church. There was thus for Congregationalists an equipoise between a critical investment in the Bible, the authority vested in personal faith, and churchmanship—a concept which must find room for tradition and doctrine and order.[4] Forsyth most keenly celebrated that equipoise. That it was seldom other than an ideal, seldom even to be approximated, is as beside the point as the fact that Forsyth has been presented as a man out of joint with his age, a conservative smothered by liberals, so persistently ignored that he has needed constant rediscovery.[5] Forsyth was no more out of joint with his times than he was then or thereafter ignored or forgotten. As minister, trainer of ministers, and writer for ministers he criticized keenest what almost enthralled him, those criticisms and grand enthusiasms mediated like his turns of phrase through the manse studies of two decades of pupils and into their pulpits to rest in who knows whose pews.

But Forsyth's foundation was the particular discipline imposed by responsible congregational ministry. That discipline was as consistent in its elements as it was also consistent in its antitheses. Here, as with all the Victorian prophets, was a balancing of the boxes.

The consistency in antithesis can be observed most easily in the incidentals of Forsyth's calling. This latter-day proponent of ministerial authority stood none the less in his days of London suburban ministry in his pulpit 'wearing a short black coat, shepherd's-plaid trousers, turndown collar and a brilliant tie'. He took to a preaching gown only to hide a sling after he had broken his collar-bone when figure skating on the Serpentine.[6] This apparently casual pulpiteer, more widely known in his earlier prime for his skills in lecture, debate, and after-dinner speech, where culture must be worn lightly and with wit (precisely those rare skills which are soonest forgotten), nevertheless concentrated his emotional energies in his words of life in the time-honoured manner of preachers. He left his pulpit drenched and limp with perspiration (what was his metabolism? He was preternaturally sensitive to the draughts which infested every chapel), as drained as he had left his preparation:

> at these times he was wrestling with thoughts almost beyond human expression; and he wrote with a physical and nervous intensity which

[4] W. B. Glover, *Evangelical Nonconformists and Higher Criticism in the Nineteenth Century* (London, 1954), pp. 22–3, 138, 273 ff.

[5] Miller, *passim*.

[6] Jessie Forsyth Andrews, introduction to P. T. Forsyth, *The Work of Christ* (1938 edn.), p. xiv.

shook the desk, and which after an hour or two left him utterly spent, stretched out white and still upon his study couch, until the spirit drove him back to pen and paper.[7]

These antitheses—those of a man who in his prime seemed tall and handsome when really he was neither—can be demonstrated in three quite separate consistencies: his appeal to the young; his drawing on art and the social conscience—that is to say, the culture of the race; and his sense of that race, of society as organism. Each issued from his experience of the Congregational dynamic.

Forsyth's appeal to the young long survived his reputation as a denominational Young Turk. His first book was for children and his Sunday ministry regularly included children's services and addresses.[8] In July 1878, at Shipley, his first pastorate, he preached one of his first published sermons.[9] It was to schoolgirls. He began with a picture which hung 'in the dining-room of one of my tasteful friends'. It was of a flaxen-haired girl, paddling. Inevitably Forsyth quoted George MacDonald, the brother-in-law of his unorthodox theological college tutor J. H. Godwin.[10] In his own Aberdeen student days MacDonald had lodged in the house where Forsyth's mother was keeper.[11] But the MacDonald whom Forsyth now quoted was not here in story-telling vein. This was a sermon to schoolgirls, daughters of the Yorkshire middle-classes who, should trade take a down-turn, would have to work for a living as well as for their own good. 'I wish every woman like every man were brought up to the view that work of some real and earnest kind was to be a necessity for them'.[12] And the Forsyth who was newly married to a clever London governess, whom he had met in Brixton and married in Bayswater, could not resist an almost epigram: 'A clever woman's real conversation is one of the best delights and highest stimuli I know'.[13]

Children were men and women in preparation moving, God willing, into the Church. Proportion fascinated Forsyth for whom life, which made sense only in relation to eternity, was best grasped as shape, with due proportion. 'The soul of man', he told Shipley's Congregational girlhood, 'cannot expand and leave the soul of woman behind. Both sides of the

---

[7] *Ibid.*, p. xxvi.
[8] P. T. Forsyth and J. A. Hamilton, *Pulpit Parables for Young Hearers* (1886).
[9] P. T. Forsyth, '*Maid Arise*', preached in Shipley Congregational Church, 28 July 1878.
[10] John H. Godwin (1809–89), *Congregational Year Book* (1890), pp. 143–5.
[11] Jessie Forsyth Andrews, p. viii.
[12] *Maid Arise*, p. 12.
[13] *Ibid.*, p. 10.

sphere must expand symmetrically. God himself is more than a man. The Divine is part womanly. Hence the divine call, "Maid arise".[14]

But Forsyth's admiration for clever women sharpened his mounting suspicion of the effeminate in contemporary religion. The effeminate was unwomanly, the more so for its verbal association with woman. Similarly Forsyth's concern for children was a box which needed balancing. In 1900, towards the end of his Cambridge ministry, he addressed a Sunday School Union meeting and deplored the shapelessness which passed for Sunday School teaching:

> The Sunday School is too much left to well-meaning and hard-working people, who, with all their earnestness, have no experience of controlling others, and no sense or power of discipline. The teachers are ... gentle and fear to hurt feelings; or they are too tender about ejecting black sheep ... They have young ideas about what Christian love means. They are too anxious to be loved and not enough concerned to be obeyed ... I am afraid that many teachers have more interest in the affections of their scholars than in their souls.[15]

That Cambridge Forsyth was entirely consistent with the Shipley Forsyth of twenty-two years back, and that was so because of the realities of congregational ministry. Between 1878 and 1900 Forsyth had undergone a deepening of religious experience, almost an overturning, even a further conversion. His own health had collapsed temporarily at the point of the most critical of his moves from one pastorate to another and his wife's had collapsed totally at the same point. Her death left him with an adolescent daughter, his only child. But these things, though unique to each sufferer, are unique to no ministry. Even in his Shipley days, thirty years young, just ordained, newly married, and careless of convention, Forsyth sounded the depths which every minister must sound. His sermon to those girls, 'Maid Arise', was grounded on the story of Jairus's daughter (Luke 8 vv. 52–6). It was based on a story of family tragedy, a fact to be faced even by school leavers. It was completed by a prayer which is not to be dismissed as a young liberal's natural meliorism. This prayer conveys that young minister's pastoral power. It is mannered indeed, conventional in form. It is also a true leading in prayer, congregational yet individualizing each member of that congregation, properly extempore therefore, yet above all

---

[14] *Ibid.*, p. 5.
[15] *The Sunday School Chronicle*, 13 December 1900, pp. 850–2.

401

things shapely—or at least striving after such shape as schoolgirls might glimpse whose reach must exceed their grasp:

> Almighty Father, who dost school us by life and try us by pain and reward us by death, we give Thee thanks for Thy kind discipline of patience and Thy rich gifts of grace. We gather in Thy house to forget ourselves and remember Thee, to lay by our rivalry and take up our prayer, to lose our fears and feel Thy comfortable thoughts. Put out the noisy world from the chamber where we meet with Thee. We are not dead utterly to things divine. Our souls do but sleep, and the crowd of soulless comforters would mock Thy power to rouse and save. Quicken our drowsy spirits lest we sleep away into the second death. Bid us arise and eat heavenly food, restore us to simple life and homely love, and give us back to faith and our Father again. Clothe us in all the charities that minister and bless. Consecrate duty and sanctify grief. For sin give penitence, from passion give us rest, and for ambition and vanity teach us divinely to serve, through the cross of Jesus Christ our Lord. Amen.[16]

Forsyth the exponent of religion in art is better known than Forsyth the pastor for women or children. Here too, however, is a similarly sustained consistency in antithesis. In part this is the reflection of an educated yet arguably self-cultivated Scotsman's temperament, in part the reflection of the enlarging sub-culture which formed him. It is also, and this is what shaped it, a reaction to the culture to which he ministered. There is a clue in 'Maid arise': the gentle irony which enjoyed, even valued, without displacing that picture in the dining-room of one of his tasteful friends. There is more than a clue in the genesis of his first considerable work, *Religion in Recent Art*.[17] These lectures, published during his Leicester ministry (with Forsyth eventually drafted onto the Museum and Art Gallery Committee), were delivered in the wake of that most significant of English provincial cultural explosions, the Manchester Art Treasures Exhibition of 1887. That was the prime cultural event of his Manchester pastorate.

In each of his pastorates Forsyth encountered church members who were educated in art and architecture, especially their technicalities. In his Sunday morning pews and at dinner parties he met the moral purpose of

---

[16] *Maid Arise*.
[17] P. T. Forsyth, *Religion in Recent Art: Being Expository Lectures on Rossetti, Burne Jones, Watts, Holman Hunt and Wagner* (Manchester and London, 1889).

mental art men whose interests were the next logical extension from the restlessly inquisitive concerns of Shipley wool and worsted men or Cheetham Hill cottontots. And he mediated their moral purpose to the Sunday evening gallery pews of the mutual improvement, university extension, institute and settlement age, to young men at several removes from Shipley or Hackney dinner parties. So his lectures on recent art were to Charles Rowley's Ancoats Brotherhood. They were masterpieces in moral story-telling with Wagner as climax.

There are still few more suggestive overtures to *Parsifal* than Forsyth's exposition of 1889, fresh as he had experienced it at Bayreuth with a rich Hackney friend seven years before. Here was redemption music. Here, perhaps, with the exception of *The Messiah* (and how pedagogically impeccable to annex to the *Messiah*, which all knew in their sleep, *Parsifal* which none would probably ever know save in their dreams),

> we have ... the greatest Redemption music in the world ... It is long since a work of first-class art took its stand upon the almost extinct sense of sin, and made its central motive the idea of Redemption.

Forsyth was almost bowled over, but not quite. Even here there were boxes to be balanced, for this was only one side of Redemption music:

> It is not so much a message from the delivering God as a representation of deliverance in man's soul. It is the soul singing its own deadly sins, its own mortal agony, and its own regenerate beauty. Wagner sang one side of the truth. 'Work out your own salvation' ...

And he sang from this side of it, this 'most gifted and passionate expositor of that semi-religious philosophy and semi-Christian atheism'; he sang from the manward side, inevitably pessimistic:

> There is one principle in Christianity which separates it by an impassable gulf from every form of Pessimism ... We can never know things at their worst till we stand where they are at their best.[18]

The Cross was that standpoint.

Forsyth was a Germanophile, like so many educated Dissenting Ministers; and the increasingly perceived formlessness of German culture was growing agony to him. We are back to shape.

There was nothing formless about Forsyth's grasp of Christianity. Election forbade that. So did the Trinity. Here too we begin in Manchester for

[18] *Ibid.*, pp. 287, 292, 287, 237, 280.

consistency in antithesis with a Forsyth who is assumed not to have lasted the course: Forsyth the socialist, whose first political pamphlet was called *Socialism and Christianity in some of their Deeper Aspects* (1886), bold with its reference to 'the greatest Socialist thinkers, like Marx'. It must be doubted whether the socialist Forsyth ever voted other than Liberal. W. L. Bradley, whose biographical study remains the best guide to Forsyth, is clear that what drew him was less socialism than 'that aspect of Christianity which makes a social ethic essential', and that aspect lay at the heart of Evangelical orthodoxy: God as Trinity, the society of persons in the Trinity, sign and seal of the organic solidarity of society and arguably 'the religious base of a Socialism as far from Egoism on the one hand as from Communism on the other'.[19]

But if the Trinity is ultimate form, matters cannot be left at that. Forsyth ministered successively to five independent aggregations of atoms. Where was their place in the form of things? How might the solitary soul be set within the church Congregational and the church Congregational be set within the Church catholic? Forsyth's answer is an organ note from his own experience set in a passage which reads as a hymn of the Evangelical Revival, delivered from the Chair of the Congregational Union when he was at last, though only for the time being, recognized as its representative figure:

> I have found my rock, my reality, my eternal life in my historic Redemption. And what is moral rock, real existence, and spiritual mastery for me is also the authority and charter of the Church, the living power in all history, the moral foundation of society, and the moral warrant of an infinite future for the race.[20]

That sense of Church and soul is breathtaking:

> All history exists for the church, but for a Church of living souls as the distillation of history . . . Apart from these souls the Church is an abstraction . . . Truly election contemplates a vast totality of souls as the direct object of God's choice and work, but the election . . . is apprehended by individual faith, sure that the believing soul is thus in the eternal thought of God. There alone have we due ground for realising the unspeakable value of a soul.[21]

---

[19] Bradley, pp. 63, 67–9, quoting *Socialism and Christianity*, p. 3.
[20] 'The Grace of the Gospel as the Moral Authority in the Church', *Congregational Year Book* (1906), p. 97.
[21] P. T. Forsyth, *The Principle of Authority* (1913), p. 354, quoted in Bradley, p. 217.

But what was to shape this relationship? Authority was. And sacrament. And ministry. In 'every true Church the note of authority must be uppermost. To put liberty, which is a secondary matter, before authority, which is primary and frontal even for liberty itself, is to confess a sect and not a Church'.[22] Those were bold words for Congregationalists, and there were bolder:

> The Sacraments are the acted Word—variants of the preached Word.
> They are signs, but they are more than signs. They are the Word, the
> Gospel itself, visible, as in preaching the Word is audible. But in
> either case it is an act. It is Christ in a real presence giving us anew His
> Redemption.[23]

And it was the minister who mediated that Word, that *act*, to the Church, commissioned by God thus and thus alone to recreate the souls of his people. And Forsyth was such a minister. All his writings have in common with his Shipley prayer that elusive, exasperating, but most comforting quality of breathing life, unexpected and often outrageous, into traditional language. The resonances are always impeccable. This quality was forged and tempered by his years as a Congregational minister.

Forsyth ministered in Shipley (Springwood), London (St Thomas's Square, Hackney), Manchester (Cheetham Hill), Leicester (Clarendon Park) and Cambridge (Emmanuel). Each church save the last was suburban. Yet each church was in the denominational mainstream. Shipley was in the most Congregational part of the West Riding; Hackney was London's most Congregational suburb; Cheetham Hill was set firm in Manchester's immensely prosperous Congregational confederacy; and Emmanuel, Cambridge, was still more of an East Anglian county town's leading Congregational church than it was anything else. The pulse of each church was a denominational pulse, and successful ministry in each would depend on fidelity to the denominational culture. And Forsyth's were successful ministries. At Hackney and Cheetham Hill he discovered Wagner, corresponded with G. F. Watts, communicated with working men and refined his power over words. At Shipley, Hackney and Cheetham Hill, moreover, he moved within the orbit of the Congregational theological colleges. Then came Leicester where, at Clarendon Park, he savoured an aldermanic culture, coaxing into being such a

---

[22] P. T. Forsyth, *Faith, Freedom and the Future* (1912), p. 290, quoted in Bradley, p. 218.
[23] P. T. Forsyth, *Lectures on the Church and the Sacraments* (1917), p. 176, quoted in Bradley, p. 240.

church as must (to use a phrase from a poem of his) turn civic life into a liturgy. Cambridge followed.

The call was almost unique in Congregational ministry. The Leicester Press swiftly spelt out its possibilities. Indeed their leaking of the new precipitated Forsyth's decision. As the *Evening Mercury* put it, Emmanuel Church was 'the chief if not practically the only Congregational church in Cambridge'; more Nonconformist students graduated at Cambridge than Oxford; and 'the principal Nonconformist training college for teachers has been removed to Cambridge, and thus from that town large numbers of young students and teachers are continually going out over the whole country'. That was hyperbole on all three counts but the scope of the call was underlined by the eight nationally known ministers who urged on Forsyth that here was 'a case where the field was measured rather by the university and the opportunities it supplied than the city and its boundaries'.

That was the new fact in an old situation. Emmanuel Church was unusually conscious of its past.[24] Its minute books were headed by the succession of ministers, their names incorrectly transcribed, from Joseph Hussey who had settled in 1691.[25] The church had suffered, and at times enjoyed, every tension natural to an urban congregation but it had sustained its order more clear-headedly than most. It was not yet Cambridge's leading Nonconformist church, although it was the oldest, and in Forsyth's time it was not the town's largest Congregational church though its membership was solid and its deacons were the sort whose businesses dignified Market Hill. What was new was the opening up of the university as a source of intellectual stimulus and evangelical mission rather than commercial opportunity for keen-eyed tradesmen. Emmanuel's building witnessed to that novelty. Its sturdy, dominating, fourteenth-century gothic thrust through the carapace of Peterhouse, Pembroke and the Pitt Press.

That building was twelve years older than Clarendon Park. It too held seven hundred. Forsyth was the third to minister in it. One of his predecessors still lived in Cambridge as a philosophy don at Trinity.[26] His

---

[24] This section relies chiefly on Emmanuel Congregational Church, Cambridge, Church Meeting Minute Book 1892–1922, in the possession of Emmanuel United Reformed Church, Cambridge.

[25] Joseph Hussey (1660–1726), minister at Cambridge, 1691–1719. G. F. Nuttall, 'Cambridge Nonconformity from Holcroft to Hussey', *Journal United Reformed Church History Society*, 1, no. 9 (April, 1977), pp. 241–58.

[26] James Ward (1854–1925), first Professor of Mental Philosophy and Logic, 1897, *DNB*.

ministry had been terrible for him. So it was at first for Forsyth, plunged into the abyss of personal despair and physical prostration. He emerged. He remarried. He grew fond of the people who had sustained his collapse. His church's membership reached two hundred for the first time in its history and his stipend reached £500. And his ministry was uttered on a deeper note. The whole denomination heard it when he preached his assembly sermon, 'God the Holy Father', and in one memorable passage cuttingly outlined such styles of ministry as had so closely engaged his own recent energies:

> He might take the genial cultured way of a natural goodness with philanthropy for repentance, an easy optimism, a beautiful Fatherhood, tasteful piety, social refinement, varied interest, ethical sympathies, aesthetic charm, and a conscience more enlightened than saved. Or he might take the pietist's way. And then is the risk fanciful of his sinking, perhaps, in the ill-educated cases, though a fluent religionist into a flimsy saint, lapped in soft airs, taking a clique for the Kingdom, and sold to the religious nothings of the hour with all their stupefying power; with no deepness of earth, no pilgrim's progress, no passion of sacred blood, no grasp on real life, no grim wrestling, no power with God, no mastery of the soul, no insight, no measure of it, no real power to retain for himself or for others, to compel a belief in the soul, its reality or its Redeemer.[27]

Emmanuel's regulatory arrangements were not too different from Clarendon Park's, though there was more liturgical conservatism. At his first Emmanuel church meeting Forsyth worried over

> the lack of response of the Amen at the close of the prayers during service, he trusted that it would be more general, failing which he · would have to suggest a remedy.

Emmanuel was not to be steam-rollered. It was much the same with the serving of communion. At Emmanuel the deacons were served with the bread and wine after they had served the communicants seated in the body of the church. Forsyth preferred it the other way round. He said that it was more usual; but he would of course, 'follow the custom of the Church till the church members themselves express a contrary desire'. It was an easier matter to introduce another Leicester practice, which was to link monthly church meetings with weekly worship, as when he gave a

---

[27] P. T. Forsyth, *God the Holy Father* (reissued London, 1957), pp. 14–15.

'short address dwelling upon the hymn of Luther which had been sung at the Sunday morning service'.

The pastor's concerns were for the church as sacramental community. In June 1897, for example, church meeting discussed the Sunday service. Forsyth had preached on baptism (shades of Shipley, 1879) and then he had baptized seven infants, '*most of the congregation staying and taking part* in an exceptional unique and edifying service which will be long remembered . . .'.[28] Then, with wounded *amour propre*, he 'referred to the lack of Church esprit de corps, as evinced by the smallness of the congregation, in his absence, on the previous Sunday evening and pointed out that it was . . . apt to give strangers an erroneous impression of the condition of the Church'. How could he ask country ministers to take his pulpit in such circumstances?

By January 1900 it was perhaps clear that Forsyth's Cambridge days were numbered. The church noted 'The growing recognition within and beyond the Church of his worth, and his conception of the power and dignity of the Pulpit'. In March, as if to demonstrate the point, Forsyth read out a soldier's letter from the South African front. It was about Forsyth's address to the International Congregational Council in Boston, Mass. At the same meeting a minister from Nova Scotia prayed and Forsyth spoke on 'the offerings made by the Wise Men from the East'. By now Emmanuel's conservatism was almost mellowing. Though a sung amen after each prayer was too much to take, worship now closed with a 'Musical Amen' and it opened (as at Clarendon Park) with the worshippers standing in readiness, as they now stood at church meetings when new members were received.

Forsyth left Emmanuel in the summer of 1901 to take over the college which had been so close to his former church in Hackney, though it was now bright and beautiful in Hampstead.[29] Emmanuel did not, could not, longer detain him. His last church meeting as a minister in congregational charge was thankful for such harmonious and faithful ministry:

> The Doctor replied . . . it was his hope and desire to do for the men whom he expected to train for the ministry at Hackney College what he had tried to do for this Church—strike a deeper note and expound the teaching of the Gospel, that nothing good could come but by

[28] My italics.
[29] C. Binfield, 'Hackneyed in Hampstead: The Growth of a College Building', *Journal United Reformed Church History Society*, 4, no. 1 (October, 1987), pp. 58–68.

sacrifice, for it was true of all that without shedding of blood there was no forgiveness of sins.

And Mr Almond, the church secretary, suitably noted:

With singing and prayer the church meetings of a unique and memorable ministry was [sic] brought to a close.

There had never been a time when undergraduates had not sometimes worshipped in Emmanuel's predecessors. From the 1850s an undergraduate presence, continuous yet transient, was a chapel fact of life. From the 1870s it was a church fact of life and it was not just an undergraduate presence. Senior members of the university from Nonconformist families joined the church. Some worshipped there in their gowns. This was the prayed-for consequence of the relaxation of university tests. Emmanuel Church was built to celebrate that relaxation and to institutionalize its consequence. Thus even the bazaar book which celebrated two hundred years of church life in 1891 was a splendidly academic production. The future Downing Professor of the Laws of England wrote on Emmanuel's earlier history.[30] A Fellow of Trinity Hall contributed two poems.[31] A recent Fellow of King's contributed a string of verses.[32] A Caius man described the rigours of Elizabethan university life and a Peterhouse man outlined the evolution of the bazaar.[33] This was the side of Emmanuel which had clinched Forsyth's acceptance of the call.

It is tempting to see Forsyth as minister to two Emmanuels, town and gown. Town was prominent enough: Mathers and Munsey the jewellers, Almond the outfitter, Thrussell the bootmaker, Macintosh the ironmonger, Wright the physician, Few the solicitor, Bond the grocer, men whose solidity was never in doubt. But this town became gown or married gown: Flora Mathers was at Newnham, Henry Bond at Trinity Hall; Mary Munsey and Beatrice Macintosh married young men whose apprenticeship was as undergraduates. By Forsyth's time there was a resident nucleus of university families: the Neville Keyneses of Pembroke, the Courtney Kennys of Downing (the most devoted attender never to become a member, for he was a Unitarian), the A. S. Ramseys of Magdalene (who

---

[30] Courtney Kenny (1847–1930), *DNB*.
[31] (Sir) A. W. W. Dale (1855–1921), Fellow of Trinity Hall 1886–99, J. A. Venn, *Alumni Cantabrigienses*, pt II, 2, p. 213.
[32] Arthur Reed Ropes (1859–1933), Fellow of Kings 1884–90, subsequently known to theatre goers as 'Adrian Ross'. Deacon at Emmanuel 1889–96, J. A. Venn, 5, p. 355.
[33] G. E. Green (1863–1931) and F. J. C. Hearnshaw (1869–1946), J. A. Venn, 3, pp. 128, 311.

were none too fond of Forsyth's paradoxes), the A. J. Wyatts of Christ's.[34] The young Baptist T. R. Glover was an associate member.[35] A. W. W. Dale of Trinity Hall was on the diaconate.[36] That was the key. Dale, Glover and Ramsey were sons of the manse. Keynes was a manse son-in-law. Where it did not repel (and the social and cultural presuppositions of Cambridge life made it a powerful repellent) the manse cousinhood made Emmanuel a natural home, especially for that first generation of married dons. For such households Emmanuel's was an inclusive fellowship. Thus, of the four deacons elected during Forsyth's ministry, one was town, two were gown (Joseph Reynolds Green FRS, of Downing, and German Sims Woodhead, the professor of pathology)[37] and one was neither town nor gown, since as a lecturer at Homerton he belonged to higher education's intermediate rung. As for the transients, the undergraduates, the stream was steady, most as sermon-tasters but a core as associate members, from at least a dozen colleges and most strikingly from the two women's colleges. Some were exotic, like the two Russian Lutherans from Emmanuel College, but most were children of the manse and the diaconate. A few came from grander backgrounds, held by traditionary loyalties. At Forsyth's first meeting John Evan Spicer of Trinity, from the papermaking family, was received as an occasional member recommended by his minister A. A. Ramsey, whose son was at Magdalene.

Their concerns were felt at church meeting. When Forsyth mooted the idea of a Sunday morning communion two views were expressed. One was that the Sunday school teachers would find it inconvenient. The other was that 'the lady students of Homerton would be glad to avail themselves of such an opportunity, being forbidden by the rules of the College to be out in the Evening . . .' Homerton won.

The essence of the relationship was distilled at Forsyth's welcome social when Lewis Gaunt of Clare

---

[34] Mrs Neville Keynes, her sister and mother-in-law, were members; her husband was an attender. Her daughter, Mrs A. V. Hill, was married at Emmanuel in June 1913. A. S. Ramsey was a member, and became a deacon and church secretary. His wife was an attender. A. J. Wyatt was an Anglo-Saxon scholar and University Coach.

[35] Glover (1869–1943), Fellow of St John's 1892–8, 1901–43, became a leading Baptist layman and a pillar of St Andrew's Street Baptist Church. In September 1892, however, he became an associate member of Emmanuel, which remained his Cambridge church for the rest of the decade.

[26] Deacon, 1886–1900.

[37] Green (1848–1914), FRS 1895. Venn, 3, p. 130; Woodhead (1855–1921), *Who Was Who 1916–1928*.

was called to express the opinion of the undergraduates: this he did
not hesitate to do saying he envied the very freshest of the freshmen
by reason of the lengthened opportunity they would have to sit
under Mr. Forsyth's teaching: he further raised considerable
enthusiasm by saying that his experiences were such that though
called to speak for the undergraduates he had no hesitation in
saying that his interest was first with Emmanuel and secondly with
the university members.

That, for most of the regular University members, was Emmanuel's
attraction. Forsyth made his position clear to them:

> The pulpit must necessarily be the test of his work: it was natural to
> him and the power of preaching a faithful Gospel was to be felt still,
> particularly in Cambridge where he hesitated not to say that his
> desire was to influence for good the members of Nonconformist
> families who were here for a time and thence departed to make their
> influence felt.

In Cambridge these young men and women were Trinity, Jesus, Christ's,
St John's, Newnham, Girton ... At Emmanuel they were also Dulwich,
Highgate, Stoke Newington, Islington, Kensington, Tollington Park, as
well as Cheetham Hill or Edgbaston, Sunderland, Lincoln, Bradford,
Birkenhead, Colchester, even Belfast or Cape Town, congregating still in
family pews, experiencing Forsyth's twin aims: beautiful worship and
church meetings to reflect 'the highest ideals of family life'.

At Forsyth's church meetings women regularly spoke: Homerton's
Miss Farren on behalf of her students; Mrs Neville Keynes about her
mothers' meeting or Dr Barrett's Congregational Union Lecture on
worship. At the annual church meetings it became the custom for young
gown to play a formal part. In 1898, W. H. Austin, the Senior Wrangler,
moved the adoption of the church reports, and F. H. Pyman, of the
Hartlepool shipping family, seconded him. That June Pyman wrote to
express his sadness at leaving Cambridge and sent £10. In December he
repeated the gift.

Emmanuel was thus Forsyth's greatest opportunity as it was certainly
his grandest frustration. Never before had he been so much the outsider
looking in. At last Emmanuel had a minister whose intellect filled the
building and the purpose; and he was excluded, save by courtesy, from the
community of Christian scholarship to which that intellect entitled him.
That frustration met Forsyth's fidelity to his call. The result was sermons

and lectures hammering out for him and his people why they stood as they did:

> If I am asked why I do not belong to the Established Church, I reply that my chief reason is, because I am such a Churchman—a High Churchman—with such a high ideal of the Church.[38]

That paradox became a commonplace for Congregationalists. He announced it in the first of two published lecture series, delivered from Emmanuel: *The Charter of the Church* and *Rome, Reform and Reaction*.[39]

At one level these works are in the exasperated tradition of anti-catholic polemic. Forsyth overboils as a latter-day Edward Miall, surveying Anglicanism, that 'great, godly, and unfortunate Church'; seeing in its monopoly 'a relic of Protection ... [bringing] in its train the torpor, neglect, and corruption of monopoly'; doubting 'whether all of us have really measured ... and with a statesman's eye, the depth, intimacy, and passion with which the Established Church interpenetrates, happily or unhappily, our social system and our national life'.[40] There is Miallite sarcasm at Anglicanism's yearning for the Greeks and Latins who discounted it rather than for the Reformed who would value it:

> For the rich madame, who will not recognise people in business because she is set on being recognised by the old aristocracy who snub and ignore her, is not only amusing, but, when she parades her religion as the reason, she is—let us say—pathetic.[41]

Forsyth's history was forcefully Whiggish made gloomier by fear of 'the awful Armageddon which awaits Europe sooner or later'.[42] Anglicanism was demoralizing. Romanism was the antithesis of all that had made Britain. Were it ever to return, Rome 'would in course of time reduce it from the most free, adventurous, powerful and righteous nation on the earth to the timid, vainglorious, petulant, cruel, pleasure-loving and bankrupt race which it has made Spain'.[43] He turned to empire:

> It is not the English Parliament nor the English Constitution that is felt in the English proconsul on the skirts of the Himalayas, but the

---

[38] P. T. Forsyth, *The Charter of the Church: Six Lectures on the Spiritual Principal of Nonconformity* (London, 1896), p. 7.

[39] *Ibid.*; *Rome, Reform and Reaction: Four Lectures on the Religious Situation* (London, 1899).

[40] *The Charter of the Church*, pp. 58, 59, 60.

[41] *Ibid.*, p. 55.

[42] *Rome, Reform and Reaction*, p. 167.

[43] *Ibid.*, p. 159.

English *man* ... An empire like ours could not hang together for a century ruled simply as a magnificent and compact organisation, and worked like a gigantic post office. But what does that mean? It means that our power is in its nature and genius Protestant and not Catholic, that its salvation is the development of individual resource and responsibility; that its doom would be to settle down into mere officialism ... and to regard the ideal Englishman more as a machine to obey orders than as a living moral centre of freedom, confidence, · and power. Make our religion Catholic, and above all things institutional, and in due time you reduce English enterprise to something in the nature of a Jesuit mission ...[44]

Cambridge could take that sort of thing in its stride, save that Forsyth admired what he excoriated and appropriated its language because it was his mother tongue: 'The whole history of the Church up to the Reformation at least is as much ours as theirs'; 'we recognize that the nation is a unity. It is a moral unity. It has a sanctity. It cannot dispense with a religion'; 'the living Christ is only realizable on an historic scale by His action through the living and historic community of the church ... the moving area of the Cross'.[45]

Here is Forsyth, protestant for the church catholic: 'This Church where I preach is a priest much more than I am, more than any member of it is, more than any clergyman. The great visible priest on earth is the Church in its various sections ...'[46] As for that preaching, it was 'spiritual struggle, the Lord's controversy. He has been wrestling with men—at grips with their souls, their fugitive, reluctant, recalcitrant soul'.[47] Who dare preach when a sermon has been so defined? Or sup, when 'In that act the Church identifies itself ... in a ceremonial way with Christ in His sacrificial act. It offers Christ, the one eternal sacrifice to God. And Christ dwelling in His Church body offers Himself, preaches Himself to the world as Crucified Redeemer'.[48]

This was not, after all, the usual vein of Dissenting polemic. It came naturally from a minister forced to relate his present position to the cumulative weight of all the Christian centuries since that act of the Cross, for whom none the less the Reformation must remain their

---

[44] *Ibid.*, pp. 168–9.
[45] *The Charter of the Church*, pp. 9, 10, 61.
[46] *Rome, Reform and Reaction*, p. 212.
[47] *Ibid.*, p. 217.
[48] *Ibid.*, p. 219.

crucible for modern man. Here, consequently, was a Free Churchman who would accept dogma as the church's footing, doctrine as its grasp, theology as its reach.[49] For the Church, not the individual, 'is the correlate of Christian truth. The great music needs orchestra and chorus round the conductor and round a theme'.[50] For this minister Emmanuel Church provided orchestra and chorus; and he was just within sound of the great music.

University of Sheffield

[49] P. T. Forsyth, *Theology in Church and State* (1915), p. xiii, in J. W. Grant, *Free Churchmanship in England 1870–1940* (London, n.d., c.1952), p. 232.
[50] Forsyth, *Church and State*, p. xviii, in Grant, p. 236.

FISHING FOR THE SOUL
'NOR'ARD OF THE DOGGER'

by JOHN R. GUY

T HE waters of the North Sea are shallow, and the weather there can be severe. On and around the Dogger Bank sudden gales cause high and heavy seas. The smacksmen of the fishing fleets in the 80s and 90s of the last century were there throughout the year on voyages which could last eight weeks, and their 50-80 ton yawl-rigged smacks were entirely at the mercy of the weather. Their fishing grounds were too far from land for them to run for shelter. They were compelled to ride out the heaviest gales or founder. In 1881 it was estimated that the North Sea fishing population numbered upwards of 12,000, the 'Short Blue' fleet alone consisting of 220 smacks crewed by 1,500 men.[1]

In that year a 32-year old market gardener, Ebenezer Joseph Mather, visited one of the fleets, and saw for himself the isolation of the smacksmen, and their vulnerability to both temptation and injury. It was his vision of a ministry at sea to these men which became reality in the work of the Mission to Deep Sea Fishermen.[2] When in the following year the Yarmouth yawl *Ensign* first sailed under that Mission's auspices, the voyage marked the inauguration of a practical Christian work which was—as it remains—a predominantly lay endeavour. But in one sphere of that work the 'professional' very quickly became dominant, to a degree that threatened to distort the very nature of the mission. This paper is an attempt to examine the work of the Mission to Deep Sea Fishermen in its first twenty years, and to explain how this situation arose.

E. J. Mather was himself a member of the Church of England,[3] but although supported by that Church, the Mission employed no ordained men. An account of worship at sea, published in Number One of the Mission's magazine, *Toilers of the Deep*, in 1886, recorded the reading of Morning Prayer and the Litany by a 'clergyman, who has devoted his holiday to service amongst trawlers'.[4] The services of clergymen were

---

[1] E. J. Mather, *'Nor'ard of the Dogger' or Deep Sea Trials and Gospel Triumphs* (London, 1888), pp. 2–3, 6, 7, 8.

[2] For the foundation of the Mission, see Mather, *'Nor'ard of the Dogger'*, pp. 49–66.

[3] Mather, *'Norard of the Dogger'*, p. 325.

[4] *Toilers of the Deep: A Record of Mission Work amongst them* [hereafter cited as TOD], 1, no. 1

voluntary, and confined to the summer months. For the rest of the year the spiritual work was largely in the hands of the skippers of the Mission ships. Inevitably—and it would seem by popular demand—the emphasis upon the Prayer Book slackened, and testimony or 'experience' meetings 'when plain, unlettered men tell how they found the Lord', bible classes, where the lessons were 'talked over' by those present, each giving his idea of the meaning, and hymn singing took over. The weekday services were always of this type, and known on occasion to last for up to ten hours, from 4 pm until 2 am.[5] By 1895 it was said that the services 'were distinctly evangelistic; the gospel message . . . set forth in all its simplicity and beauty'.[6] Seven years earlier, Mather had reported that the donor of a Mission ship had made the gift conditional upon the preaching 'of a full, free and present salvation through simple faith in the finished work of the Lord Jesus Christ' and that 'Christians . . . lay and clerical, of all denominations, may be free to preach the gospel in this vessel, so long as as they do so without putting forward any views which may be called distinctly "sectarian" and avoid proselytising'.[7] Mather had accepted the conditions.

Distinctions were not made between denominations, but between the 'converted' and the 'unconverted', and as a result there were tensions. Visiting clergy occasionally administered holy communion aboard the mission ships.[8] The sacrament was normally offered only 'when those who are known to be true believers are invited'.[9] The presence of others could result in distress. In 1891 Mather's successor, Thomas Miller, reported a fisherman telling him 'We had a clergyman here, sir, and there was just such a company as we've had today, and when he offered the bread and the wine to every one of us, it gave me such a turn . . . When I see the precious emblems offered to ungodly men, all my joy was gone'.[10] Miller approved of this 'line of demarcation' as he called it,[11] but celebrations of holy communion remained a cause of such tension, and as time passed they are mentioned less frequently in the Mission's records.

(January, 1886), p. 5. The editor of this monthly magazine was G. A. Hutchison, who also edited *The Boys Own Paper*.

[5] *TOD* 1, no. 1 (January, 1886), p. 5.

[6] 'What others say of us', *TOD* 10, no. 5 (May, 1895), unpaginated.

[7] Mather, *'Nor'ard of the Dogger'*, p. 312.

[8] *TOD* 1, no. 1 (January, 1886), p. 5; no. 6 (June, 1886) carried an illustration on p. 154 of a clergyman in surplice and hood celebrating holy communion in the hold of a mission ship.

[9] *TOD* 1, no. 1, p. 5.

[10] *Ibid.*, 6 (1891), p. 275.

[11] *Ibid.*

The problem of 'ungodly men' was to vex for some time. Mather had been determined from the outset to equip his floating 'bethels' with a Christian skipper and crew, for in the absence of ordained missioners, such were essential if a 'gospel ministry' was to be provided. The skippers played a key role, as leaders of worship, prayer and bible meetings, dispensers of Christian literature, and visitors to the other trawlers on behalf of the Mission. As the work expanded, however, with the provision of more 'bethels' which had to be kept almost constantly at sea, so the problem of staffing them with sufficient godly men became more acute. Matters came to a head in 1895, when the question of employing 'unconverted' men was raised. Miller's response was that while every effort was made to secure 'converted' crews, 'the ships must be manned, and manned by proper seamen'.[12] Although there was no compromise in respect of the skippers, crews were another matter. Men rarely transferred to the fishing fleets from other branches of the mercantile marine,[13] so the Mission had to draw its crews from the pool of available labour, converted or not.

The undenominational ministry of the Mission was, in the same year, challenged from another direction. The Revd Forbes Phillips, vicar of Gorleston, attacked its 'Salvation Army type of service' and its missioners 'full of Pentecostal fire'. Phillips spearheaded attempts to found a rival North Sea Church Mission—another fruit of the Anglo-Catholic revival. He was answered by the Revd Charles Hicks, vicar of Seething, Norwich, who frequently acted as an honorary chaplain on the mission ships. Hicks pointed out that the Mission had the support of churchmen and members of the episcopate, but conceded that 'the Council have fondly imagined that the Church has sons enough amongst its 23,000 clergy to work out on the North Sea simply for the love of souls ... [but] when the supply has not been equal to the demand for ten or eleven mission ships, Church laymen and ministers or men of other denominations have sought to further the work ...' The clergy had not risen to the challenge, and so the work was sustained primarily by the skippers of the 'bethels', men untrained for their role, but selected on the basis of their Christian commitment. The gospel ministry therefore had remained ad hoc and amateur.[14]

If the ministry was lay, it was also largely nondiscriminatory on

---

[12] *Ibid.*, 10 (1895), unpaginated.
[13] 'Counting Seafarers', *Mariner's Mirror*, 71 (1985), p. 310.
[14] The dispute between Phillips and the Mission is detailed in *The Eastern Daily Press* of 12 October 1895.

grounds of sex. Women achieved prominence both on shore and at sea. They were visiting the North Sea fleets in the summer months by 1886, within five years of the Mission's foundation.[15] These visits extended over several weeks, living aboard the Mission's smacks, in the cramped and rudimentary accommodation available. Mrs A. M. Wilson, a daughter of David Livingstone, published an account of one such visit in 1891 to the trawlers of the Great Northern fleet.

Accompanied by her husband (a poor sailor) Mrs Wilson set out on 23 May from Yarmouth, taking four days to reach the fleet. The Wilsons stayed until 16 June, a period which included six days of rough weather which kept the Mission ship double reefed fore and aft. Mrs Wilson recorded her impressions of the constant rolling and pitching, the cold, and the shipping of water. When the weather permitted, she assisted her husband, playing the harmonium at services, leading Bible classes, and giving magic lantern shows. She also visited other trawlers, which involved clambering aboard from small, open rowing boats.[16]

This ministry was purely voluntary, but on shore the work of women could be permanent and salaried. In 1890 Miss C. Wilkes was appointed Lady Visitor at Gorleston, at a salary of £80 per annum.[17] In the ensuing five years, she built up a network of related activity, visiting the wives and children of the smacksmen, holding services, prayer meetings, and Bible classes.[18] Her successor in 1895 was another woman, Helena Wright. By the end of the century, with the establishment of more Institutes in the home ports, women were taking a leading role. A photograph published in 1900 showed ten of the Mission's lady workers, some evidently in their twenties or thirties.[19] When in February 1895 the Mission established a Sailors' Home at Ymuiden in Holland, Miss Edith Woodman was put in charge. She learned Dutch to enable her to work with local fishermen and their families on shore, and also frequently visited on board Dutch and English trawlers.[20]

In contrast to the gospel ministry, the medical and surgical work undertaken by the Mission was quickly professionalized. At the outset

---

[15] *TOD* 1, no. 2 (February, 1886), pp. 41–2.

[16] Mrs A. M. Wilson, 'With the Great Northern trawlers again', *TOD* 6 (1891), pp. 250–3.

[17] Royal National Mission to Deep Sea Fishermen archives, Personal Index. I am grateful to Mr Bernard Clampton, Secretary of the Mission, for permission to consult its records, and files of *Toilers of the Deep*.

[18] *TOD* 6, no. 10 (October, 1891), pp. 261–2.

[19] *Ibid.*, 15 (1900), p. 20.

[20] *Ibid.*, 10 (1895), unpaginated. The Ymuiden Home closed in 1905.

Mather had responded to the needs of the smacksmen by equipping the *Ensign* with a properly stocked medicine chest.[21] Nevertheless it was appreciated that greater skill in the treatment of injury would not only further alleviate suffering, but also provide 'increased opportunities for preaching the Lord Jesus Christ as the Great Physician'.[22] The first step towards a professionally managed medical service was taken early in 1886, when Alfred Schofield was appointed 'Physician and Surgical Instructor to the Mission'.[23] Mather's personal influence is detectable here. Schofield was a friend and former schoolfellow, and his connection with the Mission terminated with Mather's own enforced retirement in 1889.[24]

Schofield instituted a training course for the skippers and mates of the Mission ships, leading to a certificate of proficiency in the treatment of ordinary medical and surgical cases. The first certificates were presented in May 1886 by Princess Christian at Kensington Town Hall.[25] At the same time the Mission provided better equipped Dispensary Closets on its ships, in place of the medicine chests. Schofield had trained at the London Hospital in Whitechapel, and a connection with this institution was to be crucial in the further professionalization of the medical service.[26] When Schofield was appointed, T. Gilbart-Smith and Frederick Treves joined the Mission's council. Both were to serve continuously for twenty years. The former was a physician at the London, the latter a surgeon. The influence of Treves was to predominate. He was energetic, and an enthusiastic sailor, obtaining his Master Mariner's 'ticket' in 1892. He successfully pressed for the provision of properly equipped hospital ships, with facilities for in-patients and carrying a qualified doctor. By 1890 there were three such vessels. In December 1889 Treves' erstwhile House Surgeon, Wilfred Grenfell,[27] was appointed Superintendant of the Mission's work at Sea, and this medical leadership meant—inevitably—that this aspect of the North Sea work should become almost predominant.

[21] Mather, *'Nor'ard of the Dogger'*, p. 53.
[22] *TOD* 1, no. 4 (April, 1886), p. 53.
[23] *Ibid.*
[24] Alfred Taylor Schofield, M. D. Brussels, 1884, M.R.C.S., L.R.C.P., 1883. Mather, *'Nor'ard of the Dogger'*, p. 324.
[25] *TOD* 1, no. 6 (June, 1886), p. 98.
[26] A. E. Clark-Kennedy, *The London. A Study in the Voluntary Hospital System*, 2 vols (London, 1962).
[27] For Treves, see S. Trombley, *Sir Frederick Treves: The Extra-ordinary Edwardian* (London, 1989). For his work at The London (especially with the celebrated 'Elephant Man') see Clark-Kennedy, *The London*, 2, pp. 85–7. For Grenfell's association with Treves, pp. 87–90. Grenfell recorded his work with the Mission in his autobiography, *Forty Years for Labrador* (London, 1934), pp. 59–70. See also J. Lennox Kerr, *Wilfred Grenfell, His life and work* (London, 1959).

When in 1891 an appeal was launched for a new ship, the *Alice Fisher* was described as a 'hospital trawler' whereon there would be 'room for gospel services',[28] and when the statistics for the Mission's work in 1890 were tabulated medical and surgical patients treated came top of the list, some way above temperance pledges taken or religious services held.[29] Within a decade of its foundation, the Mission was becoming dominated by its well equipped, highly organized, professional medical service.

It is fair to say that Mather had forseen these developments, and to some extent encouraged them. He regarded the free medical service as an opportunity for evangelism, but accepted that it had an economic dimension, and one which could gain the Mission support from both trawler owners and smacksmen. 'The prompt treatment of disease and injuries on the fishing grounds had [a] most important result. Numbers of men who without the aid of the mission ship must have gone home for cure in the hospital were able after a few days to resume their duties aboard the smacks, and this . . . was in aggregate an enormous gain both to the men and their families and also to the employers'.[30] Clearly a ministry which conserved life and returned hands to work in as short a time as possible had its attractions to the fleet owners. It could favourably affect a company's dividend. Directors came increasingly to support it. Mather was sufficiently worldly-wise to appreciate that this was 'conversion viewed from a business standpoint'.[31] It did not stop him taking companies' donations, nor from developing those aspects of the Mission's work, such as the medical, which further encouraged the growth of such support.

Another reason for such support was the Mission's endeavours to counteract the influence of the *copers*. These were yawls, mainly Dutch, which mixed with the fleets, and from which tobacco, alcohol and what was coyly called 'literature' was sold to the smacksmen. Tobacco in the English home ports retailed at 4s. a pound, from the *coper* the cost was 1s. 6d.[32] It was thus easy to lure the fishermen on board, where they could also be induced to purchase the cheap liquor that was available. Mather appreciated the implications and dangers of this trade. Men parted with their wages, to the impoverishment of their wives and families. They sold the fishing gear from their vessels to purchase alcohol, to the pecuniary

[28] *TOD* 6 (1891), p. 49.
[29] There were 8,904 medical and surgical patients treated during 1890.
[30] Mather, *'Nor'ard of the Dogger'*, pp. 95–6.
[31] *Ibid.*, p. 97.
[32] *Ibid.*, p. 29.

loss of the owners. And drunken fishermen put not only their own lives at hazard, but also risked the loss of their boat.[33]

From the outset the Mission took an uncompromisingly 'Temperance' stand. Seamen were urged to 'sign the pledge'. To Mather—and the fleet owners—this made good economic as well as moral sense. The question of tobacco was more difficult, but, as the Revd Newman Hall, addressing the AGM in 1886 confessed,[34] non-smoker as he was, he felt that the Mission was fully justified in taking the action it had, the selling of good quality but cheap tobacco on board its ships. Mather had enlisted the support of W. H. Wills, MP, of the family and firm of W. D. & H. O. Wills of Bristol, and a ready supply of tobacco was thereafter forthcoming.[35] The smokers thus went aboard the 'bethels' for their supplies and not the *copers*, where they could be influenced by the missioners, introduced to alternatives to the 'literature' and kept away from the alcohol. Mather thus turned the *copers*' methods against them, and finally succeeded in driving them out of business. The tobacco sales also benefitted the Mission. The sum realized in 1886 was £2,928.[36]

In its first twenty years of life, the Mission undertook a variety of work, a pastoral and gospel ministry, the promotion of temperance, and the maintenance of health. In all of these spheres of activity, the role of the Christian layman was not, to use our president's words, 'defined negatively'. The clergy, the 'professionals', wielded little influence, perhaps by design, perhaps through an unwillingness to actively engage in the North Sea work. The role of lay men and women was thus crucial in the development of an undenominational and evangelistic ministry. But in one area of that ministry, to the sick, professionalization quickly became dominant. The influence of a leading practitioner, Frederick Treves, resulted in the speedy development of seagoing hospital work, and by the late 1890s there was a real possibility of the Mission becoming a medical service, albeit one founded on Christian principles. It may be that the concurrent revolution in fishing techniques, with an accompanying change from sail to steam trawlers, which resulted in shorter voyages and 'single boating', prevented this taking place.

---

[33] *Ibid.*, pp. 31, 37.

[34] *TOD* I, no. 12 (December, 1886), p. 199.

[35] Mather, '*Nor'ard of the Dogger*', pp. 220–2.

[36] The *copers* still plied their trade in fleets where there was no mission ship. Mather discusses this, and international attempts to outlaw it, in '*Nor'ard of the Dogger*', pp. 224–7.

Evangelization at sea became increasingly difficult, and the Mission responded by concentrating more on shore-based work, which was largely non-medical. It was the ministry of the lay worker which ultimately survived, and still flourishes.

Department of Community Medicine,
Yeovil District Hospital

MINISTRY TO *ALL* THE PEOPLE?
THE ANGLICAN CHURCH IN MALAYSIA

by W. JOHN ROXBOROGH

S INCE Independence in 1957 the Anglican Church in Malaysia has disavowed any inclination towards Malay evangelism in concert with a general climate of Christian opinion which sees such efforts as not only legally difficult, if not actually illegal following enactments in a number of states, but also politically impossible and threatening to the stability of the nation. This is the background to the claim in a Singapore Anglican history written in 1963 that 'In the Peninsular . . . no missionary work among the Muslim Malays was considered and their faith always has been respected.'[1]

There is no doubt that the repetition of this observation has served the interests of Anglican leaders as an aid to good relationships with a Muslim government, but as history it is seriously flawed. In fact at various times in the earlier history of Anglicanism in what is now Malaysia and Singapore, the leaders of the church made few apologies for their assumption that their ministry ought to be to all, including Malays. Although slow, spasmodic, and not particularly fruitful as far as Malays were concerned, Anglican commitment to ministry to all the people was considered, deliberate, and real. Only over a long period was it finally abandoned having first being transposed into an effort to gain a greater measure of constitutional religious freedom than was attained, so that rights of propagation might be recognized as well as freedom of choice for people of all ethnic groups genuinely provided for.

It is possible, of course, that for some this had at its heart a sense of the superiority of English culture and therefore of English religion more than a commitment to the 'Great Commission'. And similarly when this vision faded it may have had as much to do with a loss of grip on empire as with a new appreciation of other faiths. But for others a commitment to sharing the Christian Gospel with Malays was something born of the love of God which they had experienced and which they believed it was their duty to propagate. It was also believed that the introduction of Western culture without Christianity was morally dangerous.

[1] Loh, Keng Aun, *Fifty years of the Anglican Church in Singapore Island, 1909–1959* (University of Singapore, 1963), p. 5.

423

It is true that Malay converts were few, certainly by contrast with Chinese and Tamil, although a good number of the Chinese and Indian congregations were migrants who were Christian before they came to Malaya and whose own evangelistic efforts were largely responsible for their subsequent growth. Some Malays retained their Christian commitment, most returned to Islam. Yet there were more efforts in this direction than either the meagre results or present perceptions and sensitivities suggest.

The beginnings of the Anglican Church in the area are associated with the East India Company's provision of chaplains for the British who were in Penang from 1786, Melaka from 1795, and in Singapore from 1819. Only slowly were the horizons of the church extended to others, and missions when they began were not integral to the English congregations. However in Penang, for fourteen years until his death in 1827, the Revd Robert Hutchings exercised an energetic and notable ministry which was not to be emulated for many decades. He saw to the building of St George's Church (Melaka was provided with Anglican facilities for worship simply by taking over the Dutch Reformed building, Singapore took many years to get its cathedral permanently erected), started the Penang Free School, worked on a Malay translation of the Prayer Book, and spent considerable time revising Leidekker's Malay New Testament as well as compiling a dictionary and grammar. In 1818 he was in Calcutta assisting the Bible Society with the oversight of the printing of a Jawi Old Testament.

In Singapore what outreach there was beyond the European congregation was directed towards Chinese and Tamils and only got off the ground properly in the 1860s with SPG assistance, although in 1846 the bishop of Madras, visiting on behalf of the bishop of Calcutta in whose diocese Singapore lay, had reported the deficiency that 'no missionary operations against heathenism are directly carried on at this station'.[2]

In what is now Sarawak the first missionary and later bishop, Francis McDougal, arrived in Kuching in 1848 and began a school for Malays. This made some progress until an Islamic revival stimulated by his presence led to these pupils being withdrawn and McDougal's work as it developed was with Dyak tribespeople and with Chinese.

On the peninsular during the rest of the nineteenth century mission among the Malays, such as it was, was undertaken by the LMS on Penang without much understanding and with less success, and on a rather more

---

[2] Singapore Record Book 3, 1838–63, Diocese of Singapore.

sustained and informed basis in Singapore by the ex-LMS missionary, B. P. Keasberry. Yet there was also some Anglican commitment. In particular more work was done on the Malay Prayer Book by the Revd W. H. Gomes. The task was supported by Bishop Hose, who is sometimes credited with the result, and was finally completed in 1901. Who exactly was expected to use the Prayer Book is not clear, but it may well have relevance in the 1990s, at least as the basis of liturgy in the national language which is now the medium of most education if not yet of very much Christian worship.

However, the most serious effort at a Malay mission was the opening in 1911 of an SPG sponsored medical mission of four dispensaries in the Melaka area. This was consolidated into one hospital in 1914 and the following year another dispensary for Malays was opened near Singapore. Interest in Malay work was also reinforced by the visit of J. R. Mott to Singapore where, from 21–3 January 1913, he held one of his series of follow-up conferences to take the message of the Edinburgh 1910 Missionary Conference to Asia.[3] It is striking how this ecumenical gathering which took as its region Indonesia as well as present-day Singapore-Malaysia was unhesitating in its commitment to mission among Muslim peoples. There was no doubt or question recorded; the task before them was simply to survey the work to be done and to co-ordinate its progress as they strove together 'to stem the advance of Islam'.[4] The committee appointed included the Anglican bishops of Singapore and Borneo as well as Methodist and Open Brethren leaders.

Strong support was given by the then bishop of Singapore, Ferguson-Davie, and by his wife who, as a medical doctor, took a special interest in the work of the Malay dispensaries. In 1921 she published an account of the Church in Malaya. The book is laced with artless and derogatory racial comments, yet also evident sincerity. Outside the Straits Settlements the Pangkor Treaty of 1874 had laid the basis for the extension of British influence through the Peninsular but was quite specific in excluding 'religion and custom' from the advice that it was competent for British residents to give and which the Sultans of the different Malay states were obliged to receive. This treaty was to become a focus of Christian concern because of the constraints that it at least appeared to impose on Malay evangelism. Although the SPG clinics were not in the area covered by the treaty, being within the Straits Settlements, the general position of the

[3] *The Continuation Committee Conferences in Asia, 1912–1913* (New York, 1913), pp. 171–83.
[4] *Ibid.*, p. 173.

treaty that the British would protect Malay custom, tended to apply to them also. And from their connection with the administration in India prior to 1867 the long standing tendency not to do anything with regard to religion which might interfere with trade was also true of the Straits Settlements. In addition the credibility of the British in the Malay States would have been badly strained if, just outside them in the Straits Settlements, they encouraged Malays to become Christian. The greater degree of freedom for evangelism in Penang, Melaka, and Singapore has never been more than relative as later events were to indicate. Yet in the last decades of the nineteenth century the Church was following the British flag into Perak, Selangor, and Negri Sembilan. How wide the scope of the mission of the Church could and should be was a question which had to be faced. Mrs Ferguson-Davie's commitment is as clear as her information is inadequate. It may be that she provides her own explanation.

> The climate of the Malay Peninsula makes accuracy of thought very difficult, and so there has sprung up the idea that the Government has in some treaty or other bound itself to keep the highest of all truths from the Malays. This, one is glad to say, is a false idea, as all who have studied the treaties know. Anyone who holds the Christian faith and who really cares for the Mohammedans (and they have some very attractive qualities which show themselves even in the very imperfect Mohammedanism of Malaya) must wish to give to the Malays what is so dear to himself. Will it be the privilege of the English Church? ... our race and Church seem to have been given something of the qualities which are necessary if we are to be successful.[5]

By the 1930s the medical work was proving ineffective. Wards had been opened to Chinese and Indians and this, combined with general caution, conspired to keep Malays away from a Christian hospital. Difficulties in obtaining finance and staff finally led to its being closed in 1933.

Ferguson-Davie's successor as bishop of Singapore, Bishop Roberts, shared the sense that nevertheless something ought to be done for the Malays, and with the closing of the medical work he took a number of steps to resolve the problem. Legal opinion was sought privately as to just what the restrictions of the Pangkor Treaty amounted to. Strictly speaking Malay evangelism was not illegal, but it was clear that this was not how it

---

[5] C. E. Ferguson-Davie, *In rubber lands. An account of the work of the Church in Malaya* (London, 1921), p. 85.

might be regarded in practice. At the same time Dr Laurence E. Browne, previously of the Henry Martyn School of Islamics in Lahore, was invited to visit Malaya, meet with other Christian leaders and prepare a report.

The results of Browne's investigations were published by the SPG and SPCK in 1936. *Christianity and the Malays* was written with the express purpose of 'stirring up missionary interest in this most attractive people'.[6] He estimated that of the 1,644,000 Malays in the peninsular, 'probably not more than six'[7] were Christian. Although Browne was commissioned by Roberts to investigate 'a possible mission to Malays' he was not overly optimistic. He wrote as an outsider aware that there was 'a strong feeling amongst many of the English residents ... against a mission to the Malays'.[8] Although there was a prayer fellowship overseas to support the work there was among the various churches 'not a single missionary able to devote the greater part of his time to the Malays'.[9]

There it seemed the matter rested. The bringing together of Methodists and Presbyterians with Anglican leaders to meet with Browne survived as the nucleus of the Malayan Christian Council as it was eventually constituted after the War, but for Malay evangelism as such there was no evidence of progress. In 1946 the SPCK's 'War and after series' reported that the Malays 'in many cases educated, able and cultured ... have scarcely been touched by Christian teaching. The Church will have to consider very seriously ... what attitude it is to adopt towards the whole question of evangelistic work among the Malays'.[10] However from 1948 the churches in Malaya, scarcely recovered from the devastation of the War, were faced with the fresh challenge of the Emergency which was to last till 1960. The years of terrorism brought new challenges and opportunities, for which the Malayan Christian Council provided the focus of action for the English speaking churches at least. Bishop Wilson from 1941 had been central to its formation. Bishop Baines from 1949 also took a leading role and the Malay question was one which continued to be considered as an ecumenical issue.

But it remained also a sensitive one. Anglican work among Malays in Penang, such as it was, had to cease in 1951 when Malay political organizations protested over the baptism of some Malay children.[11] In

---

[6] L. E. Browne, *Christianity and the Malays* (London, 1936), p. v.

[7] *Ibid.*, p. 9.

[8] *Ibid.*, p. 77.

[9] *Ibid.*, p. 54.

[10] J. Hayter and J. Bennitt, *Singapore*, The War and after series, No. 2 (1946), pp. 35 *seq.*

[11] G. E. Marrison, 'A Christian approach to the Malays', mss prepared for the Conference of

December 1950 there were riots in Singapore in which several Europeans were killed and a member of the executive of the Christian Council injured. The riots were in protest at the annulment of the Muslim marriage of Bertha Hertog, a Dutch girl whose Catholic parents left her in the care of a Malay Amah during the War.

Perhaps arising out of publicity given to the Hertog case, in 1952 the question of religious freedom in Malaya was raised with the Commission of the Churches on International Affairs. It was discussed at the meeting of the International Missionary Council at Willingen in July and a process of enquiry begun which was soon directed back to Malaya. At that time the only missionary with any Malay involvement, and probably the only one with a good knowledge of the language, was the semi-retired Methodist Robert Blasdell.[12] Despite his gifts and experience he did not seem the best person to deal with the finer points of the legal and political situation and it was clear that Methodists saw their future as lying with the Chinese, least of all the Malays.

In any case an 'Approach to the Malays' committee was formed whose membership included Bishop Baines and once again expert legal opinion was sought. In 1954 it was reported that a list of all Malay Christian literature had been commissioned and it was noted that 'a considerable number' of gospels and testaments had been 'sold to Malays on their initiative'.[13]

That year the issue was also raised at the second World Council of Churches Assembly at Evanston and the study material prepared for the Assembly commented that 'the failure to evangelize the Malays is due to obscure reasons, but it represents a very definite unfinished, unattempted task'. In 1955 an Anglican, G. E. Marrison, prepared a report for the Christian Council which, quoting the Evanston comment, observed that the reasons were 'not so much obscure as peculiarly recalcitrant'. The Churches recognized their 'failure and obligation'.[14]

Marrison's paper drew on the most recently acquired legal opinions and was used as the basis both for a report by Sir Kenneth Grubb to the

---

British Missionary Societies Asia Committee, p. 2; International Missionary Council Archives, World Council of Churches, Geneva, IMC 26.5.116(19), Malaysia Papers. See also G. E. Marrison, 'Islam and the Church in Malaya', *Muslim World*, 47 (1957), pp. 290–8.

[12] J. Fleming to S. H. Dixon, 6 November 1952; Council of British Missionary Societies Archives, London, Asia Committee, Malaya—religious liberty, 1952.

[13] Malayan Christian Council, Standing Committee meeting minutes, 21 October 1954.

[14] G. E. Marrison, 'Islam and the Church'.

Commission of the Churches on International Affairs and for a short memo issued by the Malayan Christian Council. Together these three documents present a very complete view of the realities of the situation. Grubb considered Malays 'tenacious rather than fanatical' although 'dangerous feelings could be very easily evoked'.[15] The fact that in the Malay states the British administrators were regarded as Christians meant that activity by the Church would be seen to have the sanction of authority. What the Treaty of Pangkor meant was that in matters of religion the British were not to interfere. It was the prerogative of the Sultans, and there could be little doubt as to what their attitude would be, especially with the reduction of their other traditional areas of authority.

Once again there seemed to be little that the Churches could do. Archdeacon Robin Woods was among those who looked across to Indonesia where a very considerable indigenous church had developed and was continuing to grow through Muslim converts and wondered what they could learn from that example.[16]

With this background, by the time of the 1956 annual meeting of the Christian Council, held in February in Kuala Lumpur, the focus of Christian concern for Malays had shifted from the question of evangelism to that of freedom of religion in the soon to be independent Malaya. In July the Council sent a memorandum to the Reid Constitutional Commission and in August a delegation met with the Commission to further press their concerns. They based their case on clause 18 of the United Nations Universal Declaration of Human Rights and drew attention to clauses in the constitutions of India and Pakistan which prescribed freedom both to change and to propagate one's religion. In their meeting with the Commission they expressed their fears about the possibility of Islam being the state religion and voiced their preference for a secular constitution.

In the event they were disappointed. The constitution provided for freedom to 'profess and practice' one's religion, but there was no specific provision for freedom to change one's faith and propagation was subject to a clause empowering states to restrict propagation among Muslims. It was a masterly piece of drafting. It had to be conceded that it did not actually prevent a Malay changing his or her religion. The provisions for

[15] K. G. Grubb, 'The Christian approach to the Malays', Commission of the Churches on International Affairs, London, 16 December 1955; Conference of British Missionary Societies Archives, Malayan Christian Council General correspondence, 1951–9.
[16] Malayan Christian Council Standing Committee, minutes 9 March 1956.

the restriction of religious propaganda were only of an empowering nature, however clear their implications for the future and however much it might be maintained that without explicit provision for religious change social pressures would continue to put any convert in a vulnerable situation. The Reid Commission had succeeded in giving the Malays the religious protection they sought, while at the same time not of itself formally limiting the religious freedom of others.

When the details became known a special meeting of the Council executive was held on 18 July, six weeks before independence and, not without discussion, the consensus was in favour of accepting the situation. The Methodist educationalist Dr Ho Seng Ong considered the constitution 'reasonable and even from the Malay point of view a concession'. Bishop Baines counselled against taking 'any steps tending to rouse world opinion'. Others felt that if they failed to protest then, or even just to express regret, their silence could be taken as acquiescence.[17] Baines stated the need for Christians to study the Muslim religion and the Malay language and for greater contact between Christians and Malays, and moved the motion which decided not to take 'action to register Christian protest or regret' either locally or internationally.[18] The Commission of the Churches on International Affairs which had been closely following the situation, had no alternative but to comply with the request. Not subject to the same constraints the *Manchester Guardian* editorial written to mark Malayan Independence commented on the restrictive religious clauses, but was speedily rebuked by Malaya House, London which claimed that 'the position of Islam is similar to that of the Anglican Church in relation to England, that and no more'.[19]

The campaign if one can call it that for Malay religious freedom may easily be accused of self-interest, yet it is clear that Bishop Baines and others of the Malayan Christian Council believed that such freedoms as they sought were in the best interests of all people, they were not just a matter of facilitating Christian conversion. However it also betrayed a lack of understanding of what the Malay community was all about and what the Treaty of Pangkor meant, quite apart from what it happened to say. The position of the British in Malaya was in terms of a contract with Malay rulers; whatever happened the country remained theirs. If they

[17] Malayan Christian Council Executive, minutes, 18 July 1957.
[18] *Ibid.*
[19] Mohamed Sopie, Information Officer, Malaya House London, letter to the editor, *Manchester Guardian*, 6 September 1957.

could not be persuaded as a community to weaken what they regarded as necessary safeguards for their religious identity then it was their prerogative to do so. The process of Westernization which for some church people had reinforced their sense of obligation to share the benefits of the Gospel not just of commerce, was to the Malays all the more reason for insisting on some protection against religious invasion as much as secular imperialism. To them Islam was a far better safeguard against the acids of modernity than the religions of peoples who had either invaded or dominated their country over many centuries. To be Malay was to be Muslim, and in the new Malaysia those who opted out of the faith would necessarily opt out of the community as well.

Whatever the possibility which might theoretically still remain for such conversion to take place, Anglicans and others recognized that they themselves had come to the end of the road in their efforts to have a ministry and a mission to all the people of Malaysia. Even the staff of the Overseas Missionary Fellowship, working with the Anglicans as well as with others, capitulated and required their staff to sign their consent to the law of the land in respect of evangelism amongst Muslims.

After Independence the Churches' evangelism was confined to Hindus, Buddhists, and Animists, though even here the freedom only continues to exist because Islam wishes to exercise the same goal. Anglicans, like the other older Churches in the country, are no longer able to say that their ministry is to all the people. But they were once.

Seminari Theoloji, Malaysia

A TRIUMPH OF PATIENCE AND PURPOSIVENESS: LINTON OF BETONG

by BRIAN TAYLOR

ROM 1869 until the founding of the diocese of Singapore in 1909, the missions and chaplaincies in Singapore and what is now West Malaysia were within the jurisdiction of the diocese of Labuan, which itself had been founded as a legal fiction in 1855 as the stock onto which the bishopric for Rajah James Brooke's Sarawak could be grafted.[1] Although the diocese and the bishopric were constitutionally distinct, as succeeding bishops were often reminded by the rajahs of Sarawak, the bishops looked at the whole area of their spiritual leadership, and regarded the staffing of it as one problem—or opportunity. G. F. Hose himself, bishop of Labuan 1881–1908, and of Sarawak 1882–1908, had served in the Straits Settlements from 1868, and had been archdeacon of Singapore for his predecessor, Bishop Chambers. For sixty-two years the St Andrew's Church Mission in Singapore, the base for work among Asians, had as superintendent two priests, W. H. Gomes, 1872–1902, and Richard Richards, 1902–34. Both had previously worked in Borneo, for more than fourteen and twelve years respectively. In the opposite direction Bishop Hose transferred to Kuching in 1898 A. F. Sharp, who had worked for six years in Singapore.

Sharp was the first priest in Borneo with the inclination, opportunity and initiative to introduce a sub-tractarian style of ministry, which he combined with a flair for finding and training Chinese and Dyak[2] workers, and giving them extended responsibility. The change in churchmanship, which was to be developed under Bishop Mounsey, 1906–16, was not welcomed by Rajah Charles Brooke, and marked a loosening of the links between the Church and government in Sarawak. In one of the few *morceaux* of ecclesiastical history in his book on Sarawak, Sir Steven Runciman mentions the Rajah's annoyance at processions of witness which Sharp organized through the streets of Kuching. This was more significant of the rift than perhaps the author realized.[3]

Sharp was invalided to England in 1910. He recovered to enjoy a long

---

[1] See B. Taylor, 'Church and State in Borneo: the Anglican Bishopric', *SCH* 12, pp. 357–63.
[2] This spelling is adopted for consistency with quotations that follow.
[3] S. Runciman, *The White Rajahs* (Cambridge, 1960), p. 211.

incumbency at St Stephen's Hampstead, 1913–48, and in three ways continued to influence the affairs of the Church in Borneo. (His spiritualist activities came later, and do not seem to have affected his judgement while he was active in missionary business.[4]) He was secretary of the Borneo Mission Association for eighteen years, 1912–30; he was an adviser to Archbishop Davidson on matters concerning the Church in Borneo;[5] and he helped to prepare missionaries who were to work in Sarawak. The most important of these was Wilfrid Linton.

Wilfrid Linton was born in 1890, the son of a Croydon book-keeper. He was educated at Oxford House School Croydon, where he became a junior master when his own school days ended. His church was St Andrew's, where he was confirmed at the age of thirteen, and where he was a server and Sunday school teacher. None of the priests there had been missionaries, though one curate left in 1904 to become organizing secretary in England of the South African Church Railway Mission, and another, who arrived that year, was an American from Tennessee. When he was about eighteen Linton began to think about being a missionary, and received extra coaching from the vicar of St Andrew's, and, in Greek, from a curate at St Michael's. He was recommended to St Augustine's College Canterbury by Bishop Montgomery, secretary of SPG, and admitted in 1910. In that year a new vicar had arrived at St Andrew's, G. M. Thompson, who had been SPG chaplain in Selangor in the Federated Malay States, and that may have turned Linton's mind to that part of the world. At St Augustine's the warden was A. M. Knight, who had been bishop of Rangoon. The subwarden from 1912 was R. U. Potts, who had worked for nine years in India, and who became a lifelong friend of Linton. He studied for the LTh of Durham, and went on to University College Durham to complete his BA degree.

It was arranged that Linton should work for Sharp in Hampstead—but he went there with doubts. They did not have a daily eucharist, and they did have pew rents. He was ordained deacon at Michaelmas 1914 and priest a year later. During his curacy he took a missionary medical course. Within three years he was eager to set out for Borneo, but there were delays in obtaining a passport. Bishop Montgomery wrote to Linton, 'I think the office of the Rajah in London would help. If a foreign potentate makes a request it surely ought to be granted.'[6] This stratagem did not

[4] See A. F. Sharp, *The Spirit Saith* (London, 1954).
[5] See, for example, correspondence in Lambeth Palace Library, Davidson: 1912 L1 Labuan; box 1 Labuan 1916.
[6] Oxford Rhodes House, USPG CLS 58, 26 October 1917.

succeed, and Linton, wearied by the passing of time, volunteered for the YMCA and served in Mesopotamia, followed by six months in India. On his release he travelled on to Sarawak, and reached Kuching on 6 March 1919. By this time Bishop Mounsey had been replaced by the popular Logie Danson, who licensed Linton on 15 March. It was intended that he should work among the Sea Dyaks of the Saribas river.

The Saribas was in the territory which James Brooke added to his state in 1853. The Dyaks of the Saribas were fierce and piratical, and energetic head-hunters. As early as 1850, F. T. McDougall, the first missionary, had included the area in his hopes for Church expansion. It was agreed that the Saribas Dyaks were likely to respond to evangelism. They showed interest in education, and enterprising boys found their way to schools in other districts. But because their land was remote, it never had priority for the placing of a missionary. There were catechists, and chapels were built. There were rare episcopal visits for confirmation—as many as seventy-seven candidates in 1904, who then had very infrequent opportunities to receive holy communion. As the long episcopate of G. F. Hose drew to a close, the number of priests shrank, and the pastoral care of the rural areas became hard to maintain. Great responsibility fell upon a Eurasian priest, born in Labuan, William Howell. He had lived at Sabu on the Undop, a tributary of the Batang Lupar, since 1878, acquiring an unrivalled knowledge of Iban[7] language and custom. When other Church workers failed he added their districts to his own, for longer or shorter periods, making long journeys by river and jungle path.

The new emphasis on the sacraments that came with Sharp and Bishop Mounsey made the wider deployment of priests an imperative need, and the Saribas was chosen as a mission centre. W. E. Weighill, a priest sent by SPG, reached Kuching in 1910, and was sent to Howell to be trained for the work. Within two months he had left Sarawak, overcome by jungle life and travel. The Saribas, where even some women were now asking for confirmation, had to wait longer. Bishop Danson agreed that this district should be given priority, and wrote in 1919, 'This is a district full of promise, for the Saribas Dyaks are the most progressive of all'.[8]

In May 1919 Danson made his first tour of the Sea Dyak area of the Second Division of Sarawak, and took Linton with him. They were joined by Howell, who walked long distances with the bishop. Linton missed much of this because of sore feet, but he was with them for a fortnight in

---

[7] 'Iban' is synonymous with 'Sea Dyak'.
[8] Borneo Mission Association Report for 1919, p. 10.

Betong, a well-established government centre where the Church had already built a house. Plans were made for building a church and a school. This roused the enthusiasm of the people, who started saving to build up a fund, and 'contrary to all precedent', as Danson later reported to SPG, 'subscribed about £120 towards this'.[9] In July 1919 Linton went to live at Sabu, to learn from Howell, and it was expected that he would be there until 1922, when the buildings at Betong might be ready for use. There is no record of any quarrel between Linton and Howell. Later Howell wrote, 'He is the right man in the right place', adding, 'A government official is stationed at Betong and Mr. Linton will not feel lonely'.[10] None the less he was perhaps glad that Betong was fifteen miles or so away as the hornbill flies, and much further as the journey had to be done. Linton may well have thought that much had moved on in the forty-one years since Howell had completed his studies at St Augustine's College Canterbury. For his part, Howell had never met anything like Linton, with his austere, disciplined churchmanship, and the frequent weekday services that he insisted on at Sabu, including the astonishing novelty of observing All Souls' Day. The Sabu registers show that Howell continued to spend much of his time away from home, in pastoral visits throughout the Sea Dyak area, administering the sacraments, encouraging the catechists, and looking after Church property. Linton was left at Sabu in charge of the school, which gave him the opportunity to learn from his pupils. He paid several visits to the Saribas and it was decided that he should be given charge there from 1 November 1920, well ahead of expectation. His district also included the Krian river, where there had been occasional missionary work for many years. Sometimes there had been a resident priest, but more recently catechists had struggled to keep the stations alive, with visits from the tireless but overworked Howell.

The second part of this paper is not a narrative account of Linton's mission in the Saribas. That can be found elsewhere.[11] None the less, while bishops and diocesan synods may adopt policies for evangelism and patterns of ministry, the results depend more than anything else on the priests and other workers in the parishes and districts, and on their attitude to work, especially in remote places where communications are poor, and on their ability to resist the temptations which beset them.

[9] USPG CLR 77, 3 July 1922.
[10] *Historical Notes* (typescript c1928), p. 41.
[11] See B. Taylor, *The Anglican Church in Borneo 1848–1962* (Bognor, 1983) under Betong, Linton, Saribas; also accounts in *The Chronicle* (quarterly report of the Borneo Mission Association) and the annual Reports of the BMA.

These are, for those who work alone, drink, and for those who have fellow-workers, quarrelsomeness.

Linton set to work, and soon built a temporary church and boys' school. The bishop was there in May 1921, and blessed the new buildings and confirmed twenty-two candidates. The mission was dedicated to St Augustine of Canterbury. A girls' school was started a year later. In 1921 two retreats were held. Village work and the development of outstations took up much of his time, but Linton considered that his main work was to build up a strong base for the mission, and that is what will be dealt with here. In the jungle people's bodies had to be cared for. He wrote, 'I think you know that in Borneo I am entirely alone and that I have to be doctor as well as Priest to the people. I am able to do this owing to the training I had at the London Missionary School of Medicine. But I have felt the need of some training in the use of the microscope for the diagnosis of disease. . . . instruction has been offered me at the London School of Tropical Medicine at very small cost.'[12] SPG gave him four guineas towards the fees, and someone gave him a microscope.

In 1923 the Rajah gave a site for permanent buildings, a few minutes' walk from the bazaar. Slowly the land at Munggu Lalang was cleared, and drains laid down. The temporary buildings were moved there in 1926, and new ones were begun. The compound included two hilltops. On one of these the boys' school was built. On 21 September 1926 the school was blessed, and also the mission house. On the same day Howell set the corner post of the new church, on the other hilltop. The great wooden basilica was consecrated on 16 October 1929. It stood until 1979. Lower down were built a girls' school, houses for workers, and a dispensary. The old church was converted into a rest house for Dyaks who came in from the villages.

More important than buildings was the development of an Iban ministry. The maintenance of a catholic pattern of worship depended on the provision of priests, but no Sea Dyak had been admitted to holy orders when Linton arrived in Sarawak. Bishop Danson entrusted Linton with the work of fostering vocations among those who had served the Church well. He considered four men to be suitable candidates. With his liking for formal arrangements he called them the College of the Holy Spirit, and gave them a strict routine of mass, manual work, reading, meditation, and the offices. The two younger candidates did not persevere, but the two experienced workers did. Matius Senang, aged about forty-five, had

---

[12] USPG CLR 77, 1 June 1923.

been a catechist, and had worked closely with Linton, accompanying him on all his journeys. A younger man, Lawrence Angking, was also a proved catechist and teacher. Senang was ordained deacon on 25 April 1925, 'the first instance on record of the Ordination of a Sea Dyak for work among his own people', as Danson observed.[13] On the same occasion, Angking was made a subdeacon, the first that the diocese had had. Senang was ordained priest in September 1926, and went to minister in the Krian part of the district. Angking's ordination as deacon was in October 1929, and as priest in 1932. Both of these men gave long service to the Church, and held positions of responsibility, especially during the Japanese occupation, when they were able to continue a quiet ministry. Senang died in 1952. Angking lived until 1966, honoured by the Church with a canonry and by the state with a decoration.

The Church in Betong was severely tested with respect to its acceptance of sacramental religion. Because of his time of preparation at Sabu, Linton was only at Betong for twenty-six months before his leave. He was away for nine months in 1923, during which time the sacraments could be administered only infrequently by visiting priests. The bishop was confident. 'Catechist Lawat and Angking, the headmaster of S. Augustine's School, have risen to the occasion, and I fancy that Mr Linton will find that there is not much in the way of arrears to make up.'[14] More testing was to follow. Linton's health had always given concern. A doctor's report to SPG towards the end of his leave observed that he was 'distinctly run-down', and that there was 'some question as to the condition of his lung'.[15] In March 1924, only three months after his return, he fell seriously ill with typhoid. A wireless message brought a launch to carry him to Kuching, where his condition was complicated with rheumatism and sciatica. After eleven weeks in hospital he went for convalescence to Western Australia, so once again Betong had to rely on visiting priests for the sacraments.

When he returned, in October, he found in Kuching a priest who was to be his assistant, W. G. Illingworth. He was an old friend of his, also from St Augustine's College Canterbury, eager to join the Saribas mission. Linton put him in charge of the boys' school, so that he himself could have more time for mission work and for his theological students. Before

[13] BMA Report for 1925, p. 6. Thomas Buda had been ordained in 1924, for work among the Bukar Land Dyaks at Tai-i.

[14] BMA Report for 1923, p. 23.

[15] USPG CLR 78, 10 October 1923.

very long, Illingworth had to go to Kuching to see the doctor. He carried on until February 1926, but then left to return to England with a strained heart. Linton was again the only priest—but not for long, as Senang's ordination to the priesthood followed later that year. When Linton was on leave in 1928, Senang was recalled from the Krian, and continuity was maintained.

One major hope of both Danson and Linton has still to be mentioned. The idea that the Saribas should be staffed with a community of missionaries was attributed to Bishop Mounsey. Danson endorsed this even before his arrival in Sarawak as bishop, and Linton was chosen to lead the experiment. The mission house at Betong was designed with this in mind, with cells for the brethren. During his leave in 1928 Linton looked for priests to join him, and found two men, still students at St Augustine's College. They were M. W. Bradshaw and A. J. Sparrow. It was necessary for them to serve as curates in England, but their intentions were maintained. Linton spent part of his leave at Kelham with the Society of the Sacred Mission. In Kuching, on 18 November 1928, he was admitted as a novice of the Community of the Holy Cross, and then returned to Betong. Bradshaw reached Sarawak early in 1931, and went to Betong in April, when community life began. Three weeks later Linton wrote to SPG, 'We have begun our life together. We cannot officially start the Community before the bishop comes, but we are living under a simple rule regulating our hours of prayer, study, silences etc & we shall find gradually how to adapt this to our needs.'[16] Danson visited Betong, and was doubtful about Linton's health, as he was beginning to suffer from filaria. He decided not to admit any more novices until after Linton's next leave. Undeterred, Linton built a chapel, connected to the mission house by a covered way, and dedicated it to the Holy Cross on 31 October 1931. Sparrow reached Sarawak in February 1932 with the new bishop, N. B. Hudson, who took him to Betong, where he joined Linton and Bradshaw in a common life and common purse.

By 1930 Linton was well established at Betong. He had completed his building programme, and the schools were running successfully. An Asian ministry was being developed and hopes for the community were high. In the absence of Danson for the Lambeth Conference of 1930, followed by his resignation, Archdeacon Champion sent reports to England. 'Fr. Linton's work at Betong was a triumph of patience and purposiveness.'[17]

[16] USPG E 86, 6 May 1931.
[17] *Chronicle*, August 1931, p. 5.

He wrote glowingly about life in the compound, 'the Sunday evening games, the "Dyak dancing", and what not. . . . it is not easy to express in words the distinctively Catholic ethos, but it is certainly very evident at Betong'.[18] Mass was said daily, and the sacrament was reserved. Incense had been used from the time of the temporary church. 'Mr Linton' had become 'Fr Linton', even in the bishop's reports, by 1929. Priestliness was emphasized by the habitual wearing of the biretta in and out of church. The devotion of stations of the cross was introduced, and retreats were regularly held, in Holy Week and at other seasons, even sometimes in village chapels. Travel to the outstations was made much easier when the parish of St Mary Stafford gave a motor launch in 1929, named after itself. The main development was at Saratok on the Krian, and at Debak on the Rimbas, a tributary of the Saribas. Valuable work was done in the schools in both of these places by Martin Nanang, who had worked for Howell, and who later became a priest. Another tributary, the Paku, had a number of villages with Christian families, where intermittent evangelism had occurred since late in the nineteenth century. Linton tried to build up the faithful there, but that was not easy.

His ministry is well illustrated from his report for 1931.

> I once carried to a sick man, and found the man out of his mind and unable to make his communion. I had made a journey of eight hours, walking over hills and through rivers, and the last part of it was in the dark. I placed the Blessed Sacrament in the small chapel, and next day carried It back to Betong. Later the sick man was brought to Betong, made his confession, was anointed, made his communion, and died in penitence and peace.

Sacramental confession was widely used.

> Our young people are brought up to make their confessions regularly, but quite old people who have not been taught to use the Sacrament, also find the benefit of it. Last Easter I had an old woman, a great-grandmother, who had never made her confession who came and made her first confession of her own will, without any urging on my part.

> The people are taught to baptise in case of emergency, and on several occasions when a newly-born child has been in danger of death it has been baptised by one of the Christians present, or even by a schoolboy

[18] BMA Report for 1930, p. 22.

of eleven or twelve years of age, home for his holidays. I know of one boy who during his holidays baptised several children, and afterwards took the funeral services, as there was no one else who could read or knew what to do.[19]

There were problems and setbacks, which were not surprising, as the village people could not understand the principles taught by the missionaries, especially when their children came home convinced that they must defy long-established custom. Marriage was a main cause of difficulty. Linton wrote,

> This is due to the clash of Christian principles with age-long customs, or with the personal likes and dislikes of people. Some of our boys have felt that they must stand out against the Eastern custom of having their wives chosen for them by their parents, and choose their own, as the parents wished them to marry heathen wives, and they of course wished for Christian ones.[20]

So Linton was accused of teaching disobedience to parents. Gambling was another contentious issue. Danson followed the example of Hose and Mounsey, and held conferences for Dyak catechists and the clergy working in Dyak areas. Cockfighting was condemned, and Linton felt obliged to obey this decision. In the Paku especially this was resented, and caused several longhouses to abandon Christianity. Bishop Howes, who served in the Saribas when he first arrived in Sarawak in 1937, recalls that Sparrow then 'took the line that we could not logically ban cockfighting while still allowing people to bet at horse racing.' Race week in Kuching was well known as one of the main events in the social year for Europeans.

> Had the ban been on the grounds of cruelty then there was a case; but it was not. There were Puritan objections to the gambling that went on at cock fights, with men the worse for drink gambling away their land, school fees and alms. Most agreed that cockfighting was a bad thing, but went on engaging in it anyway. But the Paku communities had not done this: they had lapsed 100% and were then, in '37, very anti-Mission.[21]

The clergy still preach against cockfighting, but in these more relaxed times the people just ignore them, and do not go to the lengths of

---

[19] *Ibid.*, 1931, pp. 23–4.
[20] *Ibid.*, 1928, p. 36.
[21] P. H. H. Howes to the author, 12 December 1987.

apostasy. Linton was saddened by the opposition, and the falling away, and the small number of converts—only six adult baptisms in 1930, and two admissions to the catechumenate. None the less, in his report to SPG for 1929 he wrote, 'It is not good that everyone whould speak well of us and the hostility is searching out the people, so that we are beginning to know who is in earnest'.[22] He was convinced that much of the trouble had been caused by hasty baptism with inadequate preparation in the past, and he repeatedly urged the need for the increase of the Dyak priesthood. In 1931 he wrote to the Warden of St Augustine's College,

> I feel more and more as I am longer out here that results do not really matter. It is nice to have them, but what matters really is whether we are doing the Divine Will. And if we feel certain about this, we need not get discouraged by apparently no results being achieved or by hardship or difficulty or apparent failures.[23]

Linton, Bradshaw, and Sparrow were together in Betong for only two months in 1932 before Linton left for England. His state of health caused him to cut short his four-year tour of duty, and so he lost a month of his leave entitlement. The rest of his story is briefly told. He was ordered to rest completely, because of high blood pressure, and was not even allowed to speak at the Borneo Mission Association meeting in June. He begged to return to Sarawak, 'even if it means a shorter life, or periods of ill-health alternating with good health',[24] but he was persuaded that his precarious health would place a burden on others. His resignation was at the end of 1932. He secured the appointment of chaplain to St Mary's House Buxted, a children's home run by the Wantage sisters. He was there from April 1933 until 1939, when he moved to Wantage, to be chaplain of the same community's St Helen's School. In 1945 St Augustine's College presented him to the small parish of Kingston near Canterbury, where he is remembered with respect, 'though he made a number of changes in the Church and Services (not appreciated by many). The childen were very fond of him and he was a good teacher.'[25] Several heart attacks made it impossible for him to remain there, and in 1947 he went to be chaplain of All Saints' Home Hawley, a guest house owned by the Clewer sisters. He died after a stroke on 22 October 1948, aged only fifty-eight. His ashes

---

[22] USPG E 84, 17 November 1929.
[23] Canterbury Cathedral, City and Diocesan Record Office, SAC Linton file, 2 July 1931.
[24] USPG D 45 Linton to SPG, 26 September 1932.
[25] Miss M. C. Rogers to the author, 30 January 1988.

were taken and buried under the altar at Betong. After Senang's death in 1952, a chapel of All Souls was formed in the church, as a memorial to the two priests.

After his return to England Linton's interest in Borneo continued, and he was secretary of the Borneo Mission Association from 1935 until his death—succeeding Illingworth, who had held the position after Sharp. His main concern at first was the future of the Community of the Holy Cross. When he came to England in 1932 he visited the Community of the Resurrection as soon as he could, with Bishop Hudson's permission. Discussions led to two Mirfield fathers being sent to Sarawak in 1933 to assess the opportunities there. For a few months they were at Betong with Bradshaw and Sparrow. More fathers followed them, and had a house in Kuching until they were withdrawn in 1937. Linton hoped that his community would become a branch of the Community of the Resurrection, but this did not come about. When Bradshaw left in 1934 he decided to try his vocation at Mirfield. He was professed in 1937, and worked in the community's African missions. Sparrow decided to remain a secular priest, and so the plans for a community came to an end.

Wilfrid Linton was certainly 'the right man in the right place' at Betong, as Howell said. His strong personality matched well the forceful character of the Saribas people, and he won their respect, even when they did not do as he wanted. It was fortunate that Sparrow maintained the standard of ministry that Linton established. Bishop Howes writes, 'My impression is that Sparrow continued the Linton tradition: that Services, Time-Table, School syllabus, Dispensary hours, everything had originated from Linton, and that Sparrow was pleased to carry on that tradition.'[26]

Linton's Betong continued to set the standard of ministry and Church life, and the pattern which has been the ideal in the Sea Dyak missions. There has been response to his insistence on the need for a Dyak priesthood. Senang and Angking have been mentioned, and also Nanang. One of Linton's catechists, Barnabas Jamban, a very holy man who spoke no English, was ordained in 1938. The Saribas and the Krian have continued to supply a large proportion of the ordination candidates. Of the eighteen Iban priests working in Sarawak now, eight are from those rivers; and the same area produced all four Sea Dyaks who have held the office of archdeacon. It may also be mentioned that the only Dyak woman so far to persevere in the religious life, Sister Prisca Nasa of the Community of

[26] P. H. H. Howes as n. 21 above.

Companions of Jesus the Good Shepherd, also came from Betong district, and was educated in the schools there. One final name must be given. Linton visited a non-Christian village, Kampong Pasa, and noticed a small boy, and took a snapshot of him. He persuaded the parents to let him go to school at St Augustine's, and he was one of those baptized in October 1929 when the new church was consecrated. On 6 December 1968, in St Thomas's Cathedral Kuching, Linton's protégé, Basil Temengong, was ordained bishop of the diocese.

Guildford

ABBREVIATIONS

Abbreviated titles are adopted within each paper after first full citation. In addition the following abbreviations are used throughout the volume.

BIHR	*Bulletin of the Institute of Historical Research* (London 1923–)
BL	British Library, London
CC	*Corpus Christianorum* (Turnhout 1952–)
CSer	*Camden Series* (London 1838–)
CYS	*Canterbury and York Society* (London 1907–)
DNB	*Dictionary of National Biography* (London 1885–)
DRev	*Downside Review* (London 1880–)
EETS	*Early English Text Society*
EHR	*English Historical Review* (London 1886–)
FStn	*Franziskanische Studien* (Münster/Werl 1914–)
GCS	*Die griechischen christlichen Schriftsteller der erste drei Jahrhunderte* (Leipzig 1897–)
HE	*Historia Ecclesiastica*
HJ	*Historical Journal* (Cambridge 1958–)
HL	C. J. Hefele and H. Leclercq, *Histoire des Conciles*, 10 vols (Paris 1907–35)
HMC	Historical Manuscripts Commission
JEH	*Journal of Ecclesiastical History* (London 1950–)
JRH	*Journal of Religious History* (Sydney 1960–)
Le Neve	John LeNeve, *Fasti Ecclesiae 1066–1300*, rev and exp Diana E. Greenway, 1, St Pauls (London 1968); 2, Monastic Cathedrals (1971), *Fasti Ecclesiae Anglicanae 1300–1541*, rev and exp H. P. F. King, J. M. Horn, B. Jones, 12 vols (London 1962–7), *Fasti Ecclesiae Anglicanae 1541–1857*, rev and exp J. M. Horn, D. M. Smith, 1, St Pauls (1969); 2, Chichester (1971); 3, Canterbury, Rochester, Winchester (1974); 4, York (1975)
LRS	Lincoln Record Society
MGH	*Monumenta Germaniae Historica inde ab a.c. 500 usque ad a. 1500*, ed. G. H. Pertz and others (Berlin, Hanover 1826–)
SRG	*Scriptores rerum germanicarum in usum scholarum*
SRGns	*Scriptores rerum germanicarum in usum scholarum, new series*
SRM	*Scriptores rerum merovingicarum*
MS	Manuscript
OMT	*Oxford Medieval Texts*
PG	*Patrologia Graeca*, ed. J. P. Migne, 161 vols (Paris 1857–66)
PIMS	Pontifical Institute for Medieval Studies
PL	*Patrologia Latina*, ed. J. P. Migne, 217 + 4 index vols (Paris 1841–64)
P & P	*Past and Present* (London 1952–)
PRO	Public Record Office
RS	*Rerum Brittanicarum Medii Aevi Scriptores*, 99 vols (London 1858–1911), *Rolls Series*
SCH	*Studies in Church History* (London 1964–)

ABBREVIATIONS

SVRG	*Schriften des Vereins für Reformationsgeschichte* (Halle/Leipzig/Gütersloh 1883–)
TRHS	*Transactions of the Royal Historical Society* (London 1871–)
VCH	*Victoria County History* (London 1900–)
WA	*D. Martin Luthers Werke*, ed. J. C. F. Knaake (Weimar 1883–) [*Weimarer Ausgabe*]